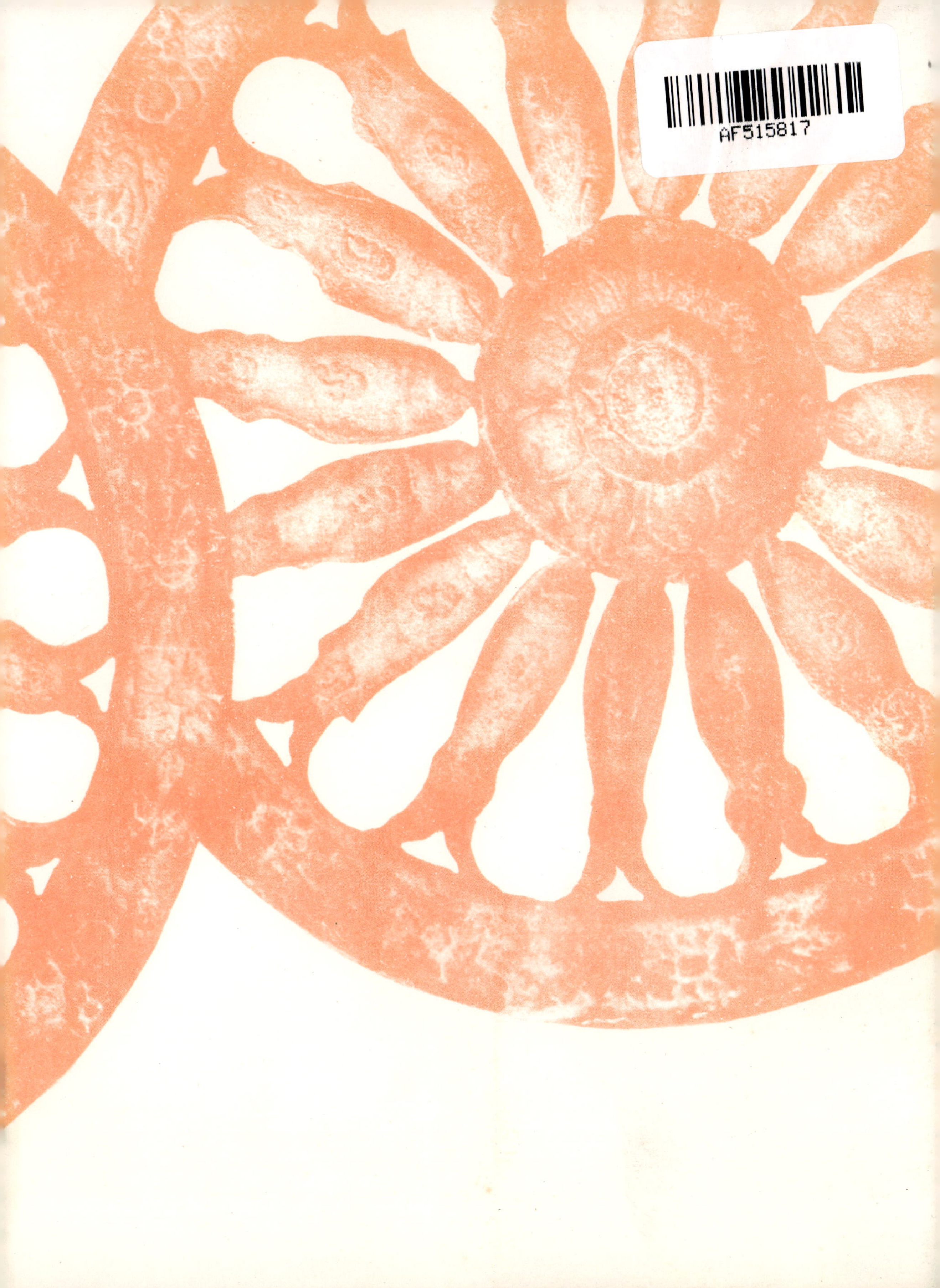

कलातत्त्वकोश
KALĀTATTVAKOŚA

कलातत्त्वकोश

KALĀTATTVAKOŚA

A LEXICON OF FUNDAMENTAL CONCEPTS OF THE INDIAN ARTS

General Editor
Kapila Vatsyayan

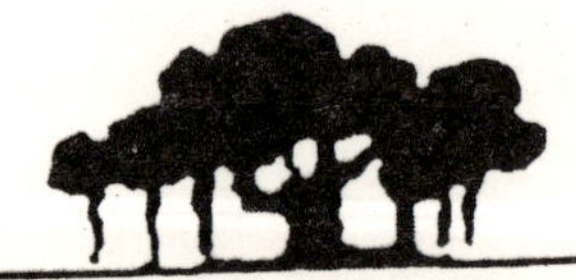

कलातत्त्वकोश खण्ड - २

KALĀTATTVAKOŚA VOL. – II

SPACE AND TIME
DEŚA-KĀLA

KALĀTATTVAKOŚA
VOLUME – II

Editor
Bettina Bäumer

INDIRA GANDHI NATIONAL CENTRE FOR THE ARTS
NEW DELHI
and
MOTILAL BANARSIDASS PUBLISHERS PVT. LTD.
DELHI

First Published: 1992
Revised Edition: 2003

Published by
INDIRA GANDHI NATIONAL CENTRE FOR THE ARTS
Central Vista, Janpath, New Delhi - 110 001

in association with
MOTILAL BANARSIDASS PUBLISHERS PVT. LTD.
Bungalow Road, Jawahar Nagar, Delhi - 110 007

ISBN : 81-208-1044-9 (Vol. II)
ISBN : 81-208-1045-7 (Set)
Price : Rs. 950/-

Typeset by
The Indira Gandhi National Centre for the Arts,
Varanasi Office : B-1/3, E-7, Lane No.2,
Ravindrapuri Extension, Varanasi-221 005

Printed in India
at Shri Jainendra Press
A-45, Naraina Industrial Area Phase - I
New Delhi - 110 028

FOREWORD

It was with both optimism as also apprehension that the Indira Gandhi National Centre for the Arts had released the First Volume of the **Kalātattvakośa**. In the Foreword to the First Volume I had given the rationale behind launching a programme of a multi-volumed publication which would serve as a lexicon for comprehending the complexities of meaning of certain fundamental terms which are pervasive in all disciplines and are crucial for understanding the Indian artistic traditions.

The vision and guidance of Tarkatīrtha Laxman Shastri Joshi with his monumental scholarship and access to primary sources, his perceptivity and wisdom had made it possible to agree upon an approximately 250 such terms. In these four years, the nature of the undertaking has expanded: the *bīja* that was sown at the meeting held in Sarnath has already begun to sprout and the *bindu* is expanding to a series of concentric circles. It was our endeavour to place the results of this exploration before scholars in the first volume. The terms had been chosen on account of their pervasiveness, universality, their multilayered meanings and the central position they occupy in intellectual discourse of all disciplines of the Indian tradition. As has been remarked by the Editor in her Introduction, this Volume was received with enthusiasm and naturally, some criticism by the international community. She has taken into account all criticisms and suggestions received. In her Introduction Bettina Bäumer has explained the methodology, the selection of the primary sources, the terms, their groupings, and sub-groupings within the larger category of space and time. There is little for me to add on the primary sources, the reasons for restricting them to Sanskrit, Pali and Prakrit and the decision to concentrate the presentations in order to reveal the interlocking and interpenetrative system rather than attempt "challenging interpretative essays".

It remains for me to place this project of the **Kalātattvakośa** in the larger context of the programmes of research, publications, exhibitions, seminars and performances of the Indira Gandhi National Centre for the Arts. In all its programmes the Institution has endeavoured to focus attention and throw light on the distinctively Indian interdisciplinary and holistic system where the textual and the oral, the verbal and the visual, the scientific and the metaphysical, the transcendental and the functional were and are parts of a 'whole'. They are segments of a single circle closely interlocked, and not autonomous units to be viewed as aggregation or as polarities in a linear order. Also, the Centre's emphasis is on comprehending the Arts not as finished products but to view them against the background of an Indian world-view , within a socio-cultural context and interdisciplinary system of form and technique and a creative process where the ideational and the functional, the sacred and the secular, vision and skill merge. Further, each of the programmes aim to bridge the recent artificially created 'schisms' between theory (*śāstra*), the prescriptive and the practical application(*prayoga*). With a view to concretize this approach, the Indira Gandhi National Centre for the Arts has endeavoured to initiate a number of complementary programmes around related concepts. In this context notions of space and time (*ākāśa* and *kāla*) have been the first concerns of the search. Four years ago, a Seminar on "CONCEPTS OF SPACE" (*ĀKĀŚA*) was held. Here, although the Sanskrit term *ākāśa* was used, the exploration was neither restricted to Sanskrit and Pali sources nor to verbal articulation in ancient texts. So also it was with the Seminar on "TIME" (*KĀLA*) which was held in 1990. Here, the notions of 'Time' were explored through all cultures and disciplines. In each case, there was confluence of those who had viewed the universe as 'matter' and 'physical space and time' as also others who comprehended the notions at the metaphysical level and as inner psychical states. There were no boundaries of the disciplines, cultures, civilizations and the Arts. In the **Kalātattvakośa** the boundaries of our endeavour have been clearly demarcated by the terms intrinsic to one tradition and as elucidated in primary texts.

Further, the two Seminars were complemented with exhibitions where notions of Space and Time were explored visually and orally as primordial stillness and as exploration leading to the expanse of the galaxies in one case and the silence of the void, in the other. The exhibitions were multimedia presentations for evoking experience of a 'totality' which is here and now, not forgetting civilizations past and the worlds dead or telescoped of astrophysics and of a new science. Judging from the response, the *prayoga* was complete as it had utilised the tools of intellectual discourse and artistic manifestation to re-evoke experience. Also, many other publications were released, in particular: 'Concepts of Space'; 'Time and Eternity'; 'Time and Eternal Change'; 'Sṛṣṭi: Its Philosophical Entailment'; 'Temporality and Logical Structure'. Notwithstanding this larger context, the necessity, one may add *sādhanā* and *svādhyāya* of investigating each tradition and each discipline in its own terms as an essential prerequisite is obvious. This is what this volume of the **Kalātattvakośa** has sought to do.

The perseverance, diligence, co-ordinating skills of sifting through hundreds of cards along with perceptions and sensitivity of the Editor and her dedicated team is exemplary. For all this I am grateful. I am now more hopeful that this approach as also structure will mark the beginning of a different method of viewing and comprehending the Indian tradition.

Kapila Vatsyayan

CONTENTS

LIST OF ILLUSTRATIONS

Pūrṇa

INTRODUCTION

sarvaṃ sarvātmakam
Everything is related to the whole.

I. General Background

The Indian Arts are like the branches of a vast tree of culture, thought, science, ritual and spirituality, and they cannot be understood in isolation. They are based on fundamental Indian conceptions of the cosmos and of man, of space and time, of the body, mind and self. These have crystallized in the Sanskrit tradition as specific concepts which pervade virtually all disciplines. Theories of aesthetics rest on philosophical concepts but are also deeply linked with medical thought and with mystical experience. The wide range of Indian art forms are interrelated through shared aesthetic theories, and there are also basic principles of form manifested in the various media employed, so that the Arts themselves are interdependent in much the same way that interrelationships exist between the sciences, religions and philosophies. The Arts form an integral part of the total culture.

So far, the Indian Arts have been largely studied in isolation, with much emphasis being given to chronologies and stylistic analysis along Western lines. The questions of meaning and the interdependence between the Arts and other disciplines have received relatively less attention. Literary and art-historical studies have rarely been combined, so as to do justice to both. There is a vast literature containing theoretical texts on the Indian Arts (Śilpa-Śāstra, Vāstu-Śāstra, Saṅgīta-Śāstra) which has not yet been sufficiently investigated and applied to the interpretation of the Arts themselves. The self-interpretation of the tradition in which the Arts have developed has yet to be carried out, partly because an adequate method of understanding the texts has been lacking.

In the context of a Seminar on "Shastric Traditions in Indian Arts"[1] T. S. Maxwell has thrown light on the interrelationship of *śāstra* and *prayoga*, of theoretical literature and practical application. Against the view that the śāstras are dry classifications which are often contradicted by artistic practice, he asserts : "Those texts epitomised and consolidated the culture in which the artist lived and worked, and from which he drew his inspiration; Śilpaśāstra, as the body of texts which effectively legitimised his calling within the culture, has endeavoured to preserve parts of this vision... All art-forms

---

1. A. L. Dallapiccola (ed.): Shastric Traditions in Indian Arts, Stuttgart: Steiner, 1989.

are practical and symbolic expressions of cultural intelligence; they carry a passive burden of assumed or inherited knowledge and an active burden of conscious knowledge which is intentionally communicated. Once one becomes aware of these two interpenetrating levels, the chaotic background of archetypes and the ordered foreground of didacticism, the methods and skills of the artist are defined, just as they are defined by shastric precept: the master *śilpin* must have (without claiming another's province for his own) knowledge of all the arts, from metrics and poetic imagery to music and dance, painting and sculpture, in increasing detail, his own field being placed last in the list, emphasising its juniority but also the legitimacy of its traditional descent; and he must be able to mobilise this knowledge in connexion with yoga and meditational techniques in order to visualise fully, from brief descriptions, the forms he will create. As an actor in and an agent of his society, he must be open to the cultural sources of that society." (pp. 11-12). Thus the texts present various kinds of sources for the artist, and to interpret art without them means to reduce our understanding of the total context in which art has its meaning.

The **Kalātattvakośa** project aims to bridge a serious gap in the understanding of Indian culture by selecting 250 fundamental concepts (based on Sanskrit) from the various disciplines, schools and texts and focussing on their occurrence and their significance in the Arts. Presented in the form of a lexicon, **Kalātattvakośa** gives each concept in its various contexts and provides the textual sources, both in the original and in translation. It is a research tool for scholars and all who are interested in penetrating to the meaning contained in artistic creativity, expression, form and purpose.

The criteria of selection are based on the frequency of interdisciplinary occurrence and the wide-ranging importance of the terms. Only concepts having meaning in a range of disciplines and associated literatures have been selected : *rasa*, for example, is used in the Vedas, and in medical (Āyurvedic) and chemical (Rasaśāstric) contexts, as well as in aesthetics. Purely technical terms within a particular tradition have thus been omitted; these will be treated in separate Technical Glossaries (for example on Saṅgīta-Śāstra and Śilpa-Śāstra). The lexicon concentrates on terms of fundamental and widespread significance in the primary sources, and thus avoids both tacit interpretation by partiality of selection, and the ongoing interpretive controversies of the secondary literature.

The criteria governing the selection of primary sources are two: the texts must be considered representative of a discipline or school of thought, and they must be the oldest available sources of that school complete with commentaries. The texts quoted do not pretend to be exhaustive, but aim to represent the most important literatures and disciplines. Thus in addition to the Vedas, Vedāṅgas, Smṛti, Itiāsa, Purāṇas, Darśanas, Tantras and Āgamas, the **Nāṭyaśāstra** along with Abhinavagupta's commentary, for example, plays a central role in establishing links between concept and art, drama(*nāṭya*) being the origin of the different Arts and of aesthetic theory.

The limitation of Sanskrit sources and related material (Prakrit, Pali), including cognates(Greek, Latin), results from the nature of the undertaking. It is the intention to cover the entire Indian tradition, and **Kalātattvakośa** is the Sanskritic section of the project. The editors are fully aware that the Arabic-Persian sources require an equal treatment of their basic aesthetic, philosophical and artistic concepts, and that the Sanskrit sources must be complemented by their counterparts in the Dravidian languages. Indeed, to present as complete a picture as possible of the development of a concept in the Indian tradition, it should be traced through the Middle Indian to modern Indian literatures, with indication of the more important semantic developments. This is not feasible at the present stage, and restraint has had to be exercised within the articles presented here.

The entries cannot therefore pretend to be exhaustive. The tradition is so rich and the source material so varied, that it is not possible to present a complete historical picture of each and every concept with all its variations; and as the focus is on the Arts, philosophical discussion has had to be limited to a minimum to prevent overbalance. Within these limitations, the absence of a preconceived interpretive scheme should enable the reader from any discipline to identify interconnections between basic concepts from the original texts in pursuit of his own specific interest, and to spread his research beyond the immediate confines of the lexicon.

The first volume of **Kalātattvakośa** received both criticism and very positive responses. Criticism has been taken into account as far as possible, and every effort will be made to improve future volumes to meet the high expectations which have been expressed.

II. Method and Use

1. The lexicon is not *organised alphabetically* but thematically by concepts. Groups of related terms are assembled in each volume, and the logic of their arrangement is explained in the introduction. Alphabetical reference is facilitated by the **List of Terms** which gives the complete list of entries for the whole lexicon, mentioning the volume in which an article has already appeared. The **Index** directs the reader to the occurrence of the terms throughout, and also refers him to other significant terms in Sanskrit and English. Arrows⟶ refer to an entry, in the same or another volume, where the term in question is treated more extensively.

2. Within a desirable flexibility of *structure,* the content of an entry generally follows the sequence as under :

Overview
Etymology and related/cognate terms
Layers of meaning
Development of the concept
Manifestation in the Arts
Classification
Process
Conclusion

Quick identification of a section which may interest the reader specifically is thus facilitated.

In some cases where a concept has a distinct meaning in different fields, an article has been divided into two or three parts assigned to different authors.

3. All *Sanskrit quotations* are given in *devanāgarī* with a full English translation; Sanskrit words or phrases occurring in the running text are transliterated and accompanied by a translation at least once. This is designed to provide access for those having limited knowledge of Sanskrit, and for non-readers of the *devanāgarī* script.

4. *Text references* are abbreviated; full titles appear only in the running text of the entry (in bold face).The **List of Abbreviations** provides the full titles, and the **General Bibliography** notes the text editions and translations used.

5. A **Select Bibliography** is appended to each article; this contains references to secondary literature to which the author refers. These references are not exhaustive but are relevant to tracing further information about the concept.

6. The *etymologies,* whether traditional or based on modern linguistics, represent the opinion of the author; they have sometimes been edited, and in cases of doubt or difference of opinion the reader is referred to Manfred Mayrhofer, *Etymologisches Wörterbuch des Altindoarishchen,* Heidelberg (Carl Winter) 1986 ff.

7. All *translations* are acknowledged, whether published(see **Bibliography**) or unpublished. If a translator's name is not given, the text has been translated by the author. Where the author has amended a previous translation, this is indicated.

8. The lexicon is *illustrated with line-drawings* only, representing fundamental diagrams, *yantras,* symbols etc. Full photographic illustration of art-historical developments and variations falls outside the purview of these volumes.

III. Concepts of Space and Time

Concepts in any given system of thought are never isolated entities; they belong to a network of larger structures and contexts. A concept could be compared to an architectural motif on a Hindu temple: it occurs at different places, in various sizes and shapes, giving the temple a structural and symbolical unity; this motif may be studied separately, its style, shape and occurrence analyzed, but unless it is placed in the context of the temple as a whole, its significance cannot be grasped. Concepts have to be understood similarly, in their interconnectedness and place in a total universe of meaning. It is for this reason that the concepts are grouped under the most important topics, instead of by the mechanical structure of alphabetical sequence.

The first volume of **Kalātattvakośa** presented some basic and pervasive concepts. This, the second volume, is devoted to concepts of space and time. The basic concepts of any culture acquire meaning only when seen against the background of its cosmology, its understanding of space and time. These conceptions determine the concrete and symbolic forms of the Arts.

The selection of concepts here is in accordance with the formal symbolism of the interrelationship between space and time. Indeed, many of the concepts have a meaning equally important in both dimensions (for example *bindu, krama, sandhi, tāla*). Others have either a predominantly spatial sense (*nābhi, kṣetra, loka*) or a chiefly temporal meaning (*kāla, kṣaṇa*). Apart from terms clearly denoting concepts of space (*deśa, loka*) and time (*kāla*), others are necessarily related to form, structure and measure (*cakra, sūtra, tāla, māna*). There is also a necessary overlap with cosmological concepts: *bindu* is not only a geometrical point, it is also the energy of creation itself; *pūrṇa* is not only the fullness of space, but also the origin and final fulfilment of the whole universe.

An important concept has been omitted here, because it will be treated in the context of the elements (*mahābhūta*) in Volume III: This is *ākāśa,* empty space, with its 'synonyms' *kha* and *vyoman.* Here we have another case of overlapping of meanings and groupings. *Ākāśa/kha/vyoman* is the void of space in its macrocosmic, microcosmic, mental and spiritual sense (*mahākāśa, ghaṭākāśa, cidākāśa, hṛdayākāśa*), it is that which provides space and opportunity (*avakāśa*) for living beings. This is the outer, unlimited firmament as well as the inner, not less unlimited space of the heart [2]. In the human body it is the void of the sense-openings (*khāni*). Thus the concept of *ākāśa* which will be treated fully in the next volume, is presupposed here in the context of space and time.

In this volume, the entries follow a cosmological and symbolical sequence: instead of starting from abstract concepts, the starting point is the point(*bindu*), the creative centre from which manifestation begins. Another, more physiological concept of the centre is *nābhi*, meaning both navel of the body and nave of the wheel, as well as centre of the universe. It is from the centre – which is still and yet contains within itself the whole dynamism of expansion – that the spokes of the wheel are conceived as emerging, the whole circle as forming, and movement beginning : *cakra*. *Cakra* is also the most ancient and pervasive symbol of time, being related to the sun. Once expansion in space and time has begun, space opens out. The most concrete concept of space is *kṣetra*, the field, in architecture, geometry, sacred geography, and in the human body. The cosmic as well as human concept of space is *loka*, world, and *triloka*, the universe consisting of three realms. *Deśa* is the directional and geographical concept of space, along with *diś*, the directions of space, which are fundamental to the Arts, particularly to architecture. The complementary concept of time is *kāla*, which is both the fullness of time as well as the divisible and ordered cosmic and human time. Other concepts denoting various aspects and divisions of time have been included in the over-all concept of *kāla*. Because of its complementary meaning and importance in Buddhism, *kṣaṇa*, the moment, has been given a separate entry.

There is no time without movement and action. The concepts of action(*kriyā*) will be treated in a future volume, but one concept of movement, which combines space and time, has been included here: *krama*, step, succession, sequence, order. With this concept, space-time begins to be structured. In any structure, the parts are related to the whole by means of junctures and joints : *sandhi* is an important concept showing the qualitative significance of points of juncture in space, time, in the body, in drama and architecture.

Structure also means measure. Here, the point of beginning has expanded, forming a line : *sūtra*, thread, is an instrument for measuring, the line in space, and continuity. In drama and architecture the *sūtradhāra* is he who holds the "thread", controlling the whole activity. "Measure" is not treated in this volume as separate topic, but as an inseparable component of the space-time concept. Hence the importance of *tāla*, measure, both in

---

2. Cf. K. Vatsyayan(Ed.), Concepts of Space, Ancient and Modern, New Delhi, IGNCA, 1991.

space and time (in sculpture, for example, and music); and of *māna*, the very concept of measure involved in creation (*mā-*, *māyā*). Temporal structure is what is called rhythm, *laya* in music; *laya* also means dissolution, and that is where spatio-temporal measure and structure end.

Space and Time are only possible against the background of the void on the one side, and fullness as the origin and end of all on the other: *śūnya*(emptiness) and *pūrṇa*(fullness) are thus complementary concepts. Since *śūnya* plays a central role in Buddhism, the two distinct meanings have been treated separately : *śūnya* in mathematics, and *śūnyatā* in Buddhist philosophy.

The concepts presented here make it evident that space, time and cosmology are deeply interrelated with the Indian Arts. The forthcoming Volume III will be dedicated to the theme of the elements(*mahābhūta*).

Acknowledgments

Many scholars were involved in drawing up the scheme at its inception; in selecting the terms and the texts; and in scanning many texts for collecting quotations. Their names have been acknowledged in the first volume.

A preliminary second volume containing seven articles was distributed among the participants of the International Seminar on Time(*Kāla*) at the Indira Gandhi National Centre for the Arts, New Delhi, in November 1990. The response and criticism received have been taken into account while preparing this final volume.

I am particularly thankful to Prof. T. S. Maxwell for his valuable suggestions for improving the style of the series, and to Dr. P. L. Sharma, who has always been ready to assist me in providing references on music and drama (particularly from the **Nāṭya-Śāstra**) and in editing the sections on the Arts. Most of the drawings have been prepared by Sri S. Dorai, the drawing on p.74 by Sri Shashank Singh. I am very grateful to Ms. J. Donatowicz and Mr. G. Houdek of the University of Technology, Vienna, for their generous help with the computer and for solving many initial problems. The volume has been entirely computer set and formatted by Sri D. K. Sahoo at the Varanasi office of the Indira Gandhi National Centre for the Arts. It is thanks to their dedicated work and to the assistance of the staff of the Varanasi office that this volume could be completed.

Varanasi **Bettina Bäumer**
21 November 1991

ABBREVIATIONS

General principles in forming abbreviations, concerning the last part of the title:

Ā	Āgama
Ār	Āraṇyaka
Bh	Bhāṣya
Br	Brāhmaṇa
Ca	Carita
Dh	Dharma (e.g. DhŚ Dharmaśāstra)
G	Gītā
H	Hṛdaya
Ins	Inscription
Kā	Kārikā
K	Kathā
Ko	Kośa
L	Lakṣaṇa
Ms	Manuscript
Nik	Nikāya
P	Paddhati
Pari	Pariśiṣṭa
Prad	Pradīpikā
Pr	Prakaraṇa
Prak	Prakāśa
Prāt	Prātiśākhya
Pur	Purāṇa
R	Ratnākara
Sam	Saṃhitā
Samu	Samuccaya
Saṅg	Saṅgraha
Sā	Sāra
Ś	Śāstra
Śa	Śataka
Sm	Smṛti
Sū	Sūtra
T	Tantra
Ṭī	Ṭīkā
Up	Upaniṣad

Vā	Vārttika
V	Veda
Vim	Vimarśinī
Vi	Vivaraṇa
Vṛ	Vṛtti
Y	Yāmala

Sections of Āgamic Texts:

cp	caryāpāda
jk	jñānakhaṇḍa
kp	kriyāpāda
vp	vidyāpāda
yp	yogapāda

Sections of Ayurvedic Texts:

CiSthā	Cikitsā Sthāna
ISthā	Indriya Sthāna
KaSthā	Kalpa Sthāna
NiSthā	Nidāna Sthāna
ŚāSthā	Śārīra Sthāna
SiSthā	Siddhi Sthāna
SūSthā	Sūtra Sthāna
UtT	Uttara Tantra
ViSthā	Vimāna Sthāna

List of commentators/commentaries:

Kṣ	Kṣīrasvāmin
Rāmā	Rāmāśramī

Major Texts

AbhidhKo	Abhidharma Kośa
AbhidhSamu	Abhidharma Samuccaya
AbhŚāk	Abhijñānaśākuntala
Abhil	Abhilaṣitārtha-Cintāmaṇi (also Mānasollāsa of Someśvara)
AbhiBhā	Abhinava Bhāratī
AbhDar	Abhinaya Darpaṇa
Abhis	Abhisamayālaṅkāra

AbhNāṭ	Abhiṣeka Nāṭaka
ĀcD	Ācāra Dinakara
AdhSū	Adhyayana-Sūtra
AghŚP	Aghoraśivācārya Paddhati
AgPur	Agni Purāṇa
AhSam	Ahirbudhnya Saṃhitā
AitĀr	Aitareya Āraṇyaka
AitBr	Aitareya Brāhmaṇa
AitUp	Aitareya Upaniṣad
AjKo	Ajaya Kośa
AjitĀ	Ajitāgama
ĀlP	Ālāpa Paddhati
AmKo	Amara Kośa
Amṛto	Amṛtodaya (Gokulanātha)
AneSaṅg	Anekārtha Saṅgraha
AṅgNik	Aṅguttara Nikāya
AniSam	Aniruddha Saṃhitā
AnnaUp	Annapūrṇopaniṣad
AparPṛ	Aparājita Pṛcchā
ĀpDhSū	Āpastamba Dharma-Sūtra
ĀpGṛhSū	Āpastamba Gṛhya-Sūtra
ĀpŚrSū	Āpastamba Śrauta-Sūtra
ĀpŚulSū	Āpastamba Śulba-Sūtra
ArthŚ	Artha-Śāstra
ArthViSū	Arthaviniścaya-Sūtra
ArthaViSūNib	Arthaviniścayasūtranibandhana (Vīryaśrīdatta)
Ārya	Āryabhaṭīya
ĀryaMS	Āryamañjuśrīnāmasaṅgīti (with Amṛtakaṇikānāma... comm.)
ĀśCū	Āścaryacūḍāmaṇi (Śaktibhadra)
AṣṭH	Aṣṭāṅga-Hṛdaya (Vāgbhaṭa-I)
AṣṭSaṅg	Aṣṭāṅga-Saṅgraha (Vāgbhaṭa-II)
AṣṭPrPār	Aṣṭasāhasrikā Prajñā Pāramitā
ĀśvaGṛhSū	Āśvalāyana Gṛhya-Sūtra
ĀśvaŚrSū	Āśvalāyana Śrauta-Sūtra
AV	Atharvaveda (Śaunaka)
AV(P)	Atharvaveda (Paippalāda)
AVPari	Atharvaveda Pariśiṣṭa
AtSam	Atri Saṃhitā
Aṭṭh	Aṭṭhasālinī (on Dhammasaṅgaṇi)
Aucitya	Aucityavicāracarcā (Kṣemendra)
AvaŚa	Avadānaśataka
AvK	Avantisundarī Kathā

ĀNi	Āvassaya Nijjuti (Āvaśyaka Niryukti)
Avim	Avimāraka
BālCa	Bālacarita
BDhSū	Baudhāyana Dharma-Sūtra
BGṛhSū	Baudhāyana Gṛhya-Sūtra
BŚrSū	Baudhāyana Śrauta-Sūtra
BŚulSū	Baudhāyana Śulba-Sūtra
BhG	Bhagavad-Gītā
BhGŚBh	Bhagavad-Gītā Śaṅkara Bhāṣya
BhāgPur	Bhāgavata Purāṇa
BhSi	Bhaktirasāmṛtasindhu (Rūpa Gosvāmin)
BhRas	Bhaktirasāyana (Madhusūdana Sarasvatī)
BhārGṛhSū	Bhāradvāja Gṛhya-Sūtra
BhārSam	Bhāradvāja Saṃhitā
BhārŚrSū	Bhāradvāja Śrauta-Sūtra
BhaBh	Bharata Bhāṣya (Nānyadeva)
BhāCam	Bhārata Campū
BhāT	Bhārgava Tantra
BhāPari	Bhāṣāpariccheda
BhPrak	Bhāva Prakāśana (Śāradātanaya)
BhṛSam	Bhṛgu Saṃhitā
BhuPr	Bhuvana Pradīpa
BoPā	Bodha Pāhuḍa
BoCar	Bodhicaryāvatāra
BoBhū	Bodhisattvabhūmi
BraPur	Brahmāṇḍa Purāṇa
BrPur	Brahma Purāṇa
BrSū	Brahma-Sūtra
BrSūŚBh	Brahma-Sūtra Śaṅkara Bhāṣya
BṛUp	Bṛhadāraṇyaka Upaniṣad
BṛD	Bṛhaddeśī (Mataṅga)
BṛDev	Bṛhaddevatā (Śaunaka)
BṛJā	Bṛhat Jātaka
BṛSaṅg	Bṛhatkathāśloka Saṅgraha
BṛSam	Bṛhat Saṃhitā (Varāhamihira)
BudCa	Buddhacarita
CaRām	Campū Rāmāyaṇa
CāVyā	Cāndra Vyākaraṇa
CarSam	Caraka Saṃhitā
Cāru	Cārudatta
ChāgUp	Chāgaleya Upaniṣad
ChaSū	Chandaḥ-Sūtra

ChUp	Chāndogya Upaniṣad
Chan	Chandomañjarī
CiL	Citra-Lakṣaṇa
Cit	Citsukhī
DakMūSt	Dakṣiṇāmūrtistotra
DaPā	Darśana Pāhuḍa
DBhūSū	Daśabhūmika-Sūtra
DUVṛ	Daśapādī Uṇādi Vṛtti
DaRū	Daśarūpaka
DaSū	Daśavaikālika-Sūtra
Datti	Dattilam (Dattila)
DBhāgPur	Devī Bhāgavata Purāṇa
DPur	Devī Purāṇa
DhPad	Dhammapada
DhSaṅ	Dhammasaṅgaṇi
Dhav	Dhavalā (comm. on ṢaṭĀ) (Vīrasenācārya)
Dhū	Dhūrtaviṭasaṃvāda
DhvĀl	Dhvanyāloka
DhvĀlLoc	Dhvanyāloka-Locana (Abhinavagupta)
DīghNik	Dīgha Nikāya
DīĀ	Dīptāgama
Divyāv	Divyāvadāna
DSaṅg	Dravyasaṅgraha (Nemicandra)
DSaṅgVṛ	Dravyasaṅgraha Vṛtti (Brahma Deva)
DuSapta	Durgā Saptaśatī
Dūta	Dūtaghaṭotkaca
Dūt	Dūtavākya
EpInd	Epigraphica Indica
GāSa	Gāhā Sattasai (Gāthā Ṣaptaśatī)
Gaṇar	Gaṇaratnamahodadhi
GanT	Gandharva Tantra
GarbhUp	Garbhopaniṣad
GarPur	Garuḍa Purāṇa
GauDhSū	Gautama Dharma-Sūtra
GGṛhSū	Gobhila Gṛhya-Sūtra
GomJīv	Gommaṭasāra Jīvakāṇḍa (Nemicandra)
GoBr	Gopatha Brāhmaṇa
GuhyaT	Guhyasamāja Tantra (with Guhyasamāja-Pradīpa ... comm.)
HaiKo	Haima Kośa
HBVil	Haribhaktivilāsa
HarPur	Harivaṃśa Purāṇa
HaCa	Harṣacarita

HyPrad	Haṭhayoga Pradīpikā
HayaPāñc	Hayaśīrṣa Pāñcarātra
HT	Hevajra Tantra
Hit	Hitopadeśa
ĪśGP	Īśānaśivagurudeva Paddhati
ĪśUp	Īśa Upaniṣad
ĪPraKā	Īśvara Pratyabhijñā-Kārikā (Utpaladeva)
ĪPraVim	Īśvara Pratyabhijñā Vimarśinī (Abhinavagupta)
ĪPraVivVim	Īśvara Pratyabhijñā Vivṛti Vimarśinī
ĪśSam	Īśvara Saṃhitā
JaimBr	Jaiminīya Brāhmaṇa
JaimUpBr	Jaiminīya Upaniṣad Brāhmaṇa
Jā	Jātaka
Jāmā	Jātakamālā
JāUp	Jāvālopaniṣad
JaySam	Jayākhya Saṃhitā
JinSam	Jina Saṃhitā
JīvPradṬī	Jīvatattvapradīpikā Ṭīkā (on GomJīv)
Jñān	Jñānārṇava (Śubhacandra)
Kād	Kādambarī
KāCaT	Kālacakra Tantra
KāPur	Kālikā Purāṇa
KāmKVil	Kāma Kalā Vilāsa
KāNīSā	Kāmandakīya Nīti Sāra
KāmSū	Kāma-Sūtra
KāmĀ	Kāmikāgama
KāVṛ	Kāśikā Vṛtti
KāśSam	Kāśyapa Saṃhitā
KāśŚi	Kāśyapa Śilpa
KāVyā	Kātantra Vyākaraṇa
KāṭhSam	Kāṭhaka Saṃhitā
KaṭhUp	Kaṭha Upaniṣad
KātBhāSū	Kātyāyana Bhāṣika-Sūtra
KātŚrSū	Kātyāyana Śrauta-Sūtra
KātŚrSūBh	Kātyāyana Śrauta-Sūtra Bhāṣya (Karka Bhāṣya)
KātŚulSū	Kātyāyana Śulba-Sūtra
KauśSū	Kauśika-Sūtra
KauṣUp	Kauṣītaki Upaniṣad
Kāvyād	Kāvyādarśa
Kāvyāl	Kāvyālaṅkāra (Bhāmaha)
KāvyālSū	Kāvyālaṅkāra-Sūtra (Vāmana)
KāMīm	Kāvya-Mīmāṃsā

KāPrak	Kāvya Prakāśa
KeUp	Kena Upaniṣad
KhGṛhSū	Khādira Gṛhya-Sūtra
KhudNik	Khuddaka Nikāya
Kir	Kirātārjunīya
Kod	Kodaṇḍamaṇḍana
KulT	Kulārṇava Tantra
Kum	Kumārasambhava
KūrPur	Kūrma Purāṇa
Kuva	Kuvalayānanda
LYVās	Laghu Yoga-Vāsiṣṭha (Abhinanda)
LT	Lakṣmī Tantra
Lalitā	Lalitā-Sahasranāma (with Bhāṣya)
LVi	Lalitavistara
LaSū	Laṅkāvatāra-Sūtra
Līlā	Līlāvatī (Bhāskarācārya)
LPur	Liṅga Purāṇa
Lok	Lokavibhāga
MāDhā	Mādhavīyā Dhātuvṛtti
MVy	Madhyamavyāyoga
MāKā	Mādhyamaka-Kārikā
MBh	Mahābhārata
Mahābh	Mahābhāṣya
MNUp	Mahānārāyaṇa Upaniṣad
MNPrak	Mahānaya Prakāśa
MNT	Mahānirvāṇa Tantra
MPur	Mahā Purāṇa
MaMa	Mahārtha Mañjarī
MSSaṅg	Mahāsubhāṣita Saṅgraha (Ed. L. Sternbach)
MVas	Mahāvastu
MaCa	Mahāvīracarita
Mahāv	Mahāvyutpatti
MSūAl	Mahāyāna Sūtrālaṅkāra
MaViṃ	Mahāyānaviṃśaka
MahāUp	Mahopaniṣad
MaitSam	Maitrāyaṇī Saṃhitā
MaitUp	Maitrāyaṇī Upaniṣad (Maitrī Upaniṣad)
MajNik	Majjhima Nikāya
MālMā	Mālatīmādhava
Māla	Mālavikāgnimitra
MVT	Mālinīvijayottara Tantra
MāMey	Mānameyodaya

MāSā	Mānasāra
MānŚrSū	Mānava Śrauta-Sūtra
MānŚulSū	Mānava Śulba-Sūtra
MāṇḍKā	Māṇḍūkya-Kārikā
MāṇḍUp	Māṇḍūkya Upaniṣad
MMK	Mañjuśrīmūlakalpa
Manu	Manu Smṛti
MarSam	Marīci Saṃhitā (Vaikhānasa Āgama)
MārkPur	Mārkaṇḍeya Purāṇa
MPĀ	Mataṅgapārameśvara Āgama
MatPur	Matsya Purāṇa
Mayam	Mayamata
MedKo	Medinī Kośa
Megh	Meghadūta
MilPañ	Milinda Pañha
MīmNyPrak	Mīmāṃsānyāya Prakāśa (Āpodeva)
MīmSū	Mīmāṃsā-Sūtra (with Śābara Bhāṣya)
MKā	Mokṣa-Kārikā
Mṛcch	Mṛcchakaṭika
MṛgĀ	Mṛgendra Āgama
Mudrā	Mudrārākṣasa
MuktUp	Muktikopaniṣad
Mūl	Mūlācāra (Ācārya Vaṭṭakera)
MūMāKā	Mūla Mādhyamaka-Kārikā
MuṇḍUp	Muṇḍaka Upaniṣad
NādaKā	Nāda-Kārikā (Bhaṭṭa Rāmakaṇṭha)
Nāgā	Nāgānanda
NaiCa	Naiṣadhīyacarita
NāMa	Nānārtha Mañjarī
Ṇāsā	Ṇāṇasāra (Jñānasāra) (Padmasingh Munirāja)
NārBhSū	Nārada Bhakti-Sūtra
NārPur	Nārada Purāṇa
NārSam	Nārada Saṃhitā
NārŚik	Nāradīya Śikṣā
NārŚiŚ	Nārada Śilpa-Śāstra
NN	Nartana Nirṇaya
NLRKo	Nāṭakalakṣaṇaratna Kośa (Sāgaranandin)
NŚ	Nāṭya-Śāstra
Nay	Nayacakra (Mailladhavala)
NT	Netra Tantra
Nigh	Nighaṇṭu
Nir	Nirukta (Yāska)

NīŚa	Nītiśataka
NiṢo	Nityaṣoḍaśikārṇava
NiSā	Niyamasāra (Kundakundācārya)
NṛpūUp	Nṛsiṃhapūrvatāpanīyopaniṣad
NṛKo	Nṛtyaratna Kośa
NṛtRat	Nṛttaratnāvalī (Jayasenāpati)
NyDīp	Nyāyadīpikā (Dharma Bhūṣaṇa)
NyKu	Nyāyakusumāñjali
Nyā	Nyāyamañjarī
NySū	Nyāya-Sūtra
NySūBh	Nyāya-Sūtra Bhāṣya
Pādtāḍ	Pādatāḍitaka
PadMa	Padmānanda Mahākāvya
PPrā	Padma Prābhṛtaka
PPur	Padma Purāṇa
PSam	Pādma Saṃhitā (Pāñcarātra School)
Pañcad	Pañcadaśī
Pañ(P)	Pañcādhyāyī (Pūrvārdha) (Rājamalla)
Pañ(U)	Pañcādhyāyī (Uttarārdha) (Rājamalla)
Pañca	Pañcarātra
PkāSā	Pañcāstikāya Sāra (Kundakundācārya)
Pañc	Pañcatantra
Pā	Pāṇini Aṣṭādhyāyī
PāDhā	Pāṇinīya Dhātupāṭha
PāŚik	Pāṇinīya Śikṣā
PPraṬī	Parama Prakāśa Ṭīkā
ParSā	Paramārthasāra
PPra	Paramātma Prakāśa (Yogīndu Deva)
ParSam	Parameśvara Saṃhitā
PāSū	Pārānanda-Sūtra
PārāŚik	Pārāśara Śikṣā
PārGṛhSū	Pāraskara Gṛhya-Sūtra
PTrī	Parātrīśikā (Tantra)
Paribh	Paribhāṣenduśekhara
PāśuSū	Pāśupata-Sūtra
PauṣSam	Pauṣkara Saṃhitā
PSā	Pavayaṇasāra (Pravacanasāra) (Kundakundācārya)
PiṅgUp	Piṅgalopaniṣad
PraCan	Prabodhacandrodaya
PraPañ	Prakaraṇapañcikā
PraṁMīm	Pramāṇamīmāṃsā (Hemacandrācārya)
PraRat	Prameya Ratnāvalī (Baladeva Vidyābhūṣaṇa)

PSāT	Prapañcasāra Tantra
PP	Prasannapadā
PrSam	Praśna Saṃhitā
PraUp	Praśna Upaniṣad
PrR	Prasthāna-Ratnākara
PraYau	Pratijñā Yaugandharāyaṇa
PraNāṭ	Pratimā Nāṭaka
PLSSamu	Pratiṣṭhālakṣaṇa-sāra-samuccaya
Prati	Pratiṣṭhātilaka (Nemicandra)
PrH	Pratyabhijñā-Hṛdaya
PravBh	Pravacana Bhāṣya (on SāṃSū) (Vijñānabhikṣu)
PraBr	Pravargya Brāhmaṇa
Pri	Priyadarśikā
Pug	Puggalapaññatti
Rāga	Rāgavibodha (Somanātha)
Ragh	Raghuvaṃśa
RājTar	Rājataraṅgiṇī
RāVā	Rājavārtika (Bhaṭṭa Akạlaṅkadeva)
RāmPUp	Rāmapūrvottaratāpinī Upaniṣad
Rām	Rāmāyaṇa
RāmCam	Rāmāyaṇa Campū
RāmUttUp	Rāmottaratāpinī Upaniṣad
RasGa	Rasagaṅgādhara (Jagannātha)
RP	Ratna Parīkṣā (Īśvara Dīkṣit)
RaPa	Ratnatraya-Parīkṣā
Rat	Ratnāvalī
RauĀ	Raurava Āgama
RauUtĀ	Rauravattara Āgama
Rāya	Rāyapasenīya-Sutta
ṚV	Ṛgveda
ṚVPrāt	Ṛgveda Prātiśākhya
Ṛtu	Ṛtusaṃhāra
Rūp	Rūpamaṇḍana (Maṇḍana)
ŚaKal	Śabdakalpadruma
ŚaRa	Śabdaratnāvalī
SaddhPuSū	Saddharma Puṇḍarīka-Sūtra
ṢaḍBr	Ṣaḍviṃśa Brāhmaṇa
SāDar	Sāhitya-Darpaṇa
ŚĀPM	Śaivāgama Paribhāṣāmañjarī
ŚPar	Śaiva Paribhāṣā
Sakala	Sakalādhikāra (Agastya)
SamāRājSū	Samādhirāja-Sūtra

SamSūt	Samarāṅgaṇa-Sūtradhāra (Bhoja)
SV	Sāmaveda
SViBr	Sāmavidhāna Brāhmaṇa
ŚāmPañcā	Śāmba Pañcāśikā
SāṃKā	Sāṃkhya-Kārikā
SāṃSū	Sāṃkhya-Sūtra
Samū	Samūrtārcanādhikaraṇa
SaṃNik	Saṃyutta Nikāya
SanSam	Sanatkumāra Saṃhitā
SDām	Saṅgīta-Dāmodara
SDar	Saṅgīta-Darpaṇa
SMak	Saṅgīta-Makaranda
SRāj	Saṅgītarāja
SR	Saṅgīta-Ratnākara (Śārṅgadeva)
SUpSā	Saṅgītopaniṣat-sāroddhāra
SaṅkSūr	Saṅkalpasūryodaya (Veṅkaṭanātha)
ŚāṅkhĀr	Śāṅkhāyana Āraṇyaka
ŚāṅkhBr	Śāṅkhāyana Brāhmaṇa
ŚāṅkhŚrSū	Śāṅkhāyana Śrauta-Sūtra
ŚāTil	Śāradā-Tilaka
Sark	Sarasvatīkaṇṭhābharaṇa (Alaṅkāra-Śāstra)
SākāT	Sārdhatriśatīkālottara Tantra
SarDSaṅg	Sarvadarśana-Saṅgraha
Sar	Sarvānukramaṇī
SaSi	Sarvārthasiddhi (on TaSū) (Ācārya Pūjyapāda Devanandī)
ŚBr	Śatapatha Brāhmaṇa
ṢaṭĀ	Ṣaṭkhaṇḍāgama (Puṣpadanta & Bhūtabali)
ṢaṭSan	Ṣaṭsandarbha (Śivagosvāmin)
SātSam	Sātvata Saṃhitā
Saun	Saundarananda
SLah	Saundaryalaharī
SeṬī	Sekoddeśaṭīkā
SiKau	Siddhānta Kaumudī
SiddhSaṅg	Siddhāntaleśa-Saṅgraha
SiddhŚir	Siddhānta-Śiromaṇi
ŚikSamu	Śikṣāsamuccaya
ŚiL	Śilpalakṣaṇa
ŚiPrak	Śilpa Prakāśa (Rāmacandra Kaulācāra)
ŚiRa	Śilparatna
ŚiRaKo	Śilparatnakośa (Sthāpaka Nirañjana Mahāpātra)
Śiśu	Śiśupālavadha
ŚDṛ	Śiva Dṛṣṭi

ŚMSt	Śivamahimnastotra
ŚPur	Śiva Purāṇa
ŚSam	Śiva Saṃhitā
ŚSto	Śiva Stotrāvalī
ŚSū	Śiva-Sūtra
ŚSūVā	Śiva-Sūtra Vārttika (Varadācārya)
ŚSūVim	Śiva-Sūtra Vimarśinī (Kṣemarāja)
SkaPur	Skanda Purāṇa
ŚlVā	Ślokavārttika
SP	Somaśambhu Paddhati
SpKā	Spanda-Kārikā
SpNir	Spanda Nirṇaya
ŚrīBh	Śrī Bhāṣya (on Brahma-Sūtra)
ŚHMu	Śrīhasta Muktāvalī
ŚrīkBh	Śrīkaṇṭha Bhāṣya (on Brahma-Sūtra)
ŚrīSam	Śrīpraśna Saṃhitā
ŚTaCi	Śrītattvacintāmaṇi
ŚṛPrak	Śṛṅgāra Prakāśa
ŚNSā	Śukranītisāra
SupĀ	Suprabheda Āgama
SūrSiddh	Sūrya-Siddhānta
SuSam	Suśruta Saṃhitā
SutNip	Sutta Nipāta
SuSū	Suvarṇaprabhāsa-Sūtra
SvT	Svacchanda Tantra
Svap	Svapnavāsavadatta
ŚvUp	Śvetāśvatara Upaniṣad
Syād	Syādvādamañjarī
TĀr	Taittirīya Āraṇyaka
TBr	Taittirīya Brāhmaṇa
TSam	Taittirīya Saṃhitā
TUp	Taittirīya Upaniṣad
TāṇḍMBr	Tāṇḍya Mahābrāhmaṇa (Pañcaviṃśa Brāhmaṇa)
TĀl	Tantrāloka (Abhinavagupta)
TSāSaṅg	Tantrasāra Saṅgraha
TVā	Tantra Vārttika
TSamu	Tantrasamuccaya
TSā	Tantrasāra (Abhinavagupta)
TaBhā	Tarka Bhāṣā
TarkSaṅg	Tarka-Saṅgraha
TaKau	Tattva Kaumudī
TaPrak	Tattva Prakāśa

TaSū	Tattvārthādhigama-Sūtra (Tattvārtha-Sūtra)
TaSā	Tattvārthasāra (Amṛtacandra)
TaVā	Tattvārtha Vārttika
TaSaSū	Tattvasamāsa-Sūtra
TaSaṅg	Tattva-Saṅgraha
TaVai	Tattva Vaiśāradī
Til	Tilakamañjarī
TiPa	Tiloya Paṇṇattī (Vṛṣabhācārya)
Trik	Trikāṇḍaśeṣa
TRa	Tripurārahasya
UbhSā	Ubhayābhisārikā
UjNīl	Ujjvalanīlamaṇi
UṇSū	Uṇādi-Sūtra
Urbh	Urubhaṅga
USū	Uttarādhyayana-Sūtra
UttCa	Uttararāmacarita
VaiKo	Vaijayantī Kośa
VaiĀ	Vaikhānasa Āgama
VaiGṛhSū	Vaikhānasa Gṛhya-Sūtra
VaiŚa	Vairāgyaśataka
VaiśSū	Vaiśeṣika-Sūtra
VaiśSūBh	Vaiśeṣika-Sūtra Bhāṣya
VaitSū	Vaitāna-Sūtra
VaJī	Vakroktijīvita
Vāk	Vākyapadīya
VāPur	Vāmana Purāṇa
VŚrSū	Vārāha Śrauta-Sūtra
VaCa	Varāṅga Carita
VŚ	Vāstu-Śāstra (Viśvakarman)
VSUp	Vāstusūtra Upaniṣad
VVid	Vāstuvidyā (Viśvakarman)
Vasu	Vasudevahiṇḍī
VPur	Vāyu Purāṇa
VedPar	Vedānta-Paribhāṣā
VedSā	Vedānta-Sāra
Veṇī	Veṇī Saṃhāra
Vibh	Vibhaṅga Pāli
ViBhai	Vijñāna Bhairava
Vik	Vikramorvaśīya
VinPiṭ	Vinaya Piṭaka
Vīrmi	Vīramitrodaya
VirPañcā	Virūpākṣa Pañcāśikā

VDhPur	Viṣṇudharmottara Purāṇa
ViPur	Viṣṇu Purāṇa
ViSahasrBh	Viṣṇu-Sahasranāma Bhāṣya
ViSam	Viṣṇu Saṃhitā
ViSm	Viṣṇu Smṛti
ViMag	Visuddhimagga
ViśKo	Viśva Kośa
VSam	Viṣvaksena Saṃhitā
ViśSam	Viśvāmitra Saṃhitā
ViKo	Viśvaprakāśa Kośa
VivR	Vivādaratnākara
ViPSaṅg	Vivaraṇaprameya Saṅgraha
Vicū	Vivekacūḍāmaṇi
VyVive	Vyaktiviveka (Mahimabhaṭṭa)
YājŚik	Yājñavalkya Śikṣā
YājSm	Yājñavalkya Smṛti
YV	Yajurveda (Vājasaneyi Saṃhitā)
YSū	Yoga-Sūtra
YSūBh	Yoga-Sūtra Bhāṣya (Vyāsa)
YVās	Yoga-Vāsiṣṭha
YYāj	Yogi Yājñavalkya
YoH	Yoginī-Hṛdaya
YuDīp	Yuktidīpikā (on Sāṃkhya-Kārikā)

LIST OF TERMS

aṃśa
agni (agni-soma) (Vol. III)
aṅga-aṅgin
adhikaraṇa/ādhāra
adhikāra
adhibhūta-adhidaiva-adhyātma (Vol. IV)
adhiṣṭhāna
anukīrtana/anukṛti/anukaraṇa (Vol. VI)
antaḥkaraṇa (Vol. XIII)
ap/udaka/jala (Vol. III)
abhinaya (Vol. X)
abhiprāya (Vol. IX)
amṛta
arcā (Vol. V)
artha-vācya-lakṣya-vyaṅgya (Vol. XII)
alaṅkāra (Vol. IX)
avatāra
avadhāna (Vol. XIV)
avasthā
avyakta-vyakta-vyaktāvyakta (Vol. VI)
asura
ahaṃkāra (Vol. XIII)
ākāra/ākṛti (Vol. V)
ākāśa (kha, vyoman) (Vol. III)
ākhyāna (Vol. XII)
āgama-nigama
ātman (Vol. I)
ānanda (Vol. XIII)
ābhāsa (Vol. VI)
āyudha/āyudha-puruṣa (Vol. IX)
ālambana/āśraya
āsana (Vol. X)
indriya (Vol. IV)
īśvara
ugra-saumya
ucita/aucitya
utsava (Vol. XV)
uddhata-sukumāra
upacāra (Vol. XV)
upamā
upāya
ṛta-anṛta
ojas
karaṇa-aṅgahāra (Vol. X)
karaṇa/kāraṇa
karuṇā
karman
kalaśa (kumbha, ghaṭa) (Vol. VIII)
kalā (Vol. IX)
kalā-pramāṇa (Vol. IX)
kalpanā
kavi
kāma (Vol. XIII)
kāla (Vol. II)
kāvya (Vol. XII)
kīrtimukha/grāsa (Vol. VIII)
kuṇḍa (Vol. VII)
kuśala/kauśala
koṇa/aśra/vṛtta (Vol. VII)
krama (Vol. II)
kriyā/kṛti
kṣaṇa (Vol. II)
kṣetra (Vol. II)
gandharva-apsaras-yakṣa
garbha/garbha-gṛha (Vol. VII)
gavākṣa (Vol. VIII)
guṇa-doṣa (Vol. IV)
guru/guru-laghu
cakra-paridhi (Vol. II)
catura/cāturya
camatkāra/camatkṛti
cāru/cārutā

cit/caitanya (Vol. XIII)
citi/caitya/stūpa (Vol. VII)
citta (Vol. XIII)
citra (Vol. IX)
citrakara (Vol. IX)
chandas-mātrā (Vol. XII)
chāyā (Vol. VI)
jāti-vyakti
jīva
jñāna-vijñāna (Vol. XIV)
jyotis/tejas/prakāśa (Vol. III)
tattva (Vol. XIV)
tantra
tanmātra
tāla (Vol. II)
triratna (Vol. VIII)
tīrtha (Vol. VII)
darśana (Vol. XIV)
dik/dikpāla
dīkṣā (Vol. XV)
dṛṣṭa-adṛṣṭa (phala) (Vol. XV)
deva/devatā
deśa (Vol. II)
dravya (Vol. IV)
dharma-dharmin
dhātu (Vol. IV)
dhyāna (Vol. XIII)
dhvaja (Vol. VIII)
dhvani (Vol. XII)
nāṭya
nāḍī
nāda (Vol. XII)
nābhi (Vol. II)
nāma(-rūpa) (Vol. XIV)
nāyaka-nāyikā (Vol. XI)
nṛtta/nṛtya
nyāsa (Vol. XV)
paṅkti/avali/mālā (Vol. IX)
patra-racanā (Vol. IX)
pada (Vol. XII)
padma/kamala (Vol. VIII)
pariṇāma
pāda (Vol. VI)
pāpa-puṇya
pīṭha (Vol. VII)
puruṣa (Vol. I)
puruṣārtha
pūjā/upāsanā/saparyā (Vol. XV)
pūrṇa (Vol. II)
pṛthivī/bhūmi/bhūmikā (Vol. III)
prakṛti (Vol. III)
praṇava
pratibhā (Vol. XI)
pratimā-pratikṛti (Vol. V)
pratīka (Vol. VIII)
pratīti/anumiti (Vol. XIII)
pramāṇa
prayoga
pravṛtti-nivṛtti
prasāda
prastāra (Vol. VII)
prāṇa (Vol. I)
prāsāda (Vol. V)
preman/prīti
bandha-prabandha (Vol. V)
bahumukha/bahubhuja (Vol. IX)
bindu (Vol. II)
bimba-pratibimba (Vol. VI)
bīja (Vol. I)
buddhi/dhī/prajñā (Vol. XIII)
brahman (Vol. I)
bhakti (Vol. XIII)
bhagavān
bhāva-vibhāva/anubhāva (Vol. XI)
bhāvanā
bhūta-mahābhūta (Vol. III)
bhoga
makara/mīna (Vol. VIII)
maṅgala (Vol. VIII)
maṇḍapa (Vol. VII)
madhura/mādhurya
manas/mānasika (Vol. XIII)
mantra (Vol. XII)
marman

mãna (Vol. II)
mānuṣa
māyā
mārga-mārgin /deśi (Vol. X)
mithuna (Vol. VIII)
mudrā (Vol. X)
mūrti (Vol. V)
mokṣa
yajña (Vol. XV)
yantra/maṇḍala (Vol. VII)
yūpa (Vol. VII)
yoga (Vol. XIII)
yoni (Vol. VII)
raṅga
racanā/ālekhana (Vol. IX)
ratha (Vol. VII)
ram-/ramaṇīya
rasa (Vol. XI)
rāga-anurāga-rāgiṇī (Vol. XI)
ruci
rūpa-pratirūpa (Vol. V)
rekhā (Vol. V)
lakṣaṇa (Vol. I)
latā (Vol. VIII)
laya (Vol. II)
lalita/lālitya
liṅga/cihna/lāñchana (Vol. VI)
līlā/krīḍā (Vol. X)
loka/triloka (Vol. II)
laukika-alaukika
varṇa/mātṛkā/mālinī (Vol. XII)
vastu (Vol. XII)
vākya (Vol. XII)
vāc/vācika (Vol. XII)
vāda-vādin
vādya (ātodya) (Vol. X)
vāyu (Vol. III)
vāsanā/tṛṣṇā (Vol. XIII)
vāstu
vigraha (Vol. V)
vidyā (Vol. XIV)
vidhi/vidhāna
viniyoga (Vol. XV)
vimarśa
viśrānti (virāma)
viśva-viśvarūpa
viṣaya (Vol. XIV)
vṛkṣa (Vol. VIII)
vṛtti-rīti-pravṛtti (Vol. VI)
vedī/vedikā/sthaṇḍila (Vol. VII)
vyakti/abhivyakti
vyāla/īhāmṛga (Vol. VIII)
vrata (Vol. XV)
śakti
śaṅkha (Vol. VIII)
śabda (Vol. XII)
śarīra/kāya (Vol. I)
śānti/śānta (Vol. XIII)
śālabhañjikā (Vol. VIII)
śāstra (Vol. XIV)
śilpa/śilpin (Vol. I)
śuci-aśuci
śuddha-vikṛta-miśra
śubha-aśubha
śūnya/śūnyatā (Vol. II)
śobhā
śraddhā (Vol. XIII)
śrī
śrīvatsa (Vol. VIII)
śruti/veda
saṃskāra/saṃskṛti (Vol. XV)
saṃsthāna/sanniveśa (Vol. VII)
sakala-niṣkala (Vol. V)
saṅketa (Vol. X)
saṅgīta/gāna/gīta (Vol. X)
sat-asat/sattā (Vol. XIII)
sattva/sāttvika
satya
sandhi (Vol. II)
sama-viṣama/samatā (Vol. XIV)
samādhi (Vol. XIII)
sahṛdaya/rasika/bhāvaka (Vol. XI)
sādṛśya-sārūpya (Vol. VI)
sādhanā/tapas (Vol. XV)

sādhāraṇīkaraṇa (Vol. XI)
sāhitya (Vol. XII)
siddhi-vibhūti (Vol. XV)
sukha-duḥkha (Vol. XIII)
sundara/saundarya (Vol. XI)
sūtra/sūtradhāra (Vol. II)
sṛṣṭi-sthiti-saṃhāra (Vol. IV)
skandha
skambha/stambha (Vol. VII)
sthāna/āyatana (Vol. VII)
sthāpatya/sthapati
sthūla-sūkṣma-para (Vol. IV)
spanda
sphoṭa(Vol. XII)
svatantra/svātantrya
svar/svarga
svara-vyañjana (Vol. XII)
svarūpa/svabhāva (Vol. XIV)
svastika/nandyāvarta (Vol. VIII)
haṃsa (Vol. VIII)
hasta (Vol. X)
hṛdaya (Vol. XIII)

BINDU

Overview

Bindu, literally meaning a drop, or a point, *drapsa* in Vedic Sanskrit, and *avayava*, body according to Pāṇini, pre-eminently refers to the point which goes to form a material body of the universe, hence it also connotes the virile semen. In the beginning *bindu* describes a circle or a triangle which is thought to be the symbol of the universe and at the same time it represents the Supreme Reality. Therefore *bindu* is not only the source, the base, the abode of rest, but also pure illumination as well as vibratory sound, ever expressing itself in forms of concepts (*pratyaya*) and objects (*bhūta*), while it remains in its pristine glory of condensed or unconditional consciousness (*bhānapiṇḍa*). It means also the bright spark. *Bindu* also means zero and the symbol for zero →*śūnya*.

Though a point, *bindu* actually consists of a unity of two, the one static and the other dynamic. It is the dynamic aspect that expresses itself as the universe of multiplicity, but the base remains one – the epitome of all (*sarvātmakam*). Due to agitation in *bindu*, the one becomes dual and after becoming dual it becomes plural. Symbolically *bindu* is represented as the central point of a circle or triangle, and its corners, the meeting points of each side, are constituted of two pairs of *bindus*.

According to Vaiśeṣika the atom (*aṇu*) does not share directly in the composition of matter, but it is from a triad (*trasareṇu*), consisting of pairs or dyads (*dvyaṇuka*) that a material body comes into being. Hence the figure of the triangle (*vaindavaṃ cakram*) which is born of *bindu* is highly significant for spiritual aspirants.

The *bindu* as the creative droplet is related to *soma*, the nectar of life, the seed of creation (*sṛṣṭibīja*) – the essence of the entire creation. The *bindu* in its limited aspects is further viewed as three distinct visible lights: the moon, the sun and fire. Still it is said to shine as pure knowing subject, bestowing light to everything (*jyotiruttamam*).

Etymology and Cognate Words

The term *bindu*, dot, point, spot, drop, semen, can be derived from the verbal root *bid- (bidi avayave)*, meaning 'to cleave, to split', (cf. PāDhā I.65). According to Yāska it is derived from the verbal root *bhid-*, 'to pierce', hence 'hole', the initial part being altered from *bh* to *b* following the rule *ādiviparyaya*.

In Pāṇini's **Aṣṭādhyāyī** *bindu* is used as *anusvāra* (cf. *mo'nusvāraḥ*, Pā 8.3.23), being the nasal sound which in Devanāgarī script is marked by a dot above the syllable. The *anusvāra* is called *bindu* in **Harināmāmṛta-Vyākaraṇa** (on I.14). In Sanskrit, dots are used in *anusvāra* and *visarjanīya* specially, and *upadhmānīya, jihvāmūlīya* and the *yamas* secondarily, though they are not found in the Māheśvara-Sūtras as quoted by Pāṇini. The sound element of *bindu* as *anusvāra* is clear as nasalization.

Synonyms and cognate terms of *bindu* are: *drapsa, pṛṣat, vipruṣ* (all meaning drop, cf. AmKo); *śūnya, kha, vyoman* (all meaning empty space); *indu, soma* (bright drop and the moon); *retas* (in the sense of semen). Śrīkaṇṭhasūri mentions the following synonyms:

> शब्दतत्त्वमघोषा वाग्ब्रह्म कुण्डलिनी ध्रुवम् ॥
> विद्या शक्तिः परा नादो महामायेति देशिकैः ।
> बिन्दुरेवं समाख्यातो व्योमानाहतमित्यपि ॥
>
> RaTParī 70-71
>
> *Bindu* is variously described by teachers as the essence of speech (*śabdatattva*), unsound word, *Brahman*, *kuṇḍalinī*, the stable, knowledge, energy, the transcendent one, the primal sound, the great *māyā*, the void and unstruck sound.

According to modern geometry the point is the minutest unit with which a line is drawn. The point is indivisible and is without length and breadth. When we think of *bindu* as minutest unity we are reminded of the Vaiśeṣika's concept of *paramāṇu* as defined thus: *mūrtatve sati niravayavaḥ*. Being limited, *paramāṇu* is without any component part. In the same way, though the point lacks a concrete body, somehow or other it becomes the component unit of a physical body either as a mass or a combination of three *aṇus*.

In **Yogabhāṣya** of Vyāsa (III.52) we find that a substance when reduced to its minutest unit is called *paramāṇu*, and in the same way the minutest time unit is → *kṣaṇa*. *Bindu* apparently is neither a time unit like *kṣaṇa* nor a space unit like *aṇu*. It is a unit of consciousness, and at the same time becomes the body of the material world. Therefore, it is a synthesis of matter, space and time, shining as the very life of them but transcending them as the spirit.

Bindu is also derived from the verbal root *ind-*, meaning 'to be powerful' (Goldstucker), perhaps *vund-*, 'to drop'? In later language it is frequently written as *vindu*, a detached particle, drop, globule, dot, spot, a pearl (AV XIX.30.5), a symbol representing the *anusvāra*, a coloured mark made on the forehead between the eyebrows. In drama, it is the sudden development of a secondary incident which like a drop of water expands and furnishes an important element.

Some compounds formed with the prefix *bindu* are as follows: *Binducitraka*, a spotted deer; *bindujālam*, spots seen on an elephant's trunk; *bindupatra*, a spotted birch leaf; *bindutantra*, dice; *bindurekhaka*, a line of points, a kind of bird;

bindusara, a lake borṇ of the semen of Śiva; *bindumādhava*, a name of Viṣṇu; in names of Upaniṣads, e.g. *Dhyānabindu*, *Nādabindu*, *Amṛtabindu*, *Tejobindu*, *bindu* connotes the shining mystic spark.

Layers of Meaning

Bindu or *drapsa* literally means a drop, meaning a small quantity of a liquid such as *soma*, rain, semen. It also means *indu*, a bright drop, a spark. In another sense it means *avayava*, a limb, member, part, portion, the component of a whole. In yet another sense *bindu* is the knowing subject. But it pre-eminently signifies the point which goes to form a body describing itself as → *nābhi*, the navel or the hub in the centre of a triangle or circle. From the *bindu*, the starting point, a triangle or a circle makes its appearance. For this reason the point or *bindu* is considered to be the primary source of everything whether it is a physical form or a concept. According to some it consists of the unity of two *bindus*, that is, the unity of two opposing energies - the one static and the other dynamic, the one representing the male principle and the other the female.

The universe seen analytically consists of knowable objects, the instrument of knowledge and knowledge itself. When these three elements are shorn off, what remains is nothing but condensed or unconditioned consciousness (*bhānapiṇḍa*). As consciousness cannot possibly be thought of as devoid of self-awareness, self-reflection of consciousness is considered to be the very life of everything, and for this reason it is called *bindu*, the autonomous agent of the activity of knowing. It is the very life of all things in whatever way they may be classified under any doctrinal scheme.

Bindu does not only constitute the thought-element but also serves as the material of all the elements of matter and speech, that is, everything is made of *bindu* whether it is the physical body or a metaphysical principle. Hence *bindu* is the meeting point of spirit and matter.

The phenomenal aspect of the universe is perceived as multiple but essentially this multiplicity has a source which is nothing but a single body, known as *mahā-bindu*, the coalesced unity of two pulsating *bindus*. This unity is single but in its creative upsurge it divides itself into two, and after becoming dual it gives rise to the universe of multiplicity. This descending order (single → dual →multiple) is called *anuloma-krama*. The reverse order (*pratiloma-krama*: multiple →dual →single) also holds true.

The Vaiśeṣika thinkers explain that the atom (*paramāṇu*) is the component entity of the *dvyaṇukas* and the body of the *trasareṇu*, the constituents of which are three atoms (*aṇus*). The point (*bindu)*, an atom (*aṇu)*, the constitutive element of the physical body, is the source from which any tangible or concrete body emerges. For example, a line is nothing but a radiation of a single point expressing itself in points moving constantly towards a particular direction. Tāntric thinkers explain that the universe has its source in *bindu*. The expanding *bindu* itself, either in the form of a triangle or a circle, manifests itself as the universe. For instance, if we take a triangle we see that it has three sides each of which has a pair of *bindus* in each corner while *mahābindu* remains in the centre.

The human body itself consists of powerful centres of consciousness. Generally they are known as →*cakras* (wheels). Being wheels they have an inmost centre known as *bindu*. These pulsating points are both centrifugal and centripetal – one leaving the circumference for the centre and the other leaving the centre towards the exterior.

The emergence of *bindu* has been interpreted from various view points. The Śaiva Siddhānta thinkers upheld the view that *bindu* is the outcome of *nāda* which again is the resultant of *śakti*: *śakternādo'bhavat binduḥ*. When the *anāhata* sound becomes condensed in the inner recess of the mind as inner cogitation (*antaḥsaṃkalpa*), it gradually becomes well-shaped like a round ball of speech (*sampiṇḍitavāgrūpaḥ*). It is named **bindu** because it is nothing but a drop (*binduriva binduḥ,* MṛgĀkp I.2.).

While describing Śiva as pervading the entire universe in six different forms, Abhinavagupta equates *jyotis* with *bindu*, a bright spark which reminds us of the *indu* of the Veda. He defines *bindu* as the sparkling pupil of the eye, round in shape like a *kadamba* flower (TĀl I.63).

Bindu in Śaiva Siddhānta doctrine has been stated to have two aspects: one is *parabindu*, the supreme, in which the subtle materials called *kalās* (*nivṛtti* and others) remain merged, while it functions in the pure region to serve as the material of worlds. It is also said that *parabindu* gives rise to the body of *Ananta* who in his turn agitates *māyā* to become the material of the impure world.

Bindu is also stated to be the material of speech which partakes of both its aspects, *parabindu* and *aparabindu*. In its *apara* aspect of speech *bindu* creates in the limited self determinate concepts by means of intermixing different modes (*svavṛttibheda saṃbhedaiḥ*). It also becomes the material of impure worlds.

Perfect knowledge regarding the reality can only be born of *bindu* in the form of scriptures. *Bindu* characterized by four *kalās* is said to be the womb (*garbha*) of the four-formed bonds of *prakṛti* consisting of *prakṛti, guṇa, mahat* and *ahaṃkāra* (MṛgĀkp I.13.196cd).

According to Kashmir Śaiva doctrine *bindu* though single, assumes the character of *visarga* and thus pervades the entirety of the universe by 'over-stepping' all (*bindunā kramitāḥ sarve*), for it is the autonomous agent of the activity of knowing. It should be meditated upon in the core of the lotus of the heart (*hṛtpadmamaṇḍalāntaḥsthaḥ*) with the characteristic of *nara*, the object, *śakti*, the power and *Śiva*, the absolute, in accordance with the distinctions of rest (*laya*). It is pure and the agent of release (*vimalatāraka*).

Bindu shines always as an undivided light (*avibhāgaprakāśa*). Even though it assumes or imposes over itself the impurities of knowability (*jñeya kāluṣya*), it always remains *bindu*, the knowing light.

The real nature of *bindu* is that of *parāmarśanīya*, the object denoted by speech, which in the above connotation assumes the body of the universe.

Yoginīhṛdaya I-10 states that *bindu* is the coalesced unity of *Śiva-Śakti* and it is called *kāma*, the sun, from which the flow is set in motion. This flow is of the character of fire and moon, that is, two *bindus*, one white and the other red. These two *bindus* when united become the coalesced unity of the sounds *a* and *ḥ*, that is *aham* from which *citkalā*, minute consciousness, emerges.

In the **Nāṭya-Śāstra** *bindu* is defined as a thread of continuity running through subsidiary episodes like a drop of oil on water.

Development of the Concept

In the Veda *bindu* is related to *indu*, the drop, spark, and also the moon. The Vedic synonym for *bindu* is *drapsa*. It also figuratively means *śukra*, semen, according to the **Nirukta** (V.14). The term has the sense of water or clarified butter which flows fast (*drutagamanaśīlaḥ*) and which can readily be offered into the sacred fire (*drutahavanaśīlaḥ*). In the **Ṛgveda** the word *drapsa* has been used in the meaning of a drop, mostly of the *soma* juice:

पवमानः संतनिः प्रघ्नतामिव मधुमान् द्रप्सः परि वारमर्षति ।

ṚV IX.69.2

And *pavamāna*, like the shout of combatants, the drop rich in sweet juice, is flowing through the fleece. (Tr. R.T.H. Griffith)

Drapsa or *indu* meaning the moon is well-known:

अव सिन्धुं वरुणो द्यौरिव स्याद् द्रप्सो न श्वेतो मृगस्तुविष्मान् ।

ṚV VII.87.6ab

Like Varuṇa from heaven he sinks in Sindhu, like a white shining spark, a strong wild creature. (Tr. R.T.H. Griffith)

In the **Atharva-Veda** the word *bindu* occurs meaning drops of water. It is described as all-refreshing and golden.

यत् समुद्रो अभ्यक्रन्दत् पर्जन्यो विद्युता सह ।
ततो हिरण्ययो बिन्दुस्ततो दर्भो अजायत ॥ AV XIX.30.5

What time cloud (*parjanya*) roared to it with lightning flashes in the atmosphere.
Thence came the drop, the golden drop, thence grass into being sprang. (Tr. R.T.H. Griffith)

The mystic element of *bindu* as the moon that has its location on the summit of the head, which in the later Tāntric and Buddhist traditions has been given much importance, may be hinted at in the following **Atharva-Veda** verse:

ऊर्ध्वो बिन्दुरुदचरद् ब्रह्मणः ककुदादधि ।
ततस्त्वं जज्ञिषे वशे ततो होता अजायत ॥

AV X.10.19

From Brahma's summit there went forth a drop that mounted up on high.
From that wast thou produced, O Cow, from that the Hotā sprang to life. (Tr. R.T.H. Griffith)

In support of the above view it may be stated that *bindu* as the absolute is the moon which melts in the summit of the head and flows through the body and finally pervades the whole body with bliss. The image of *bindu* as the moon is very significant, for some scholars are of the opinion that *bindu* has its origin in *indu*, the moon.

Ātman, the self or more precisely self-consciousness, is the essence of existence, the nectar (*amṛta*). It shines like a drop of water on a lotus leaf.

अथामृतोऽस्यात्मा बिन्दुरिव पुष्करा इति ।

MaitUp III.2

Now, the immortal soul (*ātman*) is like the drop of water on the lotus leaf. (Tr. R.E. Hume)

The above quote uses *bindu* in the sense of the drop of water. The term *puṣkara* reminds us of the Upaniṣadic concept in which it means *ākāśa*, the void, where *agni*, fire, or *āditya*, the sun, resides like a drop (cf. *idaṃ vāva tat puṣkaraṃ yo'yamākāśaḥ*, MaitUp VI.2).

Bindu signifying a drop of water was a common concept in earlier texts. In the **Nirukta** the term is derived from *bhid-*.

अथाप्यादिविपर्ययो भवति ... बिन्दुः ।

Nir II.1

Further, there is alteration in the initial part (of the root) as in *binduḥ* (*bhid* 'a drop'). (Tr. L. Sarup)

In Āyurveda *bindu* can mean drops of medicine, or spots on the body. While prescribing doses of liquid medicine to be taken through the nostrils Suśruta uses the term *bindu* to mean drops.

तस्य प्रमाणमष्टौ बिन्दवः प्रदेशिनीपर्वद्वयनिःसृता प्रथमा मात्रा ।

SuSam Cikitsāsthāna XL.28

Doses of an oily nasal drop (*sneha-nasya*) eight drops of oil trickling down the two upper phalanges of the forefingers should be regarded as the proper quantity for the smallest (lit. first) dose. (Tr. K.L. Bhisagratna)

The commentator, Ḍalhaṇa, defines *bindu* as "that which falls down from two nodes of the index finger."

Bindu meaning spots of various colours is mentioned in secular texts like Caraka and various other Śilpa texts.

आमाशयं प्रविष्टे वैवर्ण्यं स्वेदसदनमुत्क्लेदः ।
दृष्टिहृदयोपरोधो बिन्दुशतैश्चीयते चाङ्गम् ॥

CarSam Cikitsāsthāna XXIII.114

When the poison enters into the stomach, the symptoms are: abnormality of complexion, excessive sweating, lassitude, lack of proper functioning of the eye and the heart and appearance of hundreds of spots on the body.

In the **Mahābhārata** the meaning of water seems to become more common than other connotations.

अश्रुबिन्दूद्भवा तस्याः प्रावर्तत महानदी ।
अनुवर्तती सृतिं तस्या भृगोः पत्न्या यशस्विनः ॥

MBh.I.6.6

The drops of tears which fell from her eyes were formed into a great river. And that river began to follow the foot-steps of the wife of the great ascetic Bhṛgu. (Tr. P.C. Roy)

Bindu is essentially multi-dimensional. In the philosophy of language it not only signifies a drop which becomes the material of a flowing river, but it shines as Supreme Speech or *śabdabrahman* which appears to the seer as *maṇḍalam* ('round' implying perfection). The reason is that all the *śakti*s remain merged in the highest *vāc* (*sarvaśaktīnāṃ tatra samāveśānmaṇḍalam*).

यदेतन्मण्डलं भास्वत् धामचित्रस्य राधसः । Vṛṣabha's Paddhati on Vāk I.112

> The luminous globe that shines, is the wonderful and blissful abode that belongs to the liberated souls *(muktātmanām parama ānandaḥ)*.

In the above quote the specific character of *bindu* as the knowing subject has been hinted at. As the term has been derived from the verbal root *vid-*, to know, it is quite logical to equate *bindu* with *vāc*. Therefore Bhartṛhari stresses the point by saying that knowledge in its pure essence is speech (*avabodhasya vāgrūpatā*, Vāk I.116).

Bindu shines in a dual aspect: One is its sound element, pronounced as a nasal sound (*anusvāra*). The other aspect is its form or shape (*ākṛti*). The latter is written as a dot after a syllable.

The **Prapañcasāra Tantra** gives a short view about how *bindu* emerges and how pure consciousness (*cinmātrā*) becomes condensed and solidified to shine as *bindu*, to be the material of the universe.

> सा तत्त्वसंज्ञा चिन्मात्रा ज्योतिषः सन्निधेस्तदा ।
> विचिकीर्षुर्घनीभूता क्वचिदभ्येति बिन्दुताम् ॥
>
> PraSāT I.41
>
> That *prakṛti*, the Supreme Reality, which is consciousness in essence, when coming in contact with the light (*jyotis*), becomes intent on creativity and thus solidifies itself as a drop.

The internal nature of *prakṛti* is the reality which remains identical with the absolute, but when it becomes externalized (*bahirmukha*) it becomes as if condensed and solidifies itself – only then it is called *bindu*. But it should be remembered in this context that this *bindu* is *parabindu*, the highest *bindu*. When time interacts, that is, when the ripening of the latent *karma* occurs, three distinctive forms make their appearance. They are called *bindu*, *nāda* and ***bīja***.

> कालेन भिद्यमानस्तु स बिन्दुर्भवति त्रिधा ।
> स्थूलसूक्ष्मपरत्वेन तस्य त्रैविध्यमिष्यते ॥
> स बिन्दुनादबीजत्वभेदेन च निगद्यते ।
>
> PraSāT I.42-43ab
>
> When pierced by time that *bindu* becomes threefold, for its threefoldness is explained by the wise as having the forms of gross, subtle and transcendent. This is known as *bindu*, *nāda*, and *bīja*.

The above quote from the **Prapañcasāra** whose authorship is ascribed to Śaṅkara, is cryptic in expression. The above theme has been slightly elaborated in the **Śāradātilaka** of Lakṣmaṇadeśikendra.

सच्चिदानन्दविभवात् सकलात् परमेश्वरात् ।
आसीच्छक्तिस्ततो नादो नादाद्बिन्दुसमुद्भवः ॥

ŚāTil I.7

From the glorious Lord who is being, consciousness and blissful by nature and who is inseparably associated with *Śakti*, *śakti* emerged, from which *nāda*, the primal sound was born. From *nāda* the emergence of *bindu* occurred.

It is evident that the above verse explains the creative process which proceeds from the Lord in his *sakala* aspect, who is associated with *kalā* which is synonymous with *śakti*. This *śakti* has two aspects, one in which it remains latent (*pralīnāvasthā*), and the other in which it is ready to manifest (*ucchūnāvasthā*). With the beginning of activity in *śakti*, *nāda* makes its appearance, and *bindu* only becomes manifest when *nāda* whose essence is activity solidifies.

Though *bindu* is essentially *śakti* herself, when she descends as it were a little lower for starting creation she is also called *bindu*. The higher aspect is called *parabindu* while the lower is known as *aparabindu*. In the higher state *bindu* is agitated. Then, taking on its lower aspect it assumes three distinct forms:

परशक्तिमयः साक्षात् त्रिधासौ भिद्यते पुनः ।
बिन्दुर्नादो बीजमिति तस्य भेदाः समीरिताः ॥

ŚāTil I.8

Bindu is in essence the transcendent *śakti*, which again breaks into three. Its division is called *bindu*, *nāda* and *bīja*.

In the above context *bindu* represents *Śiva*, while *bīja* stands for *śakti* and the union between the two is *nāda*. The central dot in an equilateral triangle is the *bindu* which stands for the unity of *Śiva-Śakti*, i.e. it is the unity of consciousness and bliss. The three lines of the triangle are nothing but the extension of the central point representing *icchā*, *jñāna* and *kriyā*. In another aspect these three lines are *raudrī, jyeṣṭhā* and *vāmā*, born of *bindu*, *nāda* and *bīja* respectively.

In Āgama literature *bindu* is stated to be closely associated with *nāda* and sometimes it has been stated to have emerged out of the void.

नादाद् बिन्दुः समुत्पन्नः सूर्यकोटिसमप्रभः ।
स चैव दशधा ज्ञेयो दशतत्त्वफलप्रदः ।
दशधा वर्णरूपेण दशदैवतसंयुतः ॥

SvT XI.9

From *nāda bindu* is born. It is luminous like crores of suns. It is known to be of ten types and the bestower of ten sorts of attainments. Its ten colours are associated with ten divinities.

The power of activity (*kriyāśakti*) is the predominant characteristic of *bindu*, but will and knowledge (*icchā* and *jñāna*) remain merged in it. The entire universe both internal and external held within the gamut of the knowable (*vācya*) is the very nature of *bindu* (*samagravācyābhedaprakāśa*). Being such it is the light which shines identically with everything that is denoted by *nāda*.

The **Mālinīvijaya Tantra** also gives a description of *bindu* which has ten different aspects (*daśadhā bindurucyate*, MVT XII.10). The text also describes its shape:

कदम्बगोलकाकारः स्फुरत्तारकसन्निभः ।
शुक्लादिभेदभेदेन एकोऽपि दशधा मतः ॥

MVT XII.11

It is round-shaped like the *kadamba* flower and bright like a luminous star. Though it is one, having the distinctions of colours like white and others, it is considered to be of ten different forms.

The **Svacchanda Tantra** views *nāda* and *bindu* in a different way:

बिन्दुनादात्मके द्वे वै मध्ये शक्त्यात्मिका स्मृता ।

SVT VII.19cd

Among the *nāḍīs* two are of the characteristic of *bindu* and *nāda*, while that which is in their midst is of the nature of *śakti*.

While commenting upon the above verse Kṣemarāja elaborates the concept saying that the vital energy flowing through the right channel of the body is called *piṅgalā*. The purified channel of the right side is the energy of *bindu* where *jñānaśakti* functions predominantly (*bindu jñānaśaktipradhāna*). We see a similar concept in the **Śivadṛṣṭi** with its commentary by Utpala where it has been stated that *prāṇa* and *apāna* are named *bindu* and *nāda* (ŚDṛ II.6).

According to Buddhist Tāntric tradition *bindu* represents *śukra* and *rakta* flowing through the channels called *lalanā* and *rasanā*, the left and the right. This twofold nature of *bindu* is in essence *bodhicitta* in its relative aspect, while in its absolute aspect (*vivṛti*) *bodhicitta* abides in the summit of the head as the moon which when melting in the thousand petalled lotus flows down along the channels and enlivens the body with blissfulness.

चण्डाली ज्वलिता नाभौ दहति पञ्चतथागतान् ।
दहति च लोचनादिः दग्धेऽहं स्रवते शशी ॥

HT I.I.31

Caṇḍālī blazes up at the navel.
She burns the Five Buddhas.
She burns *Locanā* and the others.
Haṃ is burnt and the Moon melts. (Tr. D.L. Snellgrove)

Kṛṣṇācārya comments on the above verse: *locanādīn pṛthivyādīn dagdhe sati... haṃkāra svabhāvaḥ śaśī vajrasattvaḥ sravate.*

Bindu connoting semen (*śukra*) has been given much importance in **Haṭha-yoga** texts, for the seminal fluid is considered to be a portion of the moon (*soma*) which nourishes the body and if properly purified it leads one to attain imperishable nature and immortality of the body. It is considered to be a means for transmutation of the physical body.

> मरणं बिन्दुपातेन जीवनं बिन्दुधारणात् ।
>
> HyPrad III.88
>
> When the semen is expended death ensues (in due course), but there is (prolonged) life for him who preserves it. (Tr. S. Iyengar)

Mahāsukha, the great bliss which is the goal of human attainment is changeless, but in the lower material plane it manifests itself as sex-pleasure which is restless. It is in this plane that the seed, *bindu*, transforms itself into the physical body. When *bindu* is arrested in the physical plane it moves upward proceeding towards higher planes. In this upward movement it casts off the defilements of the elements of earth, water, fire, air and ether with which it has been associated. When *bindu* finally becomes fully free from defilements it reaches the summit of the head and attains the Absolute as great bliss.

According to Śaiva Siddhānta doctrine, reality is said to consist of three aspects. These three are *Śiva, Śakti* and *bindu*, the three jewels. The dynamic aspect of *Śiva* is *Śakti* and the aspect which becomes the material of the universe is *bindu*. While *Śakti* remains inseparably united with *Śiva, bindu* has its connection to *Śiva* only through the medium of *Śakti* (*parigraha śakti*). Both of them have *Śiva* as their base and for this reason *Śiva* is called *adhiṣṭhātṛ* and these two are superintended by the former, one directly and the other indirectly.

Bindu is the material of creation and the dynamic *Śakti* is the efficient cause. *Śakti* being impelled by the will of the Lord activates *bindu* which then assumes the form of *nāda*, the primeval Sound. This sound is called *Paranāda*, the sound.

> जायतेऽध्वा यतः शुद्धो वर्तते यत्र लीयते ।
> स बिन्दुः परनादाख्यः नादबिन्दूर्णकारणम् ॥
>
> RaTParī 22
>
> That from which the pure path emerges, remains abiding, and where it finally dissolves is *bindu* (*parabindu*) termed as *Paranāda*. It again becomes the cause of *nāda* and *bindu* (*aparanāda* and *aparabindu*).

Bindu is the cause of the pure path and it is said to be its material. Moreover, *nāda* is the first expansion (*prathamaprasararūpaḥ*) of *bindu*.

paranāda	*parabindu*	
vācya	*vācaka*	
śuddhādhvā	*nāda* and *vācaka* (*apara*) *nāda*	*bindu* *rācya* (*apara*) *bindu*

Ananta being an embodied person, its body is made of the material of *bindu*. It is for this reason his body is known as *baindavaṃ śarīram*.

Nāda in the level of ordinary human beings goes on operating, therefore it is not uncreated but created and as such it has its end (*utpattyapavargayoginaḥ*). As it is created (an effect or *kārya*) it must have some cause.

ततश्चैषां कार्यत्वेनोपादानकारणं वाच्यम् ।
तत्सिद्धो नादः परः सुमङ्गला मालिनी महामाया ॥
समनानाहतबिन्दुरघोषावाग्ब्रह्मकुण्डलिनीतत्त्वं
विद्याख्यं तत्त्वमित्युक्तं तैस्तैस्तदागमेष्वित्थम् ॥

NādaKā 16-17

Therefore as they (*nāda* in its various aspects functioning on individual levels) are caused, it is essential for them to have a material cause. Therefore the existence of *Nāda* is established which is synonymous with *sumaṅgalā*, *mālinī*, *mahāmāyā*, *samanā*, *anāhata*, *bindu*, *aghoṣā*, *vāgbrahma*, *kuṇḍalinītattva* and the category of *vidyā*. These names have been stated in different Āgamas.

Moreover, when the material of *māyā* and others is agitated, it becomes the cause of the body and senses of living beings which being subordinate to the agent (*māyā*) are able to function properly. The material from which the body and senses are born is known as *bindu*. Moreover, every human concept is closely associated with speech. No speech can emerge without having a cause. It is *bindu* which is its cause. Therefore it consists of multifarious modes (*bahuvṛttikaḥ*).

सा च कुण्डलिनी शम्भोः शक्तिः शुद्धा जडात्मिका ।
न तादात्म्यात् स्थिता किन्तु वर्तमाना परिग्रहे ॥
शिवे कर्तरि तादात्म्यान्नेयं कुण्डलिनी स्थिता ।
उपादानत्वतो हेतोः कुलाले मृत्तिका यथा ॥

PauṣĀ Bindu Pāda 10cd-12

The coiled *śakti* here equated with *bindu* belonging to Lord Śiva is pure, but it is in essence insentient. It abides in Śiva not inseparably but remains there as 'adopted'. This coiled *śakti* does not abide inseparably in Śiva the agent, but functions as a material cause as clay is for the potter.

The dwellers of the pure path (*śuddha adhvā*) have bodies and sense organs made of the material called *bindu*, and the region (*loka*) in which they enjoy existence is also made of the same material.

शिवः संकल्पमात्रेण बिन्दुक्षोभकरः सदा ।

PauṣĀ PatiPāda 30ab

Lord Śiva by means of his mere will is the agent who causes agitation in *bindu*.

Bindu is the material of speech (*vāc*) and pure principles (*tattva*). As it is insentient (*jaḍarūpa*) it is considered to be an assumed energy of the Lord (*parigrahaśakti*), the synonym of which is *kuṇḍalinī*. In *bindu* the triple state occurs, namely *adhikāra*, *bhoga* and *laya* (with reference to *Rudrāṇu* souls). In addition, their awakening (*prabodha*) and release occurs in *bindu*.

लयादिभेदः प्रागुक्तो यदुपाधौ शिवस्य तु ।
स बिन्दुरिति मन्तव्यः सैव कुण्डलिनी मता ॥
किञ्च रुद्राणवो येन बध्यन्ते यत्र वा स्थिताः ।
विमुच्यन्ते यतो वायं स बिन्दुरिति गम्यताम् ॥

PauṣĀ Bindu Pāda 3

The divisions of *laya* (rest) and others which exist as accidental attributes in Śiva have been given an account earlier. It (the distinctions) should be known as the manifestation of *bindu* or *bindu* itself. It is known as *kuṇḍalinī*, the coiled *śakti*. Moreover, the souls known as *Rudrāṇus*, are bound by it (*bindu*), have their stay in it and finally get their release from it – it is that which should be taken as *bindu*.

According to Tanpra *bindu* is not simply a mathematical point but rather the absolute in which all sorts of attributes are absent (*nirastanikhilaprapañca*), therefore it is of the nature of the void.

शून्याकाराद् विसर्गान्ताद् बिन्दोः प्रस्पन्दसंविदः ॥
प्रकाशपरमार्थत्वात् स्फुरत्ता लहरीयुतात् ।
प्रसृतं विश्वलहरीस्थानं मातृत्रयात्मकम् ॥

YoH I.10cd-11

Bindu which is empty of content, which is *anuttara*, the transcendent, and which has its end in *visarga*, is of the characteristic of vibrating consciousness and is essentially light itself. It is by its association of its light (*prakāśa*) with its self-reflection (*sphurattā*) that the Reality rolls on like waves as from the universe consisting of three levels of speech and the objects denoted by them.

Amṛtānanda, the commentator, explains the above verse in the following way:

शिवशक्तिसामरस्यरूपकामाख्यस्य बिन्दोः संसारः प्रस्पन्दो दहनेन्दुरूपसित-
शोणबिन्दुद्वयात्मकः अकारहकारसामरस्यबिन्दोः प्रस्पन्दात् संसारात्
सितशोणबिन्दुयुगलात् संविच्चिन्मयी दहनेन्दुरूपा चित्कला जायते ॥

YoHDīp I.10

From *bindu* named *kāma* which is of the nature of the coalesced unity of Śiva and Śakti the flow is set into motion. This *bindu*, the coalesced unity (*sāmarasya bindu*), is of the character of fire and moon, one white and the other red respectively. From the vibration of the unified I-consciousness (*ahaṃ*) a small portion of consciousness emerges.

Puṇyānanda elaborates the above idea thus:

परशिवरविकरनिकरे प्रतिफलति विमर्शदर्पणे विशदे ।
प्रतिरुचिरुचिरे कुड्ये चित्तमये निविशते महाबिन्दुः ॥

KāmKVil Verse 4

Upon the mass of the rays of the sun Paraśiva being reflected in the pure *vimarśa*-mirror, the *mahābindu* appears on the *citta*-wall illumined by the reflected rays. (Tr. A. Avalon)

When the Lord being all-luminous experiences self-awareness (*svasvarūpavimarśa sambandhe jāte*), then *mahābindu* with the characteristic of the concept "I am full!" (*pūrṇo'hamityevaṃrūpaḥ*) shines forth.

Mahābindu is considered to be the seat of Sadāśiva.

सदाशिवासनं देवि महाबिन्दुमयं परम् ।

YoH I.56ab

The seat of Sadāśiva, oh goddess, is composed of great *bindu.*

The above view refers to the idea that *mahābindu* is nothing but the unity of the phonemes *a* and *h*. The manifest form of the coalesced unity of *a* and *h* is *aham* (*suvyaktāhārṇasamarasākāra*).

Mahābindu or simply *bindu* is said to be the seed of creation. It is this manifest form of 'thisness' (*sphuṭedantābhāsātmā*) from which the whole creation receives its nourishment. *Mahābindu* has two aspects, one being that of evolution from which everything proceeds, is maintained and nourished, while the other is that of involution in which everything goes back to the source and finally merges in I-consciousness.

The **Netra Tantra** observes that *bindu* is the source of creation, and the semen of Śiva:

तस्मात् प्रवर्तते सृष्टिर्विक्षोभ्य परमं शिवम् । NT VII.42ab

From him creation proceeds after the great Śiva is agitated.

The above Tantra goes on describing how this virile energy can be directed to flow along the middle path (*madhyamārga*) upward passing through different stages and finally how it reaches the summit of the head. After that, in its outgoing flow, it nourishes and purifies all the pulsating points and finally makes the body immortal (like nectar, *amṛta*).

In Kṣemarāja's commentary on the **Śiva-Sūtra** the following is stated:

इयत्पर्यन्तविश्वैकवेदनरूपं बिन्दुमुन्मील्य युगपदन्तर्बहिर्विसर्जनमयबिन्दु-द्वयात्मानं विसर्गभूमिमुद्दर्शितवती ।

ŚSūVim II.7

Then the Supreme I-consciousness expresses the undivided knowledge of the universe in the form of a dot (*bindu*) in the letter *aṃ*. It shows further the *visarga* stage in the form of two (perpendicular) dots indicating simultaneously inner and outer manifestation. (Tr. J. Singh)

In the **Tantrāloka** Abhinavagupta elucidates the concept of *visarga* as composed of two dots in the following way:

ककारादिसकारान्ता विसर्गात् पञ्चधा स च ॥
बहिश्चान्तश्च हृदये नादेऽथ परमे पदे ।
बिन्दुरात्मनि मूर्धान्तं हृदयाद् व्यापको हि सः ॥

TĀl III.222-223

The letters from *ka* to *sa* are produced by the creative energy (*visarga*) of Śiva. That *visarga* is manifested in five ways, one outside (in the form of expansion of the universe), and four inside (i) in the heart, (ii) in *nāda* i.e. in the throat, (iii) in the great stage (*parame pade*), between two eye-brows, (iv) in *Brahmarandhra*. It pervades from the heart up to the top of the skull. (Tr. J. Singh)

Jayaratha, the commentator on the **Tantrāloka**, refers to the **Siddhayogeśvarī Tantra** which states that *bindu* is specifically termed as such because it remains established after pervading the entire universe (*tadevaṃ binduruddiṣṭo vyāpnuvan sa jagatsthitaḥ*). He further explains the theme thus (TĀl III under verse 222):

यतः स विसर्ग एव बिन्दुः विदिक्रियायां स्वतन्त्रः प्रमाता, बहीरूपतया हृदये नरतया बहीरूपत्वेऽपि अन्तारूपतायामेव विश्रान्तेः नादे शक्तितया, अन्तारूपतया परमे पदे, द्वादशान्ते शिवतया प्रस्फुरन् पञ्चप्रकारः ।

That *visarga* is *bindu*, the autonomous subject of the activity of knowing manifesting itself externally as *nara*, the universe, in the heart but resting in the core internally in *nāda* as *śakti*. Internally it has its rest in the highest abode (*parame pade*) and at the end of the twelve (that is in *dvādaśānta*) it shines as Śiva. Thus it remains manifest in the body in five different locations.

These five locations are the heart, the throat, the forehead, *nāda* and *brahmarandhra*. It may be asked, 'while being one how is it possible for it to abide in five different locations?' The answer is that it is pervasive. *Bindu* though one, that is, one single knowing subject, becomes manifest as an individual subject externally inclined (*bāhyātmā*). Then it shines slightly internally (*antarātmā*). When it further internalizes in the core of the heart it is called *hṛdayātmā*, that is, of the nature of the heart. Its fourth state is of the nature of *nāda* (*nādātmā*) characterized by the primal sound. The fifth state is the supreme (*paramātmā*), that is, the knowing subject (*vidikriyāyāṃ svatantraḥ pramātā*). Thus in its innate luminosity it shines in five distinct places in the body.

As *visarga* is essentially *bindu* considered to be the seed of creation, it is not different from *anuttara*. After making itself manifest externally in its gross form (*sthūlaṃ rūpam ābhāsya*), it does not disappear. In its ingoing move it rests in *anuttara* (that is in the phoneme *a*), and thus takes the form of '*a ha*'. Finally it becomes associated with the *bindu* or dot and shines as '*ahaṃ*'.

The above view has its support in the **Aitareya Āraṇyaka:**

अः इति ब्रह्म, तत्रागतमहमिति ।

AitĀr II.3.8

Visarga is *Brahman* from which I-consciousness has come forth.

In addition, the entire universe is the extension of *visarga* composed of two *bindus*, and music is pleasant because it gives nourishment to the virile energy of *Brahman* and helps the aesthete to attain steadiness in pure consciousness. Therefore Abhinavagupta writes:

शब्दोऽपि मधुरो यस्माद्वीर्योपचयकारकः ।
तद्धि वीर्यं परं शुद्धं विसिसृक्षात्मकं परम् ॥

TĀl III.229

Thus sound is sweet, for it is the agent which gives nourishment to the virile energy (in the form of *Brahman*) of the Lord. That *vīrya* is highly pure and is considered by all as having the character of creative impulse.

Moreover, it has been emphasized that everything, in whatever form of manifestation, is a form of the virile energy of the Lord.

तद्बलं च तदोजश्च ते प्राणाः सा च कान्तता ।
तस्माद् वीर्यात् प्रजास्ताश्च वीर्यं कर्मसु कथ्यते ॥

TĀl III.230

That is strength, that is virility (*ojas*), the very life, and that is pleasantness. It is from that virile energy that offspring issues forth and it is considered to be the potency in activity.

These quotes affirm the idea that *visarga* is all-pervading.

The **Yoginī-Hṛdaya** equates *bindu* with the Supreme *Liṅga*:

सूक्ष्मरूपं समस्तार्णवृतं परमलिङ्गकम् ।
बिन्दुरूपं परानन्दकन्दं नित्यपदोदितम् ॥

YoH I.47

The Supreme *Liṅga* being exceedingly luminous, is very subtle in form. It is surrounded by all phonemes and is of the form of *bindu*. It is the source of supreme bliss. It is considered to be the bulb (*kanda*) from which all sounds emerge (like creepers).

Bindu arising from the eternal abode in its first pulsation (*prathamaspanda-tayā*) is considered to be of the nature of transcendent speech (*parāvāk*), other levels of speech, viz. *paśyantī*, *madhyamā* and *vaikharī* evolve out of it. Therefore it is the source of words.

Abhinavagupta thus interprets *bindu* to mean heart and awareness (*vedana*) in the **Parātrīśikā-Vivaraṇa**:

भैरवात्मवेदनतया बिन्द्वात्मकं हृदयम् ।

PTrīVi p.82

Hṛdaya is of the nature of *bindu* which cognizes *Bhairava*, the Lord as non-different from it. (Tr. J.Singh)

But while interpreting all the phonemes, Abhinavagupta takes *bindu* as the fifteenth vowel *aṃ* which denotes awareness.

परित्यज्य तथाविधोपाधिपरिस्पन्दसत्तामभेदसत्तारोहणचिन्मयपुरुषतत्त्व-वेदनारूपबिन्दुमात्रावशेषेण वपुषा तथानुत्तरपदलीने अमिति ।

PTrīVi p.61

After the full development of *kriyāśakti*, they abandon the variations of those *śaktis* and mounting to the state of non-difference, get immersed in the remaining form of a *bindu* i.e. *aṃ*, a dot which represents awareness (*vedanā*) of the very nature of the Reality that is pure consciousness (*cinmaya puruṣatattva*) and get immersed in the *anuttara* state. (Tr. J. Singh)

In the above context *bindu* is viewed as of the nature of a phoneme, but at the same time it is the knowing subject. It remains closely linked with the supreme *anuttaraśakti* as the very life of it. Therefore it is stated in the **Tantrāloka** that though *anuttaraśakti* while developing itself puts on the garb of limitations, it never loses its pristine nature of autonomy of awareness of knowing subjecthood.

अत्रानुत्तरशक्तिः सा स्वं वपुः प्रकटस्थितम् ।
कुर्वन्त्यपि ज्ञेयकलाकालुष्याद् बिन्दुरूपिणी ॥
उदितायां क्रियाशक्तौ सोमसूर्याग्निधामनि ।
अविभागः प्रकाशो यः स बिन्दुः परमो हि नः ॥

TĀl III.110-111

Even at this stage that transcendent power though making its form clearly manifest and taking on limitations of the impurities of objectivity, it is yet always of the form of *bindu*. When *kriyāśakti* develops fully in the realm of knowable objects, the instrument of knowledge, and the experiencing subject, the undifferentiated light (*prakāśa*) which pervades all is our Supreme *Bindu*.

In the above context *bindu* is defined as the undifferentiated light which permeates objects of knowledge, the means of knowledge and the knower (*grāhya, grahaṇa* and *grāhaka*). The light of *bindu* is defiled due to its limitations, but the supreme, integral light (*prakāśa*), though associated with all, never loses its pristine purity.

Kṣemarāja in his commentary on **Śiva-Sūtra** (II.2) quotes a verse from the **Tantrasadbhāva** in which *bindu* is defined as a spark of the light of consciousness towards which the mind of the yogin can be drawn (*manobinduṃ vikarṣayet*). Through intensive awareness of this on the part of the yogin the self expands (*uccāreṇaiva dhāvati*).

The **Mataṅga-Pārameśvara** (III.21-22) defines *bindu* as *sphurad raśmi sahasrāḍhyam*, rich with brilliant rays one thousand in number, all-pervasive and great.

We have spoken above about the multidimensional nature of *bindu*, therefore it is interesting to note that *bindu* though all-pervading is essentially of the nature of dissolution or withdrawal (*saṃhāra*).

बिन्दुः संहार इत्युक्तो विसर्गः सृष्टिरुच्यते । AhSam XVI.66cd

Bindu (*anusvāra*) is said to be dissolution, and *visarga* (emission) is known as creation.

It is clear from the above view that creation starts from *visarga*, and not from *bindu*. The series of phonemes begins with *a* (*anuttara*) and extends up to the fourteenth vowel sound *au*. Here ends the development of *kriyāśakti*. Then its innate ingoing force activates it to roll it up so that it may finally rest in *a*, the *anuttara*. The condensed consciousness is symbolically known as *bindu*.

According to Pāñcarātra doctrine *bindu* not only shares in the formation of the body of the universe but also of names:

नामनामिस्वरूपेण स बिन्दुर्भिद्यते द्विधा ।
तत्र नामोदयं प्राप्य शब्दब्रह्म प्रवर्तते ॥

AhSam XVI.38

That *bindu* is divided into two, viz. in the form of name and the bearer of the name. *Brahman* as sound (*śabdabrahma*) begins to function after it has given rise to names.

In the Arts

Bindu denoting a point is a salient feature in geometry. In temple architecture and in drawing holy diagrams *bindu* is the central point from which everything proceeds, or rather, it expresses itself in multifarious forms. It is also called *madhyabindu* or *marman*.

ब्रह्मासनपदे मध्येऽम्बुरुहं स्थाप्यमेव च ।
तस्मिन् मध्ये तदोङ्कारं यज्ञसूत्रावृतं तु तत् ॥

Mayam XII.49cd-50ab

At the centre the lotus should be set down at the place of Brahmā's throne, in its centre *Om* is drawn encircled by the sacrificial thread. (Tr. B. Dagens)

In order to ascertain direction from the central *bindu* a thread is spread out towards two points where the shadow of the *śaṅku* (gnomon) has fallen. Thus one can know the exact direction of east and west.

तद्बिन्दुद्वयगं सूत्रं पूर्वापरदिशीष्यते ।
बिन्दुद्वयान्तरभ्रान्तशफराननपुच्छगम् ॥

Mayam VI.9

The line which passes through the space between these two points and (which is like that which) connects the head and the tail of a carp, is the north-south axis. (Tr. B. Dagens)

In temple architecture *bindu* has been taken as a hole in the centre of the *āmalakī* installed over the summit.

मध्ये गर्भकबिन्दुं च प्रतिशाला समानतः ।
एतेन क्रमभेदेन अमलक्या कृतं महत् ॥

ŚiPrak II.94

The *bindu* (hole) in the centre (of the *amalakī*) should be on one line with the *garbhayantra*. This is the order in which the different parts of the great *amalakī* are made. (Tr. A. Boner)

The centre-point on top of the temple-spire (*śikhara*) coincides in one line with the centre of the *garbha-yantra* in the *garbhagṛha* or sanctum.

अन्ते नीत्वा मध्यबिन्दुं गर्भबिन्दुं समाचरेत् ।

ŚiPrak I.78ab

Finally, after ascertaining the centre-point, the point of the garbha (the inner sanctum) of the temple should be undertaken. (Tr. A. Boner)

The central point of the ground-plan coincides with the *garbhabindu* when the entire structure is completed.

In Indian sculpture the image of the deity has specific centres known as *bindu*, situated at the crossing-points of the diagram, as in the case of the image of Nāṭāmbara (see Fig. 11, p.83):

छेदोर्ध्वे बिन्दुसंख्यातः त्रिकूटबिन्दुसंज्ञकः ।
त्रिकूटास्थानयुक्तेन भ्रूमध्यस्थलमुत्तमम् ॥

* * *

हृदयं दक्षिणे छेदे नाभिश्च मध्यबिन्दुगा ।

ŚiPrak II.209,211ab

The *bindu* on the upper *cheda* is known as the *trikūṭa bindu* . This place of the *trikūṭa* is best for setting the middle of the brow.

* * *

The chest is on the oblique (on the right side), the navel on the *madhyabindu*. (Tr. A. Boner)

Madhyabindu, the central point, is a very important concept in architecture which guarantees the exact proportion of the entire structure. All measurements are ascertained only when the central point is established.

अत्र शृणु मुखशाला वाडक्रियादिनिर्णयम् ।
मध्यबिन्दुं समाश्रित्य भागनिर्धारणं महत् ॥ ŚiPrak I.81

Now hear about the construction of the wall of the *Mukhaśālā*, the principal building. Proceeding from the centre-point all parts should be established. (Tr. A. Boner)

In the **Nāṭya-Śāstra** *bindu* is mentioned as one of the five constituent elements of a plot.

बीजं बिन्दुः पताका च प्रकरी कार्यमेव च ।
अर्थप्रकृतयः पञ्च ज्ञात्वा योज्या यथाविधि ॥

NŚ XIX.21

Five constituent elements of the plot should first be known and then application of them should be made properly in the dramatic composition.
These elements are beginning, sign of continuity, episode, incident and end. (Tr. P.L. Sharma)

According to **Nāṭya-Śāstra** *bindu* is a thread of continuity running through the drama when many subsidiary and allied issues develop the main plot. This runs to the end (NŚ XIX.23).

Abhinavagupta explains *bindu* as *anusandhāna*, the process of unification.

सकलोपायप्रतिजागरणनिमित्तं ह्यनुसन्धानं यावद्धि मुख्यनायकेन प्रत्यनुसन्धानेन न क्रियते तावज्जडाजडरूपः सर्वोऽप्युपायवर्गोऽनुपायकल्प इव, तथा हि तापसवत्सराजे वासवदत्ताप्रेमानुसन्धानं राजमुखेन प्रत्यङ्गदर्शितं —
"तद्वक्त्रेन्दुविलोकनेन दिवसो नीतः प्रदोषस्तथा" ।

AbhiBhā on NŚ XIX.23

The unification is verily the cause characterised by persisting awareness regarding all the means – so long as re-unification is not performed by the main hero, then all the means either insentient or sentient can serve little purpose. For example in **Tāpasavatsarāja** love for Vāsavadattā that lies deeply in the heart has been expressed by the author in every act in the mouth of the prince:
"I have spent my day and evening only looking at the moon-like face of yours."

Anusandhāna being the salient feature of *bindu*, it is all-pervading by its presence like the knowing subject, but it is to be consciously re-unified by the hero (*pratyanusandhāna*). Since both, *bindu* and *bīja* have the similar characteristic of being pervasive, the distinction between the two is difficult to ascertain. Therefore Abhinavagupta differentiates *bīja* and *bindu* in the following way:

बीजं च मुखसन्धावेव प्रवर्त्यमानमुन्मिषति, बिन्दुस्तदनन्तरमिति विशेषो-ऽनयोः, द्वेऽपि तु समस्तेतिवृत्तव्यापके ।

AbhiBhā on NŚ XIX.23

The *bīja* should be made to originate in the very *mukhasandhi*, and subsequently the *bindu* should be made to originate. The difference between them lies there. Otherwise both of them spread over the entire plot.

Abhinavagupta adopts the simile of the drop of oil on water, using this as an illustration to explain the spreading of *bīja*. Bhoja compares *bindu* to drops of water dripping continuously or drops of ghee falling at intervals in the flames of a fire which they keep burning without a break:

बिन्दुरिव च बिन्दुः । पयोबिन्दुश्च्योतन् पयोऽभिष्यन्दलक्षणायाः क्रियाया अविच्छेदहेतुः, यथा वा घृतबिन्दुः अग्निज्वलनलक्षणायाः, एवं विच्छिन्नाविच्छिन्नेषु कथाशरीरेषु योऽनुसन्धाता स बिन्दुरित्युच्यते ।

ŚṛPrak p.578

It is like a drop, therefore it is called *bindu*. As drops of water while falling become the cause of the activity of the continuity of the flow or as drops of ghee falling into the fire keep the fire blazing, the unifying agent which remains present in the body of the plot diversified with episodes as a unity is called *bindu*.

Sāgaranandin in his **Nāṭakalakṣaṇaratna-Kośa** defines *bindu* in the following way:

बिन्दुरिव बिन्दुः । विच्छिन्नायामपि धारायां यथा जलबिन्दुः पटल-पर्यन्तेष्वन्तरा लब्धनिजनिपातः पयसां पतनमभिव्यञ्जयति तथायमपि प्रयोजनमित्यर्थः ।

NLRKo 24 p.17-18

Bindu is like a drop. As the drops of water dripping from the side of the thatch indicate the fall of water even after the cessation of the shower of rains, in the same way the fall of drops indicates the fall of water. *Bindu* also indicates the purpose and maintains the continuity of the main action when it is interrupted by secondary issues.

The same text gives an illustration of *bindu* from **Veṇīsaṃhāra** to support the view how it spreads over the entire surface of the water like a drop of oil:

लाक्षागृहानलविषान्नसभाप्रवेशैः
प्राणेषु वित्तनिचयेषु च नः प्रहृत्य ।
आकृष्य पाण्डववधूपरिधानकेशान्
स्वस्था भवन्तु मयि जीवति धार्तराष्ट्राः ॥

Veṇīsaṃhāra I.8

Bhīmasena utters in rage: The sons of Dhṛtarāṣṭra caused so many harmful deeds to us by setting fire to the house made of lac, by serving me poisoned food, insulting me in the assembly hall, robbing us of money and wealth, by pulling the hair and cloth as worn by the wife of Pāṇḍavas – will they live in peace when I am still living?

In the above illustration the series of acts committed by Duryodhana keep the unity of the play alive in the mind of the hero. Though the purpose of the theme is apparently broken, the *bindu* serves as a link (*avicchedakāraṇam*).

प्रयोजनानां विच्छेदे यदविच्छेदकारणम् ।
यावत्समाप्तिर्बन्धस्य स बिन्दुः परिकीर्तितः ॥

NŚ XIX.23

प्रयुज्यते फलं यैरुपायानुष्ठानैः तेषामितिवृत्तवशादवश्यकर्तव्यतादिभिर्विच्छेदेऽपि सति यदनुसन्धानात्मकं प्रधाननायकगतं सन्धिद्रव्यज्ञानं बिन्दुः, ज्ञानविचारणं फललाभोपायत्वात् । यावदविच्छेदः प्रत्यनुसन्धानेन न कृतस्तावन्न किञ्चिदपि कार्यं निर्वहति ।

AbhiBhā on above

In case the causes (that lead to the result) are interrupted, that which maintains continuity of the composition until the end, is called *bindu*.

Commentary:

The performance of activities as causes (*upāyas*) connect them with the result (the dénouement of the plot), but their continuity may be broken by the burden of the plot and essentiality of enactment of deeds and others, even in that position the knowledge regarding the substance (*sandhi*) characterised by unification abiding in the principal hero, is *bindu* denoting reflection of knowledge, for it is a means for attaining the result. But (in this context it should be kept in mind) that so long as continuity is not maintained by the series of re-unificatory process of threading with conscious effort nothing can be possible to attain.

Process

As a minute unit of space *bindu* occupies a unique role. As a point it moves in a given direction and as a result of this movement a straight line is formed. The inner impulse which drives it forward has an ingoing pull which finally brings it back to the place of rest. Thus *bindu* has two aspects, one being its outward drive, the other its inward pull. The former is known as *bahirmukhatā*, the latter as *antarmukhatā*. The external reality that shines as a projection of *bindu* is inwardly withdrawn to become one with pure consciousness. There is a play of swinging (*dolālīlā*) which continues between *bindu* and *visarga* the result of which is two *bindus*. Then all the multiplicity is obliterated to be flooded with pure light of *Mahābindu.*

Conclusion

Bindu as a drop of life-giving substance has a dynamic nature, which persists even in its nature as the still centre-point. As the autonomous knowing subject it first assumes objectivity and finally achieves rest in pure consciousness. Literally *bindu* in its *adhibhūta* aspect is a drop which is the material or source of the gross universe. In its celestial aspect (*adhidaiva*) it is known as *indu*, the moon. In Tāntric symbolism it is *soma* representing objectivity (*māyā*). In spiritual *sādhanā bindu* occupies a unique position. It is the ever-pulsating point which is considered to be the source and the abode of rest for everything. It has centres in the human body where consciousness shines in relative brightness. These centres are of the *adhyātma* aspect of *bindu.* Another aspect of *bindu* is its association with speech, which is considered a manifestation of *bindu. Bindu* expresses itself in determinate knowledge.

In short, *bindu* as a drop or a central point is in every sphere a point charged with creative energy, whether it be the human body, the universe, language, the visual arts, or drama.

H.N. Chakravarty

Select Bibliography

Kaviraj, M.M. Gopinath: "Nāda, bindu and kalā" in: Selected Writings of M.M. Gopinath Kaviraj. Varanasi: Gopinath Kaviraj Centenary Celebration Committee, 1990.

— Aspects of Indian Thought. Burdwan: The University of Burdwan, 1966.

— Bhāratīya Saṃskṛti aur Sādhanā (in Hindi), Vol. I. Patna: Bihar Rāṣṭrabhāṣā Pariṣad, 1977.

— Tāntrik Vāṅmay men Śāktadṛṣṭi (in Hindi). Patna: Bihar Rāṣṭrabhāṣā Pariṣad, 1978.

NĀBHI

Overview

Nābhi, the navel, stands for the centre of the body and of the universe. It is also the hub of a wheel (→*cakra*).

The symbolical aspect of the navel represented as a lotus has been derived from the Viṣṇu myth depicting Viṣṇu with a lotus navel (*padmanābha*). The lotus thus symbolizes Viṣṇu, the base of the universe, and Brahmā emerging from the navel of Viṣṇu symbolizes the phenomenal universe. The lotus representing the central portion of the wheel shows three distinct divisions – the one is the *karṇikā* (pericarp), the second is *kesara* (filament) and the third is its petals. The hub of a wheel similarly consists of three parts – the first is the central point, which is called →*bindu*, around which all else revolves, the second is the thick round part into which spokes are inserted, and the third are the spokes (*aras*). The hub itself is nothing but a point, and the circle is its self-manifestation. The radii that emanate from the point or the hub, are its spokes. The spokes proceed towards a certain point but they have the propensity to recede back. The point from which they begin to recede cannot naturally remain the same, therefore it forms a curve. As all the points behave in a similar way the circumference comes into view. According to the Tāntric tradition, *nābhi* is of the shape of a lotus with ten petals. The yogin makes an effort with concentration to arrive at the central point of the navel from where he may be able to catch the direct path connected with higher planes of consciousness. To a common man of phenomenal vision the navel, being the centre of activity, pulls him down to the world of work and activity.

Etymology and Cognate Words

The word *nābhi* (f.) and *nabhya* (n.) are traditionally derived from the verbal root *ṇah-*, "*bandhane*" (PāDhā IV.57), to bind, tie or fasten. They may also be derived from the root *ṇabh-*, meaning to injure (PāDhā IV.130), to tear open (*nahyate badhnāti vipakṣādīnīti, naha bandhe naho bhaśca*, Uṇā 4.125, *iti iṇya bhaścāntādeśaḥ*).

The **Nirukta** defines *nābhi* thus: *nābhiḥ saṃnahanāt* (Nir IV.21), to fasten together. *Nābhi* is used in two genders, in masculine it signifies the principal king, the centre of the wheel, the *kṣatriya* race, and certain names; but in the feminine it means a particular limb of the body (*prāṇyaṅgam*). According to Gaṇa-Sūtra (*nābhi nabhaṃ ca*) the term *nābhi* takes the form *nabha* when the suffix *ya* (*yat*) is added to it (cf. Gaṇapāṭha under Pā V.1.2). Patañjali defines *nabhya* thus:

यदेव हि तन्मण्डलचक्राणां मण्डलचक्रं तन्नभ्यमित्युच्यते ।

Mahābh V.1.2

That which is the circular centre of each circular wheel is called *nabhya*, the hub. (Tr. S. Chattopadhyay)

Pañcatantra gives a clear view of both the hub and the spokes of a wheel and states how they mutually help each other.

अरैः सन्धार्यते नाभिर्नाभौ चाराः प्रतिष्ठिताः ।

Pañc I.93

The hub is firmly supported by spokes while the spokes are steadily fixed in the hub.

The synonyms of *nābhi* are *udarāvarta, piṇḍikā* (the nave of the wheel in which the spokes remain fixed); *tundakūpī*, (the depression on the belly) and the centre called *maṇipūra.*

Some of the compounds formed with *nābhi* are the following:

nābhikaṇṭaka = *āvarta*, whirlpool
nābhiguḍaka = *sphītanābhi*, swollen navel
nābhija = *pṛthivī*, the earth, and Brahmā
nābhibhū = Brahmā
nābhināla = the umbilical cord
nābhimaṇḍala = the circular navel
nābhipadma = the lotus of the navel

Nābhi also signifies the centre (*madhya* or *kendra*) in any geometrical, metaphorical or symbolical sense. (Cf. the centre of a circle: *vṛttasya madhyaṃ kila kendram uktam*, **Siddhānta-Śiromaṇi**, *Golādhyāya, Chedyakādhikāra* 41.) *Nābhi* is considered to be the middle of the body (*dehamadhya*).

Layers of Meaning

Nābhi is the central part of a wheel, from which spokes radiate. The spokes remain fixed in the hub and at the other end they go to the rim of the wheel, keeping always the same distance to describe the arc of the circumference. The body of the hub is generally round in shape and solid. The appropriate number of holes for fixing the spokes are made in it. The number of spokes radiating from the hub may vary according to local tradition and design.

Every human being has a navel seen as a small depression in the middle of the surface of the belly left by the severance of the umbilical cord. It is considered to be the central part of the body from which innumerable veins emerge and go to different directions of the body, some downward, some slanting, some upward. It is described to be of the shape of a wheel. Due to its centrality and the presence of the vital energy called *samāna* (balancing energy), it helps the body to remain in balance.

According to the spiritual tradition of India *nābhi* occupies a unique position. It is not only the central point of the body but cosmologically it is the point from which creation originates. For this reason Brahmā, the superintending divinity of creation, is described to have been born of the navel of Viṣṇu, the superintending divinity of maintenance as referred to in the **Mārkaṇḍeya Purāṇa**:

स नाभिकमले विष्णोः स्थितो ब्रह्मा प्रजापतिः ।

MārkPur LXXXI.51ab

Brahmā, the creator and the Lord of beings is established in Visṇu's lotus navel.

The universe has not only its source of creation (*utpattibhūḥ*) but also its steady support (*pratiṣṭhā-bhūmi*) in the navel; therefore the navel of the Cosmic *Puruṣa* as representing the universe, is said to have given birth to the hemisphere (*antarikṣa*).

For kindling fire in the Vedic rituals *araṇī* (fire sticks) are used* The central point of the lower *araṇi* is the *nābhi*, for it is supposed that fire remains latent there.

In the body microcosm, *nābhi* occupies a very unique position. The body of a foetus remains attached to the cavity of the vein of the mother with the umbilical cord (*nābhinādī*) by which the foetus gets its nourishment. It is thought to be one of the delicate points (*marman*) of the body.

According to Yoga and Tantra, *nābhi* is considered to be the central point where *ātman* remains predominantly present (*nābhāvaśeṣanāḍicakrabhūtāyāṃ prādhānyenātmā sthitaḥ*, SvT VII.7. Comm. Kṣemarāja). From the centre of the navel seventy two thousand *nāḍīs* emerge among which three are known as *iḍā, piṅgalā* and *suṣumnā*. In the Upaniṣad (BāMaUp) we find mention of ten *nāḍīs*: seven inside the head, while two function as down-going currents, and the tenth abides in the navel (*nābhyāṃ daśamaḥ*, BāMaUp II. 5.10). This tenth may easily be interpreted to be *suṣumnā*, the radiant one, which after having emerged from the centre of the navel goes straight to the heart, the joint of the eye-brow, and finally reaches *brahmarandhra*.

The Buddhist Tāntric doctrine attaches great importance to the navel where *caṇḍālī*, the spiritual fire, blazes up by the contact of sun and moon, wisdom (*prajñā*) and means (*upāya*), and ascends directly to reach the heart, the throat and finally the head where *bodhicitta* abides in its absolute state.

In **Yoga-Sūtra**, *nābhi* is envisaged as of the shape of a wheel, while to some it is of the shape of a lotus with thirty-two petals. But to the Tāntric thinkers it

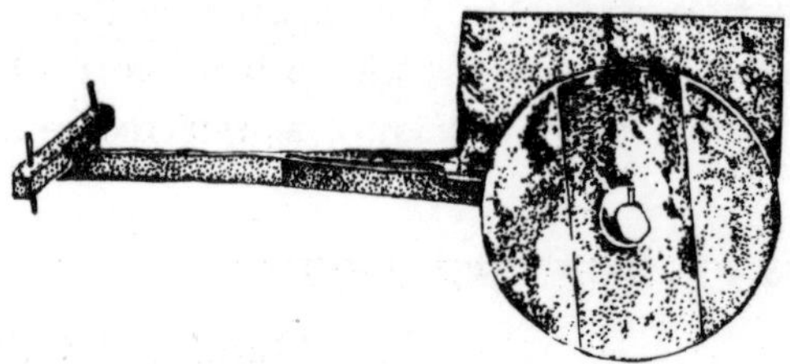

Figure 1: Vedic cart with *nābhi* (for Havirdhāna Soma)

is the place known as *maṇipūra cakra* with lotus having ten petals, considered to be the abode of fire.

With reference to the sacrificial pit of different shapes (*kuṇḍa*), *nābhi* is drawn in the middle of the *kuṇḍa* where all oblations are offered so that they may reach the divine being.

It is generally believed that the limbs below the navel are impure and limbs above it are comparatively pure. When the knot (*granthi*) of the navel is penetrated properly, the aspirant's journey towards spiritual advancement becomes certain.

During the sacred thread ceremony the teacher touches different limbs of the initiand, the navel, the heart and so on, chanting *mantras* to facilitate the disciple's vital energy flowing upward along the middle current.

Development of the Concept

Nābhi being both the centre of the wheel and the centre of the earth is conceived both physically and metaphysically. The hub in an ordinary wheel of a chariot, a bullock cart or any vehicle, though it may undergo a slight change of shape and size with age, yet occupies the central position in the wheel and directs the energy in a balanced way through the spokes to its circumference to move on. In the early Vedas the navel is considered to be the origin of rays of the sun representing a wheel (→*cakra*). The seven primal rays of the sun symbolizing the spokes, have their source in the navel. The concept that the navel of the cosmic Man is the source of the firmament (*antarikṣa*) has been hinted at in the Puruṣasūkta:

नाभ्या आसीदन्तरिक्षम् ।

ṚV X.90.14

From his (Puruṣa's) navel came the firmament. (Tr. J. Eggeling)

The firmament is the navel or the centre of →*Puruṣa*. When the cosmic *Puruṣa* is visualised as standing, the mid-space between the earth where his feet are, and heaven, his head, is his navel, the centre. Prajāpati, the creator, is also said to have his navel in the *antarikṣa* above the earth (*nābhidaghnam utthitam*, ŚBr V.1.5.2). Similarly, the sanctum of a temple (*garbhagṛha*) is the navel of *Puruṣa*, and thus may also be called *nābhi*, being the centre of the entire edifice.

In the **Ṛgveda** *nābhi* has also the meaning of kinship:

अमी ये सप्तरश्मयस्तत्रा मे नाभिरातता । ṚV I.105.9

Where those seven rays are shining, thence my house and family extend. (Tr. R.T.H. Griffith)

अजः पुरो नीयते नाभिरस्यानु ।

ṚV I.163.12

The goat who is his kin, is led before him. (Tr. R.T. H. Griffith)

A common prayer is uttered to Tvaṣṭṛ for the longevity of line and kindred (*nābhi*):

प्रजां त्वष्टा विष्यतु नाभिमस्मे अथा देवानामप्येतु पाथः ।

ṚV II.3.9

May Tvaṣṭar lengthen out our line and kindred, and may they reach the place which Gods inhabit. (Tr. R.T.H. Griffith)

The term *nābhi* has been given in **Nirukta** to connote relationship.

नाभिः संनहनात् । नाभ्या सन्नद्धा गर्भा जायन्ते इत्याहुः ।
एतस्मादेव ज्ञातीन् सनाभय इत्याचक्षते ।

Nir IV.21

Uterine is (so called) from being fastened together. It is said: children are born fastened to the umbilicus. Hence the near relatives are called as having a common umbilicus or a common tie. (Tr. L. Sarup)

The wheel, its hub, and the spokes are closely related. Therefore, it is surmised that where there is the wheel the navel and the spokes are invariably present. Their close association gives rise to the idea of kinship as *nābhi*; being the source or origin of everything, every entity is firmly fastened to the navel. Therefore the primary meaning of *nābhi* (to bind, to fasten), is very accurate. When the universe is represented as a wheel, whether it is *viśvacakra* or *kālacakra*, the former symbolizing space and the latter time, it is evident that everything, whatever it may be, is considered akin to each other, because it is closely related. Both the idea of kinship and source has been hinted at in the following verse:

दिव्यन्यः सदनं चक्र उच्चा पृथिव्यामन्यो अध्यन्तरिक्षे ।
तावस्मभ्यं पुरुवारं पुरुक्षुं रायस्पोषं वि ष्यतां नाभिमस्मे ॥

ṚV II.40.4

One (Pūṣan) in the heaven on high hath made his dwelling, on earth and in the firmament the other (Soma).
May they disclose to us great store of treasure, much longed for, rich in food, source of enjoyment. (Tr. R.T.H. Griffith)

Here we find the development of the literal sense of *nābhi*, navel, to the figurative meaning 'relationship' or source.

Similarly, the sacrificial altar from where the offerings are carried to the divine through Vaiśvānara, the sacred fire, is also considered to be the navel. The cavity of the fire-pit has a similarity to the cavity of the navel in the body:

वैश्वानर नाभिरसि क्षितीनां स्थूणेव जनाँ उपमिद् ययन्थ ।

ṚV I.59.1

Centre art thou, Vaiśvānara, of the people, sustaining men like a deep-founded pillar. (Tr. R.T.H. Griffith)

The above verse gives evidence to the idea that the fire is the navel which gives nourishment to the people and keeps them firmly fastened like a pillar.

When the fire is envisaged as a person its forehead is the sky and the centre of the earth is its navel (*nābhi*):

मूर्धा दिवो नाभिरग्निः पृथिव्या अथाभवदरती रोदस्योः ।

ṚV I.59.2

The forehead of the sky, the earth's centre, Agni became the messenger of earth and heaven. (Tr. R.T.H. Griffith)

Nābhi is the centre of the sacrificial pit and the sacred altar. It is also considered to be the centre of the earth.

देवान्यजन्तावृतुथा समञ्जतो नाभा पृथिव्या अधि सानुषु त्रिषु ।

ṚV II.3.7

Worshipping Gods, at ordered seasons decking them at three high places at the centre of the earth. (Tr. R.T.H. Griffith)

In a hymn to Varuṇa the Ṛgvedic seer praises the god as the one who "knows the secret names of the cows" and who is the seer-poet unfolding his poetic gifts (*kāvyā*). In the following verse he asserts:

यस्मिन् विश्वानि काव्या चक्रे नाभिरिव श्रिता ।

ṚV VIII.41.6

The gifts of poetic inspiration (*kāvyā= kavikarmāṇi*) inhere in Him who is as it were the hub within the wheel. (Tr. A.K. Coomaraswamy, combined with Geldner)

This means that the god is the dynamic centre of all poetic gifts and works.

Interrelatedness of the hub with the wheel is referred to in the **Atharva-Veda**. Time is here represented as a chariot with seven wheels:

सप्त चक्रान्वहति काल एष सप्तास्य नाभीरमृतं न्वक्षः ।

AV XIX.53.2

This Time hath seven rolling wheels and seven naves, immortality is the Chariot's axle. (Tr. R.T.H. Griffith)

The wheel may have a single hub or seven symbolizing seven regions of the universe or the seven days of the week.

While emphasising the idea of the relation between the spokes and the circumference, the **Atharva-Veda** states that both have their steady base in the central hub to which they remain firmly fixed. The nave of a wheel is the point of concentration.

यथा प्रधिर्यथोपधिर्यथा नभ्यं प्रधावधि ।
यथा पुंसो वृषण्यतः स्त्रियां निहन्यते मनः ॥

AV VI.70.3

Close as the felly and the spoke, fixt as the wheel-rim on the nave,
As an enamoured man's desire is firmly set upon a dame.
(Tr. R.T.H. Griffith)

The famous *brahmodya* (riddle) of **Ṛgveda** I.164 asks about "the navel of the earth":

पृच्छामि त्वा परमन्तं पृथिव्याः पृच्छामि यत्र भुवनस्य नाभिः ।
* * *
इयं वेदिः परो अन्तः पृथिव्या अयं यज्ञो भुवनस्य नाभिः ।

ṚV I.164.34ab-35ab (cf. also YV XXIII.62)

I ask you about the furthest limit of earth;
Where, I ask, is the centre of the world?
The altar is the furthest limit of earth;
this sacrifice of ours is the world's centre... (Tr. R. Panikkar)

Sacrifice is the vital centre (*nābhi*) of the earth because it connects earth and heaven, and makes humans reach the gods. Earth herself is the altar on which oblations are offered to the gods.

होतायक्षत्समिधेन्द्रमिडस्पदे नाभा पृथिव्या अधि ।

YV XXVIII.1

On the earth's centre, at libation's place let the priest worship Indra with the kindling-stick. (Tr. R.T.H. Griffith)

This earth also stands for relationship between man and cosmos. This relationship is expressed by the terms *nābhi*, *bandhu* (friend), *yoni* (source) and *garbha* (the embryo) (cf. Geldner).

द्यौर्मे पिता जनिता नाभिरत्र बन्धुर्मे माता पृथिवी महीयम् ।

ṚV I.164.33

Dyaus is my father, my begetter, kinship is here.
This great earth is my kin and mother. (Tr. R.T.H. Griffith)

While praising the earth the Vedic seers conceived of her as the mother. She was considered as the centre and the navel from which issued forth all the forces.

यत्ते मध्यं पृथिवि यच्च नभ्यं यास्त ऊर्जस्तन्वः संबभूवुः ।
तासु नो धेह्यभि नः पवस्व माता भूमिः पुत्रोऽहं पृथिव्याः ॥

AV XII.1.12

O Pṛthivī, thy centre and thy navel, all forces that have issued from thy body -
Set us amid those forces, breathe upon us. I am the son of Earth.
Earth is my mother. (Tr. R.T.H. Griffith)

The earth, the centre of all human activities serves as a common bond like the spokes about the chariot nave.

समानी प्रपा सह वोऽन्नभागः समाने योक्त्रे सह वो युनज्मि ।
सम्यञ्चोऽग्निं सपर्यतारा नाभिमिवाभितः ॥

AV III.30.6

Let what you drink, your share of food be common together, with one common bond I bind you.
Serve Agni, gathered round him like the spokes about the chariot nave. (Tr. R.T.H. Griffith)

In one context of the **Atharva-Veda** the gods are represented as a wheel where they remain firmly fixed in the hub, symbolizing unity in diversity.

दृढो दृंहस्थिरो न्यो ब्रह्म विश्वसृजो दश ।
नाभिमिव सर्वतश्चक्रमुच्छिष्टे देवताः श्रिताः ॥

AV XI.7.4

The firm, the fast, the strong, the hard, Brahma, the all-creating Ten.
Gods as a wheel about the nave, are fixed all round the Residue.
(Tr. R.T.H. Griffith)

Both gods and men are firmly fixed in the mysterious centre of the earth (*nābhi*):

यत्र देवाश्च मनुष्याश्चारा नाभाविव श्रिताः ।

AV X.8.34

Thereon the Gods and men are set as spokes are fastened in the nave. (Tr. R.T.H. Griffith)

The sacrificer's stool (representing a throne) in the context of the Sautrāmaṇi ritual is addressed as *nābhi.*

क्षत्रस्य योनिरसि क्षत्रस्य नाभिरसि ।

YV XX.1

Birthplace of princely power art thou, centre art thou of princely power. (Tr. R.T.H. Griffith)

The sacrificer's stool is addressed here as *yoni*, the source, and *nābhi*, meaning the place where everything remains firmly fixed. Prayer is addressed to it, so that the sacrificer may go directly to heaven to be born among the gods and become *sarvatanu*, i.e. with his entire body. The above two terms are symbolical for the new birth, reminding us of the uterus and the navel relating mother and child.

The revolving wheel represents sacrifice lasting for six days. Two *agniṣṭomas* are its circumference, the libations in the morning and the midday are its navel. The following description of the wheel shows that by means of sacrifice one can go to any place one likes. Just as the wheel serves the worldly purpose, similarly sacrifice leads the sacrificer to his goal.

एतदेव चक्रं यदभिप्लवः षळहस्तस्य यावभितोऽग्निष्टोमौ तौ प्रधीये,
चत्वारो मध्य उक्थ्यास्तन्नभ्यं गच्छति । वैवर्तमानेन यत्र कामयते तत्स्वस्ति ।

AitBr IV.3.15

Abhiplava ṣaḍaha (sixdays sacrificial work) is the revolving wheel of the gods. Two *Agniṣṭomas* form the circumference (of this wheel), the four *ukthyas* in the midst are then the nave. By means of this revolving (wheel of the gods) one can go to any place one may choose. (Tr. M.Haug)

It is thus clear that the term *nābhi* has been used in the Vedas not only to denote the hub of the wheel, but the centre, as in **Yajur-Veda**:

जिह्वा देवानाममृतस्य नाभिः ।

YV XVIII 89d

The God's tongue is the centre of Amṛta. (Tr. R.T.H. Griffith)

While constructing the altar in the shape of a chariot-wheel (*rathacakracit*), the priest lays bricks in such a way that it should have spokes and a circumference. The middle portion of the wheel consisting of sixteen bricks is known as the hub. The **Baudhāyana Śulbasūtra** describes it in the following way:

नाभिः षोडशमध्यमाः ।

BŚulSū V.19

The sixteen middle bricks form the nave of the wheel. (Tr. G. Thibaut)

The commentary elaborates the idea thus:

मध्ये पञ्चेष्टकापार्श्वमानीकं पञ्चविंशेष्टका चतुरस्रं परिगृह्य तस्य चतुरस्रस्या-वान्तरदिक्षु स्रक्तिषु या इष्टकाः तासां मध्येषु शङ्कुन्निहत्य स्पन्दया परितनोति। एवं षोडशेष्टकं चतुरस्रं भवति सा नाभिः ।

Comm. by Dwārakānātha Yajvan on BŚulSū V.19

In the middle one should place five bricks placing them diagonally and horizontally. From the directions of corners of the square one should ascertain the centre by placing a peg in the middle of them and then cover the entire space by means of movement. The space covered by sixteen bricks thus becomes a square. That is called *nābhi.*

The above text describes very simply where *nābhi* is to be located in the wheel.

नाभिमन्ततश्चतुर्थवेलायां परिकृषेत् ।

BŚulSū V.31

A circle is to be described in the nave of the distance of a quarter from the edge. (Tr. G. Thibaut)

In the Upaniṣads (cf. ChUp VII.15) *prāṇa* is compared to the hub of the wheel in which the spokes are fastened, being the centre of life. The **Kauṣītaki Upaniṣad** uses the same simile while speaking about the inter-relatedness of the elements of intelligence (*prajñāmātrāḥ*) and the elements of being (*bhūtamātrāḥ*):

यद्धि भूतमात्रा न स्युर्न प्रज्ञामात्राः स्युर्यद्वा प्रज्ञामात्रा न स्युर्न भूतमात्रा स्युः। न ह्यन्यतरतो रूपं किंचन सिध्येत् । नो एतन्नाना, तद्यथा रथस्यारेषु नेमिरर्पितो नाभावरा अर्पिता एवमेवैता भूतमात्राः प्रज्ञामात्रास्वर्पिताः प्रज्ञा-मात्राः प्राणेऽर्पिताः । स एष प्राण एव प्रज्ञात्मानन्दोऽजरोऽमृतः ॥

KauṣUp III.8

For, truly, if there were no elements of existence, there would be no elements of intelligence. Verily, if there were no elements of intelligence, there would be no elements of existence. For from either alone no form whatsoever would be possible. And this (the self of intelligence) is not many. For as in a chariot the felly is fixed on the spokes and the spokes are fixed on the hub, even so these elements of existence are fixed in the elements of intelligence and the elements of intelligence are fixed in the breathing spirit. This same breathing spirit is, truly, the intelligent self, bliss, ageless, immortal. (Tr. S. Radhakrishnan)

In the physiology of Āyurveda, *nābhi* occupies a very important role. **Suśruta Saṃhitā** deals elaborately with *nābhi* thus:

मातुस्तु खलु रसवहायां नाड्यां गर्भनाभिनाडी प्रतिबद्धा। सास्य मातुराहाररसवीर्यमभिवहति । तेनोपस्नेहेनास्याभिवृद्धिर्भवति। असञ्जाताङ्गप्रत्यङ्ग-प्रविभागमानिषेकात् प्रभृति शरीरावयवानुसारिणीनां रसवहानां तिर्य्यग्गतानां धमनीनामुपस्नेहो भवति ।

SuSam Śārīrasthāna III.31

The umbilical chord (*nāḍī*) of the foetus is attached to the cavity of the vein or artery of its maternal part through which the essence of lymph-chyle (*rasa*) produced from the assimilated food of the mother, enters into its organism and fasten its growth and development, (a fact which may be understood from the analogy of percolation or transudation of blood). Immediately after the completion of the process of fecundation, the vessels (*dhamanī*) of its maternal body which carry the lymph-chyle (*rasa*) and run laterally and longitudinally in all directions through it, tend to fasten the foetus with their own transudation all through its continuance in the womb. (Tr. K.L. Bhisagratna)

The navel, being the centre of all the veins (*nāḍī*), is one of the most delicate points (*marmasthāna*).

The most controversial views regarding the foetus and which part of it first starts to show its development have been discussed and it is categorically stated that it is from the navel that it begins to develop.

गर्भस्य खलु संभवतः पूर्वं...नाभिरिति पाराशर्यः, ततो हि वर्धते देहो देहिनः।

SuSam Śārīrasthāna III.32

Parāśara says that the navel portion of the foetus that will be born (*saṃbhavataḥ*) first shows its appearance before other parts of the body. Through the umbilical cord an embryo draws its substance from mother's body. (Tr. K.L. Bhisagratna)

It has also been stated that the navel being one of the softer parts of the body originates from mother.

It has been observed by the early physiologists such as Suśruta that the umbilical region is the locality of fire (*jyotisthānam*).

तस्यान्तरेण नाभेस्तु ज्योतिः स्थानं ध्रुवं स्मृतम् ।
तदाधमति वातस्तु देहस्तेनास्य वर्धते ॥

SuSam Śārīrasthāna IV.58

Be it clearly understood that there exists fire or heat (*jyoti*) in the umbilical region (of the foetus) which is found by its bodily *vāyu* and thus contributes to the growth of its body. (Tr. K.L. Bhisagratna)

As regards the existence of heat or fire in the navel according to the view of the physiologist, it is traditionally accepted by most Āgamas and Tantras that the navel called *maṇipūra* is the place from where fire emerges (cf. HT).

Moreover it has also been emphasized that *nābhi* is the source of all *dhamanīs*, according to Suśruta, from which place they go to spread out to reach different parts of the body.

नाभिप्रभवाणां धमनीनामूर्ध्वगा दश, दश चाधोगामिन्यः, चतस्रस्तिर्य्यग्गाः।

SuSam Śārīrasthāna IX.4

Of the twentyfour *dhamanīs*, which (originally) have their roots in the navel region (*nābhi*), ten have upward course, ten have downward course, and four flow laterally or transversely.
(Tr. K.L. Bhisagratna)

The above view is further elaborated by saying *nābhitaḥ prasṛtāḥ śirāḥ* (SuSam Śārīrasthāna VII.23) – the nerve vessels originating from the navel spread over the whole organism. The specific characteristic of *nābhi* denoting 'fastening' is referred to, along with the Upaniṣadic concept that the navel is the very life of beings.

यावत्यस्तु शिराः काये सम्भवन्ति शरीरिणाम् ।
नाभ्यां सर्वा निबद्धास्ताः प्रतन्वन्ति समन्ततः ॥

नाभिस्थाः प्राणिनां प्राणाः प्राणान्नाभिर्व्युपाश्रिता ।
सिराभिरावृता नाभिश्चक्रनाभिरिवारकैः ॥

SuSam Śārīrasthāna VII.4-5

All the *śirās* (vessels) that are found in the organisms of embodied beings, originate from and are fastened to the navel and (being rooted thus) they spread all over the bodies. The life (*prāṇa*) of an organic being has its seat in the vessels and on the other hand it is in *prāṇa* the navel remains well-established. The navel is surrounded by veins like the hub of a wheel is with its spokes. (Tr. K.L. Bhiṣagratna)

The body does possess some cavities of which the navel is one. They are considered to be gates of the body (cf. *navadvāre pure dehī*, BhG V.13c). Of these gates or outlets some are helpful for the body to receive light and some located in the lower part of the body are used for sending out impure substances from the body. These gates of the body lie below the navel, therefore, they are considered impure. The **Manu Smṛti** supports the above view:

ऊर्ध्वं नाभेर्यानि खानि तानि मेध्यानि सर्वशः ।
यान्यधस्तान्यमेध्यानि देहाच्चैव मलाश्च्युताः ।

Manu V.132

All these cavities (of the body) which lie above the navel are pure, (but) those which are below the navel are impure, as well as excretions that fall from the body. (Tr. G. Bühler)

It is probably due to this central position of the navel that a deep navel is considered to be an auspicious sign, as Kālidāsa describes in **Raghuvaṃśa**:

उन्नाभ इत्युद्गतनामधेयस्तस्या यथार्थोन्नतनाभिरन्ध्रः ।
सुतोऽभवत्पङ्कजनाभकल्पः कृत्स्नस्य नाभिर्नृपमण्डलस्य ॥

Ragh XVIII.20

He (Śīla) had a son celebrated by the name Unnābha, the space of whose navel was really deep, and who, looking like Viṣṇu, became the supreme ruler of the entire circle of kings. (Tr. R.G. Nandargikar)

The king as described in the above quote was called Unnābha because his navel was exceedingly deep, for it is a general view that three characteristic signs are highly appreciated in men and are supposed to be deep:

स्वरः सत्त्वं च नाभिश्च गाम्भीर्यं त्रिषु शस्यते ।

Comm. by Mallinātha on the above verse

Depth in three is appreciated (in man). They are voice, strength of character and the navel.

As in human physiology the navel is considered to be the centre of the body, in the same way according to the view of the ancient geographers the centre of the earth was Jambūdvīpa.

The **Mṛgendra Āgama** lends support to the above view:

जम्बूद्वीपं क्षितेर्नाभिस्तद्वृत्तम् ।

MṛgĀ vp 40cd

The navel of the earth is Jambūdvīpa and it is circular in shape.

Nābhi is the centre both in space (in cosmography) as well as in time. In **Mahābhārata** the navel is mentioned with reference to *kālacakra* in which the days of the year consisting of seven hundred and twenty in all are represented by the spokes of the wheel firmly fixed in the hub (*ekaṃ nābhiṃ saptaśatā arā śritāḥ*, MBh I.3.64).

The **Svacchanda Tantra** states that though the limited self, the energy belonging to the Lord (*prabhuśakti*) and the vital energy have their seats in the body permeating it everywhere, yet they have their own specific centres. The *śakti* known as *madhyaśakti* has its place below the genital organ called *mūlādhāra*, while in the navel the limited self has its seat.

नाभ्यधो मेढ्रकन्दे च स्थिता वै नाभिमध्यतः ।
तस्माद्विनिर्गता नाड्यस्तिर्यगूर्ध्वमधः प्रिये ॥

SvT VII.7cd-8ab

The limited self, the energy belonging to the Lord and the vital energy remain below the navel and still below the genital organ in the bulbous root and in the centre of the navel respectively. From the navel, o dear, veins emerge and proceed obliquely, upward and downward.

It is from the centre of the navel that all the principal nerve vessels (*nāḍīs*) remain firmly rooted where ten principal vital currents flow.

चक्रवत्संस्थितास्तत्र प्रधाना दश नाडयः ।

SvT VII.8cd

Ten principal nerve vessels remain fastened in the navel as spokes in a wheel.

The navel is considered to be the centre from which the upward current flows and it is for this reason the adept makes a daily practice of concentrated meditation on Brahmā seated on the lotus of the navel in the morning *sandhyā* prayer. Symbolically the syllable *a*, representing the first component of *Om* is located in the navel; moreover *nābhi* also represents *jāgrat*, the waking state.

The **Yoga-Sūtra** of Patañjali contains an interesting Sūtra:

नाभिचक्रे कायव्यूहज्ञानम् ।

YSū III.29

[As a result of concentration] upon the wheel of the navel [there arises the intuitive] knowledge of the arrangement of the body. (Tr. Woods (adapted))

Nābhi being the centre, the source of all *nāḍīs*, one is able to know the constitutive elements of the body like *dhātus*, wind, bile, phlegm, blood, semen and others (cf. **Vyāsa-Bhāṣya** on the above).

According to Buddhist Tāntric tradition *nābhicakra* is of the shape of a lotus with thirty-two petals, but in other Tantras it is known as *maṇipūra* in the shape of a lotus having ten petals. According to both the schools it is considered to be the place of fire in a latent form.

The **Hevajra Tantra** states:

चण्डाली ज्वलिता नाभौ दहति पञ्च तथागतान् ।

HT I.1.31

Caṇḍālī blazes up at the navel.
She burns the five Buddhas. (Tr. D.L. Snellgrove)

Kṛṣṇācārya in his commentary interprets the above verse in various ways. He takes *nābhi* to mean the centre (*nābhiśabdo madhyavācī*), and the unity of voidness and compassion to mean *caṇḍālī*. As the compact unity of both which represents fire, blazes up, it consumes five *skandhas* with the result that the *haṃkārasvabhāva śaśī*, located at the summit of the yogin's body, begins to melt. As it melts, it flows downwards through the central vein, pervading the whole body through the various *cakras* as it goes. It reaches the lowest *cakra* and *A* and *Haṃ* become *AHAṂ*.

The navel is one of the six *cakras*, as described in the **Netra Tantra**. This wheel is the wheel of *māyā*, the deluding power, and is considered to be the discerning ability of man and is also the cause of the phenomenon of creation. This *māyācakra* causes limited knowledge in the self which remains entangled in the net of *māyā*. To the yogin, the navel is not simply a particular part of the body, it is really the centre (*madhya*) of the microcosm. This centre is attained only when the yogin is able to have a firm hold of the vibrative energy of the vital air functioning through the body. Kṣemarāja interprets the verses of **Netra Tantra** VII.16.18 thus:

प्राणस्पन्दात्माक्रियाशक्तिरुत्तमातिशयेनोद्गता सती मध्यमा भवति समस्त-देहस्य नाभिर्मध्यं तत्र प्राप्ता जायते ।

When power of activity with the characteristic of the pulsative vibration of the vital energy becomes exceeding, that is excellently intent on uprising, it becomes the middlemost (*madhyamā*). Then it is said to have reached the middle of the entire body.

The **Mālinīvijaya Tantra** emphasises that from the centre of the navel a perpendicular shaft is meditatively conceived as standing erect like the stalk of a lotus. The shaft is to be conceived as steadily supported by the *ādhāraśakti*, representing the earth four fingers in breadth below the navel (*nābhyadho caturaṅgulam*). The other end of it has reached the opening of the palate.

ततो नालमनन्ताख्यं दण्डमस्य प्रकल्पयेत् ।

MVT VIII.56cd

The stalk is called Ananta representing the shaft.

In the above context the body is the source and the base of the central current, though the current originates from *mūlādhāra*, yet in the navel the *prāṇaśakti* assumes the form of *daṇḍa*. This shaft becomes well-manifest only to the yogin, therefore *nābhi* is the centre from where the dynamic energy goes straight up to reach *lambikā* in the shape of a shaft.

Jayākhya Saṃhitā deals with *nābhi* as the central place of the sacrificial pit.

दिङ्मध्येऽप्यथ कुण्डस्य नाभिं कुर्याद् द्विजोत्तम ।
अश्वत्थपत्रसदृशीं मेखलोपरि संस्थिताम् ॥

JaySam XV.22

O excellent among the twice born, in the middle of the quarters the *nābhi* of the sacrificial pit should be made. It is like the shape of the leaf of a fig tree (peepal) and remains established above the girdle.

The navel occupies the central place inside the pit (*kuṇḍa*) over which sacrificial offerings are made. When fire blazes up in the navel inside the sacrificial pit one should conceive it as *brahmāgni*, the original fire. It has been stated in **Jayākhya Saṃhitā**:

स्वकारणाग्नौ नाभिस्थे य ऊर्ध्वेन्धनवत्स्थितः ।
स्वभावदीप्तब्रह्माग्नौ परितश्चोदरोज्ज्वलम् ॥
स्मृत्वा मन्त्रं तु तन्मूर्ध्नि पतमानं द्विजाम्बरात् ।
चिन्तयेदमृतं त्वाज्यं पुरा यच्चाहृतं द्विज ॥

JaySam XII.121-122

The fire which is blazing as the fire of Brahmā in the navel is rising upward. This primal fire is self-luminous and is of the characteristic of the fire of Brahman. One should remember the *mantra* as exceedingly brilliant on all sides and the core of it is also of the same

> nature. Then one should meditate that the clarified butter which he has collected before, is of the nature of nectar as falling from the void over the fire of the navel.

From the above description it is clear that the navel is the place of fire.

Śāradā-Tilaka gives a description of the navel inside the *kuṇḍa* in the following way.

> मुष्ट्यरत्न्येकहस्तानां नाभिरुत्सेधतारतः ।
> द्वित्रिवेदाङ्गुलोपेता कुण्डेष्वन्येषु वर्धयेत् ॥
> यवद्वयक्रमेणैव नाभिं पृथगुदारधीः ।
> योनिकुण्डे योनिमब्जकुण्डे नाभिं विवर्जयेत् ॥

ŚāTil III.79-80

> The navel should be one fist in elevation and one cubit in width with reference to sacrificial pits with the measurement of one cubit square. The *nābhi* should be extended by the wise in other pits by two, three and four *aṅgulas*. The pit in the shape of a womb of the lady and that of the shape of a lotus *nābhi* should not be made.

The **Ahirbudhnya Saṃhitā** states that Lord Viṣṇu resides in the body of beings and drives the body of each individual by means of the wheel of the navel (*dvādaśāreṇa nābhicakreṇa*, AhSam XXXIII.112cd).

In the Arts

by B. Bäumer

In the context of the Arts, *nābhi* has a symbolic, a physical, as well as aesthetic aspect, in which the physical becomes symbolic. Symbolically, *nābhi* stands for a concept of centrality which is derived from the human body and from cosmogony/cosmology. It is not a static centrality as an immobile point, but an organic and hence dynamic centre (→*bindu*) on which the growth of the whole structure depends. If the texts insist that *nābhi* is the centre of the body, though in another context it may be the heart, this is significant for the continuum of micro- and macrocosm.

Nābhi as a symbol of centrality can be demonstrated in the following fields:

1. Ritual: e.g. the centre of the sacrificial altar symbolized by a lotus, one of the common symbols of the navel. According to Āgamic tradition this centre is the place where the sacred fire is taking its birth from the womb of the goddess of speech (*vāgīśvarī*).

2. Architecture: In secular architecture, whether town-planning or construction of a house, and in sacred architecture, a *maṇḍala* is first drawn with *nābhi*

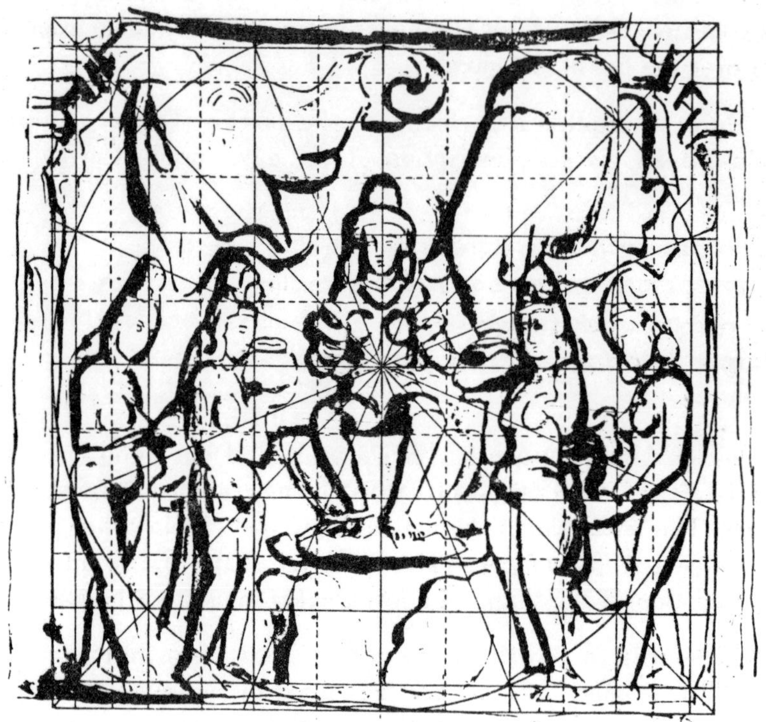

Figure 2: Mahālakṣmī, Mahabalipuram

as the centre. This is considered as the navel of the *vāstupuruṣa* (→*puruṣa*) according to Śilpa and Vāstu texts (e.g. Mayam VII.43cd). This centre should not be 'injured' at the time of construction, being a vulnerable point:

> सर्वेषां ग्रामाणां नाभिं न प्रोतयेन्मतिमान् ।
>
> Mayam IX.54cd
>
> In every village the sage should not pierce the navel. (Tr. B. Dagens (adapted))

This centre or navel is often symbolized by a lotus:

> ब्रह्मासनपदे मध्येऽम्बुरुहं स्थाप्यमेव च ।
>
> Mayam XII.49cd
>
> At the centre of the seat of Brahmā a lotus should be placed. (Tr. B. Dagens)

3. In sculpture, the navel of the main deity often coincides with the geometrical centre of the whole composition set in a circle, and hence becomes

the centre of concentration and radiation. This is particularly true in the case of images representing creative or generative deities such as Lakṣmī, Viṣṇu in various forms, and some images of Śiva, as has been analyzed by Alice Boner. As examples we can mention Mahālakṣmī at Mahabalipuram, Mahālakṣmī at Ellora Cave XIV and Viṣṇu on Ādiśeṣa at Ellora Cave XV. In these and many other images, the central position of the navel of the deity suggests concentrated creative energy ready to expand. Viṣṇu is in a state of rest before creation when a lotus grows from his navel with Brahmā seated on it. His designation as *padmanābha* clearly indicates this relationship of navel and lotus, of cosmic rest and new creation. The Śilpa texts speak of the central thread measuring the images as *nābhi-sūtra*, since it touches the navel of the image (cf. RauĀ kp XXXV.114,etc.). Apart from the symbolical place of the navel in the divine image, its physical description is given as follows:

नाभिः प्रदक्षिणावर्तस्तद्विस्तारं तु षड्यवम् ।
निम्नं यवद्वयं विद्यात्.. ।

AjitĀ kp XXXVI. 98ab

The navel should be made as turning to the right (clockwise). Its width measures six *yavas* (one *yava* = 1/8 of an *aṅgula*). The depression should be known to have the measurement of two *yavas.*

The navel is a small depression in the middle of the surface of the belly. The central point of the navel should be incised in such a way that it may move clockwise.

4. In dance, the navel also occupies a central position. The **Nāṭya-Śāstra** does not deal explicitly with *nābhi*, but it is founded on the āyurvedic and yogic conception of the navel as the centre of bodily movement and as seat of energy. It is significant that a text dealing with music and dance like **Saṅgīta-Ratnākara** describes *nābhi* in detail, and calls it *brahmagranthi*, 'the knot of brahman', because of its central position (→*brahman*).

आधाराद् द्व्यङ्गुलादूर्ध्वं मेहनाद् द्व्यङ्गुलादधः ॥
एकाङ्गुलं देहमध्यं तप्तजाम्बूनदप्रभम् ।
तत्रास्तेऽग्निशिखा तन्वी चक्रात्तस्मान्नवाङ्गुले ॥
देहस्य कन्दोऽस्त्युत्सेधायामाभ्यां चतुरङ्गुलः ।
ब्रह्मग्रन्थिरिति प्रोक्तं तस्य नाम पुरातनैः ॥
तन्मध्ये नाभिचक्रं तु द्वादशारमवस्थितम् ।
लूतेव तन्तुजालस्था तत्र जीवो भ्रमत्ययम् ॥

SR I.2. 145cd-148

Two finger-length above the base and two finger-breadth below the genitals in the space of one finger-breadth is the centre of the body,

shining like mother gold.
There is located a slender flame of fire at a distance of nine fingers that the life-source of the body is found, four fingers in elevation as well as in extension. This has been called *brahmagranthi* by the ancients.
Right in its centre is situated the 'cycle of the umbilicus' (*nābhi-cakra*) with twelve spokes, and like the spider caught in (its own) net, yonder there wanders the self-conscious being. (Tr. R.K. Shringy and P.L. Sharma)

While describing the fourteen locations for the movement of the hands (*karakṣetra*) in dance, the same text describes the movement of the hands held at the level of or touching the navel (SR VII.546-547ab). The central position of the navel in dance has to do with the balance of the human body (*sama*). "The *sama* has another concomitant in visual and aural terms. This is the continual awareness of the centre. The centre of the wheel (*cakra*) of the Vedic and Upaniṣadic image corresponds to the navel of the human body. Thus we have the pictorial image of Man set in a framework of a circle with the navel at its centre and a vertical median corresponding to one diameter of the circle... From the position of the standing man in the circle with the navel as the centre and the spinal cord as the vertical median, various positions are evolved." (Kapila Vatsyayan, The Square and the Circle of the Indian Arts, pp. 52-53).

5. In music the navel is important as a centre for the production of voice.

आत्मेच्छया महीतलाद् वायुरुद्यन् निधार्यते ।
नाडीभित्तौ तथाकाशे ध्वनी रक्तः स्वरः स्मृतः ॥

BṛD 15

By the will of the *ātman*, the *vāyu* (that is moving upward) from the base of the 'earth' (*nābhi*, navel) (and) is held on the 'wall' of the *nāḍīs* and in the space, is known as *svara*, the delightful sound. (Tr. P.L. Sharma)

The **Bṛhaddeśī** elsewhere also talks of *nābhi* as the starting-point of the upward movement of the vital air in sound production (BṛD 1: *tatrādautāvadihāgnipavanasaṃyogāt puruṣaprayatnapreritordhvam nābherūrdhvadeśamākrāmad...*). The **Saṅgīta-Ratnākara** also describes the process of the manifestation of sound in the human body:

आत्मा विवक्षमाणोऽयं मनः प्रेरयते, मनः ।
देहस्थं वह्निमाहन्ति स प्रेरयति मारुतम् ॥

ब्रह्मग्रन्थिस्थितः सोऽथ क्रमादूर्ध्वपथे चरन् ।
नाभिहृत्कण्ठमूर्धास्येष्वाविर्भावयति ध्वनिम् ॥

SR I.3.3-4 (also cf. PāŚik 6-7)

Desirous of speech, the individuated being impels the mind, and the mind activates the 'fire' (battery of power) stationed in the body, which in turn stimulates the vital force. The vital force stationed around the root of the navel rising upwards gradually manifests sound (*nāda*) in the navel, the heart, the throat, the cerebrum and the cavity of the mouth as it passes through them. (Tr. R.K. Shringy and P.L. Sharma)

The centre of energy being situated below the navel, the navel is itself the first point that is touched by the vital air moving upwards. The deep breathing in the production of voice is even today spoken of as *nābhi kā svara* (Hindi, navel voice) in oral tradition.

It is thus clear that each of the Arts in its own context depends on the organic and creative centre of energy of the navel (*nābhicakra*) for its unfoldment.

Process

The navel (*nābhi*) means the centre where energy remains concentrated and directed to different directions. As it is both a static symbol and centre of dynamism, it is represented as a hub in a wheel. In its creative process it acts in two different ways, the one pushing the energy to become externalized, while the other bringing the subtle energy to follow a direct and upward course in order to reach some other centres of more subtle energy. The former way may be designated as extroverted but the latter is introverted. Though the navel is commonly thought to be the centre of activity, it is also to be conceived as the abode of rest.

The navel thus conveys both movement and rest. Even in rest it is moving. The wise one can see the centre through which he can reach the real goal. If one fails in one's effort, one is sure to remain entangled in the meshes of the wheel of time.

Conclusion

We have discussed above how the concept of *nābhi* has developed in different dimensions and how it has assumed the concrete shape of a hub of a chariot wheel, the navel of the body of the human being, and the centre of an edifice. Its meaning has passed from abstract to subtle, i.e. from the concept of a cosmological centre to the spiritual centre of the body. In whatever sense it has been used in philosophical, spiritual and secular texts, its basic meaning, namely 'fastening' is always present. The navel fastens the world as if firmly established in Dhruva, the polar star, as its axis. This is its terrestrial character. So long as it remains intact, either in the wheel of a cart or the wheel of the body, the cart or body moves freely.

The central point of the navel is the source and the body as a whole is the passive recipient of the energy which has been released by the central source. The aspirant in Yoga makes an active effort to utilize the energy from the central point of the navel which proceeds along the course of *suṣumnā*.

In conclusion, it may be stated that *nābhi* stands for the centre of a living organism, whether it is the human body, the sacrificial altar, the *maṇḍala*, or the temple. It stands for stability (*dhṛti*) and movement (*gati*). The fire remains always present in the navel, it propels, but does not allow its energy to go astray. The navel does not only fasten tightly but allows everything to move in order with discipline. It is the centre which gives life.

H.N. Chakravarty

Select Bibliography

Coomaraswamy, A.K. : "Kha and other words denoting zero in connection with the Metaphysics of Space" in: Selected Papers, Vol. 2 ed. by Lipsey, Roger. Princeton: Princeton University Press, 1977.

Dharmadhikari, T.N.: Yajñāyudhāni. Pune: Vaidika Saṃśodhana Maṇḍala, 1989.

CAKRA

Overview

Cakra, disk or wheel, is one of the central symbols of Indian civilization, manifested in Art and Yoga. *Cakra*, which has been etymologically derived from the root *kṛ-*, to make, implying the idea of movement, denotes a wheel, or a circular disk. The wheel consists of a circular frame which turns on an axle, with a hub or nave in the centre (→*nābhi*) with which a number of spokes are attached, connecting it with the outer rim. It may be a cart-wheel, or the potter's wheel, or the spinning-wheel, all of which are known from the dawn of Indian civilization and are still in use today.

Cakra denotes the solar disk which is a symbol of Time since the Veda, and the emblem of the solar deity Viṣṇu. It is also a powerful weapon (e.g. *sudarśana cakra*).

The entirety of the universe has been conceived as a cosmic wheel, *viśvacakra*, or the wheel of Brahman, *brahmacakra*, since it is moved from within by the indwelling power of Brahman. In the sense of the wheel of existence (*bhavacakra*) it refers to the law of nature as ever moving and rotating, implying a cyclical view of the course of history. The *saṃsāracakra* is the ever-rotating wheel causing the beings to continually pass through a cyclic change. In its microcosmic meaning it denotes the human body or the individual soul (*cakrapuruṣa*).

In the Vedas *cakra* represents the wheel of Time wherein twelve are the fellies and three are the naves, in which three hundred and sixty spokes are tightly fixed. The solar chariot is sometimes described as one-wheeled (*ekacakra*), symbolizing the disc of the sun.

The Buddha is said to have set the *dharmacakra* in motion, the wheel of the Law, in contradistinction to *bhavacakra*, the wheel of existence and early Buddhist art has represented the wheel as a powerful symbol. The Aśokan *cakra* has been chosen as an emblem for the Indian Republic, for it signifies movement and order. The spokes fixe‘ in a hub imply unity in diversity.

In the yogic and tāntric context, *cakra* assumes a very important role denoting subtle spiritual centres in the body, or an aggregate of divinities (e.g. *śakticakra*). It is also used as a synonym of →*yantra* or →*maṇḍala*, e.g. the *śrīcakra*, the body of the lady divine and the temple of goddess Śrī.

Etymology and Cognate Words

Cakra can be derived from the following roots: *kṛ-*, to do, to make, with the suffix *-ka*; or from *kram-*, to step, to go towards; or *cak-*, to be satiated or satisfied with the suffix *-ra*; or *car-*, to move, to stir, with metathesis.

Thus the **Nirukta** defines *cakra*:

> चक्रं चकतेर्वा । चरतेर्वा । क्रामतेर्वा ।
>
> Nir IV.27
>
> *Cakram* (wheel) is derived from (the root) *cak* (to repel) or *car* (to move), or *kram* (to go). (Tr. L. Sarup)

The Pāṇinian school derives *cakra* from the reduplicated root *kṛ-*, to do, with the suffix *-ka* (i.e. *a*) (cf. Vārttika on Pā VI.1.12). The action of *cakra* is said to be *purogamana*, moving forward.

Abhinavagupta gives a hermeneutical etymology, following Yāska, which throws more light on the term:

> विकासात्तृप्तितः पाशोत्कर्तनात्कृतिशक्तितः ।
> चक्रं कसेश्चकेः कृत्या करोतेश्च किलोदितम् ॥
>
> TĀl XXIX.106cd-107ab
>
> The term *cakra* signifies expansion, satisfaction, cutting of bonds, the energy of activity.
> The verbal roots that are involved (in the formation of *cakra*) are *kas, cak, kṛt* and *kṛ*, which mean to shine, to satisfy oneself, to cut and to do respectively.

From the above etymologies it is clear that Abhinavagupta gives a detailed and deep significance to the verbal root *kas-*, meaning to go, move, approach, beam, shine, to denote expansion, and *cak-*, satiation (*tṛpti*) and so on.

Cakra is semantically related to *vṛtta* and *maṇḍala*, denoting a circular shape. The parts of the wheel are designated as *nābhi* (nave), *ara* (spoke), *nemi* or *pradhi* (felly, circumference, rim). The **Amarakośa** defines *cakra* as follows: "The wheel is a part of the chariot, at whose end is the felly, *nemi* being feminine and *pradhi* masculine" (*cakraṃ rathāṅgaṃ tasyānto nemiḥ strī syāt pradhiḥ pumān*, AmKo *kṣatravarga* 502).

Innumerable compounds are formed with *cakra*, as e.g.: *cakravartin* (universal ruler), *cakrapāda* and *cakrayāna* (vehicle), *cakrapāṇi* or *cakradhara* (the one holding the discus as his emblem, i.e. Viṣṇu), *cakravyūha* (circular array of troops), *cakravāla* (circle, horizon); *cakraka* (arguing in a circle), *cakravṛddhi* (compound interest), *ekacakra* (a name of a village known in the **Mahābhārata**); and as last part of a compound: *rāśicakra* (zodiacal cycle), *saṃsāracakra* (cycle of birth and death), *yoginīcakra* (circle of *yoginīs*), etc. In all such compounds, apart from the meaning of wheel, the following meanings are implied: any circular arrangement, a group or host of beings or divinities, a circular shaped design, a dynamic and ordered centre and circumference.

Layers of Meaning

The *cakra* is essentially a rotating wheel with a centre and a circumference. It is the single disk of the sun which travels over all lands and sheds glory over all. The centre of the disk is supposed to be a point which is pulsating and always intent on movement (→*bindu*). The centre of the wheel is a hollow nave (→*kha*, cf. *sukha, duḥkha*). The central point being dynamic it naturally gives birth to a second one and the second also by its innate dynamism gives birth to another. Therefore, in this way a line becomes manifest. The shortest distance that is covered by two points is a straight line. Because of its urge for expansion the points go on extending as radii which finally are arrested at the circumference of a circle.

The hub or the →*nābhi* of a wheel does indeed have a centre where the *aras* or spokes remain fixed and go to every point on the circumference. The centre is equidistant from every point on the circumference.

Symbolically the wheel represents the universe, *viśvacakra*, in both of its aspects known to be Time and Space. The central point (→*bindu*) being ever pulsating is thought of to represent the luminous self abiding in the centre of the physical sun and esoterically abiding in the core of the heart. While the wheel functions in the whole body as *dehacakra*, as an individual, *cakras* function as conscious centres in different locations of the body. The all-inclusive macrocosm of this very wheel is variously named as *kālacakra*, *sudarśanacakra*, *dharmacakra, saṃsāracakra* and so on.

The wheel is the support (*ādhāra*, in the sense of Space) in which everything becomes manifest. It has two aspects, the one is static and the other dynamic. The dynamic *cakra* does not only have its own innate pulsation but it propels others to move on. The Pāñcarātra doctrine considers the movement of the cosmic wheel as being propelled by the divine Will by whose dynamism it is continuously in movement and manifests itself as creation, maintenance and dissolution. At one end, the periphery, appear all the pictures of creation and at the other end everything goes to rest in dissolution. Between these two ends *sthiti*, the state of existence shines. It is a wheel with a hub in the middle representing dissolution. The outer rim is creation. As it revolves, the spokes appear as existence.

According to the **Ahirbudhnya Saṃhitā** (III.48 ff.), the cosmic wheel is the sun beautiful in appearance (*sudarśana*). With the creative upsurge of the will it shines as *darśana*, viewing or in other words it is only *dṛk*, seeing, but soon it manifests itself as a pulsative will (*saṃkalpaḥ spandanātmakaḥ*) and later it evolves as activity, *kriyā*, which in the form of a disk becomes one with all beings (*sarvabhāvātmikā)*. As a dynamic energy it controls the universe and also protects it. It shines as a *cakra* in the hand of Viṣṇu. It not only illumines but delights, and at the same time adds heat and thus bestows good to the world in the form of the sun, the moon and the fire. It is this wheel which serves as weapons (*śastra*) and scriptures (*śāstra*) which only remain as the directive principle in the heart of the real knower (*śāsanaṃ hṛdayasthitam*). For the good of the universe *śāstra* emerges from the *kriyā* aspect of Sudarśana (cf. AhSam III.49-51).

Development of the Concept

Cakra, the round disk of the sun, is first referred to in the Vedas to mean the luminous object moving like a wheel in the firmament. The *cakra* represents Viṣṇu, the all-pervading Divine, striding over three regions (fire, lightning and sun).

इदं विष्णुर्विचक्रमे त्रेधा नि दधे पदम् ।

ṚV I.22.17

Through all this world strode Viṣṇu; thrice his foot he planted.
(Tr. R.T.H Griffith)

The disk of the sun revolves in the upper sky unwastingly like a wheel. It has all the characteristics of the chariot-wheel with a felly (*sanemi*) and car-poles.

सनेमि चक्रमजरं वि वावृत उत्तानायां दश युक्ता वहन्ति ।
सूर्यस्य चक्षू रजसैत्यावृतं तस्मिन्नार्पिता भुवनानि विश्वा ॥

ṚV I.164.14

The wheel revolves, unwasting, with its felly, ten draw it, yoked to the far-stretching car pole.
The sun's eye moves encompassed by the region: on him dependent rest all creatures. (Tr. R.T.H. Griffith)

The bright eye of the sun, the impeller of the wheel, is the eye of all, the eye of Mitra, of Varuṇa, of Agni and of the universe (cf. *cakṣur mitrasya*...ṚV I.115.1, etc.). The cosmic eye is the disk of the sun which makes strides (*kram-*) over three regions.

Sometimes the disk of the sun is referred to as a chariot or a chariot-wheel but more so as a wheel with all its common characteristics, viz. hub and felly (*nābhi* and *nemi*). The wheel is attached underneath a car which is drawn by horses.

सप्त युञ्जन्ति रथमेकचक्रमेको अश्वो वहति सप्तनामा ।
त्रिनाभि चक्रमजरमनर्वं यत्रेमा विश्वा भुवनाधि तस्थुः ।

ṚV I. 164.2

Seven to the one-wheeled chariot yoke the Courser; bearing seven names the single courser draws it.
Three-naved the wheel is, sound and undecaying, whereon are resting all these worlds of being. (Tr. R.T.H. Griffith)

The car which moves on a single wheel represents here the sun itself and the rays, though one, having seven names, draw it. According to Yāska the second hemistich chiefly describes the year, with three seasons on which all created beings rest together. With reference to the above passage Yāska has given the etymological derivation of *cakra* as : *cakraṃ cakatervā, caratervā, krāmatervā* (Nir IV.27).

The sun's disk (*cakra*) representing Time has been referred to in a good number of Vedic verses.

द्वादश प्रधयश्चक्रमेकं त्रीणि नभ्यानि क उ तच्चिकेत ।
तस्मिन्त्साकं त्रिशता न शङ्कवोऽर्पिताः षष्टिर्न चलाचलासः ॥

ṚV I.164.48

Twelve are the fellies, and the wheel is single, three are the naves. What man hath understood it?
Therein are set together spokes three hundred and sixty, which in nowise be loosened. (Tr. R.T.H. Griffith)

The translator adds a note in order to elucidate the meaning: The single wheel is the year; the twelve spokes are the months; the three naves are the three seasons (hot, wet and cold) of four months each and the spokes are the days of the luni-solar year.

The car (*ratha*) to which the wheels are set is derived from the verbal root *raṃh-* (*raṃhater gatikarmaṇaḥ*), to speed, to move on, and it stands for the Sun, the disk which moves along and is yoked with seven horses.

इमं रथमधि ये सप्त तस्थुः सप्तचक्रं सप्त वहन्त्यश्वाः ।

ṚV I.164.3

The seven who on the seven-wheeled car are mounted have horses, seven in tale, who draw them onward. (Tr. R.T.H. Griffith)

In several places the sun seated on a chariot (*cakra*) represents the luminous eye which sees the world below. Therefore the prayer is uttered by the seers thus:

तच्चक्षुर्देवहितं शुक्रमुच्चरत् । पश्येम शरदः शतम् ।

ṚV VII.66.16

A hundred autumns may we see that bright Eye, God-ordained, arise. (Tr. R.T.H Griffith)

The chariot (*ratha*) of the sun because of its luminosity and radiating light, is viewed as golden:

हिरण्ययी वां रभिरीषा अक्षो हिरण्ययः । उभा चक्रा हिरण्यया ।

ṚV VIII.5.29

Golden is its supporting shaft, the axle also is of gold, and both the wheels are made of gold. (Tr. R.T.H. Griffith)

Cakra does not only mean the sun's disk that floods the whole region with light and life, but it serves as the weapon in the form of a discus. Deviation from one connotation to another is amply found in the Vedas.

सूरश्चक्रं प्र वृहज्जात ओजसा प्रपित्वे ।
वाचमरुणो मुषायतीशान आ मुषायति ॥

ṚV I.130.9

Waxed strong in might at dawn he (Indra) tore the Sun's wheel off. Bright red, he steals their speech, the Lord of Power their (of Asuras) speech he steals away from them. (Tr. R.T.H. Griffith)

In the above context the wheel of the sun has been used as a discus to harm the enemies which in the Epic is attributed to Viṣṇu.

The seven-wheeled chariot (*saptacakram*) symbolizing the year is referred to in the following hymn:

सोमापूषणा रजसो विमानं सप्तचक्रं रथमविश्वमिन्वम् ।
विषूवृतं मनसा युज्यमानं तं जिन्वथो वृषणा पञ्चरश्मिम् ॥

ṚV II.40.3

Soma and Pushan, urge your chariot hither, the seven-wheeled car that measures out the region.
That stirs not all, that moves to every quarter, Five reined and harnessed by the thought, ye mighty. (Tr. R.T.H. Griffith)

In the **Atharva-Veda** also the symbolism of *ratha* (chariot) and *cakra* is contained in a riddle:

अष्टाचक्रं वर्तत एकनेमि सहस्राक्षरं पुरो नि पश्चा ।
अर्धेन विश्वं भुवनं जजान यदस्यार्धं कतमः स केतुः ॥ AV XI.4.22

It rolleth on, eight-wheeled and single-fellied, and with a thousand eyes, forward and backward.
With one half it engendered all creation, what sign is there to tell us of the other? (Tr. R.T.H. Griffith)

The chariot of the sun is referred to here. Its movement – one forward and the other backward – refers to day and night. The wheel of Pūṣan is referred to in one **Ṛgveda** hymn. It can be interpreted both as a wheel and a discus, for it has a felly which rotates but does not waver. By the force of the term *riṣyati* (injures) it can easily be interpreted as a weapon of Pūṣan.

पूष्णश्चक्रं न रिष्यति न कोशोऽव पद्यते ।
नो अस्य व्यथते पविः ।

RV VI.54.3

Pūṣan's wheel is not injured, the well (of his car) falls not down, nor does its felly waver. (Tr. A.A. Macdonell)

In a singular **Atharva-Veda** hymn the disk of the sun or the human body is represented as a fort of gods. This very hymn has been in later Tantra texts interpreted as the divine abode of Mother Śrī.

अष्टाचक्रा नवद्वारा देवानां पूरयोध्या ।
तस्यां हिरण्ययः कोशः स्वर्गो ज्योतिषावृतः ॥

AV X.2.31

The fort of Gods, impregnable, with circles eight and portals nine, contains a treasure-chest, celestial, begirt with light. (Tr. R.T.H. Griffith)

The Vedic seers realised that the rotating wheel representing the disk of the sun remains ever fresh only because it goes on moving. The verbal root *car-* meaning to move on is very apt for the wheel which is the Sun itself. The following passage of the **Brāhmaṇa** speaks highly of movement thus:

चरन्वै मधु विन्दति चरन्त्स्वादुमुदुम्बरम् ।
सूर्यस्य पश्य श्रेमाणं यो न तन्द्रयते चरंश्चरैवेति चरैवेति ॥

AitBr 7.15

The wanderer finds honey and sweet *udumbara* fruit. Behold the beauty of the sun, who is not wearied by his wanderings.
Therefore, wander, wander. (Tr. Martin Haug)

In another hymn of the **Atharva-Veda** we find that *cakra* is the symbol of Time.

सप्त चक्रान्वहति काल एष सप्तास्य नाभीरमृतं न्वक्षः ।
स इमा विश्वा भुवनान्यञ्जत्कालः स ईयते प्रथमो नु देवः ॥

AV XIX.53.2

This Time hath seven rolling wheels and seven naves, immortality is the chariot's axle. This Time brings hitherward all worlds about us, as primal Deity is he entreated. (Tr. R.T.H. Griffith)

Time as represented here by the wheel is a divinity. It rides over the world causing seasonal changes; but the axle bestowing immortality is highly desirable to the mortal.

The same tune is heard when the following hymn is read carefully:

द्वे ते चक्रे सूर्ये ब्रह्माण ऋतुथा विदुः ।
अथैकं चक्रं यद्गुहा तदद्धातय इद्विदुः ॥

AV XIV.1.16

Two wheels of thine the Brahmans know, Sūrya, according to their time.
That which is hidden only those who know the highest truths have learned. (Tr. R.T.H. Griffith)

The concept of time causing change, decay and death is closely related to the wheel, but the wheel which is endless is the wheel-divine (*devacakram*) riding on which the gods wander about through the worlds of mortals and finally lead the sacrificer to the luminous abode of Brahman. Thus states **Śāṅkhāyana Brāhmaṇa**:

देवचक्रं वा एतत्परिप्लवं यत्संवत्सरस्तदमृतत्वम् ।

ŚaṅkhBr XX.1

The year is a revolving divine wheel. That is immortality. (Tr. S. Chattopadhyay)

The **Nirukta**, while giving the etymological meaning of *cakra*, describes the chariot of the sun.

सप्त युञ्जन्ति रथम् । एकचक्रमेकचारिणम् ।
चक्रं चकतेर्वा । चरतेर्वा । क्रामतेर्वा ।

Nir IV.27

Seven yoke the one-wheeled car, i.e. the car which moves on a single wheel. *Cakra* (wheel) is derived from (the root), *cak-* (to repel) or *car* (to move), or *kram* (to go). (Tr. L. Sarup)

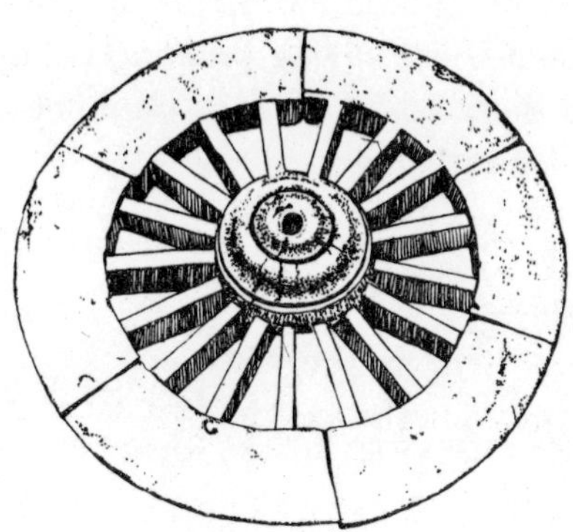

Figure 1: Vedic Wheel: *Ratha-cakra*

In the context of the ritual called *ādhāna*, i.e. depositing three fires, the *ratha-cakra*, the chariot-wheel is made to rotate by a brahman priest along the ground, from the place of *gārhapatya* fire to the *dakṣiṇā* and lastly to the *āhavanīya* fire place.

> स ब्रह्मा रथचक्रमधिरोहति – नाभिदघ्नऽउद्धितम् ।
>
> ŚBr V.1.5.2
>
> The Brahman (priest) mounts a cart-wheel, set up on (a post) as high as navel. (Tr. J. Eggeling)

According to Taittirīya ritualists the wheel after being mounted by the brahman is to be turned thrice in a sun-wise motion.

According to Āpastamba the wheel is described to be made of *udumbara* wood with seventeen spokes.

> तस्मिन्नौदुम्बरं रथचक्रं सप्तदशारं प्रतिमुञ्चति ।
> औदुम्बरं रथचक्रं ब्रह्मारोहति ॥
>
> ĀpŚrSū XVIII.4.3.11
>
> The chariot-wheel consisting of seventeen spokes made of udumbara wood is fixed (on a peg dug firm, in the *cātvāla*). The Brahmā priest mounts the chariot wheel made of *udumbara* wood.

In the **Śulba-Sūtra** we find how the physical *cakra* is fashioned.

> रथचक्रचितं चिन्वीतेति विज्ञायते । द्वयानि तु खलु रथचक्राणि भवन्ति ।
> साराणि च प्रधियुक्तानि ।
>
> BŚulSū V.1-3
>
> He is to construct the *agni* in the shape of a chariot-wheel: such is

the tradition. There are indeed two kinds of chariot wheels. Namely those with spokes and those having *pradhis* (i.e. massive wheels consisting of a square piece to which four segments of a circle are attached). (Tr. G. Thibaut)

The same text states how to prepare the *rathacakraciti.*

चतुःषष्टिरराश्चतुःषष्टिर्वेदिः ।

BŚulSū V.20

(In a *Rathacakraciti*), sixtyfour bricks form the spokes of the wheel, sixtyfour the *vedi* (that means the empty interstices between the spokes). (Tr. G. Thibaut)

Mahābhāṣya of Patañjali (V.1.2) speaks of two types of wheels: *aravanti*, with spokes and *anaravanti*, without spokes, but in every case wheels should have *nābhis*, hubs.

The **Chāndogya Upaniṣad** makes use of the symbol of the wheel to clarify a point. The chariot which was known to the people of old had two wheels.

स यथोभयपाद् व्रजन् रथो वोभाभ्यां चक्राभ्यां वर्तमानः प्रतितिष्ठत्येवमस्य यज्ञः प्रतितिष्ठति यज्ञं प्रतितिष्ठन्तं यजमानोऽनु प्रतितिष्ठति । स इष्ट्वा श्रेयान् भवति ।

ChUp IV.16.5

As a two-legged man walking, or a chariot proceeding with both wheels, is well supported, so his sacrifice is well supported. The institutor of the sacrifice is well supported after the sacrifice which is well supported. (Tr. R.E. Hume)

The above quote uses the analogy of two wheels of a car in order to bring home to the idea how the sacrificer and the sacrifice are mutually inter-related like the two wheels making the steady movement of the chariot possible.

The view which is implicit in the Saṃhitās, becomes vividly explicit in the Upaniṣads. The *cakra* retaining all the physical characteristics of a wheel now signifies the indwelling soul of the body.

तमेकनेमिं त्रिवृतं षोडशान्तं शतार्धारं विंशतिप्रत्यराभिः ।
अष्टकैः षड्भिर्विश्वरूपैकपाशं त्रिमार्गभेदं द्विनिमित्तैकमोहम् ।

ŚvUp I.4

We understand him (as a wheel) with one felly, with a triple tire, with sixteen end-parts, fifty spokes, twenty counter-spokes, with six sets of eight, whose one rope is manifold. Which has three different paths, whose one illusion (*moha*) has two conditioning causes. (Tr. R.E. Hume)

The verse quoted above is interpreted to mean a wheel with a felly and spokes, applied to the soul generally interpreted as the indwelling self. Following the Śāṃkhya philosophy, the felly stands for *ātman*, its three tyres are three *guṇas*, the sixteen end-parts are the five elements, five organs of perception and five organs of action. In the above way everything has been explained.

By the intuitive sicht of the seers *cakra* is now viewed as not only all-inclusive, all-abiding, but as one integral principle.

सर्वाजीवे सर्वसंस्थे बृहन्ते तस्मिन् हंसो भ्राम्यते ब्रह्मचक्रे ।
पृथगात्मानं प्रेरितारं च मत्वा जुष्टस्ततस्तेनामृतत्वमेति ॥

ŚvUp I.6

In this Brahma-wheel the soul (*haṃsa*) flutters about, thinking that itself (*ātmānam*) and the Actuator are different. When favoured by Him, it attains immortality. (Tr. R.E. Hume)

Any series of actions or the relation of cause and effect is generally presented with the simile of wheels, to explain the cosmic law or the law of nature. Viewed in this perspective, the beauty of interrelatedness becomes manifest.

अन्नाद्भवन्ति भूतानि पर्जन्यादन्नसम्भवः ।
यज्ञाद्भवति पर्जन्यो यज्ञः कर्मसमुद्भवः ॥
कर्म ब्रह्मोद्भवं विद्धि ब्रह्माक्षरसमुद्भवम् ।
तस्मात्सर्वगतं ब्रह्म नित्यं यज्ञे प्रतिष्ठितम् ॥
एवं प्रवर्तितं चक्रं... ।

BhG III.14-16a

Living beings are born of food. Food is produced by rain. Rain is due to sacrifice. Sacrifice is the offspring of rituals. Know that the rituals are born of the Vedas, and that the Vedas are born of imperishable Reality. Therefore, the all-pervading Vedas are eternally rooted in sacrificial rites. So was the wheel in motion set. (Tr. A.G.K. Warrier)

The cycle in the form of food and sacrifice goes on rotating endlessly.

तस्मादन्नात्पुनर्यज्ञः पुनरन्नं पुनः क्रतुः ।
एवमेतदनाद्यन्तं चक्रं सम्परिवर्तते ॥

YājSm III.4.124

Then from the food the sacrificial fire is born. Then food is born again and again comes sacrifice. Thus the wheel of food and sacrifice goes on moving in a cyclic order.

The **Viṣṇu Purāṇa** also refers to the sun as a potter's wheel which rotates continually and thus causes day and night for the earth.

कुलालचक्रपर्यन्तो भ्रमन्नेष दिवाकरः ।
करोत्यहस्तथा रात्रिं विमुञ्चन् मेदिनीं द्विज ॥

ViPur II.8.29b-30a

... and whirling round like the circumference of a wheel of a potter, he (sun) distributes day and night upon the earth. (Tr. Wilson)

Certainly from the time of the **Mahābhārata**, *cakra* came to signify the wheel of Time. Time shows itself symbolised as a wheel with all its physical characteristics and it is eulogised as divine.

चतुर्विंशतिपर्व त्वां षण्णाभि द्वादशप्रधि ।
तत्त्रिषष्टिशतारं वै चक्रं पातु सदागति ॥

MBh III.133.22

May that ever-revolving wheel (Time) that has twentyfour joints, six naves, twelve peripheries and 360 spokes protect you. (Tr. M.N. Dutt)

The wheel as a symbol of the universe (*saṃsāracakra*) goes on rotating continually and all beings remain enmeshed in it.

एवं संसारचक्रेऽस्मिन् व्याविद्धे रथचक्रवत् ।
तमेति भूतग्रामोऽयं भूतग्रामेण कार्यवान् ॥

MBh III.9.32

(Yudhiṣṭhira said:) Even thus, endued with actions, creatures come into this wheel of existence that is continually turning like the wheel of a chariot, and even thus, coming thither, they meet with their fellow creatures.

For **Mahābhārata**, in continuation of the **Kaṭha Upaniṣad**, the car symbolizes the body of living beings (cf. KaṭhUp III.3 *ātmānaṃ rathinaṃ viddhi śarīraṃ rathameva ca*, "know thou the soul (*ātman*) as riding in a chariot. The body is the chariot"). The limited self experiences pleasure and pain in a cyclic order while remaining entangled in the wheel of existence (cf. MBh XI.7.14cd: *sa tu saṃsāracakre'smiṃścakravat parivartate*).

The **Mahābhārata** also refers to the potter's wheel using the simile in the context of living beings.

यथा च मृण्मयं भाण्डं चक्रारूढं विपद्यते ।
...एवं देहाः शरीरिणाम् ॥

MBh XI.9ab, 11d

As an earthen pot placed on the potter's wheel undergoes misfortunes, ... so it is in the case of the embodied soul.

In the **Mahābhārata** *cakra* is also mentioned as the dreadful weapon of Nārāyaṇa or Kṛṣṇa (cf. MBh I.19.6)

In the context of Āyurveda, in the **Suśruta Saṃhitā**, we find a short description of veins of the human body which remain fastened steadily in the navel like the spokes of the wheel from where they proceed to different parts of the limbs (→*nābhi*).

यावत्यस्तु शिराः काये सम्भवन्ति शरीरिणाम् ।
नाभ्यां सर्वा निबद्धास्ताः प्रतन्वन्ति समन्ततः ॥

* * *

शिराभिरावृता नाभिश्चक्रनाभिरिवारकैः ॥

SuSam Śārīrasthāna VII.3,6

The veins that are situated in the body of embodied people, are all fastened in the navel from where they pervade every part of it... The navel is surrounded by the veins as the hub of the wheel is enclosed by its spokes.

Caraka Saṃhitā uses the term *cakra* with its rotational movement in order to explain how the circulation of blood and other fluids function in the body.

संतत्या भोज्यधातूनां परिवृत्तस्तु चक्रवत् ।

CarSam Cikitsāsthāna XV.21

The gradual conversion of *dhātus* runs incessantly in a cyclic order. (Tr. P.V. Sharma)

The comparative superiority of destiny and human effort (*daiva* and *puruṣakāra*) is explained by the instance of the wheel of a chariot:

यथा ह्येकेन चक्रेण न रथस्य गतिर्भवेत् ।
तथा पुरुषकारेण विना दैवं न सिध्यति ॥

YājSm 1.351

As the movement of the chariot is not possible only by a single wheel, in the same way destiny never becomes fruitful without human effort.

Patañjali describes that *nābhicakra*, being the centre of the body, and the primary source of veins, can be made the centre of attention for the yogin. It is not only the central part of the body but also the central point where all the subtle ingoing and outgoing currents meet.

नाभिचक्रे कायव्यूहज्ञानम् ।

YSū III.19

When one practises concentration (*saṃyama*) in the wheel of the navel, one is able to know the structure of the whole body.

In support of the above view Bhoja, the commentator, writes that the navel is the centre of the body structure. It is from here where all the nerves and veins emanate and spread throughout the body. He further states that this *cakra* is of the shape of a lotus having ten petals, but according to some it consists of sixteen petals.

The **Yogasūtra Bhāṣya** also refers to the wheel of existence (*saṃsāracakra*) constituted of six spokes.

ततः पुनर्धर्माधर्मौ सुखदुःखे रागद्वेषाविति प्रवृत्तमिदं षडरं संसारचक्रम् ।

YSūBh IV.11

From that again arise piety and impiety, happiness and misery, attachment and hatred. Thus revolves constantly the six-spoked wheel of existence. (Tr. H. Aranya)

Bhartṛhari refers to *alātacakra*, the fire-brand which goes on rotating when motion is applied to it only once.

स्पर्शप्रबन्धो हस्तेन यथा चक्रस्य सन्ततः ।
न तथालातचक्रस्य विच्छिन्नं स्पृश्यते हि तत् ॥

Vāk II.291

Just as it is possible to have continuous contact of the hand with the wheel, that is not possible in the case of the fire-brand which can be touched only with interruption. (Tr. Iyer)

In Buddhism the symbol of the wheel is central. It signifies either the wheel of existence (*bhava-cakra*) or the Wheel of Law (*dharmacakra*). The implication of the *dharmacakra* is the dynamic nature of the Buddha's teaching, which moves from one person to another, and also the symbolism of the centre, the spokes and the periphery. It is by virtue of *dharmacakra* that people are able to attain *nirvāṇa*.

त्रिपरिवर्तं द्वादशाकारमनुत्तरं धर्मचक्रं प्रवर्तयन्तम् ।

LVi XIII p.111

He (Lord Buddha) turned the highest *dharma*-wheel thrice with twelve aspects of (four noble truths).

The four noble truths (*āryasatya*) are: 1. Life is suffering, 2. desire of life is the cause of suffering, 3. extinction of that desire is the cessation of suffering, 4. the eightfold path leads to that extinction.

धर्मचक्रं तु दृङ्मार्गः

AbhidhKo VI.54

The wheel of *Dharma* is the path of insight.

The commentary gives an etymological meaning thus: as it moves on (*caṅkramaṇāt*) it is called *cakra*, that is wheel. Because of its identity of nature the path of seeing (the truth) is called the wheel of *dharma*.

The text further elaborates the idea thus:

आशुगत्वाद्यरादिभिः

AbhidhKo VI.54

It moves on fast by means of its spokes and other elements.

It moves on quickly, leaving one place and occupying another. It moves on in such a way that the place that has not been covered yet (*ajita*) is made to come under its sway (*jita*). Esoterically the movement of the wheel signifies victory over affliction born of wrong views regarding the body etc. and when it is won over, the knower of the truth is placed in the path of liberation. The wheel moves on to cover a high ground and then comes down to the lower. In this way the path of liberation comes to the view of the aspirant over and over again. The **Sphuṭārthā** Commentary further throws light on the concept of the wheel of *Dharma* in the following way:

एवमाशुगत्वादिभिः अरादिभिः साधर्म्यादार्याष्टाङ्गो मार्गश्चक्रमिति ।

AbhidhKoBh VI.54

Thus an account of its identity of nature of having speedy movement of its spokes the eight-fold right path is known as the wheel.

The right insight, the right vow, the right effort and the right memory are its spokes; the right speech, the right activity and that which ends in right occupation (*karmānta*) represent the hub of the wheel, and *samādhi* stands for the rim of the wheel.

As the wheel revolves thrice it assumes twelve forms. Suffering is the sublime truth (*āryasatyam*), this is the first movement. It is to be known, that is the second movement. It has already been understood rightly, this is the third movement. These three circular movements of the wheel are known as *darśanamārga.* A single complete movement of the wheel brings forth right view, then follows knowledge free from doubts (*jñāna*), then follows *vidyā* which is the true nature of the reality, followed by *buddhi* which gives the right understanding. Relating these four, *cakṣu, jñāna, vidyā* and *buddhi* to the above three movements, the wheel assumes a twelve-fold form (summary of **Sphuṭārthā** Commentary).

The **Lalita-Vistara** clearly explains the *Dharma-cakra-pravartana* of the Buddha as *dharma-yajña* or *dharmavarṣa*, showers of *dharma.* The wheel of *dharma* is called *amṛta-cakra*, the wheel of immortality (LVi 26.17) and *anuttara-cakra* (LVi 26.12), the wheel transcendent.

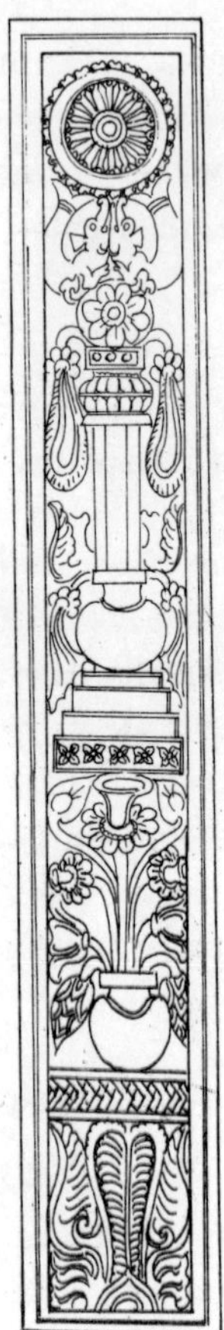

Figure 2: Cakradhvaja on Sarnath Railing Pillar

प्रवर्तयतु भगवान् धर्मचक्रं प्रवर्तयतु सुगतो धर्मचक्रं बहुजनहिताय बहुजनसुखाय लोकानुकम्पायै महतो जनकायस्यार्थाय सुखाय देवानां च मनुष्याणां च ।

LVi 26.p.301

The great preacher of divine majesty set in motion the *Dharma Cakra* for the welfare of many, for the happiness of many, as compassion to the whole world, for the good and happiness of all gods and men. (Tr. V.S. Agrawala)

Lalita-Vistara further describes the concrete form of the wheel thus:

सहचित्तोत्पादधर्मचक्रप्रवर्ती नाम बोधिसत्त्वो महासत्त्वस्तस्यां वेलायां चक्रं सर्वरत्नप्रत्युप्तं सर्वरत्नप्रशोभितं नानारत्नालंकारव्यूहविभूषितं सहस्रारं सहस्ररश्मिसनाभिकं सनेमिकम् ।(LVi p.302)

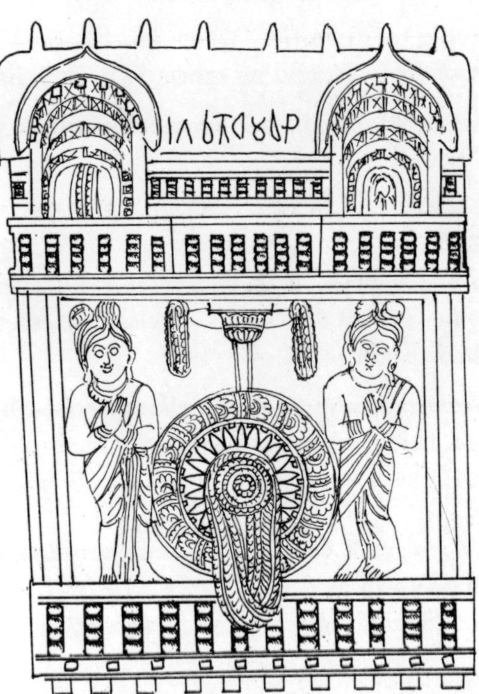

Figure 3: Worship of the *dharmacakra*, Bharhut

Then at that time the Bodhisattva of great strength named *Dharmacakra-pravartī*, with the quickening of *citta* set in motion the *cakra*, that was studded with many jewels, adorned with many gems, decorated with a variety of bejewelled ornaments, of thousand spokes, of thousand rays, having a navel, with a felly. (Tr. V.S. Agrawala)

The Saddharmapuṇḍarīka Sūtra eulogizes the wheel of Law thus:

अविवर्त्तिचक्रं हि प्रवर्तयन्ता ॠद्धीवलस्मिन् स्थित ये च धीराः
प्रमोचयन्तो बहुप्राणिकोटी महाद्रुमो सो च प्रवुच्चते हि ॥

SaddhSū V.33

Those who move forward the wheel that never rolls back, and with manly strength stand firm in the exercise of miraculous power, releasing many *koṭis* of beings, those are called great trees. (Tr. H. Kern)

In the Buddhist Tantras, *cakra* has two meanings, one is an assembly of divinities, the other refers to the centres in the subtle body. Thus the **Hevajra Tantra** defines *cakra* as an assembly of divinities which purifies the senses.

चक्रं निवहं खधात्वाख्यं विषयादीनां विशोधनम् ।(HT II.3.28ab)

> *Cakra* is an assembly (of divinities) which purifies the sphere of sense and so on, and thus it is as void as space. (Tr. D.L. Snellgrove)

Kānhapāda, the commentator, in his **Yogaratnamālā** interprets the verse in a different way.

> चक्रमिति महासुखलक्षणं, निवहं, करुणा खधातुः सर्वधर्मशून्यता विषयादीनां विशुद्धिः ।
>
> In the context of the wheel it is characterised by supreme bliss, while *nivaha* means mercy (*karuṇā*), which is in essence the void. That signifies purification of all objects.

With reference to *cakra* he says that it is characterised by supreme blissfulness, *nivahaṃ* is *karuṇā*, the essence of which is the void and purification of the objects is nothing but of the nature of voidness i.e., *śūnyatā* which is free from all attributes.

The four centres of consciousness in the body are generally named *cakra*, but specifically they are known as:
(a) *nirmāṇa-cakra*, (b) *dharma-cakra*, (c) *saṃbhoga-cakra*, and (d) *mahāsukha-cakra*.

> निर्माणचक्रे पद्मं चतुःषष्टिदलं धर्मचक्रे अष्टदलम् ।
> सम्भोगचक्रे षोडशदलं महासुखचक्रे द्वात्रिंशद्दलम् ॥
>
> HT I.1.23
>
> In the *nirmāṇacakra* located in the navel the lotus has sixtyfour petals, in the *dharmacakra* in the throat the lotus has sixteen petals, in the *mahāsukhacakra* on the head the lotus has thirtytwo petals. (Tr. D.L. Snellgrove)

The above *cakras* are also known as *kāyacakra*, the wheel of the body, *cittacakra*, the wheel of mind, *vākcakra*, the wheel of speech, the unity of body, mind and speech. They are *cakras*, for they help the adept to attain gradual perfection or development of spirit (in accordance with the verbal root *kasī* = *vikāse*).

Another meaning of *cakra* in Buddhism is the cycle of existence. The phenomenal world, according to the Buddhist, rotates like a wheel. Every being is caught in the spokes of the wheel of existence and everyone is bound to pass through different states. Thus *cakra* is known as *bhavacakra* consisting of twelve phases. The chain of existence runs thus: *avidyā - saṃskāra - vijñāna - nāmarūpa - ṣaḍāyatana - sparśa - vedanā - tṛṣṇā - upādāna - bhava- jāti - jarāmaraṇa*.

This *cakra* veils those who have been born in the womb, but for the Buddha there is no veil (*nirāvaraṇa*). That is, the cycle of *avidyā* and others constitute a chain of existence, one following the other as cause and effect, but the enlightened one is not bound by this chain of relations.

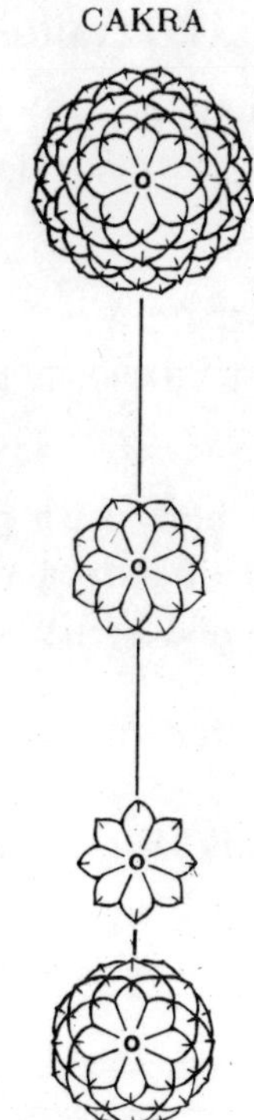

Figure 4: Yogic *cakras* according to Buddhist Tantras

Vimalaprabhā, a Buddhist Tāntric commentary on **Kālacakra Tantrarāja** gives a definition of *kālacakra* in the following manner.

काकारो कारणे शान्ते लकाराच्च लयोऽत्र वै ।
चकाराच्चलचित्तस्य क्रकारात्क्रमबन्धनात् ॥

Vimalaprabhā I-2 p17

The syllable *kā* signifies the tranquil cause, and the syllable *la* means dissolution in it. The syllable *ca* denotes unsteady modalities of the mind and *kra* signifies gradually fastening the unsteady mind in it.

Vimalaprabhā gives another interpretation of *kālacakra* thus:

कालः परमाक्षरो महासुखलक्षणः, तेनोत्पादितं निरावरणं स्कन्धधात्वादिकं चक्रं यस्य शरीरमसौ कालचक्रः ।

Vimalaprabhā I-2 p17

Time (*kāla*) is the Supreme immutable one which is characterised by the highest bliss (*mahāsukhalakṣaṇam*) which gives birth to the wheel in the form of *skandha* and *dhātu* as are free from any veil - and this wheel itself is its body and that is known as *kālacakra*.

In the Śaiva Tantras too the human body itself is to be meditated upon as a *cakra* consisting of sixteen radii, the central point of which is the self located in the core of the heart as the Supreme I.

षोडशारं स्मरेच्चक्रमात्मदेहमनन्यधीः ।
एषोऽहमिति संचिन्त्य स्वकार्यपरिवारितम् ॥

MVT XVI.2

One should meditate on his body with perfect concentration of intellect as a wheel consisting of sixteen radii. 'This is me' meditate thus even when it is surrounded by its evolutes.

Aham (Ego), the central subject, remains well-attended by five *jñānendriyas*, five *karmendriyas* and five subtle elements along with the mind, all these sixteen are presided over by *ahaṃkāra*, only then the body machine functions properly like a wheel, represented with sixteen spokes.

The **Netra Tantra**, takes the body as the centre of *cakras* where consciousness vibrates.

जन्माख्ये नाडिचक्रं तु नाभौ मायाख्यमुत्तमम् ॥
हृदिस्थं योगिचक्रं तु तालुस्थं भेदनं स्मृतम् ।
बिन्दुस्थं दीप्तिचक्रं तु नादस्थं शान्तिमुच्यते ॥

NT VII.28cd-29

In the *mūlādhāra* (*janmādhāra*) the wheel of all the channels (veins) is located. In the navel the wheel called *māyā* is located, from where the delusive *māyā* functions. In the heart the wheel of yogis is located. The *cakra* named *bhedana* is located in the palate. In the *bindu*, a little above the joint of the two eyebrows, the *dīpticakra* is located. The sixth *cakra* is *śānti* which is located in *nāda* and which bestows tranquillity.

The commentator explains the meaning of the names of the various *cakras*: One is named *yogicakra* because in this centre the yogin attains concentration of mind. The next is called *bhedana-cakra* because it is crossed with much effort. The *dīpticakra* is so called because it is luminous. Thus the pulsating centres of consciousness are six according to the Tantra. To an awakened yogi these centres or wheels have each of them a central point. When the yogi arrives at the centre of the lowest *cakra*, through a radius he soon finds himself functioning in the wheel next above it. Then by his continuous effort he reaches the sixth leaving the five *cakras* behind.

Abhinavagupta's **Tantrāloka** throws enough light on the concept of *cakra* and *cakreśvara*, the yogin who becomes the lord of the wheel.

आनन्दचक्रवह्न्यश्रि

TĀl V.111a

The blissful wheel is a triangle of fire.

Jayaratha explains the term *vahnyaśri* as the fiery triangle (*vahnyaśri iti trikoṇam*). When one realises absorption in a particular centre of consciousness like the one stated above it is viewed as triangular in shape and its location is *mūlādhāra*. Here the adept experiences bliss, therefore the name *ānandacakra* is quite apt for it. When the adept experiences fullness of bliss, it is supposed that he has attained lordship over that specific centre.

... आनन्दप्रभृतौ पञ्चके यदा ॥
योगी विशेत् तदा तत्तच्चक्रेशत्वं हठाद् व्रजेत् ।

TĀl V.108cd-109ab

When the yogi enters the five wheels beginning with *ānanda* and so on, then he attains immediately lordship over them.

However, there is a wheel called *anuttara* which transcends each of the *cakras* but at the same time remains linked with all.

एतदानुत्तरं चक्रं हृदयाच्चक्षुरादिभिः ।
व्योमभिर्निसरत्येव तत्तद्विषयगोचरे ।

TĀl V.27cd-28ab

This transcendent wheel (consisting of twelve forms) indeed emerges outside from the heart through the outlets (void) of the eyes and other senses to reach each individual object.

The transcendent wheel constituted of ten inner and outer sense organs along with the mind and intellect, has its seat in the heart. While the sense organ is engaged in knowing the object, the wheel as it were, goes outside through the outlet of the organ and assumes a particular mode (*vṛtti*). This is the function of the *cakra* in its *adhibhūta* level, but when it is viewed in its *adhidaiva* aspect, it is observed that the *cakras* have all the characteristics of deities (*dṛgādidevīs*). They emit their rays outside through different channels and perform five functions like creation and others. The *ādhyātmika* aspect of the *cakra* is when one experiences the delight of fullness after identifying oneself with all in integral unity.

Abhinavagupta gives a clear definition of the principal *cakra* and subsidiary ones. According to the Kaula doctrine some *cakras* in the body used to be called the principal and the others which help the principal are called subsidiary.

यदेवानन्दसन्दोहि संविदो ह्यन्तरङ्गकम् ।
तत्प्रधानं भवेच्चक्रमनुचक्रमतोऽपरम् ॥ (TĀl XXIX.105cd-106ab)

The thing that yields bliss is very close to consciousness (*saṃvid*). That is to be known as the principal *cakra* but the others are called *anucakra*, that is, subsidiary *cakras.*

The sense organs like the eyes, ears and others are known as *anucakras.* For bestowing full satisfaction to the principal *cakra* other sense organs are to be given befitting offerings. The above difinition gives two characteristics of *cakra*, the one is its blissfulness and the other is closeness to consciousness.

The supreme wheel of the Lord is hinted at by Abhinavagupta in his **Tantrāloka** thus:

भैरवीयमहाचक्रे संवित्तिपरिवारिते ।

TĀl V.32ab

The great wheel belonging to the Supreme Lord (Bhairava) is surrounded by the divinites superintending over the inner and outer sense organs.

The highest Lord (*cakreśvara*) known as *parapramātā*, the supreme subject, is considered to be the sovereign. The divinities called *dṛgādidevīs* which are shining and representing eyes and other senses are merely his extension. They emerge from the highest source when his function of creation starts, but they remain dissolved in pure consciousness at the time of dissolution. When the universe becomes dissolved with no trace of impression left (*saṃskārasyāpi parikṣaye*), it should be meditated upon as an inner surge, expressing itself in delight. It should be meditated upon as a great expanding wheel (*mahatcakram*) revolving continuously and blossoming in diverse forms of the universe.

Yoginī-Hṛdaya, another Tāntric text, describes beautifully how *cakra* becomes manifest from the supreme *śakti*:

यदा सा परमा शक्तिः स्वेच्छया विश्वरूपिणी ।
स्फुरत्तामात्मनः पश्येत्तदा चक्रस्य सम्भवः ॥

YoH I.9cd-10ab

When the supreme dynamic energy by means of her will wants to assume the form of the universe, she sees her own effulgent pulsation, and then the wheel (*cakra*) emerges.

In the above context *cakra* means *śrīcakra* which essentially is the body of the divine, that is, the unity of *ahaṃ*, I, and its self-reflection that is, of *prakāśa* (light) and *vimarśa* (self-reflection).

When this *cakra* manifests itself it is thought to be composed of *kāmakalā*, and everything, whatever it may be, is in essence *kāma* = *prakāśa* and *kalā* =

vimarśa, that is light and its self-reflection. *Śrīcakra* consists of nine triangles. The central *cakra* known as *Baindavacakra*.

चक्रं कामकलारूपं प्रसार परमार्थतः ।

YoH I.24cd

The *cakra* (born of *bindu*, a point or dot) is essentially of the nature of *kāmakalā* and the expansion of it is of the same nature (therefore, the entire universe is *kāmakalā* in essence).

The *cakra* of Mother Śrī emerges out of the union of Śiva and Śakti.

पञ्चशक्तिचतुर्वह्निसंयोगाच्चक्रसम्भवः ।

YoH I.8cd

The holy *cakra* originates out of the union of five *śaktis*, (i.e. five triangles with the apex downward) and four *vahnis* = Śiva (the apex of the triangle going upward).

The total *cakra* consists of nine such triangles. *Śrīcakra* as a complex geometrical figure is described in an anonymous *Yāmala* work in the following way.

बिन्दुत्रिकोणवसुकोणदशारयुग्ममन्वश्रनागदलसंयुतषोडशारम् ।
वृत्तत्रिभूपुरयुतं परितश्चतुर्धा श्रीचक्रमेतदुदितं परदेवतायाः ॥

quoted in KāmKVil

Śrīcakra belonging to the Supreme divinity has been stated to consist of a *bindu*, triangle, eight triangles, the pair of ten triangles, fourteen triangles, eight petals along with sixteen petals, three circles and three *bhūpuras*.

In the above context *bindu* is considered a *cakra* from which the entire *cakra* with all its constituents emerge. The aggregate of triangles, petals of lotuses and other constituents is known as *cakra*. If in a particular figure there is the absence of a triangle, even then inside the filament of the lotus a triangle is generally thought to be present. In that case the entire diagram is considered a *cakra*. The great Lord Śaṅkara is lauded by a devotee as the source of the host of *śaktis* (*śakticakra-vibhavaprabhava*).

यस्योन्मेषनिमेषाभ्यां जगतः प्रलयोदयौ ।
तं शक्तिचक्रविभवप्रभवं शंकरं स्तुमः ॥

SpKā I.1

We laud that Śaṅkara by whose mere opening of the eye lids there is the appearance and dissolution of the world and who is the source of the glorious powers of the collective whole of the Śaktis.
(Tr. Jaideva Singh)

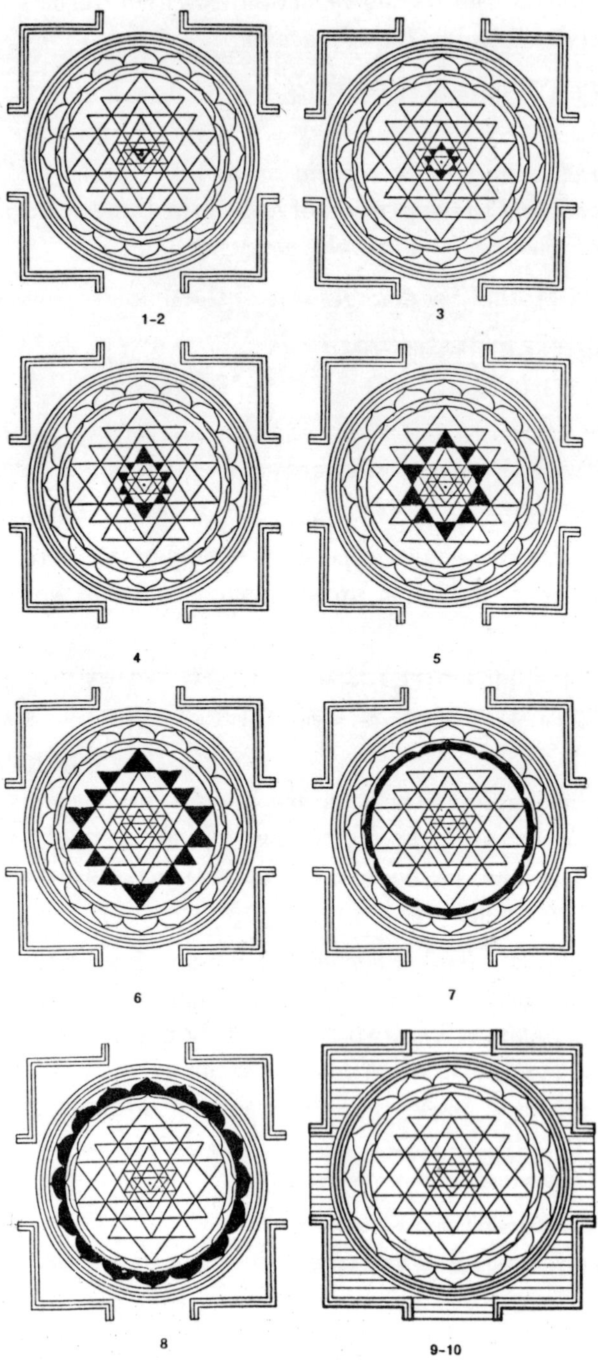

Figure 5: Śrīcakra in the order of manifestation (*sṛṣṭi-krama*)

In the above context the energies that function in the body as sense organs are also called *cakras*. They are *khecarīcakra*, *gocarīcakra*, *dikcarīcakra* and *bhūcarīcakra*, which function in the void of consciousness, in the centres of the sense and motor organs and finally in the level of external objects. They are known as *cakra* only because they shine, extend and the yogin experiences fullness.

The sage Durvāsā says in **Tripuramahimna Stotra** (28):

श्रीचक्रं श्रुतिमूलकोश इति ते संसारचक्रात्मकम् ।

> *Śrīcakra* is the source of the Vedas. The root of the Vedas is *Oṃkāra*. The inmost triangle is the treasury of *praṇava*. The *cakra* is the universe symbolised by the wheel.

According to Śaiva doctrine six centres of consciousness are generally accepted. They are known as *cakras* but they are different from the current *haṭhayogic* view of *cakras* known as *mūlādhāra*, *svādhiṣṭhāna*, *maṇipūra*, *anāhata*, *viśuddha* and *ājñā*. Instead Abhinavagupta takes the heart to be the first pulsating location of consciousness. The locations of the *cakras* with their superintending deities are the heart, the throat, the palate, the joint of the two eyebrows, the forehead and *brahmarandhra* (*hṛdādiṣaṭkasthān brahmādīn*, TĀl XV.495).

Kaulas practice a certain form of rituals which is known as *cakrapūjā*. Though it has become obsolete nowadays, we try to state very briefly what it exactly means. In **Kulārṇava** we have a description of it as shown below.

स्त्रीणामन्यतमं स्थानं पुंसामन्यतमं पृथक् ।
अथवा मिथुनं कृत्वा क्रमात्समुपवेशयेत् ॥
पङ्क्याकारेण वा सम्यक् चक्राकारेण वा प्रिये ।
शिवशक्तिधिया सर्वं चक्रमध्ये समर्चयेत् ॥

KulT VIII.104-105

> The place of the ladies and that of male members is separate. Or O dear, they should take their seats in pairs either in rows or in a perfect circle. They should worship each of them conceiving them as Śiva and Śakti while they are in the circle (*cakra*).

As the performance of the ritual takes place among members seated in a circle the ritual is known as *cakrapūjā*, but really it means something else. The *pūjā* relates to the principal *cakra* of the human body therefore it is termed so.

The Vaiṣṇava conception of the *sudarśana cakra* contains the whole concept of time, or rather, Time itself is the most powerful weapon:

वरायुधोऽयं देवेश सर्वायुधनिवर्हणः ।
सुदर्शनो द्वादशारो यो मनः सदृशो जवी ॥

VāmanaPur LXXIX

O Lord of divine beings, this is an excellent weapon and more powerful than all weapons. This Sudarśana consists of twelve spokes, speedy like the mind. These divine beings are stationed in its spokes, gods, months, signs of the zodiac and the six seasons. They are abiding in it for the protection of people of good conduct.

Cakra as Sudarśana is used by a faithful Vaiṣṇava as a mark in the body.

द्वादशारन्तु षट्कोणं वलयत्रयसंयुतम् ।
हरेः सुदर्शनं तप्तं धारयेत्तद् विचक्षणः ॥

Haribhaktivilāsa XV.50

The wise should bear in his person the hot mark of Hari's sudarśana which consists of twelve spokes. The central hub is hexagonal. It consists of three rings.

A *cakra* of the above description is also placed on a golden jar and set above the top of the Vaiṣṇava temple.

According to Pāñcarātra doctrine *śakti* threads through all the entities whether they are positive or negative. From it arise activity (*kriyā*) and *bhūti*, the object, by the sportive will (*saṃkalpa*) of Lord Viṣṇu. The activity represents Sudarśana which is activated by the will of Lakṣmī.

संहृताखिलभूतस्य स्तैमित्यं ब्रह्मणो हि यत् ।
अप्ययः सा महारात्रिस्तत् संकल्पेन धार्यते ॥
महारात्रिधरोनाम तदरं वै सुदर्शनम् ।
तदेकारं महच्चक्रमद्यत्वे चिन्त्यते सुरैः ॥

AhSam VIII.38-39

The tranquillity of Brahman which occurs after the dissolution of all the beings, is the great night and it is upheld by the will of the Lord. Thus this wheel is the bearer of the Great Night. It is said to be of one spoke related to Sudarśana and to be meditated upon by the sages.

The vibrative motion that activates the great Sudarśana to act as creation and others, is propelled by the will of the Lord.

प्रभवे चाप्यये वापि स्थितौ वापि महामुने ।
चलत्तापूर्वरूपं यः संकल्पस्तत्र वर्तते ॥
चलनं नाम तच्चक्रं सुदर्शनमयं महत् । AhSam IX.41-42ab

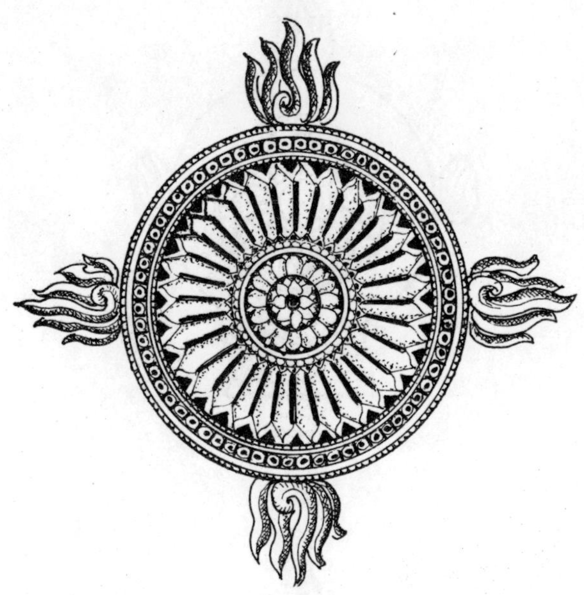

Figure 6: Viṣṇu cakra (Cola bronze)

O great sage, the will that exists prior to vibrative motion causing creation, dissolution and maintenance, is known as the great wheel of motion made of Sudarśana.

In the above Saṃhitā we find that every principle is symbolised by a wheel consisting of a distinctive number of spokes. For example *mahārātridharacakra* consists of a single spoke, while *uṣaścakra* has two, *udayacakra* three and so on.

त्रिनाभियुक्तं षण्नेमि पञ्चारं चक्रमव्ययम् ।
संवत्सरमयं यत्तत्कालचक्रमिति स्थितम् ॥

AhSam XXXIII.9

The wheel named *kālacakra* (the wheel of Time) consisting of the year is attached with three hubs, six fellies and five spokes. It is immutable. Thus the wheel consisting of the year is established.

In a similar way the wheel of the universe symbolizing *Puruṣa* has been described.

अव्यक्तादिविशेषान्ततत्त्वरूपैररैर्वृतम् ।
चतुर्विंशतिसङ्ख्याकैः पुरुषात्मकनेमियुक् ॥

AhSam XXXIII.11

The wheel representing the universe (*jagaccakram*) is attached with twenty four spokes beginning from *avyakta* (*prakṛti*) to the earth and its felly represents *Puruṣa*, the soul.

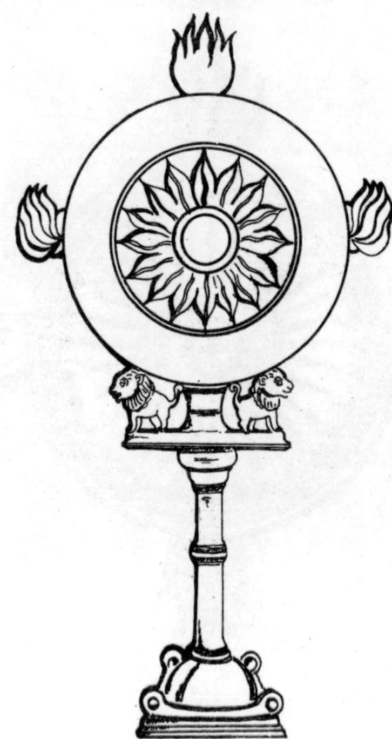

Figure 7: Viṣṇu's cakra as processional symbol

As in the above verse the wheel symbolises time, the verse quoted just above stands for the universe as space.

Sudarśana cakra, the discus is the weapon (*āyudha*) of Viṣṇu:

> चक्रं सुदर्शनं नाम सा भवत्यरिदारणम् ।
> अस्त्रं परमतेजिष्ठ आग्नेयं नाम वैष्णवम् ॥
>
> LT XXIX.42
>
> She (Śakti) is (identical with) the disc named sudarśana, which destroys enemies. This highly powerful weapon made of fire belongs to Viṣṇu. (Tr. Sanjukta Gupta)

The following verse also refers to *cakra* as a weapon:

> अध्वषड्कमये चक्रे चक्रिणं चक्रमुत्तमम् ।
>
> LT XXXI.60ab
>
> One should meditate on the possessor of the disc and the disc itself consisting of six paths (*adhvas*) (at the time of great fear). (Tr. Sanjukta Gupta)

According to Śaiva doctrine the universe as the disc symbolises it as consisting of six divisions. They are known as *varṇa, mantra* and *pada.* These three are a group signifying word (*vācaka*) and the next three, *kalā, tattva* and *bhuvana*, are placed under the group of signified objects (*vācya*). In short they are known as six paths.

Cakra is also used to symbolise syllables beginning from *a* and ending in *h*.

तत्र वर्णमयं चक्रं प्रथमं शृणु वासव ।

LT XXIX.47ab

Among these, O Vāsava, listen first to the description of the cycle of creation consisting of letters. (Tr. Sanjukta Gupta)

Thus the syllables moving along the ingoing and outgoing vital energy imitate the endless circular movement of the wheel.

In conclusion we may say that *cakra* as a concept is present in multifarious dimensions in the history of Indian literature, though one or the other meaning may have predominated in a certain school, but the pre-eminent notion of cyclic order and constant movement conveyed by the term is present everywhere.

In the Arts

by Kapila Vatsyayan

The Indian Arts imbibe the essence of some fundamental concepts, reflect their multi-dimensional nature and, in turn, provide verbal and visual imagery which crystallizes as the symbol of the concept. The wheel then comes full circle. As has been mentioned in the beginning of this article, *cakra* denotes an idea, is concretized as form, especially circular form, and suggests movement. In this respect *cakra*, both in the context of speculative thought, philosophic discussion and the varied schools of Tantra, is connected with two other terms treated in this volume, namely, *bindu* and *nābhi*. The relationship of the point (*bindu*), the hub or the nave, the conceptual centre (*nābhi*) and the circumference (*vṛtta*) along with the spokes (*aras*) is near universal.

1. The earliest evidence of the transformation and representation of the idea of *cakra* as physical form, has undoubtedly to be traced back to the Vedic *yajña* and the construction of the *śālā* and the altars. The circular and the semi-circular altar shapes, known by their familiar names of *gārhapatya* and *dakṣiṇāgni*, is indicative of the importance that is attached to the geometrical forms of the square, the circle and the semicircle. The symbolic significance of the circular and the semi-circular form as also the actual wheel with its hub (nave), spokes and circumference in the *yajña* provides the basis for a language of form in the Indian Arts. As has been mentioned earlier, the **Śulba-Sūtra** enjoins the priest to construct the *agni* in the shape of a chariot wheel. It is

added that there are two kinds of chariot wheels, namely, those with spokes and those having *pradhis* (felly).

The metaphor of the wheel (*cakra*) is pervasive in the Vedas and Upaniṣads. In the **Atharva-Veda** there are many significant references to the form of the wheel. Each of these represents a form as also a metaphor for comprehending the movement of time. Perhaps, the most significant amongst these are the following:

दृढो दृंहस्थिरो न्यो ब्रह्म विश्वसृजो दश ।
नाभिमिव सर्वतश्चक्रमुच्छिष्टे देवताः श्रिताः ॥

AV XI.7.4

The firm, the fast, the strong, the hard, Brahma, the All-creating Ten. Gods, as a wheel about the nave, are fixed all round the Residue. (Tr. R.T.H. Griffith)

Here in the context of glorification of the Residue of the sacrifice, the Gods are compared with a wheel fixed on the axle, in which all the Gods come together.

पञ्चारे चक्रे परिवर्तमाने यस्मिन्नातस्थुर्भुवनानि विश्वा ।
* * *
सनेमि चक्रमजरं वि वावृत उत्तानायां दश युक्ता वहन्ति ।

AV IX.9.11ab, 14ab

Upon the five spoked wheel revolving ever, whereon all creatures rest and are dependent.
The wheel revolves, unwasting with its felly: ten draw it, yoked to the far-stretching car-pole. (Tr. R.T.H. Griffith)

Here the five-spoked wheel means the year with five seasons, the dewy and the cold seasons being counted as one. The wheel is also compared with the globe.

Finally, the metaphor is used for communicating the all-inclusive quality of life:

त्वं स्त्री त्वं पुमानसि त्वं कुमार उत वा कुमारी ।
त्वं जीर्णो दण्डेन वञ्चसि त्वं जातो भवसि विश्वतोमुखः ॥ 27 ॥
* * *
यत्र देवाश्च मनुष्याश्चारा नाभाविव श्रिताः ।
अपां त्वा पुष्पं पृच्छामि यत्र तन्मायया हितम् ॥ 34 ॥

AV X.8.27,34

You are man and woman, boy and girl; you are the old man tottering about with a staff, and you are the child new born. You are of all forms.

That in which gods and men are set, like spokes in the hub of the wheel, I ask you about the flower of the waters, where it has been placed.

The metaphor of the *cakra* permeates the discussions in the Upaniṣads. Sometimes, the relationship of the senses, body, mind and soul is compared to the chariot wheel as in the **Kaṭha Upaniṣad** (III.3-6) or when it is used to explain the relationship of the micro and the macro (the individual and the all-pervasive) as in the case of the **Śvetāśvatara Upaniṣad**, quoted earlier in the article (ŚvUp I.6).

It will be clear from the above quotations that the metaphor of the point, hub (nave), spokes and circumference is used to describe the body, both physical and psychical. In each case the network of relationships between centre and periphery is underlined. The navel denotes a centre, the spokes and circumference suggest conceptual and virtual space and time.

It will also be clear that the metaphor of the wheel (*cakra*) is overlayered on the concept of →*puruṣa* as both physical body and as the coordinate of the micro and the macro. The physical navel and the geometrical centre coalesce as much as the limbs of the body and the spokes of the wheel (*cakra*) coalesce. The circumference suggests conceptual and virtual space of a standing man; the geometrical circle with a centre, spokes, radii, circumference becomes a code as also a metaphor for life phenomenon.

2. The Arts coalesce the essence of the concept in the Upaniṣads and the forms used in the Brahmanical ritual of the three Agnis. Consequently, whether Hindu, Buddhist or Jaina architecture, the wheel and the spokes, the *bindu* and the hub (nave) are near universal. These are concretized in architectural plans throughout the country over a period of nearly 12 to 14 centuries. Vāstu texts, although late, in fact incorporate an ancient tradition. The circular form in temple architecture is mentioned in texts ranging from the **Bṛhat-Saṃhitā, Agni Purāṇa, Aparājita-Pṛcchā, Mānasollāsa, Śilparatna-Kośa, Tantra-Samuccaya** and others. In short, in all architectural traditions from North to South and East to West, *Vesara* as a generic category denotes circular temples.

कुण्डलान्तमुपानादि वृत्तं वेसरमुच्यते । RauĀ XXXIX. 24

Vesara is said to be circular in shape, from the lowest base (*upāna*) to the end of the *kuṇḍala*, the summit. (Tr. H.N. Chakravarty)

कण्ठात्प्रभृति वृत्तं यत् वेसरं परिकीर्तितम् ।

KāmĀ I.49.108b

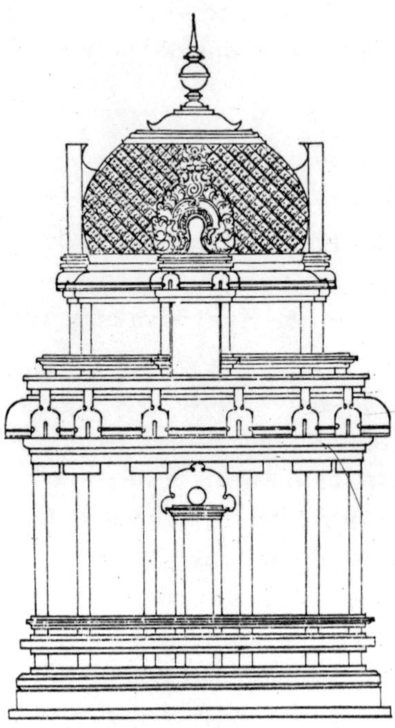

Figure 8: Vesara Vimāna

Vesara is that type of edifice which is circular from the neck upwards. (Tr. H.N. Chakravarty)

3. In actual construction, one of the earliest and finest examples is the Stūpa of Nāgārjunakoṇḍa. The foundations of the Stūpa give a clear idea of the plan of the Stūpa with its centre, the hub, the spokes, the circumference. In most instances, the *cakra* is a basic geometrical motif. *Stūpas* based on the *cakra* as a principal motif are found throughout India and Sri Lanka. The greatest example of the *cakra maṇḍala* in architecture, undoubtedly, is Borobudur of Indonesia. In India, the most important circular temples with a clear structure of the *bindu*, the hub (nave), the navel (*nābhi*), *garbha* and *vṛtta* are in Trichur, Palaghat and Ernakulum.

The late Shri H.R. Sarkar has given a full account of the circular temples of Kerala. Most important amongst these are: Perumpaludur, Polpulli, Kaviyur

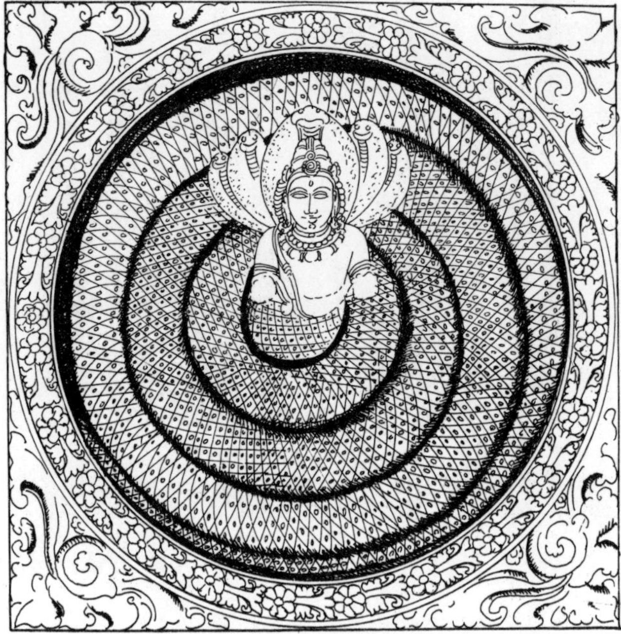

Figure 9: A Nāga on ceiling (Bādāmī Cave)

and Ramantali. (See H.R. Sarkar: Encyclopaedia of Indian Temple Architecture: 1983).

4. While architecture accepts the *cakra* as a fundamental design in architectural ground plan, it is incorporated in the architectural edifice as a sculptural motif. Examples are innumerable. They range from the delineation of the *cakra* in ceilings to the depiction of *cakra* as sculptural form on the outer and inner walls of the temple. One amongst the earliest and most impressive examples is the coiled serpentine *nāga* seen in the ceilings of Bādāmī. An equally important panel in Bādāmī is where the hub, the wheel and the circumference are transformed into a beautifully designed fish, lotus and the circumference. The 16 spokes of the wheel consist of fishes, the lotus is the hub – all are contained within the circumference (see Fig.10). Examples can be seen throughout the Indian continent. Mention may be made only of two great examples of the chariot wheels of the temple of Konarak and the ceiling of the temple of Mt. Abu. Here there is clear evidence of the transformation of the fundamental concepts transformed in stone through a remarkable visual imagery. The metaphor of the Upaniṣads and the geometrical motifs of the Vedic *yajña*, are manifested as symbolic form of great significance.

5. In *Śilpa*, the *cakra* assumes another kind of importance. This time, it is not the ground plan of the **Vāstu Śāstra**, but it is the very basis of the armature

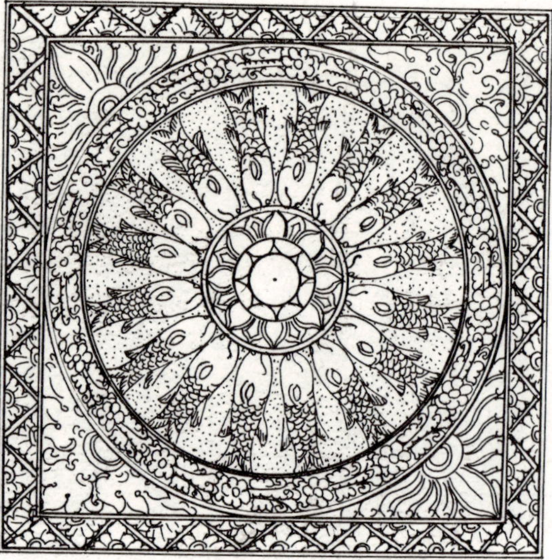

Figure 10: Ceiling with fish design (Bādāmī Cave)

of the sculptural form. The system of the verticals and horizontals, known as the *sūtras*, all evolve and develop physically as also conceptually and, of course, metaphorically by identifying a *bindu* (point), a centre as the *nābhi* (the navel). The identification of *nābhi* as centre with an hypothetical *cakra* around it, is near universal, particularly from the 4th century onwards. It constitutes the fundamentals of the principles of composition of Hindu, Buddhist and Jaina sculpture. The system of proportion and measure as mass, volume, distribution of weight, is evolved from the concept of *bindu*, *nābhi*, spokes and circumference, in short, the *cakra*. The central vertical axis mundi, the *brahma-sūtra*, passes through the *nābhi* (navel) beginning from the middle of the head, fore-head and touching a mid-point between the two feet of the standing figure. This provides the diameter of the hypothetical circle. The sculptural composition develops from these fundamentals.

Other vertical axes pass through the shoulders and outstretched arms. Similarly, a principal horizontal axis passes through the *nābhi* (navel). Other horizontal chords pass through the neck, chest, pelvis, knees and ankles. The configuration of principal vertical and horizontal diameters and chords constitutes the basis of the elaborate system of *sūtras* (medians) and *bhaṅgas* (deflections). Alice Boner analyzed the reliefs of Ellora not only on the basis of the fundamental concepts of the *nābhi* and *vṛtta* but also on the basis of the identification of the point as centre with the five elemental *cakras* spoken of in the context of the Tāntric conception. In her words:

"The importance and significance of the central point (*bindu*) of the composition is in many cases demonstrated also by the fact that it is identified with one or the other of the five elemental *cakras* (centres of energy) of the deity represented. It is identified either with the Maṇipūra cakra, the creative Fire-centre at the navel, or with the Anāhata or Prāṇa-cakra in the chest, the centre of breath and vital energy, or with the Viśuddha-cakra at the base of the throat, the centre of speech and discriminative knowledge, occasionally also with the Svādhiṣṭhāna cakra." And she interprets the *yantras* as follows:

"Since the concentric figurations, as exemplified by the groundplans of temples, by yantras and *maṇḍalas*, are of cosmic order, and since the diagrams underlying the sculptures are also concentrically organized, the possibility of their too representing cosmic symbols cannot a priori be discounted. One may even venture the hypothesis that, if *yantras* of abstract lines correspond in the language of signs to the *bīja-mantras*, the *mantras* of seed-syllables in the language of sounds, these diagrams of figurative compositions may correspond to those mantras in which the divinity is invoked in fully articulated words set in verses. If they can be considered as cosmic symbols, the central *bindu*, the hub of the composition would here also take the place of the Brahman or Ātman, the surrounding circle would embrace the totality of Manifestation, and the space within the circle would be the field (*kṣetra*), the universe with cosmic and human existence, in which the operations of divine powers take place. The subtle states of being would be near the centre, while the grosser states would be towards the circumference. The space-directions would impart their specific character and function to movements on all planes of existence. Such movements may run across the entire field, when determined by entire diameters or their parallels. They may be centrifugal or centripetal, when determined by the radii. When flowing outwards they would indicate expanding stresses, either creative or destructive, when ebbing inwards, collecting, integrating tendencies, and thus refer to processes of evolution or involution, of manifestation or dissolution. Movements running around the circumference of the circle would refer to the rotation of the world-wheel, the *saṃsāra-cakra*, sustained but unredeemed." (Principles of Composition in Hindu Sculpture by Alice Boner, p. 28).

Her intuitive findings of the identification of *bindu, nābhi* and *cakra* as fundamental principles is supported and reinforced by evidence, since the concept of the *cakra* as a principle of composition in sculpture has been elaborated in texts such as **Śilpa Prakāśa** and **Śilpasāriṇī**. The descriptions of the *Nāṭāmbara* in the **Śilpa Prakāśa** are as relevant to the concept of the *bindu* discussed elsewhere as the concept of the *cakra*. Describing the *Nāṭāmbara yantra* (see Fig. 11) the **Śilpa Prakāśa** says:

समचतुरस्रक्षेत्रे मध्ये मण्डलवर्त्तने ।
कारयेत् युगं भागन्तु त्रिरेखायुक्तमध्यमे ॥ 203 ॥

लम्बाकारे तदा मध्ये मध्यरेखा सुविस्तरे ।
मध्यरेखानिम्नविन्दुमारभ्य प्रस्थ मध्यमे ॥ 204 ॥
कीलयेत् प्रथमा छेदद्वये पार्श्वसमन्वये ।
तद्युक्तरेखमालम्ब्य रेखावेद गुणांकिते ॥ 205 ॥
मध्ये लम्बाकृतौ वेदमध्यरेखा समाश्रिते ।
पार्श्वदेशे द्वयाकर्षि ऊर्ध्वदेशांगचालनम् ॥ 206 ॥
एतत्तु तांडवं यंत्रं सर्वतांडवलक्षणम् ।
सर्वनृत्यगतां मूर्त्तिं कारयेत् शिल्पिपुंगवः ॥ 207 ॥

ŚiPrak II.203-207

Inside a square field there is a circle, in which four divisions should be made in length and in breadth.
There two diagonals (*koṇa-cheda*) touch the middle line. Starting from the *nimna-bindu* (lowest bindu) on the *madhya-rekhā* upto the *madhya-prastha*,
Draw two lines equally to both sides. Above this, starting from the (next) *bindu* two lines touching the third (*prastha*).
Above the *madhya-prastha* ij the middle, across the third and the middle vertical lines, the lateral upper fields are divided by two (oblique) lines.
In the upper middle, in two parts, make lines in the form of a triangle. This is the *Tāṇḍava Yantra* on which the *Nṛtya mūrtis* will be made. (Tr. Alice Boner)

6. Indian sculpture explores all possibilites within the circular form as diameters, radii, rombuses, hexagons. The framework of the verticals and horizontals, of the oblique diameters or cords, all evolving from a central point, provides the complex structural basis for different types of configuration in the Indian sculpture. The acceptance of the idea of the converging of energies in the centre (*nābhi*) or radiating out hold the key to symmetrical and asymmetrical compositions. The Naṭarāja in *bhujaṅgatrāsita* (see *Sūtra*, Fig.3) is a supreme example of the application of the principles of the *cakra* in sculptural composition. The principle of centre, spokes and circumference, constitute the underlying structure of suggesting incessant movement figuratively. (For a fuller analysis, see "The Square and the Circle of the Indian Arts"). The *Cakrapuruṣa* as a personification of Viṣṇu's emblem, is a visual representation of these conceptions (Fig. 12).

7. *Cakra*, as a principal form, is fundamental to theatre, dance and music. While **Nāṭya-Śāstra** does not use the word '*cakra*', it is obvious that Bharata based the ground plan of the three types of theatre on the *yajña-śālā* and the three *agnis*. It is significant that the **Nāṭya-Śāstra** does not speak of a circular theatre. Later texts on theatre do mention circular theatres, called *Vṛtta*.

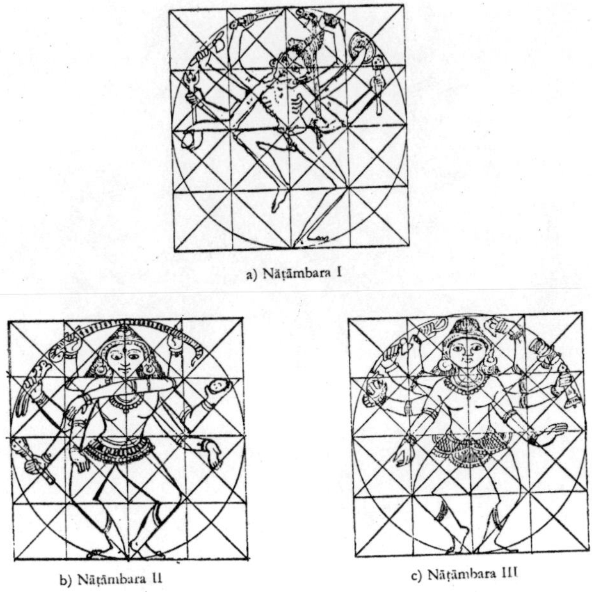

a) Nāṭāmbara I

b) Nāṭāmbara II

c) Nāṭāmbara III

Figure 11: Nāṭāmbara yantra from Śilpa Prakāśa

Śāradātanaya's **Bhāva Prakāśa** says that the king should have three types of theatres in his palace and assigns the circular theatre for the *citra* and *miśra* type of dance, specially where *mārga* and *deśī* are mixed. (See Śāradātanaya **Bhāva Prakāśa** Chapter X). There is archaeological evidence which points to the existence of circular theatres in India. Of significance are the descriptions relating to the space of the stage. The **Nāṭya-Śāstra** identifies a *brahma maṇḍala* as the centre of the stage. This is the cognate of the *nābhi* (navel) of the **Vāstu** and **Śilpa-Śāstra**.

Chapter V of the **Nāṭya-Śāstra** repeatedly refers to the centre of the stage in the context of the preliminaries or *pūrvaraṅga*. While the word *cakra* does not occur, the word *maṇḍala* is used here both as square and circle. Later in Chapter XV, the **Nāṭya-Śāstra** enunciates the principle of *kakṣyā vibhāga* (stage space denoting areas closer to the centre and those on the periphery and sides). Behind this structure is the tacit acceptance of a point, a *nābhi* or *brahmasthāna* (centre). The different areas of the stage suggesting different directions are conceived as radii emanating from the centre. Each section of the preliminaries makes a ground pattern, either of a *svastika*, or a square or a circumambulation, i.e. the circumference of the circle, here called *vṛtta*. In Chapter IV entitled *Nṛtya Tāṇḍava Lakṣaṇam*, after the descriptions of the

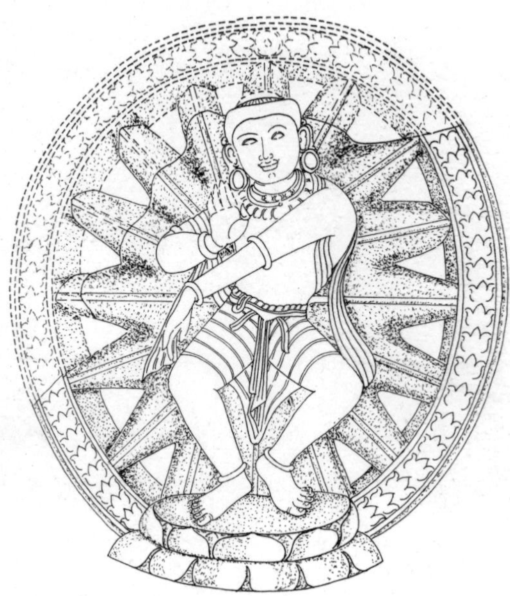

Figure 12: Cakra-puruṣa, Patna Museum

cadences of movements, called *karaṇas* and *aṅgahāra* choreographical patterns, called *piṇḍībandha*, are elucidated upon. The technical term suggests a centre (*piṇḍa*, a micro mass) and interlockings. Despite differences of opinion on these terms, it would appear that the *gulma* pattern suggests all performers gathering towards the centre (centripetal) and the *bhedyaka* is the opposite where rows of dancers form radii emerging from a centre. The *śṛṅkhalā* (chain formation) suggests interlocking of arms around the circumferance.

In the context of the four *abhinayas*, the concept of *cakra* becomes basic. The system of movement as unit and cadence, specially movements denoted by the terms *cārīs*, *karaṇas* and *aṅgahāra*, have a logic only when understood as using the upper and lower limbs as spokes emerging from a hypothetical centre and covering a spatial circumference. Bharata is also conscious of a principal category of physical movement which is circular in nature, called by the term *recaka*. In Chapter IV it is described as follows:

चतुरो रेचकांश्चापि गदतो मे निबोधत ।
पादरेचक एकः स्यात् द्वितीयः कटिरेचकः ॥
कररेचकस्तृतीयस्तु चतुर्थः कण्ठरेचकः ।
रेचिताख्यः पृथग्भावे वलने चाभिधीयते ॥

NŚ IV.248-249

Listen carefully about four types of *recaka* as spoken by me. The first among them is *pādarecaka*, rotation of feet along with tip of the toes, the second is *kaṭirecaka*, rotation of the waist, the third is *kararecaka*, rotative motion of hands, and the fourth is *kaṇṭharecaka*, the rotation of the neck. It is named as *recita* when it is rotated fully along with its four-fold divisions. When these four are performed separately, they be spoken of with reference to *valana*. (Tr. H.N. Chakravarty)

This classification suggests movements of particular parts of the body where a rotation movement is possible. In the section on the *nṛtta hastas* the **Nāṭya-Śāstra** emphasizes the fact that since the movement of the hands does not signify meaning, the path of movement covered in space is more important (cf. NŚ IX). While the word *recaka* stands for a movement of a particular part of the body, the *bhramarī* denotes pirouette to cover floor space. It is circle or half circle around the central axis, covering floor space or elevation space. There are many sub-categories of *bhramarī*. A minute analysis of the *nāṭya* and *nṛtta* texts reveals that, whether the movement is in place or space, the principle is the same as in the case of sculpture (*śilpa*): Each time a centre is identified, a hypothetical circumference is conceived and then all possibilities of concentric circles, configuration of verticals, horizontals, intersections, diagonals, rombuses, hexagons, octagons, are explored, both in movement of particular parts or limbs as also covering ground space.

8. The concept of *cakra* holds the key to an understanding of the movement of drama as conceived by Bharata, as *itivṛtta*. This time, it is not the static geometrical form, but the movement of the plot which is conceived in concentric circles or in terms of cyclic time or in terms of expanding circles. Bharata expressly uses the image of expanding circles in Chapters 21.22. There is an overlayering of concepts and structure in Bharata's discussion of the plot of a play (*itivṛtta*). Space does not allow us to delineate upon the complex structure and the interconnections of the sequences of the plot, namely, the beginning (*prārambha*), the effort (*yatna* or *prayatna*), the continuation of the effort and the hope of attainment (*prāptisambhava*), the actual possibility of attainment (*niyatāphalaprāpti*) and finally the attainment of the fruit (*phalayoga*) as a group with the concepts of *bīja, bindu, patākā, prakarī*, fulfilment (*kārya*) (cf. NŚ XIX.21). The third group comprises *mukha*, the *pratimukha, garbha*, the *vimarśa* and *nirvahaṇa* (→*sandhi*) (cf. NŚ XXI.36). The three groups are joined together in formations, called the *bandha* in the Nāṭyaśāstra terminology (cf. NŚ XVIII.5) and, of course, through the most important concept of the →*sandhis*. In the context of the *cakra* it must be remembered that, whether it is the sequential order of the movement of action in theatrical time or a spatial order, the governing choreographical pattern is based on the circle or cyclicity either as concentric circle or as centre point, the spokes and the circumference.

The concept of *cakra* constitutes a key to the structural basis of the **Nāṭya-Śāstra**. It permeates all aspects. In Chapter XXVIII.7 a significant statement sums it up:

> एवं गानं च वाद्यं च नाट्यं च विविधाश्रयम् ।
> अलातचक्रप्रतिमं कर्तव्यं नाट्ययोक्तृभिः ॥
>
> NŚ XXVIII.7
>
> ...त्रयोऽप्येते समूहा एकीभावं नेया इति यावत् ।... यस्माद् द्वि[वि]विधाश्रयं भिन्नेन्द्रियग्राह्यविविधक्रियारूपं, तस्माद्यत्नेनास्यैकता तत्सम्पाद्या, येनैक-बुद्धिविषयता[तां] सामाजिकस्य गच्छेत् । अलाततेजःकणो हि न वस्तुतो युगपदनेकदेशसम्बन्धी, लाघवयत्नेन तु तथा तथा साम्यमापादितम्।
>
> AbhiBhā on above
>
> Thus song, instruments and drama that have manifold substrata, should be made analogous to *alātacakra* (a circle of fire made by briskly rotating a firebrand) by those who put together a dramatic performance.
>
> Abhinava Bhāratī:
> These three groups (of song, instruments and drama) have to be unified, this is the purport. Because this (conglomeration) has manifold bases or substrata by way of various 'actions' perceptible by different sense-organs (eye and ear), (therefore) it should be so unified by effort so that it becomes perceptible to the aesthete with one (unitary) *buddhi* (comprehension or perception). A particle of the firebrand is not really related to many points in space simultaneously (i.e. at one given moment the particle of fire occupies only one point in space) but because of the effort towards swiftness unity is attained (so that one unified circle of fire is perceived). (Tr. P.L. Sharma)

9. It is evident that the **Nāṭya-Śāstra** evolves a complex system of movement as also a framework of the structure of drama on the basis of cyclicity of time and circular movement in concentric circles. This is the counterpart at the levels of sense perceptions and artistic expression, of the philosophy of the Upaniṣads and the concretisation of the concepts in Vedic ritual.

Of equal or greater significance is the near universality of the transformation of the concept into a language and grammar of form in the Indian musical tradition. While the **Nāṭya-Śāstra** had given it a primary importance in the classification of metrical patterns and musical structure of notes and →*tāla* (metrical cycles), the **Saṅgīta Ratnākara** incorporates the concept of the *cakras* enunciated in the Tantras as the very basis of the production of sound. Chapter I of the **Saṅgīta Ratnākara** (I. 2.120-140) speaks of ten *cakras* of the body (*daśa cakrāṇi*) and classifies them as *ādhāra, svādhiṣṭhāna, maṇipūra, anāhata, viśuddhi, lalanā, ājñā, manas, soma* and *sahasra*. Concluding the discussion the author establishes a correspondence between these and the 'moods' or states of being, and underpins the necessity of meditating on the *cakras* for attaining proficiency in music. (Cf. SR I.2.140). He also relates the emergence of sound and particular musical notes with these *cakras*, which then really become an octave in music.

The concept of the centre is made clear through the term *brahmagranthi*, which is described as:

आधाराद् द्व्यङ्गुलादूर्ध्वं मेहनाद् द्व्यङ्गुलादधः ॥ 145 ॥
एकाङ्गुलं देहमध्यं तप्तजाम्बूनदप्रभम् ।
तत्रास्तेऽग्निशिखा तन्वी चक्रात्तस्मान्नवाङ्गुले ॥ 146 ॥
देहस्य कन्दोऽस्त्युत्सेधायामाभ्यां चतुरङ्गुलः ।
ब्रह्मग्रन्थिरिति प्रोक्तं तस्य नाम पुरातनैः ॥ 147 ॥
तन्मध्ये नाभिचक्रं तु द्वादशारमवस्थितम् ।
लूतेव तन्तुजालस्था तत्र जीवो भ्रमत्ययम् ॥ 148 ॥

SR I.2.145-148

Two finger-length above the base and two finger-breadth below the genitals in the space of one finger-breadth is the centre of the body, shining like molten gold. (145c-146b).
There is located a slender flame of fire at a distance of nine fingers from that centre, and it is there that the life-source of the body is found, four fingers in elevation as well as in extension.. This has been called *brahma-granthi* by the ancients. (146c-147)
Right in its centre is situated the cycle of the umbilicus (*nābhi cakra*) with twelve spokes, and like the spider caught in (its own) net, yonder there wanders the selfconscious being. (148) (Tr. P.L. Sharma)

10. The *cakra* is basic to musical structure. The *sama* or beginning of a rhythmic cycle (→*tāla*) is not a beginning in a linear order; it is the *centre* both as point and as vertical diameter.

There are many musical compositions which denote circularity, e.g. in the *Varṇālaṅkāra* Section the form called *vyāvṛtta* and in the *Prabandha* Section the composition called *cakravāla*.

पूर्वपूर्वाक्षरव्राते योऽन्त्यो वर्णचयः स चेत् ॥
उत्तरोत्तरसङ्घादौ चक्रवालस्तदोच्यते ।
गद्यपद्यप्रभेदेन स द्विधा गदितो बुधैः ॥ SR IV.219c-220

Cakravāla (*prabandha*) is called as such when the last group of syllables of the preceding syllabic structure (comparable to a sentence)

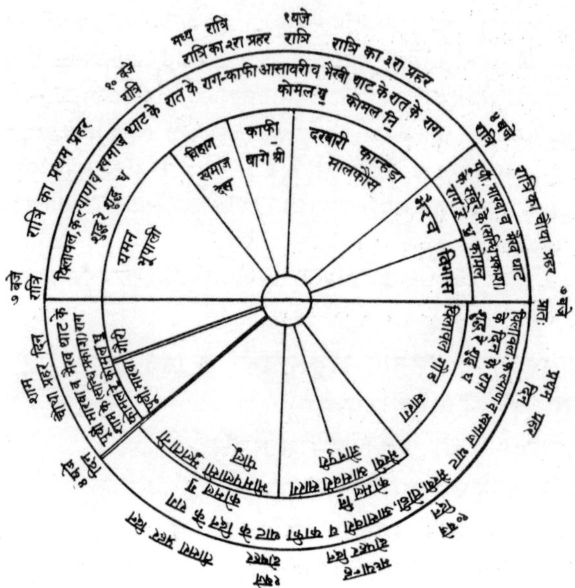

Figure 13: Rāgasamaya cakra

> forms the beginning of the succeeding structure. That (*prabandha*) has been said to be two-fold through the distinction of prose and poetry.
> The circular movement of textual units has been conceived here, because the ending unit of the preceding phrase forms the beginning of the next one. (Tr. P.L. Sharma)

Some of these are analogous to the dance compositions mentioned in the **Nāṭya-Śāstra**, called *piṇḍībandha*.

In time to come the Indian musical system evolved a multilayered pattern of correspondences between the notes, micro-tones and the phenomenal world of vegetation, birds and animals as also the temporal movement of the earth. All these culminate in the notion of *rāga-samaya-cakra* where the *rāga* and the notes correspond to particular moments of day or night, *muhūrta prahara*, all moving in cyclicity.

11. The *tāla* system, unique to Indian Arts, particularly music and dance, imbibes, embodies and manifests the concept of *cakra* in self-evident terms. The structural framework evolves invariably from the identification of a point (*bindu*), centre (*garbha* or *nābhi*) and the circumference (*vṛtta*). While the centre (*sama*) is invariable – still and immutable and the general perimeter of the circumference is predetermined, within it are near infinite possibilites of permutations and combinations. In geometrical terms, this is analogous to the *yantras* (basic design) of Indian architecture and sculpture, with their centre, diameters

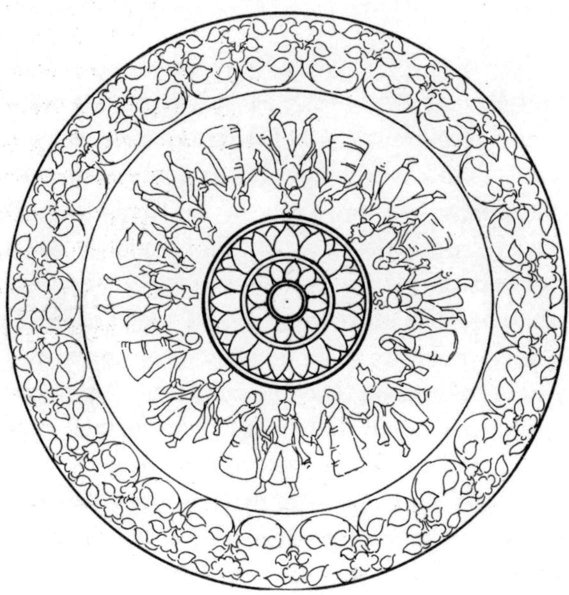

Figure 14: Rāsamaṇḍala, after Chamba Rumal

and radii. From the most abstract to the concrete or figurative, the Indian Arts at the level of theory and practice (*śāstra* and *prayoga*) codify and articulate the concept.

The *hallīsaka* and the *rāsa* with the *rāsamaṇḍala* are the kinetic and visual expressions of this fundamental concept with a potential for multiple interpretation. Each represents in artistic terms the complementarity of the unmanifest and manifest, the mutual dependence of the one and the many, and the dynamics of stillness and movement. Besides the theoretical conceptions, the more important aspect is the development of the circular form in dance which acquires mystical significance in the *rāsa-līlā*. The most important amongst these is the dance of Kṛṣṇa and the Gopīs in a circular formation. At one plane the area of the dance and the circular formation is the universe (*bhūmaṇḍala*), at another it symbolizes the principle of the One and the Many, the centre and the periphery in their aspects of interchangeability. The *rāsa-maṇḍala* is the artistic counterpart of the centripetal and centrifugal processes implied and sometimes described in the Upaniṣads through the all-pervasive metaphor of the *nābhi* (hub), the spokes (*aras*) and circumference (*vṛtta*). The *cakra* holds a key also to understanding the phenomenon of continuity and change in the Indian Arts. Had they subscribed to a concept of linearity and movement only in a single direction, there could be little possibility of affirming the still-immutable centre and incessant flux.

Process

The wheel represents infinity: endlessness on the one hand and beginninglessness on the other. Therefore it is a befitting representation of the world-cycle which when analysed, exhibits a perpetual flux. As it is ever in movement it moves on from one unmanifest and ends in another unmanifest but it shows a minute stop, a steady motionlessness only for a subtle moment between two movements, the past and the future, and thus manifests itself as the state known as the present. Otherwise the movement of the wheel is nothing but moments of appearance and disappearance. The movement of the wheel being cyclic, it is involved with two types of motion, the one is known as *anuloma*, forward movement, and the other is *pratiloma*, backward. The former explains the creative process and the later signifies the process of withdrawal.

The wheel conveys the simple idea of motion when it is viewed from outside but as everyone remains involved or enmeshed in the wheel therefore one fails to find real peace. As the wheel represents all that is fullness, decidedly it has some subtle points which leads one to arrive at the centre which is free from upheavals of worldly activities. In some doctrines the wheel representing endless movement of time consists of subtle time units called →*kṣaṇa* or the intermediate juncture (→*sandhi*) of two movements. The spokes of the wheel are nothing but radiating rays which go on functioning, and everything consciously or unconsciously remains ever in contact with the Supreme, the centre of the wheel of existence. These rays of the wheel emanating from the disc of the sun are beneficial for transmuting everything into divine being. Thus the wheel conveys two ideas: the one points to life, its reality and beauty and the other signifies and shows the way how to get rid of the tangles of the wheel and become one with the Lord (*cakreśvara*).

Conclusion

We may sum up the wide spectrum of the meaning of *cakra* in the Indian tradition in the words of V.S. Agrawala: "The worship of the *cakra* as representing the supreme ideals underlying the cosmic manifestation on the one hand and of the individual life on the other has been a part of Indian tradition from the most ancient times... . The *cakra* has a two-fold aspect, viz., the centre and the circumference. There is rest at the centre and movement in the circumference, unity in the centre and diversity in the circumference. The complete *cakra* presents a synthesis or harmony between the two. There is no better symbol than the Wheel, showing the law of unity in diversity. The *cakra* implies an aggregation of spokes, all of which emanate from a common source and represent so many points on the periphery of the wheel... .

The essential feature of the *cakra* is cyclic movement (*gati*) in a rhythmic order which brings with it great blessings and happiness; for example, the cycle of six seasons (*ṣaṭ-ṛtu-cakra*) presents a charming poetry of flowers, plants, singing birds and many other harmonies. The tiller of the soil witnesses the miracle of the Wheel in the sprouting of the seed and then its bursting into flowers and fruition. Boyhood, youth and age depend on the potency of the *cakra*, unfolding in each life. Thus the meaning of the *cakra* has a universal appeal. It stands for the Supreme Law of the cosmos and human life. " (V.S. Agrawala, The Wheel Flag of India (Chakra-Dhvaja), pp.i-ii).

H.N. Chakravarty

Select Bibliography

Agrawala, V.S.: The Wheel Flag of India *cakradhvaja.* Varanasi: Prithivi Prakashan, 1964.

Begley: Viṣṇu's Flaming Wheel: The Iconography of the Sudarśana Cakra. New York, 1973.

Boner, A.: New Light on the Sun Temple of Konarka. Varanasi: Chowkhamba Sanskrit Sansthan, 1972.

Cirlot. J.E.: A Dictionary of Symbols. London: Routledge and Kegan Paul, 1962.

Deloche, Jean: Contribution à l'histoire de la voiture en Inde. Paris: Ecole Francaise d'Extreme-Orient, 1983.

Dharmadhikari, T.N.: Yajñāyudhāni. Pune: Vaidika Saṃśodhana Maṇḍala, 1989.

Hopkins, Jeffrey: The Kālacakra Tantra. London: Wisdom Publications, 1985.

Jhalakīkar, M.M: Bhīmācārya, (Revised by V.S. Abhyankar): Nyāyakośa. Pune: Bhandarkar Oriental Research Institute, 1928.

Rao, T.N. Gopinatha: Elements of Hindu Iconography (Vol. I, Part-I). Madras: The Law Printing House, 1914.

Vatsyayan, Kapila: The Square and the Circle of the Indian Arts. New Delhi: Roli Books International, 1983.

KṢETRA

Overview

The Sanskrit word *kṣetra* (Pāli *khetta*), with a particular degree of generality, refers to physical space of all types: field, landed property, enclosed spot of ground, portion of space, place of origin, dominion, region, etc. The core meaning is extended to a conglomerate of wide-ranging aspects, from geometric forms to metaphysical expressions: plane figure as triangle, circuit, superficies, a house, a town, seat, sphere of activity, source, extent, wife, womb, body, primeval soul or matter. The total field of spatial meaning is transformed when used in psychical and spiritual contexts.

There is, thus, a vast accumulation of the word *kṣetra* and its cognates in various traditional texts: the Vedas, the Upaniṣads, the Smṛtis, the Purāṇas and the Epics, Āyurveda, Jyotiṣa, Śilpa, Saṅgīta, Sāhitya, and so on.

How did this diversity of meanings come about? What is its nature? How is the word *kṣetra* related with its given meaning? What kind of worldview emerges from its grammatical treatment?

In a consideration of these questions the following aspects of the semantic treatment are essential: etymology and cognates, meanings, conceptual development, and usage in specific contexts.

Etymology and Cognate Words

Kṣetra (neuter) is derived from the verbal root *kṣi-* or *kṣay-* to dwell (Nir X.14), to abide, to reside, to remain (AV XIX.10.10), to inhabit (ŚBr XIII.2.3.2). It is used to denote the field, ground, land, region and country, even from the Ṛgvedic period. As a first part of a compound form, it mostly occurs in *kṣetrapati* 'the lord of the soil or ground' in the **Ṛgveda** (IV.57.1). In later texts *kṣetrapati* is worshipped as a god; it is also used to denote property and in the **Yajur-Veda** it means 'belonging to the lord of the soil'. Again *kṣetrapatya* is used in **Atharva-Veda** (Paippalāda recension I.99.4) to denote landlordship. As a derivative of *kṣetra* the adjective form *kṣetriya* is used in **Atharva-Veda** to denote an organic and incurable disease; its plural form means the environs of a place. Again *kṣetriya-nāśana* is used in the **Atharva-Veda** (II.8.5) to denote 'removing a chronic disease'.

By the use of singular or combined suffixes, the spatial semantics turns into new categorical sets: *kṣetra-adhidevatā*, the tutelary deity of a sacred place; *kṣetradevatā*, the deity of the field; *kṣetra-padam*, a place sacred to deity; *kṣetra-pāla* a deity protecting fields (an epithet of Śiva); *kṣetra-vid*, a sage; *kṣetrajña*, embodied spirit, expert, knowing the locality; *kṣetrajñā*, a fifteen-year-old girl impersonating Durgā at a festival; *kṣetrastha* or *kṣetrasannyāsa*, residing at a sacred place as recluse; and so on.

By postpositions another set of qualifying terms is found: *dharmakṣetra*, the field of righteousness; *śubhakṣetra*, auspicious ground for temple; *samakṣetra*, even surface; *buddha-kṣetra*, Buddha-field or region, and so on.

The synonyms for *kṣetra*, are *valaja, niṣkuṭa, rājikā, pāṭīra, vapra, kedāra*. Fields collectively are *kaidārya*. Other synonyms for *kṣetra* are *sthāna* (place), *bhūmi* (land), and *deśa* (country). *Maṇḍala* is a broader spatial term for *kṣetra*. *Tīrtha* as a class of sacred place is *kṣetra*.

The term *kṣetra* is also notable in a number of languages almost homophonous and with the same connotation. Indo-iranic (Iir), old Avestan *šōiθra* means district, Modern Avestan *šōiθra* means place; of Modern Avestan, Yasna II.16 *šōiθrahe paiti* = Vedic *kṣetrasya pati*. Mostly. Avestan *šōiθra gaoiiaoiti* is compared to Ṛgvedic *agavyūti kṣetram*. Avestan *šōiθriia*, Vedic *kṣetriya*. Khotaneese *kṣīra* (*tumšuq xšera*) means country, kingdom, etc.

Dimensions of Meaning

Kṣetra as a generic term refers to the field you plough, the land you subsist on, the ground you stand on, the house, the town you live in, and so on. A core identification of meaning can be sought in a set of four generalizing expressions.

1) A perceptual distinctive unit of physical space. Example: Field and plough lands (ṚV IV.38.1).

2) A model characterized by geometric form. Example: diagram for an image panel (VSUp II.12).

3) A biological category indicating generative process. Example: woman (Manu IX.33a).

4) A conceptual construct of body, and/or mind as a spiritual sphere. Example: body and the knower of the body, that is Self (BhG XIII.1).

As a categorical term, it reflects various layers of conceptual thinking: physical, metaphysical, mathematical, mystical, inner, outer, micro, macro, and so on.

a) Physical-Metaphysical: In the **Bhagavad-Gītā** the term *kṣetra* has been used both for the physical body (XIII.1) and for the phenomena of mind (XIII.6).

b) Mathematical-Mystical: *kṣetra* refers to spatial phenomena measured and drawn up in relations of forms. The **Vāstusūtra Upaniṣad** (II.11) mentions a perfect geometric form and calls it *rūpakṣetra*, 'the cosmic image panel'.

c) Inner-Outer: The body is called *kṣetra,* the soul that dwells in the body is *kṣetrajña*, 'the knower of the body' (BhG XIII.1). The **Suśruta Saṃhitā** has used the word *kṣetra* for the uterus (Śārīrasthāna II.33) as also for the body (Sūtrasthāna XXXV.5).

d) Macrocosm-Microcosm: The **Bhāgavata Purāṇa** (IX.6.37) points out that the whole earth is *kṣetra.* The position of stars in the sky is also *kṣetra.* But a *tīrtha kṣetra*, 'place of pilgrimage', such as Kāśī, is conceptualized as a microcosm, the sacred universe (SkaPur).

While the basic sense of space is maintained throughout its use, the word *kṣetra* moves on from the concrete to the abstract in its manifold dimensions. Perhaps it is the wordplay of Sanskrit that has made such diversity of meanings possible.

Development of the Concept

Kṣetra is a powerful word, initially used to denote fertile land and gross physical space and, subsequently, applied to subtler forms and processes. The visionaries of the transcendental world of forms allowed its simultaneous growth of both concrete and abstract representations.

No rigid technical frame can be applied to determine its exact sequence of meanings. However, a visible order of categorical sets can be discussed under two broad classes: a) the geographical, geometric and abstract space; and b) the human body and its physical, psychical and spiritual attributes.

A) Geographical, geometric, abstract space:

Kṣetra and its derivatives occur one hundred seventyfive times in the Vedic texts alone, with wide-ranging meanings. For the first time it finds mention in the **Ṛgveda**, most commonly, to denote geographical space, land, field, region or expanse of country.

Indra is described as the winner of land, the sunlight and the waters (ṚV I.100.18). Distinct from the ordinary land is the *bhadra kṣetra*, 'auspicious land' (ṚV V.62.7), and the *mahikṣetra*, 'great, splendid, rich dominion' (ṚV III.31.15). The country void of pasture is also mentioned (ṚV VI.47.20). *Kṣetra* stands for the field and not the forest (AV XIV.2.7). Land is precious and hence we find the following expressions: *kṣetrāsām*, 'procuring land' (ṚV IV.38.1), *kṣetrapatyam*, 'possession or ownership of land' (TSam I.8.20.1), *kṣetra-jeṣe* refers to 'contest for landed property' (ṚV I.33.15), *kṣetrasātā* 'acquisition of land' (ṚV VII.19.3), *kṣetrajitya* 'victorious in battle', 'acquisition of land' (YV XXXIII.60), *kṣetrañ-jaya* 'acquiring, or gaining landed property' (Mait-Sam II.2.11), and so on. There are indications of 'fertile field': *apnasvati* and 'barren land' *ārtana* (ṚV I.127.6), proparly irrigated and manured agricultural field (ṚV VII.49.2; AV I.6.4; XIX 2.2; III.14.3; XIX.31.3). The other related terms are *kṣetra-tara* 'a good fertile field' (ŚBr I.4.1.16), *kṣetra-sādhas* 'one making the field fertile', 'he who divides the field' (ṚV III.8.7; VIII 31.4), *kṣetrika*, 'a farmer' (YSū IV.3), and *kṣetra-vitrūṇi* 'furrow' (Agniveśa GṛSū III.8.2). The wider sense of place is retained in several subsequent texts such as Upaniṣads (ChUp VII.24.2; VIII.1.5) and Purāṇas (ViPur IV.2.65; 51).

The **Ṛgveda** indicates that the field (geographical space) was carefully measured (I.110.5). In the later texts, *kṣetra* is a technical term for geometric figures. We shall return to this usage in the subsequent section.

As the cosmocentric worldview began influencing the semantic field, the word *kṣetra* was used for a larger dimension, and deeper meanings of space.

The notion of auspicious place originated in the Vedas, in the context of describing the sacrificial hall.

हिरण्यनिर्णिगयो अस्य स्थूणा वि भ्राजते दिव्यश्वाजनीव ।
भद्रे क्षेत्रे निर्मिता तिल्विले वा सनेम मध्वो अधिगर्त्यस्य ॥

ṚV V.62.7

Adorned with gold, its columns are of iron: In heaven it glitters like a whip for horses; or stablished on a field deep-soiled and fruitful. So may we share the meath that loads your car seat. (Tr. R.T.H. Griffith)

The whole conception of sacred place has found its greatest development in the Purāṇas.

The *saptadvīpā pṛthivī*, seven-island earth, is described as *kṣetra*.

यावत्सूर्य उदेति स्म यावच्च प्रतितिष्ठति ।
सर्वं तद्यौवनाश्वस्य मान्धातुः क्षेत्रमुच्यते ॥

BhāgPur IX.6.37

From the point from which the sun starts to the point where he stops (breaks his journey) all that under the sun is called the land of Māndhātṛ, son of Yuvanāśva. (Tr. S. Subbarau)

Tīrtha kṣetra was eulogised as a microcosm. *Kṣetra* now stands for spiritual space.

तद्वीरासीत्पुण्यतमं क्षेत्रं त्रैलोक्यविश्रुतम् ।
नाम्ना सिद्धपदं यत्र सा संसिद्धिमुपेयुषी ॥

BhāgPur III.33.31

The place where Devahūti achieved her perfection, my dear Vidura, is understood to be a most sacred spot. It is known all over the three worlds as *Siddhapada*. (Tr. Swami Prabhupada)

गंगायमुनयोर्नद्योरन्तराक्षेत्रमावसन् ।
आरब्धानेव बुभुजे भोगान्पुण्यजिहासया ॥

BhāgPur IV.21.11

The great saintly sage Maitreya told Vidura: My dear Vidura, king Pṛthu lived in the tract of land between the two great rivers Gaṅgā and Yamunā. Because he was very opulent, it appeared that he was enjoying his destined fortune in order to diminish the results of his past pious activities. (Tr. Swami Prabhupada)

All sacred places are not *kṣetra*. As a place of pilgrimage, they are *tīrthas*. Of these only a cluster of *tīrthas* of special spiritual significance is given the categorical term *kṣetra*. Kāśī, Kāmarūpa, Bhāskara, Puruṣottama, Nārāyaṇa, Gayā and Prayāga are the *siddhakṣetras*, the places of supreme attainment; Kurukṣetra, Kedāra, Varāhamūla, Gajakṣetra and Puṇḍarīkakṣetra are *puṇya-kṣetras*, meritorious places. There are other places of supreme importance. Kurukṣetra is sacred to Brahmā and hence called *Brahmakṣetra*; Purī is *Viṣṇu-kṣetra*, sacred to Viṣṇu; Bhuvaneśvara is *Śivakṣetra*, sacred to Śiva; Jajpur in Orissa is *Śaktikṣetra*, sacred to the goddess Pārvatī. The *kṣatras* are listed in the **Mahābhārata** and several of the eighteen Purāṇas. In them everything of the cosmos that is powerful and auspicious finds a place. The example of *Kāśīkṣetra* is appropriate at this point.

In the Purāṇic literature Kāśī has been described as a place (*kṣetra*) greater than crores of holy places. It is conceived as a symbolic circle with a radius of five *krośas* (about 16 km), divided into three *khaṇḍas* (segments), each having a presiding deity. The boundaries of the *Kāśīkṣetra* are marked by the pilgrim's clockwise circumambulation of the inner and outer sacred zones, respectively called the *antargṛha* and the *pañcakrośī parikramā*. Pilgrimage within the *kṣetra* is further intensified by intricate networking of the *yatra*, sacred journey, both in space and time.

All the *tīrthas*, all the gods, all the planets and all the seven stars (*saptarṣi*) are enshrined within the physical space marked by the *pañcakrośī parikramā* route. The *antargṛha*, the *āyatana* and the *trikoṇa yātrā* routes together with the sacred spots of the *kuṇḍa* make *Kāśīkṣetra* a perfect model of the Tāntric *maṇḍala*. However, as the **Kāśī-Rahasya** reveals, its physical appearance has been changing through the ages. In the Kṛta Yuga, *Kāśīkṣetra* looked like a trident (Śiva's *triśūla*); in the Tretā it assumed a circular form like Viṣṇu's *cakra*; in the Dvāpara it took the form of a chariot, symbolic of the Sun; and in the Kali Yuga it has a conchlike shape. *Kāśīkṣetra* has been depicted as the body of Śiva (Fig. 1), and *Puruṣottamakṣetra* (Purī) is represented as the conchshell (Fig.2). Further, *Kāśīkṣetra* is an earthly representation of a transcendental model. It is a replica of the paradigmatic universe. As the name suggests, *Kāśī*,

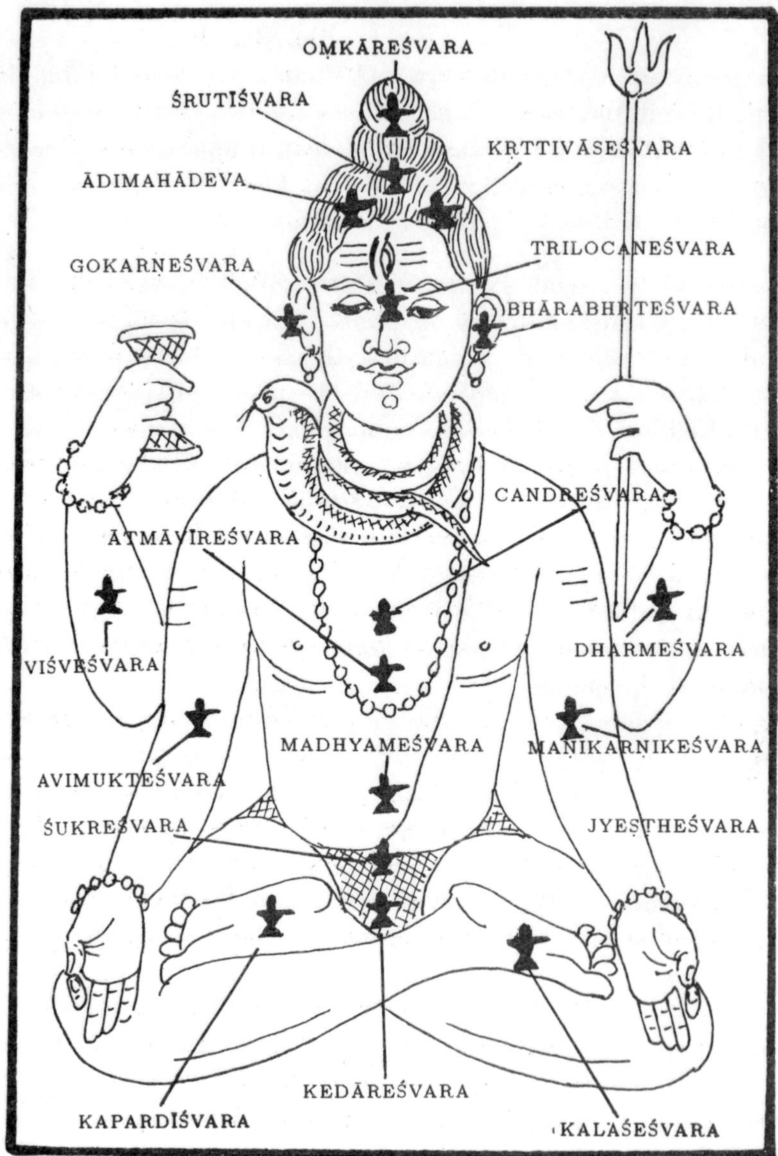

Figure 1: Vārāṇasī-Svarūpa Śivamūrti: The body of Śiva as the sacred field of Varanasi

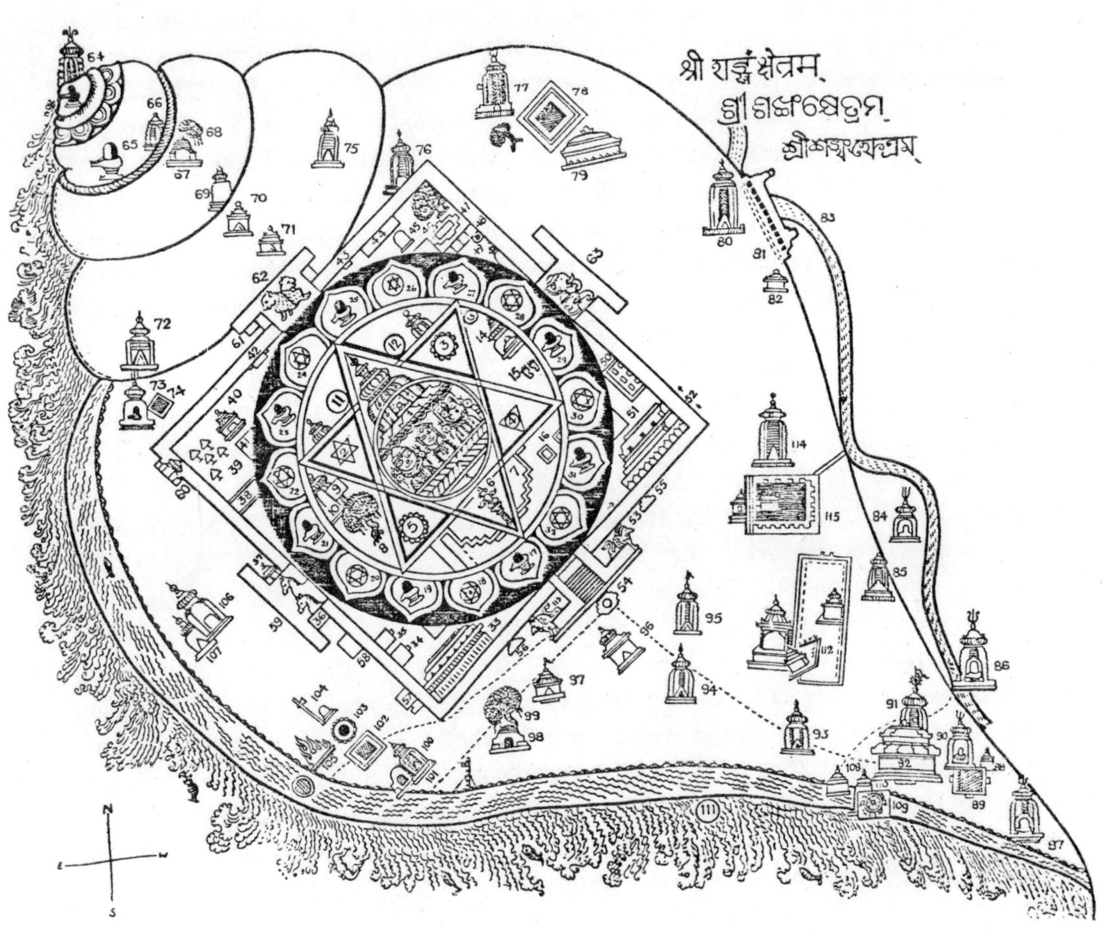

Figure 2: Puri as Śaṅkha-Kṣetra: In the shape of a conch

Legend to Śaṅkha Kṣetra:

1. Śrī Balabhadra, Jagannātha, Subhadrā and Sudarśana 2. Śrī Kṣetreśvarī Vimalā 3. Śrī Mahālakṣmī 4. Uttarā Durgā 5. Baṭamaṅgalā 6. Garuḍastambha 7. Bhogamaṇḍapa 8. Kalpavṛkṣa 9. Rohiṇī Kuṇḍa 10. Baṭa Gaṇeśa 11. Ucchiṣṭa Gaṇapati 12. Śrī Sarasvatī Devī 13. Navagraha 14. Koṇārk Sūryadeva 15. Pādapadma 16. Yajñabaṭa 17. Agñeśvara 18. Indrāṇīdevī 19. Kṣetrapāla 20. Svana Bhairavī 21. Mukteśvara 22. Citrakālī 23. Baṭamārkaṇḍeya 24. Kātyāyanī 25. Gopeśvara 26. Veda Kālī 27. Pātāleśvara 28. Bhuvaneśvarī 29. Vaikuṇṭheśvara 30. Yajñeśvarī 31. Īśāneśvara 32. Śītalā Devī 33. Pākaśālā 34. Dakṣiṇeśvara 35. Kuṇḍaleśvara 36. Ram Chaitanya Temple 37. Barābhaya Hanumāna 38. Nirmālya Hanumāna 39. Alakā Bāṭikā 40. Cakra Nārāyaṇa 41. Rāmeśvara 42. Caturdhāma 43. Kānapātā Hanumāna 44. Nīlādri Bihāra 45. Vāyavyeśvara 46. Śiālilatā 47. Koili Baikuṇṭha 48. Tapasvī Hanumāna 49. Suvarṇakūpa 50. Ānanda Bazār 51. Devasnānamaṇḍapa 52. Meghanāda Pācirī 53. Siṃhadvāra (Eastern Gate) 54. Aruṇa Stambha 55. Baḍachatā Maṭha 56. Chāuni Maṭha 57. Pejaṅalā 58. Praharī Hanumāna 59. Dakṣiṇadvāra (Southern Gate) 60. Durgāmādhava 61. Maṅgaleśvarī 62. Paścimadvāra (Western Gate) 63. Uttaradvāra (Northern Gate) 64. Śrī Lokanātha 65. Yameśvara 66. Kaṇḍunṛsiṃha 67. Kaṇḍu Āśrama 68. Nikumbhilābaṭa 69. Haracaṇḍī 70. Cāmuṇḍeśvarī 71. Vanadurgā 72. Baśelī 73. Kapālamocana 74. Maṇikarṇikā Tīrtha 75. Ghaṭamaṅgalā 76. Bhagavatī 77. Mārkaṇḍeyeśvara 78. Mārkaṇḍeya Tīrtha 79. Saptamātṛkā 80. Ālambā Devī 81. Aṭhara Nalā 82. Makaradhvaja Hanumāna 83. Bhārgavī Nadī 84. Mukteśvara 85. Baṭamaṅgalā 86. Kapoteśvara 87. Vilveśvara 88. Siddha Hanumāna 89. Indradyumna Tīrtha 90. Nīlakaṇṭheśvara 91. Ādinṛsiṃha 92. Guṇḍicā Maṇḍapa 93. Ardhaśoṣaṇī (Māusīmā) 94. Marcikā Devī 95. Carchikā Devī 96. Ṣoḍaśa Putrī 97. Nārāyaṇī 98. Aṅgirāśrama 99. Aṅgirābaṭa 100. Dakṣiṇā Kālī 101. Ugreśvarāśrama 102. Śvetagaṅgā 103. Muktiśilā 104. Ādiśānkara Pīṭha 105. Svargadvāra 106. Vārāhī Devī 107. Śyāmā Kālī 108. Beḍī Hanumāna 109. Cakra Tīrtha 110. Cakra Nārāyaṇa 111. Mahodadhi (Tīrtha) 112. Jagannātha Ballava 113. Kāśī Viśvanātha 114. Viśveśvarī 115. Narendra Sarovara.

luminous, *kṣetra*, represents the primeval egg of golden colour wherein Brahmā, the progenitor of all creatures and regions, himself was born. Herein the eight directions as well as the Lords of the planets, sun and moon had their origin. *Kāśīkṣetra* is situated on Śiva's *triśūla*, at the centre of space and time, the meeting place of heaven and beyond. The cosmological structure of the *pañcakrośātmaka kṣetra* represents the five subtle and transforming *tanmātras* of which this universe was created. The *pañcakrośī* stands for the five fundamental levels of reality: *annamaya kośa, prāṇamaya kośa, manomaya kośa, vijñānamaya kośa*, and *ānandamaya kośa*. Its three segments signify *triloka*, the 'three-world' totality of the universe, consisting of three realms: earth, atmosphere and heaven. Here *pralaya* is ovarcome and all beings rest for ever. It is Brahman itself of which this turning world is but an expression.

The spiritual notion of *kṣetra* is found also in the Jain and the Buddhist tradition. The Jain *tīrthas* are of two classes: one is *siddhakṣetra*, the places where the Tīrthaṅkaras and other holymen have attained *nirvāṇa*; and the other *atiśayakṣetra*, those places which have assumed importance because of temples, idols, or certain miraculous events.

In the Buddhist scriptures, the *buddhakṣetra* means Buddha-field, region or, usually, world or world system in which a particular Buddha lives and operates.

सर्वाणि च तानि बुद्धक्षेत्राणि बोधिसत्त्वस्याभया स्फुटानि संदृश्यन्ते स्म ॥

LVi XIX. p.202

All the Buddha fields were enlightened by the Bodhisattva's rays.

The *upakṣetra* or subordinate (Buddha) field has been stated to be four times the size of a (Buddha) *kṣetra*. According to the **Hevajra Tantra** (I.7.12) the *kṣetras* are Munmunī, Kāruṇyapāṭaka, Devī-Koṭya and Karmārapāṭaka, and the *upakṣetras* are Kulatā, Arbuda, Godāvarī and Himādri.

The field also means the spiritual soil on which the yogin has to toil in order to bring fruit.

भन्ते नागसेन, खेत्तस्स तीणि अङ्गानि गहेतब्बानी'ति यं वदेसि, कतमानि तानि तीणि अङ्गानि गहेतब्बानी'ति? यथा महाराज, खेत्तं मातिकासम्पन्नं होति, एवमेव खो महाराज, योगिना योगावचरेन सुचरितवत्त पटिवत्तमातिकासम्पन्नेन भवितब्बं । इदं महाराज, खेत्तस्स पठमं अङ्गं गहेतब्बं । पुन च परं महाराज, खेत्तं मरियादसम्पन्नं होति, ताय च मरियादाय उदकं रक्खित्वा धञ्ञं परिपाचेन्ति, एवमेव खो महाराज योगिना योगावचरेन सीलहिरिमरियादासम्पन्नेन भवितब्बं, ताय च सीलहिरिमरियादाय सामञ्ञं रक्खित्वा चत्तारि सामञ्ञफलानि गहेतब्बानि । इदं महाराज, खेत्तस्स दुतियं अङ्गं गहेतब्बं । पुन च परं महाराज, खेत्तं उट्ठानसम्पन्नं होति; कस्सकस्स हासजनकं, अप्पं पि बीजं वुत्तं बहु करोति, बहु वुत्तं बहुतरं होति, एवमे'व खो महाराज, योगिना

योगावचरेन उट्ठानसम्पन्नेन विपुलफलदायिना भवितब्बं, दायकानं हासजनकेन भवितब्बं, यथा अप्पं दिन्नं बहु होति, बहु दिन्नं बहुतरं होति । इदं महाराज, खेत्तस्स ततियं अङ्गं गहेतब्बं। भासितं पे'तं महाराज, थेरेन उपालिना विनयधरेन -

खेत्तूपमेन भवितब्बं उट्ठानविपुलदायिना ।
एस खेत्तवरो नाम यो ददाति विपुलं फलं'ति ॥

MilPañ VII.64

Revered Nāgasena, three limbs of the field are to be known. Which are these three limbs as mentioned by you that should be known? O Lord, just as the field is made of soil, so O lord, the yogin who has applied himself to the path of *yoga*, should be well-disciplined in moral conduct in reciprocal way like the soil is turned carefully over and over again. This, O Lord, is the first limb of the field which is to be known. Then again, O Lord, the field consists of a boundary wall where, storing water, the tiller of the field causes the paddy to grow and ripen, in the same way the person who follows the course of *yoga* should be possessed of good moral conduct. By virtue of non-transgression of the bounds of morality and propriety one is able to protect one's asceticism and obtains four-fold fruit of being as an ascetic. This, O Lord, is the second limb of the field. Then again, O Lord, the field is equipped with prosperity yielding plenty of fruits and causes delight in the heart of some. A small quantity of seed when sown, yields abundantly, when sown more in quantity, it yields more. The ascetic should be endowed with exertion yielding plenty of fruits so that to whom they are given, they may gladden them. When a small gift gives plenty of fruits, plenty of gifts being presented yield bigger results. This, O Lord, is the third limb of the field. This has been stated by the venerable Upāli, the master in Vinaya.

One should follow the nature of the field consisting of big and tall trees yielding fruits imitating them in height and expanse. This is the excellent field which gives fruits abundantly. (Tr. H.N. Chakravarty)

The Tāntric texts deepen the meaning of *kṣetra* by identifying the external holy places with specific centres within the subtle body. Abhinavagupta's **Tantrāloka** describes the mystical *kṣetras* within the body.

क्षेत्राष्टकं क्षेत्रविदो हृदम्भोजदलाष्टकम् ।
प्रयागो वरणा पश्चादट्टहासो जयन्तिका ।
वाराणसी च कालिङ्गं कुलूता लाहुला तथा ।

TĀl XV.89-90ab

To the knower of *kṣetras* located inside the body the *kṣetras* are eight. They are the eight petals of the heart-lotus. The names of the *kṣetras* are Prayāga, Varaṇā, Aṭṭahāsa, Jayantikā, Vārāṇasī, Kaliṅga, Kulūtā and Lāhulā. (Tr. H.N. Chakravarty)

According to Abhinavagupta, these *kṣetras* are the means to attain some sort of *siddhi*, but they are decidedly not the means to attain liberation (*sādhakānām upāyaḥ syāt siddhaye na tu muktaye*, TĀl XV.82ab). The *kṣetra* or *pīṭha* that may shine internally inside the body is to make them manifest by conscious effort of the yogin. He does this by means of associating the vital energy to the specific spots.

In the **Lalitā-Sahasranāma**, Lalitā's body is described as of the nature of *kṣetra* (*kṣetrasvarūpā*, Lalitā 127a). Bhāskararāya's commentary on this text explains this epithet in the following way:

क्षेत्रं कामरूपादिकं वसुधादिशिवान्तषट्त्रिंशत्तत्त्वात्मकं शरीरं वा । तत्स्वं निजं रूपं यस्याः सा । तथा च लैङ्गे - 'बिभर्ति क्षेत्रतां देवी त्रिपुरान्तक-वल्लभा । क्षेत्रज्ञत्वमजो धत्ते भगवानन्तकान्तकः' ॥

Bhāskararāya on above

Kṣetra, Kāmarūpa and other abodes or thirty-six categories from earth to Śiva, these form her body. **Liṅga Purāṇa** says, 'Devī, the wife of the destroyer of the three cities (i.e. Śiva) becomes *kṣetra* (matter). The divine and eternal lord, the death is the knower of the bodies'. (Tr. A.N. Sastry)

In Hindu astronomy, the word *kṣetra* occurs in the context of the ecliptic circle with its various subdivisions. Varāhamihira's famous work **Bṛhat-Saṃhitā** uses the word *kṣetra* to describe angles, etc.

...कालस्य क्षेत्रस्य च वेत्ता ।

BṛSam II.4

(An astrologer should be) conversant with the subdivisions of time and with those of the ecliptic circle. (Tr. M.R. Bhat)

The parallelism in the division of time and circle has been noted by other writers also (cf. Āryabhaṭa, Āryabhaṭīya, Kālakriyāpāda 2).

The lord of the ascendent is called *kṣetreśvara* (cf. BṛSam XCVI.12).

केन्द्रे यथास्थानबलप्रकर्षं क्षेत्रस्य तत्क्षेत्रपतेश्च बुद्ध्वा ।
कार्योऽक्षराणामनुपूर्वयोगो मात्रादिसंयोगविकल्पना च ॥

BṛSam XCVI.13

The order of the letters as well as the joining of the *mātrās* (upper, lower and transverse), conjunct consonants at the beginning or the end should be fixed, only after ascertaining fully the extent of the positional strength of the *kendra* houses and their lords. (Tr. M.R. Bhat)

B) Biological, physical, psychical, spiritual:

The spectrum of *kṣetra* impinges on another area, viz. the human body and its generative functions. The common metaphor of seed-and-soil is further applied to the complex metaphysics of body-and-soul.

Examples: Woman has been widely referred to as the soil (*kṣetra*)

क्षेत्रभूता स्मृता नारी ।

Manu IX.33

By the sacred tradition the woman is declared to be the soil. (Tr. G. Bühler)

कृष्णद्वैपायनाज्जज्ञे धृतराष्ट्रो जनेश्वरः ।
क्षेत्रे विचित्रवीर्यस्य पाण्डुश्चैव महाबलः ॥

MBh I.57.95

From Kṛṣṇadvaipāyana was born, in the soil of Vicitravīrya, Dhṛtarāṣṭra, the lord of men, and Pāṇḍu of great strength. (Tr. P.C. Roy)

क्षेत्रे विचित्रवीर्यस्य कृष्णद्वैपायनः पुरा ।
त्रीनग्नीनिव कौरव्याञ्जनयामास वीर्यवान् ॥

MBh I.1.54

Formerly, the spirited and virtuous Kṛṣṇadvaipāyana (by the injunctions of Bhīṣma, the son of Gaṅgā) caused birth to three boys, who were like the fires by the wife of Vicitravīrya. (Tr. P.C. Roy)

एवं ह्यात्मा जायते स्त्रीषु भूयः कश्चित्तस्मिन्क्षेत्रयोगाद्विशेषः ।

BṛSam LXXV.2

...even so is the soul reborn in woman. But as a result of the influence of the soil or mother, slight difference does occur in the fruit or child. (Tr. M.R. Bhat)

Kālidāsa also refers to Śakuntalā's mother as *kṣetra*:

अपि नाम कुलपतेरियमसवर्णक्षेत्रसम्भवा स्यात्?

AbhiŚāk I.(before 20)

Can she (Śakuntalā) be the daughter of the patriarch by a woman of an inferior (lit. dissimilar) caste? (Tr. M.R. Kale)

The **Mahābhārata** uses *kṣetra* in a wider metaphysical sense, in the context of life itself:

क्षेत्रं पुरुषकारस्तु दैवं बीजमुदाहृतम् ।
क्षेत्रबीजसमायोगात् ततः सस्यं समृध्यते ॥

MBh XIII.6.8

The field is human effort and destiny is the seed. By the association of both the field and the seed crops come up. (Tr. H.N. Chakravarty)

The medical sense of *kṣetra* meaning body occurs already in the **Bṛhad-Devatā**:

शरीरमिन्द्रियैर्युक्तं क्षेत्रमित्यभिधीयते ।

BṛDev IV.40

The body joined with the organs of sense is designated by *kṣetra*. (Tr. A.A. Macdonell)

A more intricate and technical meaning is found in Āyurveda. As a generative organ the womb (*garbhāśaya*) comes to be regarded as *kṣetra*. The seed-and-soil metaphor continues in scientific works.

बलवृद्धिकरास्त्विमे भावा भवन्ति, तद्यथा - बीजक्षेत्रगुणसंपच्च...

CarSam Śārīrasthāna VI.13

These factors lead to increase of strength such as ... excellence of seed and soil... (Tr. P.V. Sharma)

Fertility of the soil and fertility of the mother's womb have always been related to each other:

ध्रुवं चतुर्णां सान्निध्याद्गर्भः स्याद्विधिपूर्वकम् ।
ऋतुक्षेत्राम्बुबीजानां सामग्र्यादङ्कुरो यथा ॥

SuSam Śārīrasthāna II.33

A co-ordination of the four factors of menstrual period (*ṛtu*), healthy womb (*kṣetra*), nutrient liquid i.e. chyle of digested food (*ambu*), healthy semen (*bīja*) and the proper observance of the rules is necessary for the conception and development of a healthy child just as the season (*ṛtu*), good soil (*kṣetra*), water (containing nutrient matter) and vigorous seeds (*bīja*) together with proper care, help the germination of strong and undiseased sprouts. (Tr. K.L. Bhisagratna)

The elements constituting the human body (*kṣetra*) are enumerated:

खादीनि बुद्धिरव्यक्तमहङ्कारस्तथाष्टमः ।
भूतप्रकृतिरुद्दिष्टा विकाराश्चैव षोडश ॥
बुद्धीन्द्रियाणि पञ्चैव पञ्च कर्मेन्द्रियाणि च ।
समनस्काश्च पञ्चार्था विकारा इति संज्ञिताः ॥
इति क्षेत्रं समुद्दिष्टं सर्वमव्यक्तवर्जितम् ।

CarSam Śārīrasthāna I.63-65

Ākāśa etc. (*ākāśa, vāyu, tejas, ap* and *pṛthivī*), *buddhi, mahat* (intellect), *avyakta* (the unmanifest primordial nature) and *ahaṃkāra* (ego), the eighth one, constitute *bhūtaprakṛti* (original source of creatures). *Vikāras* (products) are sixteen – five sense organs, five motor organs, mind and five objects (*bhūtas*). This (aggregate) except the unmanifest one is known as *kṣetra* (body). (Tr. P.V. Sharma)

The location of piles is also termed as *kṣetra.*

सर्वेषां चार्शषां क्षेत्रं गुदस्यार्धपञ्चमाङ्गुलावकाशे त्रिभागान्तरास्तिस्रो गुदवलयः क्षेत्रमिति ।

CarSam Cikitsāsthāna XIV.6

The site of all the piles – the site of piles is the three anorectal folds situated in the space of five and a half fingers each at the distance one-third (of the above measurement). (Tr. P.V. Sharma)

In the context of Yoga *kṣetra* relates to the breeding ground of the *kleśas* or afflictions:

अविद्या क्षेत्रमुत्तरेषां प्रसुप्ततनुविच्छिन्नोदाराणाम् ।

YSū II.4

Avidyā is the breeding ground for the others (i.e. *asmitā* etc.) whether they be dormant, attenuated, interrupted or active. (Tr. H. Aranya)

In a positive sense, it means the fertile soil of Yoga that is to produce spiritual fruit:

तत्त्वं बीजं हठः क्षेत्रमौदासीन्यं जलं त्रिभिः ।
उन्मनी कल्पलतिका सद्य एव प्रवर्तते ॥

HyPrad IV.104

Mind (*tattva*) is the seed. Haṭhayoga is the soil and complete desirelessness is the water. With these three, the *kalpavṛkṣa*, which is the *unmanī avasthā* springs up immediately. (Tr. S. Iyangar)

The emergence of the metaphor of *kṣetra* as body and *kṣetrajña* as soul or Brahman can be traced back to the Upaniṣads.

The **Chāndogya Upaniṣad** refers to the one "who does not know the field" (*akṣetrajña*), in the following context:

तद्यथापि हिरण्यनिधिं निहितमक्षेत्रज्ञा उपर्युपरि सञ्चरन्तो न विन्देयुः ।
एवमेवेमाः सर्वाः प्रजा अहरहर्गच्छन्त्य एतं ब्रह्मलोकं न विन्दन्त्यनृतेन हि
प्रत्यूढाः ॥

ChUp VIII.3.2

So, just as those who do not know the field might go over a hidden treasure of gold again and again, but not find it, even so all creatures here go day by day to that Brahma-world (*brahma-loka*), but do not find it; for truly they are carried astray by what is false. (Tr. R.E. Hume (adapted))

R. C. Zaehner, in his translation of the **Bhagavad-Gītā** comments on this passage: "The *kṣetra-jña*, then, is the 'man who knows the local country', the 'man who knows his own field' as we would say in English meaning the 'man who knows his own subject'. And it is interesting to note that in secular language this is precisely what *kṣetra-jña* means (e.g. MBh I.84.12: I.85.13: I.87.8 *kṣetrajñaṃ tasya dharmasya*, 'an expert in this matter': cf. ibid. I.87.13: I.88.I, etc.). One's 'field', then one's 'subject' is oneself as a psychosomatic complex, but under the field there is a 'hidden hoard of gold', the Brahman-world, which lies latent in the heart of all of us, and so one can only be said to be a true 'knower of the field' if one has discovered this treasure. The treasure is, of course, the self." (p.334).

The later **Maitrī Upaniṣad** has cited the word *kṣetrajña* twice (2.5; 5.2). But the full development of the idea is found in the **Mahābhārata** and the **Bhagavad-Gītā**.

The key to the mystery of *kṣetra* is provided in the **Bhagavad-Gītā**'s opening verse itself. The whole setting of the teaching of the **Bhagavad-Gītā** takes place at two levels of *kṣetra:*

धर्मक्षेत्रे कुरुक्षेत्रे...

BhG I.1

On the field of Rightekusness, on the grounds of *kurukṣetra*...

Abhinavagupta explains these two terms thus:

कुरूणां करणानां यत्क्षेत्रंमनुग्राहकम् अतएव सांसारिकत्वधर्माणां सर्वेषां क्षेत्रमुत्पत्तिनिमित्तत्वात् । "अयं स परमो धर्मो यद्योगेनात्मदर्शनम्" इत्यस्य च धर्मस्य क्षेत्रं समस्ताधर्माणां क्षयादपवर्गप्रास्या त्राणभूतं

तदधिकारि- शरीरं सर्वक्षेत्राणामक्षादेर्हिंसार्थत्वात् परस्परबाध्यबाधकभावेन वर्तमानानां रागवैराग्यक्रोधक्षमाप्रभृतीनां समागमो यत्र तस्मिन्.

Gītārthasaṅg I.1

The 'field' is that which favours the Kurus representing sense-organs and instruments of knowledge. Therefore it is the field of all sorts of worldly conducts (entailing virtue and vice), because it (the body) is the source from which they emerge.

Self-realization which is attained by means of yoga, is the Supreme *dharma*, the summum bonum.

According to the dictum the body is the field of such a *dharma*, the absolute. The body of the adept becomes the redeemer on account of total absence or declining of all soils of relative *dharmas* and becomes fit for salvation. The verbal root *kṣad-* signifies violence from which the term *kṣatra* is derived. The body is the meeting place of attachment and non-attachment, anger and mercy where they exist in the form of the killer and the killed. (Tr. H.N. Chakravarty)

The nature of the complex relationship between body, mind and soul in space-time order is explained thus:

इदं शरीरं कौन्तेय क्षेत्रमित्यभिधीयते ।
एतद्यो वेत्ति तं प्राहुः क्षेत्रज्ञ इति तद्विदः ॥
क्षेत्रज्ञं चापि मां विद्धि सर्वक्षेत्रेषु भारत ।
क्षेत्रक्षेत्रज्ञयोर्ज्ञानं यत्तज्ज्ञानं मतं मम ॥

BhG XIII.1-2

The body is called the 'field' and he who knows it is the 'knower of the field', or so it has been said by those who know it.
And know that I am the 'knower of the field', in every field; knowledge of (this) field and (this) knower of the field I deem to be (true) knowledge. (Tr. R.C. Zaehner)

Śaṅkara comments on these two verses in the following way:

क्षतत्राणात्क्षयात्क्षरणात्क्षेत्रवद्वास्मिन् कर्मफलनिर्वृत्तेः क्षेत्रमिति ।

* * *

सर्वक्षेत्रेषु यः क्षेत्रज्ञः ब्रह्मादिस्तम्बपर्यन्तानेकक्षेत्रोपाधिप्रविभक्तः तं निरस्त-सर्वोपाधिभेदं सदसदादिशब्दप्रत्ययागोचरं विद्धि इति अभिप्रायः ।हे भारत! यस्मात् क्षेत्रक्षेत्रज्ञेश्वरयाथात्म्यव्यतिरेकेण न ज्ञानगोचरमन्यदवशिष्टमस्ति तस्मात्क्षेत्रक्षेत्रज्ञयोः ज्ञेयभूतयोः यज्ज्ञानं क्षेत्रक्षेत्रज्ञौ येन विषयीक्रियेते, तज्ज्ञानं सम्यग्ज्ञानमिति मतं अभिप्रायः मम ईश्वरस्य विष्णोः।

1.It is called the field (*kṣetra* is from *kṣata trai* (to protect) as it protects from wound (injury) from *kṣi* (destruction) as it perishes or disintegrates, or as it gives rise to fruits of works just as a field does.
2. The idea is that the field-knower, present in and variegated by these countless fields, beginning from Brahma and extending down to clumps, is devoid of all differences derived from the adjuncts and is beyond the range of expressions like being and non-being. Since there is nothing to be known other than the truth of the fields, field-knower and God, my view – the view of Lord Viṣṇu – is that the content of right knowledge is fields and field-knowers. (Tr. A.G.K. Warrier)

Nīlakaṇṭha comments on the first verse:

इदमनात्मत्वेन भास्यं घटाद्यहंकारान्तं शरीरं विशरणधर्मि हे कौन्तेय, क्षेत्रं क्षिणोत्यात्मानमविद्यया त्रायते च विद्ययेति क्षेत्रं कर्मबीजप्ररोहस्थानं क्षेत्रशब्देन उच्यते ।

O son of Kuntī, this body, not being the Self, appearing like a jar, including the ego-sense, is of perishable nature. The *kṣetra* (body) destroys the Self by ignorance and saves it by knowledge. This germinating place of the seed of works is called by the word *kṣetra*. (Tr. S. Chattopadhyay)

इच्छा द्वेषः सुखं दुःखं सङ्घातश्चेतना धृतिः ।
एतत्क्षेत्रं समासेन सविकारमुदाहृतम् ॥

BhG XIII.6

अथ इदानीमात्मगुणा इति यानाचक्षते वैशेषिकास्तेऽपि क्षेत्रधर्मा एव न तु क्षेत्रज्ञस्य इत्याह भगवान् - इच्छा इति । इच्छा यज्जातीयं सुखात्मकमर्थमुपलब्धवान् पूर्वं पुनः तज्जातीयं समुपलभमानः तमर्थं समादातुमिच्छति सुखहेतुरिति, सा इयमिच्छा, अन्तःकरणस्य धर्मः ज्ञेयत्वात् क्षेत्रम् । तथा द्वेषः - यज्जातीयमर्थं दुःखहेतुत्वेन अनुभूतवान् पुनः तज्जातीयमर्थमुपलभमानः तं द्वेष्टि, सोऽयं द्वेषः ज्ञेयत्वात् क्षेत्रमेव । तथा सुखम् - अनुकूलं प्रसन्नं सत्त्वात्मकं ज्ञेयत्वात् क्षेत्रमेव । दुःखं प्रतिकूलात्मकं ज्ञेयत्वात् तदपि क्षेत्रम्। सङ्घातः देहेन्द्रियाणां संहतिः । तस्मिन् अभिव्यक्तान्तःकरणवृत्तिः तप्ते लोहपिण्डे अग्नि इव, आत्मचैतन्याभासरसविद्धा चेतना, सा च क्षेत्रं, ज्ञेयत्वात् ।धृतिः यया अवसादं प्राप्तानि देहेन्द्रियाणि ध्रियन्ते सा च ज्ञेयत्वात् क्षेत्रम् । सर्वान्तःकरणधर्मोपलक्षणार्थमिच्छादिग्रहणम् । यदुक्तं तदुपसंहरति - एतत् क्षेत्रं समासेन सविकारं सह विकारेण महदादिना उदाहृतमुक्तम् ।

Śaṅkara on above

Desire, antipathy, pleasure, pain, the group, awareness, austentation – these, briefly, are said to be the field and its transformations.

Śaṅkara:

The Lord Kṛṣṇa says that what the Vaiśeṣikas call the qualities of the self also are the attributes of the field only and not those of the field-knower: desire etc.

Here 'desire' is taken as an attribute of the inner sense. Due to it one seeks to acquire, once more, the object that yielded pleasure earlier. Being an object of knowledge, it is part of the field. So too 'antipathy'. The kind of thing which was once experienced as a source of pain is hated when it is met with again. This 'antipathy' too is part of the field, being an object of knowledge. Similarly 'pleasure' or that which is agreeable and essentially, *sattva*, is also field only for the same reason. What is antagonistic, i.e. pain too is field being knowable. The 'group' refers to the body and the senses. 'Awareness' is a modification of the inner sense manifested within the 'group'. Like fire manifest in heated metal the 'group' is pervaded by the quintessence of Self's intelligence as 'awareness'. That, too, being a knowable is field. 'Sustentation', by which are upheld the depleted body and the senses also, being a knowable, is field. Desire, etc. are cited here to connote all the attributes of the inner sense. What was stated is concluded in the words: 'Briefly thus has been set forth the field together with its transformations like the universal mind'.
(Tr. A.G.K. Warrier)

Elsewhere in the **Mahābhārata** the term is used in a similar sense:

अव्यक्तं क्षेत्रमुद्दिष्टं गुणानां प्रभवाप्ययम् ।
सदा पश्याम्यहं लीनं विजानामि शृणोमि च ॥

MBh XIV.43.35

(Brahman said this): 'The unmanifest lives in the symbol called *kṣetra*, and is that in which the qualities are produced and absorbed. I always see, know, and hear it (though) it is hidden.' (Tr. M.N. Dutt)

Kṣetra denotes here the eternal universe.

यं तं व्यक्तस्थमव्यक्तं विचिन्वन्ति महर्षयः ।
क्षेत्रे क्षेत्रज्ञमासीनं तस्मै क्षेत्रात्मने नमः ॥ MBh XII.47.33

(Bhīṣma, thus praised Lord Kṛṣṇa). The great Ṛṣis seek thy unmanifest self within the manifest, called *kṣetrajña* phou sittest in *kṣetra*. Salutations to thee in thy form of *kṣetrajña*. (Tr. P.C. Roy)

The **Brahma-Sūtra** explains both the terms *kṣetra* and *kṣetrajña* with unfaltering clarity.

सत्त्वशब्दो जीवः क्षेत्रज्ञशब्दः परमात्मेति यदुच्यते, तत्र सत्त्वक्षेत्रज्ञशब्दयोरन्तःकरणशारीरपरतया प्रसिद्धत्वात् ।

BrSūBh I.2.12

The objection that the word *sattva* might denote the individual soul, and the word *kṣetrajña*, the highest soul, is to be met by the remark that in the first place the words *sattva* and *kṣetrajña* had the settled meaning of internal organ and individual soul. (Tr. G. Thibaut)

In other texts also the word *kṣetrajña* has been used to denote Self.

According to **Lalitā-Sahasranāma**, *kṣetrajña* is the protector of matter and the knower of matter (127b) while *kṣetrapāla* is the one worshipped in the precinct of the sacrificial ceremony (*kṣetrapālasamarcitā*) (127d). Following Bhāskararāya's commentary, *kṣetrajña* is the *jīva*. The **Viṣṇu-Smṛti** says: "The body O Earth, is called *kṣetra*; one who knows this is called *kṣetrajña*. O fair one, know me as the *kṣetrajña* in all bodies".

In the **Yogasūtra-Bhāṣya** (II.17), *kṣetrajña* is described as the self who is beyond action and mutation.

In a secular context the kingdom of a mighty king has been described as *cakravartī kṣetra*.

देशः पृथिवी । तस्यां हिमवत्समुद्रान्तरमुदीचीनं योजनसहस्रपरिमाणं तिर्यक् चक्रवर्तिक्षेत्रम् ।

ArthŚ IX.1.17-18

Place means the earth. In that the region of the sovereign ruler extends northwards between the Himavat and the seas one thousand *yojanas* in extent across. (Tr. R.P. Kangle)

But the king himself, as protector of *kṣetra*, is not *kṣetrajña*. In **Lalitā-Sahasranāma** as we have seen *kṣetrajña* means the protector of matter (*jīva*). Obviously, *kṣetrajña* stands exclusively for individual or Universal Self. It thus transpires that the semantic relationship between *kṣetra* and *kṣetrajña* cannot be understood by a simple structural analysis bereft of grammatical philosophy.

Manifestation in the Arts

Sculptors, architects and painters cannot do without imaginative realization of multiple forms and their variations in terms of precise measurement. Bhāskara's **Līlāvatī,** a classic in geometry, provides adequate knowledge of *kṣetravyavahāra.* Texts dealing exclusively with the Arts also offer technical details of the various geometric forms. Most commonly, the term *kṣetra* stands for surface.

दीर्घचतुरस्रस्याक्ष्णया रज्जुस्तिर्यङ्मानी पार्श्वमानी च यत्पृथग्भूते कुरुतस्तदुभयं करोतीति क्षेत्रज्ञानम् ।

KātŚulSū II.11

The (area of the) square drawn on the diagonal of a rectangle is equal to the sum of (the areas of) the squares drawn separately on its breadth and length: this is the property of plane figures (concerning rectangles). (Tr. S.N. Sen and A.K. Bag)

This rule is the same as the Pythagoras theorem, but in the **Śulbasūtras** it is enunciated separately for the rectangle and for the square.

In the context of temple architecture, the **Śilpa-Prakāśa** has used the word *kṣetra* in a number of verses, mostly denoting a geometric surface. Attributional aspects have also been indicated.

a) *Śubhakṣetra*, auspicious ground:

सूत्रविस्तारमात्रेण सुगन्धादिः भवेद्यदि ।
शुभक्षेत्रमिति ख्यातं प्रासादार्थं मनोहरम् ॥

ŚiPrak I.54

If at the time of stretching the string some sweet smells arise, that ground is called auspicious and is a beautiful site for a temple. (Tr. A. Boner)

b) *Samakṣetra*, even surface:

शृण्वत्र तु लताभेदान् गुणच्छेदांस्तथैव च ।
दण्डाकारे समक्षेत्रे ह्यथवा पट्टिसन्निधौ ॥

ŚiPrak I.288

Hear about this creeper variety, its characteristics and its lines. It can be made on a vertical even surface (*daṇḍākāra*) or on a horizontal band (*paṭṭi*). (Tr. A. Boner)

c) Describing the field for a panel or frieze:

चतुरस्रसमाकारमाद्ये क्षेत्रे समाचरेत् ।
वर्तुलैकमथान्यं च समक्षेत्रे यथाविधि ॥

ŚiPrak I.299

First carve the surface into equal squares, one is a *vartula* and in the other square field above, according to rules. (Tr. A. Boner)

d) In the description of the *śikṣādāna yantra* the geometrical field is referred to as *kṣetra*:

विषमवर्गक्षेत्रे च करणीयाः मीमांसकाः ।
मध्यत्रिकोणक्षेत्रे च कर्त्तव्या उपचारकाः ॥

ŚiPrak I.385

In the sides of the rhomb make students (*mīmāṃsakas*). In the middle triangular field place (two) attendants (*upacārakas*).
(Tr. A. Boner)

e) *Viṣamakṣetra*, uneven surface:

वैतालविषमक्षेत्रे विषमं चतुरस्रकम् ।
तत्स्थाने सिंहं कूर्मं वा पीठे रम्ये दृढे तथा ॥

ŚiPrak II.45

The Vaitāla temple is rectangular on a rectangular ground. That building is on a *siṃha* or *kūrma-pīṭha*, beautiful and strong.
(Tr. A. Boner)

For obvious reasons, even the technical texts dealing with subjects like geometry of material Arts have not remained unaffected by metaphysical thinking. Examples:

चतूरेखाबद्धक्षेत्रमिति ।यथा सरित्कुण्डे तथा रूपक्षेत्रे चतुरस्रं सर्वमापादविश्वं प्राजापत्यमार्गेण श्रुतिर्दर्शयति ।तथा हि रूपक्षेत्रे तद्रूपस्याधारः ।

VSUp II.11

The area is enclosed by four lines. Like a water-tank, so also the relief panel is a square. The Vedas show that the entire world including all its quarters, follows the way of Prajāpati (cosmic laws). Thus in the panel too that (cosmic) form is contained. (Tr. A. Boner)

Here the diagram for an image-panel, the whole field on which lines are drawn and the image will be carved is called *kṣetra*. The square (rectangular) field is compared to a water-tank. The panel is called *rūpakṣetra*.

Another verse mentions the *karṇikakṣetra* or rhomb.

धरेव कर्णिकक्षेत्रमाकर्षयन्ति स्थापकाः ।

VSUp II.13

The *sthāpakas* trace the *karṇikakṣetra* (rhombus) as the earth. (Tr. A. Boner)

In the field of music, *kṣetra* is used as a referent to generative process. In the appropriateness of specific expression, the *rāga* producing human organism is *kṣetra* and the specific individual inflection of tone known as timbre today is *kṣetrakāku.*

शरीरं क्षेत्रमित्युक्तं प्रतिक्षेत्रं निसर्गतः ।
रागे नानाविधा काकुः क्षेत्रकाकुरिति स्मृता ॥

SR III.124

The body is said to be the *kṣetra* (field) and in the singing of *rāga*, naturally there are various tonal inflections (*kāku-s*) related to every *kṣetra* (producing organism). This (shade of *rāga*) is known as *kṣetrakāku* (individual inflection of tone). (Tr. R.K. Shringy and P.L. Sharma)

Saṅgīta-Ratnākara(II.120c-121b) defines *kāku* as *chāyā* (lit. reflection or shade) which could roughly be understood as equivalent to that quality of sound for which the word timbre or tone-colour stands. The passage under reference speaks of six varieties of *kāku*, qualified by *svara, rāga, anya-rāga, deśa, kṣetra* and *yantra.* The first three are highly technical, but the last three are easy to comprehend; they stand for regional intonation (*deśa*), special quality of individual human voice (*kṣetra*) that gives a distinct identity to the *rāga* performed timbre of musical instruments (*yantra*).

An elaborate description of the bones, nerves, organs and limbs of the body is given. The imagery of the nave and the wheel is employed to explain the system of the nerves.

धमन्यो रसवाहिन्यश्चतुर्विंशतिरीरिताः ॥
कुल्याभिरिव केदारास्ताभिर्देहोऽभिवर्धते ।
एताः प्रतिष्ठिता नाभ्यां चक्रनाभावरा इव ॥

SR I.2.105cd-106

The arteries carrying lymph-chyle (*rasa*) are known to be twentyfour and like a field nourished by channels of water, the body (fed by them) also grows. These arteries are so rooted around the umbilicus as the spokes fitted into the hub of a wheel. (Tr. P.L. Sharma and R.K. Shringy)

From the biological and physical the expression moves to the psychical and spiritual. Conversely the macrocosm enters the microcosm of the body of Man.

Many verses in the musical texts describe the process of 'universal self' entering the womb and assuming a body. The word used in this context is again *kṣetrajña* and stands for the total concept of the 'self that abides in the body'.

In the context of dance, *kṣetra* refers to the location in space of the dance movements, as for example, the places where the hands are moving:

> पार्श्वद्वयं पुरस्ताच्च पश्चादूर्ध्वमधः शिरः ।
> ललाटकर्णस्कन्धोरोनाभयः कटिशीर्षके ॥
> उरुद्वयं च हस्तानां क्षेत्राणीति चतुर्दश ।
>
> SR VII.546-547ab
>
> There are fourteen *kṣetras* (locations or regions or 'fields') of the hands; viz. (i) the two 'sides' ('side' could stand for the body or the space or the left and right) i.e. the hands hanging on their respective sides or moving in the space on the sides, (ii) forward i.e. in the space away from the body, (iii) backward i.e. towards the back of the body, (iv) upwards (in space), (v) downwards (in space), (vi) head (the hands reaching the height of the head or touching the head), (vii) forehead (the hands touching the forehead or reaching the frontline of the forehead), (viii) ears (the hands touching or covering the ears), (ix) shoulders (the hands touching the shoulders or reaching the shoulder-line), (x) breast (hands touching the bosoms or reaching its frontline), (xi) navel (hands touching the navel or reaching the frontline of the navel), (xii) waist (hands resting on the waist), (xiii) top of the head (hands moving above the top of the head or resting on it), (xiv) thighs (hands beating the thighs). (Tr. P.L. Sharma)

Process

As described before, *kṣetra* is conceived in terms of a generative principle. The process of generation is implied in the given meanings in several contexts. Examples:

a) *Field*, where something grows. Indications of fertile field and pasture are found in **Ṛgveda** (I.127.6).

b) *Sacred place*, where spiritual powers are generated and sins are destroyed. The Purāṇas (SkaPur, KūrPur) have copiously eulogised the sacred places of pilgrimage.

c) *Kingdom*, where the temporal powers are produced (ArthŚ II.28.11).

d) *Body*, that grows and perishes. So suggest the **Bhagavad-Gītā** (XIII.1) and the **Suśruta Saṃhitā** (Sūtrasthāna XXXV.5).

e) *Wife*, who bears progeny, finds mention in Manu (IX.33).

f) *Womb*, wherein the child is conceived and the foetus is nourished. Technically used in the Āyurvedic texts (CarSam Śārīrasthāna VI.13).

g) *Inflection of tone*, which relates to the musical sound-producing human organism. Technically used in the musical texts (SR III.124).

h) *Phenomenon of mind*, as mind, intelligence, consciousness, and ego that arise and breed. This is how the **Mahābhārata** (XII.47.33) has used the word *kṣetra*.

Conclusion

Our treatment of *kṣetra* has highlighted four important ideas. 1) *Kṣetra* provides a ground for anyone embarking on Bhartṛhari's philosophy of Sanskrit grammar.

The ultimate reality, *Śabda-Brahman*, is of the nature of the word. The word is eternal, and so is the meaning of the word. In the framework of the Sanskritic Indian model of semantics, the entity conveyed by the word *kṣetra* is not the eternal object such as field, land, or body, that ordinarily appears as the given meaning. Instead, it conveys the conceived object with reference to the all-encompassing space-time dimension, as reflected in the secondary elaboration of the specific range of concepts pertaining to the word *kṣetrajña*.

Thus, the first obvious conclusion: the word *kṣetra* conveys things only with reference to the conceptual existence; consequently the diversity of its meanings is unified.

2) *Kṣetra* is so uniquely structured in the semantic field that it becomes central to any comprehensive view of man and space.

As explained before, this word originates in the concrete description of the physical objects and subsequently develops a fundamentally dynamic feature through intricate process of abstraction. Its meaning flows from the earth to the astral space (*kṣetra*, *kendra*, astronomical houses), from the geometric figure to the image-panel (*rūpakṣetra*), from the inner organ (womb) to the outer body (*śarīra*), from the product (object, form) to the process (generation, creation), and conversely from the macrocosm (*kṣetrajña*) to the microcosm (*tīrthakṣetra*). In this apparent paradox there is, of course, a considerable degree of logical consistency and coherence. Prajāpati Brahman created the world by self-immolation and when the space was created he asked the gods to remake him. This primary expression of the ultimate experience explains the true significance of the word *kṣetra*. From the *kṣetra* (space) emerges the *kṣetra* (body); from the *kṣetra* (womb) the *kṣetra* (body) grows. He who lives in *kṣetra* (body) is the *kṣetrajña* (individual soul). The *rūpakṣetra* (image panel) contains *kṣetrajña* (image of the Universal Self).

A general conclusion, then, is: the meanings of a word cannot be inconsistent with the cosmology of the culture in which they are born.

3) *Kṣetra* has a dynamic foundation.

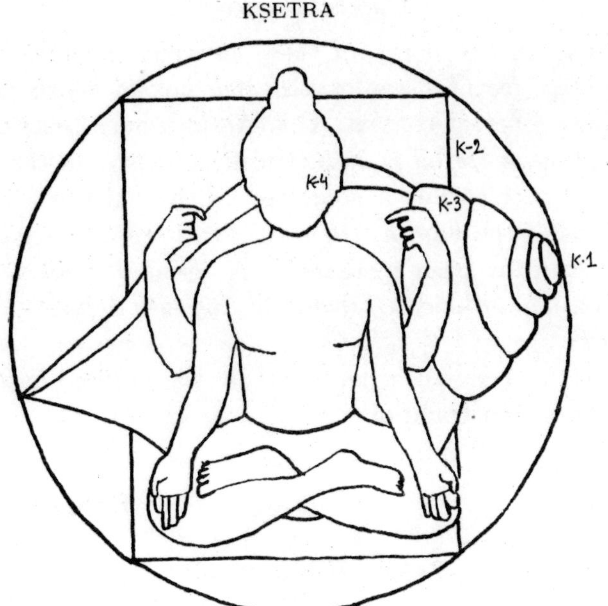

Figure 3: Kāśīkṣetra

It begins with concrete semantic reflections (physical objects), buds into abstract consideration (psychical, biological process), and blossoms with the fragrance of cosmic realities (archetypal representation, *kṣetrajña*). *Tīrthakṣetra* facilitates commonman's empirical understanding of the universe. The conception of the cosmic panorama of Kāśīkṣetra, presented in Fig.3, is an excellent example: the holy circuit of *pañcakrośī* Kāśī, the conch-shaped Kāśī of the Kali Yuga, the *āyatana yātrā* of Kāśī, and the Śiva-rūpa Kāśī together make a perfect illustration of the symbolic structure, or 'form thoughts', of Kāśī-kṣetra. Of the K-4, the circle symbolizes space (*kṣetra*), the quadrangle symbolizes time (*kāla*), the conch symbolizes life (*jīva, prāṇa*), and the anthropomorphic Śiva symbolizes the Universal Self (*kṣetrajña*). Similar manifestation of the cosmogonic theory of space is found in the iconographic representation of Viśvarūpa in the **Śilpaśāstra**, and also in the extensive treatment of *saṅgītapuruṣa* in the musical texts. Thus, the third conclusion: Transformation of grammatical meanings into symbolic structure helps the visual representation of a worldview that provides not only a live illustration but also a strong basis for experiential affirmation of the cosmic unity in the diversity of human cultures.

4) *Kṣetra* as a conceptual term cannot be fully comprehended outside India's traditional vision of the world. For, language and worldview are closely related.

The English word for *kṣetra* is the 'region' which the social sciences have defined as a cohesive and homogeneous area marked, commonly, by some such features as linguistic and cultural. Regional boundaries are marked by uniform distribution of any one, or many, of these features. A region is conceived as a nodal where these features are located and beyond which are the regions, or areas, of totally different content. This Western homocentric, ethnocentric, parochial perception of region is diametrically opposed to the Indian cosmocentric perception of *kṣetra* as a homology of the universe. But regrettably, modern India is using the word *kṣetra* in the exact sense of 'region'; its internal boundaries have already been reorganised in terms of homogeneous areas of language, religion, and ethnicity. Obviously, the new meaning contradicts the Indian worldview.

If tradition is the text, then, undoubtedly the modern usage of the word *kṣetra* betrays the Indian tradition.

Baidyanath Saraswati

Select Bibliography

Macdonell, A.A. and A.B. Keith: Vedic index of names and subjects. Delhi: Motilal Banarsidass, (1912) 1982.

Maxwell, T.S.: Viśvarūpa. Delhi: Oxford University Press, 1988.

Raja Radhakantadeva: Śabdakalpadrumaḥ, Part I. Varanasi: The Chowkhamba Sanskrit Series Office, 1967.

Saraswati, Baidyanath: The spectrum of the sacred: essays in the religious traditions of India. New Delhi: Concept Publishing Company, 1984.

— "Kashi pilgrimage: the end of an endless journey" in Makhan Jha (ed.), Dimensions of pilgrimage: an anthropological approach, pp. 91-104. New Delhi: Inter-India Publications, 1985.

— "Thinking about 'region' " in S.B. Chakrabarti (ed.). Social sciences and social realities: Felicitation volume in honour of B.K. Roy Burman, pp. 410-414. Delhi: Mittal Publications, 1988.

Suryakanta: A practical Vedic Dictionary. Delhi: Oxford University Press, 1981.

Vatsyayan, Kapila: The Square and the Circle of the Indian Arts. Delhi: Roli Books International, 1983.

LOKA

Overview

Loka is hard to translate in English as it covers different ranges of meanings and interconnected subconcepts, such as the 'world of appearance', the 'mundane world', the 'perishable phenomena' the 'cosmic divisions of space', any realm, mundane or transcendental and the common people and their behaviour.

Loka has developed as a very complex key concept in different *Śāstras*, religions, codes and practices, Arts and ritual and in mythology. This overlaps with some notions of space and yet it is different from space usually designated by →*ākāśa* (infinite absolute space) and →*diś/deśa* (direction, related space). *Loka* is a pervasive term embracing cosmic notions of space on one hand and the world of direct perception, the world of sense objects on the other. It is both space and what fills space; it is both the people and their behaviour; it is both the object of perception and the process of perception. It is because of this complexity that it has come to signify a sense of totality and therefore has come to assume an important role in every discipline, be it philosophy or language, and in every meaningful activity, creative or otherwise. It is *loka*, which is the measure of all actions, all thoughts and all speech. It is through *loka* that mystic experience is actualized as a commonly shared ordinary experience and *vice versa. Loka* pervades through the Vedic cosmogony, Vedic sacrifice, Buddhist and Jaina conceptions of the universe, Indian Art and literature, particularly *nāṭya* (drama), political science and law, grammar and logic, daily rites and rituals. It is more a process term than a static concept.

Etymology and Cognate Words

Loka is derived from *lok-* or *loc- (bhvādi)*, 'to see, to behold, to perceive' or *lok-* or *loc- (curādi)*, 'to know, to recognise'. *Loka* is phonetically associated with *roka* and *roca* which has been used in the Vedic literature in the sense of luminous body and radiant form.

दिवश्चिदा ते रुचयन्त रोका

ṚV III.6.7a

(O Agni) Even from the sky thy brilliant lights shone hither.
(Tr. R.T.H. Griffith)

The passages quoted by Gonda (see below) necessitating acceptance of the meaning of *loka* as giving room or space, can be explained easily by the meaning of the root *ruc-, roca-*, which though primarily means to shine, secondarily denotes to be pleasing, to be likable and desirable.

Some of the important compounds are *triloka, āloka, avaloka, lokeśa, lokayātrā, lokasaṅgraha, lokācāra, lokāntara, lokāyata, lokakathā, lokatantra, lokapaṅkti, lokapāla, lokaśruti, lokasthiti, lokavṛtta, lokabuddhi, loka-pratyakṣa, lokabhāṣā, loka-vijñāna, lokadhātu* (in Buddhism), *lokadharmī* (in drama), *lokottara*, another word for *alaukika* in aesthetics etc. *Loka* is generally defined as: '*lokyate iti lokaḥ*', meaning 'that which is perceived is the world.'

The second deriving root is *ruc- (bhvādi)* which means 'to shine', 'be bright or radiant or resplendent'. Its extended meaning is 'to be splendid, beautiful and good, to be agreeable, to be pleasing. In causative *rocayati-*, means to cause to shine, to illuminate, to make pleasant, to like, to make anything agreeable or pleasing, to choose, to intend. The associated words are *ruc, rucaka, ruci, roka, roca, rocana, rocamāna, rocya* etc. An important synonym of *loka* is *bhuvana*, world.

Its apposite terms are: *loka-veda* (realm of the world or common people and realm of the Veda), *loka-śāstra* (common practice and scholastic postulation), *loka-nāṭya* (life and drama) etc.

The pair of *ihaloka* (this world) and *paraloka* (the other world) is also well-known. Some other important derivatives are *laukika-alaukika* (commonplace or ordinary and extra-ordinary), *lokottara* or that which transcends the ordinary. These words have specific implications in specific contexts which will be discussed in the next section.

Levels of Meaning

Semantically, *loka* has developed a vast field of connotation in Indian literature: 1) *loka* or *aloka* (the world of light and darkness), 2) *bhūloka, bhuvarloka* and *svarga* or the earth, the middle region and the heavens; 3) *ihaloka* and *paraloka* (this world and the other); 4) seven (spheres) viz. *bhūloka, bhuvarloka, svarloka, maharloka, janaloka, tapoloka*, and *satyaloka* (the seven successively higher regions); 5) fourteen (the above seven and seven successively lower regions, viz. *atala, vitala, sutala, rasātala, talātala, mahātala* and *pātāla*; 6) Inhabitants of this world or this earth, mankind, ordinary people (as opposed to privileged class people, such as kings or noblemen). 7) Community of men and women, sharing a common tradition, common practices and common usages; 8) Common practice or usage (verbal or non-verbal); 9) Language of the common people (as opposed to language of mystic experience or language of ritual); 10) Vast space (*uruloka*); 11) Open space allowing free movement and full scope for independent living, room, freedom; 12) The sum total of the entire activity of people, human, divine and devil; of creatures, plants, of trees, rivers, hills, mountains, oceans, forests, lakes, fields; 13) The unbroken chain of experience (primarily sensory and secondarily supersensory) which has become a part of the total personality of a people.

J. Gonda in his comprehensively documented monograph, LOKA: World and Heaven in the Veda, has taken great pains to establish that the original meaning of the basic Indo-European root was to clear out space in the midst of a wood and as such the most appropriate primary meaning of the word '*loka*' is 'open space allowing freedom', and that this meaning holds good in a number of citations where some god has been said to create or make some proper place to live in for the worshipper.

Gonda has concluded that "A *loka* is not the 'world' or some arbitrary place but a place of specific and independent entity; often this place is not locally or specially definable. It is a position or situation which from the point of view of religion and life is safe, stable, steady, 'a resting place' " (*Ibid* p.35). He adds further that '*loka*' may mean 'free room', in this world or where it may be – rather than world. According to him, this connotation of *loka* is a semantic development of the earliest root '*louko*' meaning cut out the place. *Loka* has come to denote a right or proper place of an object.

Gonda's conclusion does not take into consideration the total range of meaning of *loka* in Indian literature. 'World' or 'worldly affairs' is not an adequate translation of the word *loka*.

As such the primary meaning of *loka* is manifestation out of the Unmanifest; the evolution of directions or *loka*s from the ear of the Global Being may also refer to the creation process as analogous, unmanifest sound giving birth to the manifest world cherished by the Āgamas.

The extended meaning of *loka* in Epics, Purāṇas and Śāstras posterior to the Vedic literature also corroborates that *loka* is manifestation, appearance, coming into light, sphere of direct perception, sphere of the known (as against that of the unknown), the people and their base as seen here and now and concrete wisdom (as an abstract ideation and supersensory mystic vision).

Loka primarily means light and communion with the sphere of light, and secondarily the sphere of manifestation and the process of manifestation; as the sphere of light it has another secondary meaning 'to look or appear pleasing and so be liked'. Blending these two meanings *loka* comes to mean a desirable and perceivable place. Subsequently it means being associated with that closer manifestation or creative sphere. And consequently it comes to mean the process of manifestation, process of direct perception, cumulation of such process to yield a total view of things inside or internally and in sensory experience, things mutually related and interdependent.

Ultimately it could be said that the entire totality of substantive quantitative, qualitative and actional meaning is contained in the word *loka*; so that *loka* itself is not an independent category, it is always interlinked with the correspondingly associated concept such as *loka* and *aloka*, *loka* or Veda, *loka* or *śāstra*, *loka* or *chandas* (Veda), *loka* or *nāṭya*, *ihaloka* or *paraloka*. These pairs do not denote opposition.

So it follows that *loka* is a valid concept in all spheres of creativity, as it provides a frame which not only seeks to deny the non-existence of the sphere of manifestation in desire (*kāma*), but which holds this sphere as the substratum of all creative activity. This creative activity is actually a re-enactment of the first act of creation, i.e. the first coming in existence of definite forms and names, in other words that of *loka* as well as the re-enactment of *loka*s coming into being. This *loka* stands in complementation to the vast immeasurable sphere of the unmanifest, of the breathless, of the desireless, of that which is beyond the word of prediction as Being or Non-being. This concept taken as an integrated and inter-woven concept is particularly important when one finds unexplained and blank spaces in the Śāstric traditions or in the written tradition. This concept is equally useful in relating the world of senses to the world of inner consciousness. It is a bridge concept.

The pair of *laukika-alaukika*, literally meaning that which does or does not belong to *loka* or ordinary life, has been used in various layers of meaning in different systems of philosophy, aesthetics, grammar etc. *Alaukika* or extra-ordinary has sometimes been used in a positive sense and at other times in a negative sense. A very brief review of this usage will shed some light on the multilayered meanings of *loka*.

Aesthetic experience is said to be *alaukika* or extra-ordinary in a positive sense, it will be dealt with in the section on Arts. In grammar *laukika* is that which is established in usage as being correct, whereas *alaukika* (in the negative sense), is that which is not considered to be proper in usage. (Cf. **Siddhānta Kaumudī**, *vṛtti* on *samāsaśeṣaprakaraṇa*).

In Mīmāṃsā the words used in Vedic injunctions (*vidhi*) are said to be *alaukika* and their usage is prohibited out of context as their meaning is comprehensible only in their original context. (Cf. TaVā I.2.24 and MīmSūBh I.4.10)

This system of philosophy also speaks of *dharma* as being a means of attaining *alaukika śreyas* (extra-ordinary welfare) and *alaukika* is described as that which is comprehensible only through Veda and its dependent or supportive (postulations) (**Bhāṭṭa-Cintāmaṇi** p.6). There is a different description of *alaukika pramāṇas* in Mīmāṃsā. The **Bhāṭṭa-Cintāmaṇi** of Gāgā Bhaṭṭa speaks of 31 *alaukika pramāṇas* which operate as auxiliaries of the main *pramāṇas* (p.11).

The deeds enjoined by the Vedas are called *alaukika* and their authority is contained in the Vedic texts (sentences) that are also considered to be *alaukika* (because they do not need any other authority i.e. *svataḥ pramāṇa*) (cf. BrSūBh I.1.4).

The Navya-Nyāya system speaks of three types of *alaukika pratyakṣa* (perception) viz. *sāmānyalakṣaṇa*, *jñānalakṣaṇa* and *yogaja*. *Sāmānyalakṣaṇa* is the mental extension of the perception of smoke-hood to all smokes; this is the general perception of smoke. The illustration of *jñānalakṣaṇa* is the memory of the fragrance of sandalwood, which makes possible the perception of fragrance, while looking at a piece of sandalwood without the sense of smell coming into operation. *Yogaja* perception operates in the state of *samādhi* where the combination of *ātman* and mind brings about the perception of past, future and the like (cf. **Nyāyakośa**). Nyāya also speaks of the pair of *laukika* and *parīkṣaka*, the non-expert and the expert. *Laukika* is one who has not been able to transcend the ordinary *loka* and thus has not attained excellence of intellect. *Parīkṣaka*, being contrary to *laukika*, is one who is capable of 'examining' a thing through arguments and means of valid knowledge. Being *laukika* stands for the absence of attainment of the excellence of intellect through the study of the *Śāstra* (cf. NySūBh I.1.25 and Viśvanātha's Vṛtti on the above). Thus the following shades of meaning of *laukika-alaukika* could be observed in the following brief review.

1) Accepted or established usage (*laukika*).

2) Accepted means of valid knowledge (except the 'word') (*laukika*).

3) That which is not self-evident like the Vedas (*laukika*).

4) That which is beyond all the categories of ordinary experience (*alaukika*).

5) The antonym of illusion (*laukika*).

6) The non-expert as different from the expert (*laukika*).

Development of the Concept

Let us now take up the historical development of this concept and have a close look at the growth of the contextual frame in which *loka* is used from the earliest time to the present day. Let us take two Vedic Hymns:

ऋतञ्च सत्यञ्चाभीद्धात् तपसोऽध्यजायत ।
ततो रात्र्यजायत ततः समुद्रो अर्णवः ॥
समुद्रादर्णवादधि संवत्सरो अजायत ।
अहोरात्राणि विदधद् विश्वस्य मिषतो वशी ॥
सूर्याचन्द्रमसौ धाता यथापूर्वमकल्पयत् ।
दिवञ्च पृथिवीञ्चान्तरिक्षमथो स्वः ॥ ṚV X.190.1-3

1. From blazing Ardor Cosmic Order came
and Truth; from thence was born the obscure night;
from thence the Ocean with its billowing waves.

2. From Ocean with its waves was born the year
which marshals the succession of nights and days,
controlling everything that blinks the eye.

3. Then, as before, did the creator fashion
the Sun and Moon, the Heaven and the Earth,
the atmosphere and the domain of light. (Tr. R. Panikkar)

Heaven, earth and atmosphere have been invariably grouped as *lokas.* So *Loka* in this Creation Hymn comes to mean the last link in the chain emanating from a frame of infinite time and space.

In another Hymn, Puruṣa-Sūkta, the *mantra 'nābhyā āsīd* etc. can be translated as: The middle regions came into existence from the navel of the great Being. From the head of the great Being the sky, the earth from his feet, and the first sacrificer fashioned the directions from his ear (ṚV X.90.14) (→*deśa*).

A parallel is found where it has been said that the dark was enveloped by the dark, all the cosmic waters unreconcilable were enveloped in it and out of the glory of *tapas*, the great heat, the great Being came into being.

तम आसीत् तमसा गूळ्हमग्रेऽप्रकेतं सलिलं सर्वमा इदम् ।
तुच्छ्येनाभ्वपिहितं यदासीत्तपसस्तन्महिनाजायतैकम् ॥

ṚV X.129.3

It was as if the dark lay lapped in dark,
Or the face of the flood was blank, or, if not, unformed.
Then heat, the heat of slowly swelling desire,
Cast the most primal thing on the shore of creation.

Reading these two hymns together one can easily gather that the unmanifest infinite Time and Space are visualised as the great night and the great expanse of water.

And furthermore *loka* is a manifest creation and is linked with the relative concept of direction (→*diś, deśa*), which has by its very definition combined in itself the notions of time and space (time because there is a movement, and space because there is a movement from one point to the other).

This relative notion makes *loka* as one whole divided into mutually related spheres of existence or appearance or manifestation. The notion of manifestation is much more relevant than that of making room by cutting obstructions like trees.

It is a usual trend in Vedic language that a noun is given a cognate adjective and a verb a cognate object. So the adjectives like '*uru*' (derived from *vṛ*- to choose) as already indicated is a cognate adjective, which emphasises the connotation of something preferred or desired; followed by the word *loka*.

On one hand *loka* appears to be a spatial concern, on the other it is a mental construct of the objective view of a Vedic ritual. In mid-way it is stretched out to mean all activities of people as well as people engaged in these activities, which form a bridge between man and his environment both divine and otherwise. It is quite clear that *loka* is not *deśa* , which is purely a spatial concept, no doubt it is inclusive of *deśa*, in its non-particularised sense.

The meaning of *deśa* is in some sense overlapping with that of *loka*. But it is very clear that the concept of *loka* is a more exclusive concept and it has a non-spatial component.

Deśa and *kāla* go together as two dimensions of a particular event or happening. They are the substrata par excellence, and they are mutually dependent, while *loka* is not bound physically, materially, or even have any geographical or historical dimension. In a sense, *loka* is an abstraction of certain mythical concepts.

Vedic references to *loka* could be grouped in two categories. The first, where the ideational divisions of space – both human and divine are indicated, such as *manuṣyaloka, devaloka* or *bhūloka, bhuvarloka* etc. The second where *loka* is the ideational construct of a realm of security, bliss, peace, and enjoyment. The first category is usually indicated by some particular division such as *bhūloka* (earth, 'this' *loka*), *bhuvarloka* or *antarikṣa* (mid-space), *svarloka* or *dyuloka* (heavens as referring to the region beyond). In the second category *loka* is usually referred to as a non-spatial entity. Wherever *loka* is qualified by 'this' i.e. *iha* or *adaḥ*, it is always paired with 'that' i.e. *amu-para-tatra*.

The first category of references are mostly found in the Brāhmaṇas in the context of the fusion of a particular part of a ritual, or in the context of the equation of *loka* with a particular god, metre, *mantra* or ritual. Some examples of the first category are:

कतमे ते त्रयो देवा इतीम एव त्रयो लोका एषु हीमे सर्वे देवा इति ।

BṛUp III.9.8

Which are the three gods?
They, verily, are the three worlds, for in them all these gods exist.
(Tr. R.E. Hume)

भूरिति वै प्रजापतिरिमामजनयत भुव इत्यन्तरिक्षं स्वरिति दिवमेतावद् वा
इदं सर्वं यावदिमे लोकाः सर्वेणैवाधीयते ।

* * *

त्रयो वा इमे लोकास्तदिमानेवैतल्लोकानाप्नोति ।

ŚBr II.1.4.11 and 25

Verily, with '*bhūḥ* (earth)!', Prajāpati generated this (earth); with '*bhuvaḥ* (ether)'! the ether; with '*svaḥ* (heaven)!' the sky. As far as these (three worlds) extend, so far extends this universe: with the universe it (the fire) is accordingly established.
For there are three worlds indeed; so that he (the sacrificer) thereby (i.e. by laying down the fire with '*bhūr bhuvaḥ svaḥ*') obtains these three worlds. (Tr. J. Eggeling)

स एतास्तिस्रस्तनूरेषु लोकेषु विन्यधत्त । यदस्य पवमानं रूपमासीत्, तदस्यां पृथिव्यां न्यधत्त । अथ यत्पावकं, तदन्तरिक्षे । अथ यच्छुचि, तद्दिवि ।
अयं वै लोकः प्रथमं हविः, अथेदमन्तरिक्षं द्वितीयम्, द्यौरेव तृतीयम्, बहुलेव वा इयं पृथिवी, लेलयेवान्तरिक्षम्, लेलयेवासौ द्यौः, उभे चिदेनां प्रत्युद्यामिनी स्तामिति तस्मात् समानबर्हिषी ।

ŚBr II.2.1.14 and 16

He (the sacrificer) then laid down in these (three) worlds, those three bodies of his. That 'blowing (*pavamāna*)' form of his he laid down on this earth, that 'purifying (*pāvaka*)' one in the ether, and that 'bright (*śuci*)' one in the sky.
Now the first oblation represents this world, the second one the ether, and the third one the sky. But this earth is compact; and the ether and yonder sky are, as it were trembling: and in order that these two may counterbalance that (earth) the (last) two (oblations) have one *barhis* in common. (Tr. J. Eggeling)

इदमेव लोकमृचा जयति, अन्तरिक्षं यजुषा, दिवमेव साम्ना ।

ŚBr IV.6.7.2.

By the *ṛk* he conquers this world, by the *yajus* the air, by the *sāman* the sky. (Tr. J. Eggeling)

तमसा वा असौ लोकोऽन्तर्हितः । स एतेन ज्योतिषा तमोऽपहत्य स्वर्गं लोकमुपसंक्रामति ।

ŚBr IV.3.4.8

For yonder world is shut off by darkness; and dispelling the darkness by that light he reaches the heavenly world. (Tr. J. Eggeling)

In the **Śāṅkhāyana Brāhmaṇa**, the calendar year is visualized as a revolving divine wheel and is identified with immortality. The gods ascend this wheel and wander through three *lokas* (regions or spheres) viz. *devaloka* (divine abode), *pitṛloka* (abode of the manes) and *jīvaloka* (abode of the animate ones), according to another reckoning seven spheres: *agniloka*, *vāyuloka*, *indraloka*, *varuṇaloka*, *mṛtyuloka*, *brahmaloka* and *nāka* (heaven).

> देवचक्रं वा एतत्परिप्लवं यत्संवत्सरस्तदमृतत्वं तस्मिन्नेतत्षट्तयमन्नाद्यं ग्राम्याश्च पशव आरण्याश्चौषधयश्च वनस्पतयश्चाप्सुचरं च परिप्लवं च तद्देवाः समारुह्य सर्वाँल्लोकाननु परिप्लवन्ते देवलोकं पितृलोकं जीवलोकमिममपोदकमग्निलोकम् ऋतधामानं वायुलोकमपराजितमिन्द्रलोकमधिदिवं वरुणलोकं प्रदिवं मृत्युलोकं रोचनं ब्रह्मणो लोकं नाकं सप्तमं लोकानां तद्यदभिप्लवमुपयन्ति संवत्सरमेव तद्यजमानाः समारोहन्ति ।
>
> ŚāṅkhBr XX.1
>
> A calendar year is a revolving divine-wheel. That is immortality. Within it reside six types of food – village animals, wild animals, herbs (*oṣadhi*), trees (*vanaspati*), aquatic and land animals. Ascending this calendar year, the gods wander through all the regions – those of the gods and fathers, the animate world, the waterless fiery world, the sphere of the wind which is the abode of the cosmic order, the unconquered world of Indra, the celestial sphere of Neptune, the profane mortal world, the luminous abode of Brahma and the seventh divine sphere. The sacrificers ascend the same calendar year in which the gods perform the *abhiplavaṣaḍaha* rite.
> (Tr. S. Chattopadhyay)

The heavenly abode is thus described in the **Śatapatha Brāhmaṇa**, as being related to the Sun (not the physical sun).

> इत्येवमिमाँल्लोकान्त्समारुह्य - अथैषा गतिः, एषा प्रतिष्ठा - य एष तपति। तस्य ये रश्मयः - ते सुकृतः, अथ यत्परं भाः - प्रजापतिर्वा सः, स्वर्गो वा लोकः ।तदेवमिमाँल्लोकान्समारुह्य - अथैतां गतिमेतां प्रतिष्ठां गच्छति।
>
> ŚBr I.9.3.10
>
> When one has thus ascended these worlds, that is the goal, that the safe refuge: the rays of Him (the Sun) who burns there, are the righteous (departed) and what highest light there is, that is Prajāpati or the heavenly world. Having then in this way ascended these worlds, he reaches that goal, that safe refuge. (Tr. J. Eggeling)

The idea of ascending various *lokas* (worlds) is also obvious here.

Nāka, the third *loka* is described as *jyotiṣmat* (full of splendour) in the **Atharva-Veda** (IX.5.6).

The 'world of immortality' is also associated with the Sun.

अन्तकाय मृत्यवे नमः प्राणा अपाना इह ते रमन्ताम् ।
इहायमस्तु पुरुषः सहासुना सूर्यस्य भागे अमृतस्य लोके ॥

AV VIII.1.1

Homage to Death the Ender ! May thy breathings, inward and outward, still remain within thee.
Here stay this man united with his spirit in the Sun's realm, the world of life eternal ! (Tr. R.T.H. Griffith)

The imperishable world is attained through imperishable merit.

तं वा एतं संवत्सरं स्वर्गं लोकं प्रपद्यते । सर्वं वै संवत्सरः, सर्वं वा अक्षय्यम्। एतेनो हास्याक्षय्यं सुकृतं भवति, अक्षय्यो लोकः ।

ŚBr I.6.1.19

This same year he (who going by means of the fore-offerings) enters, as the world of heaven; for, assuredly, the year is all and the All (universe) is imperishable: his thereby becomes imperishable merit, the imperishable world. (Tr. J. Eggeling)

Śabara's commentary prescribes three oblations for ascending the three worlds.

त्रीणि एतानि हवींषि भवन्ति। त्रय इमे लोकाः, एषां लोकानां आरोहणाय।

MīmSūBh IV.4.12

There are three worlds; to ascend these three worlds there are three oblations. (Tr. R.S. Bhattacharya)

Those references indicate two things. One – *loka* is an idealised division of space and this division is based on a tripartite division of the cosmos which works through:

Three gods: Agni, Indra and Sūrya
Three kinds of prayer: *ṛk, yajuḥ, sāma*
Three kinds of fires: *pavamāna, pāvaka, śuci*
Three layers of *vāk*: *tisro devī – iḍā, mahī, sarasvatī*
Three regions of space: *bhūr, bhuvar, dyaus*
Three divisions of time: *bhūta, bhaviṣya and vartamāna*

In the second category of references, the *loka* concept is a conglomeration of deity, ritual, *mantra*, incantation, and contemplation. Thus the second category in a way complements the meaning of *loka* described above, while making *loka* purely an ideal concept. Some relevant citations are:

अस्मिन् भयस्थे कृणुतमु लोकम् ।

ṚV II.30.6d

(O Indra and Soma) give us firm standing in this time of danger. (Tr. R.T.H. Griffith)

कर्तेमु लोकमुशते वयोधाः ।

ṚV IV.17.17d

...giving the suppliant vital strength and freedom. (Tr. R.T.H. Griffith)

यो वो वृताभ्यो अकृणोदु लोकम्

ṚV X.30.7a

He who made room for you when fast imprisoned. (Tr. R.T.H. Griffith)

अग्नीषोमा ब्रह्मणा वावृधानोरुं यज्ञाय चक्रथुरु लोकम् ।

ṚV I.93.6cd

Strengthened by holy prayer Agni and Soma have made us ample room for sacrificing. (Tr. R.T.H. Griffith)

आर्दयद्वृत्रमकृणोदु लोकम् ।

ṚV X.104.10c

Vṛtra he (Indra) quelled and gave men room and freedom. (Tr. R.T.H. Griffith)

Sāyaṇa has given the synonym *avakāśa* for *loka*. The word *avakāśa* means intervening space, free time or opportunity. Gonda has interpreted *loka* to mean a cut out space for free movement. Looking closely to these citations and going to the totality of the meaning one is forced to reject this development of meaning of *loka* from the reconstructed word LOURUS i.e. freedom for movement is not the real purpose of the word in the above citations. It is something which has been committed or sought as *mokṣa* or liberation from pain and misery. *Loka* is a cherished goal of the ritual activity performed here. This meaning will be very well connected with the meaning of the root of the word *roca*, 'to be liked' (as said earlier). The later words like *lokakṛt*, *lokayātrā* show the further extension of the meaning. The final goal of life is sustenance, which makes this life meaningful; as such *loka* is ordaining the way of living, in later development. It is significant that in most of the Vedic citations where *loka* means a place of security or freedom it occupies a secondary position, in view of the basic meanings discussed above.

Loka as ritual space has thus been described in the **Śatapatha Brāhmaṇa:**

तस्मा एतं पुरस्ताल्लोकं करोति - यद्दीक्षितो भवति । तं कृतं
लोकमभिजायते । तस्मादाहुः कृतं पुरुषोऽभि जायत इति ॥

ŚBr VI.2.2.27

When he (the sacrificer) becomes initiated, he makes for it (his self) that world (or place) beforehand, and he is born into the world made by him: hence they (scholars) say, 'Man is born into the world made (by him)'. (Tr. J. Eggeling)

Svarga is described as a realm where there is no fear, old age or grief.

स्वर्गे लोके न भयं किञ्चनास्ति न तत्र त्वं न जरया बिभेति ।
उभे तीर्त्वाशनायापिपासे शोकातिगो मोदते स्वर्गलोके ॥

KaṭhUp I.12

In the heavenly world is no fear whatsoever.
Not there art thou. Not from old age does one fear.
Over both having crossed - hunger, and thirst too -
Gone beyond sorrow, one rejoices in the heaven-world.
(Tr. R.E. Hume)

The **Īśopaniṣad** describes, as a contrast, the worlds covered with 'darkness':

असुर्या नाम ते लोका अन्धेन तमसावृताः ।
ताँस्ते प्रेत्याभिगच्छन्ति ये के चात्महनो जनाः ॥

ĪśUp 3

Devilish (*asurya*) are those worlds called,
With blind darkness (*tamas*) covered o'er
Unto them, on deceasing, go
Whatever folk are slayers of the Self. (Tr. R.E. Hume)

The **Bhāgavata Purāṇa** echoes the Vedic thought by associating *bhūrloka* with the feet, *bhuvarloka* with the navel and *svarloka* with the head of the Cosmic *Puruṣa* (vide II.6.42).

The Viśiṣṭādvaita system postulates *loka* as a realm, accepting three *lokas*, viz. *manuṣyaloka* (the human world), *antarikṣaloka* (the atmospheric world) and *brahmaloka* (the world of the aggregate of individuated souls), instead of the Vedic *bhūḥ*, *bhuvaḥ* and *svaḥ*.

"स यो ह वै तद्भगवन्मनुष्येषु प्रायणान्तमोङ्कारमभिध्यायीत, कतमं वाव स तेन लोकं जयति" इति प्रक्रम्य एकमात्रं प्रणवमुपासीनस्य मनुष्यलोकप्राप्तिमभिधाय, द्विमात्रमुपासीनस्यान्तरिक्षलोकप्राप्तिमभिधाय, त्रिमात्रमुपासीनस्य प्राप्यतया अभिधीयमानो ब्रह्मलोकोऽन्तरिक्षात् परो

जीवसमष्टिरूपस्य चतुर्मुखस्य लोक इति विज्ञायते । तद्गतेन चेक्ष्यमाणस्तल्लोकाधिपतिश्चतुर्मुख एव ।

ŚrīBh I.3.12

For, he argues, on the introductory question, "He who here among men should meditate until death on the syllable Om, what would he obtain by it?" The text first declares that he who meditates on that syllable as having one *mātrā*, obtains the world of men; and next, that he who meditates on it as having two *mātrās* obtains the world of the atmosphere. Hence the Brahma-world, which the text after that represents as the object reached by him who meditates on Om as having three syllables, must be the world of Brahmā Caturmukha who is constituted by the aggregate of the individual souls. What the soul having reached that world sees, therefore, is the same Brahmā Caturmukha. (Tr. G. Thibaut)

In the **Viṣṇu Purāṇa** *loka*, the terrestrial world, has been visualised as a lotus (*lokapadma*) and various regions as its petals:

भारताः केतुमालाश्च भद्राश्वाः कुरवस्तथा ।
पत्राणि लोकपद्मस्य...

ViPur II.2.39

The countries of Bharata, Ketumāla, Bhadrāśva and Uttarakuru lie, like leaves of the lotus of the world... (Tr. Wilson)

Sometimes the seven *lokas* are divided into two categories as 'created' (*kṛtaka*) or 'artificial' and hence 'perishable' and 'uncreated' (*akṛtaka*) and hence imperishable; the first three *lokas* falling under the first and the last three under the second, *mahar-loka*, the middle one being described as a mixed category.

त्रैलोक्यमेतत् कृतकं मैत्रेय परिपठ्यते ।
जनस्तपस्तथा सत्यमिति चाकृतकं त्रयम् ॥
कृतकाकृतयोर्मध्ये महर्लोक इति स्मृतः ।
शून्यो भवति कल्पान्ते योऽत्यन्तं न विनश्यति ॥

ViPur II.7.19-20

These three spheres are termed transitory: the three highest, Jana, Tapa, and Satya are styled durable: *Mahar-loka*, as situated between the two, has also a mixed character; for although it is deserted at the end of the Kalpa, it is not destroyed. (Tr. Wilson)

Sometimes, in the Vedic stream only two *lokas* are spoken of viz. *pitṛloka* and *devaloka*, associated with the 'south' and the 'north' (vide ŚBr XII.7.3.7).

Brahman is the 'seat' of all the *lokas* and thus is their basic unity postulated in **Kaṭha Upaniṣad**. The image of the inverted tree is also conspicuous in this passage (KaṭhUp VI.1).

In the Indian mind *prakāśa* (light) is associated with enveloping knowledge, liberation from all sorts of narrow outlooks, so expansion is the most cherished concept in almost all the layers of meaning of *loka*. The entire life is a journey from *tamas*, darkness, to *jyoti*, light. This is the cherished *lokayātrā*.

There is hardly any necessity for going into the narrower meanings of the word *loka* in the citations discussed above.

To conclude, *loka* is an idealised concept of incessant meaningful research of the purpose of life. In other words, the *loka* concept is one of deep concern for life here and now, and this life is a whole life, not only the life of human beings, it is shining, vibrating and resplendent in both sentient and insentient beings.

Thus far we have treated *loka* in Vedic thought. Coming to the later development of the concept, where these three distinct developments of the *loka* concept are found, the first *loka* is the behaviour – here and now, often translated as worldly behaviour but its appropriate translation will be life here and now. The second *loka* is a category of cosmic divisions enumerated earlier in this essay. The third *loka* as juxtaposed to or paired with *śāstra* is a continuously and consistently structured interrelated life-pattern, the validity of which is not questioned because of its dominance and has been held in high esteem by the scholastic tradition. It has been prescribed that philosophical postulations should adhere to the experience of *loka* and should not deviate from it.

तस्माद् यद् यथालोके दृष्टं तत् तथैवानुमन्तव्यं निरूपकैर्नान्यथा ।

BrSūBh II.3.26

Logicians must shape their inferences in such a way as to make them agree with ordinary observation, not in any other way.
(Tr. G. Thibaut)

Śaṅkarācārya has described *loka* as the guide of *śāstra*:

मुख्यमेव ह्यात्मानम् उपदिदिक्षु शास्त्रं लोकबुद्धिम् अनुसरत्...

BrSūBh I.1.12

The *śāstra*, wishing to convey information about the primary Self, adapts itself to common notions ...(Tr. G. Thibaut)

The king is also advised to learn from *loka*:

वार्तारम्भांश्च लोकतः (राजा लभेत्)

AgPur CCXXV.22

(Let the king learn) various trades and professions from the people.

The famous *sūtra* of **Brahma-Sūtras** reading as follows analogises the creative energy of *Brahman*, the supreme reality to *loka*:

लोकवत्तु लीलाकैवल्यम् ।

BrSū II.1.33

But (Brahman's creative energy) is mere sport, such as we see in ordinary life. (Tr. G. Thibaut)

धर्मस्य चाव्यवच्छिन्नाः पन्थानो ये व्यवस्थिताः ।
न ताँल्लोकप्रसिद्धत्वात् कश्चित् तर्केण बाधते ॥

Vāk I.31

Nobody can violate, on the basis of reasoning, those paths of Dharma which have come down without a break, because they are accepted in the world. (Tr. K.A.S. Iyer)

The importance of *loka* is so great that **Mahābhāṣya** has spoken of an independent discipline called '*lokavijñāna*'. Here *loka* signifies the primacy of man's relationship in terms of immediacy, manifested in the linguistic usage current in the behaviour of people (Mahābh VI.2.36 and I.1.21)

According to Mīmāṃsā, the relation between word and meaning is based on *loka* and not on *śāstra*:

शब्दार्थसम्बन्धः लोकतः न शास्त्रतः ।

MīmSūBh III.2.4

The relation existing between word and its meaning is to be known from worldly behaviour, and not from the scriptures. (Tr. R.S. Bhattacharya)

प्रत्यङ्गवर्ती लोको लक्ष्यते। तद्यथा पुरुषोऽयं प्रातरुत्थाय यान्यस्य प्रतिशरीरं कार्याणि तानि तावत् करोति ततः सुहृदां ततः सम्बन्धिनाम्।

Mahābh I.1.57

In the world one acts according to the nearness of relation. As for example a man after rising in the morning performs whatever is concerned with his own body, afterwards (what concerns) his friends and then (what concerns) his relatives. (Tr. R.S. Bhattacharya)

In the sphere of human relationship one acts according to what is immediate i.e. a man after getting up first performs whatever is concerned with his own body, afterwards that which is related with his dear ones and lastly what is concerned with his (distant) relatives.

Loka also determines the transference of primacy to the person who takes the place of another to perform the duties of that person, in the same way as in śāstric ritual, whatever symbolic presentation serves as a substitute for the symbolized, has the same importance for the period in which that replacement is ordained.

लोके यो यस्य प्रसंगे भवति लभतेऽसौ तत्कार्याणि । तद्यथा - उपाध्यायस्य पुत्रो याज्यकुलानि गत्वा अग्रासनादीनि लभते ।

Mahābh I.1.56

In the worldly behaviour it is found that one who comes in the place of another takes to his work. As for example the pupil of a teacher receives the front seat (i.e. the seat of honour) etc. when he goes to the house of the sacrificer (in whose sacrifice the teacher acted as a priest). (Tr. R.S. Bhattacharya)

This principle of transference in *śāstra-loka* does not necessarily act in an identical manner, because they are not replicas of each other. They stand in type-token relationships, *loka* provides the token, while *śāstra* makes out types of these tokens:

सिद्धे शब्दार्थसंबन्धे । लोकतोऽर्थप्रयुक्ते शब्दप्रयोगे शास्त्रेण धर्मनियमः ।

Mahābh (Paspaśā)

Sound and sense and the relationship subsisting between the two being established as eternal, the use of words being determined by the sense current in popular speech, the science (of grammar) enjoins restrictions (i.e. the use of correct words to the exclusion of corrupt ones) for religious merit. (Tr. K.C. Chatterjee)

Nevertheless it is the '*loka-vyavahāra*' or the everyday life-behaviour which is the basis of scholastic generalisation and codification. The ordinariness of *loka* is transformed into something extraordinary if that ordinariness is completely surrounded irrespective of what could be its consequence here, or hereafter, to the universal being and then completely identified with the other and the only creative one.

In Buddhist philosophy, the aspect of decay is emphasised in '*loka*'.

लुज्यत इति लोकः ।

AbhidhKoBh I.8cd, p.29

The word *loka* is so-called because it is in the process of decomposition. (Tr. L.M. Pruden)

लुज्यते प्रलुज्यते तस्माल्लोकः । लुज्यते विनश्यतीत्यर्थः लुजिरिह गृहीतः, न लोकिः । नैरुक्तेन तु विधानेन गकारस्य स्थाने ककारः कृतः, तस्माल्लोक इति भवति ।(Comm. Sphuṭārthā on the above)

> Because it is in the process of dissolution and decomposition. 'Dissolves' means 'is destroyed'. Here the root *luji* has been accepted and not '*loki*', (*luji* would form the word '*loga*'). According to the prescription of etymology, the letter '*ga*' is replaced with '*ka*', hence it becomes '*loka*'. (Tr. N.H. Samtani, modified).

Loka is also identified with the body or *yoni* i.e. 'form of existence or station fixed by birth'.

> कर्मजं लोकवैचित्र्यम् ।
>
> AbhidhKo IV.1a
>
> The variety of *loka* i.e. the various forms of existence (like animals, birds, human beings etc.) is form of *karma* (action).

One whole chapter (IV) in the above text deals with the pains and pleasures 'enjoyed' or undergone by respective 'bodies' or forms of existence collectively termed as *loka*. The Buddha is said to have taught the Abhidharma for the '*loka* that whirls about in this great ocean of transmigration' (cf. AbhidhKoBh I.3d, p. 14, 15).

The **Abhidharma-Kośa** III, and its Bhāṣya also describes in detail twenty spheres or *sthānas*, including eight *mahānarakas* (big hells), four *dvīpas* (islands), one category of *tiryak* (lit. horizontal standing for sub-human creatures in general), another category of *preta* (lit. one who has 'gone' for ever or far, used for the dead ones), i.e. the dwellings of *tiryak* and *preta* categories, and six *devanikāyas* (divine dwellings). The first chapter of this text (pp. 507-512) gives a detailed description of islands, mountains, oceans etc. All this is description of *loka*, the manifest state. Apart from the idea of constant crumbling and disintegration (*lujjana-palujjana*) of *loka*, three *lokas* are accepted in Buddhist thought; viz. *saṅkhāraloka* (the world of formation), *sattāloka* (the world of beings) and *okāsaloka* (the world of location). The constant 'dissolution' of the phenomenal world on the one hand and 'continuity' or 'permanence' in the constancy of this change on the other hand together constitute the totality of the Buddhist concept of *loka* (cf. ViMag XIII, p. 926, VII, p. 434, 435 and p. 168).

The ephemeral nature of *loka* is poetically described by Aśvaghoṣa in the following passage:

> लोके प्रकृतिभिन्नेऽस्मिन्नकश्चित्कस्यचित् प्रियः ।
> कार्यकारणसंबद्धं बालुकामुष्टिवज्जगत् ॥
>
> Saun XV.35a
>
> In this world, which is by nature separate, no one is really the beloved of anyone else; it is cause and effect that hold the world

together, like a hand holding a ball of sand together. (Tr. E.H. Johnston).

To be in the world and yet remain unaffected by its nature is visualised as an ideal. The world is full of suffering through cold, heat, disease etc.:

क्वचिच्छीतं क्वचिद्घर्मः क्वचिद्रोगो भयं क्वचित् ।
बाधतेऽभ्यधिकं लोके तस्मादशरणं जगत् ॥

Saun XV.45c

In one place cold, in another heat, in one place disease, in another danger afflicts men excessively. Therefore the world is without refuge. (Tr. E.H. Johnston)

क्षयं जन्म निरस्तजन्मन्सद्धर्मचर्यामुषितोऽस्मि सम्यक् ।
कृत्स्नं कृतं मे कृतकार्य कार्यं लोकेषु भूतोऽस्मि न लोकधर्मा ॥

Saun XVIII.10d

O Conqueror of birth, birth for me is destroyed; I dwell rightly in the practice of the good Law. O Accomplisher of the task, I have done all that is required, I exist in the world and yet am free from its elements. (Tr. E.H. Johnston)

The variegated objects of this world (*lokacitra*) are forbidden as objects of desire:

दुःखं सर्वत्र सर्वस्य वर्तते सर्वदा यदा ।
छन्दरागमतः सौम्य लोकचित्रेषु मा कृथा ॥

Saun XV 50d

Since suffering is the lot of everyone everywhere at all times, do not, my friend, hanker after the glittering object of the world. (Tr. E.H. Johnston)

Lokadhātu is an important concept in Buddhist thought. This word stands for *loka* as a category, translated as 'world' or 'world of beings' (Cf. SaddhSū XVIII.66, XI.34).

Lokadhātu is a compound standing for a particular division of the world, (vide AbhidhKo I, p.7). Worldly pleasures are called *lokasaukhya* (Cf MSūAl XVII, p. 123).

In Jaina philosophy *loka* is conceived as the conglomeration of five *astikāyas* *viz. dharma, adharma, ākāśa, jīva*, and *pudgala.*

पञ्चास्तिकायसमुदायो लोकः । धर्माधर्माकाशजीवपुद्गलाः पञ्चास्तिकाया-
स्तत्समुदायो लोकः । आकाशमाधारो भवति, धर्मादयस्त्वाधेयाः,

आधाराधेयभावेन यदवस्थानमनाद्यमेषां स लोकः। ...स च लोकः क्षेत्रविभागेन त्रिविधः – अधस्तिर्यगूर्ध्वं चेति । धर्माधर्मास्तिकायौ लोकव्यवस्थाहेतू । तयोरवगाहनविशेषाल्लोकानुभावनियमात् सुप्रतिष्ठक-वज्राकृतिर्लोकः ।

TaSūBh III.6

अधोलोको गोकन्धरार्धाकृतिः ।... गोग्रीवायास्त्वधरमर्धमुपरिष्टात् सङ्क्षिप्तम् अधस्तात् क्रमवृद्ध्या विशालं विशालतरं च भवति तद्वदधोलोकसन्निवेशः, उपरि तनुकोऽधस्तु विशालो विशालतरश्चेति । ... तिर्यग्लोको झल्लर्याकृतिः। ऊर्ध्वलोको मृदङ्गाकृतिरिति । ... झल्लरी सर्वत्र समतला तुल्यविष्कम्भायामा वादित्रविशेषस्तद्वत् तिर्यग्लोकसन्निवेशः ... मृदङ्गो वादित्रविशेष उपरिष्टादधश्च संक्षिप्तो मध्ये पृथुस्तद्वदूर्ध्वलोकः ।

Ṭīkā on above

Loka is the mass, aggregate or totality of the five *astikāyas* (ontological categories); viz. *dharma* (nature or attribute), *adharma* (that which is not the nature or attribute of a given thing), *ākāśa* (space or ether), *jīva* (creature) and *pudgala* (material object including atoms). (Out of these *jīva* is sentient and the other four are insentient). *Ākāśa* is the *ādhāra* (substratum) and the others such as *dharma* and the like are *ādheyas* (those that are supported or sustained). *Loka* is the beginningless *avasthāna* (standing together) of these (*astikāyas*) in the relationship of *ādhāra* (the recipient) and *ādheya* (the thing to be received). That *loka* is threefold according to the division of *kṣetra* (lit. field, here realm); viz. low or below, *tiryak* (horizontal or transverse) and high or above. The *astikāyas* (known as) *dharma* and *adharma* are the cause of *vyavasthā* ('order' or establishment) of *loka* i.e. they bring about a regular system. *Loka* has a form similar to that of *supratiṣṭhaka* (the string tied on crossed bamboos for incensing clothes and *vajra* (Indra's weapon) shaped like a circular discus or like two transverse bolts crossing each other, the former is relevant here) on account of *lokānubhava* (the definite ascertainment of *loka*) form of the specific plunging into these two (*dharma* and *adharma*). (The idea seems to be that the positive and negative attributes of the accepted entities bring about a definite system of *loka*).

The lower *loka* is in the shape of half of *gokandhara* (the neck of a cow or bull). The lower half of the neck of a cow or bull is small on the higher side (towards the head) and gradually grows bigger and bigger on the lower side (towards the body); similar is the configuration of the lower *loka*. The horizontal or transverse *loka* is of the shape of

> *jhallarī* (a kind of drum). The upper *loka* is of the shape of *mṛdaṅga* (another kind of drum). *Jhallarī* is of even shape everywhere i.e. equal in breadth and length (throughout); the configuration of the horizontal *loka* is similar (to that of *jhallarī*). *Mṛdaṅga* is a special instrument (drum) that is small on top and in the bottom and big in the middle; the higher *loka* is similar.

The 'placement' (*viniveśa*) of *loka* is said to be eternally expanding (*nitya-santati*) and in a beginningless state of change or transformation (*anādi-pariṇā-mika*) which rests on the *lokasthiti* (the continued existence or permanence of *loka*). That is to say, *loka* is both a process without a beginning and a permanent configuration. The fact that elements like water and earth keep their identity intact is evidence of a permanence in the configuration that is *loka* (cf. TaSūBh III.6).

The concept of *lokapuruṣa* is also basic in Jaina thought, who is visualised as a human being standing in the *viśākha* posture (*sthāna*) with the two hands resting on the waist. This posture is described in **Nāṭya-Śāstra** (X.61cd-64), the details are not relevant here.

A brief account of the treatment of *loka* in the Purāṇas, Smṛtis and the like would be relevant here.

Loka is the world of light and manifestation and *aloka* is the world of darkness and the unmanifest. In between them, there is a *lokāloka* mountain, where four *lokapālas* reside – according to **Matsya Purāṇa** (CXXIV.93, 94).

To be desirable by this whole manifest universe comprising both sentient and non-sentient, is a cherishable goal, and it is a person of that stature who acquires the capacity to transcend this world of manifestation.

It is notable that the Purāṇic universe in consonance with Vedic tradition, has given supreme importance to the realm of Truth, because standing there alone one could watch the different milestones in the great journey of the person.

The place of *bhūloka*, and there too the place of Bhāratabhūmi, the land of active involvement with the supreme being, is held very high, because Truth by itself has no relevance except through a continuous quest for it, irrespective of all obstacles and all temptations. The Purāṇas, therefore, highly extol the virtue of such an overpowering quest of Truth and subsequently the virtues of the place, where such a quest is.

Śāstra differs from *loka*, in other words, formulation of the 'token' into interrelated distinctive categories, acts in a different manner from the universe of the 'token' in as much as it requires the use of a meta-language, a language which is marked by clarity, unambiguity, consistency, brevity, universality, unquestionability and perfection. This is also called Sūtra language (→*sūtra*).

This language is an abstraction of the structured multilayered reality and is

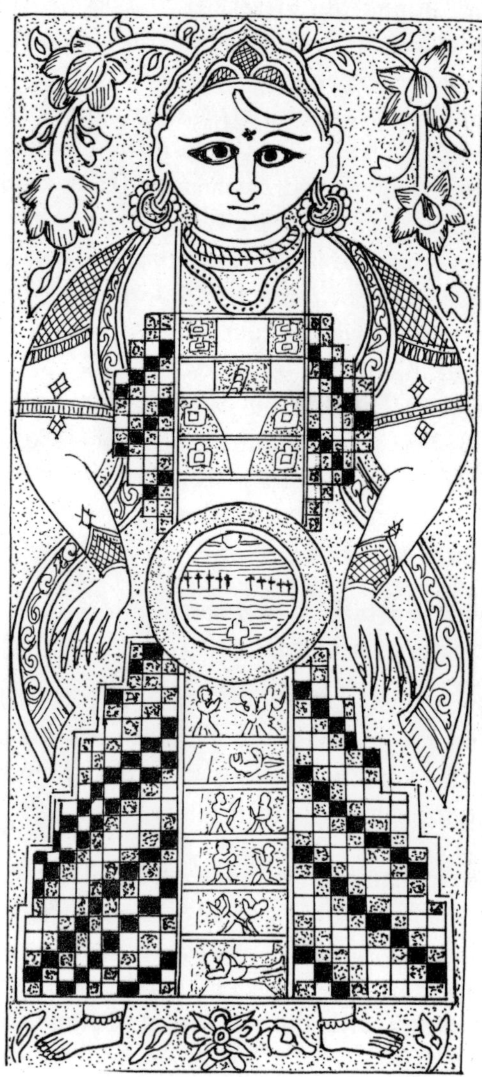

Figure 1: Jaina Lokapuruṣa, XVI cent. Gujarat

a universe in itself to the extent that for purpose of absolute clarity, universality and transcendence beyond the world of perception into the realm of the possible but imperceived, it has to make its own rules analogous to but different from those of the natural language. This much about *loka* and *śāstra*. So is the case with the language of mystic experience and the language of poetic creation. *Loka* is the main ingredient of all such seemingly unworldly supramundane even supramental experience and is never lost sight of even on the peak of such a unique experience beyond words, because that unique experience has to be shared with *loka*, and has to permeate in the *loka*, for its furtherance and enrichment. Unless someone is dear to *loka*, his transcendence over *loka* is not a matter of surprise, is not a matter of aesthetic wonder or pleasure. It is involvement in *loka* (*raktalokatā*) which makes the act of transcendence or extraordinariness pleasurable to the ordinary.

This is one of the aspects of *loka*, something within perception, the opposite of which is *aloka* the sphere of unmanifest, the sphere of darkness. But this binary division, if looked at as two aspects of the same whole, necessitates the existence of an observant plane, *lokāloka*, the mid or high point of the manifest-unmanifest which controls the action-interaction of these two.

लोकालोको बहिस्तस्या लोकालोकनियामकः ।
योजनायुतविष्कम्भस्तुङ्गशृङ्गपरिच्छदः ॥

MṛgĀ vp XIII.110b-111a

Outside that land there stands the mountain *lokāloka* which is the controller of both (*loka* and *aloka*). It is ten thousand *yojana* in extension with tall peaks. (Tr. B. Bäumer)

So *loka* by extension of meaning takes within its fold the entire cosmos, the derivation of meaning of *loka* is extended from *lokyate* (which is seen) to that which makes perception possible – *lokyate aneneti* – so that *Brahman*, the infinite, as well as space, air, fire, water and earth – are the holders (*dhārakas*) and thus *lokas*, which along with the self, bring into manifestation the mobile and immobile:

ब्रह्मखानिलतेजांसि जलं भूश्चेति धातवः ।
इमे लोका एष चात्मा तस्माच्च सचराचरम् ॥

YājSm III.4.145

Brahman, the self, ether, air, fire, water and the earth are called *dhātu* because they pervade the whole body and keep on holding it (*dhārayanti*). These five and the self are seen, therefore they are *lokas*. From them the mobile and immobile worlds are born. (Tr. H.N. Chakravarty)

Loka is thus not only a conglomeration of all these five elements and the universal being, but it is also a concept which is shared by the different levels of beingness, the concept of becoming. This becoming is made possible internally through a journey through *Bhūr, Bhuvaḥ, Svaḥ, Mahaḥ, Janaḥ, Tapaḥ, Satyam* and externally through a journey through *manuṣyaloka, pṛthvīloka, pṛthvī, antarikṣa, pitṛloka, devaloka*, and *brahmaloka*.

It is noteworthy that Truth is the highest in the Vedic tradition as well as the Purāṇic one. The quest for *satya* does not indicate lack of involvement in mundane human activity, because it is through delight or through charged human acts alone that visualisation of the higher truth is made possible here and now. 'This' world is described in **Atharva-Veda** as beinc 'the most beloved' of all.

अयं लोकः प्रियतमो देवानामपराजितः ।
यस्मै त्वमिह मृत्यवे दिष्टः पुरुष जज्ञिषे ।
स च त्वानु ह्वयामसि मा पुरा जरसो मृथाः ।

AV V.30.17

This living world, unconquered of the Gods, is most beloved of all.
To whatsoever death thou wast destined when thou wast born, O man,
This death and we call after thee. Die not before decrepit age!
(Tr. R.T.H. Griffith)

The highest cherished goal is not a renouncement but acceptance of this manifest sensiate world as the '*līlādhāman*', as the playground of the highest truth i.e. the Universal Being.

कल्पायुषां स्थानजयात् पुनर्भवात् क्षणायुषां भारतभूजयो वरम् ।

BhāgPur V.19.23ab

(Nay,) securing (birth in) the land of Bhāratavarṣa on the part of men with a short span of life is preferable to the attainment of the abode (the spheres higher than Indra's heaven, viz., Maharloka, Janaloka, Tapoloka and Satyaloka or Brahmaloka) of those who live for a (whole) Kalpa (the lifetime of the three worlds, covering a thousand revolutions of the four Yugas, or 4,320,000,000 human years) – an abode which leads to rebirth (after one has enjoyed one's allotted span of life there). (Tr. C.L. Goswami)

प्राप्ता नृजातिं त्विह ये च जन्तवो
ज्ञानक्रियाद्रव्यकलापसम्भृताम् ।
न वै यतेरन्नपुनर्भवाय ते
भूयो वनौका इव यान्ति बन्धनम् ॥ BhāgPur V.19.25

> Those Jīvas (embodied souls) however, who do not strive to secure immunity from rebirth (even) after attaining birth in the human race – fully equipped with knowledge (discrimination), capacity for actions leading to knowledge and substances helpful to such activities – fall into bondage again like wild birds (disentangled from the fowler's net, yet carelessly sporting on the same tree where they were once entrapped). (Tr. C.L. Goswami)

As regards the composition of *lokas*, Śaṅkarācārya says that they are specific configurations of elements or *mahābhūtas (mahābhūta-sanniveśa-viśeṣaḥ)* (cf. BrSūBh III.3.16).

Another meaning of *loka* given by Śaṅkarācārya is the abode of 'enjoyment' or experience for the living beings.

> लोकशब्दश्च प्राणिनां भोगायतनेषु भाष्यते ।
>
> BrSūBh IV.3.4
>
> Now the term 'world' is used to denote places of enjoyment of living beings. (Tr. G. Thibaut)

Rāmānujācārya has given the name *bhogabhūmi*, 'the ground of enjoyment' for *loka* (vide ŚrīBh IV.3.4).

The description of transcendental realms is a special feature of Śaiva and Vaiṣṇava texts. The description of Rudraloka in **Svacchanda Tantra** (X.547-548,572-588b) is full of architectural imagery in the form of temples, palaces, chariots, seats (*siṃhāsanas*), towers, lakes, streets, gardens, water-tunnels etc., ornamental richness in terms of jewels or precious stones and all imagery in terms of musical instruments, recitation of *sāman*, emotional outbursts of devotees, cries of animals like the elephant, horse and bull.

The Gauḍīya Vaiṣṇava (Caitanya school) texts also abound in similar descriptions of *goloka*, the eternal abode of Kṛṣṇa (cf. **Brahma-Saṃhitā**). The basic idea behind all such descriptions is that whatever obtains 'here' in the phenomenal world is one-fourth (*ekapāda*) of what is eternally present in the divine abode of Rudra or Viṣṇu or Kṛṣṇa. Whatever is not 'there' is not here; if something is 'here' it is definitely 'there' in infinite richness and exuberance. All this imagery is inseparably connected with the concept of *līlā*, the *rudraloka* or *goloka* is divine 'stage' of *līlā*. In **Lalitāsahasranāma** (227c) one of the names of Devī is *lokātītā* (beyond the worlds). Bhāskararāya's commentary on this name says that she resides in the Supreme Śaivapura which is beyond all *lokas*, beginning with Indraloka and ending with Viṣṇuloka.

The meaning of *loka* as a concept has another connotation, more concrete, namely worldly behaviour:

लोकवृत्तं लोकः ।

KāvyalSū I.3.2

The world means the behaviour of the world consisting of movable and immovable objects.

This is further extended to the cumulative experience of the knowledgeable ones. It is a great source of knowledge established throughout the three regions of the world. It is possessed by the twice-born both in detailed and compendious form.

This experience is inclusive of pain, pleasure and is as valid an experience as the experience gained through the contemplation of Vedas or through the contemplation of Self (*adhyātma*). The **Yoga-Sūtra** identifies the tangible aspect of *loka* with animate and inanimate objects, like cow and the jar (Cf. YSūBh I.43).

Lokapratyakṣa is spoken of in the **Yoga-Sūtra Bhāsya** (I.49) in the sense of ordinary perception and *lokabuddhi* for common sense (Cf. YSūBh III.17).

In Āyurveda *loka* is conceived as an aggregate of (i) six *dhātus* (the five *bhūtas* and *Brahman*) or (ii) three constituents, viz. mind, self and body.

षड्धातवः समुदिताः "लोक" इति शब्दं लभन्ते, तद्यथा - पृथिव्यापस्तेजो वायुराकाशं ब्रह्म चाव्यक्तमिति ।

CarSam V.4

The aggregate of six constituents is termed as 'universe' (macrocosm) such as *pṛthivī, ap, tejas, vāyu, ākāśa* and unmanifest Brahman (Principle of consciousness). (Tr. P.V. Sharma)

सत्त्वमात्मा शरीरं च त्रयमेतत्त्रिदण्डवत् ।
लोकस्तिष्ठति संयोगात्... ॥

CarSam Sūtrasthāna I.46

Mind, self and body – these three make a tripod on which the living world stands. (Tr. P.V. Sharma)

Puruṣa has been equated with *loka* by Caraka; whatever obtains in the *puruṣa*, also obtains in *loka*. Here *puruṣa* could be identified with the human being as a type and *loka* with vegetable and animal life.

"पुरुषोऽयं लोकसंमितः" इत्युवाच भगवान् पुनर्वसुरात्रेयः । यावन्तो हि लोके मूर्तिमन्त भावविशेषास्तावन्तः पुरुषे यावन्तः पुरुषे तावन्तो लोके ।

CarSam Śārīrasthāna V.3

Lord Punarvasu said – Person is equal to the universe. Whatever formed entities are in the universe, the same are in the Person and vice-versa. (Tr. P.V. Sharma)

In the Arts

In *nāṭya* (drama) which is a total art, the crucial test is the *loka*, the cumulative awareness and receptiveness of all beings, human and others.

लोको वेदास्तथाध्यात्मं प्रमाणं त्रिविधं स्मृतम् ।
वेदाध्यात्मपदार्थेषु प्रायो नाट्यं प्रतिष्ठितम् ॥
वेदाध्यात्मोपपन्नं तु शब्दच्छन्दःसमन्वितम् ।
लोकसिद्धं भवेत् सिद्धं नाट्यं लोकात्मकं तथा ॥
न च शक्यं हि लोकस्य स्थावरस्य चरस्य च ।
शास्त्रेण निर्णयं कर्तुं भावचेष्टाविधिं प्रति ॥
नानाशीलाः प्रकृतयः शीले नाट्यं प्रतिष्ठितम् ।
तस्माल्लोकप्रमाणं हि विज्ञेयं नाट्ययोक्तृभिः ॥

NŚ XXV.120-123

Loka, Veda and *adhyātma* (inner vision) – these form the threefold *pramāṇa* (testimony) (in *nāṭya*) (the threefold means of right knowledge viz. perception, inference and truth conveyed verbally is *loka*; Veda the revealed texts and *adhyātma* intuitive knowledge of the self). Drama is virtually based on the content of Veda and *adhyātma*. Drama is composed of Veda and *adhyātma*, is couched in words and metres; it (drama) is testified by *loka*, only then it is testified; it is *lokātmaka* (made up of *loka*). Śāstra (discipline) cannot codify the *bhāva* (inner attitude) and *ceṣṭā* (outer action) of mobile and stationary beings. The characters (*prakṛtis*) in drama have diffarent *śīlas* (dispositions), drama is based on disposition; hence the producers of drama should realise the testimony of *loka*.

Similarly, *loka* has been accepted as one of the *pramāṇas* or means of valid knowledge (the others being *nyāya, smṛti, śruti, āgama* etc.) and it has been described as the behaviour (*pravṛtti*) of the mobile and immobile beings (cf. SarK I.146)

Though *loka* presents the transient aspect of existence marked by pain and pleasure, by instability, by afflictions and clingings, by suffering as frequently lamented in monistic literature (be it Buddhism, Jainism or other monistic systems like Vedānta) and is etymologically explained as:

सो सब्बो पि लुज्जनपलुज्जनट्ठएन लोको ति अयं वचनत्थो ।

ViMag XIII.926

All that is a world (*loka*) in the sense of crumbling and disintegrating (*lujjan-palujjan*). (Tr. Ñyāṇamoli)

It is still the centre of all activities, including the activity of ascending it.

कर्मशिल्पानि शास्त्राणि विचक्षणबलानि च ।
सर्वाण्येतानि नश्यन्ति यदा लोकः प्रणश्यति ॥

NŚ XIX.151

When *loka* (collective human talent or calibre) is destroyed, all the practical Arts, disciplines and sources of strength of experience and proficiency are lost. (Tr. P.L. Sharma)

Thus *loka* is the substratum of creative activity. Manifestation and aesthetic appeal is impossible without a total comprehension of *loka* here and now. **Saṅgīta-Ratnākara** lays down that *loka* is to be followed, so that delightful blooming of a musical note (*svara*) is assured. *Loka* is also more elaborate than *śāstra.*

यथा यथा स्वरे व्यक्ती रक्तेः प्रचुरता भवेत् ।
तथा तथा विधातव्यं ततं लोकानुसारतः ॥

SR VI.418cd-419ab

The *tata* (stringed instruments) should be constructed (and played) in accordance with *loka* (current practice) so that the *svara* becomes manifest and *rakti* (delightfulness) becomes abundant.

सन्त्यन्यान्यपि वाद्यानि लोके भूयांसि यानि च ।
तेषु विस्तारसन्त्रासादुदास्ते सोढलात्मजः ॥

SR VI.1207cd-1208ab

There are many other musical instruments also in *loka* (current usage), but the son of Soḍhala (Śārṅgadeva, the author of **Saṅgīta-Ratnākara**) refrains from describing them, because of fear of elaboration.

दुष्टं लोकेन शास्त्रेण ...
... इत्येवं दशधा गीतदुष्टता ।

SR IV.379a-380cd

There are ten blemishes of *gīta* (song); the first two blemishes are ... the song is faulty according to *loka* (current taste) or according to *śāstra* (formulated prescription).

Loka is one of the three limbs of *kāvya*, the other two being *vidyā* (learning) and *prakīrṇa* (miscellaneous objects) (cf. KāvyālSū I.3.1).

This idea of consonance with *loka*, the behaviour as perceived, does not exclude the potentiality of its being systematised or idealised. Therefore the two categories of dramatic presentation (*abhinaya*), the *lokadharmī* or *nāṭyadharmī* are not exclusive categories.

The evolution of *nāṭyadharmī* itself is based on what is happening in this *loka*. Any abstraction for that matter presupposes something concrete. Moreover a *nāṭyadharmī* (an ideational presentation) is aimed at giving the essence of what one finds at the concrete level and is necessitated by the impossibility of presenting the whole activity of all times and spaces in a physically bound time and space. The idea behind this twofold split of either *lokadharmī* and *nāṭyadharmī* or *deśī* and *mārga* is that mutual interaction of these two has to be ensured, so that the performance continues to be a process, rather than to be a dead end, and still it has to be ideational in order to be able to communicate, to people of all time and space.

Sometimes there is an apparent contradiction in the treatment of the extraordinary, the extrasensory, the supermental reality. On one hand *nāṭya* (drama) has to concern itself with *trailokya* as its sphere of performance, whatever has happened, is happening and is likely to happen in these three worlds (NŚ I.107cd). And on the other hand it has to be different from the *laukika* or the ordinary, being distinct in this respect.

> तत्र नाट्यं नाम लौकिकपदार्थव्यतिरिक्तं तदनुकारप्रतिबिम्बालेख्यसादृश्या-
> रोपाध्यवसायोत्प्रेक्षा-स्वप्नमायेन्द्रजालादिविलक्षणं तद्ग्राहकस्य सम्यग्ज्ञान-
> भ्रान्तिसंशयानवधारणानध्यवसायविज्ञानभिन्नवृत्तान्तास्वादनरूपसंवेदन
> संवेद्यं वस्तु रसस्वभावमिति वक्ष्यामः ।
>
> AbhiBhā on NŚ I.1 (Vol. I, p.3)
>
> *Nāṭya* (drama) is different from *laukika* (pertaining to everyday life) things; it is distinct or distinguished from imitation, reflection, painting, similitude, imposition, apprehension, metaphor, dream, illusion or deception, magic etc.; the instrument of its perception is *āsvādana* (tasting) of a *vṛttānta* (happening or situation), which is different from valid perception, illusion, doubt, indecision, non-apprehension, knowledge or understanding; thus drama is of the nature of *rasa* which is perceived through the process of *āsvādana*; this will be explained later.

It is notable here that **Nāṭya-Śāstra** propounds that *nāṭya* is the presentation of *loka-vṛtta* (happenings of this world).

> ग्राम्यधर्मप्रवृत्ते तु कामलोभवशं गते ।
> ईर्ष्याक्रोधादिसम्मूढे लोके सुखित-दुःखिते ॥
>
> NŚ I.9
>
> When the people (*loka*) became engaged in *grāmya-dharma* (sub-cultural life-pattern), were in the grip of desire and greed, were infatuated by jealousy and anger (and) were overwhelmed with pleasure and pain (then the *devas* approached Brahma).

नानाभावोपसम्पन्नं नानावस्थान्तरात्मकम् ।
लोकवृत्तानुकरणं नाट्यमेतन्मया कृतम् ॥

NŚ I.112

This *nāṭya* (drama) has been created by me which is rich with various *bhāvas* (mental states), is full of many situations and is representational of the totality of human life (*loka-vṛtta*).

योऽयं स्वभावो लोकस्य सुखदुःखसमन्वितः ।
सोऽङ्गाद्यभिनयोपेतो नाट्यमित्यभिधीयते ॥

NŚ I.119

The nature of *loka* (people) associated with pleasure and pain, when that is presented through *abhinaya* (acting) with *aṅga* (body) etc., it is called *nāṭya* (drama).

लोकस्वभावं संप्रेक्ष्य नराणां च बलाबलम् ।
संभोगं चैव युक्तिं च ततः कार्यं तु नाटकम् ॥

NŚ XIX.149

Nāṭaka (drama) should be composed after observing the nature of people and the strength and weakness of men, as well as their enjoyment and usage.

त्रैलोक्यस्यास्य सर्वस्य नाट्यं भावानुकीर्तनम् ॥

NŚ I.107cd

Nāṭya (drama) is the *anukīrtana* (restatement) of the *bhāva* (mental or inner state) of the totality of the three worlds.

Transcending the ordinary is accepted as a criterion of artistic beauty.

अपरा सहजाहार्यकविकौशलशालिनी ।
निर्मितिर्नूतनोल्लेखलोकातिक्रान्तगोचरा ॥

VaJī III.2

There is also another kind of artistic beauty. It glows with the natural as well as the acquired skills of the Poet. It results in imaginative original creations which are extraordinary. (Tr. K. Krishnamoorthy)

This apparent contradiction between that which pertains to *loka* and that which transcends it is easily dissolved when we look at it from the angle that there is a two level operation as indicated earlier in this essay. The reality of the universe of perception is not realised in parts, and it is through an intense but impersonal contemplation of the essence of this reality, that a transcendence into the reality of aesthetic abstraction is made possible. This transcendence makes the process of communication more effective, because contemplation leads to a universally acceptable ideational universe, which has the potential of appeal to the audience of today as well as that of tomorrow provided that the audience is prepared to receive the transcendental experience. So *loka* is a channel inevitable and yet transcendable in its own interest.

The more one is ordinary, the more propensity one has to go beyond the ordinary, the more one is engrossed in ordinary human relationships, the more one is likely to transform this involvement into an extraordinary relationship, caring neither for the consequences of this involvement either in this world or in the world beyond. Such a complete surrender makes one equated with the other one, the one who is pervasive and who is everywhere, who is so intimate and yet is always a stranger and outsider. Rūpa Gosvāmin in **Ujjvalanīlamaṇi** sums up beautifully this transcendence and complete identification with the stranger:

रागेणैवार्पितात्मानो लोकयुग्मानपेक्षिणा ।
धर्मेणास्वीकृता यास्तु परकीया भवन्ति ताः ॥

UjNīl III.16

The unmarried heroines (not accepted by Kṛṣṇa through *dharma* or code of conduct in the form of marriage) who being devoid of the worries regarding the two worlds (this and the next one), offer themselves through love alone are called *parakīyās*. (Tr. S. Punjani, modified by P.L. Sharma)

An extra-ordinary feat is called *alaukika-kriyā* (vide **Bhaktirasāmṛtasindhu** IV.2.6,7).

In poetics *alaukika* has been explained as the distinct or unique (experience) born of *laukika* (pertaining to life) apparatus (*sāmagrī*) (vide Vamana Jhalakikara's commentary on KāPrak, P.93). Thus the mutation of *laukika* into *alaukika* takes place in aesthetic experience.

The words *camatkāra* (lit. wonder) and *carvaṇā* (rumination) standing for the uniqueness of aesthetic experience and the process of this experience bearing analogy with chewing or ruminating in the enjoyment of food (ordinary in nature) have been explained by later poeticians as being beyond the ordinary (*lokottara*).

लोकोत्तरत्वं चाह्लादगतचमत्कारत्वापरपर्यायोऽनुभवसाक्षिको जाति-विशेषः ।

RasG P.4,5

अनुभवसाक्षिक इत्यनेन तदन्यप्रमाणनिरासः । स चानुभवः सहृदयानामेव ।

Nāgeśa's Commentary on the above

The state of being beyond the ordinary is a specific category the evidence of which lies in experience (and) which is synonymous with being of the nature of *camatkāra* (wonder) inherent in (aesthetic) delight.

Commentary:

By saying that this category (of being beyond the ordinary) has experience as its evidence, other evidence is ruled out; and that experience accrues only to the *sahṛdayas* (aesthetes).

Carvaṇā, the process of aesthetic experience is also beyond the ordinary.

न चात्र लौकिकप्रत्यक्षादिप्रमाणव्यापारः । किन्त्वलौकिकविभावादिसंयोग-बलोपनतैवेदं चर्वणा ।

AbhiBhā on NŚ VI.31

Nor is a process of ordinary means of valid knowledge like perception (*pratyakṣa*) etc. applicable here. But this process of *carvaṇā* ('chewing') is brought about by the combination of extraordinary (*alaukika*) *vibhāvas* etc.

सा च चर्वणा न प्रमाणान्तरतो जाता पूर्वं येनेदानीं स्मृतिः स्यात् । न चाधुना प्रमाणान्तरादुत्पन्ना, लोकोत्तरे प्रत्यक्षाद्यव्यापारात् । स्वयं तु नाप्रामाणिकी, स्वसंवेदनसिद्धत्वात् । चर्वणावबोधरूपैव, ज्ञानविशेषस्यैव चर्वणात्वात् ।

KāPrak, Saṅketa Commentary, p.51

That *carvaṇā* (rumination) is not born previously of any other means of valid knowledge so that it could become memory, nor is it now born of any other means, because the means of knowledge such as perception and the like do not operate in the *lokottara* domain. It is not without any evidence, by itself, because it is proved by the self-evident knowledge. *Carvaṇā* is indeed of the nature of knowledge, because a specific (category of) knowledge itself is *carvaṇā.*

Thus the transformation of the ordinary into the extraordinary or beyond the ordinary is accepted as the basic condition of aesthetic experience. The culmination of *carvaṇā* is *rasa* which is *alaukika* par excellence.

तेन विभावादिसंयोगाद्रसना यतो निष्पद्यतेऽतस्तथाविधरसनागोचरो लोकोत्तरोऽर्थो रस इति तात्पर्यं सूत्रस्य ।(AbhiBhā on NŚ VI.31)

The process of 'tasting' (*rasanā*) is accomplished through the blending (*saṃyoga*) of *vibhāva* etc. (which themselves are extraordinary);

hence the object of experience through *rasanā* viz. *rasa* is something that is extraordinary (*lokottara*); this is the purport of the Sūtra (expounding *rasa*).

Loka in the Visual Arts

Though we find elaborate descriptions of the different worlds (*lokas* and *bhuvanas*) in early literature, Vedic, Jaina, Buddhist as well as Āgamic, the visual material depicting the various *lokas* is much less. Direct pictorial representations of the *lokas* in painting and miniature that have come down to us are late, mostly dating from the XVIth to the XIXth centuries. This may also be due to the fact that such drawings, manuscript illustrations or paintings were earlier made on perishable material. Most of the extant representations of *lokas/bhuvanas* belong to Jaina and Buddhist (Tibetan) sources (see Bibliography W.Kirfel and C. Caillat).

However, the representation of *loka(s)* has to be taken in a wider context which includes the cosmic symbolism of sculpture and architecture. Many an iconographic form can be understood in cosmological or cosmogonic terms. We may only give some examples.

The conception of the *triloka* – earth, mid-space and heaven, or nether-world, earth and heaven – has been depicted in the figure of Viṣṇu Trivikrama (→ *krama*), who with his three steps covers all the three worlds. In sculpture he is represented with one foot stepping firmly on the earth, or pressing down the demon-king Bali in the nether-world, and the other foot raised high to indicate his highest step (*parama pada*). The third, or rather intermediary step is not visible. In painting, however, we find an exceptional image of Trivikrama showing him with three legs. The sequence of taking three strides throughout the three worlds is here shown in simultaneity, and yet the dynamism is evident. (Fig. 2)

We find some iconographic varieties of the Varāha avatāra of Viṣṇu which contain all the *lokas* in his body cf. Ādivarāha of Eraṇ). The Varāha myth is also cosmogonic in nature and embraces the three worlds: Viṣṇu in the form of a boar dives down in the nether-world to rescue Bhū, the Earth, and to raise her above the primordial waters.

Another important form of Viṣṇu which contains in itself the whole cosmos with all its *lokas* is his manifestation as *Viśvarūpa*, "of universal form". Its scriptural sources are the 11th chapter of the **Bhagavad-Gītā** where Kṛṣṇa reveals himself to Arjuna in his all-embracing form, and the **Bhāgavata Purāṇa** (X.39.44-57 – X.40.1-3) (→*viśva*). Some of the later miniature paintings (cf. Rajasthan, XVIth – XVIIth cent.) represent Viśvarūpa as containing all the *lokas* in his body which is contained within the *brahmāṇḍa* ('cosmic egg').

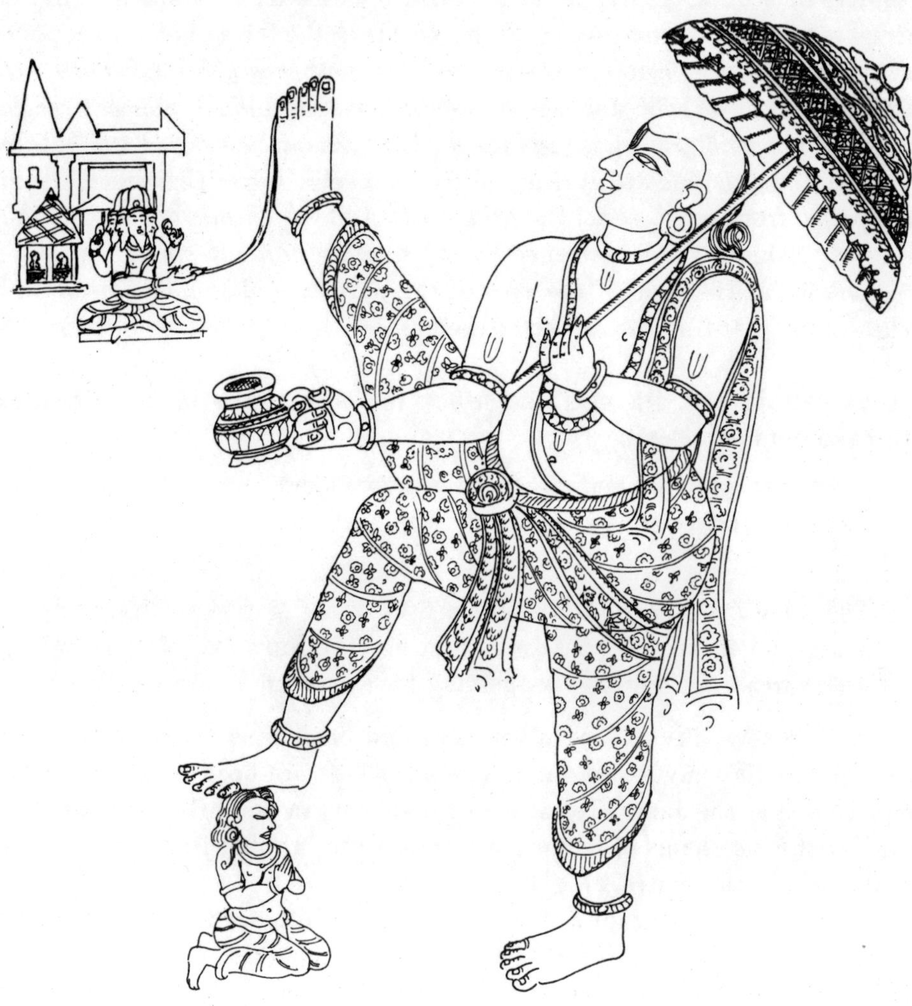

Figure 2: Viṣṇu Trivikrama, Deccani painting, XVII cent.

The most elaborate representations of the *lokas* are found in Jaina cosmographic depictions. Most of this material is not older than the XVIth cent., but its sources date back as early as the 1st cent. B.C. The conception of *lokapuruṣa* represents the cosmos comprising all the worlds in the form of an anthropomorphic standing figure: below the waist are the nether-worlds (*adholoka*), consisting of the seven hells and nether regions; in the middle, called *tiryagloka* (horizontal) or *madhyaloka*, is the region where human beings and animals live, and above the waistline are in rising order the twelve *kalpas* (heavens), the nine *graiveyakas* (from *grīvā*, neck) the neck-portion of the cosmic being where nine classes of 'divinity' reside, crowned by the five *anuttaravimānas* or unsurpassable domains at the level of the eyes of the *puruṣa*, and the *siddhaśīla* on his forehead, the place of the perfected beings on the top of the universe. (See Fig.1)

Umāsvāti in the 4th cent. describes the *lokapuruṣa* in his **Praśamaratiprakaraṇa** as follows:

> जीवाजीवा द्रव्यमिति षड्विधं भवति लोकपुरुषोऽयम् ।
> वैशाखस्थानस्थः पुरुष इव कटिस्थकरयुग्मः ॥
>
> v.210
>
> The *lokapuruṣa* (cosmic being) consists of the sixfold substance of living and inert beings. Like a man he (the universe) is standing with spread-out legs and supporting his hands on his waist.

Out of this totality of the universe we find depictions of the middle world only, which is the only world where human beings are born (*manuṣyaloka*). It is represented as the Jambūdvīpa, with the salt ocean and other continents and oceans, with long chains of mountains, great rivers flowing from the peaks and Mount Meru in the centre. (Fig. 3)

The Buddhist iconography of Tibet and other Himalayan states has a clear representation of the cosmos in its frescoes and thangkas. Without going into details, in a schematic way the worlds with Jambūdvīpa, the seven oceans and islands are depicted with the world mountain Meru rising from the centre and supporting the upper worlds. (Fig. 4)

Leaving aside the visual depictions of the *lokas* in sculpture and painting, the Hindu temple is itself an image of the cosmos with all its layers and parts. Though the temple in one sense symbolizes the Divine Being (→*puruṣa*), this is inclusive of the cosmos. "Not only is the cult object (be it an image or a symbol) an abode for the numinous power for which the temple is built; after its presence is ensured by consecration rites, the entire cosmos is next invoked to come down and pervade the physical body of the temple.

The cosmos is conceived to be present abstractly and is apart in conception from the images inside the temple and outside on its walls. It is also apart

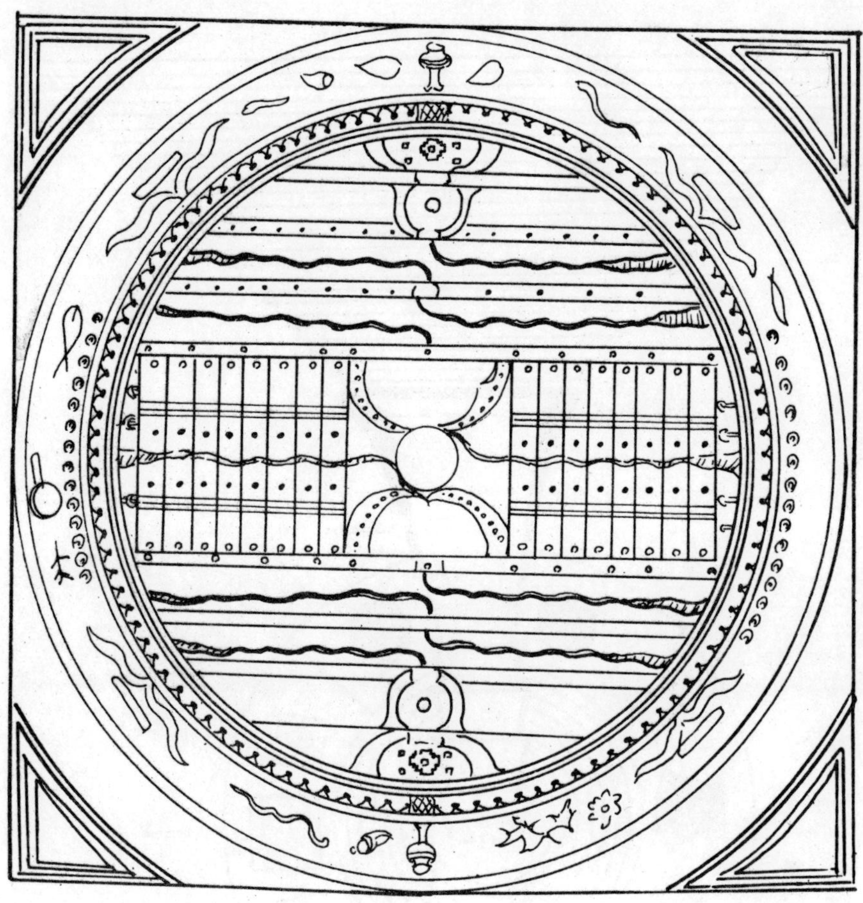

Figure 3: Manuṣyaloka, the world of Men, with Jambūdvīpa, in Jaina cosmography (XVI cent., Gujarat)

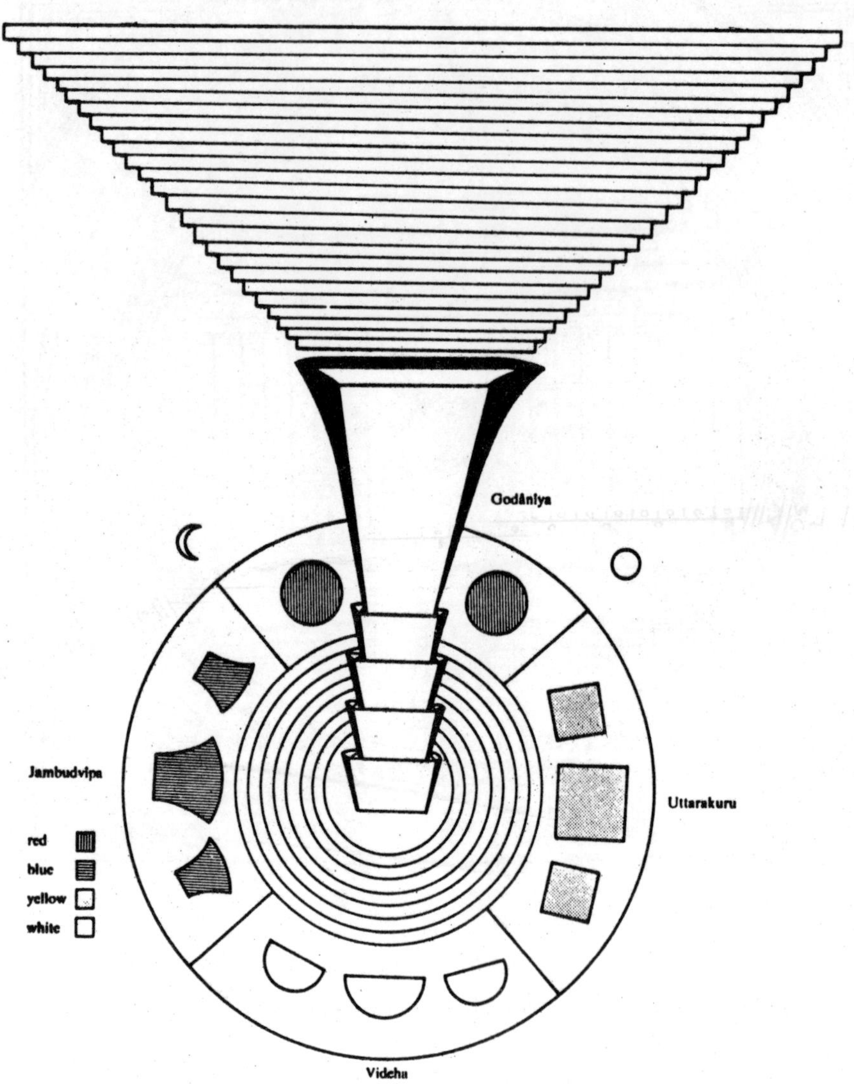

Figure 4: Buddhist cosmology, after a fresco from Lahul

from the dynamic forces of matter and space and of the static Consciousness beyond time, which are summoned to stay and be stabilized in the cosmic configuration, the *vāstupuruṣamaṇḍala*, on which the temple stands. What is implied, without a diagram being involved, is the descent into the mouldings and ornamented members of the sacred building, of the emanations of Cosmic Power – the entire hierarchy of the Hindu cosmology." (M.A. Dhaky, "Prāsāda as Cosmos", pp. 211-212). The **Vāstuśāstra** of Viśvakarman quoted by Dhaky in the same article, invokes for example the earth in the lower part of the wall portion (*khuraka*), the mountains in the pillars and the sky in the ceiling (*karoṭaka*, **Vāstuśāstra**, *prāsādastaradevatānyāsādhikāra*, vv.4, 10).

A similar conception is found in the **Agni Purāṇa** (*dhvajārohaṇavidhi*). The meaning of this invocation of the divinities, elements and parts of the cosmos in the various parts of the temple is not only to assume protection of the particular

Conclusion

Summing up, *loka* is a generalised concept of space filled up primarily with activity of various kinds now and here, but secondarily of possible transformations at a higher or lower level. It can neither be equated with the world nor with common people, nor with the sphere of direct perceptions or the manifest, nor the folk or rustic as against the elite; nor the oral unformed tradition as against the codified written tradition nor the real as against the ideal. And yet it covers all these ranges of meaning interrelated to each other. Unfortunately the term *loka* has been devalued during the last 150 years in India as folk, and has come to mean a subterranean flow of collective consciousness forgotten and rediscovered. Its attraction, if any, is either academic or exotic, but the recent studies in performing arts or the ritualistic arts of India have amply shown that *loka* is the eye to see the whole tradition, because it is in *loka* that we find a continuous flow of creative activity in consonance with the world view of the timeless Indian tradition.

Loka, though a spatial concept to a certain degree, is not a particular space, concrete or idealised, but is the continuous flow of activity which fills not one but many analogous such spaces. This *loka* provides the thread for scholastic formulation and also validates the applicability of that formulation in common man's everyday behaviour. It is thus the beginning and end of all creative thought and activity in India.

Vidya Niwas Misra
Prem Lata Sharma

Select Bibliography

Caillat, C. and Ravi Kumar: The Jain Cosmology. New Delhi, 1981.

Dhaḳy, M.A.: "Prāsāda as Cosmos" in: The Adyar Library Bulletin, Vol. XXXV, Parts 3-4, pp. 211-226, 1971.

Gonda, J.: Loka – World and Heaven in the Veda. Amsterdam: N.V. Noord-Hollandsche Uitgevers Maatschappij, 1966.

Kirfel, W.: Die Kosmographie der Inder. Hildesheim: Gg. Olms, 1967.

Jhalakikar, M.M. Bhimācārya (Revised by V.S. Abhyankara): Nyākośa. Pune: Bhandarkar Oriental Research Institute, 1928.

Misra, V.N.: Bhāratīya Paramparā (in Hindi). Bhopal: Madhyapradesh Hindi Grantha Academy, 1989.

DEŚA

Overview

The concept of *deśa* (space, region) has two aspects: 1) it is a part of the total space-time dimension and is usually visualized as a complementary unit in the twin concept of *deśa-kāla* (space-time); 2) the second aspect is its geographical notion, when the word *deśa* denotes either a country, a region or the home country, the home region and this notion is irrespective of the notion of time. The earlier synonym of *deśa* is *diś*, direction, quarter, which again, paired with *kāla* (time), signifies a relative concept of space. But the concept of *deśa* differs from this as a static notion, *diś* being related to movement. Nevertheless the pairs *deśa-kāla* are process terms and are not absolute entities, unrelated to any other entities. The twin concept has a great bearing on activity, be it of daily worship, of creative Art, of poetry, of craft, or of some vocation such as agriculture, carpentry and the like. Whatever happens happens in some *deśa-kāla* which is usually reckoned from the point of the first act of Creation, taking time in the space of that act as the zero point beyond which no reckoning of time and space can be made.

The term *diś* is contrasted with →*ākāśa*, both carrying a spatial notion. *Ākāśa* is the infinite space, the great expanse, while *diś* is finite space perceived as something covered through movement from one point to the other. One knows the beginning and one knows the end and so can measure the interval or scan the direction of the movement. Here we can safely state that *deśa* is the measured finite space while *diś* is the perceived direction of the process of movement. Furthermore, *diś* is closely related with another very charged term →*loka. Loka* is more of a non-physical notional space than physical space itself, while *diś/ deśa* or even *ākāśa* relate to actual physical space. *Diś/ deśa* has been conceived as the substratum of all happening, which stands at any given time or space related to some other point. In other words, every worldly happening is within the frame of relative time and space and as such every happening is necessarily linked with the other in a chain of succession (→*krama*). Whenever there is a performance of sacrifice, worship, dance, drama, versification, seasonal festival or everyday ritual, this is to be integrated into the total act of creation. So it has on one hand to relate itself to that act and be bound by it, while on the other hand it has to transcend this boundary and enter into an absolutely free time and space. To achieve this freedom every such performance has a pre-requisite of creating so to say suspended time or space, which can also be conceived as timeless and spaceless. The ritual of remembering the present time and space at the moment of entering into the performance (*saṃkalpa*) is followed by the ritual of *digbandha* (suspension of space) and *prāṇāyāma* (suspension of breath process), that is time. As a consequence every creative act is in time and space and yet has an a-temporal and a-spatial abstraction made out of its temporal and spatial body. Here and now is a must for this intense interaction with the realm of divinity, purity and enlightenment. (See also →*kāla*).

Etymology and Cognate Words

The root from which *deśa* is derived is a very significant verb: *diś-* 'to direct', 'to instruct', 'to indicate'. It has a cognate in the Greek word, *dike*, which is the governing principle of human order, more or less analogous with the concept of *ṛta*. Hence the notion of *dikpāla* and *lokapāla* has evolved, the divinities presiding over the quarters of space who carry great weight in sculpture and architecture as well as in performing arts and ritual worship.

Other terms for 'space', partly synonyms, partly overlapping and partly larger in meaning are: *āśā, bhuvana, loka.* Another synonym is *varṣa.* This word is strangely an important focal unit of time, i.e. the year. *Varṣa* etymologically means a giver or a showerer of gifts, strengthener, energiser. This aspect of *deśa* is an indicator of deriving strength from geo-historical identity. By derivation the root *diś-* means 'to give instruction' but this sense is usually carried in Skt. where there is a prefix like *upa-*, *anu-*, *ā-*, *sam-*, *ati-* etc. *Deśanā* means a religious instruction – an instruction into right path of action, and *deśika* the teacher who shows the right direction. *Loka* is a wider concept which covers the meaning of *diś*, but not vice-versa. Thus the transcendental world may be called *paraloka* or *brahmaloka*, but never *deśa*, which is bound to the known universe.

Levels of Meaning

The idea of space has been visualized in three different ways in Indian thought. There is space as one of the five elements where it is designated as *ākāśa* and space as indicator of relative proximity or distance and relative direction of movement in relation to the focal point which seems to be constant for that reckoning. And lastly, space as a geographically bound physical notion. Besides, there is a notion of →*loka* which is spatial as well as non-spatial, which is of the nature of experience as well as the nature of object.

Semantically, *diś* and *deśa* have developed as notions of clarity and distinctiveness. The notion of *diś* has different classifications as dependent on the different facets of relativity, as dependent on the visual placement of the Sun from the observer's point from the earth and dependent on the placement of the observer and his right hand or left hand, his front or his back, his upper side or his lower side. There is a third dependence on the geographical placement of different parts of one region which has an imaginary centre and directional divisions which are measured with respect to that centre. *Diś* has an extended meaning of clarity, clear exposition, and is a synonym of *spaṣṭa*. The measurable aspect of *deśa* makes it in the beginning a geographically bounded area and thence by extension it means an integrated whole, of which *pradeśa* is a part. *Ekadeśa* is one side of the whole. *Deśa* also means country of one's origin, the home country and so a source of inspiration. The notion of rightness is inherent in *deśa*. *Deśa* is an idea, one's action has to conform to that idea. The words formed by this root cover a large area of śāstric operations and have a great role in shaping and reshaping the Indian culture.

There is a subtle distinction between *diś* and *deśa*. *Diś* is purely direction which can be enumerated as left-right or east-west, north-south (*prācī, pratīcī, udīcī, avācī*, or the four corners, etc.). Together with the intermediate directions there are eight, to which two directions, up and down, or zenith and nadir, are added.

These ten directions have been quoted in **Śatapatha-Brāhmaṇa** (VI.8.2.12). The main directions are also called *pradiś*, the corner direction *ādiś*, the mid direction *vidiś*, the upper direction *uddiś* in **Śukla-Yajurveda Saṃhitā**.

Diś is a relative term. *Diś* or direction is a concept through which the location of a point as related to an observer is indicated. *Deśa* is unrelated to the observer and is a division of finite space. This is not merely a geographical concept, it is also a historical fact, because it is not only bound by physical boundary but also by tradition, ideas, customs, ways of life and collective memory shared by the people living in that space who are simultaneously living in history and tradition.

A very important term *deśī* (complementary term of *mārgī*) is derived from the word *deśa*. (see → *mārga*). *Deśī* is not merely local colour or regional variation but is also of the nature of something raw, innate, or unhewn, inherent in the collective entity of a people. And as such it has a great bearing in the dynamic interaction between Art and nature, between craft and skill, between conscious and subconscious and between scripture and *loka-vidyā* (popular lore).

Development of the Concept

The term *diś* occurs in the Puruṣa-Sūkta. Here the ears of the Great Being become the origin of both *diś* and *loka*, while the same hymn views the genesis of the earth from his feet, of the mid-region from the navel and that of the sky from the head.

नाभ्या आसीदन्तरिक्षं शीर्ष्णो द्यौः समवर्तत ।
पद्भ्यां भूमिर्दिशः श्रोत्रात् तथा लोकाँ अकल्पयन् ॥

ṚV X.90.14

From his navel issued the Air;
from his head unfurled the Sky,
the Earth from his feet,
from his ear the four directions.
Thus have the worlds been organized. (Tr. R. Panikkar)

In this description *diś* and *loka* have been put together, the first being associated with the faculty of hearing, receiving communication, internalising and extending outside, the second being all-comprehensive and related to the total Being of the *puruṣa*. *Diś* is a key concept in ritual because offerings are made to all directions so that a wholesome fulfilment is achieved.

दिशः प्रदिश आदिशो विदिश उद्दिशो दिग्भ्यः स्वाहा ।

YV VI.19

The regions, the fore-regions, the by-regions, the intermediate and the upper regions – to all the regions Hail! (Tr. R.T.H. Griffith)

Every direction is invoked as a mother, the fulfiller as described in the **Yajur-Veda**.

प्रागपागुदधराक् सर्वतस्त्वादिश आधावन्तु अम्ब निष्पर समरीर्विदाम् ।

YV VI.36

From east, from west, from north, from south – from every side may the regions resort to thee (soma)! O mother, satisfy (him)! may the noble meet together! (Tr. J. Eggeling)

Diś has been integrated into the time-frame by making every quarter, every direction one of the seven rays of the sun and the totality as the all-absorbing resplendent white ray.

स दिग्भिरेव सप्तविधः ये प्राच्यां दिशि रश्मयः सैका विधा । ये दक्षिणायां सैका । ये प्रतीच्यां सैका । य उदीच्यां सैका । य ऊर्ध्वायां सैका । येऽवाच्यां सैका । मण्डलमेव सप्तमी विधा ।

ŚBr X.2.6.3

By the regions it (Prajāpati) is sevenfold – the rays which are in the eastern region are one part, and those in the southern are one, and those in the western are one, and those in the northern are one, and those in the upper (region) are one, and those in the lower (region) are one, and the disk itself is the seventh part. (Tr. J. Eggeling)

Another passage in **Śatapatha Brāhmaṇa** describes the evolution of finite space from infinite space which again is a consummation of the creator, the infinite time (reckoned with sun) and infinite space.

> सा आदित्येन दिवं मिथुनं समभवत् । तत आण्डं समवर्तत ।...अथ यः कपाले रसो लिप्त आसीत् । ता अवान्तरदिशोऽभवन् । अथ यत् कपालमासीत् ता दिशोऽभवन् ।
>
> ŚBr VI.1.2.4
>
> By means of the Sun he (Prajāpati) entered into union with the sky: thence an egg arose... And the juice which was adhering to the shell became those intermediate quarters; and that which was the shell became those (chief) quarters (points of the compass). (Tr. J. Eggeling)

The word *deśa* has a few occurrences in the Vedic literature. In an **Aitareya Brāhmaṇa** passage *deśa* is the intervening place between two directions.

> देवासुरा वा एषु लोकेषु संयेतिरे । त एतस्यां प्राच्यां दिशि येतिरे । तांस्ततो असुरा अजयंस्तेऽवाच्यां दिशि येतिरे । तांस्ततो असुरा अजयंस्ते प्रतीच्यां दिशि येतिरे । तांस्ततो असुरा अजयंस्त उदीच्यां दिशि येतिरे। तांस्ततो असुरा अजयंस्त एतस्मिन्नवान्तरदेशे येतिरे । य एष प्राङ्ुदङ् ते ह ततो जिग्युः ।
>
> AitBr VIII.10
>
> The Devas and Asuras were fighting in these worlds. They fought in the eastern direction, then the Asuras defeated them. They then fought in the southern direction, and the Asuras defeated them again; and likewise they were defeated by the Asuras when fighting in the western and northern directions. They were then fighting between the eastern and northern directions, and remained victors. (Tr. M. Haug)

In **Yajur-Veda** there is a reference to *deśa* meaning land, which is now called *pañcasindhu.*

> पञ्चनद्यः सरस्वतीमपियन्ति सस्रोतसः ।
> सरस्वती तु पञ्चधा सो देशेऽभवत् सरित् ॥
>
> YV XXXIV.11
>
> Five rivers flowing on their way speed onward to Sarasvatī. But then became Sarasvatī a fivefold river in the land. (Tr. R.T.H. Griffith)

These are the earliest records of *deśa* in Vedic literature.

However, in Upaniṣadic literature the distinction between *diś* and *deśa* has become clear. In a **Praśna Upaniṣad** passage experiences are related to two types of spatial notions, *deśa* and *diś.*

अत्रैष देवः स्वप्ने महिमानमनुभवति यद् दृष्टं दृष्टमनुपश्यति । श्रुतं श्रुतमेवार्थमुपशृणोति, देशदिगन्तरैश्च प्रत्यनुभूतं पुनःपुनः प्रत्यनुभवति ।

PraUp IV.5

There, in sleep, that god experiences greatness. Whatever object has been seen, he sees again; whatever has been heard, he hears again. That which has been severally experienced in different places and regions, he severally experiences again and again. (Tr. R.E. Hume)

In the Upaniṣads, the totality of space, mostly called *ākāśa* or *vyoman*, is fullness (*pūrṇa* or *bhūman*). This fullness encompasses all the directions of space, not only exterior but also interior. When consciousness expands in all directions, it conquers total freedom:

स एवाधस्तात् स उपरिष्टात्, स पश्चात् स पुरस्तात्, स दक्षिणतः स उत्तरतः । स एवेदँ सर्वमिति । अथातोऽहङ्कारादेश एव । अहमेवाधस्तादहमुपरिष्टादहं पश्चादहं पुरस्तादहं दक्षिणतोऽहमुत्तरतोऽहमेवेदँ सर्वमिति ।

अथात आत्मादेश एव । आत्मैवाधस्तादात्मोपरिष्टादात्मा पश्चादात्मा पुरस्तादात्मा दक्षिणत आत्मोत्तरत आत्मैवेदं सर्वमिति । स वा एष एवं पश्यन्नेवं मन्वान एवं विजानन्नात्मरतिरात्मक्रीड आत्ममिथुन आत्मानन्दः स स्वराड् भवति । तस्य सर्वेषु लोकेषु कामचारो भवति । अथ येऽन्यथातो विदुरन्यराजानस्ते क्षय्यलोका भवन्ति । तेषां सर्वेषु लोकेष्वकामचारो भवति ।

ChUp VII.25.1-2

1. That [Plenum], indeed, is below. It is above. It is to the west. It is to the east. It is to the south. It is to the north. It, indeed, is this whole world.–

Now next, the instruction with regard to the Ego (*ahaṃkārādeśa*).–

I, indeed, am below. I am above. I am to the west. I am to the east. I am to the south. I am to the north. I, indeed, am this whole world.–

2. Now next, the instruction with regard to the soul (*ātmādeśa*).–

The Soul (Ātman), indeed, is below. The Soul is above. The Soul is to the west. The Soul is to the east. The Soul is to the south. The Soul is to the north. The Soul, indeed, is this whole world.

Verily, he who sees this, who thinks this, who understands this, who has pleasure in the Soul, who has delight in the Soul, who has intercourse with the Soul, who has bliss in the Soul – he is autonomous (*sva-rāj*); he has unlimited freedom in all worlds. But they who know otherwise than this are heteronomous (*anya-rājan*);

they have perishable worlds; in all worlds they have no freedom. (Tr. R.E. Hume)

Pāṇini has used the term in various connotations – in the sense of locality and country (Pā V.2.135), country or region and people of that country (Pā VII.4.9), home-land (Pā I.1.75) as a separate entity (Pā V.3.27) and *ekadeśa* to denote the portion of a whole (Pā III.3.79). He has traced the word *diṣṭa* from *diś-* (Pā IV.4.60).

Deśa and *diś* have been extensively used in post-Vedic Sūtra literature, in the Epics, Purāṇa and Smṛti literature. There are copious references to *deśa* both in combination and isolation, in the context of cosmography.

Mahābhārata has described the various waters and their presiding deities. The space-directions are mentioned along with their qualities:

एतद् द्वितीयं धर्मस्य द्वारमाचक्षते द्विज ।
त्रुटिशो लवशश्चात्र गण्यते कालनिश्चयः ॥

MBh V.107.4

This direction is said to be the second gate to virtue, O twice born one, and here does the king of death, with a sure hand, calculate the life allotted to men, in *Truṭis* and *Lavas* (periods of time). (Tr. M.N. Dutt)

इयं दिग्दयिता राज्ञो वरुणस्य तु गोपतेः ।
सदा सलिलराजस्य प्रतिष्ठा चादिरेव च ॥
अत्र पश्चादहः सूर्यो विसर्जयति भाः स्वयम् ।
पश्चिमेत्यभिविख्याता दिगियं द्विजसत्तम ॥

MBh V.108.1,2

This direction is the favourite one of king Varuṇa, lord of the seas. In fact this has been the region of birth of the king of the waters and even the region of his influence. Here does the sun abandon his rays himself last of all in the day; this is known as the western direction, O best among the twice born. (Tr. M.N. Dutt)

यस्मादुत्तार्यते पापाद् यस्मान्निःश्रेयसोऽश्नुते ।
तस्मादुत्तारणफलादुत्तरेत्युच्यते बुधैः ॥

MBh V.109.1

Since a man is absolved from his sins in this quarter and since he attains salvation here, by the wise it is called North (*uttara*), from its power of absolution (*uttāraṇa*). (Tr. M.N. Dutt)

The epics also speak of *digvijaya*, a conquest or march in all directions, where the king becomes an incarnation of the Sun conquering all directions of space. Hence the sovereign is called *cakravartin*. This concept is also applied to a saint who conquers the land in a spiritual way (e.g. Buddha or Śaṅkara).

Caraka indicates in one of his Sūtras that *deśa* means both the land and the body of the patient. This is an extension of the word *deśa*:

देशश्च भूमिरातुरश्च ।

CarSam Vimānasthāna VIII.92

Place is land as well as patient. (Tr. P.V. Sharma)

This meaning has a great relevance in the Āgama literature where the human body is understood as a microcosm.

Each part of the body is visualised as a *deśa* as referred in **Mṛgendra Āgama**.

क्व देशे धारणारूपं चिन्तनीयं विपश्चिता ।

MṛgĀ yp 39cd

In which region (of the body) should the wise meditate (on the qualities of the five elements)...?

Deśa-kāla play an important role in the composition of **Rāmāyaṇa** where the story starts with the question posed by Vālmīki to Nārada who is the ideal person here and now. This concern with the present time and place marks the birth of a new poetry and that is perhaps the reason why **Rāmāyaṇa** is called *ādikāvya*. Due attention to time and place is essential in all action, ritual or otherwise.

Manu (II.8) lays down that propriety of every action has to be decided in consonance with the scripture on one hand and applying one's discretion (the third eye, *jñānacakṣu*) within the scope of the time and place of action on the other.

सर्वं तु समवेक्ष्येदं निखिलं ज्ञानचक्षुषा ।
श्रुतिप्रामाण्यतो विद्वान् स्वधर्मे निविशेत वै ॥

Manu II.8

But a learned man after fully scrutinising all this with the eye of knowledge, should, in accordance with the authority of the revealed texts, be intent on (the performance of) his duties. (Tr. G. Bühler)

This is supported by Patañjali in his **Mahābhāṣya**:

आम्नायशब्दानामान्यभाव्यं स्वरवर्णानुपूर्वीदेशकालनियतत्वात् ।

Mahābh V.2.59

Vedic words are different in nature (from secular or popular speech) for these words are regulated by accent, the order of letters, place and time (for reading the Vedas). (Tr. R.S. Bhattacharya)

Viṣṇudharmottara Purāṇa describes *deśa-kāla* as the two arms of the creator. It is to be noted that the same reference speaks of *kāla* in isolation as embodied in the rosary of the creator. It is obvious that this rosary representing time is infinite time, while joined with *deśa* it is finite.

अक्षमाला स्मृतः कालः पुस्तकं चागमं स्मृतम् ।
यज्ञः सत्यं तपो दानं तस्य वक्त्रचतुष्टयम् ॥
देशकालौ तथा शौचं शुद्धिश्चास्य भुजाः स्मृताः ।
श्रुतिः स्मृतिः सदाचारः स्वस्य च प्रियमात्मनः ॥

VDhPur III.77.5-6

The rosary string should be known as Time, and the book as Tradition. His four faces represent Devotion, Truth, Austerity, and Liberality. His arms are known as place, period, purity, and purification. Oh upholder of the law, the four feet of the beloved god should be known as Revelation, Recollection, Righteousness, and Self-dependence. (Tr. D.C. Bhattacharya)

Coming to philosophical literature *diś* and *kāla* are substances (*dravyas*) according to the Nyāya-Vaiśeṣika and Mīmāṃsā systems. The Vaiśeṣika system in consonance with its realistic attitude holds that *diś* is an objective reality and exists independent of experience; while some Naiyāyikas as referred to by Jayanta Bhaṭṭa in **Nyāyamañjarī** hold that *diś* is an object of perception. It is cognised by the notion of east, west and the like.

समानन्यायत्वात् पूर्वापरादिप्रत्ययगम्या दिगपि प्रत्यक्षा वेदितव्येति ।

Nyāyamañjarī I, p.125

Following the same reasoning (i.e. *kāla* as a perceptible substance) the space is also an object of perception cognised by the notions of the east and the west etc. (Tr. H.N. Chakravarty)

The Naiyāyika view finds support in **Mānameyodaya**, in Mīmāṃsā triad. All these systems interpret space in terms of directions which are demarcated by the reference to the movements of the Sun. In other words *diś* serves as the connecting link between the solar motion and the object. *Diś* is an eternal ubiquitous unitary substance. Its different divisions are the qualities of the bodies which are in space. Space and time are conceived as the efficient cause of the entire universe. Later Naiyāyikas like Raghunātha Śiromaṇi do not admit the separate existence of *diś* and *kāla.* According to him they are subsumed in *Īśvara.*

According to both Yogācāra and Mādhyamika systems time and space are not real. According to Yogācārins these objects appear as substrata of consciousness and they explain it on the analogy of dream which is non-existent.

In dream though there are no gods, no men or women and the like existing in reality, yet these are experienced in a particular time and place. So spatio-temporal determination can be conceived even if there is no objective reality.

यदि विज्ञप्तिरनर्था नियमो देशकालयोः ।
सन्तानस्यानियमश्च युक्ता कृत्यक्रिया न च ॥

VijMSi(Viṃśatikā) 2

If consciousness (is the only truth) without the external objects (then) their spatial and temporal determination as well as the in-determination of the streams of consciousness and their action (or usefulness) should all be unfounded. (Tr. K.N. Chatterjee)

देशादिनियमः सिद्धः स्वप्नवत्... ।

VijMSi (Viṃśatikā) 3

The determinations of space etc. are established as in a dream. (Tr. K.N. Chatterjee)

The Mādhyamika holds that space and time have no objective existence even from the empirical standpoint. It is just by force of habit that we posit objective existence to these two mental concepts:

आकाशादिं कल्पान्ते नित्यानीति पृथग्जनैः ।
लौकिकेनापि तेष्वर्थान् न पश्यन्ति विचक्षणाः ॥

Catuḥśataka IX.5

Ether and others are viewed by the people of worldly vision as eternal persisting to the end of a *kalpa* but a worldly man sees in them substantiality and those who have insight do not see any essence in them. (Tr. H.J. Chakravarty)

Sāṃkhya, Yoga and Vedānta systems do not admit space as reality beyond the Self. Space and time are a necessity of human thinking, they are conditioning factors which influence the varying changes and growth. Advaita Vedānta philosophy treats both *diś* and *deśa* as appearance and accepts these entities at the level of delusion. *Deśa* and *kāla* are superimposed for understanding appearance of fruition.

अस्य जगतः ..... प्रतिनियतदेशकालनिमित्तक्रियाफलाश्रयस्य ।

BrSūBh I.1.2

Of this world which is the abode of the fruits of actions, these fruits having their definite places, and causes. (Tr. G. Thibaut)

Rāmānuja's Viśiṣṭādvaita system considers space, *diś* or *ākāśa*, as an evolute of *prakṛti* (Nature). Space is a distinguishing attribute (*viśeṣaṇa*) which makes distinctions between various parts and between different objects possible (cf. ŚrīBh II.3.45).

The Vaiṣṇava Āgamas like **Ahirbudhnya Saṃhitā** modify this view by saying that the pure creation is differentiated into four *vyūhas*. One of them is created by the illusions of *sudarśana* and assumes the forms of space.

शुद्धा पूर्वोदिता सृष्टिर्या सा व्यूहादिभेदिनी ।
सुदर्शनाख्यात् सङ्कल्पात् तस्या एव प्रभोज्ज्वला ॥
ज्ञानानन्दमयी स्त्याना देशभावं व्रजत्युत ।
स देशः परमं व्योम निर्मलं पुरुषात् परम् ॥
निःसीमसुखसन्तानमनवद्यमनाकुलम् ।
तत्रानन्दमया भोगा लोकाश्चानन्दलक्षणाः ॥
ज्ञानानन्दमया देहाः मुक्तानां भवितात्मनाम् ।

AhSam VI.21-24ab

The pure creation of which we have spoken before is differentiated into four *vyūha*s. From the desire of Sudarśana its brilliant rays consisting of knowledge and bliss become extended and assume the form of space. That space, the highest *vyoman* is free from impurity and even transcends *puruṣa*. It is the source of limitless flow of happiness. It is free from all blemishes and unmixed with other elements. The experience there is blissful and the regions are made of bliss. The bodies of liberated souls who are absorbed in the truth of the self consist of knowledge and bliss. (Tr. H.N. Chakravarty)

However, practically all the spiritual schools assert that the ultimate state of the soul has to transcend space and time. *Deśa* as limited, relative space has no 'place' in the transcendental state, but it is the unlimited space (*ākāśa* or *vyoman*) which comes closest to the experience of limitlessness. This is clearly expressed in the **Vijñāna-Bhairava Tantra** of Kashmir Śaivism:

व्योमाकारं स्वमात्मानं ध्यायेद्दिग्भिरनावृतम् ।
निराश्रया चितिः शक्तिः स्वरूपं दर्शयेत् तदा ॥

ViBhai 92

When one concentrates on one's self in the form of vast space, unlimited by any direction whatsoever, then the power of consciousness freed of all props reveals herself. (Tr. Jaideva Singh (amended))

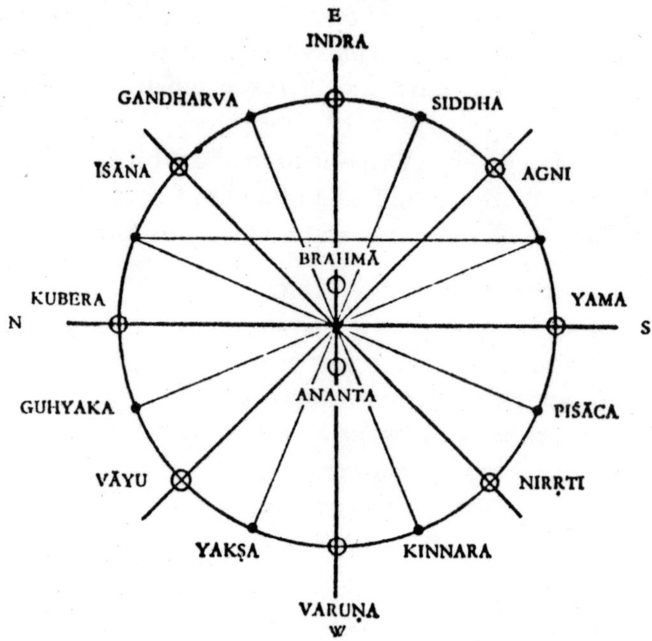

Figure 1: Space-Directions and Dikpālas

Classification

According to some reckoners there are four quarters of space, according to others seven, eight or ten (the four main directions, the four intermediate quarters, zenith and nadir). The presiding deities of these quarters are also bearing different names in different texts. Presiding deities are called *dikpāla*, *lokapāla* or *āśāpala*. The most accepted pattern is as follows:

dik	*dikpāla*	*dik*	*dikpāla*
prācī (east)	Indra	*vāyavya* (north-west)	Vāyu
agnikoṇa (south-east)	Agni	*udīcī* (north)	Kuvera
avācī (south)	Yama	īśāna (north-east)	Īśāna
nairṛta (south-west)	Nirṛti	*ūrdhva* (upward)	Brahmā
pratīcī (west)	Varuṇa	*adhas* (downward)	Ananta

There are also some twin concepts in the divisions of *diś*: 1) *dakṣiṇa-vāma* (right-left), 2) *dūra-antika* (far-near), 3) *purastāt-parastāt* or *paścāt*, (4) *agrataḥ-pṛṣṭhataḥ* (in front-behind).

The divisions of space with measurement according to Kauṭilya's Arthaśāstra (II.20.2-27) are as follows (cf. also the article *māna*):

8	*paramāṇus* (atoms)	=	1 *rathacakravipruṣ* (chariot-wheel particle)
8	*rathacakravipruṣes*	=	1 *likṣā* (nit)
8	*likṣā*	=	1 *yūkā* (louse)
8	*yūkās*	=	1 *yavamadhya* (barley-middle)
8	*yavamadhyas*	=	1 *aṅgula* (finger)
4	*aṅgulas*	=	1 *dhanurgraha* (a bow-grip)
8	*aṅgulas*	=	1 *dhanurmuṣṭi*
12	*aṅgulas*	=	1 *vitasti* (span) (equivalent to *tāla* as in Visual Arts)
14	*aṅgulas*	=	1 *śama* (yoke-pin), or 1 *śala* (dart), or 1 *parigraha* or 1 *pada* (foot)
2	*vitastis*	=	1 *aratni* (cubit), the *hasta* of Prajāpati
1	*hasta* + 1 *dhanurmuṣṭi*	=	1 *kiṣku* or 1 *kaṃsa*
42	*aṅgulas*	=	1 carpenter's sawing – *kiṣku*
54	*aṅgulas*	=	1 *hasta* for measuring forest produce
84	*aṅgulas*	=	1 *vyāma* (a measure for ropes) or 1 *pauruṣa* (man's height)
4	*aratnis*	=	1 *daṇḍa*, or 1 *dhanus*, or 1 *nālikā* or 1 *pauruṣa* for the house holder
108	*aṅgulas*	=	1 *dhanus* (measure for roads) or 1 *pauruṣa* for measuring the piling of fire-altars
6	*kaṃsas*	=	1 *daṇḍa*, a measure for gifts to Brahmins
10	*daṇḍas*	=	1 *rajju* (rope)
2	*rajjus*	=	1 *parideśa* (pointing out)
3	*rajjus*	=	1 *nivartana*
32	*daṇḍas*	=	1 *bāhu*
2000	*dhanuses*	=	1 *goruta*
4	*gorutas*	=	1 *yojana*

Measure of space according to Abhidharmakośa (III.86-87):

7	*Paramāṇus*	=	1 *aṇu*
7	*aṇus*	=	1 *loharaja*

7	*loharajas*	=	1 *apraja*
7	*aprajas*	=	1 *śaśaraja*
7	*śaśarajas*	=	1 *eḍakaraja*
7	*eḍakarajas*	=	1 *goraja*
7	*gorajas*	=	1 *vātāyanachidraraja*
7	*vātayanachidrarajas*	=	1 *likṣā*
7	*likṣās*	=	1 *yūkā*
7	*yūkās*	=	1 *yava*
7	*yavas*	=	1 *aṅgulīparva*
3	*aṅgulīparvas*	=	1 *aṅgulī*
24	*aṅgulīs*	=	1 *hasta*
4	*hastas*	=	1 *dhanus*
500	*dhanuses*	=	1 *krośa* or 1 *araṇya*
8	*krośas* or *araṇyas*	=	1 *yojana*

In both cases, the last space-measurement is *yojana.*

In the Arts

by P.L. Sharma

The aesthetic space (*deśa*) is a micro-construct of the total space as borne out by this passage in **Nāṭya-Śāstra** which divides the space of theatre in outer, middle and inner, clearly demarcating the initiate from the non-initiate and bringing the semi-initiate in the middle from the point of view of receptive keenness.

बाह्यं वा मध्यमं वापि तथैवाभ्यन्तरं पुनः ।
दूरं वा सन्निकृष्टं वा देशं तु परिकल्पयेत् ॥
पूर्वप्रविष्टा ये रङ्गं ज्ञेयास्तेऽभ्यन्तरा बुधैः ।
पश्चात् प्रविष्टा विज्ञेयाः कक्ष्याभागे तु बाह्यतः ॥
तेषां तु दर्शनेच्छुर्यः प्रविशेद् रङ्गमण्डलम् ।
दक्षिणाभिमुखः सोऽथ कुर्यादात्मनिवेदनम् ॥

NŚ XIII.8-9

भागत्रितये सति कस्मिंश्चिद्भागे देशादि कल्पयित्वा तत्रैव दूरादिभेदं परिकल्पयेत्, भूयस्त्वाल्पत्वादिभिन्नेन परिक्रमेण कल्पयेदित्यर्थः । ...पूर्वभूताः प्रधानभूताः सन्तः पूर्वं ये प्रविष्टास्तेऽभ्यन्तरा इति । अधिष्ठितो देशविशेषोऽभ्यन्तरकक्ष्या ...पश्चात्प्रविष्टानां तु स्थानं बाह्यकक्ष्या ते तु येन स्थानविशेषेण प्राक्प्रविष्टमुपसर्पन्ति स देशो मध्यमा कक्ष्या । एतदुक्तं भवति - पूर्वप्रविष्टस्य स्वस्थान एवेतिवृत्तोचितगृहोद्यानादिविभागः । पश्चात्प्रविष्टस्यापि पूर्वप्रविष्टेन सह यावन्न सम्मिलनं तावत्प्रेक्षायामेव

मध्यमकक्ष्यायां तु गतिपरिक्रमादिः तत्सम्मेलनार्थं, सम्मिलितानां तु कक्ष्याविभागो विच्छिद्यत इति सम्मेलन इतिकर्तव्यतामाह ...पूर्वप्रविष्टस्य यो दक्षिणो भागस्तं वीक्षमाणः स्थितो यथा प्रेक्षकस्य स पराङ्मुखीभवतीत्यर्थः।

AbhiBhā on above

Text:

One should construe space as outer, middle and also inner, again as far or near. Those who enter the stage earlier are known as the inner ones i.e. they would occupy inner space. Those who enter later are known to be in the outer zone of the stage. He who enters the stage-arena with a desire to see those who have entered earlier, should deliver his message, facing the south.

Commentary:

Having (established) three divisions (inner, middle and outer), one should construe definite location and the like (*deśādi*) and there itself should one construe the distinction of far (and near) and the like through *parikramā* (moving around on the stage by the actor) distinguished by abundance or paucity (i.e. if a bigger distance is to be suggested, the movement should be bigger both in terms of space and time and if a smaller distance is to be suggested, the movement should be smaller). Those who have entered earlier, are inner, being primary and main. The space occupied by them is the inner zone. Those who enter later, their space is the outer zone. The middle zone is that space through which the later ones approach those who have entered earlier. This is being said – one who enters first occupies his own place such as house, garden and the like, according to the plot; the one who enters later, keeps moving in the middle space in order to meet the one who has entered earlier, until he meets him, remaining in the very sight of the audience. When the meeting takes place, the above division of space breaks down, i.e. the earlier and later entrants cross each other's zone. The author is explaining how this meeting should be enacted. One (who enters later with a desire to meet the one who has entered earlier) should stand (or sit) facing the right (southern) side of the one who has entered earlier so that he turns his back to the audience i.e. the later one will stand or sit on the left side of the earlier one, facing his right side.

In drama, according to **Nāṭya-Śāstra**, one and the same space gets transformed into different places through the movements of the actors. No sets are required to represent different places.

कक्ष्याविभागो निर्देश्यो रङ्गपीठपरिक्रमात् ।
परिक्रमेण रङ्गस्य ह्यन्या कक्ष्या भवेदिह ॥

कक्ष्याविभागे ज्ञेयानि गृहाणि नगराणि च ।
उद्यानारामसरितस्त्वाश्रमा अटवी तथा ॥
पृथिवी सागराश्चैव त्रैलोक्यं सचराचरम् ।
वर्षाणि सप्तद्वीपाश्च पर्वता विविधास्तथा ॥
अलोकश्चैव लोकश्च रसातलमथापि च ।
दैत्यनागालयाश्चैव गृहाणि भवनानि च ॥
नगरे वा वने वापि वर्षे वा पर्वतेऽपि वा ।
यत्र वार्ता प्रवर्तेत तत्र कक्ष्यां प्रयोजयेत् ॥

NŚ XIII.3-7

परिक्रामन्त्यनेनेति परिक्रामः चार्यादिसंनिवेशः तद्वशादेकस्यापि रङ्गदेशस्य स्थानभेदेनापरित्यागः, यथा "आरोढुमुद्वहेद् गात्रम्" "अतिक्रान्तेन पादेन" (XII.102) इत्यादिना विशेषे तु प्रासादपर्वतादिरूपत्वमस्यैव। ननु भाण्डवाद्यविनिर्मुक्ते रङ्गपीठदेशे क्रमविशेषस्थानभेदक्लृप्तिः । तत्रेत्याह – कक्ष्याविभाग इत्यादि विशिष्टे शिष्टे देशे स्थानान्पराणि कल्पनीयानि कविजनस्मरणार्थमुपलक्षणत्वेन पठन्ति(ति) । गृहादीनि पृथिवीस्वर्ग-पातालभेदात् पुनरुदाहृतानि सर्वसंग्रहाय त्रैलोक्यमित्युक्तेऽपि स्मरणार्थं वर्णनोद्देशः।
ननु सर्वत्र प्रयोगे सर्वे त्रैलोक्यवर्तिनः स्थानभेदात् किं सम्भाविनः, नेति दर्शयति नगरे वेत्यादि ।...यत्र यत्र वार्तावृत्तान्त इतिवृत्तबलायातः प्रकर्षेण वर्तते तत्र मध्ये यो देशविभागस्तमेव प्रवर्तयेद् रङ्गपीठे दर्शयेत् न सर्वमित्यर्थः।

AbhiBhā on above

Text:

The divisions of zones (on the stage) should be indicated by circular movement on the stage; through circular movement on the stage a different zone comes into being.

According to divisions of zones, should be known houses, cities, gardens, rivers, hermitages and forests, earth, oceans, all the three worlds with mobile and immobile (creatures), the *varṣas* (division of earth as separated by certain mountain ranges), seven islands and various mountains, visions (or lustres), spheres or regions, and also *rasātala* (a lower *loka* or sphere), the abodes of demons and *nāgas* (lit. snakes), houses, buildings etc. The same zone should be established (on the stage), wherever an 'episode' is being enacted, whether it is a city, forest, *varṣa* (a division of the earth), or a mountain.

Commentary:

Parikrāma is that by which (the actors) move around i.e. the arrangement of *cārīs* (movements of limbs below the waist); on account of those (movements) one and the same space on the stage gets transformed into different places; e.g. "for ascending (a higher place) the body should be raised up" or "one should move with a leaping foot" (NŚ XII.102) – through these movements and the like, the particular part of the stage is transformed into a palace or mountain. (Objection:) Is it so in the space on the stage minus the place for *bhāṇḍa* (lit. drum, here musical ensemble) the distinction of specific places is construed in a definite order? No, hence it has been said that the division of zones on the stage (has to be established through movements of the actors). Various places have to be construed on the remaining space (minus the musical ensemble); these places are being enumerated by the author for prompting the poets; this enumeration is only representative, not exhaustive (in the form of *upalakṣaṇa*). Houses and the like have been enumerated once again according to the distinction of *svarga* (higher sphere) and *pātāla* (lower sphere); although *trailokya* (three worlds, viz. higher, middle and lower) that covers everything has already been spoken of, just for the sake of prompting or reminding.

(Objection:) Everywhere (in dramatic performance) is it possible to present all the places that are covered in the three worlds? No, hence (the author) says – "in a city or" etc. wherever the '*vārtā*' (incident or episode) is being enacted, that specific portion of space (like palace, garden or forest) should be shown, not all (places).

The directions on the stage are identified on the basis of the direction of the seating-place of the musical ensemble. The prescription of the **Nāṭya-Śāstra** is as follows:

यतो मुखं भवेद् भाण्डं द्वारं नेपथ्यकस्य च ।
सा मन्तव्या तु दिक् पूर्वा नाट्ययोगेन नित्यशः ॥

NŚ XIII.11

That is known as the eastern direction towards which faces the *bhāṇḍa* (lit. drum, but here musical ensemble) and the door(s) of *nepathya* (back-stage); this is always (the understanding) in relation to theatre.

The context is that of establishing the directions which the actors will face while acting on the stage. Immediately preceding this verse is the injunction that one who enters later, delivers his message, facing the south. Abhinavagupta says that the subsequent verse (given above) establishes the east so that the other directions could be located.

These doors face the audience; thus the audience is seated in the east and is facing the west. The left and right parts of the stage are south and north respectively. The idea is that the stage has its own system of establishing the directions, independent of the directions regulated by the sun.

The concept of *pravṛtti* (mode of dramatic presentation) is closely linked with region (*deśa*), because attire, language, patterns of behaviour and even vocations owe their specific nature to their respective regions. The following extracts from **Nāṭya-Śāstra** explain this concept.

> चतुर्विधा प्रवृत्तिश्च प्रोक्ता नाट्यप्रयोक्तृभिः ।
> आवन्ती दाक्षिणात्या च पाञ्चाली चोढ्रमागधी ॥
> ....प्रवृत्तिरिति कस्मात् ? उच्यते – पृथिव्यां नानादेशवेषभाषाचारा वार्ताः
> ख्यापयतीति वृत्तिः प्रवृत्तिश्च निवेदने ।
>
> NŚ XIII.37
>
> Fourfold *pravṛtti* has been spoken of by the performers of drama; viz. *āvantī, dākṣiṇātyā, pāñcālī* and *oḍhramāgadhī*. How does the *pravṛtti* (come into being?) It is being answered. *Vṛtti* is that which announces (makes known) the various modes of behaviour, vocations (etc.); *pravṛtti* makes (the message of *vṛtti*) concrete or obvious.

The various regions covered by the form *pravṛttis* are enumerated in **Nāṭya-Śāstra** XIII.39-50.

> एकीभूताः पुनश्चैताः प्रयोक्तव्याः प्रयोक्तृभिः ।
> पर्षदं देशकालौ चाप्यर्थयुक्तिमवेक्ष्य च ॥
>
> NŚ XIII.55
>
> These (*pravṛttis*) could again be used by the performers in a combined way, keeping in view the assembly (of spectators led by the patron), the *deśa* (region to be represented), time and the design of *artha* (objective, justified by the behaviour of various characters).

The performing arts and for that matter any performance lays emphasis on *digbandha* as indicated earlier. This act is symbolic of a total comprehension of space in all its aspects.

While theatrical space is in some sense imaginary, the arts that deal directly with space are architecture and sculpture. Here the space-directions (*diśaḥ*) assume their full cosmic and symbolical significance, and nothing is left to chance: the direction of a temple in relation to the rising Sun, the placement of the *dikpālas* or presiding divinities of the quarters on the eight corners of the temple, all this implies the qualitative importance of the space-directions. Why the South is associated with Death (Yama), the North with the gods and liberation, the East with new life and inspiration, all this has its deeper cosmic, mythological, symbolical and geographical reasons. "The fundamental character of space-directions can never be altered and their functions cannot

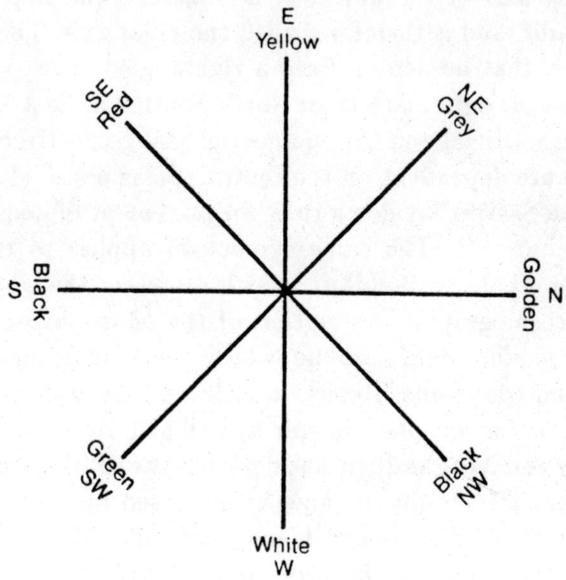

Figure 2: The colours associated with the directions. After the Mahānirvāṇa Tantra (XIII.90-95)

be interchanged." (Alice Boner, Principles of Composition p. 30). All sacred architecture, but even secular architecture, follows the same basic principles:

"A sphere with three rectangular diameters directed towards the six cardinal points has from the dawn of human history been understood to represent the plan on which the Great Architect of the Universe has built this Cosmos. All traditional cultures have based their architecture on this fundamental plan, in accordance with the immanent significance of space-directions. When building a dwelling place or a sanctuary the basic idea was always and everywhere to recreate symbolically the shape of the universe. It was intended to adequately circumscribe a consecrated piece of ground, on which to maintain, during the sojourn on earth, a living contact with the transcendent Principle. Therefore the central nucleus from where emanate all developments in space and the vertical axis had to be emphasized." (Ibid. p. 21)

About the origin of the space-directions from the central point (→*bindu*) and their inherent qualities Alice Boner writes:

"The three dimensions of space emanating from the centre are not equivalent. One, the vertical dimension dominates over the two others and holds them together. It represents the primary extension the Bindu and is central with respect to the two other dimensions that lie horizontally across it. As the central, immovable axis of the universe, it joins the two opposite poles, the Zenith and the Nadir, and is therefore called the polar axis. The two horizontal dimensions or axes that lie across, form a rightangled cross, whose arms run forward and backward, right and left, or North-South and East-West. These two axes are called the solsticial and the equinoctial axis respectively, they stand in opposition to and are dependent on the central, polar axis." (Ibid. p. 20)

Hence the Śilpa-Śāstras lay down rules for placement of gods and goddesses in the respective quarters. The same symbolism applies to the *yantras* and *maṇḍalas*, whether Hindu or Buddhist, which represent the whole universe.

The Purāṇic cosmographic description of the *bhuvanakośa* has the image of a focal point, mount Meru, around which there are concentric circles of different oceans and continents. Depiction of features as well as ethnic features of a region has an important place in epic as well as lyrical poetry. Kālidāsa, in his **Raghuvaṃśa** and **Meghadūta** has depicted the different parts of India in a sequence in a very picturesque manner unsurpassed by any poetry.

Deśa as extension of the idea of home looms large in the creative mind. So much so that the presiding deity of creative Arts is called Bhāratī. The nomenclatures of styles, moods, *rāgas* and usages in different spheres are named after the regions where they are dominant. That is why *deśī* has come to stay as an important mood in music as well as dance-drama along with the *mārgī*, *deśī* giving bent to the original fancies and memories, and *mārgī* to the classical and the intellectually integrating aspects.

अबलाबालगोपालैः क्षितिपालैर्निजेच्छया ।
गीयते सानुरागेण स्वदेशे देशिरुच्यते ॥

BṛD 14

(The songs that) women, children, cowherds and kings sing out of their own will with love and pleasure in their own lands are known as *deśī*.

एतद्देशी तु विख्यातं तत्तद्देशजने यथा ।

NṛtRatnā I.54

That is known as *deśī* which is done according to the local taste. (Tr. M. Bose)

The details will be discussed in the article on →*mārga* including *deśī*.

Conclusion

Summarising this article it can be safely concluded that absolute reality, dependent reality or appearance, whatever may be its place in the metaphysical structure of any Indian philosophical system, time and space have an important role to play and they are a basic part of any ritual or Art. The Indian mind is awake to the space and time here and now as well as to time and space beyond. Time and space beyond is pure consciousness. All the time Man interacts with *deśa-kāla*, the creative mind creates an aesthetic time and space through concretisation, through consecration and deification and through configuration in colour, sound, letters, architectural shapes or gestures and movements in the respective art genres.

Vidya Niwas Misra

Select Bibliography

Boner, Alice: Principles of Composition in Hindu Sculpture (Cave Temple Period). Delhi: Motilal Banarsidass, 1990.

Mandal, Kumar Kishore: A Comparative study of the concepts of space and time in Indian thought. Varanasi: The Chowkhamba Sanskrit Series Office, 1968.

KĀLA

Overview

Kāla, 'time', is a concept that has assumed many meanings in the different systems of philosophy, spirituality, the sciences and the Arts. *Kāla* has been conceived either as a divine power or as a limiting factor of existence. It is represented in art and myth as one of the major aspects of Śiva and his female counterpart Kālī, the Great Devourer, the Great Destroyer and the beginningless beginner. As such *kāla* cannot be easily explained unless we put together its different connotations and usages. *Kāla* as an absolute category is denied by the idealist systems, and some philosophies such as Kashmir Śaivism have accepted it as one of the five covers or enveloping forces (*kañcukas*) which conceal the supreme reality or which seem to delimit it. The space-time pair, *kāla* and *diś* (→*deśa*) has been no doubt accepted by such systems as Nyāya-Vaiśeṣika, Jaina philosophy and Mīmāṃsā. These concepts have a great influence on everyday life and on rituah activity (daily or occasional) and for that matter on other creative activities as well. *Kāla* is geometrically represented by a circle while *deśa* as a square. Symbolical representations of *kāla* are the wheel (of a chariot), disc, handdrum (*ḍamaru*), a snake eating its tail, conch-shell etc. The earliest metaphor of *kāla* is a steed representing movement (*kālo aśvo vahati* etc., AV XIX.53.1). Like so many other concepts *kāla* has two aspects – creative, as well as destructive. Every etymology of the word indicates this double aspect.

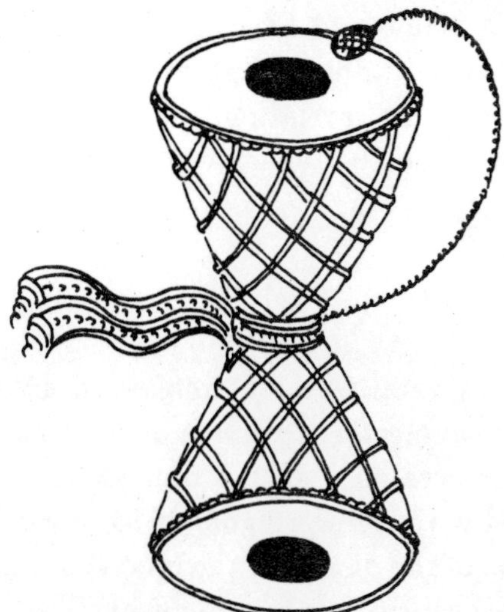

Figure 1: Ḍamaru: beating the rythm of creation

Kāla is derived from *kal-*, 'to calculate', or from *kala-*, 'to devour'. The role of *kāla* in shaping things is made possible by its potential to dissolve all shapes into itself. Every activity has to take place in time (*kāla*) and at the same time it has to transcend the limitations of finite time. A *pūjā* ritual starts with the reckoning of finite time and space placed within the frame of the entire creation and moves into the sphere where time and space are being suspended. In other words, finite time and finite space have been sacrificed to create unending time and space. A similar situation is created in a performance – visually in drama, music and dance. Historical time and geographical space are mythically transformed in the Purāṇas with the result that past and future are subsumed in the present. The present moment becomes the most important centre of existence. It may appear incongruous on the surface that the Indian reckoning of time goes into the minutest detail, calendars go into the hoariest antiquity, the day is divided into 21,600 units of breath and yet it is the boundless time which is sought for through these subtle divisions of time.

The contradiction of this bi-aspectual notion of time is soon resolved when it is juxtaposed against the act of sacrifice which is nothing but reintegration through dismemberment. The minute divisions of time by themselves have relevance so far as they make the whole appear in all its possibilities. This fits in well with the apt definition of time '*kālo gati-nivṛtti-sthitiḥ saṃdadhāti*' (ŚāṅkhĀr VII.20): *kāla* makes a coalescence of all movement, all drives and all processes. The translation of the passage as given by A.K. Coomaraswamy is as follows: "Time (*kāla*) unites procession, recession and stasis, and by these All this (world or universe) is united". He further elaborates it by saying that "subjectively, psychologically, the past (*bhūtam*) is the prior and the future (*bhavyam*), the posterior form and the present (*bhavat*) is their union (*saṃhitā*) or product". (Cf. A.K. Coomaraswamy, 'Time and Eternity', p.9). This unifying characteristic of time is best observed in flashes of lightning, flashes of creativity and for that matter any manifestation or revelation.

The treatment of *kāla* cannot be separated from that of →*deśa*, space, and of activity (→*kriyā*).

Etymology

Kāla can be derived in several ways: (i) *kalyate iti kālaḥ* - from *kal-*, means to calculate, to reckon, to enumerate, to give a definite name. Thus *kāla* means the reckoned one, the enumerated one, the named one. This in fact is finite time and this is associated with the word *kāla* which means a division, a part, a measure (of time as well as of the phases of the moon) and the capacity to create or transfer. (ii) *Kāla* is derived from *kala-*, 'to devour', 'to absorb' or from *kala-(curādi)*, 'to drive', 'to impel'. Hence *kāla* is death, the great devourer as well as the great driver and so becomes associated with Śiva, the great destroyer, and the sun, Sūrya the impeller. (iii) *Kāla* can also be an *l* form of ***kāra*** (***kar***), meaning the time of success, decisive action, hence the right time. (iv) It can be related to *car-*, to turn, to move (*kālacakraṃ pravartate*, in Lat. *volventibus annis*). (See M. Mayrhofer, Etymological Dictionary, new revised ed., sub voce).

Kāla is also related with *kalyam*, 'day-break, morning, yesterday, as well as tomorrow' (Hindi *kal*, yesterday and tomorrow).

To sum up all these possible derivations refer to movement or passing and so all refer to changing time. Non-Sanskrit words do not carry the sense of its two aspects, infinite time and finite time and of *kāla* or *ananta* which is the devourer, the dissolver, the absorber and ultimately the reckoner and the starter of a new life. It is the substratum of all substrata.

Layers of Meaning

It would be relevant to discuss at some length the different connotations of *kāla* and its synonyms. The primary meaning of *kāla* is a fixed or right point of time, the proper time, occasion, circumstance, season, meal time. The secondary meaning of time is the end, death, time of death, god of death. The third range of meaning is also covered by another word *diṣṭa* (that which has been ordained). *Kāla* is thus defining both finite and infinite aspects of time as well as the imperceptive causal factor in every event. Infinite time has been equated with *akāla* (beyond time or beyond death).

The driving aspect of *kāla* is also covered by the word *samaya* which also denotes agreement, directive principle, convention, oath, covenant:

समयः शपथे भाषासम्पदोः कालसंविदोः ।
सिद्धान्ताचारसंकेतनियमावसरेषु च ।
क्रियाकारे च निर्देशे ... ।

Haimakośa 3.541-542

Kāla as driving force is an important dimension of all happenings and has as one of its connotations historical time. This connotation is based on the pre-19th century western concept whereas historical time has a limited role in traditional Indian thought. Though historicity has not been rejected yet it has been always overshadowed by the notion of trans-historicity. That is why the image of the rotating wheel or spiral-like formation as one finds in a conch-shell or the image of a serpent eating its tail is an oft-repeated motive in Indian pictorial art. The beginning of a tale with a verb *asti*, 'there is' is also an indicator of reckoning of event patterns. The notion of rebirth through a ritual death is another illustration of eternity of time or in other words trans-historicity of

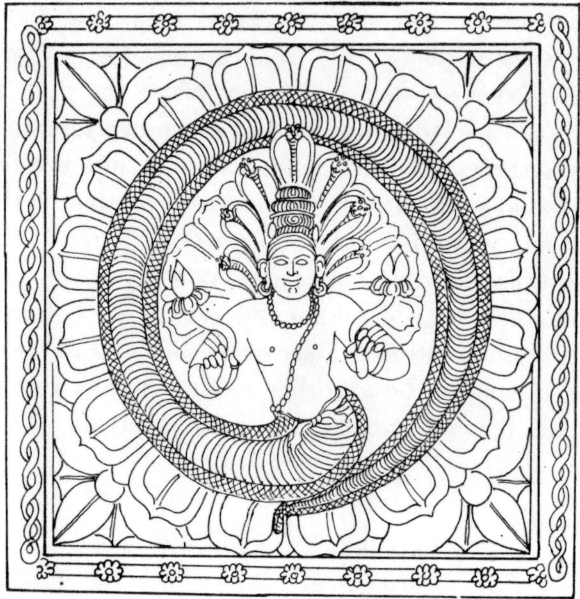

Figure 2: Nāga, Bādāmī cave-temple ceiling

time. This notion observes a continuum of ever-changing but ever-integrating wholes. It is the whole which is more important than the chain of changing units. In *sādhanā* it is →*laya* (falling into a rhythm pattern, immersion into eternity), in drama it is →*rasa*, in worship it is *naivedya* (offering of the essence of oneself), in sacrifice it is the *avabhṛtha* (postsacrificial bath, a preparation for fresh sacrificial activity); it is always the renewable aspect of time which is in the focus of a creative act. All the aspects are covered by the term →*līlā*, divine sport, which entails immortality of mortal form and mortality of the immortal.

Kāla as a creative dimension is usually paired with →*deśa*, space. *Deśa* again is not absolute space. For that matter there is no absolute space, even *ākāśa* (the vast illumined space), →*vyoman* (the great protector or cover), *kha* (the vast hole) or →*śūnya* (the void filler and not void itself) are all manifestations of the Great One's heated desire (*tapas*). The distinction between *deśa* and *vyoman* is analogous to that between *akāla*, *mahākāla* and *kāla* (between Great Time and limited time). *Deśa* is relative space as well as a marked geographical region, a specific area related to another such area. In other words *deśa* is in the same way unit in a spatial continuum as a period of time is in a temporal continuum. Nevertheless this specific *deśa-kāla* is an important setting for not only an event but also for an action. These two validate the action concerned. Every action has to be preceded by a recollection of *deśa* and *kāla*. In other words, every action has to be placed on the axis of *deśa* and *kāla*, *kāla* being the vertical axis and *deśa* horizontal. The rules of good conduct and the paths of richness have to be in consonance with the demands made by specific *deśa* and *kala*. They govern the entire sphere of desire – action and comprehension. And yet by themselves they are not independent categories, but they are dependent on the great chain of continuum. Conceptually, *deśa* and *kāla* are mutually dependent and mutually transformable. *Kāla* (time) can be represented by a geometrical space and *vice-versa*, space can be represented by measures of time. Both are substrata of all manifest things and both are end in all, of all manifested activity.

Another concept, →*loka* is indirectly related to *kāla* and is directly linked with *deśa*. *Loka* is non-specific space of manifestation, it is not an absolute dimension but the manifested stage of creation holding all together.

Measurement of time has been one of the most important preoccupations of the Indian thinkers. This measurement has been in terms of space, covered by a ray of light (*trasareṇu*) or in terms of inhalation or exhalation of breath, or in terms of a wink of eye, or in terms of articulation of a sound or beat of a drum, or passing of a shadow from one point to the other, or a ripple in water. Indians were among the first measurers of time on the basis of astronomical positions. 27 star-conjunctions were minutely observed and pictorially described by Indians. The year-rotation (*saṃvatsara*) and the cycle of seasons (*ṛtu*), the divisions of day and night (*ahorātra*), the transition of dawn and twilight (→*sandhi*), the rise of moon and sun, equinoxes and solstices, midpoints of night and day, all were closely observed and described; and life pattern was matched with them, so that there is perfect harmony between the cosmic and micro-cosmic chain of change, as will be elaborated hereafter.

Development of the Concept

The concept of *kāla* is symbolically represented by the Great Night in the Creation Hymn in the **Ṛgveda** X.190. This Night is a bridge between two intense heats of desire, recreated in an orderly fashion and the expanse of creation which is represented by the primordial creators.

ऋतं च सत्यं चाभीद्धात् तपसोऽध्यजायत ।
ततो रात्र्यजायत ततः समुद्रो अर्णवः ॥
समुद्रादर्णवादधि संवत्सरो अजायत ।
अहोरात्राणि विदधद्विश्वस्य मिषतो वशी ॥

ṚV X.190.1-2

1. From blazing Ardor Cosmic Order came and Truth;
from thence was born the obscure night;
from thence the Ocean with its billowing waves.
2. From Ocean with its waves was born the year
which marshals the succession of nights and days,
controlling everything that blinks the eye. (Tr. R. Panikkar)

This is infinite time enveloping infinite space. The creation takes place in this time and then finite time is manifested by a chain of actions, cosmic actions at both the macro and micro levels. This equation of infinite time as great darkness and the space with the great primordial waters is further supported by the famous creation hymn, Nāsadīya-Sūkta.

तम आसीत्तमसा गूळ्हमग्रेऽप्रकेतं सलिलं सर्वमा इदम् ।
तुच्छ्येनाभ्वपिहितं यदासीत्तपसस्तन्महिनाजायतैकम् ॥
कामस्तदग्रे समवर्तताधि मनसो रेतः प्रथमं यदासीत् ।
सतो बन्धुमसति निरविन्दन् हृदि प्रतीष्या कवयो मनीषा ॥

ṚV X.129.3-4

3. It was as if the dark lay lapped in dark,
Or the face of the flood was blank, or, if not, unformed.
Then heat, the heat of slowly swelling Desire,
Cast the most primal thing on the shore of creation.
4. Desire it was that lifted out at the start
That very first seed, thrusting the spirit up, and
Desire that thinkers found as the bridge that led back
From Being to Absence of Being, when they sounded their hearts.

A fuller treatment of Time is found in the **Atharva-Veda** where *kāla* has been conceived as the prime mover and the great progenitor. A metaphor of the horse with seven reins to control, its thousand eyes and great virility and strength, the great knowers and composers ride on it.

कालो अश्वो वहति सप्तरश्मिः सहस्राक्षो अजरो भूरिरेताः ।
तमारोहन्ति कवयो विपश्चितस्तस्य चक्रा भुवनानि विश्वा ॥

AV XIX.53.1

Time drives like a horse with seven reins,
a thousand-eyed unaging Stallion.
Him the inspired poets mount
All beings are his chariot wheels. (Tr. R. Panikkar)

This great horse carries the chariot-wheel of the universe. The seven seasons (*vasanta-grīṣma-varṣā-śarat-hemanta-śiśira* and the whole year itself) are the seven wheels (cf. ŚBr X.2.6.1) and seven are its naves. Immortality (the wheel signifying death) is the axis. *Kāla* gives shape to all manifestation. He is approached as the first god.

सप्त चक्रान्वहति काल एष सप्तास्य नाभीरमृतं न्वक्षः ।
स इमा विश्वा भुवनान्यञ्जत्कालः स ईयते प्रथमो नु देवः ॥

AV XIX.53.2

This Time hath seven rolling wheels and seven naves, immortality

is the chariot's axle.
This Time brings hitherward all worlds about us:
as primal Deity is he entreated. (Tr. R.T.H. Griffith)

The pitcher of fullness (→*pūrṇa*) is placed on time and we see this pitcher from all sides; that fullness brings forth all becoming. That infinite time is wrapped in the great infinite space.

पूर्णः कुम्भोऽधि काल आहितस्तं वै पश्यामो बहुधा नु सन्तः ।
स इमा विश्वा भुवनानि प्रत्यङ्कालं तमाहुः परमे व्योमन् ॥

AV XIX.53.3

Above time is set a brimful vessel.
Simultaneously we see Time here, there, everywhere.
Set face to face with all existences,
Time is throned, men say, in the loftiest realm. (Tr. R. Panikkar)

Time fills all the becoming and transcends it. Hence he is the father and he is the son of all becoming. No energy is higher than this expansion.

स एव सं भुवनान्याभरत् स एव सं भुवनानि पर्यैत् ।
पिता सन्नभवत् पुत्र एषां तस्माद् वै नान्यत् परमस्ति तेजः ॥

AV XIX.53.4

Time has gathered together all beings that are;
he has passed through all the gathered beings.
He who was father has become their son
There is no glory higher than this. (Tr. R. Panikkar)

In this Sūkta (AV XIX.53) *kāla* is described poetically as the creator of three *lokas* and the substratum of past and future, of all activities, of all contemplation, of all vitality, of all pleasure, of all births, of all desires. He is the lord of all and father of whatever is impelled, is born and is securely placed through him. *Kāla* takes the role of supreme reality and carries the great being seated in the highest heaven. Another hymn (AV XIX.54) is also devoted to *kāla* wherein *kāla* is the substratum of all phases of creation, all activities, all sequences, all ritual happenings and all celestial beings. *Kāla* transcends this *loka* and the *loka* beyond and the great truths with its power of pervasiveness. He is approached as the Supreme God by all.

Time and creation becoming identical make the finite aspects of time, important for all activities. So that the year, the period taken by the earth to make the rotation of the sun (the cycle of seasons marking physical and psycho-somatic changes), the month, particularly the lunar month (the period of completing one full cycle of rotation of the moon), lunar *tithi* (period taken by the moon going round the earth), day and night, sunset and sunrise, the midpoints of day and night, and dawn and twilight, all these assume a great significance in performance of rituals. In the Puruṣa-Sūkta (ṚV X.90) the seasons have been likened to sacrificial materials, the spring being the clarified butter (*ghṛta*), the summer being the fuel to kindle the fire on the altar, and autumn being the offering to propitiate the universal Being (*virāṭ*).

यत्पुरुषेण हविषा देवा यज्ञमतन्वत ।
वसन्तो अस्यासीदाज्यं ग्रीष्म इध्मः शरद्धविः ॥

ṚV X.90.6

Using the Man as their oblation
The Gods performed the sacrifice.
Spring served them for the clarified butter,
Summer for the fuel, and Autumn for the offering. (Tr. R. Panikkar)

The year-cycle is an image of the life-cycle and the recurrence of the cycle reflects renewal of life at each stage for a new function to perform. The renewal of the year is a re-enactment of the moment of creation and is rekindling of the fire of desire to live. This juxtaposition of life-cycle against the cycle of the year is made possible through linking them to the ritual of sacrifice (*yajña*). Sacrifice and ritual is aimed at reintegration of the whole being through dismemberment, so that the entire cycle of existence is made purposeful through this ever renewed desire to be one with the act of creation as well as the main actors of creation. Passage after passage in Brāhmaṇas and Upaniṣads refer to such equation that *saṃvatsara* is an equal measure with the sacrifice, and with Man.

संवत्सरसंमितो वै यज्ञः । पञ्च वा ऋतवः संवत्सरस्य ॥

ŚBr III.4.1.14

The sacrifice is of equal measure with the year, and five seasons there are in the year. (Tr. J. Eggeling)

These equations make succesion of cycles of temporal movements, one of the coordinates of purposeful activity – purpose being integration into a whole, and for that reason a big moment of rejoicing is called →*utsava* (overflowing of the juice obtained from the pressing of *soma*). It is through offering of one's life to the All-Being or his powers and manifestations that real rejoicings can be obtained.

The significant role assigned to this regenerative aspect of time in Vedic literature is further developed by philosophical systems. They take time as one of the nine substances, *dravyas* in the Nyāya-Vaiśeṣika, one of the eleven in the Pūrvamīmāṃsā, one of the five *kañcukas* (covers) in Kashmir Śaivism, one of the *śaktis* of the Lord in the Vaiṣṇava Āgamas and one of the aspects of the supreme reality named either as Viṣṇu, Śiva, Durgā etc. Thus Mahākāla is identified with Śiva, Kāla is identified with Yama (the controller), *Kālī, Kālarātri, Mahārātri, Moharātri*, the epithets of mother goddess, and Sūryanārāyaṇa is also called *kālapriya. Kāla* also became identified with several *yantras* and *cakras* in esoteric systems, and an independent system of mystic *sādhanā* came to be called by the name *Kālacakra* in later Buddhism.

Sciences relying on regular observations and deductions such as Āyurveda, astrology, astronomy, chemistry or alchemy and metallurgy also place a great premium on proper time, ripe time and auspicious time as indicated by suitable conjunctions of planets, stars and psychosomatic movements such as *svara* (breath-movement), image reflections and the like. Such a pre-occupation with time developed into a fusion of ideas and practices in everyday life to an extent that Indian people show an ahistorical attitude and yet have developed such a keen awareness of the changing rhythm pattern of time, so much so that *kāla* came to be considered as the main cause of all creation or manifestation by some philosophical schools while others propounded *svabhāva* (inherent nature), *niyati* (necessity), *yadṛcchā* (chance), *bhūta* (elements), the female womb or the matrix (*yoni*) or →*puruṣa*, the Great Being, as the primordial Cause.

कालः स्वभावो नियतिर्यदृच्छा भूतानि योनिः पुरुष इति चिन्त्यम् ।

ŚvUp I.2

Time (*kāla*), or inherent nature (*svabhāva*) or necessity (*niyati*) or chance (*yadṛcchā*).
Or the elements (*bhūta*), or a (female) womb (*yoni*), or a (male) person (*puruṣa*) are to be considered (as the cause).
(Tr. R.E. Hume)

But the Upaniṣads concluded that such theories are mere delusions spread out by the great God who is the mover of the wheel of the universe and who is himself the Time of time, the Reckoner of the reckoner.

This Upaniṣadic position became the foundation of the Indian idea of time notwithstanding the positions taken by the pluralistic philosophical systems.

स्वभावमेके कवयो वदन्ति कालं तथान्ये परिमुह्यमानाः ।
देवस्यैष महिमा तु लोके येनेदं भ्राम्यते ब्रह्मचक्रम् ॥
येनावृतं नित्यमिदं हि सर्वं ज्ञः कालकारो गुणी सर्वविद्यः ।
तेनेशितं कर्म विवर्तते ह पृथिव्यप्तेजोऽनिलखानि चिन्त्यम् ॥
तत्कर्म कृत्वा विनिवर्त्य भूयस्तत्त्वस्य तत्त्वेन समेत्य योगम् ।
एकेन द्वाभ्यां त्रिभिरष्टभिर्वा कालेन चैवात्मगुणैश्च सूक्ष्मैः ॥

ŚvUp VI.1-3

Some sages discourse of inherent nature (*svabhāva*); others likewise, of time. Deluded men!
It is the greatness of God in the world
By which this Brahma-wheel is caused to revolve.
He by whom this whole world is constantly enveloped
Is intelligent, the author of time, possessor of qualities (*guṇin*), omniscient.
Ruled o'er by Him, (his) work (*karman*) revolves –
This which is regarded as earth, water, fire, air, and space!
He creates this work, and rests again.
Having entered into union (*yoga*) with principle (*tattva*) after principle,
With one, with two, with three, or with eight,
With time, too, and the subtile qualities of a self. (Tr. R.E. Hume)

Kāla **and** ***akāla*** **are two forms of Brahman:**

द्वे वाव ब्रह्मणो रूपे कालश्चाकालश्च ।अथ यः प्रागादित्यात् सोऽकालोऽकलः । अथ य आदित्याद्यः स कालः सकलः । सकलस्य वा एतद्रूपं, यत् संवत्सरः संवत्सरात् खल्वेवेमाः प्रजाः प्रजायन्ते । संवत्सरेणेह वै जाता विवर्धन्ते । संवत्सरे प्रत्यस्तं यन्ति । तस्मात्संवत्सरो वै प्रजापतिः कालोऽन्नं ब्रह्मनीडमात्मा च । इत्येवं ह्याह –

कालः पचति भूतानि सर्वाण्येव महात्मनि ।
यस्मिंस्तु पच्यते कालो यस्तं वेद स वेदवित् ॥

विग्रहवानेष कालः सिन्धुराजः प्रजानाम् । एष तत्स्थः सविताख्यः । यस्मादेवेमे चन्द्रर्क्षग्रहसंवत्सरादयः सूयन्ते । अथैभ्यः सर्वमिदम् ।... तस्मादादित्यात्मा ब्रह्म । अथ कालसंज्ञमादित्यमुपासीत ।

MaitUp VI.15-16

There are, assuredly, two forms of Brahman: Time and the Timeless. That which is prior to the sun is the Timeless (*a-kāla*), without parts (*a-kala*). But that which begins with the sun is time, which has parts. Verily, the form of that which has parts is the year. From the year, in truth, are these creatures produced. Through the year, verily after having been produced, do they grow. In the year they disappear. Therefore the year, verily, is Prajāpati, is time, is food, is the Brahma-abode and is Ātman. For thus has it been said:

'T is Time that cooks created things,
All things, indeed, in the Great Soul (*mahātman*).

In what, however, Time is cooked – who knows that, he the Veda knows!
This embodied Time is the great ocean of creatures. In it abides he who is called Savitṛ (etymologically, the Begetter), from whom, indeed are begotten moon, stars, planets, the year, and these other things.... Therefore Brahman is the soul (*ātman*) of the sun. So, one should reverence the sun as a name of Time. (Tr. R.E. Hume)

The ethical and political systems also evolved a time-oriented world-view. Some are taking time as one of the factors of fruition, others consider time as the supreme factor on which depend all happening of events; as in the **Mahābhārata**:

गतिं हि सर्वभूतानामगत्वा क्व गमिष्यसि ।
यो धावता न हातव्यस्तिष्ठन्नपि न हीयते ।
तमिन्द्रियाणि सर्वाणि नानुपश्यन्ति पञ्चधा ॥ 51 ॥
आहुश्चैनं केचिदग्निं केचिदाहुः प्रजापतिम् ।
ऋतुमासार्धमासांश्च दिवसांस्तु क्षणांस्तथा ॥ 52 ॥
पूर्वाह्णमपराह्णं च मध्याह्नमपि चापरे ।
मुहूर्तमपि चैवाहुरेकं सन्तमनेकधा ।
तं कालमवजानीहि यस्य सर्वमिदं वशे ॥ 53 ॥

MBh XII.217.51-53

Time is the destiny (flux: *gati*) of everything; if one does not follow it, where can one go? Whether you try to flee from it or remain motionless, you cannot escape from time. The five senses cannot grasp it. Some say that (*kāla*) is Fire, and others that it is the Lord of the creatures (Prajāpati). Some conceive of time as a season, others as a month, a day or even an instant.... There are those who say that it is the hour (*muhūrta*): but that which is uniquely One has many forms. Time must be acknowledged as that which controls everything that exists.

In the **Bhagavad-Gītā** Kṛṣṇa reveals himself as Time: "Among those who reckon I am Time" (*kālaḥ kalayatām aham*, BhG X.30). He is not limited but imperishable Time (*aham evākṣayaḥ kālo*, ... X.33). When he reveals his universal form (*viśvarūpa*), he says:

कालोऽस्मि लोकक्षयकृत्प्रवृद्धो लोकान्समाहर्तुमिह प्रवृत्तः ।

BhG XI.32ab

Time am I, wreaker of the world's destruction, matured – resolved here to swallow up the worlds. (Tr. R.C. Zaehner)

Here it is again the destructive aspect of Time which absorbs everything.

A brief survey of different positions in the philosophical systems with regard to *kāla* and its place in the universe is given below:

(i) Time is nothing but sequence and the perception of reality as consciousness itself relates to both, sequence and non-sequence, as described by the Kashmiri Śaiva thinker Abhinavagupta:

अध्वनः कलनं यत्तत्क्रमाक्रमतया स्थितम् ।
क्रमाक्रमौ हि चित्रैककलना भावगोचरे ॥
क्रमाक्रमात्मा कालश्च परः संविदि वर्तते ।

TĀl VI.6-7a

The effecting (*kalana*) of limitations in paths (*adhvas*) is set up in sequence and without any sequence. These sequences and non-sequences regarding the reality (*bhāva*) shine simultaneously like a painting. Time with the characteristic of *krama* and *akrama* abides in the Supreme Consciousness. (Tr. H.N. Chakravarty)

(ii) The highest stage of bliss transcends time, as in Śaṅkara's Vedānta:

यत्र धर्माधर्मौ सह कार्येण कालत्रयं च नोपावर्तेते तदेतदशरीरत्वम् ।

BrSūBh I.1.4

That bodiless entity in fact, to which merit and demerit with their consequences and threefold time do not apply, is called release. (Tr. G. Thibaut)

Transcendance or irrelevance of time is perceived in the dream phenomena where the dream time in terms of both, manifestation and duration, is in conflict with the concept of physical time.

(iii) *Kāla* is succession of moments (→*kṣaṇa*), as in the Yoga system of Patañjali:

यावता च समयेन चलितः परमाणुः पूर्वदेशं जह्यात् उत्तरदेशमुपसंपद्येत स कालः क्षणः ।

YSūBh III.52

As the minimal object is an atom, so minimal time is a moment. In other words, the time taken by an atom in motion in leaving one point in space and reaching the adjacent point, is a moment. (Tr. H. Aranyaka)

This position has been further supported by the **Śaiva Pratyabhijñā** which maintains that time as succession is determined by the multiplicity of actions:

कालः सूर्यादिसञ्चारस्तत्तत्पुष्पादि जन्म वा ।
शीतोष्णे वाथ तल्लक्ष्यः क्रम एव स तत्त्वतः ॥

ĪPKā II.1.3

Time in reality is nothing else than the succession, observable in the movement of the sun etc., in birth of different flowers and in (seasons like) summer and winter. (Tr. K.C. Pandey)

Time as a power has been concretised as the Goddess Kālī:

क्रमाक्रमकलनैव कालः स च परमेश्वर एव अन्तर्भाति तद्भासनं च देवस्य काली नाम शक्तिः ।

TSā VI

Time is the creative impulse characterised by the manifestation of sequence and non-sequence. That (time) shines as the very nature of the Great Lord. The shining of time in the form of sequence and non-sequence is due to the energy of the Lord named Kālī. (Tr. H.N. Chakravarty)

(iv) *Kāla* is the cause of transformation as successive development. This is the position taken by Vaiṣṇava Āgamas:

कालः कलनरूपस्य परिणामस्य कारणम् ।

LT XVI.4ab

Kāla is the incentive to transform in the form of impulse and effective development (*kalana*). (Tr. Sanjukta Gupta)

(v) Time is not a separate substance independent of space, as in Sāṃkhya. There is no separate category of time because it is action or movement which gets the designation of time. And these actions are functions of organs. So time is subsumed in the functions of the organs.

प्रागेवैतदुपादिष्टम् – न कालो नाम कश्चित्पदार्थोऽस्ति । किं तर्हि क्रियासु कालसंज्ञा । ताश्च करणवृत्तिरिति प्रतिपादितम् ।

YuDīp on SāṃKā 50, p.132

It has been already established that there is no category (*padārtha*) named time. On the contrary the name 'time' is given to actions or movements (*kriyā*). These are the functions of the organs. (Tr. R.S. Bhattacharya)

(vi) Time is not manifested by space. It is manifested by action and therefore past and present are inconceivable without the action in the present. Thus the Nyāya system maintains:

तयोरप्यभावो वर्तमानाभावे तदपेक्षत्वात् ।

NySū II.1.40

नाध्वव्यङ्ग्यः कालः । किं तर्हि ? क्रियाव्यङ्ग्यः ।

NySūBh on above

If there is no present tense, the other two, the past and the future, also would be inconceivable, as these are relative to that.

* * * *

As a matter of fact, time is not manifested by space, it is manifested by action. (Tr. G. Jha)

This is also the position of Āyurveda:

खादीन्यात्मा मनः कालो दिशश्च द्रव्यसङ्ग्रहः ।

CarSam Sūtrasthāna I.48

In short, *ākāśa* etc. (*ākāśa, vāyu, tejas, ap* and *pṛthivī*), self, mind, time and place are *dravyas* (substances). (Tr. P.V. Sharma)

(vii) Time is the cause of growth and decay in the universe, as the Mahābhāṣyakāra says:

येन मूर्त्तीनामुपचयाश्चापचयाश्च लक्ष्यन्ते तं कालमाहुः ।

Mahābh II.2.5

Time is that because of which growth and decay of concrete objects are processed.

This is also supported by Bhartṛhari in his **Vākyapadīya**:

उत्पत्तौ च स्थितौ चापि विनाशे चापि तद्वताम् ।
निमित्तं कालमेवाहुर्विभक्तेनात्मनास्थितम् ॥
तमस्य लोकयन्त्रस्य सूत्रधारं प्रचक्षते ।
प्रतिबन्धाभ्यनुज्ञाभ्यां तेन विश्वं विभज्यते ॥
नैको न चाप्यनेकोऽस्ति न शुक्लो नापि चासितः ।
द्रव्यात्मा स तु संसर्गादेवं रूपः प्रकाशते ॥

Vāk III.9.3-4,7

It is Time, differentiated (though one) which has been declared to be the cause of the origin, existence and destruction of objects which go through these states.

Time has been called the wire-puller of the world Machine. It regulates the universe through prevention and permission.

Nothing is one or many, nothing is white or non-white in itself. It is due to association with other things that substance appears in this way or that. (Tr. K.A.S. Iyer)

This is an aspect of *avidyā* or *māyā* (ignorance) and so it is the substratum of all, appearance being a part of it.

> कालो भावानामवभासनानवभासनात्मा क्रमः, मायीयमलान्तर्भूता कालशक्तिः।
>
> Kālasiddhāntadarśinī, H.C. Bhattacharya, p. 70
>
> Time is the sequence of manifest and unmanifest becoming and is a part of the impurity belonging to *māyā*, the delusive power of the great Lord.

(viii) According to Mīmāṃsā, time is one of the *dravyas* (substances) or *padārthas*, it is eternal and all-pervasive. It is preceded by the six senses and is cause of all cognition.

(ix) The Yogadarśana accepts the reality of the moment (→*kṣaṇa*) and treats all other manifestations of time as imaginary (cf. YSūBh III.52).

(x) According to the Gauḍīya Vaiṣṇava school, time is one of the four eternities, the other three being the Lord, *jīva* and *māyā*, and it is dependent on the Lord. Furthermore, time is by itself devoid of any of the three *guṇas* and is the cause of prediction of past, present and future.

(xi) The Buddhist concept of time is inseparably linked with the basic conceptions of the unsubstantiality (*anicca*) of the world, and of dependent origination (*pratītya-samutpāda*). The only reality of time is the instant (→*kṣaṇa*), which is also the moment of enlightenment.

Nāgārjuna in his **Madhyamaka-Kārikā** refutes the view of *kālavādins*, that is of those who hold the view that time is a substance. In short the view of the opponent is that time has three aspects, viz. the present, the past and the future. But Nāgārjuna asks:

> प्रत्युत्पन्नोऽनागतश्च यद्यतीतमपेक्ष्य हि ।
> प्रत्युत्पन्नोऽनागतश्च कालेऽतीते भविष्यतः ।
> प्रत्युत्पन्नोऽनागतश्च न स्तस्तत्र पुनर्यदि ।
> प्रत्युत्पन्नोऽनागतश्च स्यातां कथमपेक्ष्य तम् ।
>
> MaKā XIX.1-2
>
> If 'the present' and 'future' exist presupposing 'the past', 'the present' and 'future' will exist in 'the past'.
> If 'the present' and 'future' did not exist there (in 'the past'), how could 'the present' and 'future' exist presupposing 'the past'?
> (Tr. F.J. Streng)

With this argument he refutes the existence of time as an entity. If the *kālavādins* emphasise that time being eternal it does not require anything for it to depend. But Nāgārjuna refutes:

अनपेक्ष्य पुनः सिद्धिर्नातीतं विद्यते तयोः ।
प्रत्युत्पन्नोऽनागतश्च तस्मात्कालो न विद्यते ॥

MaKā XIX.3

Without presupposing 'the past' the two things ('the present' and 'future') cannot be proved to exist. Therefore neither present nor future time exist. (Tr. F.J. Streng)

It is further stated with sound argument that time cannot be postulated to exist as an absolute which is known through subtle time unit (*kṣaṇa*) and others and which is quite distinguished from *kṣaṇa* itself. But this view is not tenable for without taking recourse to *kṣaṇa* any other time cannot be known (*kṣaṇādivyatirekeṇāgṛhyamāṇatvāt*, MaKā under verse XIX.5).

भावं प्रतीत्य कालश्चेत्कालो भावादृते कुतः ।
न च कश्चन भावोऽस्ति कुतः कालो भविष्यति ॥

MaKā XIX.6

If depending on something time is said to exist, how can time exist without a thing?

There is not anything which exists; how, then, will time become (something)? (Tr. F.J. Streng)

The commentator throws light on the above quote saying that the following five are only in names, *saṃvṛtimātram*, relative alone, *vyavahāramātram*, serving only worldly purpose. They are not at all real or absolute. These five are, the past, the future, the ether, *nirvāṇa* and *pudgala*.

As everything, according to Buddhist doctrine, is momentary, it is quite irrelevant for it to accept time as an absolute. Therefore it is said that time is not a reality:

तं तं उपादाय पञ्ञत्तो कालो वोहारमत्तको ।
पुञ्जो फस्सादिधम्मानं समूहो ति विभावितो ।

Aṭhṭhasālinī, p.49

Taking into account every individual activity, time is conceived and it only serves worldly purpose. Just as the aggregate of attributes like touch and others is considered to be a substance.

Therefore emergence, maintenance and dissolution which show themselves as activity are time and nothing else. But time is only conceptual, not real.

"The suddenness of the Awakening contrasts with the length of the Way, the aeonic time that is *now*, and once for all escaped." This is called *ekakṣaṇābhisambodhi* (cf. A.K. Coomaraswamy, Time and Eternity, p.45). This is further developed in Tāntric Buddhism where "the instant or timeless Wakefulness from which generation (the descent of spirit into matter) proceeds is not only the first but also the last moment of the temporal cycle (*kālacakra*) of existence (*saṃsāra*) when consciousness returns to its source; evolution (*utpattikrama*) and involution (*utpannakrama*) representing the two halves of the cycle of existence, whether cosmic or individual." (Ibid. pp. 46-47).

(xii) In the available Jaina ontological literature, the earliest reference to time as an associative of the actuality of the world phenomena is found. In the **Uttarādhyayana-Sūtra** (XXVIII.10), which succinctly states *vattanālakkhaṇo kālo* ... (Skt. *varttanālakṣaṇaḥ kālaḥ*): "Time's intrinsic characteristic is 'change-conducivity"'. This conceptual definition was accepted by Vācaka Aśvasena (5th Cent. A.D.): *kālastu varttanā liṅgam*", "change-conducivity is the distinguishing characteristic of time".

It was, however, Vācaka Umāsvāti who in his **Sabhāṣya Tattvārthādhigama-Sūtra** (c. A.D. 375) enlarged upon the inferences derived from the Āgamic perception of *kāla*; he defined the operational aspect of 'time' as change-conducivity, accidence – consequencing, movement and temporal ordering. This helps to clarify the role (*upakāra*) of 'time'. Umāsvāti defines time:

> अथ कालस्योपकारः क इति ? अत्रोच्यते – वर्तना परिणामः क्रिया परत्वापरत्वे च कालस्य ॥
>
> TaSūBh V.21-22
>
> Now, what is the role of 'time'? It is said: change-conducivity, accidence – consequencing, motion and temporal ordering (constitute the role) of 'time'. (Tr. M.A. Dhaky.)

Apropks of *kāla*, in his second work, the **Praśamaratiprakaraṇa**, Umāsvāti mentions *pariṇāma, varttanā, vidhi* (instead of *kriyā*) and *parāparatva* and identifies them as the inherent properties of *kāla* (*pariṇāmavartanāvidhiparāparatvaguṇalakṣaṇaḥ kālaḥ* - Ibid XIV. 218ab).

Time was thus recognized not only as an 'experiential reality' but also as a potent factor, to the extent of being an auxiliary cause, in bringing about the phenomena and the continual charges in the manifest modes.

There is another view which considers time not as an existentiality but as a 'substance', and hence it is a 'substantiality' though a formless one like space, ether and gravity. For this notion the Āgamas present two distinct views: the first view makes 'time' a conditional substantiality, connected with the internal and external modal changes of other substantialities; in which case, particularly for 'matter', it may imply either that time is matter's 'dimension' or has a 'mass' that is related to the substance of matter. This perception is close enough to the contemporaneous views on 'time' in physics. The second view concerning 'time' tends to make it an unconditional substantiality which, though possessing eternality and singularity, is monodimensional in disposition. This view embraces a concept that time-substance possesses particles – chronosons – which, unlike the material particles, – atoms – do not combine. They pervade the entire material universe. Just as there are 'space-points' so there are 'time-points' and, like the 'spatial extension', there is 'temporal extension' (sensed particularly in relation to matter.) Whether 'time' is atomic (chronotomic) or not, is a debatable point and this aspect of the postulate on 'time' is unknown in the writings of the Northern Jaina teachers, excepting of Hemacandra (c. 2nd-3rd quarter of the 12th cent. A.D.) who apparently had conceded to it.

The Jaina concept of 'time' thus differs from those ancient Indian schools (like Sāṁkhya) which took 'time' as unreal: at the other end of the scale, it also differed from those who advocated its absolute paramountcy, – 'time', according to them, being the causal agent of all happenings, generative or destructive. The Jaina philosophers accepted phenomenic time as 'real' and hence a 'reality'; but its operation, according to their perception, is relegated to an auxiliary status, as an axis of potter's wheel helps turning of the wheel and with it the shaping a vessel, and thus is not the cause of the causality. On 'time' it thus adopts a middle position between the two extreme views, it accepts neither its unreality nor its total supremacy.

Some incidental observations, made more poignantly by the relatively later texts, are that 'time' moves only in a vertical (forward) direction; the 'present' is only a micro-moment which diminishes '1' from infinity which is future and adds '1' to the infinity which is past. The infinitesimal, unanalysable, hence the ultimate unit of 'time' is *samaya* or *addhā*, a sort of chronon as viewed in the Āgamas of the second and third century A.D. The mensurable categories of conventional time (*vyavahāra-kāla*) range from a single moment to the computations leading to mind-boggling megacycles containing transfinite aeons of time. (Based on M.A. Dhaky, "The Concept of 'Time' in Nirgrantha Darśana".)

(xiii) According to Jyotiṣa there exists a close relationship between cosmic and human time. Hence all human actions, but especially ritual, i.e. sacred actions, have to be in harmony with cosmic time. Thus the origin of Jyotiṣa is explained:

वेदा हि यज्ञार्थमभिप्रवृत्ताः
कालानुपूर्वा विहिताश्च यज्ञाः ।
तस्मादिदं कालविधानशास्त्रं
यो ज्योतिषं वेद स वेद यज्ञान् ॥ Vedāṅga-Jyotiṣa 3

> The Veda exists for the purpose of performing sacrifice; sacrifices are prescribed according to the order of the times; thus he who knows astronomy (*jyotiṣa*), which is the science that regulates time, knows the times of sacrifices.

But not only ritual, the whole human life is governed by the idea of finding the 'right time' for everything, which is precisely *kāla* or, more specifically, *muhūrta*. Time of work and time of festival, time of marriage and time of birth and death, all are in correspondence with a cosmic order of things whose science is astrology.

Jyotiṣa speaks of two dimensions of time (1) destruction and (2) reckoning. The reckoning dimension of time is of two categories – gross and subtle, concrete and abstract.

लोकानामन्तकृत्कालः कालोऽन्यः कलनात्मकः ।
स द्विधा स्थूलसूक्ष्मत्वान्मूर्त्तश्चामूर्त्तसंज्ञकः ॥
प्राणादिः कथितो मूर्त्तः त्रुट्याद्योऽमूर्त्तसंज्ञकः ।
षड्भिः प्राणैर्विनाडी स्यात्तत् षष्ठ्या नाडिका स्मृता ॥
नाडी षष्ठ्या तु नाक्षत्रमहोरात्रं प्रकीर्तितम् ।
तत्त्रिंशता भवेन्मासः सावनोऽर्कोदयैः स्मृतः ॥

Sūrya-Siddhānta, madhyamādhikāra I.10-12

Time is the destroyer of the worlds: another Time has for its nature to bring to pass. This latter, according as it is gross or minute, is called by two names, real (*mūrta*) and unreal (*amūrta*). That which begins with respirations (*prāṇa*) is called real; that which begins with atoms (*truṭi*) is called unreal. Six respirations make a *vināḍī*, sixty of these a *nāḍī*; and sixty *nāḍīs* make a sidereal day and night; of thirty of these sidereal days is composed a month; a civil (*sāvana*) month consists of as many sunrises. (Tr. E. Burgess)

The chart of time divisions according to **Sūrya-Siddhānta** will be given in the appendix. The concrete time starts with the minimal unit of breath and the abstract time with *truṭi*.

In the reckoning of time, *yuga* (age) takes an important role as cosmic time. In **Sūrya-Siddhānta** the measurement of Ages is described as follows:

युगस्य दशमो भागः चतुस्त्रिद्व्येकसंगुणः ।
क्रमात्कृतयुगादीनां षष्ठांशः सन्ध्योः स्वकः ॥ Sūrya-Siddhānta I.17

The tenth part of an Age, multiplied successively by four, three, two and one, gives the length of the Golden (*kṛta*) and the other Ages, in order: the sixth part of each belongs to its dawn and twilight. (Tr. E. Burgess)

The entire discussion on the concept of *kāla* may be philosophically summarised and categorised as given below:

(1) *Kāla* as an independent category:

The Nyāya-Vaiśeṣika system treats *kāla* as an independent substance among its nine substances.

The Prabhākara school of Pūrva-Mīmāṃsā is in agreement with the Nyāya-Vaiśeṣika system so far as the number of substances is concerned. The Kumārila School adds two more substances, darkness and sound to the above mentioned nine substances of the Nyāya-Vaiśeṣika system.

The classical Sāṃkhya does not recognise time as an independent category. But Vijñānabhikṣu maintains *prakṛti* itself as eternal and infinite space and time (SāmKāBh p.2-12). Thus we find that in this system absolute space and time are forms of *prakṛti* itself. So far as relative space and time are concerned they are mental conceptions.

The Jaina school treats *kāla* as an independent substance among its five insentient substances.

The concept of *kāla* assumes a very significant position in Buddhism due to its emphasis on the concept of momentariness and action, except in the school of the Madhyamaka which declares Reality beyond the four categories of logic.

(2) *Kāla* as Absolute Reality:

Gauḍapāda has examined different theories of creation in his **Māṇḍūkya-Kārikā** and one of these theories maintains creation out of Time (*kālātprasūtiṃ bhūtānāṃ manyante kālacintakāḥ*, I.8). However, in the following *kārikā* he negates all theories of creationists and provides his own theory of *ajātivāda* or non-origination as the final one. But the very mention of *kāla* as Absolute Reality as conceived by some previous thinkers provides meaning to the subsequent theories where the Absolute Reality has been identified with Viṣṇu, Śiva, Durgā *etc.*, and they in turn have been identified with *kāla* . It is mostly found in the Āgamic traditions of Indian philosophy, where the Absolute Reality is termed as Mahākāla or Akāla, as Kālī, etc. Most of the Āgamic traditions believe in the *kālaśakti* through which the Absolute creates this universe. Their system is a dynamic absolutism. They have to accept the absoluteness of Time along with that of Ultimate Reality whether it is Viṣṇu or Śiva or Śakti.

(3) *Kāla* as appearance:

Gauḍapāda's theory of *ajātivāda* declares everything as appearance or unreal except the →*ātman* which is identical with →*Brahman*. Śaṅkara follows his grand teacher, Gauḍapāda, on the theory of *ajātivāda* and holds *kāla* as unreal.

Summing up, time both as appearance or as a causal dimension is necessarily a process, which dissolves in itself the relative notions of past, present and future, and it is the present which is most significant in all systems of Indian thought.

Classification

Coming to the divisions of time there are two types of classification: (1) based on the relative notion, namely past, present and future (*trikāla*), (2) based on seemingly absolute measure such as *kalpa, manvantara, yuga* etc. And there is a third classification of finite and infinite time, finite time being *kāla* and infinite time being *Mahākāla* or *akāla* as stated earlier.

Different terms for past are *atīta*, past beyond our perception, *bhūta*, lit. 'what has become', the process of becoming having reached the peak, the term *bhūta* also stands for the five elements as well as for departed souls, lying in a state of suspension. The terms for present are *vartamāna* (rotating), *sat* (existence), *pratyutpanna* (just born or produced before the viewer). The terms for future are *bhaviṣyat* or *bhaviṣya* (likely to become), *bhavya* (expected or hoped to become, taking shape), *anāgata* (which has not arrived). These different designations indicate two things: (i) existence is in the present, and past and future are aspects of becoming; (ii) phe immediate is the most important. Thus the present moment is the focal point of all meditations and of all creations. The classifications or divisions according to measurement of time as in Vedic literature, Purāṇas, Dharmaśāstras and Jyotiṣa-Śāstra are given in the appendix. There is some variation in terminologies of the Buddhist and the Jaina systems.

If we take the year as the central point for dividing two *ayanas, māsas, ahorātras, ghaṭikās, kāṣṭhā, muhūrta, pala* etc., and for multiplication into *yuga, manvantara, kalpa, brahmadina, viṣṇudina, rudradina, brahmākṣaradina* and even beyond; a few more Sanskrit words would need elaboration as regards their etymological meaning and cosmic significance. The terms for year are *saṃvatsara* (which is of five kinds – *saṃvatsara, parivatsara, idāvatsara, idvatsara, vatsara). Amongst the synonyms are *hāyana, samā, varṣa, śarada. Vatsara* means the calf of a cow which makes the udder of the cow to brim with milk. This metaphor implies that the time taken by the earth in completing its rotation around the sun from one vernal equinox to the other is like a catalytic agent in drawing out the flow of cosmic energy for the benefit of all beings. The year is thus a continuum of seasonal sacrifices. The completion of that cycle of sacrifices marks the fulfilment of the preceding cycle and the beginning of a new cycle with new hope and new energy. The beginning of the *saṃvatsara* is a great cosmic event and is celebrated as a festivity. The date of celebration varies according to the reckoning of the year. In hoary antiquity the year ended with the autumn. So the year is also called *śarada* and the new year started with the first day of *mārgaśīrṣa* or *agrahāyana* ('the foremost of the year'). The first day according to the lunar calculation is the first day of the bright half of *caitra*. While according to the solar reckoning the first day is the first day of *meṣa* transition (*saṅkrānti*). The word *abda* means that which does not fall off with the fall of leaves. In other words, the year does not die though the cycle of one year has been completed, yet it springs forth as a new existence after the completion of that cycle. The word *varṣa* indicates either the importance of the rainy season in India or it implies the gift showering aspect of the year. Every year brings the shower of new gifts. The word *samā* is equated with Brahma, the bare existence, so that *samā* stands for year as the recurring presence.

The word *māsa* is derived from the root *mā-* 'to measure', 'to traverse'. It also means the moon (the traverser). A month is usually reckoned from the first day of the dark half to the full moon day but there is another reckoning according to which the first day of the bright half is the first day of the month. The months of the Indian calendar are named after the name of the *nakṣatra* which falls on the full moon day of the month. Two months make a *ṛtu* (season) (cf. *dvau hi māsāvṛtuḥ*, ŚBr VII.4.2.29). The word *ṛtu* is derived from *ṛ-*, 'to go', 'to be in perpetual motion'. There are mainly six seasons: *vasanta, grīṣma, varṣā, śarat, hemanta* and *śiśira*. Each month is presided over by one of the *ādityas*, the solar deities. Each season is marked by a change in the weather pattern, life pattern and ritual pattern. This chain of change has fascinated the Indian mind from ancient time in poetry, drama, dance, music, painting or all forms of creative activities, it delineates the cycle of seasons as an integral part of all life and so naturally of human life. The names of *rāgas*, dance forms, lyrical forms and colours have also been formed on the names of seasons.

The word for fortnight (*pakṣa*) means a wing so that every month is conceived like a two-winged bird – one wing is dark and the other bright. A lunar month is +29 days and the solar +30 days. The adjustment between the lunar month and the solar month is made through the insertion of the leave-months after every 35 months, called variously: *adhimāsa, malamāsa, adhikamāsa, puruṣottama-māsa*. There is another month which is stellar and which is completed by the cycle of the 27 lunar *nakṣatras*. The *ahorātra* (day-and-night unit) starts with sunrise while the *tithi* (lunar day) starts with the change in the phase of the moon. The days are named after the planets while the *tithis* are named after the phases of the moon. Each has two names – one numerical and the other mystic. The fifteenth day of the dark fortnight is called *amāvāsyā*, while the fifteenth day of the bright fortnight is called *pūrṇimā* or *pūrṇamāsa*. *Amāvāsyā* is also called *darśa* and *kuhū*, *pūrṇimā* is also called *rākā* and *sinīvālī*. The two basic Vedic rituals performed on the *amāvāsyā* and *pūrṇimā* day are called *darśapūrṇamāsa*.

The *darśa* ritual is symbolic of complete merger of the *somatattva* into *agnitattva*, while the *pūrṇamāsa* ritual is the full blooming of the newly sprung *somatattva* after the *darśa* merger. The word *amāvāsyā* means the cohabitation, the complete consummation of *soma* with *sūrya*.

The division of day and night into *prahara, nāḍikā, ghaṭikā*, and of *ghaṭikā* into further subdivisions is varied but usually accepted nowadays is a day = 16 *ghaṭikās* grouped into 8 *praharas. Ghaṭikā* is divided into 60 *palas* and one *pala* into 60 *vipalas*. There is disagreement on the minimum unit which is more a psychosomatic construct than a physical measurement.

The multiplication of the year varies slightly in the Buddhist and the Jaina theologies but the patterns remain the same. All the Indian systems of thought treat time as a stretched out and yet contractable and dissoluble phenomenon. It is not exactly the return of the same cycle but a coming into action of a similar cycle. The Indian historians had for that reason postulated that after the completion of one *ayana* (aeon) comprising the completion of 27 cycles of the rotation of the vernal equinox, there is a suspension, reversal and going forward motion like that of a pendulum for a brief adjustment as expounded by **Sūrya-Siddhānta**:

> त्रिंशत्कृत्यो युगे भानां चक्रं प्राक्परिलम्बते ।
> तद्गुणाद् भूदिनैर्भक्ताद् द्युगणाद्यदवाप्यते ॥
> तद्दोस्त्रिघ्ना दशाप्तांशा विज्ञेया अयनाभिधाः ।
> तत्संस्कृताद् ग्रहात्क्रान्तिच्छाया चरदलादिकम् ॥
>
> Sūrya-Siddhānta III.9-10
>
> In an Age (*yuga*), the circle of the asterisms (*bha*) falls back eastward thirty score of revolutions. Of the result obtained after multiplying the sum of days (*dyugaṇa*) by this number, and dividing by the number of natural days in an Age,
> Take the part which determines the sine, multiply it by three, and divide by ten; thus are found the degrees called those of the precession (*ayana*). From the longitude of a planet as corrected by these are to be calculated the declination, shadow, ascensional difference (*caradala*), etc. (Tr. E. Burgess)

The rotational cycle of the constellations under this formula is suspended in a pendulum 600 times in one *yuga*. This suspension of macrocosmic Time generates an adjustment in *ayanāṃśa*. An analogus suspension of microcosmic Time is also made possible through the process of contemplation, assuming the basic unity of the micro and the macro levels.

This view has not been accepted by the scientists in the West. But the recent theories of time indicate a change. Stephen W. Hawking in his book, A Brief History of Time has beautifully summarised this: "The laws of science do not distinguish between the forward and backward directions of time. However, there are atleast three arrows of time that do distinguish the past from the future. They are the thermodynamic arrow, the direction of time in which disorder increases; the psychological arrow, the direction of time in which we remember the past and not the future; and the cosmological arrow, the direction of time in which the universe expands rather than contracts" (p.160–161).

Manifestation in the Arts

by P.L. Sharma

The concept of time peculiar to Indian thought and myth has given rise to a theory of aesthetics distinct from that of the Greeks, and it has conditioned the Indian Arts. It is a cyclic notion of time in which the past and the future merge in an ever-new present. What is important is not a linear continuity, but a cycle – circle or spiral – with a still centre and a dynamic periphery. We shall see how this basic approach is manifested in the various art-forms.

In music, time is measured through →*tāla* composed of units of time of variable length, interspersed with variable length of pauses that determines the 'tempo' or speed. *Tāla* is a repetitive or cyclic figure of time-units, whose progression could be visualized as a spiral.

Tāla is concretised though 'action' of the hands which is either sounded or unsounded. The pair of cymbals is an extension of the human hands. Since the hands move in space, four sounded and four unsounded 'actions' were specified in the ancient system according to the movements of hands. These spatial specifications regarding concretisation of time-units in a *tāla*-cycle are a part of *Gandharva*, the ritual music described in **Nāṭya-Śāstra** and prescribed for use in *pūrvaraṅga.* They are no longer followed in current practice, but the hands do have to move in space for concretising the *tāla*-cycle. Hence there is a visual (spatial) component of *tāla*.

Pause or →*laya* is a very important concept in the context of *tāla.* The 'actions' concretising *tāla* are intermittent, incessant action cannot become a measure of time. As the *laya* or pause increases, the speed decreases and as the pause decreases, the speed increases.

Mārga is another allied concept →*tāla.* The concept of *mārga* and *laya* embodies three layers or levels, each progressing in doubles. This corresponds to the world-view where three levels of manifestation are basic. The numbers three and four have a fundamental place in the *tāla* system, and in a way, number five is also basic. Constraints of space forbid detailed treatment.

A musical piece (composed) and a musical performance (composition + improvisation) has a linear time-length which is measured with repetitive *tāla*-cycles. Regularised pauses in between time-units forming the *tāla*, drum-syllables, syllables of the song-text, tones or melodic units, steps of dance etc. create a feeling of pulsation that forms tempo or speed. The function of *tāla* is to bring about harmony (*samatva*) among song, instruments and dance.

There is bound to be a sequence or succession in the performance measured by *tāla* and in the *tāla* itself, within the small and big units of melody, text, dance-steps or movements, etc. The cycle of *tāla* and along with it the cycle of melody, text, dance-movement etc. cuts the total line of performance into cyclic units; each time there is a sense of completion and a 'beginning' and yet there is a continuum. Cycle after cycle revolves around the centre which is either the 'beginning' of the *tāla*-cycle or the point in the cycle where the melody-cum-text-cum-dance-movement 'begins'. This second point of 'beginning' that could coincide with the beginning of the *tāla*-cycle or could be placed at any other unit of that cycle, is known as '*graha*' (lit. catching). It is like a point of entry in a cycle. This '*graha*' or beginning of the melody (*gīta*) or dance has been viewed as past (*atīta*), future (*anāgata*) or present (*sama*), in relation to the 'beginning' of the *tāla*-cycle i.e. whether the melody 'begins' after the *tāla* has 'begun' or before it has 'begun' or simultaneously with the beginning of *tāla* (*sama*). Really speaking, there is no beginning or end in a cycle; but when two cycles meet i.e. one 'enters' the other, then a 'beginning' has to be imagined and that point is the beginning of the time-cycle, in other words, its first unit.

The total linear length of a composition or performance, the cycles forming part of that line, the point of meeting of twofold cycles, the pulsation or speed (fast, medium, slow) – all these temporal structures are constructed in order to bring about an experience of timelessness in the sense of cutting out sequence or succession and establishing the totality of experience that is in time and yet condensed in one total, indivisible 'moment'. 'Measure' is not possible without units that are limiting factors. But limiting is not an end in itself; it aims at transcending limitation or division. Through *tāla* one rides a 'horse' of time that runs on the path of time and the rider (both performer and listener) aims at an experience of the unextended point of time which is Now, of which temporal experience is impossible. In order to reach absolute Time, *tāla* is a path made of relative time; its cyclic conception is conducive to the realisation of the point of time which is "at once the beginning and end of time." Thus time is 'created' in music and it is also dissolved.

So far we have dealt with the organisation of time-measure in music, which is of primary importance as music embodies movement. Another aspect of the role of time in music is the tradition of relating *rāgas* (melodic configurations or melodic matrices) to different parts of the day and night cycle and to different seasons (specially spring and the rainy seasons). Although written evidence of this tradition goes back only to the **Saṅgīta-Ratnākara** (early 13th cent.), its origin could be traced back to the rendering of **Sāma-Veda**, where specific *sāmans* are prescribed for different seasons. The visual counterpart of the seasonal *rāgas* can be found in miniature painting, in the Rāgamālā representations and in painting depicting the seasons (*ṛtu*).

In literature, time is treated in a complex pattern of simultaneity and not in a linear manner. Most narratives, whether in prose or verse, start with *asti*, 'there is', indicating the everpresent event. The best example of complex simultaneity is found in the Purāṇas; in **Rāmāyaṇa** and **Mahābhārata** the pattern is similar but not identical. The co-existence of several pairs of speakers and listeners, the dialogue of each pair extending over a different length of time, could be illustrated by analysing the first two *skandhas* of **Bhāgavata-Purāṇa**. The focus keeps on changing, but at least four pairs are simultaneously constant at any given time. In the subsequent *skandhas* the chain of listeners and speakers becomes more complex and thereby the multiplicity of layers becomes stronger, but the unity is never lost. Sequentiality and simultaneity play, as though, a game of hide and seek.

Presentation of the past, future and present in one strain, in other words, presentation of the past and future as present is common to all the three *viz.* Purāṇa, **Mahābhārata** and **Rāmāyaṇa**. These three classes of texts are not presented here in the chronological order, because Purāṇa embodies the most complex pattern of plurality of timelevels and **Mahābhārata** and **Rāmāyaṇa** come in a descending order in this review of complexity.

In classical Sanskrit literature, Bāṇabhaṭṭa's **Kādambarī** is the best example of multiplicity of time-layers, which is baffling to the outsider. It may be added here that the vast literature of fables, parables and tales in India, both related primarily to moral education and entertainment (although there is no dichotomy between the two objectives) is also steeped in the Purāṇic tradition of narration in a multi-layered pattern of time described above. **Pañcatantra, Hitopadeśa** and the like pertain to the first type and **Kathāsaritsāgara, Bṛhatkathāmañjarī** and the like pertain to the second type. It may also be noted here that the profuse use of direct dialogue in narration at all levels introduces an element of drama.

The following two extracts from A.K. Coomaraswamy are relevant here, for understanding the essence of the 'present' in narration.

"There has thus been clearly established, in the Indian sources, a logical connection of Omniscience, an unbroken Memory of all things, with temporal and spatial omnipresence...., the divine life being uneventful, not in the sense that it knows nothing of what we call events, but in as much as all of the events of what are for us past and future times, are present in it now, and not in a succession." (Selected Papers, Metaphysics, Vol.2, p.60). "Hence indeed is the only seer, hearer, thinker, knower and fructuary in us... and therefore, because of His timeless omnipresence, must be omniscient. Memory is a participation of His awareness who never himself 'remembers' anything, because he never forgets." (Ibid. p.51).

The presentation of 'past' and even 'future' as 'present' in literature discussed above is designed to initiate the listener (reader) into the state of 'now' and eternal 'awareness'. Hence the 'past' and 'future' are effaced into the 'present'; events are so presented that their sequentiality merges into simultaneity and unity. To quote Coomaraswamy again for an explanation of 'now': "....the utterance *fiat lux* and the manifestation *lux erat* by no means imply a temporal succession of events, the utterance (*vyāhṛti*) of names and the appearance of the worlds is simultaneous, and strictly speaking, eternal (that is to say 'now'; that now of which a temporal experience is impossible, being only of a past and a future, and where becoming never stops to be)." (Ibid. p.193)

'*Nāṭya*' (drama, theatre) has been viewed in **Nāṭya-Śāstra** as the retelling of '*bhāvas*' of the entire universe (*trailokyasyāsya sarvasya*) in a glorifying way (*bhāvānukīrtana*). *Nāṭya* has been viewed again, as a '*yajña*' or sacrifice and as '*kriyā*', or action, which may be interpreted as rediscovering of the unity of life through action underlying all mundane, spatial and temporal multiplicity represented in theatre. *Nāṭya* is, therefore, experientially '*rasa*' or attaining of 'bliss' (*ānanda*) and 'repose in one's own self' (*sva-saṃvid-viśrānti*) by transcending time and space. From the point of view of the playwright and performer, it is retelling of the '*bhāvas*' in a glorifying way.

This concept of drama and theatre necessitates the postulation of three dimensions of time that are simultaneously present in theatre.

1) Firstly, the 'cosmic time' in which all multiplicity of creation takes place. In theatre, the multiplicity of the universe has to be retold, rather than being remade or reproduced, in a glorifying way through retelling the '*bhāvas*', which form the basis of universal experience crossing the limitations of our individual experiences in a fragmented and multiple time and space. This 'cosmic time' has been viewed as recreated in the playhouse (*prekṣāgṛha*) and the space of performance. It is also recreated in each performance by invoking the eight presiding 'eities of eight directions, Creator God and other gods and the three worlds etc. in the '*pūrvaraṅga*' or preliminaries of drama. 2) Secondly the time of performance (*prayoga*) in which the director of the play (→*sūtradhāra*) introduces the play and the performance to the spectators, who are present to relish it. This dimension of time is seen in *pūrvaraṅga* as well as *prastāvanā* (the prologue). This time of the performer and the spectator may recur in the course of performance, whenever the *sūtradhāra* chooses to relate the performance with the time of spectators. 3) Thirdly, the inner time of the play itself with all its multiple levels of past, present and future.

Presentation of the 'inner' time of drama by the poet (playwright) and director-producer is prescribed in **Nāṭya-Śāstra** in the following contexts:
(a) Each Act of the play should depict the action of one day.
(b) When an Act ends, then an interlude should be inserted for describing (not presenting) the action of the maximum duration of one year.

The following extracts from **Nāṭya-Śāstra** and Abhinavagupta's commentary will elucidate the above two points. There are two passages dealing with relationship of one day with one Act.

एकदिवसप्रवृत्तं कार्यस्त्वङ्कोऽर्थबीजमधिकृत्य ।
आवश्यककार्याणामविरोधेन प्रयोगेषु ॥

NŚ XVIII.21

अथाङ्कस्य प्रयोगकालपरिमाणमियदिति दर्शयति एकदिवसप्रवृत्तमिति । तादृशमवान्तरेणार्थेन प्रयोजनेन युक्तं बीजमुपायानुष्ठानं वर्णनीयताया अधिकृत्याङ्कः कर्तव्यो यस्य प्रकृष्टं च यद्वृतनं प्रयोगरूपं तदेकदिवसेनेति मुहूर्तपञ्चदशकेनैव, यतस्तावन्तं कालमावश्यकानि भोजनादीनि अशक्य-निरोधनानि ततः परन्तु प्रयोगकालश्चेत् तत्प्रेक्षकप्रयोक्तॄणां तदाप्यावश्यकस्य सन्ध्यावन्दन-भोजनादेरविरोधेनेत्येवं कार्यानेकत्वमेकत्राङ्के निषिद्धम् ।

AbhiBhā on above

Text:

The Act should be 'made' (organised) for covering the seed (core) of *artha* (objective or thing that is sought) operating in 'one day'. (This should be done) without involving any conflict with necessary actions (of life) in performance.

Comm.:

After this (the author) shows that this much is the time of performance of one Act, through the verse beginning with (the words) 'operating in one day'. 'Seed' is that which embodies the '*artha*' or '*prayojana*' (desired object) and the 'effort' or 'means' adopted for achieving the desired end is to be described; that Act has to cover this action and it should be so constructed as to make the performance or excellent behaviour cover only one day i.e. fifteen *muhūrtas* (1 *muhūrta* is equal to 48 minutes), because necessary action of life like taking food cannot be restrained or stopped for that long a period and if the time of performance is more than that (i.e. 12 hours) then also it should be organised without violating or obstructing actions like taking food, doing *sandhyāvandana* etc. on the part of the audience and performers. Thus the abundance of actions in one Act is prohibited.

Two points are notable in the above passage of the commentary: (i) A 'day' is defined as a period of 15 *muhūrtas* (48 minutes x 15 = 720 minutes i.e. 12 hours). (ii) The problem of avoiding obstruction of necessary actions of life like taking food and doing ablutions in the 'junctures' (*sandhyā*) of morning, noon and evening, is raised in the context of the total duration of the performance of an Act.

The above problem raises an important question and that is, – is it the actual duration of performance of an Act under consideration, or is it the duration of actions depicted in an Act which is being discussed? Keeping in view the contemporary model of performance in Kooḍiattam it could be construed that the duration of actual performance of an Act could extend upto twelve hours or so. If this view is accepted, the existence of a performance tradition similar to Kooḍiattam, in the time of Abhinavagupta could be surmised. If the duration of the actions to be depicted is accepted to be under consideration, these necessities are mentioned in the commentary. A balanced view could, perhaps accept both the durations.

ज्ञात्वा दिवसावस्थां क्षणयाममुहूर्तलक्षणोपेताम् ।
विभजेत्सर्वमशेषं पृथक्पृथक्कार्यमङ्केषु ॥

NŚ XVIII.25

एवमितिवृत्तनियममङ्के प्रदर्श्य तदितिवृत्तकालनियमं दर्शयति; क्षणयाममुहूर्त्तानां यानि लक्षणानि कर्त्तव्यान्यस्मिन् क्षणे सन्ध्यानुष्ठेयेत्यादीनि तैरुपेतां दिवसस्यावस्थां ज्ञात्वा सर्वं कार्यं प्रत्येकं सर्वात्मना परिपूर्णरूपमत एवाशेषं विभजेत् विभागेन दर्शयेत् । नाडिकाभिरष्टधा दिनं रात्रिं च विभज्य छायाप्रमाणेन वेति तेन एकदिवससंपादितमुपयोगिचेष्टितमङ्के बध्नीयादिति तात्पर्यम् ।

AbhiBhā on above

Text:

Having known the situation of the day, which is characterised by moment, *yāma* (one-eighth part of the daynight cycle i.e. three hours) and *muhūrta* (48 minute-unit), one should divide the total action into distinctly separate actions in the Acts.

Comm.:

Having shown (prescribed) the organisation of plot in the Acts, the author goes on to show the regulation of time in the plot. After knowing (ascertaining) the situation of the day characterised by moment, *yāma* and *muhūrta* i.e. in a particular moment *sandhyā* is to be performed and so on; the situation of the day has to be known (ascertained) with reference to different actions prescribed for different parts of the day. Each action is complete in itself, hence the totality has to be divided *i.e.* one should present it according to division or in a well-demarcated form. Either the day and night has to be divided as eightfold (in eight *yāmas* or *praharas*) with (water) tubes or with the measure of shadow and with that division one should compose the useful action performed in one day, in the (format of) one Act; this is the purport of the author.

The day (as a unit of time) as depicted in drama is characterised by different human actions normally associated with different parts of the day and the author of a drama text has to keep in view these different situations. One act of drama is prescribed to contain different actions performed in one day, in different parts of the same.

The description of the action of one year is dealt with in the following passage:

> अङ्कच्छेदं कृत्वा मासकृतं वर्षसंचितं वापि ।
> तत्सर्वं कर्तव्यं वर्षादूर्ध्वं न तु कदाचित् ॥
>
> NŚ XVIII.31
>
> ...तस्मादेकवचनान्तेनैव समासः । न च रामायणभारतादिचरितत्याग-प्रसङ्गः। कार्यग्रहणं ह्येतदर्थं मुनिना कृतं, यत्र हि यत्ननिष्पाद्यं सञ्चितं तदेव वर्षं गण्यते वर्षान्तराणि तु तत्र विद्यमानान्यपि अविद्यमानकल्पानि। रामचरिते हि चतुर्दशवर्षाण्यरण्यनिवासो यद्यपि कार्यः, वर्षाणि त्रिचतुराणि भवन्ति यत्र मारीचवधसुग्रीवराज्यदानादि अवान्तरकार्यं संभवति । तस्माद्वर्षादूर्ध्वमित्यनेन कार्यं वर्षद्वयादि निषिध्यत इत्येवं वर्षसहस्रायुषोऽपि वर्षशतान्तरालवृत्तचरितव्याख्यानेऽपि न किञ्चिद् दुष्यति।
>
> AbhiBhā on above
>
> Text:
>
> After ending the Act the action performed during a month or year should be presented (through the interluding sections like *praveśaka* and *viṣkambhaka*), but never should this (presentation) cover more than a year.
>
> Comm.:
>
> The compound related to 'month' and 'year' is to be understood in singular number only. This does not involve the elimination of the story of Rāmāyaṇa and Mahābhārata. With this purpose in view the *muni* (author) has included the word 'action'; that year is counted as a year where the achievement through effort is contained (lit. deposited), other years are almost non-existent, although they might 'exist'. In the story of Rāma, although residence in the forest for fourteen years is to be presented, yet there are only three or four years where 'action' like the killing of Mārīca, the gift of kingdom to Sugrīva comes into being. Hence the prescription 'beyond a year' prohibits the presentation of action extending to two years or more. Thus there is nothing wrong in presenting the action in the story of a person having a life-span of thousand years, with actions separated by a hundred years.

The concept of time in drama is presented in this passage. The Act in drama is prescribed to cover action of 'one day'. When action covering a longer period, say a month or a year, is to be depicted, the act should be ended and an interluding section like *praveśaka* should be inserted in order to present this action through narration (in dialogue), rather than through direct presentation. The time-span of this 'action' so represented should not be more than one year. Abhinava discusses the implication of this prescription. He says that 'year' is not just the calendar year, but the period corresponding to a calendar year, in which some special 'effort' is depicted. Thus the problem posed by long stories like **Rāmāyaṇa** and **Mahābhārata** is solved, because the 'years' containing special effort are not many, and one interlude could cover the action performed in one month or one year. There could be many months and years in the story that would not be marked by any 'action' depicting special 'effort'.

Thus different dimensions of time operate in Sanskrit drama and tradition of Indian theatre simultaneously. The experience in theatre is that of sequentiality in the time of the performer and the spectator on the one hand and the sequentiality in the inner time of the play on the other. But ultimately it is the experience of transcending all multiplicity of time and space and attaining indivisible, unlimited, blissful and free self, beyond all sequentiality and simultaneity, although temporarily i.e. as long as we are able to witness the drama (*vibhāvādijīvitāvadhi*). In this respect theatre experience is different from *brahmāsvāda* or relishing the state of identity with *Brahman*, which is not a temporary phenomenon.

Sanskrit theatre was able to discover a theatrical device to solve the problem of presenting the multiple levels of past, present and future of the inner time of a play simultaneously. This device is known as *nāṭyāyita* or drama within drama and *dhruva* songs included in the *sāmānyābhinaya* or the general and harmonious aspect of *abhinaya*. Sanskrit playwrights have freely used this device in their plays.

In sculpture and painting the image is a static creation insofar as it embodies only one moment of 'action' or movement and time cannot be perceived without movement. But this seemingly static nature of an image is yet full of dynamism. One of the ways of expressing the dynamic nature of a divine being is its representation with multiple arms and heads. The many-armed images express movement, sequence of actions and the powerful nature of the God. Here again it is the simultaneity of divine actions which is manifested in a single image.

The clearest example is the image of Śiva Naṭarāja which shows all the five acts of Śiva in one image: creation, preservation, destruction, veiling and liberation. This is described in a Tamil source quoted by A.K. Coomaraswamy: "O my Lord. Thy hand holding the sacred drum has made and ordered the heavens and earth and other worlds and innumerable souls. Thy lifted hand protects both the conscious and unconscious order of creation. All these worlds are transformed by thy hand bearing fire. Thy sacred foot, planted on the ground, gives an abode to the tired soul struggling in the toils of causality. It is thy lifted foot that grants eternal bliss to those that approach thee. These five actions are indeed thy handiwork." (Cidambara Mummani Kovai, quoted in A.K. Coomaraswamy, The Dance of Śiva, p. 71). Coomaraswamy's interpretation brings out the simultaneous representation of time and eternity: "If we would reconcile Time with Eternity, we can scarcely do so otherwise than by the conception of alternations of phase extending over vast regions of space and great tracts of time. Especially significant, then, is the phase alternation implied by the drum, and the fire which 'changes', not destroys. These are but visual symbols of the theory of the day and night of Brahmā...." (Ibid. p.78).

However, there is a more hidden temporal dimension of sacred images which can be revealed by analysing their composition in terms of dynamic stresses and rhythmic structure. The following extracts related to Alice Boner's analysis of 'time-division' in sculpture will illustrate this point.

"The analysis of composition accounts for the two basic factors, space and time, by two different methods: the space-division or measure consists essentially of a net of vertical and horizontal lines which fix the space, the position and the proportions of the formelements. The time-analysis or the movement-rhythm is based specially on the diagonals and all the oblique axes of the central circle, as well as their parallels, since the dynamics of a figure or a group of forms always expresses itself in the oblique lines, whereas the statics is based on the verticals or the horizontals." (Bettina Bäumer in: Alice Boner: Artist and Scholar, p.71)

The following extract from a letter of Paul Mus addressed to Alice Boner also throws light on time in sculpture in the context of divine images:

"The diagram of time, in my view, is above all a diagram of transition into action. Time is the means by which the action operates for the devotee starting with the total structure of the image and putting together certain of its spatial components. The concern is not with time, it is rather the contact of the divine image with the heart of the devotee, whereas this image will be reflected and projected back into this same image. Such is the double movement effected by the figurative *yantra* in these circumstantial details. Time becomes a factor only because it is in time that a devotee goes to the temple. He brings his time with him. It is this time belonging to him which reflects itself and reverberates in the movement of the images which 'come' towards him through the obliques and the chords which you have so well discerned. These are the ways, the progressions, the gliding bars of this movement. It will, however, slide towards the devotee without shaking the immovable and perpetual spatial structure which is the god's. Let us say – the space-diagram is the essence of a god; the time-diagram is the function of a god." (Ibid.)

All this holds good of the image in the *sanctum sanctorum* of a temple as well as relief panels in cave temples meant for meditation. But the panels on the outer walls deal with sequential time or phenomenon and are hence called *līlāvigraha*, 'playful images'. Thus the 'ephemeral' on the outside of the temple leads to the 'eternal' in the interior.

In painting what is again striking is the simultaneity of events, e.g. the different events of the life of Kṛṣṇa in a single miniature, as in the early reliefs the story of Buddha is narrated in a single panel.

We have already mentioned the depiction of time as the seasons, the twelve months, the times of the day as well as festivals in painting. Here again, it is cyclic time which is depicted, not a unique event of the past.

Let us now proceed to show the different ways how time has been symbolized in Indian Art and literature. A racing horse, a coiled thousand-hooded serpent (Śeṣanāga or Ananta = the Infinite), a rotating twenty-four spoked wheel, a vessel filled with water (the unmanifest creature), a hand-drum being beaten by Śiva during his Cosmic Dance, a *sudarśana* disc in the hand of Viṣṇu, a circular *maṇḍala*, these are some of the main symbolic representations of *kāla*. Indian myth has two distinct foci: one is the Sun, the prime merger and generator of finite time, with whom Viṣṇu, the sustainer, Buddha, the awakened one and Mahāvīra, the wanderer, are equated; the other, the unmanifest Infinite Time (the merger of all processes) is represented by the figures of *Mahākāla*, Kālī, River, Ocean, *Ananta*, *Śeṣanāga* or *Dharma-cakra*, the *Nāga* and the *Śiśumāra* figure (described in the **Bhāgavata Purāṇa**). This second aspect of *kāla* is destructive only in appearance, it is essentially a precondition of creation; so that Mahākāla and Śiva are identical, *kāla* and Viṣṇu (according to **Bhagavad-Gītā**) are identical, Kālī and *yogamāyā* (the creative energy) are identical and *mātra vindu* (the ultimate drop) and *mahālaya* (the ultimate merger) are identical. Creation presupposes annihilation or transcendence over Time. Immortality (*amṛta*) presupposes crossing the stream of Death (passing through Time).

Let us now take some illustrations. A figure of Viṣṇu lying on the body of Ananta (Śeṣa) visualises transcendence over time and conception of the creation in primordial dream. This conception includes in itself both the creation and the creator.

The figure of Kālī (the female counterpart of Mahākāla Śiva) is seen mounted on Śiva as corpse. In other words, she is condensed consciousness, holding in one hand a blood vessel and in the other a head (*muṇḍa*) symbolising human ego and wearing a garland of human skulls. Here Kālī is personified Time, Time as absorber of limitation (*kālasaṃkarṣiṇī*), Time as beyond time.

The *kālacakra* or the wheel of existence in Buddhism marks twelvefold cycles of existence (→*cakra*). The wheel of life in Buddhist art, particularly in

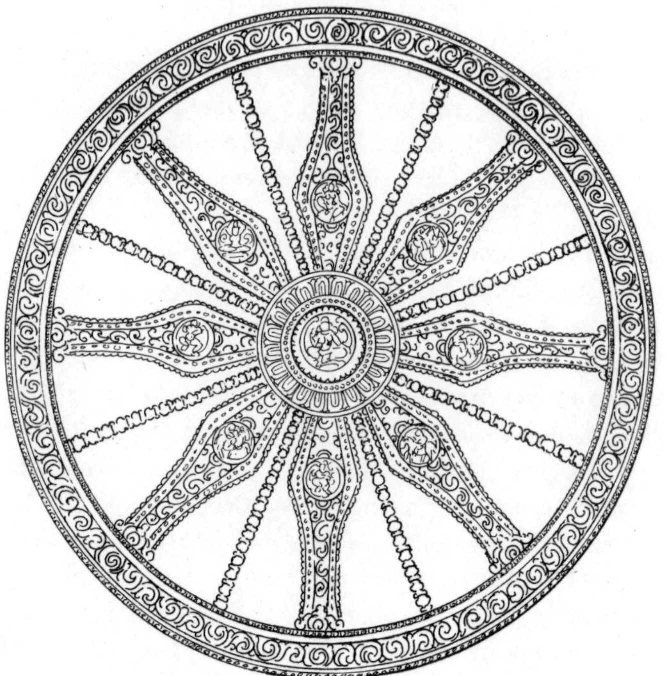

Figure 3: Wheel of the Sun-Temple at Koṇārka

Vajrayāna, depicts a cyclic process of existence. In other words time as flux – the upper sector in the realm of gods, dedicated to aesthetic nature. But there is a limitation of their existence and they sink again into the lower existence when their moral merits are exhausted. The lower sector of the wheel shows the realm of inferno (*niraya*). Here *kāla* as Dharmarāja or as Amitābha appears with the mirror of knowledge. Both these aspects benign and fierce are not opposites there, but complementary.

The chariot wheels in Koṇārka temple show cosmic time as movement and time as a great eraser of pain and pleasure. The whole temple is a metaphor of Time frozen in stone.

There is a poetic description of the Infinite subsuming within itself both time and space in **Bhāgavata Purāṇa**(V.23) as a Śiśumāra (as a great dolphin). It is of the nature of a light, quite as a dolphin, the polar star *dhruva* being the point of its tail, the creators, Agni, Indra and Dharma form its tail, Dhātā and Vidhātā the root of the tail. The seven sages make the girdle of the breast. The right fold of the coil is *uttarāyaṇa* and the right side are the constellations of the northern sky. The southern fold and the southern side present *dakṣiṇāyana* and the constellations of the southern sky. The whole body has symmetrically balanced right and left paths. The milky way forms the belly, *punarvasu* and *puṣya* form the two sides of the hip. By the 27 *nakṣatras* are formed the various limbs of the nine planets – Mars in the mouth, Saturn in the genitals, Jupiter in the hump, the Sun on the chest, the Moon in the mind, Venus in the navel, Mercury in the breath, Rāhu in the throat and Ketu spread over the entire body. Nārāyaṇa is in the heart, the twin gods Aśvins in the breast and the other stars are in all the pores of the body.

This picture of cosmic time and space unity is the picture of unknown supreme reality revealing itself through its unfolding, its potential of *līlā*. It is frenzied action of creation, of sacrifice, of love, or of *samādhi*, frenzied movement which deems the moment of the momentlessness, the great moment. *Mahārāsa* of Śrī Kṛṣṇa is one such moment but the most unique one. It is not mere coincidence that the word *kṣaṇa* in Sanskrit means moment as well as joy or release.

A reference to the role of time in ritual (both Vedic and Āgamic), festivals, spiritual culture (*sādhanā*), charity etc., will be relevant.

In temple ritual, there are various *pūjās* to be performed during different parts of the day with some differences among the various schools, different festivals round the year, e.g. *rathayātrā, snānayātrā, candana-yātrā* etc., some events prescribed after every twelve years e.g. the change of the 'body' of the images in the Jagannātha temple at Puri, or the Kumbha Melā.

In the Vaiṣṇava cult, specially among the Gauḍīya Vaiṣṇavas (Bengal school founded by Caitanya), the contemplation of divine sports (*līlās*) according to eight *praharas* (units of three hours each) is prescribed. Special worship, *japa* (almost silent chanting of a *mantra*), *vrata* (fasting and other vows) etc. are prescribed in *Navarātra* (unit of nine days) falling twice a year in *vasanta* (spring) and *śarat* (fall) and also in the months of *Māgha, Vaiśākha* and *Kārtika*. The full moon and the darkest day of the lunar calendar, as well as *ekādaśī* (eleventh day) and monthly *saṅkrānti* (lit. transition) of the solar calendar; all these are considered very important for *vrata, dāna* (alms giving), *snāna* (holy dip) etc. The solar and lunar eclipses are also special occasions for the above activities.

The 'creation' of an image for special worship for a specific period of time and then the *visarjana* (immersion) of that image i.e. dissolution of that time is embodied in the tradition of *Durgā-pūjā* and *Gaṇapati-pūjā*.

Thus right from Vedic to Āgamic ritual to common festivals of the people, the 'creation' and 'dissolution' of time and an integral view of the time-cycle in nature forming part of cosmic time as related to harvest of different grains, fruits and the like, as well as to milch and draught animals is uniformly reflected. Thus there is a striking unity of basic approach in the festivals observed at various levels.

Conclusion

The symbol of *Śiśumāra* gives a bird's eye view of the Indian perception of time on the one hand and on the other goes back to the first moment of creation, the moment of coming into action. It goes on to integrate the entire transhistorical passage of time coming to the instantaneous moment marking every cosmic position not merely in terms of the position of the solar planet but also in terms of their relation to the positions of stars going upto the galaxies. This attempts at striking a balance between time beyond and time within, at internalising all time in the control of breath in yoga (communion of the macrocosm within the microcosm) and at externalising the seemingly rhythmic recurrent time into either the ritual space or the theatrical space. All this attempt is towards integration through dissection.

Human creativity has for its substratum a perpetual tension between eternal and temporal. The creator experiences every limitation, spatial, temporal or cognitional, painful and cumulative. Therefore such a situation throws a challenge to him to transcend this limitation. The Buddhist way denies the existence of the patient or experiencer through the theory of *anātmavāda.* The other way out is enlargement and expansion of the limited experiencer and ultimate realization of oneness with *Brahman.* Any act of creation in art, literature, music, dance, has for its starting point a denial of the permanent or a denial of the limitation. *Kāla* or time is one such limitation, and yet all art takes place in time and transforms time.

Space as the other creative act is on one hand an act of piercing through what is here and now and on the other is a suspension of here and now through the creation of a more real and a more essential here and now, in other words through the creation of aesthetic time and space. So that in the words of Kabir *amṛta* or immortality has to be obtained by pressing time in one's fist (*kāla niccorike amṛt pīve*).

The Indian preoccupation with minute details of subtle time on one hand and its aiming at immeasurable unmanifest infinite on the other, are not two opposites, they are complementary to each other. This explains the rejection of the historical method for comprehending reality. This also explains why historical records have been continuously transferred into mythological legends or in other words into 'a myth of eternal return'. The usefulness of linear time has not been totally rejected, it has only been marginalised. For the present, it would suffice to conclude that a sharp and pointed perception of the present is made possible through recollection of the All and its merger in a transcendental peak.

Vidya Niwas Misra

Appendix: Divisions of Time

by S. Chattopadhyay

In Vedic literature we find the beginnings of divisions of time. We can derive some divisions of real time (*mūrtakāla*) from the Vedic verses (*cf.* ṚV I.164.48). According to the **Ṛgveda** the smallest unit of time is *ahorātra*, consisting of a unit of day and night. The year (*saṃvatsara*) consisting of 360 days and nights, the divisions of time are as follows:

30 *ahorātras* (days and nights) = 1 *māsa* (month) (*cf.* ṚV I.25.8)
4 = 1 *ṛtu* (season) (ṚV X.18.5)
3 *ṛtus* or 12 *māsas* = 1 *saṃvatsara* (year) (ṚV X.190.2)

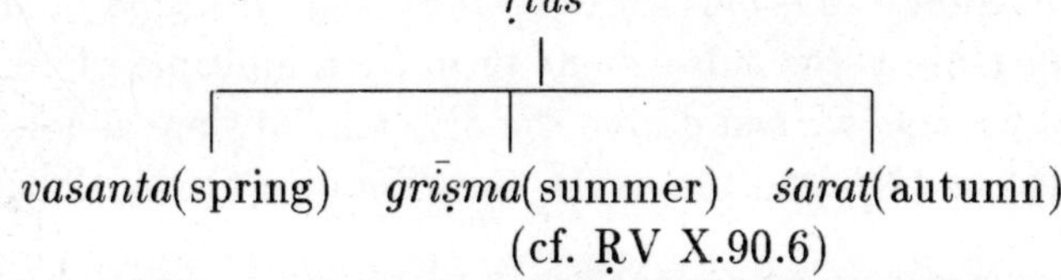

(cf. ṚV X.90.6)

In the **Yajur-Veda** the divisions of time are further differentiated. Here we find *uṣās*, the time of dawn, the starting point of one *ahorātra* (a day and a night), which is the smallest unit consisting of 48 minutes (*uṣāmuhūrta*). Hence the divisions of time are as follows:

30 *uṣās* = 1 *ahorātra* (a day and a night)
15 *ahorātras* = 1 *ardhamāsa* (half-month)
2 *ardhamāsas* = 1 *māsa* (month)
2 *māsas* = 1 *ṛtu* (season)
6 *ṛtus* = 1 *saṃvatsara* (cycle of year)
2 *saṃvatsaras* = 1 *parivatsara* (second year of cycle)
3 *saṃvatsaras* = 1 *idāvatsara* (third year of cycle)
4 *saṃvatsaras* = 1 *idvatsara* (fourth year of cycle)
5 *saṃvatsaras* = 1 *vatsara* (fifth year of cycle)

(cf. YV XXVII.45, XXII.28)

The **Atharva-Veda** equally takes *ahorātra* as the smallest unit.

15 *ahorātras* (day and night) = 1 *ardhamāsa* (half month)
2 *ardhamāsas* = 1 *māsa* (month)
2 *māsas* = 1 *ṛtu* (season)
3 *ṛtus* = 1 *ayana* (half year)
6 *ṛtus* or 2 *ayanas* = 1 *saṃvatsara* (year) (cf. AV XV.6.18)

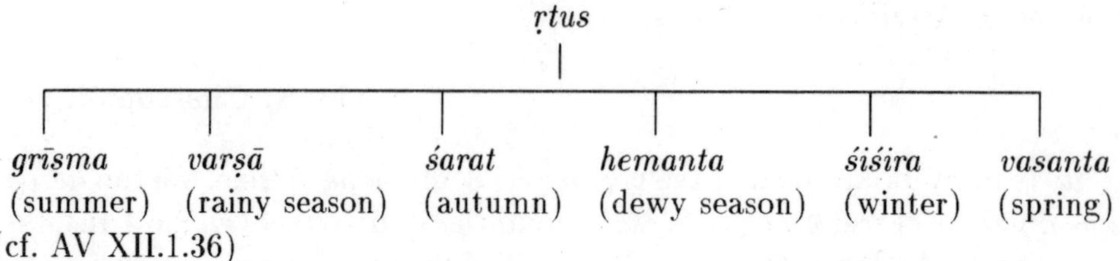

(cf. AV XII.1.36)

The Brāhmaṇa literature brings a development in reckoning time. In the **Śatapatha-Brāhmaṇa** we find a detailed description of divisions of time, including subtle time, in the context of explaining *saṃvatsara* (XII.3.2.1-5). *Saṃvatsara* as 1 year = 6 seasons, or 12 months, or 13 months, or 24 half months, or 720 days or nights, or 360 *ahorātra*s (a day and a night), or 10,800 *muhūrta*s and its subtle divisions *kṣipra, etarhi, idāni, prāṇa* or *nimeṣa* as the smallest unit, increasing the subsequent term by a multiple of 15 respectively. From the above passage we can derive the divisions of time as follows (we have made an attempt to calculate the exact duration of each division):

1 *prāṇa* or *nimeṣa* = 0.0568889 second approx.
15 *prāṇas* or *nimeṣas* = 1 *idāni* (0.8533333 second approx.)
15 *idānis* = 1 *etarhi* (12.8 seconds)
15 *etarhis* = 1 *kṣipra* (3.2 minutes or 192 seconds)
15 *kṣipras* = 1 *muhūrta* (48 minutes)
30 *muhūrtas* = 1 *ahorātra* (a day and a night)
15 *ahorātras* = 1 *ardhamāsa* (half month)
2 *ardhamāsas* = 1 *māsa* (month)
2 *māsas* = 1 *ṛtu* (season) (cf. ŚBr VII.4.2.29)

[Sometimes 4 *māsas* = 1 *ṛtu* (cf. ŚBr X.2.6.1-2) or 2 months and 12 days = 1 *ṛtu* (cf. ŚBr. I.2.5.12-13)]

6 *ṛtus* = 1 *saṃvatsara* (year of cycle)
2 *saṃvatsaras* = 1 *parivatsara* (second year of cycle)
3 *saṃvatsaras* = 1 *idāvatsara* (third year of cycle)
4 *saṃvatsaras* = 1 *idvatsara* (fourth year of cycle)
5 *saṃvatsaras* = 1 *vatsara* (fifth year of cycle) (cf. ŚBr VIII.1.4.8)

In the **Aitareya-Brāhmaṇa** (VII.15) we find the earliest reference to the divisions of *yuga*, a mythical aeon.

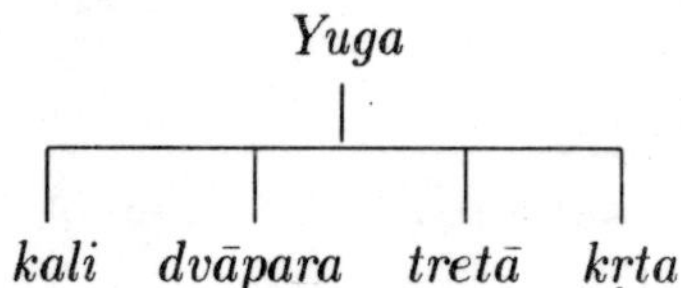

In **Śāṅkhāyana-Āraṇyaka** (VII.20) we find that *sthiti* (stasis) or the present time consists of a union of *gati* (movement) or the past time and *nivṛtti* (cessation) or the future time. The present time, combining past and future, unites the divisions of time. Every entity when it comes into being has to pass through a temporal movement (*gati*) which is also a subtle moment. Similarly after *sthiti* that entity moves towards a cessation which is also a subtle time unit. It is also supported by Vaiśeṣika thinkers that every entity should have its duration for three *kṣaṇas* and that three *kṣaṇas* are the time unit signified by the term *sthiti*, under which various divisions of time are united, taking *dhvaṃsi* as the smallest unit of time. Here we find the name of various divisions of time in proper order, without mentioning the exact measurement.

If *dhvaṃsi* is taken as the smallest unit, being $\frac{1}{100}$th part of a *muhūrta*, the divisions of time with measurement are as follows:

1 *dhvaṃsi* = 28.8 seconds
2 *dhvaṃsis* = 1 *nimeṣa* (57.6 seconds)
2 *nimeṣas* = 1 *kāṣṭhā* (115.2 seconds)
$2\frac{1}{2}$ *kāṣṭhās* = 1 *kalā* (288 seconds or 4.8 minutes)
5 *kalās* = 1 *kṣaṇa* (24 minutes)
2 *kṣaṇas* = 1 *muhūrta* (48 minutes)
30 *muhūrtas* = 1 *ahorātra* (day and night)
15 *ahorātras* = 1 *ardhamāsa* (half month)
2 *ardhamāsas* = 1 *māsa* (month)
2 *māsas* = 1 *ṛtu* (season)
6 *ṛtus* = 1 *saṃvatsara* (year)

The **Manu-Smṛti** (I.64-71) describes the divisions of time in the following order. Here we can assume the exact time of a *nimeṣa* according to the chart:

1 *nimeṣa* (twinkling of the eye) = 0.1777778 second
18 *nimeṣas* = 1 *kāṣṭhā* (3.2 seconds)
30 *kāṣṭhās* = 1 *kalā* (1.6 minutes or 96 seconds)
30 *kalās* = 1 *muhūrta* (48 minutes)
30 *muhūrtas* = 1 *ahorātra* (day and night)
15 *ahorātras* = 1 *pakṣa* (fortnight)
2 *pakṣas* = 1 *māsa* (month)
12 *māsas* = 1 *varṣa* (year)

Other divisions upto *caturyuga* are the same as in **Sūrya-Siddhānta** (see below).

Kauṭilya in his **Arthaśāstra** (II.20.29-64) gives a detailed analysis of the divisions of time, taking *tuṭa* as the smallest unit. From his explanation we can calculate the exact duration of the smallest unit *tuṭa*. The chart is as follows:

1 *tuṭa* = 0.06 second
2 *tuṭas* = 1 *lava* (0.12 second)
2 *lavas* = 1 *nimeṣa* (0.24 second)
5 *nimeṣas* = 1 *kāṣṭhā* (1.2 seconds)
30 *kāṣṭhās* = 1 *kalā* (0.6 minute or 36 seconds)
40 *kalās* = 1 *nālikā* (24 minutes)
2 *nālikās* = 1 *muhūrta* (48 minutes)
15 *muhūrtas* = 1 *divasa* (day) or *rātri* (night)
30 *muhūrtas* = 1 *ahorātra* (a day and a night)
15 *ahorātras* = 1 *pakṣa* (fortnight)
2 *pakṣas* = 1 *māsa* (solar month $30\frac{1}{2}$ days and lunar month $29\frac{1}{2}$ days)
2 *māsas* = 1 *ṛtu* (season)
3 *ṛtus* = 1 *ayana* (half year)
2 *ayanas* = 1 *saṃvatsara* (year)
5 *saṃvatsaras* = 1 *yuga* (age)

In the Purāṇas we find a further development of the divisions of time. The **Viṣṇu-Purāṇa** takes *nimeṣa* as the smallest unit whereas **Bhāgavata-Purāṇa** and **Brahma-Vaivarta-Purāṇa** accept *paramāṇu* as the starting unit in reckoning time.

Viṣṇu-Purāṇa (I.3):

1 *nimeṣa* = 0.2133333 second
15 *nimeṣas* = 1 *kāṣṭhā* (3.2 seconds)
30 *kāṣṭhās* = 1 *kalā* (1.6 minutes or 96 seconds)
30 *kalās* = 1 *muhūrta* (48 minutes)
30 *muhūrtas* = 1 *ahorātra* (day and night)
30 *ahorātras* = 1 *māsa* (month)
6 *māsas* = 1 *ayana* (half year) (the period of the sun's progress north or south of the ecliptic)
2 *ayanas* = 1 *varṣa* (year) or 1 *divya ahorātra* (divine day and night)
12,000 divine years = 1 *caturyuga* (4 *yugas*)

Bhāgavata-Purāṇa (III.11.5-15) and **Brahma-Vaivarta-Purāṇa:**

1 *paramāṇu* = 0.0000264 second approx.
2 *paramāṇus* = 1 *aṇu* (0.0000527 second approx.)
3 *aṇus* = 1 *trasareṇu* (0.000158 second approx.)
3 *trasareṇus* = 1 *truṭi* (0.0004741 second approx.)
100 *truṭis* = 1 *vedha* (0.0474074 second)
3 *vedhas* = 1 *lava* (0.1422222 second)

3 *lavas* = 1 *nimeṣa* (0.4266667 second)
3 *nimeṣas* = 1 *kṣaṇa* (1.28 seconds)
5 *kṣaṇas* = 1 *kāṣṭhā* (6.4 seconds)
15 *kāṣṭhās* = 1 *laghu* (1.6 minutes or 96 seconds)
15 *laghus* = 1 *nāḍikā* (24 minutes)
2 *nāḍikās* = 1 *muhūrta* (48 minutes)
6 or 7 *nāḍikās* = 1 *yāma* or *prahara* (144 minutes or 168 minutes).

In astronomical texts (Jyotiṣa) we find a vivid picture of the divisions of time. The **Sūrya-Siddhānta** (I.10-21) differentiates *kāla* (time) primarily in two forms (i) *mūrtakāla* (real time) and (ii) *amūrtakāla* (unreal time), taking *prāṇa* (4 seconds) and *truṭi* (atom) as the smallest units respectively, whereas Bhāskara II in his **Siddhānta-Śiromaṇi** (I.19.20) details the unreal time from some different measurement, taking *truṭi* as the smallest unit. The chart is as follows:

Divisions of time in Jyotiṣa
(**Sūrya-Siddhānta** I.10-21)

Kāla

Real Time (*mūrta kāla*)		Unreal or Abstract Time (*amūrta kāla*)	
1	*vipala* = 0.4 second	1	*truṭi* (atom) = time taken by a needle in piercing a single petal of lotus
10	*vipalas* = 1 *prāṇa* (4 seconds)	1	*reṇu*= 60 *truṭis*
6	*prāṇas* = 1 *pala*	1	*lava* = 60 *reṇus*
	or = or	1	*līkṣaka*= 60 *lavas*
60	*vipalas* = 1 *vināḍī* (24 seconds)	1	*prāṇa* = 60 *līkṣakas*
60	*palas* or *vināḍīs* = 1 *nāḍī* (*ghaṭikā*) (24 minutes)	6	*līkṣakas* = 1 *vipala* (0.4 second)
60	*nāḍīs* = 1 *ahorātra*		
(2.5	*nāḍīs* = 1 hour)		
30	*ahorātras* = 1 *māsa*		
12	*māsas* = 1 *varṣa* or 1 day of the gods		
360	days of the gods = 1 divine year		
12,000	divine years = 1 *caturyuga* (quadruple Age)		
	or = or		
4,320,000	solar years = 1 *mahāyuga* (Great Age)		

The composition of the *caturyuga* (quadruple Age) or *mahāyuga* (Great Age) is as follows:

	divine years	solar years
Dawn	400	144,000
Golden Age (*kṛta yuga*)	4,000	1,440,000
Twihight	400	144,000
Total duration of the Golden Age	4,800	1,728,000
Dawn	300	108,000
Silver Age (*tretā yuga*)	3,000	1,080,000
Twilight	300	108,000
Total duration of the Silver Age	3,600	1,296,000
Dawn	200	72,000
Brazen Age (*dvāpara yuga*)	2,000	720,000
Twilight	200	72,000
Total duration of the Brazen Age	2,400	864,000
Dawn	100	36,000
Iron Age (*kali yuga*)	1,000	360,000
Twilight	100	36,000
Total duration of the Iron Age	1,200	432,000

So the total duration of a Great Age = 4,800 + 3,600 + 2,400 + 1,200 = 12,000 divine years or 1,728,000 + 1,296,000 + 864,000 + 432,000 = 4,320,000 solar years. 71 *caturyugas* + a twilight equal to *kṛta yuga* = 1 *manvantara*
14 *manvantaras* + a twilight equal to *kṛta yuga* = 1 *kalpa.*
So 1 *manvantara* = 71 x 12,000 + 4,800 (a twilight equal to *kṛta yuga*) = 852,000 + 4,800 = 856,800 divine years or 1 *manvantara* = 71 x 4,320,000 +1,728,000 (a twilight equal to *kṛta yuga*) = 306,720,000 + 1,728,000 = 308,448,000 solar

1 *kalpa* = 14 *manvantaras* + 4,800 (a twilight equal to *kṛta yuga*) = 14 x 856,800 + 4,800 = 11,995,200 + 4,800 = 12,000,000 Divine years or 1 *kalpa* = 14 *manvantaras* + 1,728,000 (a twilight equal to *kṛta yuga*) = 14 x 308,448,000 + 1,728,000 = 4,318,272,000 + 1,728,000 = 4,320,000,000 solar years.

Division of unreal time in Bhāskara's **Siddhānta-Śiromaṇi** (I.19.20):

1 *truṭi* = 0.0000296 second
100 *truṭis* (atoms) = 1 *tatpara* (0.002963 second)
30 *tatparas* = 1 *nimeṣa* (0.0888888 second)
18 *nimeṣas* = 1 *kāṣṭhā* (1.6 seconds)
30 *kāṣṭhās* = 1 *kalā* (48 seconds)
30 *kalās* = 1 *ghaṭikā* (or 24 minutes)
2 *ghaṭikās* = 1 *kṣaṇa* (48 minutes)
30 *kṣaṇas* = 1 *ahorātra*.

Time in Buddhism

by G.C. Pande

Buddhist discussions on time began in the context of the religious quest of transcendence and in course of time moved on to metaphysical, logical and dialectical issues. They also had to reckon with the cosmological context of time which had a strong earlier tradition.

The Buddhists adopted the concept of a cosmic cycle along with the ideas of *karman* and *saṃsāra*. The ancient **Aggañña-suttanta** mentions the *saṃvaṭṭa-vivaṭṭa* of the world (→*loka*), i.e., its evolution after involution. The interval of time from creation to dissolution was called *kalpa* which is a common designation in Brahmanical and Buddhist literature of the classical age and appears to have been drawn from astronomical literature. The Buddhists distinguished between several kinds of *kalpas*. The *saṃvarta-kalpa* was the time taken in dissolution which begins when *naraka* or purgatory begins to be depleted of its denizens and is completed when the world-receptacle or *bhājana* is destroyed after the force of collective *karman* responsible for creation has been exhausted (*ākṣepake karmaṇi parikṣīṇe*). Empty space or *ākāśa* then remains of the material world. The time of creation is *vivarta-kalpa* which begins when matter characterized by motion (*vāyu*) begins to function. Cosmic time is cyclical, well-ordered and vast. In its determination and regulation the leading part is played by the working of moral law – *karman* and *vipāka-phala*, not by the mere mechanics of motion or merely physical causality (*sabhāgahetu* and *niṣyanda-phala*). Although motion is regarded as an inherent characteristic of matter in space, what regulates it in the context of cosmic evolution and dissolution is a mental force, the will (*cetanā*) which is the essence of *karman* and leads to *vipāka*.

However, cosmic time or the *mahākāla* of popular usage, is a merely conventional concept which is relevant only when we regard composite things enduring for some time as real entities. But all material objects are really compounded of atoms and all motion is ultimately reducible to atomic motion. Now the time which an atom takes to move the least distance is called a moment or →*kṣaṇa* which could be conceived as the limit towards which ever-shorter intervals of time tend (*adhvaparyanta*) i.e. as infinitesimal time. It has also been defined as the time taken in the production of a phenomenon (*dharma*) when all its causal conditions (*pratyayas*) have been completed. Both of these definitions were of the Sautrāntikas. The Vaibhāṣikas defined *kṣaṇa* as the marginal time in the production of an effect. As a unit of measuring time *kṣaṇa* was only an ideal supposition like *paramāṇu*. The fact is that in ancient science the actually used practical units for the measurement of time were different from the many extremely subtle units culminating in *kṣaṇa* which find mention.

The Antinomy of Time

It will be seen that the Buddhist views on physical and cosmological time are mostly neither original nor profound. In this respect they are in sharp contrast to the ingenuity of the Jaina views. In fact, it is certain that such views were no part of original Buddhism. They found their way into Buddhist tradition from the mythological milieu in which it developed. The cosmology of the **Aggañña-sutta** really relies on current views such as are referred to in the **Brahmajāla-sutta**. Buddha, on his part, clearly regarded speculations about their infinity or finitude of the world in time or space as *avyākṛta* or indeterminate. The *avyākṛtas* are thus stated in Pali:

सस्सतो लोको, असस्सतो लोको; अन्तवा लोको, अनन्तवा लोको ।

DīghNik IX.3.16

The world is everlasting, the world is not everlasting; The world has an end in space, the world has no end in space.

The *Sūtras* include the questions about the world in space and time in the list of the forteeen *avyākṛtas*. Now questions have been in general divided into four types – phose which can be answered categorically (*ekāṃśa-vyākaraṇīya*), those which can be answered after analysing and sub-dividing the question (*vibhājya-vyākaraṇīya*), those which can be answered by cross-questioning the questioner and eliciting his real intention (*pariprichya-vyākaraṇīya*) and, finally, those of which no answer can be given (*sthāpanīya*). The *avyākṛtas* belong to this last class. Now, as to why Buddha did not settle the questions about the eternity of the world etc., it is said he took into consideration the intention of the questioner. The latter could mean the universal Soul to be the world but such a Soul was unacceptable to Buddha. If the questioner meant by the world the whole of *saṃsāra*, i.e., the life-sequence of beings and the production and destruction of elements, every answer would again be out of place since an eternal *loka* would then exclude everyone's *parinirvāṇa* and a non-eternal *loka* lead to annihilation.

These explanations of the Ābhidhārmikas do not appear to do justice to the silence of Buddha because in effect they adduce only reasons of psychological prudence or of avoidable mislocation. They stem from a realistic pluralism in which there are in principle always definite answers to questions of existence and non-existence, *astitā* and *nāstitā*, in terms of the middle way, *madhyama pratipad*, eluded the Ābhidhārmikas. It is the Mādhyamikas who saw the deeper aspect of the silence of Buddha in terms of reality as →*śūnyatā* which is non-empirical and trans-logical. At the empirical level neither the *loka* nor *saṃsāra* has a first beginning or final end. Here time flows as a beginningless and endless cycle.

संसारोऽनवराग्रो हि नास्यादिर्नापि पश्चिमम् ।

MaKā XI.1

The cycle of existence (*saṁsāra*) is beginningless and ceaseless for it has neither a first nor a last.

These *avyākṛtas* are reminiscent of the first Antinomy in Kant. For Buddha the questions by their very nature preclude the possibility of a logical answer. They treat the 'word' which is the notional aggregate of all objects as itself a definite object. Thus they illegitimately extend the application of the concepts of space and time beyond their empirically testified proper domain. As the **Abhidharmakośa** states: "Cosmic time is of the nature of the five *skandhas*", which are empirically given as events specifiable with reference to space, time and cause. Buddha avoided the extremes of eternalism and annihilationism with respect to reality because they involve the transcendental application of empirical concepts (*saṃvṛti*).

Time in Buddhist Religious Experience

Buddha's notion of time was not derived from Cosmology or speculative metaphysics but from introspective reflection over experience. If we turn to watch ourselves we would discover a constant succession of ideas and we seem to live in this stream of consciousness. We seem to be passing away every moment and sense time as a unique and irreversible process in which being moves towards death. Temporality as the mutability or mortality of the subjective being or consciousness is the source of the deeper kinds of suffering viz., *pariṇāma-duḥkhatā* and *saṃskāra-duḥkhatā*. Both the subject and the object of desire are involved in change willy nilly and this is the reason why happiness is fleeting and turns into suffering. More basically, we desire to be without realizing that being is necessarily destined not to be. Our very being is involved in commotion and evanescence. Thus temporality is ingrained in subjective being or the self and since suffering is ultimately rooted in it, the quest of the spiritually sensitive and ambitious person can only be for Immortality or the conquest of time. So Buddha set out to discover what is eternally quiescent. The enemy he sought to conquer was *Māra* or Death. As explained above, the cycle of cosmic and individual existence (*loka-dhātu* and *saṃsārādhva*) depend on the force of *karman* which is ultimately rooted in desire. It is as desire that *Māra* lurks in the human heart.

The quest of the Buddha culminated in the experience of *Sambodhi* which illumined the Truths of *nirvāṇa* and *pratītyasamutpāda*. *Nirvāṇa* was intuited as eternally quiescent, *pratītyasamutpāda* as the process of contingency. All states of experience appear and disappear depending on causes and conditions. Human subjectivity or the individual self is an interdependent cycle of psychic events rooted in ignorance and the force of past actions and it is to this cycle of *saṃsāric* phenomena or *dhamma* that time belongs. The apprehension of *Nirvāṇa* following the dispelling of Ignorance is the apprehension of reality as timeless. This reality is logically indeterminate (*atakkāvacara*). What *pratītyasamutpāda* seeks is to restrict the attribution of being and non-being to what is given in experience and ordered in time. All such objects are designated *dharmāḥ*. They are transient (*anitya*), contingent (*pratītyasamutpanna*), synergic functions (*saṃskāras, saṃskṛta*) and aggregates (*skandhāḥ*). Heteronomy and temporality are essential to them. Since they are conceived in and through experience only, '*dharmāḥ*' may be rendered phenomena. It follows that mind and matter (*nāma-rūpa*), being radically temporal, cannot be the self. Whether the self as such is or is not, was for Buddha an unanswerable question since being and non-being apply only to contingent objects and presuppose *avidyā*. The delusion of the self in time needs to be transcended for the attainment of freedom from suffering.

Time and Reality in the Abhidharma

Early Buddhist schools generally agreed to divide *dharmas* into two classes, *saṃskṛta* or contingent and *asaṃskṛta* or non-contingent. The former are temporal, the latter eternal. The former include *nāmarūpa* or the five *skandhas*, the latter certainly included *nirvāṇa* though some schools counted several other *dharmas* too as eternal. *Dharmas* are supposed to have their distinctive natures or essences (*svabhāva*) in terms of which they are known and in accordance sith which they function. Their *svabhāva* (nature) provides their *laks̨aṇa* (recognisable character) and determines their *vyāpāra* or *kāritra* (function or activity). Buddha had spoken of impermanence as one of the three universal marks (*lakṣaṇas*) of all things, mental and material.

It is the law of dependent origination which regulates the being and non-being of a *dharma* in time. Many Ābhidhārmikas tended to identify dependent origination with the *dharmas* which thus arise and perish:

प्रतीत्यसमुत्पादः कतमः, सर्वे संस्कृतधर्मा इति ।

AbhidhKo III.25

What is dependent origination? It is the totality of contingent phenomena.

Saṃskṛtatva and *pratītyasamutpannatva* have been identified since both refer to genesis dependent on causal conditions. Time or *adhvā* has been identified with the *saṃskṛta dharmas*. A *saṃskṛta dharma* is one which may be recognized by four marks (*lakṣaṇas*) which are in effect constitutive of temporality. These were traditionally listed as *jāti* or birth, *jarā* or aging, *sthiti* or duration, *anityatā* or impermanence. This fourfold division of the *saṃskṛta-lakṣaṇas* was naturally disputed since the *Sūtras* speak of only three *lakṣaṇas* of the *saṃskṛta*.

त्रीणीमानि संस्कृतस्य संस्कृत-लक्षणानि, संस्कृतस्य भिक्षव उत्पादोऽपि प्रज्ञायते व्ययोपि स्थित्यन्यथात्वमपि ।

There are three characteristics of phenomena. Their coming into being is known as their passing away and alternation.

Here production (*utpāda*) is the same as 'birth' (*jāti*) while perishing (*vyaya*) is the same as aging (*jarā*) and change of state (*sthityanyathātva*) is identical with impermanence (*anityatā*). For this reason some schools like the Theravādins accepted only three marks (*lakṣaṇas*) of the *saṃskṛta*. With respect to the mind, however, some philosophers of the Theravāda school accepted only two *lakṣaṇas* viz., origination and cessation, but others among them argued for three *lakṣaṇas* on the ground that between origination and cessation one must postulate a neutral and static state just as when a body thrown up starts falling it must pass through a moment of zero upward motion. The Theravādins also identify the three *lakṣaṇas* mentioned in the *Sūtra* differently from what is proposed by Vaibhāṣikas. According to the Theravādins *jāti* and *utpāda* are the same but *jarā* is equated to *sthiti*. Hence the Theravādins regarded *sthiti* as one of the three aspects of *saṃskṛtatva*. As for *anityatā* it is only spelled out by these three.

Thus while the Theravādins accepted three *saṃskṛta-lakṣaṇas* or even two, the Sarvāstivādins accepted four. The Sammitīyas are said to have accepted the four as constituting four moments (*kṣaṇas*). Why *sthiti* is not mentioned in the *Sūtra* was explained in various ways. It could have been omitted or joined to *jarā* in *sthityanyathātva* so that the element of duration or stability is not emphasized lest it should encourage attachment. A distinction is also made between duration (*sthiti*) as a mark (*lakṣaṇa*) and the being (*sthiti*) which may be attributed to unconditioned elements (*asaṃskṛta dharmas*) which endure in their own nature. In other words, temporal duration has to be distinguished from the self-subsistence of the timeless.

The four marks (*lakṣaṇas*) which define the conditioned (*saṃskṛtas*) are themselves elements (*dharmas*) which the Sarvāstivādins class as *citta-viprayuktadharmas* i.e., they are distinct objects of true knowledge but of a non-mental nature. The four marks (*lakṣaṇas*) function together but successively like a band of robbers attacking a way-farer. *Jāti* pulls out the *dharma* into the present and even while *sthiti* holds it, *jarā* and *anityatā* strike it and send it into the past. They are universal and defining features of phenomena (*saṃskṛtas*) giving them a necessarily evanescent life in time (*adhvasaṃcāra*).

The Sautrāntikas rejected this whole concept as due to mistaken ramification of the *saṃskṛta-lakṣaṇa*. These *lakṣaṇas* have no real or substantial existence. They are not themselves causal factors but merely abstracted aspects of the causal process. These *lakṣaṇas* were mentioned by Buddha for a purpose. Fools cling to the series of changing states of the mind regarding it as their self. To show the conditioned nature of this stream he spoke of the *saṃskṛta-lakṣaṇas*. He did not mean that every moment has these aspects. The moment (*kṣaṇa*) is not recognized as being produced, enduring etc. These *lakṣaṇas* do not evidence the reality of the *saṃskṛtas*, nor are they like the marks of excellence etc. They are aspects of the phenomena as a series. They show that we may distinguish for each phenomenal series a beginning, a continuing duration, and a cessation. Its constant alteration is the alteration in its terms ordered in succession. There is a succession of moments as a stream. When one speaks of the phenomenon as enduring one is only speaking of it as a stream of moments. One cannot speak of the moment as arising, enduring, and perishing simultaneously. As the moment perishes by itself one cannot speak of its duration. One cannot, therefore, speak of these different aspects or *lakṣaṇas* as belonging to the moment.

It was, however, argued that one could speak of the *lakṣaṇas* with respect to the moment or *kṣaṇa* also if one did not think of them as distinct reals. Thus coming into being after previous non-being is the birth of the moment or the momentary *dharma*. Its non-being which follows being is its death. The succession of one moment by another may be called duration since the succeeding moment has a similarity to the earlier one and represents it, as it were. But since the successive moment is also dissimilar to the earlier one we can speak of the alteration of being. It is, however, admitted that a series may come to a final end in which case its last moment will have no successor to give it duration or alteration, though some argued that even the last moment could be said to have duration or *sthiti* in the sense of self-subsistence (*avasthāna*) and hence also alteration (*sthityanyathātva*). The two necessary and universal aspects are production and cessation. Duration and alteration come in only when there is a continuing series. The real teaching of the Buddha may be gleaned from the *Sūtra* when it says: "*Saṃskṛta* is that which comes into being after earlier non-being and having come into being perishes into non-being. Its duration is its continuation as a series in which there is a constant alteration"

Thus the Four Marks (*lakṣaṇas*) are regarded by the Vaibhāṣikas as real synergic factors which are responsible for actualizing the conditioned *dharmas* into a sucession of momentary phenomena in time. For the Sautrāntikas the marks are merely notional, not real (*prajñaptimātram, na dravyasat*). The real elements underlying the phenomena are momentary occurrences, *saṃskāras* or *saṃskṛta-dharmas.* As temporal successions of cause and effect they constitute *santati*:

> का चेयं सन्ततिः ? हेतुफलभूताः त्रैयध्विकाः संस्काराः ।
>
> Sphuṭārthā I, p.218
>
> What really is the continuity of lineage? The temporal successions of cause and effect passing through three paths. (Tr. H.N. Chakravarty)

Although the *dharmas* have their own distinctive nature (*svabhāva*) they are deemed to exist only for a moment in time. Does it mean that the past and the future *dharmas* are to be regarded as non-existent? The nature of the past, present and the future was extensively discussed in this context by the Sarvāstivādins and their critics. The Sarvāstivādins propounded the thesis that the past and the future have reality but they held that this does not amount to the eternalist heresy because of the acceptance of the *saṃskṛta-lakṣaṇas.*

> न संस्काराणां शाश्वतत्वं प्रतिज्ञायते वैभाषिकैः संस्कृतलक्षणयोगात्, प्रतिज्ञायते तु विशदं सर्वकालास्तिता ।
>
> Sphuṭārthā, Vol. III, pp.803-4
>
> Permanence of *saṃskāras* is not accepted by Vaibhāsikas because they are associated with the characteristic of being created. But they assert clearly the eternality of the existence of time. (Tr. H.N. Chakravarty)

There is an obvious objection to Sarvāstivāda. If the past and the future are also real, the passage of time would make no difference to reality which is not the same when past, future or present. How the epochs of time are to be correlated with changes in reality, elicited a number of responses. Some argued (*Bhāvānyathātvavāda*) that when an object passes through time its existence or temporal being (*bhāva*) changes, not its essential reality:

धर्मस्याध्वसु प्रवर्तमानस्य भावान्यथात्वं भवति नो द्रव्यान्यथात्वम् ।

Sphuṭārthā Vol.III, p.805-7

> The characteristic mark being set in motion to pass along the paths of time, the temporal being undergoes changes, not its essential reality. (Tr. H.N. Chakravarty)

A broken golden vessel still remains golden. Another view (*lakṣaṇānyathātvavāda*) was that the passage of time changes the dominant aspect (*lakṣaṇa*) of the object. When it becomes past it has the predominant aspect of the past but is not wholly devoid of its 'present' and 'future' aspects. A man loving a woman need not be devoid of love for other women. A third view (*avasthānyathātvavāda*) emphasized the change of state or condition (*avasthā*) in time. As an object becomes present or past its condition is altered, not its essence. "When an element is in a condition in which it does not yet produce its function, it is called future; when it produces it, it is called present; when, having produced it, it ceases to work, it is past, its substance remaining the same". "Just as in an abacus the same ball receives different significations according to the place it is thrown in". A fourth view (*anyathānyathātvavāda*) held that an object is past, present or future in relation to the earlier or succeeding moment, future with respect to earlier moments, past or present. The distinction between the past, future and present is, thus a relative one. No moment is in itself past, present or future but could be deemed so in relation to some other moment.

These four views point out (a) that basic object or element retains its nature as an intelligible essence (*svabhāva*) despite the passage of time; (b) that it undergoes a change of mode (*bhāva*) acquiring or losing existence with time; (c) that these changing modes reflect the predominance of one aspect (*lakṣaṇa*) over the others; (d) that the mode of existence or the aspect of presentness consists in activity (*kāritra*); (e) that the distinction between the past, present and future is a relative distinction made in the succession of events one after the other.

The Theravādins too regarded time as a notional (*paññatti*), not a real entity. The notion of time is that of an ordered series of momentary intervals (*khanas*). A series of *paccaya* – relations are involved in this ordering. On the other hand a moment includes three aspects, origination, duration and destruction. In the case of mental phenomena, as mentioned above, only two aspects were admitted by some who held that thoughts arise and perish without enduring. In the case of matter all the three aspects are to be found in the moment. In fact, while the Theravādins did not entertain the idea of a separate class of *cittaviprayakta-dharmas*, they included the *saṃskṛta-lakṣaṇas* within matter (*rūpa*) of which one of the varieties is called *lakkhana-rūpa.* This includes the production of a material element and its continuation in a series. Both of these were included in the aspect of *jāti* or *uppada*. Aging (*jaratā*) and impermanence)(corresponding to the other two *saṅkhata-lakkhanas* were also included in the *lakkhana-rūpa*. The whole point of underscoring these marks as inherent in matter is to combat the commonsense notion of its stability. Even the slightest introspection reveals the mind to be a flux of momentary states. That matter too is an incessant process of change in time, is a sophisticated notion to which only theory can give access. However, it must be kept in mind that *lakkhana-rūpa* is included in *sukhuma-rūpa* which is a part of *dhamma-rammana*. In other words, these inherent marks or matter are to be cognized by the mind, not the senses. Thus while matter and mind are temporal processes, logical entities like time, or *nibbana* are timeless.

In Sarvāstivāda as well as Theravāda the concept of moment occurs for both mind and matter. It was quickly seen that their correlation in experience poses a problem. During the time taken to perceive an object, the object itself would change. The Sautrāntikas accepted this squarely and declared the present content perception to correspond to the object of the previous moment. The Theravādins, on the other hand, realized on the basis of acute psychological analysis that perception involves a number of operations and hence psychic moments. To harmonize this with their notion of the direct perception of present objects, they developed the idea of different magnitudes for mental and material moments. The mental moment (*cittakkhana*) is much briefer than the material moment (*rūpa-kkhana*) so much so that seventeen of the former correspond to one of the latter! The Theravādins attempt detailed calculations of the number of moments involved in some important kinds of experiences or mental or physical processes.

Time and the Buddhist Logicians

That all conditioned reality is momentary, is a principle common to all Buddhist schools even though, as seen above, the concept of the moment was not the same for all of them. Originally the principle appears to have been based on the introspective awareness of experience as incessant flux, a fact on which there was a large measure of agreement among different schools, Buddhist and non-Buddhist. However, that all mental and physical reality is strictly momentary, was disputed by non-Buddhist schools. The Buddhists in classical times sought to establish the principle by strictly logical means. They argued analytically that the concept of reality is to be understood as practical efficiency (*arthakriyākāritva*). To be real is to function causally. Now a cause cannot function without alteration. In other words to be a cause, or to act is simply to produce an effect. What a cause produces it must produce immediately and since the existence of the cause consists in this productive moment, it can neither exist earlier than this moment of functioning nor survive it. Thus to be is to function causally and since causal functioning is completed without delay, it must cease in the next moment when the effect comes into being. The effect, in turn, to be real has to produce and perish. As causal efficiency, which can only be instantaneous, reality must be conceived as momentary actualizations on which is superimposed the intellectual construct of a series of such moments. Empirical objects correspond to these as pragmatically demarcated or identified. Thus 'sound' or 'fire' as empirical objects appear to endure and change over a period of time but have to be intellectually conceived as series of existentially different vibrations or flashes, each lasting for a moment and being followed by another. If all intellectual constructions were to be set aside and we could perceive bare reality, we would simply have actualizations perishing instantaneously because that is the only way in which we can conceive pure reality.

Buddhist and rival philosophers debated this doctrine of momentariness over centuries with acute and subtle arguments for and against it. Analytical arguments from pure concepts such as being or causality are often regarded as the hardcore of philosophy but they are peculiarly apt to suffer from the charges of *petitio principii.* These concepts have been interpreted in terms of rival but perennially alive perspectives. The Buddhist perspective underlying the doctrine of momentariness assumes that what is real must make a difference to experience and can only be a causally active process.

Time and the Dialecticians

Whether it is philosophically tenable to hold to the reality of the unconditioned as well as the conditioned, of eternal as well as the temporal, without either reducing the eternal to a mare idea or the temporal to a mere delusion, it is an unavoidable question. The fact that the nature (*svabhāva*) of a *dharma* cannot be conceived except by relational dependence on another shows that it is not a reality but an intellectual construction. Nor can the existence or non-existence attributed to the *dharmas* be real because these attributions cannot be made independently. The concept of reality should be that of something which is self-intelligible and self-dependent but all the elements into which empirical reality is analysable follow the Law of Dependent Origination. Their reality could only be pragmatic. Nor can there be an unconditioned reality by the side of the conditioned because that would only add to the list of relationally conceived *dharmas*. Finite objects cannot be real because they are inconceivable apart from the finitizing or determining activity of the mind. And the infinite is not an object by their side.

If the *dharmas* are devoid of reality (*śūnya*), time too becomes unreal. In fact, motion, change and causality present insuperable contradictions and time is inseparable from these. Besides, time has special problems of its own. Since what is real is only momentary, it cannot really move or change. If causality were to be real it would be impossible to explain the relationship of cause and effect as one of either identity or difference. As for time, its three divisions into past, present and future have no independent reality since each can be defined only in relation to the others. Time cannot be comprehended in itself as an unmoving whole. Nor can it be apprehended as the moving moment since that cannot be distinguished from some specific existence. Time is, thus, notional, not real.

Conclusion

At first sight it seems that since everything is held impermanent in Buddhism, time must be the most important feature of reality for it. In a way it is true because Buddhism does regard time as an aspect of causality to be the deepest feature of conditioned reality. But it does look beyond it to the attainment of the timeless, unconditioned reality. Time is phenomenally real and where it is real there is suffering and death. There is, however, an ultimate spiritual goal where time is not real and on attaining which freedom is realized. Bondage depends on the deluded sense of the self in the non-self which leads to action and its results occurring in time. It is the disillusionment about the empirical self and its craving for becoming in time that is necessary for the vision of eternity which transcends the opposites of being and non-being. Freedom comes from disengagement from the Wheel of Time.

Bibliography:

Abhidharmakośa (Patna, 1975)
Abhidharmakośa (with Vyākhyā), Varanasi, 1970.
Abhidhammatthasangaho, Varanasi, 1967.
La Vallee Pouśsin: L'Abhidharmakośa de Vasubandhu. Paris: 7 Vols., 1923-1931.
La Vallée Poussin: Vijñaptimātratāsiddhi, Paris, 1928.
Six Buddhist Nyaya Tracts, Calcutta, 1910.
La Vallée Poussin (ed.): Madhyamaka (avec Prasannapada). Bibliotheca Buddhika, reprinted 1970.
Stcherbatsky, Central Conception of Buddhism. London: 1922
G.C. Pande: Studies in the Origins of Buddhism. Delhi: 1983

Select Bibliography

Balslev, Anindita Niyogi: A Study of Time in Indian Philosophy. Wiesbaden: Otto Harrassowitz, 1983.

Bhattacharya, Haran Chandra: Kālasiddhāntadarśinī, ed. by Gaurinath Sastri. Varanasi: Sampurnananda Sanskrit University, 1984.

Bhattacharya, U.C.: Problems of time in indian thought. Calcutta review, no. 52, 1934, p. 302-9.

Das, S.R.: "Notion of Time in Indian Philosophy" in: Indian Historical Quarterly, no. 9, 1933, p. 149-53.

Eliade, M.: "Time and eternity in Indian thought" in Man and Time; Eranos Year Book 1958, p. 173-200. London: Routledge and Kegan Paul.

Coomaraswamy, Ananda K.: Time and Eternity. Ascona (Switzerland): Artibus Asiae Publishers, 1947.

Franze, Marie-Louise von: Time–Rhythm and Repose. London: Thames and Hudson, 1978.

Fraser, J.T., Lawrence, N. and Park, D.: The Study of Time III. New York: Springer Verlag, 1970.

Govinda, Lama Anagarika: Foundations of Tibetan Mysticism. London: Rider and Company, 1959.

Hawking, Stephen W.: A Brief History of Time. New York: Bantam Books, 1989.

Hiriyanna, M.: "An Indian view of Present Time" in: Quarterly Journal of the Mythic Society (Bangalore), no. 14. 1924.

Madhavatirtha: The Concept of Time in Indian Philosophy Ahmedabad: Vedant Ashram, 1951.

Mahadevan, T.M.P.: Time and the Timeless. Madras: Upanishad Vihar, 1953.

Mandal, Kumar Kishore: A comparative study of the concepts of Space and Time in Indian Thought. Varanasi: The Chowkhamba Sanskrit series office, 1968.

Misra, V.N.: Bhāratīya Paramparā (in Hindi), Bhopal, Madhyapradeśa Hindi Grantha Academy, 1989.

Panikkar, R.: Toward a typology of time and temporality in the ancient Indian tradition, Philosophy East and West, no. XXIV, no. 2, April 1974. p. 161-4.

Sastri, S.: Conception of time in Post-Vedic Sanskrit Literature, Essays on Indology. p. 149- 204. Delhi, Maharchand Lachhmandass 1963.

Schayer, S.: Contributions to the problem of time in Indian Philosophy, Cracow, Polska Akademia Umiejetności Prace Komisji Orientalistycznej, 1938.

Scheftelowitz, J.: Die Zeit als Schicksalsgöttin in der indischen und iranischen Religion, Stuttgart, Kohlhammer, 1929.

Kane, P.V.: History of Dharmaśāstra Vol. V, part-I (Vratas, Utsavas and Kāla etc.), Poona: Bhandarkar Oriental Research Institute, 1974.

KṢAṆA

Overview

The term *kṣaṇa* conveys a variety of meanings according to the lexical works. Basically it is connected with the concept of time and usually it means 'a moment', 'a certain division of time'. Various meanings conveyed by *kṣaṇa* mainly fall into two groups. One group consists of those meanings which refer to a part of time. Thus *kṣaṇa* means 'time in general', 'a certain point in time', 'a very short duration', 'a time atom' and 'a fifteenth part of a *tithi*'. Meanings belonging to the other group commonly share the concept of a state devoid of action as their basis. *Kṣaṇa* thus conveys leisure, rest, a time for enjoyment, a festival, a good time etc. A still further development is seen in the meanings 'an opportunity', 'an invitation for dinner' and 'happiness'. A few more meanings of *kṣaṇa* such as *madhya* 'middle' and *pāratantrya* 'dependence' are recorded in the lexica.

In mythological works *kṣaṇa* appears as one of the several names of deities like Indra, Śarva, Gaṇeśa and Sūrya. It is also the name of a power of a goddess. *Kṣaṇa* appears as a name of a rite in the **Śaṅkaravijaya**, whereas in the **Pārāśara-Śikṣā** it is a name of a kind of a euphonic combination.

In the philosophical works in general and in Buddhist works in particular *kṣaṇa* implies the transitory, momentary character of existence.

In the works on the Arts *kṣaṇa* is used in its ordinary sense, namely, 'a festival', 'a short time' and 'happiness'. Moreover, the derivative *kṣaṇika* appears in the compounds *kṣaṇikālaya* and *kṣaṇikabera* in the works on architecture where *kṣaṇika* denotes a temporary idol established in a temple.

Etymology and Cognate Words

Yāska in his **Nirukta** gives the derivation of *kṣaṇa* as follows:

क्षणः क्षणोतेः; प्रक्ष्णुतः कालः ।

Nir II.25

Kṣaṇa (an instant) is derived from (the root) *kṣaṇ-* (to injure); it is the injured time. (Tr. L. Sarup)

Durga comments on this derivation as follows:

क्षणः क्षणोतेः हिंसार्थस्य स हि प्रक्ष्णुतः प्रकर्षेण हिंसितः कालोऽल्पत्वात् ।

Kṣaṇa (is derived) from (root) *kṣaṇ-* which means 'to kill', because it is the *prakṣṇuta* 'excessively diminished time' since it is short.

Thus *kṣaṇa* is time chiselled to its last particle. This etymology stresses the atomic character of *kṣaṇa*.

The PW explains *kṣaṇa* as derived from *īkṣaṇa* 'eye'. Mayrhofer also traces the origin of *kṣaṇa* to the noun *akṣan* 'eye' and implies thereby that *kṣaṇa* basically referred to the winking of eyes (The Concise Etymological Dictionary p.284). Thus the common idea underlying all these etymologies is that *kṣaṇa* is the minutest time-atom equivalent to the action of the winking of eyes. In the attested usage *kṣaṇa* shows no connection with killing although one *Kośa* records killing as one of the meanings of *kṣaṇa*.

Synonyms of *kṣaṇa* are *muhūrta, nimeṣa* and *lava*. They denote short duration throughout Sanskrit literature. *Kṣaṇadā* 'night', *kṣaṇapati* 'moon', *kṣaṇabhaṅga* 'momentary existence', *kṣaṇasampad* 'good luck of getting a human birth in the middle region', *kṣaṇika* 'transient' are a few among the words derived from *kṣaṇa* which are often attested in literature. *Kṣaṇa* in these words implies different shades of its meaning such as a moment, happiness and rest.

Kṣaṇa is also used alongwith roots *kṛ-, dā-* etc. Thus *kṣaṇam kṛ-* means to 'invite' or 'to accept invitation', 'to take the opportunity', while *kṣaṇam dā-* means 'to extend an invitation for a function'.

A complete diversion from the core-meaning of *kṣaṇa* appears in the use of *kṣaṇika* as a name of a euphonic combination in **Pārāśara-Śikṣā**.

तकारान्ते पदे पूर्वे शकारे परतः स्थिते ।
क्षणिकं तं विजानीयात् तच्छकेयं निदर्शनम् ॥

PārāŚik 140

That (*Sandhi* which takes place) when preceding word ends in *t* and *ś* appears after (it) should be known as *kṣaṇika*. The example is the combination *tacchakeyaṁ*.

The *kṣaṇika sandhi* is illustrated as follows:

तच्छकेयम् = तत् + शकेयम् ।

Here the final *t* of the preceding word is replaced by *c* and the following *ś* is replaced by *ch*. Why this →*sandhi* is called *kṣaṇika* is difficult to explain.

Layers of Meaning

The core meaning of *kṣaṇa* has the following aspects:

1. Time – in general or a specific division.
2. Action – the smallest action such as the winking of the eyes.
3. Rest – state of inactivity, pause.
4. Transient character of existence.
5. Happiness resulting from rest or relaxation.

These aspects are combined into the different connotations of *kṣaṇa*. However, all different connotations of *kṣaṇa* seem to revolve round the temporal aspect of the core meaning of *kṣaṇa*. In fact, two parallel streams of the two meanings, namely, 'short duration' and 'state of inaction', seem to be current from the early times.

Development of the Concept

Although the word *kṣaṇa* is conspicuously absent in the Vedic Saṃhitās, its synonyms, namely, *muhūrta* and *nimeṣa* appear in the **Ṛgveda**, the **Taittirīya**, the **Paippalāda**, the **Mādhyandina** and the **Śaunaka-Saṃhitās**. Use of the word *nimeṣa* in these Saṃhitās clearly shows that the word *nimeṣa* originally denoted winking of the eyes and later was associated with the time required for the winking. In the **Taittirīya-Saṃhitā** various parts of the sacrifical horse which is identified with a *saṃvatsara* 'year' are compared to different divisions of time.

उषाः वै अश्वस्य मेध्यस्य शिरः ।सूर्यः चक्षुः... अहोरात्रे निमेषः।

TSam VII.5.25.1

Dawn is the head of the sacrificial horse; the sun is the eye... The day and the night are the winking of eyes.

Bhaṭṭabhāskara comments:

यस्तदीयो निमेष उन्मेषसहितस्ते उभे अहोरात्रे ।

His closing of eyes along with the opening of eyes is both the day and the night.

The word *nimeṣa* originally referred to the closing of eyes, but since the closing is immediately followed by opening, *nimeṣa* denotes both the actions together.

Various divisions of time to its smallest part appear to have been already fixed in the period of the Saṃhitās. All divisions of time are represented by the word *nimeṣa* in the following sentence:

सर्वे निमेषा जज्ञिरे विद्युतः पुरुषादधि ।

YV XXXII.2

All *nimeṣas* (parts of time) were born from the illuminating person.

Mahīdhara comments:

सर्वे निमेषास्त्रुटिकाष्ठादयः कालविशेषाः पुरुषादधि पुरुषसकाशाद् जज्ञिरे। कीदृशात् पुरुषात् ? विद्युतः । विशेषेण द्योत्यते विद्युत्, तस्मात्।

All *nimeṣas* (that is, the specific divisions of time *truṭi, kāṣṭhā* etc.) were born from the Person. From what kind of Person? He who illuminates brightly. From such illuminating Person (they were born).

The word *muhūrta* is found in the **Ṛgveda** in the sense 'a short while':

रमध्वं मे वचसे सोम्याय ऋतावरीरुप मुहूर्तमेवैः ।

ṚV III.33.5

Linger a little at my friendly bidding; rest holy ones, a moment in your journey. (Tr. R.T.H. Griffith)

Yāska in his paraphrase of the above verse mentions *kṣaṇa* as a synonym of *muhūrta.* The first attested reference to *kṣaṇa* appears in the **Gopatha-Brāhmaṇa** as follows:

पुरुषो वाव संवत्सरः ।...अहोरात्राभ्यां पुरुषः क्षणेन कतिकृत्वः प्राणिति चापानिति च ।

GoBr I.5.5

A person is *saṃvatsara* 'year'. How often does a man outbreathe and inbreathe in a moment by day and night? (Tr. H.C. Patyal)

The word *muhūrta* is also used in the same passage denoting specific time in relation to other parts of time. However, *kṣaṇa* appears undefined in relation to *muhūrta* or any other division of time.

Names of various parts of time have been already established in the **Śāṅkhāyana-Āraṇyaka** in the famous **Saṃhitopaniṣad**:

गतिः पूर्वरूपं निवृत्तिरुत्तररूपं स्थितिः संहितेति जारत्कारव आर्तभागस्तस्यामेतस्यां संहितायां ध्वंसयो निमेषाः काष्ठाः कलाः क्षणा मुहूर्ता अहोरात्रा अर्धमासा मासा ऋतवः संवत्सराश्च संधीयन्ते ।

ŚāṅkhĀr VIII.21

Movement is the symbol of the former (form), stopping, of the latter (form); rest is the Union says Jāratkārava Ārtabhāga. In this union there are united *dhvaṃsis, nimeṣas, kāṣṭhās, kṣaṇas, muhūrtas*, days and nights, fortnights, months, seasons and years. (Tr. A.B. Keith, S. Bhate)

The sequence in which the terms *dhvaṃsi, nimeṣa*, etc. occur in the above passage indicates that these divisions of time had already been measured in terms of each other. Thus *dhvaṃsi* is the smallest unit of time, whereas *saṃvatsara* is the largest unit according to the **Śāṅkhāyana-Āraṇyaka**. *Kṣaṇa* appears fifth in the hierarchy, a unit smaller than *muhūrta* and larger than *kalā*, *kāṣṭhā*, *nimeṣa* and *dhvaṃsi*.

Exact duration of a *kṣaṇa* as well as other divisions of time in terms of each other is given differently in different works (→*kāla*). In the **Bhāgavata Purāṇa** the divisions start with *truṭi* which is described as time required for the Sun to cross three *paramāṇus*. 100 *truṭis* form one *vedha* while 3 *vedhas* form 1 *lava*; 3 *lavas* are equivalent to 1 *nimeṣa* and 3 *nimeṣas* put together make 1 *kṣaṇa* (BhāgPur III.2.6-7). In the **Bhaviṣya Purāṇa** the order appears as follows:

त्रिंशत् काष्ठाः कलामाहुः क्षणास्त्रिंशत् कलाः स्मृताः ।
मुहूर्तमथ मौहूर्ता वदन्ति द्वादशक्षणम् ॥

BhaviPur I.2.87

Thirty *kāṣṭhās* are one *kalā*; thirty *kalās* are said to be one *kṣaṇa* and twelve *kṣaṇas* form a *muhūrta* as say the knowers of *muhūrta*.

Here *kāṣṭhā* is described as eighteen times winking of eyes. The **Amarakośa** gives the following distribution:

अष्टादश निमेषास्तु काष्ठा त्रिंशत्तु ताः कला ।
तास्तु त्रिंशत् क्षणस्ते तु मुहूर्तो द्वादशास्त्रियाम् ॥

AmKo I.11

Eighteen *nimeṣas* form one *kāṣṭhā*. Thirty *kāṣṭhās* make one *kalā*. Thirty *kalās* form one *kṣaṇa* and twelve *kṣaṇas* form one *muhūrta*.

While commenting on the word *nimeṣa* Maheśvara remarks:

अक्षिपक्ष्मपरिक्षेपो निमेषः परिकीर्तितः ।

Tossing of eyelashes is described as a *nimeṣa*.

These and a few other descriptions of *kṣaṇa* and other parts of time clearly show that *kṣaṇa* stood for time of a short duration but not the time-atom. In different works it is described as either shorter or longer in duration than *nimeṣa*. However, from very early period the word *kṣaṇa* was chosen to describe a very short duration or momentary appearance of an object.

In the **Maitrāyaṇī Upaniṣad** life is compared with an actor wearing a temporary costume.

नट इव क्षणवेषं ...इत्यथोक्तम् ।

MaitUp III.2

It is already said (that life in this world is) comparable to an actor temporarily wearing a costume.

The transient or momentary character of life is thus pointed out by using the word *kṣaṇa*.

In the **Tejobindu Upaniṣad** *kṣaṇika* appears along with *sthira* 'stable'.

न स्थिरं क्षणिकं नाशं न गतिर्न च धावनम् ।

TejobinduUp 6.21

There is nothing stable or momentary, there is no destruction, no going and no running. (Tr. M. Mirasdar)

The **Yoga Vāsiṣṭha** also contrasts *kṣaṇa* with *kalpa* in order to stress the relativity of time:

दुःखितस्य निशा कल्पः सुखितस्यैव च क्षणः ।

YVās III.60.22

To the afflicted person night is like an era, (the same however appears) as a moment to a happy person. (Tr. M. Mirasdar)

The **Yoga-Sūtra** defines, for example, the concept *krama* as follows:

क्षणप्रतियोगी परिणामापरान्तनिर्ग्राह्यः क्रमः ।

YSū IV.33

Succession is the uninterrupted sequence of moments cognised as distinct on the cessation of evolutionary change. (Tr. Rama Prasad)

The commentary describes *kṣaṇa* as follows:

यथापकर्षपर्यन्तं द्रव्यं परमाणुरेवं परमापकर्षपर्यन्तः कालः क्षणो यावता वा समयेन चलितः परमाणुः पूर्वदेशं जह्यादुत्तरदेशमुपसम्पद्येत स कालः क्षणः ।

YSūBh on III.52

Just as an atom is substance or matter (*dravya*) reaching the limit of minuteness, so a *kṣaṇa* (moment) is time that reaches the highest limit of minuteness, or a *kṣaṇa* (moment) is time taken by an atom in leaving the position in space it occupies or the time taken in reaching the next point in space.

The *Bhāṣya* further offers an explanation of *kṣaṇa* by saying that time being devoid of reality, is merely a mental concept (*vastuśūnya buddhinirmāṇaḥ*) which appears as if it were an actual object to awakened people or whose doctrines are divergent.

क्षणस्तु वस्तुपतितः क्रमावलम्बी । क्रमश्च क्षणानन्तर्यात्मा तं कालविदः काल इत्याचक्षते योगिनः । न च द्वौ क्षणौ सह भवतः ।... तस्माद् वर्तमान

एवैकः क्षणो न पूर्वोत्तरक्षणाः सन्तीति तस्मान्नास्ति तत्समाहारः । ये तु भूतभाविनः क्षणास्ते परिणामान्विता व्याख्येयास्तेनैकेन क्षणेन कृत्स्नो लोकः परिणाममनुभवति तत्क्षणोपारूढा खल्वमी सर्वेधर्माः ।

YSūBh III.52

But *kṣaṇa* (moment) falling among (i.e. being mixed up with) real perceptible things appears (to the human mind) as dependent on sequence (or succession). *Krama* (sequence) is of the nature of uninterrupted succession. The sequence is called *kāla* by yogins who know (the real nature of) time. For, two *kṣaṇas* do not exist together... Therefore, the present alone is a single moment. There is no existence of prior and posterior moments. Therefore, it is impossible that there should be sequence of two moments that exist simultaneously. Therefore there can be no combination (*samāhāra*) of two moments (in reality). But those moments that have passed away and those that are yet to come are to be interpreted or described as connected with the (constant) flux of changes (in the world). Therefore the whole world experiences change in each single moment. So all these (external) aspects of the world are dependent on one moment (in the present). (Tr. P.V. Kane slightly adapted, History of Dharmashastra, Vol.V, Pt.I.)

According to the doctrine of Patañjali when a mustard seed is perceived by a yogin in a particular place at a particular moment and on another occasion when that seed changes the place the question may be asked whether the seed seen earlier can be recognised by the yogin or not. Vyāsa clarifies the view by saying that every object whatever it may be – if it is a gross substance its characteristic mark will be of much help for distinguishing the object possessing the sameness of form, shape and colour. Because of similarity of characteristic marks it is quite impossible for a person of ordinary vision to recognise the object again, but a yogin in whom the discerning vision (*vivekajaṃ jñānam*) has perfectly developed is able to recognise even a small atom even though it has changed its place from the earlier one. The distinction is neither its shape, form nor colour, if there is any, but the difference of *kṣaṇa* alone which is only known to the yogin (*kṣaṇabhedastu yogibuddhigamya eva*, YSūBh III.52).

From the above discussion it is clear that every object is indelibly stamped with *kṣaṇa*, a very subtle time unit. By means of this differentiating mark the yogin is able to recognise the object by means of his discerning intuition.

Kṣaṇa as a reference to the transitory character of objects rose to eminence in Buddhist literature. The Buddhists for the first time describe *kṣaṇa* as the time atom. In Pali literature *khaṇa* is described as one millionth part of the time required for the winking of eyes.

सो पन खणो अच्छरा संघाटक्खणस्य अक्खिनिमीलनक्खणस्य च अनेककोटिसत- सहस्सभागो दट्ठब्बो ।

Paramārthadīpanī p.123

Let us imagine that the duration of time required for snapping of fingers or for closing the eyes is divided into many millions of lacs. One of such divisions may be equal to the duration of the *khaṇa*. (Tr. J.R. Joshi)

In the Buddhist Sanskrit literature also *kṣaṇa* is described as the smallest measure of time further giving rise to other measures such as *lava* and *muhūrta*. The **Abhidharmakośa** describes *kṣaṇa* as the time atom.

परमाण्वक्षरक्षणाः रूपनामाध्वपर्यन्ताः ।

AbhidhKo III.85

Atom is the extreme limit of matter; syllable is the extreme limit of names; and moment is the extreme limit of time. (Tr. M. Mirasdar)

Dharmakīrti defines the exact duration of the time atom in terms of the atom of matter.

एकाण्वत्ययकालश्च कालोऽल्पीयान् क्षणो मतः ।

PramāṇaVā 2.496

The duration of *kṣaṇa* is very small, equivalent to that required (by an atom) to cross (another) atom.

The Buddhist theory of *kṣaṇikavāda* or *kṣaṇabhaṅgavāda* 'momentariness' has this subtle character of *kṣaṇa* the time-atom as its basis. It is the Indian form of the theory of Universal Flux. *Kṣaṇa* is described by scholars as a key-word to the Buddhist ontology. According to the Buddhists in general, and the Sautrāntikas in particular, every object that comes into existence in this world is momentary. There is no time besides *kṣaṇa*. Birth is immediately followed by destruction. Nothing is permanent in this life. Whatever is born is destroyed the next moment. In fact, destruction or annihilation is nothing but a mere cessation of birth.

The Buddhists described *kṣaṇa* in relation to both, birth and destruction.

कोऽयं क्षणो नाम ? आत्मलाभोऽनन्तरविनाशी । सोऽस्यास्तीति क्षणिकः ।

Sphuṭārthā on AbhidhKo IV.2 (p.568)

What is this *kṣaṇa*? (*Kṣaṇa*) signifies the acquirement of individuality accompanied by immediate destruction. That which possesses it is called *kṣaṇika*. (Tr. J.R. Joshi)

The **Abhidharmasamuccaya** describes *kṣaṇa* in the following words:

क्षणलक्षणं कतमत् ? संस्काराणां क्षणादूर्ध्वम् अनवस्थानम् ।

AbhidhSamu p.38

What is the characteristic of a *kṣaṇa*? (It is) non-existence of any impression at the next moment. (Tr. J.R. Joshi)

In Buddhist literature the term *kṣaṇika* refers to the momentary existence of an object, whereas the term *kṣaṇabhaṅga* refers to its annihilation immediately after its birth. The *kṣaṇikavāda* further implies the transient character of human life. *Kṣaṇa* is thus not only the only reality, but it is the highest reality in Buddhist metaphysics.

The *kṣaṇabhaṅgavāda* was severely criticised by other systems such as Vedānta, Nyāya, and Mīmāṃsā by scholars like Śaṅkara and Jayantabhaṭṭa. On the other hand, some scholars are seen engaged in re-establishing the doctrine of *kṣaṇa.*

Vijñānabhikṣu refutes the views of other systems about *kṣaṇa* and expresses his own view as follows:

तस्यैव च क्षणस्यावयवविशेषैर्मुहूर्ताहोरात्रादिपरार्द्धान्त व्यवहारो भवति न त्वखण्डो महाकालोऽस्ति प्रमाणाभावात् ।

YSāSaṅg IV

The different measures of Time – days, months, etc. upto the highest time-measure are the outcome of the constituent particles of the said Moment; and there is no ground for postulating the existence of Infinite Time. (Tr. G.N. Jha)

Yet another meaning is attached to *kṣaṇa* in the Buddhist literature. It is found in the compound *kṣaṇasampad*, 'the good luck of favourable birth'. The Buddhist Hybrid Dictionary explains *kṣaṇa* as 'birth under favourable conditions'. This meaning is related to the auspicious position of stars in the sky when festive celebrations were held. The **Bodhicaryāvatāra** says:

क्षणसम्पदियं सुदुर्लभा प्रतिलब्धा पुरुषार्थसाधनी ।

BoCar 4

This rare gift of a birth in favourable conditions accomplishing the highest objective has been obtained.

In another development of the meaning *kṣaṇa* was understood not merely as a part of time but as a spare time, a leisure, time for rest. This basic concept of *kṣaṇa* which is described in the lexical works as *nirvyāpārasthitiḥ* "a state devoid of action"(AmKo III.3.47) led to a number of connotations. *Kṣaṇaṃ kṛ-* is found in the earlier Śrauta-Sūtras as well as in the **Mahābhārata** used in the senses 'to accept an invitation', 'to take an opportunity', 'to celebrate' and 'to enjoy'. The word *kṣaṇa* is used in later literature in the senses 'a festive occasion', 'enjoyment', and finally, 'happiness'.

In the **Āgniveśya-Gṛhya-Sūtra** *kṣaṇa* is used with root *kṛ-* in the sense 'to invite for dinner'.

इति वा सङ्कल्प्य ब्राह्मणान् शुचीन् श्रोत्रियान् दरिद्रान् ...क्षणं करोति ।

ĀgniveśyaGṛSū III.31

Having thus decided (he) invites pious, learned and poor Brahmins for dinner. (Tr. G.U. Thite)

The **Baudhāyana-Gṛhya-Sūtra** uses the root *grah-* alongwith *kṣaṇa.*

तेषामेव उदकं निनीय रुद्रप्रणवेन क्षणं ग्राहयति । अष्टकाश्राद्धे क्षणः क्रियतामिति ओं तथेति प्रतिवचनम् ।

BauGṛSū II.11.17

Having poured water for them (he) makes (the priests) accept the invitation with Rudrapraṇava. (He says,) "Please accept the invitation for *aṣṭakāśrāddha*". The reply is "*Oṃ tathā*". (Tr. G.U. Thite)

Kṣaṇam kṛ- in the sense "to take an opportunity" is found in the **Mahābhārata.**

श्रेयो हि ते स्यात् क्षणं कुर्वत इति ।

MBh I.3.100

(He says) "If you take this opportunity it will bring you prosperity".

In later classical literature *kṣaṇa* appears also in the sense of 'joy'. **Stavamālā** records this meaning.

क्षणादमूभिरर्चितः कृष्णः ।

Stavamālā 189

Those (ladies) worshipped Kṛṣṇa with pleasure.

The **Daśakumāra-Carita** alliterates with *kṣaṇa* as follows:

तया क्षणं क्षणहीनया तूष्णीमस्थायि ।

DKCa 5.1.(1)

Bereft of pleasure she kept quiet for a moment.

In the Arts

In the different texts on Art *kṣaṇa* is used in different shades of its ordinary meaning, for instance, 'festival', 'entertainment', 'an auspicious time, etc.

कारयेद् वै क्षणं रात्रौ नटनृत्यकथानकैः ।

SkaPur II.4.10.40

One should celebrate the night by means of acting, dancing and storytelling.

An art performance is thus nothing but a *kṣaṇa* 'a celebration'. In dramaturgy *kṣaṇa* appears in the sense of an occasion or an auspicious moment.

The **Nāṭakalakṣaṇaratnakośa** describes different times suitable for the performance of different types of drama.

प्रभातमपि कालस्य सामान्यात्कश्चिदिच्छति ।
एष क्षणः सहस्रांशोरुदयेन प्रशस्यते ॥

NLRKo 242

Some (dramatists) desire early morning (as the time suitable for performing a drama). This is regarded an auspicious time due to sunrise.

In works on literary criticism *kṣaṇa* is also used merely in its usual meaning 'moment' or 'a short time'. The **Vyaktiviveka** describes the state of the mind of the audience in the following words:

पाठ्यादथ ध्रुवागानात् ततः सम्पूरिते रसे ।
तदास्वादभरैकाग्रो हृष्यत्यन्तर्मुखः क्षणम् ॥

VyVive I.2

After the *pāṭhya* or *dhruvāgāna* when the *rasa* is overfilled (the spectator) totally immersed in its enjoyment turns inward for a moment, filled with joy.

In the works on architecture the word *kṣaṇika* is used to denote idols temporarily established in a temple. It appears compounded with *ālaya* and *bera* in the following verses from the **Mānasāra**.

सौ (सु) ग्रामे क्षेत्रसीमान्ते चान्यग्र (त्र) निरीक्षणम् ।
क्षणिकालयं संस्थाप्य पूजयेत्तन्त्रवित्तमः ॥

MāSā LXI.49

In the villages, at the end of the field and at other places frequented by people, the learned (sculptor) wellversed in the science (of sculpture) should build a temporary temple and worship him.
(Tr. P.K. Acharya)

यन्मधूच्छिष्टबिम्बस्य पञ्चवर्णैरलङ्कृतम् ।
क्षणिका (क) बेरमेवोक्तं चलं चाप्यचलं तथा ॥ MāSā LXVIII.B

> The sculptor (*vardhaki*) at the command of the chief architect (*Sthapati*) should think over (lit. meditate on) the correct image and purify with the five powders (*pañca varṇa*) the idol to be cast in wax. This process is recommended for the transitory idol, stationary or movable. (Tr. P.K. Acharya)

It appears from the above references that temporary temples were built up and temporary idols, either stationary or movable, were kept in such temples.

Conclusion

From the attested uses of the word *kṣaṇa* throughout Sanskrit, Pali and Prakrit literature it can be concluded that *kṣaṇa* originally denoted a very short duration of time. This short time characterised the transitoriness of worldly existence and led to the birth of the high philosophical doctrine of universal flux as it appears in Buddhist Philosophy. In another development short time secondarily conveyed a spare time, a time to spare for oneself or for somebody else. In the former case *kṣaṇa* connoted leisure, opportunity, festival, enjoyment and celebration, whereas in the latter case it connoted an invitation for dinner. In addition to these meanings, *kṣaṇa* also appears in the sense of joy in the classical Sanskrit literature. In the works on the Arts *kṣaṇa* is used in the sense of a short while, leisure, festivity, celebration etc. The derivative *kṣaṇika* is used in the works on Architecture to refer to the temporary character either of an idol or of a temple.

Saroja Bhate

Select Bibliography

Chakravarty, H.N.: "Kṣaṇa: Its Spiritual Significance" in The Indian Theosophist, Vol. 82, Nos. 10 and 11; Varanasi, The Theosophical Society, 1985.

L. de la Vallee Poussin: "Notes sur le moment ou kṣaṇa des bouddhistes" in Rocznik Orientalistyczny, Warsaw, 1931-32.

Sahai, M.: "Patañjali's theory of pariṇāma, krama and kṣaṇa" in Yoga-Mīmāṃsā, Kaivalyadham, Maharastra, 1968.

Silburn, L.: Instant et cause, Le discontinu dans la pensee philosophique de l'Inde, Paris, Vrin, 1955.

KRAMA

Overview

Krama, step, succession, sequence, order, method, from the root *kram-*, to step, has both spatial and temporal implications. In cosmogony it is the three gigantic steps of Viṣṇu Trivikrama which create the living space of the three worlds. This mythic act is frequently represented in art, sculpture and painting.

In the temporal sense *krama* means the orderly succession of events, actions and movements; in nature the succession of days and nights, months, seasons and years; in language the proper order of words and sentences; in ritual the orderly procedure of the ritual performance; in spiritual life the soul's progress towards liberation (*kramamukti*); and in music and dance the orderly succession of notes and steps.

The philosophical discussion of *krama* revolves around the question whether time is dependent upon sequence or not. In the *Krama* school of Kashmir Śaivism *krama* has a mystical sense and is related to the emergence of Śaktis.

In all its various connotations and usages, *krama* always refers to the right or prescribed order and never to a whimsical, accidental or merely mechanical sequence. Thus in any artistic creation it means the proper procedure which is itself a part of the work of art. In its literal sense of step, *krama* plays an important role in the visual arts and in dance.

Etymology and Cognates

Krama is derived from the root *kram-*, to step, as in the *Dhātupāṭha*:

क्रमु पादविक्षेपे ।

PāDhā I. 502

The verbal base *kramu* is used to denote 'to step'.

The primary sense of the noun is therefore the step, going, pace, course, hence sequence, order, series and succession, and also method. The spatial meaning leads to the temporal, both being inseparable. In adverbial use *kramāt, krameṇa* or *kramaśaḥ* mean 'gradually, in due order'.

Important derivatives are *parikrama* (circumambulation), *vikrama* (stride, pace, motion, course; also valour, power), *saṃkrama* or *saṃkrānti* (passage, transition), and compounds such as *kramavṛtti, kramamukti* (liberation in stages), *pariṇāmakrama* (order of transformation), *sṛṣṭikrama* (order of creation) and *saṃhārakrama* (order of dissolution), *bhāgyakrama* (the course of fate), etc.

Texts whose title starts with *Krama-* like **Kramastotra, Kramasadbhāva, Kramakeli**, belong to the *Krama* school of Kashmir Śaivism.

Layers of Meaning

Basically there are two dimensions of the concept of *krama*, the first being in space, as the placing of one step after the other in walking, and derived from this is the meaning in time, the succession and sequence of actions and events. Any succession in space and time implies order, hence *krama* also denotes the proper or prescribed order of things, in nature, in language, in human activity, and hence in the performing arts such as drama, dance and music.

Besides, there are two movements possible in any succession, one ascending and the other descending, one projecting and the other withdrawing, hence the concepts of *ārohakrama* and *avarohakrama*, of *sṛṣṭikrama* and *saṃhārakrama* which are almost universally applicable.

Development of the Concept

The expansion of space in the form of the three worlds is powerfully represented in the Vedic myth of Viṣṇu Trivikrama, 'with the three strides'. By his cosmogonic deed Viṣṇu grants living space to all beings. He is therefore often called *urukrama* in the **Ṛgveda**, 'the vast-striding one'.

विष्णोर्नु कं वीर्याणि प्र वोचं यः पार्थिवानि विममे रजांसि ।
यो अस्कभायदुत्तरं सधस्थं विचक्रमाणस्त्रेधोरुगायः ॥
प्र तद्विष्णुः स्तवते वीर्येण मृगो न भीमः कुचरो गिरिष्ठाः ।
यस्योरुषु त्रिषु विक्रमणेष्वधिक्षियन्ति भुवनानि विश्वा ॥
प्र विष्णवे शूषमेतु मन्म गिरिक्षित उरुगायाय वृष्णे ।
य इदं दीर्घं प्रयतं सधस्थमेको विममे त्रिभिरित्पदेभिः ॥
यस्य त्री पूर्णा मधुना पदान्यक्षीयमाणा स्वधया मदन्ति ।
य उ त्रिधातु पृथिवीमुत द्यामेको दाधार भुवनानि विश्वा ॥
तदस्य प्रियमभि पाथो अश्यां नरो यत्र देवयवो मदन्ति ।
उरुक्रमस्य स हि बन्धुरित्था विष्णोः पदे परमे मध्व उत्सः ॥

ṚV I.154.1-5

I will proclaim the mighty deeds of Viṣṇu
who measured out the earthly regions and propped
the heavens above, accomplishing in his course
three mighty strides.
For this his prowess Viṣṇu is acclaimed.
He inhabits the mountains, like a savage beast

wandering at will; in his three mighty paces
are set all worlds.
Now may my prayer ascend to the far-striding
Viṣṇu, the Bull, who dwells upon the mountains,
to him who unaided measured with threefold step
these far-flung spheres.
The marks of his three strides are filled with honey
imperishable; each is cause of joy.
Alone he supports the three spheres – Earth and Sky
and all things living.
May I attain to Viṣṇu's glorious mansion
where the faithful rejoice, where, close beside the Strider,
within his highest footstep springs the well
of purest honey! (Tr. R. Panikkar)

"His *trivikrama*, or three strides, have also been interpreted in a temporal way, connected with the Sun's orbit: the rising, the zenith, and the setting of the sun. In any event Viṣṇu, as the sacrificial rituals remind us, is the deity who encompasses both time and space, that is to say, past, present, and future, as well as earth, air and heaven" (R. Panikkar, The Vedic Experience, p.151). There has been much discussion on the significance of Viṣṇu's three steps, to mention only some of the most significant views: "Now it has long been clear that Viṣṇu's three strides are somehow connected with the totality of the universe, but it has never been expressly stated, what exactly is the mythical significance of the third step. Its explanation must be sought in the cosmogony, i.e. in the creation myth... But at the same moment Viṣṇu "strides out": his first step corresponds to the nether world (which includes the earth), his second step to the upper world, but his third step is a mystery, not perceptible to the human eye, for it corresponds to the totality... All that exists, is in the three steps, or in the third that represents them." (F.B.J. Kuiper, Ancient Indian Cosmogony, p. 53).

The three steps of Viṣṇu are connected with the creation of the world:

विष्णुक्रमैर्वै प्रजापतिरिमं लोकमसृजत ।

ŚBr VI.7.4.7

By the Viṣṇu-strides Prajāpati created this world. (Tr. J. Eggeling)

The step of Viṣṇu is also used in some magic rituals of the **Atharva-Veda** (cf. AV X.5.30-31, *viṣṇoḥ kramo'si*, "you are the step of Viṣṇu...").

In the Vedic ritual the steps of Viṣṇu are re-enacted. Thus in the concluding ceremony of the *darśapūrṇamāsa* sacrifice the sacrificer strides the three Viṣṇu-strides and thus obtains power:

यद्वेव विष्णुक्रमान्क्रमते । यज्ञो वै विष्णुः । स देवेभ्य इमां विक्रान्तिं विचक्रमे यैषामियं विक्रान्तिः । इदमेव प्रथमेन पदेन पस्पार, अथेदमन्तरिक्षं द्वितीयेन, दिवमुत्तमेन, एताम्वेवैष एतस्मै विष्णुर्यज्ञो विक्रान्तिं विक्रमते । तस्माद्विष्णुक्रमान्क्रमते । तद्वा इत एव पराचीनं भूयिष्ठा इव क्रमन्ते ।

ŚBr I.9.3.9

And again why he strides the Viṣṇu-strides, is: Viṣṇu, truly is the sacrifice, by striding (*vikram*), he obtained for the gods that all-pervading power (*vikrānti*) which now belongs to them. By his first step he gained this same (earth), by the second this aerial expanse, and by his last (step) the sky. And this same pervading power Viṣṇu, as the sacrifice, obtains by his strides for him (the sacrificer): for this reason he strides the Viṣṇu-strides. Now it is indeed from this (earth) that most (beings) go (upwards). (Tr. J. Eggeling)

In the ritual of the **Kṛṣṇa Yajurveda** the three steps of Viṣṇu are called *krama, krānta* and *vikrānta.*

इमे वै लोका विष्णोर्विक्रमणम्, विष्णोर्विक्रान्तम्, विष्णोः क्रान्तम् । तदिमानेव लोकान्त्समारुह्य सर्वमेवेदमुपर्युपरि भवति । अर्वागेवास्मादिदं सर्वं भवति ।

ŚBr V.4.2.6

Now Viṣṇu's outstepping (*Vikramaṇa*), Viṣṇu's outstep (*Vikrānta*), and Viṣṇu's step (*Krānta*) are these (three) worlds, thus having ascended these worlds, he is high above everything here, and everything here is below him. (Tr. J. Eggeling)

In the **Yajur-Veda** the sacrificer (*yajamāna*) is enjoined to make four strides representing the course of Viṣṇu as the sun, while addressing each stride thus:

विष्णोः क्रमोऽसि सपत्नहा गायत्रं छन्द आ रोह पृथिवीमनु वि क्रमस्व ।
विष्णोः क्रमोऽसि अभिमातिहा त्रैष्टुभं छन्द आ रोहान्तरिक्षमनु वि क्रमस्व ।
विष्णोः क्रमोऽस्यरातीयतो हन्ता जागतं छन्द आ रोह दिवमनु वि क्रमस्व ।
विष्णोः क्रमोऽसि शत्रूयतो हन्तानुष्टुभं छन्द आ रोह दिशोऽनु वि क्रमस्व ॥

YV XII.5

Thou (Ukhya Agni or Agni of the Fire-pan) art the rival-slaying stride of Viṣṇu. Mount the Gāyatra metre: stride along the earth.
Thou art the foe destroying stride of Viṣṇu. Mount the Triṣṭup metre: stride along mid-air.
Thou art the traitor-slaying stride of Viṣṇu. Mount the Jagatī metre: stride along the sky.

Thou art the foeman-slaying stride of Viṣṇu. Mount the Anuṣṭup metre: stride along the quarters. (Tr. R.T.H. Griffith)

The Soma altar is also prepared by measuring the space with steps:

तस्मात्प्राङ्प्रक्रामति त्रीन्विक्रमान् तच्छङ्कुं निहन्ति ।

ŚBr. III.5.1.1.

He (the Adhvaryu) now strides three steps forwards (to the east), and there drives in a peg. (Tr. J. Eggeling)

In fact, measuring space by steps is one of the most ancient and universal ways of measuring, of which Viṣṇu's strides represent the cosmic counterpart.

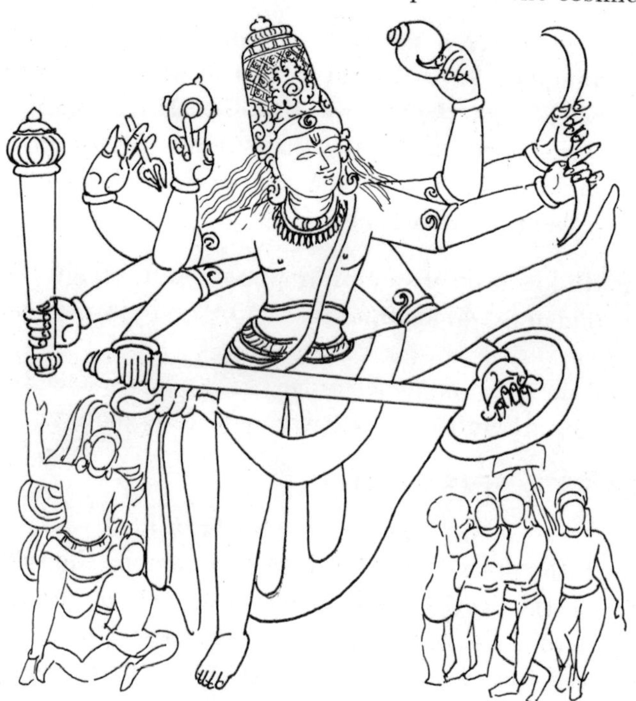

Figure 1: Viṣṇu Trivikrama, Ellora

The myth of Viṣṇu Trivikrama has been developed in the Purāṇic mythology, in the context of Vāmana Avatāra. Viṣṇu is always praised as the one who has measured, conquered, created as well as transcended the universe by his three strides.

पदक्रमाक्रान्तभुवं भवन्तम् ।

ViPur I.4.35

We praise thee, who has traversed the world by a series of steps.

While commenting on Viṣṇu's name as Trivikrama in the **Viṣṇusahasranāma**, the commentary ascribed to Śaṅkara explains:

> त्रयो विक्रमास्त्रिषु लोकेषु क्रान्ता यस्य स त्रिविक्रमः । 'त्रीणि पदा विचक्रमे' (तै॰ ब्रा॰ II.4..6) इति श्रुतेः । त्रयो लोकाः क्रान्ता येनेति वा त्रिविक्रमः ॥
> "त्रिरित्येवं त्रयो लोकाः कीर्तिता मुनिसत्तमैः ।
> क्रमसे तांस्त्रिधा सर्वांस्त्रिक्रमोऽसि जनार्दन ॥"
> इति हरिवंशे (279.50) ॥
>
> ViSahasrBh 69
>
> *Trivikramaḥ*
> Of three Steps.
> The Three steps covered the three worlds. The śruti (TBr II.4.6) says: 'He triumphed [over the three worlds] with His three steps'; or He has walked over the three worlds. The **Harivaṃśa** (279.50) says: "The sages have named the three worlds as *tri*; and as You covered them all in three steps You are named *Trivikrama.*"
> (Tr. R. Ananthakrishna Sastry)

This powerful myth has been frequently represented in art, in the cave temple reliefs of Ellora, Bādāmī, Mahābalipuram and others, upto the later miniature paintings.

In Vedic ritual the question of the order of the performance is an important matter. Thus the Śrauta Sūtras discuss *krama* in this context:

> स्याद्वानुपूर्व्यनियमः श्रुत्यर्थक्रमेभ्यः ।
>
> KātŚrSū I.5.3
>
> There may rather be a particular fixed order among the subservient rites, since, 1. the Śruti makes a mention of such an order, 2. since such order becomes essential in view of the logical sequence of the ritual acts and (lastly) 3. since such an order is expressed by the enumeration of the rites in a particular order (i.e. *Śruti-pāṭha* and *Brāhmaṇa-pāṭha*). (Tr. H.C. Ranade)

This statement seems to be a '*siddhānta*', made with reference to the previous *sūtra* (I.5.2) which says that there is no necessity to follow a particular order of the subservient rites. The present *sūtra* refutes it and says that there should be a fixed order and gives evidence from Vedic passages.

There are two types of orders (*kramas*), viz., *Śrutipāṭha-krama* and 2. *Mantra* (or *Brāhmaṇa) pāṭha-krama.* Both the *pāṭha-kramas* enumerate the rites in a particular order, e.g. in the *Darśapūrṇamāsa* sacrifice, it is said, the sacrificer should observe vows first, then offer the Agnihotra oblation; then select the

Brahman-priest and then offer the main offerings and so on. This order has to be followed for the sacrifice to be effective.

If in the Vedas the spatial dimension is predominant in the cosmogonic process, in the Purāṇic myth and philosophical discussions of creation the temporal aspect seems to move in the foreground. However, to the process of creation (*sṛṣṭi-krama*) corresponds the reverse process of withdrawal (*saṃhāra-krama*). *Krama* here implies both the mere temporal succession in which creation comes about, and the particular order in which the universe is created. This is discussed in Vedānta:

> स्रष्टा त्वेकोऽपि क्रमेणानेकं स्रष्टव्यं सृजेत् ।
>
> BrSūBh II.3.6.
>
> One creator may successively create more than one thing. (Tr. G. Thibaut)
>
> प्रतिवेदान्तं ह्यन्यान्या सृष्टिरुपलभ्यते क्रमादिवैचित्र्यात् ।
>
> BrSūBh I.4.14
>
> All the Vedānta passages which treat of the creation enumerate its successive steps in different order, and so in reality speak of different creations. (Tr. G. Thibaut)
>
> एतेनाक्रमवत्सृष्टिवादिन्यः श्रुतयो व्याख्याताः, तासां सर्वथोपपत्तेः, क्रमवत् सृष्टिवादिनीनां त्वन्यथानुपपत्तेः ।
>
> BrSūBh II.3.10
>
> Thereby those scriptural passages are accounted for which speak of the creation (on the whole) without specifying the order of creation, for they may be explained anyhow, while on the other hand the passages specifying the order of creation cannot be turned in any other way (i.e. not away from their direct sense). (Tr. G. Thibaut)

This order follows mostly the order of the →*tattvas* or principles of reality as described in Sāṃkhya. Generally, the order of manifestation moves from the subtle to the gross elements, whereas the order of withdrawal moves from gross to subtle. In fact, everything in this universe has the three states of creation (*sṛṣṭi*), maintenance (*sthiti*) and absorption (*saṃhāra*). The reverse order is discussed in **Brahma-Sūtra** II.3.14 and commentaries:

> विपर्ययेण तु क्रमोऽत उपपद्यते च ।
>
> BrSū II.3.14
>
> The order (in which the elements are retracted into Brahman) is the reverse of that (i.e. the order in which they are created); this is proved (by its agreement with observation). (Tr. G. Thibaut)

Śaṅkara, besides quoting the Śruti (TUp III.1.1) as scriptural authority, gives the simple example that corresponding to the order in which one has ascended a staircase, one descends in the reverse order (*viparītakrama*). If the evolution starts from the original cause, the reabsorption goes back to the cause (BrSūBh on II.3.14). This is also called *anulomakrama* i.e. in natural order (lit. with the hair), and *pratilomakrama*, against the natural order (cf. BrSūBh on II.3.15).

This reverse order of manifestation is described thus in the **Mahārthamañjarī** of Maheśvarānanda, a Kashmir Śaiva text:

> भावा वृत्तिषु ताश्चित्ते चित्तं संविदि सा परे ।
> व्योम्न्यस्तंगमितो यत्र क्रम उल्लङ्घनात्मकः ॥

Mahānaya Prakāśa, quoted in
Mahārtha Mañjarī Comm. on 35

> The external and internal entities go back to modalities, and they go back to the mind (*citta*) and *citta* goes back to consciousness which finally sets in the transcending void. Thus *krama* is of the characteristic of leaping or passing over from one stage to another. (Tr. H.N. Chakravarty)

In the discussion of language too, Śaṅkara observes that a particular order of the letters is essential for a word to be meaningful (*kramavattvād varṇānām*, BrSūBh I.3.28):

> सत्यपि समस्तवर्णप्रत्यवमर्शे यथा क्रमानुरोधिन्य एव पिपीलिकाः पङ्क्तिबुद्धिमारोहन्ति एवं क्रमानुरोधिन एव वर्णाः पदबुद्धिमारोक्ष्यन्ति ।

BrSūBh I.3.28

> But just as ants constitute the idea of a row only if they march one after the other, so the letters also constitute the idea of a certain word only if they follow each other in a certain order. (Tr. G. Thibaut)

Krama means progress or development also in a moral sense:

> गुणवान्निर्गुणो जात इत्यनर्थक्रमं विदुः ।
> निर्गुणो गुणवाञ्जात इत्याहुः सिद्धिदं क्रमम् ॥

LYVās usp IV.27

> From the state having good qualities the one without any qualities is born – this is to be known as the order of evil. While the one devoid of good qualities has transformed himself possessed of qualities, this is the order conferring perfection. (Tr. H.N. Chakravarty)

The **Yoga Vāsiṣṭha** gives a psychological analysis of the process of seeing in the act of consciousness:

यच्च पश्यामि तद्दृश्यं दर्शनं तु फलं ततः ॥
यदा पश्यामि कालोऽसौ यथा पश्यामि स क्रमः ।
प्रौढा नियतिरित्यस्य यत्र पश्यामि तन्नभः ॥

YVās VI (II).87.22-23

What I see is the object of seeing, the sight is its result.
When I see, it is time. The way I see is succession (*krama*) belonging to the ripe *niyati*, the restraining agent. The place where I see is the void. (Tr. H.N. Chakravarty)

Krama, succession, is here the mode of seeing, the succession in which time and space operate, following the prescribed order of things. Without order or succession time and space only refer to the 'when' and 'where' of seeing, of experience.

Bhartṛhari in his discussion of Time (*kāla*) defines sequence as an essential characteristic of all differentiation:

प्रतिबन्धाभ्यनुज्ञाभ्यां वृत्तिर्या तस्य शाश्वती ।
तया विभज्यमानोऽसौ भजते क्रमरूपताम् ॥

Vāk III.9.30

Through its eternal activity consisting of prevention and permission, it (Time) is differentiated and it assumes the form of sequence. (Tr. K.A.S. Iyer)

असतश्च क्रमो नास्ति स हि भेत्तुं न शक्यते ।
सतोऽपि चात्मतत्त्वं यत् तत् तथैवावतिष्ठते ॥

Vāk III.9.36

That, which is not, has no sequence, it cannot be differentiated. The essence of that, which is, remains always the same. (Tr. K.A.S. Iyer)

It is Time which regulates any sequential order of things, just as the vital air acts in the body:

आविश्येवानुसन्धत्ते यथा गतिमतां गतीः ।
वायुस्तथैव कालात्मा विधत्ते क्रमरूपताम् ॥

* * *

निर्भासोपगमो योऽयं क्रमवानिव दृश्यते ।
अक्रमस्यापि विश्वस्य तत् कालस्य विचेष्टितम् ॥

Vāk III.9.42,46

Just as the force called 'Air' (*vāyu*) after having entered, as it were (the joints of the body) regulates the function (*gatiḥ*) of all organs (*gatimatāṃ*), in the same way, Time brings about sequence in things.

This appearance of the Universe which is really without sequence as something with sequence is the work of Time.
(Tr. K.A.S. Iyer)

The three divisions of Time, past, present and future, are not themselves a product of sequence, but they make it possible for objects to appear in succession.

तमः प्रकाशवत्त्वेते त्रयोऽध्वानो व्यवस्थिताः ।
अक्रमास्तेषु भावानां क्रमः समुपलभ्यते ॥

Vāk III.9.52

These three paths are like light and shade, and they are without sequence. In them objects acquire sequence. (Tr. K.A.S. Iyer)

Utpaladeva in his **Īśvarapratyabhijñā-Kārikā** discusses the interrelatedness of time, action and succession (for a detailed explanation see Abhinavagupta's **Vimarśinī**):

सक्रमत्वं च लौकिक्याः क्रियायाः कालशक्तितः ।
घटते न तु शाश्वत्याः प्राभव्याः स्यात् प्रभोरिव ॥
कालः सूर्यादिसञ्चारस्तत्तत्पुष्पादिजन्म वा ।
शीतोष्णे वाथ तल्लक्ष्यः क्रम एव स तत्त्वतः ॥
क्रमो भेदाश्रयो भेदोऽप्याभाससदसत्त्वतः ।
आभाससदसत्त्वे तु चित्राभासकृतः प्रभोः ॥
मूर्तिवैचित्र्यतो देशक्रममाभासयत्यसौ ।
क्रियावैचित्र्यनिर्भासात्कालक्रममपीश्वरः ॥

IPKā II.1.2-5

The worldly action can be maintained to be successive, due to the power of time, but not the eternal activity of the Highest Lord, like the Lord Himself.
Time in reality is nothing else than the succession, observable in the movement of the sun etc., in birth (*janma*) of different flowers and in summer and winter.
Succession depends upon difference, the latter on the existence of a certain manifestation and non-existence of another, and the existence of some manifestation and non-existence of another are brought about by the Lord Himself who manifests the variety of manifestations.
The Lord makes the spatial succession manifest by means of variety of manifestations of bodies (*Mūrtivaicitrya*) and the temporal succession by means of manifestation of the variety (of forms) in action (*Kriyāvaicitrya*). (Tr. K.C Pandey)

However, the sense of difference, of before and after in time or space, cannot be present in consciousness. Without negating succession, the Āgamas state that creation is both succession and non-succession (*kramākrama*).

नित्यं कालानवच्छेदाद्वैतत्यात्र प्रदेशगम् ।
क्रमाक्रमसमुत्पत्तेः क्रमाद्युत्पत्तिशक्तिमत् ॥

MṛgĀ vp III.2b-3a

(The cause) is eternal, because unlimited by time and not localised because of its immensity. It has the power to produce progressively and otherwise, because its production (creation) is both progressive and simultaneous.

In creation, succession itself is an expression of the freedom of the Lord, hence it is not denied.

स्वातन्त्र्यशक्तिः क्रमसंसिसृक्षा क्रमात्मता चेति विभोर्विभूतिः ।
तदेव देवीत्रयमन्तरास्तामनुत्तरं मे प्रथयत् स्वरूपम् ॥

TĀl I.5

The power of freedom, the will to create sequence (*krama*) and the very sequence are the glory of the Lord, the *anuttara*. These three are the triad of the goddesses (*parā, parāparā and aparā*). May the *anuttara* while showing its diverse manifestations remain present in my heart as one with myself. (Tr. H.N. Chakravarty)

The Kashmir Śaiva thinkers hold pure consciousness (*saṃvit*) to be beyond sequence and non-sequence:

इत्थं द्वादशधा संवित्तिष्ठन्ती विश्वमातृषु ।
एकैवेति न कोऽप्यस्याः क्रमस्य नियमः क्वचित् ॥
क्रमाभावान्न युगपत् तदभावात् क्रमोऽपि न ।
क्रमाक्रमकथातीतं संवित्तत्वं सुनिर्मलम् ॥

TĀl IV.178cd-180ab

Thus pure consciousness in twelve forms remains abiding in all the subject, object and the instrument of knowledge of the universe. She (*saṃvit*) verily is one and any sort of limitations of sequential order is not possible in her. In the absence of *krama* (sequence) it is neither called simultaneous. In the absence of simultaneity, sequence is absent there. The essence of *saṃvit* is beyond *krama* and *akrama*, for it is really pure. (Tr. H.N. Chakravarty)

At the level of limited consciousness which distinguishes the knower, knowledge and object of knowledge (*jñātā, jñāna, jñeya*) as mutually exclusive, sequence is implied as long as there is a relation of subject and object, but not at the level of pure and absolute consciousness:

अक्रमता मे क्रमिकं ज्ञात्राद्यं सक्रमाक्रमा तु चितिः ।

Virūpākṣa Pañcāśikā III.33a

I-consciousness, the essence of which is light (*prakāśa*), is without any sequence and the knowing subject, the instrument of knowledge and the object of knowledge are sequential while *citi*, consciousness, is both, sequential and non-sequential. (Tr. H.N. Chakravarty)

The *Krama* school of Kashmir Śaivism is so called because there is a gradual rising of the soul to realization. It makes use of the succession of space and time for reaching the state beyond space and time. The *Krama* system analyses every act of cognition in terms of the rising of the twelve *Kālīs* or phases of the Śakti. "The outstanding characteristic of this tradition is that it worships a sequential rather than a simply concentric pantheon. A series of sets of deities (*cakras*) is worshipped in a fixed sequence as the phases (*krama*) of the cyclical pulse of cognition (*saṃvit*). These phases are Emission (*sṛṣṭikrama*), Maintenance of the emitted (*sthitikrama*) (also called Incarnation (*avatārakrama*)), Retraction of the emitted (*saṃhārakrama*) and the Nameless fourth (*anākhyakrama*) (also called the Phase of the Kālīs (*kālīkrama*)), in which all trace of the preceding process is dissolved into liberated and all-pervading consciousness." (A. Sanderson, p.683).

This sequence in the emergence of the Kālīs can be arranged in a circular way. Another aspect of the mystical meaning of *krama* in this school is the gradual rising of *kuṇḍalinī* through the *cakras*. Besides, *krama* has also ritual implications, because it refers to the sequence of actions in Kaula ritual. Here *krama* becomes "virtually synonymous with the term '*prakriyā*' " (M. Dyczkowski, p.77).

One of the early *Krama* texts (not available now), the **Krama-Siddhi**, gives a mystical meaning of *krama* as the two aspects of Rudra manifesting in an alternating way. His fierceful nature becomes manifest in dissolution and his benign nature in bestowing grace.

ककारः क्रोधरूपस्तु मकारो मङ्गलो भवेत् ।
क्रोधे तु मङ्गलं कुर्यात् क्रमः कालक्रमो भवेत् ॥
गुर्वायत्तं क्रमज्ञानमाज्ञासिद्धिकरं परम् ।
क्रमज्ञानान्महादेवि ! त्रैलोक्यं कवलीकृतम् ॥

Krama-Siddhi, quoted in
Mahārtha Mañjarī, comm. on 41

In the term *krama, kra* represents the dreadful nature and *ma* stands for auspiciousness. While in the fierceful state one should consider it to be auspicious. *Krama* is of the nature of time sequence. The knowledge of the concept of *krama* can only be known from the

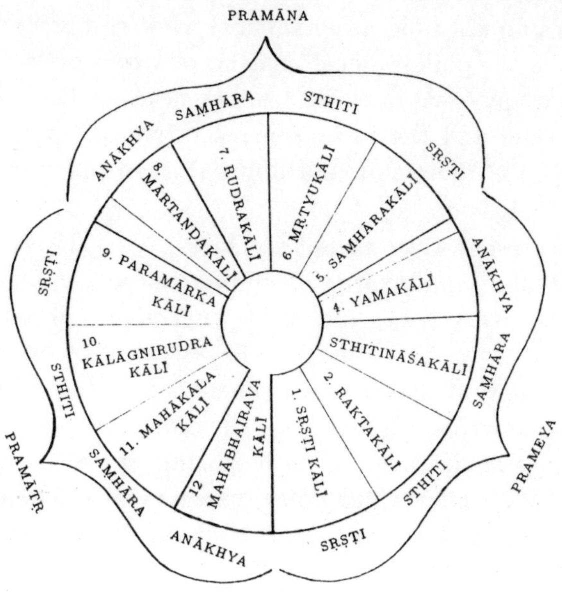

Figure 2: The Wheel of Energies, Śakticakra (after L. Silburn)

teacher for it is the highest attainment of command. O great goddess, by means of perfect knowledge regarding *krama*, the three worlds have been swallowed up. (Tr. H.N. Chakravarty)

One of the mystical terms of Kashmir Śaivism is *kramamudrā* which relates to the alternation (hence *krama*) of inner absorption (*samādhi*) and outer consciousness (*vyutthāna*). *Kramamudrā* externalises the interior and interiorizes the exterior in a succession of flux and reflux (Cf. L. Silburn). *Krama* is here not so much a temporal sequence which belongs to the realm of difference (*bheda*), but a means of integrating the totality of inner and outer experience and thus reaching a state of equality (*samatā*).

Krama in the Philosophical Systems (Āstika Darśana)

by Anindita N. Balslev

The philosophical considerations concerning the idea of *krama* or sequence in the context of the views about time in the Āstika Darśanas deserve careful attention. Is the notion of sequence an integral part of that of time?

In this section focus will be made on different aspects of the idea of *krama* especially in the light of the various conceptual models of time that have emerged in the history of Indian thought. At the outset, it may be observed that the Brahmanical schools do not hold an unanimous view regarding time. This has important bearing on the philosophical analysis of *krama* or sequence. In order to appreciate the metaphysical implications, one needs to take an over-all view of the problem of time and the various perspectives of the idea of sequence which are documented in the philosophical literature of the major Brahmanical schools.

To take some representative examples: The Nyāya-Vaiśeṣika schools advocate a view of absolute Time expressed in the concept of *Mahākāla*. This is a notion of time as unitary (*eka*), indivisible (*akhaṇḍa*), all-pervasive (*vibhu*). What is pertinent for an understanding of the idea of sequence in this conceptual structure is to note that change or movement is not ascribed to *Mahākāla* or absolute time (hence described as *niṣkriya*). This is a static view of time (*sthira-kāla-vāda*). Time, it is held, knows of no beginning or end (*anādi, ananta*). It is conceived as an independent (*svatantra*) category of existence without reference to which no change or movement is conceivable or possible (cf. *kālo hi jagadādhāraḥ kālādhāro na vidyate*). *Mahākāla* is the support, the instrumental cause (*nimitta kāraṇa*) of an event or an entity to which a beginning or an end or both can be ascribed. Hence it is said: *janyānāṃ janakaḥ kālo* etc. (**Bhāṣāpariccheda**, *kārikā* 22). However, the ideas of time-divisions and time-phases are accounted for as conventional practices (*vyavahāra*) made possible with the help of any standard motion such as the solar motion. This is the idea of *khaṇḍa kāla*. Time as such (*svarūpataḥ*) of course knows of no such divisions. Thus the notion of temporal sequence is not to be taken as integral to time as such. The metaphysical scheme of these schools thus operates with the idea that all change and becoming pertain to time but time itself does not change or flow.

The concepts of temporal priority and posteriority are not applicable to the eternal substances (*nitya-vastu*), but only to that which is generated (*janya*), that which is contingent (*kādācitka*). *Mahākāla* is ubiquitous (*niraṃśa*) and inferred on the ground (*liṅga*) of such notions as priority (*paratva*) and posteriority (*aparatva*), of simultaneity (*yaugapadya*) and succession (*ayaugapadya*), of quickness (*kṣipratva*) and slowness (*ciratva*) etc. Note that the notion of succession is not identical with that of time, rather it is identified as the *liṅga* for inferring the reality of *Mahākāla*.

The philosophical pattern with regard to the problem of time is very largely the same in the school of Pūrva Mīmāṃsā. Philosophically the most interesting dispute among the schools has been regarding the epistemological question of how time is known: by perception or by inference? The Nyāya-Vaiśeṣika schools insist on inference whereas the school of Pūrva Mīmāṃsā (Bhāṭṭa) on perception.

It may be now asked what is precisely entailed in the notion of *krama*. How is it defined in the philosophical literature?

A direct reference to *krama* can be found in the **Nyāya-Sūtra**:

> क्रमवृत्तिवदयुगपद्ग्रहणम् ।
>
> NySū III.2.6
>
> Due to successive conjunction (of the mind with the senses), objects are not simultaneously known. (Tr. M. Gangopadhyaya)

This is a concrete instance which demonstrates how the idea of sequence is employed. The commentary of Vātsyāyana indicates that the idea of *kramavṛttitva* is used in the context of a discussion about sensory knowledge as olfactory, visual etc. These arise in contact with the mind only successively, one after the other and not simultaneously (*ayugapadgrahaṇam*). Since the mind is *aṇuparimāṇa* (atomic) and not *vibhuparimāṇa* (all-pervasive), it cannot come in contact with the different sense-organs (*indriyas*) at the same time.

Nyāya-Bhāṣya clearly defines *krama* with an appropriate example:

> उपमर्दप्रादुर्भावयोः पौर्वापर्यनियमः क्रमः ।
>
> NySūBh IV.1.16
>
> The regular order of priority and posteriority of destruction and appearance is sequence. (Tr. H.N. Chakravarty)

From this it is clear that sequence (*krama*) implies the invariability of priority and posteriority in the order of events, such as, the coming into existence (of the sprout) preceded by the destruction (of the seed) constitutes their sequence. This is taken from a discussion concerning causality where Nyāya challenges the Buddhist position.

This general meaning of succession (*ānantarya*) can be seen also in the **Nyāya-Sūtra** IV.1.16, and again, in such a statement as *dravyanirūpaṇānantaraṃ krameṇa guṇādikaṃ nirūpyate* etc. **Nyāyakośa** indicates the meaning of *krama* as *arthānāṃ naiyatyena pūrvāparāvasthānam*, "the subject matters (of a system) have their position given (in the text following a regular order, some earlier and later, this is stated to be sequential order".

Now to take some representative examples from the Mīmāṃsā literature:

> इहेदानीं क्रमनियमलक्षणमुच्यते । तच्छ्रुत्यर्थपाठप्रवृत्तिकाण्डमुख्यैः वक्ष्यते। श्रुत्यादीनां च बलाबलम्। आदितस्तु श्रुतिक्रमश्चिनयते। किं यथा श्रुति पदार्थानां क्रम आस्थेय उत अनियमेन। ... श्रुतिलक्षणमानुपूर्व्यं तत्प्रमाणत्वादिति । श्रुतिः-श्रवणमक्षराणां, तन्निमित्तं यस्य क्रमस्य स साधुक्रमः । श्रुतिप्रमाणका हि वैदिका अर्थाः ।...सत्रे दीक्षाक्रमे ये

यजमानास्त ऋत्विजः इत्युक्त्वा तेषां दीक्षाक्रम विधत्ते । सामर्थ्याच्च क्रमः विधीयते । गुणभूतो हि पदार्थानां क्रमो भवति । यश्च यस्यानिर्वर्त्यमानस्योपकरोति स तस्य गुणभूतः ।...एवं प्रत्यक्षः क्रमस्य गुणभावः यत्र तत्रार्थेन स एवाश्रयितव्यः ।

MīmSūBh V.1.1-2

We now proceed to deal with the subject of 'order of sequence'; this 'order' is determined by 1) direct assertion (Śruti), 2) efficiency (utility) (*artha*); 3) verbal text (*pāṭha*), 4) commencement (*pravṛtti*) or tendency, 5) place (*kāṇḍa*) in the text, 6) the principal (*mukhya*) and among these there is comparative strength and weakness.... (The question is) Should the things laid down be done in the order in which they have been directly asserted? Or in any order without restriction?... The order of sequence should be determined on the basis of Direct Assertion as this is the sole authority. Śruti consists in the reading of the words of the text; and that order of sequence which is determined by such reading is the right one; because in all Vedic matters Śruti is the sole authority... we have an example of this in the order in which the Initiations are performed at the Satra session. Having declared that 'those same persons who are the priests are also the sacrificers', the Śruti goes to lay down the order in which these sacrificers are to be initiated....

The order of *krama* is enjoined also by *Artha* i.e. utility or efficiency. The order of sequence is only auxiliary – a subordinate factor – of things and when one thing helps in the accomplishment of another, the former is considered as an auxiliary of the latter, ... whenever the order of sequence is distinctly perceived to be an auxiliary it should be taken to be determined by the efficiency... (Tr. G.N. Jha)

This is an important use of the idea of *krama* in the context of sacrifice. *Krama* or sequence is considered under six headings: 1) *Śrauta Krama*, 2) *Artha Krama*, 3) *Pāṭha Krama*, 4) *Sthāna Krama*, 5) *Mukhya Krama*, 6) *Pravṛtti Krama*. This is a classification pertaining to the sequential order in the performance of a sacrifice. The special import of the term *krama* in this context is to emphasise the successive order demanded in a methodical practice. When the injunction is obtained from a revealed text, it is *Śrauta Krama*. Again, the sequence that is actually followed for pragmatic reasons, even if the injunction of the śruti is otherwise, is *Artha Krama* etc. The emphasis is on the idea of *paurvāparya*, the idea of what precedes and what follows in the order of the performance of a sacrifice. Thus *krama* or sequence involves succession.

Used in diverse contexts, the idea of sequence entails a notion of change and action with reference to which one could speak of a succession of one entity or an event followed by another. This is why it is said that: *kramaḥ kriyāviśeṣaṇatayā vidhīyate* ("Sequence is enjoined as the qualifier of action", **Mīmāṃsā Kośa**).

The metaphysical status of change and becoming, however, varies from system to system. The question whether sequence is an objective phenomenon or merely a subjective construction has been variously treated in the philosophical literature.

In the philosophy of Advaita Vedānta the problem of time qua change is treated as a problem of appearance. The metaphysical commitment to the Upaniṣadic idea of reality as the 'one without a second' lead to *Vivartavāda.* In this scheme the Nyāya-Vaiśeṣika model of time as an objective category is dialectically rejected (cf. Śrī Harṣa's **Khaṇḍanakhaṇḍakhādya** and Citsukha's **Tattvapradīpikā**). The immutable consciousness (*kūṭastha caitanya*) alone has an absolute status (*paramārthika*), change and duality are relative/contingent/conventional /empirical (*vyavahārika*). The idea of sequence has relevance in a context dealing with change and difference (*bheda*), hence belong to the domain of the *vyāvahārika.* Thus all references to the notion of *krama* or sequence in the Advaita discourse are to be treated accordingly, no matter whether the context is dealing with cosmology or soteriology. However, the usage of the term *krama* carries with it the ideas of *ānantarya* and *paurvāparya* as has been indicated earlier. The word *krama* appears over and over again in the **Brahma-Sūtra-Bhāṣya** conveying the notion of succession.

In the context of soteriology Advaita Vedānta distinguishes between *krama-mukti* and *sadya-mukti.* Whereas the latter implies immediate salvation, the former implies a notion of salvation to be attained by stages (cf. BrSūBh I.3.13).

For a philosophical appraisal of the idea of sequence in this conceptual structure, it is to be carefully noted that for Advaita Vedānta the *sat* is unsublatable in all three times (*trikālābādhya*). The *nitya-vastu* is *apariṇāmī,* hence any idea of a temporal order which makes room for sequence, involving duality and difference, is a problem of appearance.

Although the notion of sequence has been discussed in the philosophical literature of various Brahmanical schools, and the term is profusely used in a variety of contexts, nowhere is this notion treated with such depth as in Sāṃkhya and Yoga. Both in Sāṃkhya and Yoga philosophy the idea of *krama* forms an important part of the general theme of *pariṇāma* or change. These schools, both advocating *pariṇāmavāda,* however, differ in their respective understanding of time which has significance for the philosophical treatment of the notion of *krama.* These ideas therefore deserve a fuller treatment.

First of all, it may be noted that *nityatva* or eternality is ascribed to both *puruṣa* and *prakṛti,* the dynamic principle of matter. *Puruṣa* is *apariṇāmī,* it is the unchanging and unchangeable principle of consciousness. Thus *nityatva* or eternality, for Sāṃkhya and Yoga, is an idea applicable to that which knows of no beginning or end (*anādi, ananta*), and which never loses its essence (*svabhāva*). Thus the idea of change or *pariṇāma* – with reference to which alone one can meaningfully speak of *krama* or sequence – may or may not be combined with the idea of eternality. Note that in Advaita Vedānta the concept of *nityatva* is so rigorously formulated that it does not leave any room for change and difference. In the conceptions of *prakṛti* and *puruṣa*, the Sāṃkhya and the Yoga schools put forward a notion of eternality which can be conceived in terms of change or as bereft of it. Thus *puruṣa* is described as *kūṭastha nitya* and *prakṛti* as *pariṇāmi nitya*, translated aptly by K.C. Bhattacharya as 'unchangingly eternal' and as 'eternal in change' respectively.

Now the notion of →*pariṇāma* needs to be further explored for an understanding of the idea of *krama* or sequence. That which is *apariṇāmī*, unchanging and unchangeable, knows of no sequence (*akrama*).

The Sāṃkhya and Yoga insights into the notions of time and sequence know of subtle philosophical differences, despite the many important common features of the conceptual structures. This may be said to be due to their respective treatment of causality (*kārya-kāraṇa-bhāva*). Both the schools, however, agree in repudiating the Nyāya-Vaiśeṣika model of absolute time, the idea of *Mahākāla* as an independent (*svatantra*) category.

There is no mention of *kāla* in the Sāṃkhya list of categories (*tattva*). Vācaspati Miśra in his **Tattvakaumudī**, the commentary on the **Sāṃkhya-Kārikā** (33) of Īśvarakṛṣṇa, has argued that the limiting conditions (*upādhi*) by which the Vaiśeṣika accounts for the three time phases of past, present and future, are themselves the basis of all temporal usages, there is no necessity of postulating a distinct entity called time. The idea of an absolute time *à la* Vaiśeṣika is equally rejected by Vijñānabhikṣu in his **Sāṃkhya-Pravacana-Bhāṣya** (2.12).

If the idea of a static time (*sthira-kāla-vāda*) with reference to which the Nyāya-Vaiśeṣika philosophies accounted for change and movement, of which the idea of sequence is an integral part, how is the latter understood in Sāṃkhya?

The **Yukti-Dīpikā** interprets the Sāṃkhya view of time as an aspect of the causal process (*kāraṇa-parispanda*). Vijñānabhikṣu holds time to be nothing apart from the ubiquitious *ākāśa* or ether which is an evolute of *prakṛti*. In order to understand the Sāṃkhya view of sequence, one has to explore further the idea of *pariṇāma*. Evidently, where there is no change there can be no sequence. The questions concerning time and sequence do not arise with regard to *puruṣa*.

It is evident that the idea of *krama* is important for an understanding of the forward (*anuloma*) and backward (*pratiloma*) movement of *prakṛti*, the consequence of which is creation (*sṛṣṭi*) and dissolution (*pralaya*) respectively. The idea of the three time-phases is relevant in the context of *visadṛśa-pariṇāma*, the movement that has brought forth heterogeneity. *Sadṛśa-pariṇāma*, however, is a notion of a primordial homogeneous movement, the pre-empirical aspect of the dynamic *prakṛti*. For Sāṃkhya it is superfluous to postulate a separate, distinct *tattva* called time as in the notion of *prakṛti*. Sāṃkhya combines space, time and matter in the same principle.

Questions concerning *krama* or sequence come to play a crucial role in the Yoga discourse. It is a key idea for the Yoga analysis of *pariṇāma*. The **Yoga-Sūtra** III.13-15 and the commentary thereon elaborates on this theme indicating the three major aspects of *pariṇāma: dharma-*, *lakṣaṇa-* and *avasthā-pariṇāma*. These ideas are very important for an appraisal of the Yoga insights into the problems of time and sequence. To put it briefly, *dharma-pariṇāma* focuses on that aspect when a change is perceived as a change of quality; *lakṣaṇa-pariṇāma* emphasises the three temporal phases as different stages of the mutation of an entity, the *avasthā-pariṇāma* indicates a change of state. It is evident that each one of these three aspects of *pariṇāma* involves a sequence. The idea of *lakṣaṇa-pariṇāma* is particularly important for understanding why a notion of an absolute time is rejected in the Yoga conceptual structure. The three time-phases are seen as the potential (future), the manifest (present) and the sublatent (past) stages of an entity.

What is objective and what is only an intellectual construction in the context of the Yoga analysis of time become clear as one explores the notion of *kṣaṇa* and *krama* respectively.

The **Yoga-Sūtra** says:

> क्षणतत्क्रमयोः संयमाद्विवेकजं ज्ञानम् ।
>
> YSū III.52
>
> As a result of constraint upon moments and their sequence (there arises the intuitive) knowledge proceeding from discrimination.
> (Tr. J.H. Woods)

Vyāsa's commentary on this contains illuminating elaborations about *kṣaṇa* and *krama* i.e. the moment and the sequence. The following observations are particularly significant:

> यावता वा समयेन चलितः परमाणुः पूर्वदेशं जह्यादुत्तरदेशमुपसंपद्येत स कालः क्षणः तत् प्रवाहाविच्छेदस्तु क्रमः ।...स खल्वयं कालो वस्तुशून्योऽपि बुद्धिनिर्माणः शब्दज्ञानानुपाती, ...क्षणस्तु वस्तुपतितः क्रमावलम्बी, क्रमश्च क्षणानन्तर्यात्मा तं कालविदः काल इत्याचक्षते योगिनः । न च द्वौ क्षणौ सह भवतः ।
>
> YSūBh III.52
>
> Or that much of time by which an atom in motion gives up its previous position and reaches the next place in the moment. The

uninterruption of the flow thereof is however the succession.... It is in fact this time which, although devoid of reality, becomes an intellectual creation following the literal idea.... The moment however, falling under the head of reality, is supported by succession. Further, the succession possesses the nature of intervention of the moments. The Yogis who are the knowers of time, call it by the name of time. Again, two moments can never coexist. (Tr. Bangalibaba)

From these it is possible to read the philosophical position that the Yoga school takes on the problem of time. The school advocates a discrete view of time. What is real is the moment (→*kṣaṇa*). The idea of an unitary, objective time *à la* Vaiśeṣika or a notion of a collection (*saṃhāra*) of moments or a series of moments (*kṣaṇapravāha*) is a mental/subjective construction without having any reality. This is so because no two moments can be said to exist simultaneously. The (present) moment is not a construction; Vyāsa describes it as *vastupatitaḥ*, Vācaspati Miśra as *vāstavika* (real).

The whole universe, says Vyāsa, undergoes change in a single moment:

एकेन क्षणेन कृत्स्नो लोकः परिणाममनुभवति ...तयोः क्षणतत्क्रमयोः संयमात्
तयोः साक्षात्करणं ततश्च विवेकजं ज्ञानं प्रादुर्भवति ।

YSūBh III.52

The whole world undergoes change by that single moment... From the Saṃyama upon the moment and its succession, the direct vision of them appears. (Tr. Bangalibaba)

The notion of a sequence rests on the idea of a succession of moments, hence is considered to be a *vikalpa*, a verbal cognition with regard to a thing which does not really exist.

Allusions to *kṣaṇa* and *krama* are numerous in the **Yoga-Sūtra**, the commentary and the various sub-commentaries. It is said, to give a few more examples:

क्रमान्यत्वं परिणामान्यत्वे हेतुः ।

YSū III.15

The order of the sequence (*krama*) is the reason for the order of the mutations. (Tr. J.H. Woods)

Again

क्षणप्रतियोगी परिणामापरान्तनिर्ग्राह्यः क्रमः ।

YSū IV.33

The positive correlate to the moment, recognised as such at the final limit of the mutation, is a sequence. (Tr. J.H. Woods)

This is revealing how a sequence of mutations is perceived in the moment by a yogin.

The idea of the end of a sequence of mutations in the context of *samādhi* is expressed in the following:

> ततः कृतार्थानां परिणामक्रमसमाप्तिर्गुणानाम् ।
>
> YSū IV.32
>
> When as a result of this, the aspects (*guṇa*) have fulfilled their purpose, they attain to the limit of the sequence of mutations. (Tr. J.H. Woods)

The full philosophical import of the idea of sequence in the Indian context is connected with the various views on time that have developed in the history of Indian thought.

In the Arts

Succession, order and method (*krama*) are essential in any Art form, but more so in the performing arts like drama, music and dance. However, even the so-called static arts like painting, sculpture and architecture have to follow a regular procedure in their creation which can never be arbitrary (also →*vidhi*). Any monumental work of art like a temple, which cannot be seen at one glance like a miniature painting, also requires a procedure of viewing it. In the case of a temple or a city this is called *parikrama*, circumambulation. It is only by moving around it that the visitor or devotee can get an impression of the total monument or group of monuments. Ritual *parikrama* of a sacred place also re-creates and enlivens the space.

Especially in the case of the Arts, *krama* refers not to a neutral or mechanical sequence, but to a regular order which is part of the artistic whole. The word *anukrama* is often used, as in the description of the *rāsa* dance in the **Viṣṇu Purāṇa**:

> ततः प्रववृते रासश्चलद्वलयनिस्वनः ।
> अनुयातशरत्काव्यगेयगीतिरनुक्रमात् ॥
>
> ViPur V.13.51
>
> Then proceeded the dance to the music of their clashing bracelets, and songs celebrated in suitable strain the charms of the autumnal season. (Tr. Wilson)

In Vedic recitation *krama* also refers to the proper order:

ऋचो बह्वृचमुख्यैश्च प्रेर्यमाणाः पदक्रमैः ।
शुश्राव मनुजव्याघ्रो विततेष्विह कर्मसु ॥

MBh I.64.31

At particular places that tiger among men (Duḥṣanta) heard the chanting of Ṛk hymns by first-rate Brahmanas according to the just rules of intonation. (Tr. P.C. Roy)

In poetry *krama* is the right order of words and sentences:

यथोपदेशं क्रमशो निर्देशोऽत्र क्रमो मतः ।

Kāvyāl IV.20ab

Krama (orderly statement) is that where the things attributed (*nirdeśa*) follow the order of the first statement (*upadeśa*). (Tr. P.V. Naganatha Sastry)

गमकानि निबध्यन्ते वाक्ये वाक्यान्तराण्यपि ।
पदानीवात्र कोऽप्येष प्रसादस्यापरः क्रमः ॥

VaJī I.46

When in a sentence other sentences are made to fuse with a coherence usually possible only in the case of the constituent words, we have another variety of 'perspicuity'. (Tr. K. Krishnamoorthy)

In architecture there is a prescribed order of building the different parts of a temple:

एवं भेदे तथा कर्म क्रमभेदे तथा गुणाः ।
संप्रवक्ष्यामि संक्षेपान्निष्फलं शिल्पिभिर्विना ॥

ŚiPrak I.499

These parts and their works, their order and different properties, which I will tell in brief, are useless without the *śilpin*. (Tr. A. Boner)

शृणु त्वमाद्यच्छेदानां कोणकभागनिर्णयम् ।
अनुक्रम्य तथानर्थराहादिकं यथाक्रमम् ॥

ŚiPrak II.425

You first hear the description of the divisions of the *koṇakabhāga*, of the *anartha*, the *rāhā* and other parts in their proper order. (Tr. A. Boner)

But no doubt it is in the context of music and dance that temporal succession and spatial movement play an important role.

In music (*saṅgīta*) *krama* refers to the order of notes (*svaras*), as in the formation of *mūrchanās* the seven *svaras* have to be used in ascent and descent:

क्रमयुक्ताः स्वराः सप्त मूर्छनेत्यभिसंज्ञिताः ।

NŚ XXVIII. 32ab

सप्तेति पूर्णा इत्यर्थः । क्रमयुक्ता इति क्रमेणारोहणं तथैव स्वराणामवरोहणेन च पुनरप्याहरणमिति क्रमः । तेन युक्ताः सम्यगाहिताः ।

AbhiBhā on above

The seven *svaras* (used) in their order are known as *mūrchanā*.
Commentary:
The number seven implies that *mūrchanās* are complete. *Krama* or order implies that the seven *svaras* have to be used in ascent successively and similarly, again the *svaras* have to be taken in descent. The *svaras* having this *krama* i.e. *svaras* in which this *krama* is embedded (are *mūrchanā*). (Tr. P.L. Sharma)

In *kūṭatānas*, where the original order of notes is broken for the sake of permutation, this process is called *utkrama* or *vyutkrama*:

हन्यादनन्तरायेण पूर्वा यस्य क्रमोत्क्रमात् ।
गुणकारसमास्तत्र क्रमाच्छेषाः स्युरुत्तमाः ॥

Datti 40

In a series progressing arithmetically, multiply the last number with the preceding ones in succession. The resulting aggregate will include both *krama-tānas* (where the *svaras* are in their proper sequence) and the *vyutkrama-tānas* (the *kūṭa-tānas* where the *svaras* are not in sequence). The *krama-tānas* will equal the end-number with which the multiplication was begun. The rest will be *utkrama* (or *kūṭa-tānas*). (Tr. Mukund Lath)

The **Bṛhaddeśī** also makes the distinction between *krama* and *vyutkrama* clear:

सा ऋषभस्य (सर्षभस्य) सरीत्येक एव क्रमः । व्युत्क्रमे द्वितीयः रिसः ।

BṛD p.30

Ṣaḍja (with *ṛṣabha*) has only one *krama* (original order), the second variety, *risa* is formed by breaking the order (*vyutkrama*). (Tr. P.L. Sharma)

असंपूर्णाश्च संपूर्णा व्युत्क्रमोच्चारितस्वराः ।
मूर्छनाः कूटतानाः स्युः... ॥

SR I.4.32abc

The incomplete and complete *mūrchanās* with their notes produced in a permuatated form become permutational note-series (*kūṭa-tānas*).
(Tr. R.K. Shringy and P.L. Sharma)

The 'combinations' or sets of one, two, three, four, five, six and seven notes, derived out of *mūrchanās* of two *grāmas*, that maintain the original order of notes are also known as *krama*:

चतुः स्वरेषु न्याद्यौ द्वौ चतुर्धा द्वादशपरे ॥
क्रमाद्द्विधेति द्वात्रिंशत् ...

SR I.4.45cd,46a

Among the tetratonic (*kūṭa-tānas*), the two commencing with *ni* are fourfold, while the other twelve (original) series are twofold; these are thirty-two (*kramas*).

Besides, the series of *mūrchanās* numbering seven for each one are also known as *krama*:

प्रथमादिस्वरारम्भादेकैका सप्तधा भवेत् ।
तासूच्चार्यान्त्यस्वरांस्तान् पूर्वानुच्चारयेत् क्रमात् ॥
ते क्रमास्तेषु संख्या स्याद् द्वानवत्या शतत्रयम् ।

SR I.4.19-20ab

Each one of them (56 *mūrchanās*) becomes sevenfold by commencing with the first note and so on. In these (seven *mūrchanā-kramas* or *mūrchanā* series), the last notes having been sung, initial notes may be sung in their respective order. These are *mūrchanā* series (*kramas*) and their number is three hundred and ninety two.
(Tr. R.K. Shringy and P.L. Sharma)

One of the 25 *alaṅkāras* or embellishments of the *sañcārī-varṇa* or circular note-pattern is called *krama*:

, कला द्वित्रिचतुः स्वराः ।
आद्यस्वराद्यास्तिस्रः स्युर्द्वितीयाद्यादयस्तथा ॥
यत्रासौ क्रम इत्युक्तः ,

सरि - सरिग - सरिगम, रिग - रिगम - रिगमप ।
गम - गमप - गमपध, मप - मपध - मपधनि ॥

SR I.6.44d,45a

(The embellishment) in which there are three phrases consisting of two, three and four tones respectively, commencing with the initial tone and three (similar) phrases commencing with the second tone and so on, is called krama, e.g. *sa-ri sa-ri-ga sa-ri-ga-ma, ri-ga ri-ga-ma ri-ga-ma-pa, ga-ma ga-ma-pa ga-ma-pa-dha, ma-pa ma-pa-dha ma-pa-dha-ni*. (Tr. R.K. Shringy and P.L. Sharma)

Another *alaṅkāra* of the *sthāyi-varṇa* or steady note-pattern is *krama-recita*:

आद्यन्तयोर्मूर्च्छनादिश्चेत् स्वरोऽन्तर्द्वितीयकः ।
सैका कलाथ चेन्मध्येऽतस्तृतीयचतुर्थकौ ॥
सा द्वितीया पञ्चमाद्यास्त्रयोऽन्तश्चेत् कला परा ।
एवं कलात्रयेणोक्तोऽलङ्कारः क्रमरेचितः ॥
सरिस सगमस सपधनिस

SR I.6.11,12

The embellishment (called) *krama-recita* is described in three phrases as follows: the first tone of the *mūrchanā*, in the first phrase, is placed in the beginning as well as at the end with the second (tone) in-between; the third and the fourth (tones) are placed in-between in the second phrase; while in the third phrase the three tones commencing with *pañcama* are placed in-between, e.g. *sa-ri-sa, sa-ga-ma-sa, sa-pa-dha-ni-sa.* (Tr. R.K. Shringy and P.L. Sharma)

In the context of dance the words *krama, kramaṇa* or *saṃkramaṇa* are not used for denoting the steps and movements, however, their synonyms *sañcaraṇa* and *apasarpaṇa* are found. The past participle of *kram-* is used in the names of three *ākāśikī cārīs: atikrānta* ('over-step'), *apakrānta* ('going away') and *pārśvakrānta* ('side-step') (cf. NŚ X.30-32 and SR VII. 942-947). Sometimes the movement of one of the *cārīs* is referred to as *krama* in the **Nāṭya-Śāstra**:

अतिक्रान्तक्रमं कृत्वा चोत्प्लुत्य विनिपातयेत् ।
जङ्घाञ्चिता परिक्षिप्ता सा ज्ञेया हरिणप्लुता ॥

NŚ X.43

Having done the movement (known as) *atikrānta* (the *atikrānta cārī* described in NŚ X.30, lit. the past participle of crossing or transcending), one should 'throw down' (the foot) after a jumping movement (forward) and the (other) shank is 'thrown' (back) with an *añcita* foot (with bent or curled toes), that (total movement or *cārī*) is known as *hariṇaplutā* (*cārī*, the jump of the deer). (Tr. P.L. Sharma)

Here one could establish a connection between the steps in dance movements, the mythological steps of Viṣṇu and, for that matter, Śiva as Naṭarāja, and their representations in sculpture.

In the **Nāṭya-Śāstra** *krama* is also a technical term for one of the *sandhyaṅgas* of *garbhasandhi* (→*sandhi*), and it is related to the realization of *bhāva* (mood or mental state):

भावतत्त्वोपलब्धिस्तु क्रम इत्यभिधीयते । NŚ XIX.84cd

भावस्य भाव्यमानस्य वस्तुनो भावनातिशये सत्यूहं प्रति भावनादिबलात् स्याद् या परमार्थोपलब्धिः सा क्रमः । बुद्धिर्हि तत्र क्रमते न प्रतिहन्यते ।

AbhiBhā on the above

The realisation of the true or real state of *bhāva* is called *krama*.
Commentary:
Bhāva stands here for the object of *bhāvanā* (contemplation with love or attraction); because of excessive *bhāvanā* the object of this act which exists in the imagination or apprehension is realised as being true or real. The intellect moves forward and is not obstructed.
(Tr. P.L. Sharma)

Abhinavagupta relates here *bhāva* with *bhāvanā* as the imaginative realization, and he quotes as an example a verse describing the state of a heroine who is so immersed in the thought of her lover that she feels that everybody is talking about him and knows about her secret. Here *krama* may be so called because of a progressive identification with the object of one's imagination.

Conclusion

Though *krama* appears to have a simple meaning, that of step, course, sequence, order and process, in space as well as in time, the implications of this concept are very rich. The conquering, and thus creation of the three worlds is attributed to the three steps of Viṣṇu Trivikrama in Vedic and Purāṇic myth. In philosophy the discussion involves the concept of time as succession and change. In Tantrism *krama* has a mystical connotation.

In the Arts, method and procedure are essential. In music where sequence of notes and time sequence are central, *krama* plays an important role. In dance, the steps, their character and sequence, though called with different names, are also *krama*. Any performing art depends upon the spatial and temporal unfolding which is only possible in a proper sequence and order.

Though *krama* is essentially succession, it can in no way be equated with the modern western notion of linear time and progress, because it is always relative. It is only in the spatial sense that it has to do with the pervasion of cosmic space, as symbolised by the powerful strides of the figure of Viṣṇu Trivikrama.

Bettina Bäumer

Select Bibliography

Balslev, Anindita Niyogi: A Study of Time in Indian Philosophy. Wiesbaden: Otto Harrassowitz, 1983.

Dyczkowski, Mark S.C.: The Canon of the Śaivāgama and the Kubjikā Tantras of the Western Kaula Tradition. New York: SUNY Press, 1988.

Gonda, J.: Aspects of Early Viṣṇuism. Delhi: Motilal Banarsidass, 1969.

Kuiper, F.B.J.: Ancient Indian Cosmogony, Chapter on "The Three Strides of Viṣṇu". New Delhi: Vikas, 1983.

Panikkar, Raimundo: The Vedic Experience, Mantramañjarī. Delhi: Motilal Banarsidass, 1983.

Piantelli, Mario: "Kramamukti – a few notes" in Indologica Tourinensia Vol. II, Torino, 1974.

Rastogi, Navjivan: The Krama Tantricism of Kashmir, Vol. I. Delhi: Motilal Banarsidass, 1979.

Sanderson, Alexis: "Śaivism and the Tantric Traditions," in The World's Religions, ed. by S. Sutherland etc. London: Routledge, 1988.

Silburn, Lilian: La Bhakti. Le Stavacintāmaṇi de Bhaṭṭanārāyaṇa. Paris: Ed. De Boccard, 1964.

— Hymnes aux Kālī. La roue des énergies divines. Paris: Ed. De Boccard, 1975.

SANDHI

Overview

Sandhi, junction, joint, connection, combination, union, meeting point, etc., derived from the root *dhā-*, to place, with prefix *sam-*, together, refers to 'crucial' moments in time as well as junctures in space. *Sandhyā* is the time of twilight, of the meeting of night and day, which is particularly sacred for worship. The *trisandhyā* are the three divisions of the day: dawn, noon and dusk, which represent the three times. *Sandhi* is a combination of two elements in which both undergo a transformation while still retaining their identity. In grammar, *sandhi* is the euphonic conjunction of vowels and consonants which undergo change in their combination. *Sandhis* are also the joints in the body which give it flexibility but need special protection. In the Vedas the body of Prajāpati, the creator, gets disjoined by his act of creation, and is again reconstructed in the sacrifice and in the construction of the fire altar (*agniciti*). His body, both spatially and temporally, is thus joined again, the bricks of the altar representing the days of the year, since Prajāpati is identified with the year.

In human life there are periods of transition which are called *sandhis*, e.g. "The transition between childhood and youth is known as *vayaḥsandhi*" (UjNīl X.8, *bālyayauvanayoḥ sandhir vayaḥsandhir itīryate*). In social relations *sandhi* can have an erotic meaning, and it has a political meaning as an agreement or peace settlement between two parties.

In the conception of time, these moments of juncture and phases of transition make the measurement of time possible. They also constitute a break or rest in time as in the *sandhis* between the cosmic ages (*yuga*). These times are particularly sacred and they need special attention. In a spiritual sense the subtle intervals represent the centre (*madhya*), and attention on these moments permits penetration into the centre of consciousness.

The term *sandhyā-bhāṣā* or *sandhā-bhāṣā*, sometimes translated as 'twilight language', is an enigmatic language containing double meaning, which is used by Buddhist Tantras and found in mystical poets like Kabir.

In the Arts, *sandhi* plays an important role in drama (*nāṭya*) as the junctures of the plot, joining together the different purposes and leading to the final end. There are five *sandhis* in Sanskrit drama which are combined with *sandhyaṅgas*, because they are joined together to create a total action. In temple architecture *sandhi-sthāna* is the place of junction between the main parts of the temple and between smaller sections, which have an important functional, structural as well as symbolical meaning. Generally, intervals, transitions and junctions are important elements in any art form.

Etymology and Cognate Words

Sandhi (m.) is derived from the root *dhā-*, to put, to place, with prefix *sam-*, meaning 'to join, unite, combine, connect, reconcile, heal, etc.' Hence it is a junction, connection, union, combination, juncture or joint, both in space and in time. The root *dhā-* also implies 'to do something well', cf. *vidhi, vidhāna*, 'order, method'. (Cf. Lakṣmī comm. on **Siddhānta-Kaumudī**, on *sandhi*, p.91). The **Amarakośa** defines *sandhiḥ, śleṣe*: "*sandhi* means adhering or clinging to." Both terms are used to denote the act of joining together (*sandhāna*, cf. comm. **Padacandrikā**). Closely related and partly synonymous words are *saṃhitā, sandhā, sandhāna*, all with similar meanings. *Sandhāna* also has a spiritual sense: intense awareness, concentration and unification of consciousness (cf. Kashmir Śaivism). *Sandhyā* (f.) is derived from *sandhi* and it particularly signifies the junctures between day and night, i.e., the morning and the evening twilight, as well as the ritual and prayer performed at those times. *Trisandhyā* are the three juncture times of the day which structure time.

An interesting synonym is *parvan*, which also signifies a joint, knot, break, pause, division and a time of juncture, as in the changes of the phases of the moon; thus it means sacred time and festival. The **Amarakośa** describes *parvasandhi*:

स पर्वसन्धिः प्रतिपत्पञ्चदश्योर्यदन्तरम् ।

AmKo I.4.7

Parvasandhi is a time where the junction of the first and fifteenth of a fortnight occurs.

Another related term is *viṣuvat*, "having or sharing both sides equally, middle, central, also top, summit, equinox." It is, in effect, a *sandhi* in which both sides are equal.

The most important compounds are *sandhikāla*, the time of juncture, and *sandhisthāna*, the place of junction.

Layers of Meaning

Junctures and joints, *sandhi*, both in space and time, are mostly meeting-points between two things: two moments of time, two elements in space, two letters in language, two people or groups in society, two limbs in the body. Both in space as in time, such points or moments are particularly important, both dangerous and vulnerable. Hence they need to be protected, to be attended to and if need be, to be healed. Ritual and prayer are performed at such junctures in order to prevent the parts of the day, month or year from disintegrating, to assure continuity. Negatively, this implies the danger of the falling apart of opposite elements, e.g. day and night. Positively attention to these moments or points of juncture allows a penetration into the 'centre' between two opposites in space and time. The fact that such times are vulnerable and particularly open to 'intermediary' states of mind makes them 'sacred' time, outside the ordinary alternation of light and darkness, wakefulness and sleep. Twilight (*sandhyā*) in fact participates in both; it cannot be identified with either member of these pairs.

Sandhi is, on the one hand, a juncture of two elements in which these elements undergo a transformation due to their contact. The classical example is the euphonic combination of two vowels or consonants in Sanskrit grammar. In the human context this implies also an agreement or alliance between two people or groups, e.g. a peace settlement. On the other hand, *sandhi* also signifies the interval, the space in between, interstice, such as the horizon which separates earth and heaven (*antarikṣa* in the Vedas). In time it is a pause, which may be a moment or the cosmic interval between two ages or *yugas*. Thus *sandhi* is both, interval and junction. It is neither complete separation nor indistinct mixture, for even where the two elements merge they do not lose their distinct identity. Two words which have combined with *sandhi* can still be recognized individually. Thus the **Kāśikā** on Pāṇini (VI.2.154) gives two definitions of *sandhi: sandhir iti hi paṇabandhena aikārthyam ucyate*, "*Sandhi* is oneness of aim or intention based on an agreement"; and *kecit punar āhuḥ gṛhyamānaviśeṣa pratyāsattiḥ sandhiḥ*, "*Sandhi* is proximity or close contact having cognizable difference".

The myth of Narasiṃha Avatāra summarizes in the clearest symbolic language the meaning of *sandhi*. The demon Hiraṇyakaśipu had received a boon from Brahmā that he could be killed neither by a man, a god nor an animal, neither by day nor by night, neither inside nor outside the house, but he was overcome by Viṣṇu in the form of a man-lion, at the time of twilight and at the threshold, i.e., at the vulnerable time and space of *sandhi*.

Sandhi is manifested in the threefold division of time, *trisandhyā*, the three junctures of the day representing past, present and future (*trikāla*). The astronomical definition of the moment of twilight is given by **Bṛhat Saṃhitā** of Varāhamihira:

अर्धास्त्तमितानुदितात् सूर्यादस्पष्टभं नभो यावत् ।
तावत्सन्ध्याकालश्चिह्नरेतैः फलं चास्मिन् ॥

BṛSam XXX.1 (also cf. Manu II.101)

The interval between the periods when the sun is half-set and the stars have not yet become distinct, is called a Juncture i.e. the evening twilight. Similarly that between the period when the stars have become dim and the sun is half-risen is called dawn. (Tr. M.R. Bhat)

Development of the Concept

One of the oldest meanings of *sandhi* is joint in the body, which we find already in the **Ṛgveda** where Indra is healing, i.e. joining, the injured or dissevered parts of Etasa:

य ऋते चिदभिश्रिषः पुरा जत्रुभ्य आतृदः ।
सन्धाता सन्धिं मघवा पुरूवसुरिष्कर्ता विह्रुतं पुनः ॥

ṚV VIII.1.12

He who, without bandage, before the neck has been pierced, closed up the (dissevered) joint again, bounteous Maghavan, who makes whole the injured part. (Tr. after Geldner)

Some have understood *sandhi* to mean the wound, i.e. the place of dislocation. This verse occurs also in the **Atharva-Veda** (XIV.2.47) and **Sāma-Veda** (I.3.2.1.2).

In the creation of *puruṣa*, Man, the **Atharva-Veda** speaks about the joints of his knees:

कस्मान्नु गुल्फावधरावकृण्वन्नष्ठीवन्तावुत्तरौ पूरुषस्य ।
जङ्घे निर्ऋत्य न्यदधुः क्व स्विज्जानुनोः सन्धी क उ तच्चिकेत ॥
चतुष्टयं युज्यते संहितान्तं जानुभ्यामूर्ध्वं शिथिरं कबन्धम् ।
श्रोणी यदूरू क उ तज्जजान याभ्यां कुसिन्धं सुदृढं बभूव ॥

AV X.2.2-3

Whence did they (i.e. the agents in his creation, whoever they were) make the ankles that are under, and the knee-bones of Puruṣa above them?
What led them onward to the leg's construction? Who planned and formed the knees' articulation?
A fourfold frame is fixed with ends connected, and up above the knees a yielding belly.
The hips and thighs, who was their generator, those props whereby the trunk grew firmly stablished? (Tr. R.T.H. Griffith)

The joints in the body are vulnerable and important parts, without them the body would fall into pieces.

Equally, there are junctures in the cosmos, joining opposites in space and time. The junction in space is the atmosphere or mid-space (*antarikṣa*) which lies between earth and heaven:

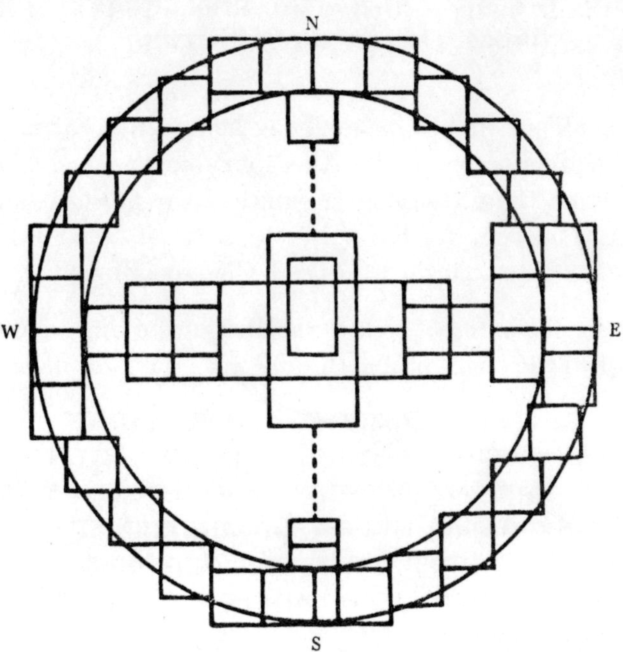

Figure 1: Central part of the Vedic fire altar

अन्तरिक्षं ह त्वेवैषोऽग्निश्चितः । तस्य द्यावापृथिव्योरेव सन्धिः परिश्रितः ।
परेण ह्यन्तरिक्षं द्यावापृथिवी सन्धत्तः । ताः परिश्रितः ।

ŚBr X.5.4.2

But indeed, that (brick built) Fire-altar also is the air: the junction of heaven and earth (the horizon) is its (circle of) enclosing-stones, for it is beyond the air that heaven and earth meet, and that (junction) is the (circle of) enclosing stones. (Tr. J. Eggeling)

The altar (*citi*) is an image of the cosmos and just as mid-space joins earth and heaven, the enclosing stones are placed at the important juncture. *Antarikṣa* is a clear illustration of *sandhi*: it is defined solely as the 'in-between', it neither merges with heaven or earth, nor is it separated from them. It prevents earth and heaven from collapsing, being propped up by Indra who holds the two worlds apart, but it also links them and bridges the gulf. Here the fire-altar (*agniciti*) is identified with *antarikṣa*, because it is by means of the sacrifice and the fire-altar that one ascends from earth to heaven.

Both space and time are created from the body of Prajāpati, the creator, as he is dismembered:

सोऽकामयत प्रजायेयेति । स तपोऽतप्यत । सोऽन्तर्वानभवत् । स

उपपक्षाभ्यामेवर्तूनसृजत । तेभ्यो रजते पात्रे घृतमदुहत् । यास्य सा तनुरासीत् । तामपाहत । सोऽहोरात्रयोः सन्धिरभवत् ।

TBr II.2.9.7-8

He (Prajāpati) desired to create living beings. He practised austerities. He became pregnant. He (then) created the seasons from the armpits. From those (seasons) he milched the purified butter in a silver pot. That was its body. He threw it off. That became the juncture of the day and night. (Tr. S. Chattopadhyay)

Prajāpati's dismemberment creates the divisions of time, and his joints (*parvan*) correspond to the times of juncture between day and night:

प्रजापतेर्ह वै प्रजाः ससृजानस्य पर्वाणि विसस्रंसु । स वै संवत्सर एव प्रजापतिः, तस्यैतानि पर्वाणि अहोरात्रयोः सन्धी, पौर्णमासी च अमावास्या ऋतुमुखानि । स विस्रस्तैः पर्वभिर्न शशाक संहातुम्, तमेतैर्हविर्यज्ञैर्देवा अभिषज्यन् - अग्निहोत्रेणैवाहोरात्रयोः सन्धी तत्पर्वाभिषज्यन् - तत्समदधुः। पौर्णमासेन चैवामावास्येन च पौर्णमासीं च अमावास्यां च तत्पर्वाभिषज्यन् तत्समदधुः । चातुर्मास्यैरेवर्तुमुखानि तत्पर्वाभिषज्य तत्समदधुः ।

ŚBr. I.6.3.35-36

After Prajāpati had created the living beings, his joints (*parvan*) were relaxed. Now Prajāpati, doubtless, is the year, and his joints are the two junctions of day and night (i.e. the twilights), the full moon and new moon, and the beginnings of the season.

He (Prajāpati) was unable to rise with his relaxed joints and the gods healed him by means of these havis-offerings: by means of the Agnihotra they healed that joint (which consists of) the two junctions of day and night, joined that together; by means of the full-moon and the new-moon sacrifice they healed that joint (which consists of) the full and new moon, joined that together; and by means of the (three) cāturmāsyas (seasonal offerings) they healed that joint (which consists of) the beginnings of the seasons, joined that together. (Tr. J. Eggeling)

The reconstruction of Prajāpati's body is done by means of the fire-altar whose bricks represent all the moments of time – the year – and whose layers correspond to the space-directions. Both in space as in time the junctures are critical points.

स सन्ध्योरुपस्पृश्य - एते यजुषी जपति । तथा द्वे यजुषी त्रीन् परिधीन्-अनुविभवतः । "दिवो मूर्धासि पृथिव्या नाभिः" (YV XVIII.54) इति दक्षिणे । "विश्वस्य मूर्धन्नधि तिष्ठसि श्रितः " (YV XVIII.55) इत्युत्तरे

मूर्धवतीभ्याम् । मूर्धा ह्यस्यैषः । अप्सुमतीभ्याम् । अग्नेरेतद्वैश्वानरस्य स्तोत्रं, यद्यज्ञायज्ञियम् । शान्तिर्वा आपः । तस्मादप्सुमतीभ्याम् ।

ŚBr IX.4.4.13

Having touched it (the fire) at the two joints, he (the sacrificer) mutters these two formulas, – thus two formulas equal in power three enclosing-sticks, – with (YV XVIII.54), 'the sky's head thou art, the earth's navel, [the essence of the waters and plants, the life of all, the ample refuge (?): homage be to the path!]' on the right, and with (YV XVIII.55), 'On the head of the All dost thou keep standing, [in the (aerial) ocean is thy heart, in the waters thy life: bestow water, send the water-store (cloud), – from the sky, from the cloud, from the air, from the earth, favour us with rain!]' on the left (joint), – thus with two (verses) containing (the word) 'head', for this is indeed its head; and containing (the words) 'in the waters': that Yajñāyajñīya doubtless is Agni Vaiśvānara's chant of praise, and water is (a means of) appeasing, – therefore (he touches them) with two (verses) containing (the words) – 'the waters'.
(Tr. J. Eggeling)

Junctures are also intervals which are necessary for breathing, which in the construction of the fire-altar is fulfilled by placing perforated bricks (*svayamātṛṇṇa*) between the solid bricks.

Again, in the context of the construction of the fire-altar, the bricks are called *rasa*, essence, and the loose soil in between the bricks is called *anna*, food. While placing the bricks and joining them with earth, it is said that the priest "joins and unites the food and its essence" (ŚBr VIII.5.3.3). The different layers of bricks are related to the cosmic worlds, and the three intermediate layers represent the air, which is their juncture (cf. ŚBr. VIII.5.4.12).

The Śulva-Sūtras prescribe:

मन्त्रव्यतिरेकेऽक्ताः शर्कराः सन्धिषूपदध्यात् ।

BŚulSū II.47

If the number of the *mantras* is greater (than that of the bricks) pebbles anointed with ghee are to be placed in the spaces between the bricks. (Tr. G. Thibaut)

Thus *sandhi* is also related to the corresponding *mantras*. In the context of the *soma* sacrifice the dangerous nature of the time of *sandhi*, between day and night, is stressed, but the same time is also important for peace or atonement:

यस्य प्रातःसवने सोमोऽतिरिच्यते। माध्यन्दिनं सवनं कामयमानो-ऽभ्यतिरिच्यते गौर्धयति मरुतामिति धयद्वतीषु कुर्वन्ति। हिनस्ति वै

सन्ध्यधीतम्। सन्धीव खलु वा एतत्। यत्सवनस्यातिरिच्यते। यद् धयद्वतीषु कुर्वन्ति। सन्धेः शान्त्यै, इति।

TBr I.4.5.1

The sacrificer whose soma-juice is left with a surplus after performing the morning libation of *soma*, (his) that *soma* is also left with a surplus after performing the midday oblation. (To avoid this vice of surplus) he has to read the Vedic verses containing the terms *dhayat* as *gaurdhayati marutām* etc. It certainly kills the person who recites this during the juncture of day and night. This (*soma*) is certainly like a juncture which is left with a surplus after the libation using the Vedic verses containing the term *dhayat* etc. By the recitation of the Vedic verse containing the term *dhayat* etc., the fault of being a *sandhi* becomes pacified. (Tr. S. Chattopadhyay)

Sandhi is the point of juncture between darkness and light, between day and night. In the *aśvamedha* various animals are sacrificed to various divisions of time. To *sandhi*, i.e. twilight, bats are offered because they move in darkness as well as in light (YV XXIV.25).

The fact that *sandhi* has also an erotic meaning even in the Veda emerges from the enumeration of victims bound to the stake in the *puruṣamedha*, where the **Yajur-Veda** mentions among others: *sandhaye jāraṃ*, "for rendezvous (or meeting) a lover (is offered)" (YV XXX.9).

In the **Atharva-Veda** the joining of cosmic and human elements is referred to (e.g. *vātaḥ prāṇena saṃhitaḥ*, " Wind is joined with vital breath", AV XIX.27.7), which has healing power:

अग्निः प्राणान्त्संदधाति चन्द्रः प्राणेन संहितः ।
व्यहं सर्वेण पाप्मना वि यक्ष्मेण समायुषा ॥

AV III.31.6

Agni combines the vital airs. The moon is closely joined with breath.
I free from every evil, from decline: I compass round with life.
(Tr. R.T.H. Griffith)

All-compassing Earth joins together night and day, darkness and dawn (AV XII.1.52).

Thus in the Veda we find the cosmic, ritual and human or bodily meanings of *sandhi*. In later Vedic texts the grammatical meaning is also found:

येन सन्धिं विवर्तयति, येन स्वरास्वरं विजानाति, येन मात्रामात्रं विभजते सा संहिता ।

AitĀr III.1.5

Saṃhitā is that by which one operates *sandhi* (juxtaposition) of the former and later (letters), by which one distinguishes vowel and non-vowel (i.e. consonant) and by which one separates *mātrā* (mora) and *amātrā* (non-mora). (Tr. R.S.Bhattacharya)

Finally, the **Nirukta** defines *saṃhitā* (synonym of *sandhi*) in the following way:

परः सन्निकर्षः संहिता । पदप्रकृतिः संहिता । पदप्रकृतीनि सर्वचरणानां पार्षदानि ।

Nir I.17

Saṃhitā is the closest conjunction by means of euphonic combination. *Saṃhitā* is based on the original form of words. The phonetic treatises of all schools are based on the original form of words. (Tr. L. Sarup)

The Upaniṣads, in continuation of the Āraṇyakas contain the great connections and correlations between macro- and microcosmic elements. Here a subtle distinction is made between *sandhāna* and *sandhi, sandhi* being the static and *sandhāna* the dynamic aspect of the conjunction. The **Taittirīya** sums it up in the fivefold combination (*saṃhitā*), which is worth quoting fully:

अथातः संहिताया उपनिषदं व्याख्यास्यामः । पञ्चस्वधिकरणेषु ।
अधिलोकमधिज्यौतिषमधिविद्यमधिप्रजमध्यात्मम् । ता महासंहिता
इत्याचक्षते । अथाधिलोकम् । पृथिवी पूर्वरूपम् । द्यौरुत्तररूपम् ।
आकाशः सन्धिः । वायुः सन्धानम् । इत्यधिलोकम् ।
अथाधिज्यौतिषम् । अग्निः पूर्वरूपम् । आदित्य उत्तररूपम् ।
आपः सन्धिः । वैद्युतः सन्धानम् । इत्यधिज्यौतिषम् ॥
अथाधिविद्यम् । आचार्यः पूर्वरूपम् । अन्तेवास्युत्तररूपम् ।
विद्या सन्धिः । प्रवचनं सन्धानम् । इत्यधिविद्यम् ।
अथाधिप्रजम् । माता पूर्वरूपम् । पिता उत्तररूपम् । प्रजा सन्धिः । प्रजननं सन्धानम् । इत्यधिप्रजम् ।
अथाध्यात्मम् । अधरा हनुः पूर्वरूपम् । उत्तरा हनुरुत्तररूपम् । वाक् सन्धिः । जिह्वा सन्धानम् । इत्यध्यात्मम् । इतीमा महासंहिताः । य एवमेता महासंहिता व्याख्याता वेद सन्धीयते प्रजया पशुभिः ब्रह्मवर्चसेनान्नाद्येन सुवर्ग्येण लोकेन ।

TUp I.3

Now next, we will expound the mystic meaning (*upaniṣad*) of combination (*saṃhitā*) in five heads:

with regard to the world;
with regard to the luminaries;
with regard to knowledge;

with regard to progeny;
with regard to oneself.

Now, with regard to the world. –
The earth is the prior form; the heaven, the latter form. Space is their conjunction, wind, the connection. – Thus with regard to the world.

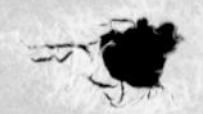

Now, with regard to the luminaries. –
Fire is the prior form; the Sun, the latter form. Water is their conjunction; lightning, the connection. – Thus with regard to the luminaries.
Now, with regard to knowledge. –
The teacher is the prior form; the pupil, the latter form. Knowledge is their conjunction; instruction, the connection. – Thus with regard to knowledge.
Now, with regard to progeny. –
The mother is the prior form; the father, the latter form. Progeny is their conjuction; procreation, the connection.– Thus with regard to progeny.
Now, with regard to oneself. –
The lower jaw is the prior form; the upper jaw,the latter form. Speech is their conjuction; the tongue, the connection. –
Thus with regard to oneself. These are the great combinations. He who knows these combinations, thus expounded, becomes conjoined with offspring, with cattle, with pre-eminence in sacred knowledge, with food, with the heavenly world. (Tr. R.E. Hume)

Here knowledge of the conjunctions means being 'conjoined' with the reality in question. The Upaniṣad, that is the mystic relationship, is precisely a matter of establishing the right combinations.

We find two more meanings of *sandhi* in the Upaniṣads. The **Kaṭha**, in a rather mysterious verse, seems to relate *sandhi* to the 'juncture' between life and death, which makes it possible to overcome both:

त्रिणाचिकेतस्त्रिभिरेत्य सन्धिं त्रिकर्मकृत् तरति जन्ममृत्यू ।

KaṭhUp I.17a

Having kindled the triple Nāciketa fire, having attained the intermediary state (or union) of the three, performing the triple work (or rite), one crosses over birth and death. (Tr. adapted from Hume)

Another meaning relates *sandhi* to the intermediary state of the soul between the ordinary consciousness of the world (*idam*) and the transcendent state (*paraloka-sthāna*):

तस्य वा एतस्य पुरुषस्य द्वे एव स्थाने भवतः ।
इदं च परलोकस्थानं च ।सन्ध्यं तृतीयं स्वप्नस्थानम् ।
तस्मिन्सन्ध्ये स्थाने तिष्ठन्नेते उभे स्थाने पश्यतीदं च
परलोकस्थानं च ।अथ यथाक्रमोऽयं परलोकस्थाने भवति
तमाक्रममाक्रम्योभयान् पाप्मन आनन्दांश्च पश्यति ।

BṛUp IV.3.9

Verily, there are just two conditions of this person: the condition of being in this world and the condition of being in the other world. There is an intermediate third condition, namely that of being in sleep. By standing in this intermediate condition one sees both those conditions, namely being in this world and being in the other world. Now whatever the approach is to the condition of being in the other world, by making that approach one sees the evils (of this world) and the joys (of yonder world). (Tr. R.E. Hume)

This Upaniṣadic passage is commented upon by Śaṅkara as well as Rāmānuja on **Brahma-Sūtra** III.2.1: *sandhye sṛṣṭirāha hi*, "In the intermediate sphere the creation (is effected by the soul); for (scripture) says (so)". (Tr. G. Thibaut). Śaṅkara comments on this:

किं प्रबोध इव स्वप्नेऽपि पारमार्थिकी सृष्टिराहोस्वित् मायामयीति ।तत्र तावत्प्रतिपद्यते सन्ध्ये तथ्यरूपा सृष्टिरिति ।सन्ध्यमिति स्वप्नस्थानमाचष्टे, वेदे प्रयोगदर्शनात् "सन्ध्यं तृतीयं स्वप्नस्थानम्" (BṛUp IV.3.9) इति। द्वयोर्लोकस्थानयोः प्रबोधसंप्रसादस्थानयोर्वा सन्धौ भवतीति सन्ध्यम् । तस्मिन् सन्ध्ये स्थाने तथ्यरूपैव सृष्टिर्भवितुमर्हति ।

BrSūBh III.2.1

(The doubt arises) whether the creation in dream is as real as in the waking state, or it is only illusory. While on this topic, it is gathered that the creation in the intermediate stage (lit. occurring at the junction) is real. By the term "Intermediate stage" is meant dream, for such a use is met with in the Vedas, as in, "The dream state, which is the third, is at the junction of the two (waking and deep sleep") (BṛUp IV.3.9). It occurs at the juncture of the two worlds (the other and this) or between the two states of waking and deep sleep; therefore it is called the *sandhya* (intervening stage). The creation that occurs in that intervening period must necessarily be real. (Tr. Swami Gambhirananda)

The Upaniṣad itself describes the importance of this state as one from which the soul can see, so to say, in both directions, from which it has a clear vision.

In grammar the meaning of *sandhi* is clearly defined as the euphonic combination of vowels and consonants in a word, compound or sentence.

The reason for this is the continuous utterance without a break or pause (cf. *pūrvottara varṇānām avirāmena uccāraṇam sandhānaṃ sandhiḥ saṃhiteti yāvat*, **Śākaṭāyana Prakriyā Saṅgraha**, where *sandhāna, sandhi* and *saṃhitā* are treated as synonyms).

The **Yājñavalkya-Śikṣā** mentions four kinds of *sandhi*:

सन्धिश्चतुर्विधो भवति । लोपागमविकाराः प्रकृतिभावश्चेति ।

YājŚik 7

Sandhi is of four kinds, it is of the nature of *lopa* (elision), of *āgama* (augment), of *vikāra* (transformation) and of *prakṛtibhāva* (remaining without any change). (Tr. R.S. Bhattacharya)

We are not concerned with *sandhi* rules, but with definitions which throw light on the meaning of the term. Thus the commentary on the **Kātantra-Vyākaraṇa** defines *sandhi*:

सन्धानं सन्धिः, उत्कृष्टो वर्णानां सन्निकर्ष उच्यते । तद्विषयमपि कार्यं समानदीर्घादिसन्धिरित्यभिमतम् उपचारात् ।

Durga on Kātantra-Vyākaraṇa I.2.18

Sandhi or *sandhāna* is the close nearness (juxtaposition) of letters. Any operation like the lengthening of vowels in the field of *sandhi* is secondarily called *sandhi*. (Tr. R.S. Bhattacharya)

वर्णानां समवायः सन्धिरिति व्युत्पत्त्या इहोच्यते । अथ तत्रापि कथं सन्धिशब्देन दीर्घादिरुच्यते, सन्निकर्षस्य धर्मपरत्वात् । सत्यम्, सन्धिविधेयकार्यं सन्धिरित्युपचारात् ।

Kavirāja on Kātantra-Vyākaraṇa I.2.18

Etymologically the word *sandhi* means the *samavāya* (union) of letters. It may be called: how the lengthening, etc. (of letters) are called *sandhi*, since *sannikarṣa* (juxtaposition) is of the nature of attribute. It is true to say so; it is the result or effect of *sandhi* which is secondarily called *sandhi*. (Tr. R.S. Bhattacharya)

Grammatically, *sandhi* is clearly a combination of letters effecting a change in them:

सर्वप्रकरणव्यापी वर्णमात्रनिमित्तकः ।
वार्णो विकारः सन्धिः स्याद् विषयापेक्षकः क्वचित् ॥

Harināmāmṛta-Vyākaraṇa I.45

Sandhi is a transformation or change (*vikāra*) of letters; it depends upon letters only; in a few places it depends upon *viṣaya* (meaning or context). It pervades all the factors of language (or it is connected with all grammatical operations). (Tr. R.S. Bhattacharya)

In Āyurveda the physiological meaning of *sandhi* as joints in the body is clear. Caraka speaks of 200 such joints, though he admits that this number cannot be definitely proved (CarSam Śārīrasthāna VII.14). Suśruta mentions 210 *sandhis* (SuSam Śārīrasthāna V.6). Caraka defines bone-joints as:

अस्थिसन्धयोऽस्थिसंयोगास्तत्रोपनिबद्धाश्च स्नायुकण्डराः ।

CarSam Sūtrasthāna XI.48

Bone-joints are those where bones meet alongwith the bound ligaments and tendons. (Tr. P.V. Sharma)

Suśruta gives a classification of the joints:

...सन्धयस्तु द्विविधाश्चेष्टावन्तः, स्थिराश्च ॥
शाखासु हन्वोः कट्यां च चेष्टावन्तस्तु सन्धयः ।
शेषास्तु सन्धयः सर्वे विज्ञेया हि स्थिरा बुधैः ॥

SuSam Śārīrasthāna V.24-25

The joints may be divided into two kinds according to as they are immovable (synarthrosis) and movable (diarthrosis). Those which are situated at the four extremities as well as in the *Kaṭi* (waist) and *Hanus* (jaws) are movable; the others are known to be unmovable by the learned. (Tr. K.L. Bhisagratna)

It is clear from other descriptions that the joints in the body are those most vulnerable parts which can easily be severed (cf. MBh XII.5.4 where Karṇa is about to sever the joint of Jarāsandha's body). They therefore need special protection.

Another meaning of *sandhi* is found in the **Arthaśāstra** and other texts related to political science: it is the agreement, peace or alliance with an enemy at the time of conflict. The **Yājñavalkya-Smṛti** mentions *sandhi* in this sense as the first of several measures to come to an agreement with an enemy.

सन्धिं च विग्रहं यानमासनं संश्रयं तथा ।
द्वैधीभावं गुणानेतान् यथावत् परिकल्पयेत् ॥

YājSm I.13.347

Let him employ as the occasion may require these (following) measures: alliance, war, marching, sitting, seeking protection and distribution. (Tr. S.C. Vidyaranya)

The **Agni Purāṇa** mentions *sandhi* as one of the six courses of action of politics (AgPur CCXXXIV.18). The **Manu-Smṛti** mentions two kinds of action in the case of an alliance:

समानयानकर्मा च विपरीतस्तथैव च ।
तदात्वायतिसंयुक्तः सन्धिर्ज्ञेयो द्विलक्षणः ॥

Manu VII.163

An alliance which yields present and future advantages one must know to be of two descriptions, (viz.) that when one marches together (with an ally) and the contrary (when the allies act separately). (Tr. G. Bühler)

The **Arthaśāstra** itself defines *sandhi* as *paṇabandha* (treaty, ArthŚ VII.1.6), and as synonyms it mentions *śama* (peace) and *samādhi.*

पणबन्धः सन्धिः ।
* * *
शमः सन्धिः समाधिरित्येकोऽर्थः ।

ArthŚ VII.1.6, VII.17.1

Entering into a treaty is peace.
* * *
Peace, treaty, hostage, these are one and the same thing. (Tr. R.P. Kangle)

Peace or agreement is always to be preferred to war, unless it is unavoidable:

सन्धिविग्रहयोस्तुल्यायां वृद्धौ सन्धिमुपेयात् ।

ArthŚ VII.2.1

If there is equal advancement in peace or war, he should resort to peace. (Tr. R.P. Kangle)

The **Arthaśāstra** contains another interesting meaning of *sandhi*, meaning the opening or hole in the wall or door through which a thief enters the house (ArthŚ IV.6. 16). The contrary meaning is implied when the joining of two pieces of metal is referred to:

तेजो हि सन्धानकरणम् ।
नातप्तं लोहं लोहेन सन्धत्त इति ।

ArthŚ VII.3.8-9

For, heat is the means of joining together. Metal that is not heated does not become joined with metal. (Tr. R.P. Kangle)

In the epics and Purāṇas, *sandhi* is mostly related to time (→*kāla*). Time can only be measured because there are junctures, which are compared to the knots of a bamboo (*parvan* in both senses), and which constitute a break and hence make divisions possible. *Sandhi* also refers to the fact that there are no sudden transitions in nature; even if they appear to be minute, there are phases of transition which partake of both sides.

The **Matsya Purāṇa** states clearly this conception of time:

अतःपरं प्रवक्ष्यामि पर्वाणां सन्धयश्च याः ।
यथाग्रथ्नन्ति पर्वाणि आवृत्तादिक्षुवेणुवत् ॥
तथाब्दमासाः पक्षाश्च शुक्लाः कृष्णास्तु वै स्मृताः ।
पौर्णमास्यास्तु यो भेदो ग्रन्थयः सन्धयस्तथा ॥

MatPur CXLI.29-30

Now the periodical junctions, *Parva-sandhis* will be described. These are like the knots of a bamboo or a sugarcane joined to one another in a circle. The year, the months, the dark and the bright fortnights and the full moon night are the knots and junctions.

In the context of the cosmic ages, *sandhi* is a period of interval between *yugas* and *kalpas* (cf. MBh I.2.3). Its measure depends on the length of the preceding and succeeding *yuga*:

दिव्यार्काब्दसहस्राणि युगेषु चतुरादितः ॥
एकैकहान्या तावद्भिः शतैस्तेष्वष्ट सन्धयः ।

TĀl VI.138b-139a

Among the *yugas* consisting of twelve thousand divine years the *kṛta* in the beginning has four thousand divine years, that is the *kṛtayuga* consists of four thousand years and the *yugas* that are following are shortened by one thousand years from the former one, that is *tretā* consists of three thousand years, *dvāpara* of two thousand years and *kali* of one thousand years. The *sandhis*, the joints are eight and they consist of twenty hundred years. (Tr. H.N.Chakravarty)

Sandhis between the *yugas* are eight. They are as follows: The end of *kali* consists of one hundred years along with the first portion of *kṛta* consisting of four hundred years, the totality being 500 years. In the same way the *sandhi* between *kṛta* and *tretā* is of the duration of seven hundred years, the duration of *sandhi* between *tretā* and *dvāpara* is five hundred years, the *sandhi* between *dvāpara* and *kali* is three hundred years. These *sandhis* are as it were a period of transition between the times showing the characteristics of both, the prior and the posterior. This period 'between the times' is symbolized in myth by the cosmic sleep of Viṣṇu in the world ocean on the serpent Ananta ('Endless', because outside time). It is as if time itself were resting from its activity.

The **Yoga-Vāsiṣṭha** gives a philosophical and mystical interpretation of the junction between times, which is difficult to apprehend. Though the point between the two times appears to be like the void, yet it partakes of the nature of both. If *sandhi* is supported to be *sama* (equal) it may signify *viṣuvat* where all-pervasiveness becomes manifest:

> तमः प्रकाशयोश्छायातपयोर्दिनरात्रयोः ।
> मध्ये विलक्षणं रूपं प्राज्ञैरपि न लभ्यते ॥
> सन्धिरप्यविलोपः स्यादेतयोरपि तद्वपुः ।
> भावाभावैर्यथैकस्था निष्ठावेतौ तथैव हि ॥

YVās VI(I).81.99-100

> Like in the juncture of darkness and light, the shadow and the sun, the day and the night, the form without any specific character becoming manifest in the middle (of the two), is unattainable even by intelligent people. If this is taken to be true, then the juncture should be a thing like the void. But really it is not so because it consists of the characteristics of both, that is its body, it has the character of both darkness and light. Just as with the concept of *bhāva* and *abhāva* which abides steadily in one single concept, that is, the concept of light and darkness, in the same way, in the juncture of light and darkness both light and darkness remain present. (Tr. H.N. Chakravarty)

The Purāṇas and Tantras as well as ritual Paddhatis also prescribe a special ritual called *sandhi pūjā* at the crucial moment between the eighth and ninth lunar day of Durgāpūjā (*mahāṣṭamī-mahānavamī-sandhi*, cf. **Kālikā Purāṇa, Durgārcanapaddhati**, etc.).

In the Āgamas, esp. in Kashmir Śaivism or Trika, *sandhi* assumes a mystical meaning, being related to *madhya*, the centre, and *viṣuvat*, the equinoxial point in a spiritual sense. This 'centre' refers mostly to the centre between the two breaths, *prāṇa* and *apāna*, and to the central vein (*suṣumṇā*) through which *kuṇḍalinī* rises. Awareness on this 'centre' leads to equality (*samatā*), beyond the constant oscillation between opposites. In this juncture, the central vein (*nāḍī*), the two veins get dissolved. The *guru* is capable of effecting this in the body of the disciple (cf. SvT III. 150). Kṣemarāja, the commentator of **Svacchanda Tantra**, explains *sandhāna* (joining) as *aikyātmaprāptiḥ* (attainment of oneness).

> रेचकस्थो मध्यनाडीसन्धिविद्गुरुरित्यदः ।

TĀl XV.435cd

> The spiritual guide being established in emitting the breath internally, is the knower of how to unite all the categories in the middle path (*madhyanāḍī*). (Tr. H.N. Chakravarty)

Here *recaka* does not mean the process of emitting the air from the lungs outside, but rather a specific form of *prāṇāyāma* known only to *yogins* in which

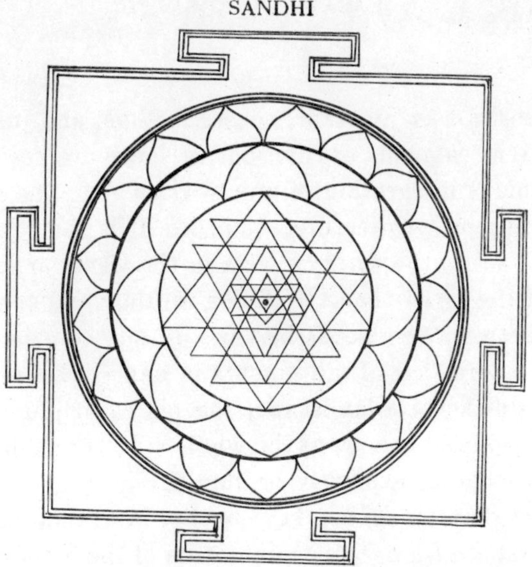

Figure 2: Śrīyantra sandhis

pūraka, kumbhaka and *recaka* are done internally. After being established in performing the *recaka*, the teacher makes an effort to push the subtle vital energy to move upward but before that he brings all the subtle *tattvas* in the middle current to have their unification. The person who is capable of doing this is called *madhyanāḍīsandhivit.*

Sandhi has also a geometrical-symbolical meaning in the drawing of a *yantra*, such as the *śrīcakra.* Thus Lakṣmīdhara in his comm. on **Saundaryalaharī** quotes a verse of unknown origin:

> द्विरेखासंगमस्थानं सन्धिरित्यभिधीयते ।
> त्रिरेखासंगमस्थानं मर्म मर्मविदो विदुः ।

Comm. by Lakṣmīdhara on SL 11

> The point in which two lines meet is called *sandhi* and the point in which three lines meet is known as *marman* according to the view of those who have knowledge about *marman.* (Tr. H.N.Chakravarty)

This definition is very revealing, because *marman* is a crossing-point, a vital point, whereas *sandhi* involves only the junction of two lines. In the Śrīcakra there are twenty-eight *marman*-points and twenty-four *sandhis.*

Thus we can say that the concept of *sandhi* unfolds in the various disciplines in its different aspects, but there is no historical development in the real sense, as in the case of other concepts.

In the Arts

Moments of transition or junction, pauses in time, and junctures or transitions between different elements or divisions in space are decisive for the completion and harmonious integration of any work of Art – be it poetry, drama, music, dance, painting or architecture/sculpture. It is sometimes said that the pauses in music or poetry, the empty spaces in the visual arts, are more telling about the genius of the artist than the 'filling' of time and space with sound or form. The silence between the words bestows gravity to a poem, the still moments enhance the expression of movements in dance, the void of the horizon gives depth to a painting of a landscape, the places of juncture between two parts of a temple reveal the beauty of the whole structure. All this is contained in the word *sandhi*, whether explicitly or implicitly.

In the **Nāṭya-Śāstra** *sandhi* is a key concept in drama, as the junctures of the plot. We may first see Bharata's enumeration of the five main *sandhis* along with Abhinavagupta's elaboration:

> मुखं प्रतिमुखं चैव गर्भो विमर्श एव च ।
> तथा निर्वहणं चेति नाटके पञ्च सन्धयः ॥
>
> NŚ XIX.37
>
> ....उद्देशं तावदाह मुखं प्रतिमुखं चैवेति । समुच्चयपदैः पञ्चानां सर्वत्रावश्यम्भावित्वं द्योतितम् । नियमवाचिभिः क्रमनियमः । नाटक इत्यभिनेयरूपक इत्यर्थः । महावाक्यार्थरूपस्य रूपकार्थस्य पञ्चांशा अवस्थाभेदेन कल्प्यन्ते ।...अर्थावयवा सन्धीयमानाः परस्परमङ्गैश्च सन्धय इति समाख्या निरुक्ता । तदेषां समानलक्षणम् ।
>
> AbhiBhā on above
>
> There are five *sandhis* or junctures in drama viz. *mukha* (lit. face), *pratimukha* (lit. the reflected image of the face), *garbha* (lit. an interior of anything), *vimarśa* (lit. deliberation, reasoning) and *nirvahaṇa* (lit. completion, attainment).
>
> Commentary:
>
> The author is enumerating (the *sandhis*) *mukha, pratimukha* and (these) alone; the conjunctive words 'and' (thrice *ca*), imply that all the five (*sandhis*) are inevitably prescribed everywhere. The restrictive (words) (*eva* twice and *tathā* and *iti* once each) prescribe the order. The word *nāṭaka* stands for the *rūpaka* that is fit to be enacted. The plot (*artha*) of *rūpaka* (drama) is like the content (*artha*) of a "big sentence" (literary composition) and five parts of the same (plot) are conceived according to the different *avasthās* (stages of the development of the plot). The limbs or components (of the

plot i.e. *avasthās*) get joined with one another and with *aṅgas* (i.e. *arthaprakṛtis*) and (these joints) are *sandhis*, thus the etymology of (the prefix) *sam* is given (i.e. proper joint or juncture is *sandhi*). This is the common definition of all of these (*sandhis*). (Tr. P.L. Sharma)

The following explanation by Kapila Vatsyayan may be helpful to clarify the whole context of *sandhi* in drama: "All these (situations) are placed in the frame of the *sandhis* (joints) whose names are expressive and significant. A strict correspondence is established between the *avasthās*, the *artha-prakṛtis* and the *sandhis*. This time Bharata uses the imagery of the architecture and not of geometrical motifs, recalling the expansion of a single primary consciousness, with subsidiary vibrations. They are the *mukha* (the opening entrance), the *pratimukha* (the architectural meaning and Bharata's interpretation slightly differ), the *garbha*, the *vimarśa* and the *nirvahaṇa*. While the first three terms indicate a structure, the last two indicate an action or happening in time. In explanation, Bharata uses the imagery of the seed, its temporary invisibility underground (*pratimukha*), and its germination (*garbha*). Again follows a time sequence of obstacle or pause and final fulfilment. While there is a seeming lack of clarity in these series, the intention is clear. Bharata is trying to relate the inner with the outer, and the movement is cyclic like that in a *yajña* with stages. The beginning is the end, and we can see an identity of approach between those who conceived of the different stages of the *yajña* and Bharata's conception of the plot.... The plot with its junctures (*sandhis*) and the different stages of development (the five *avasthās*) are the frame work for the unfolding of the dominant mood (*bhāva*) and its variation. The latter is the content (already impersonalized and archetypal) and the former is the format of the drama." (Kapila Vatsyayan, The Square and the Circle of the Indian Arts, p. 47-48).

Bharata gives definitions of each of the five *sandhis* and they are explained by Abhinavagupta who also gives illustrations from various dramas.

Here we may quote only two examples:

1. *Mukha-sandhi*:

यत्र बीजसमुत्पत्तिर्नानार्थरससम्भवा ।
काव्ये शरीरानुगता तन्मुखं परिकीर्तितम् ॥

NŚ XIX.39

तत्र मुखस्य स्वतन्त्रस्येतिवृत्ते समस्तप्रयोजनस्यात एव नायकस्य स्वमुखेन परद्वारेण वा या प्रारम्भावस्था प्रथमा व्याख्याता तदुपयोगी यावानर्थराशिः स मुखसन्धिः ।... प्रागारम्भभावित्वान्मुखमिव मुखं, यावत्क्रियावत्यर्थभाग-राशौ बीजस्य मुखोपायस्य सम्यगुत्पत्तिः शरीरेण प्रारम्भात्मना अनुगता

भवति, नानाभूतोऽर्थवशात् प्रसङ्गायातो रससम्भवो यः (?) स्यात् । एतदुक्तम् प्रारम्भोपयोगी यावानर्थराशिः प्रसक्तानुप्रसक्त्या विचित्रास्वाद आपतितः तावन्मुखसन्धिः, तदभिधायी च रूपकैकदेशः ॥

AbhiBhā on above

Where the birth of *bīja* (seed) takes place, out of many *arthas* (components of plot) and *rasas* in the *kāvya* (text of drama), followed by (the composition of) *śarīra* (body of drama in the form of plot).

Summary of the commentary:
The name of the first *sandhi* is *mukha* (lit. face), because its primacy is similar to that of the face in the body: this *sandhi* is related to the first *avasthā* (step) named as *ārambha* or *prārambha* (beginning) and the first *arthaprakṛti* (ingredient of plot) known as *bīja* (lit. seed). The beginning could be indicated by the hero himself or through somebody else. The variegated presentation forming "the beginning" made by the various components of plot interlocked with one another is in its total expanse the domain of *mukhasandhi*, and the exposition of the same is a part of the drama; the purport seems to be that although the total expanse of the 'beginning' is allocated to '*mukhasandhi*', yet a particular part or 'spot' in the drama could be said to be the exponent of this *sandhi.* The variety in the total expanse is in terms of *rasas* and *arthas* (*artha* is that which is sought and it means also the component of plot). (Tr. P.L. Sharma)

The first act of any drama contains the main *rasas* which will unfold in the course of action, and its happenings represent an 'opening' of the events to come (*mukhasandhi*). This 'opening' is again hidden in the next *sandhi.*
2. *Pratimukha-sandhi*:

बीजस्योद्घाटनं यत्र दृष्टनष्टमिव क्वचित् ।
मुखन्यस्तस्य सर्वत्र तद् वै प्रतिमुखं स्मृतम् ॥

NŚ XIX.40

Where the opening of the *bīja* (seed) 'placed' or sown in the *mukha-sandhi* takes place and this opening is sometimes 'seen' (visible or manifest) and at other times 'lost' (invisible or unmanifest) and this (hide and seek) happens everywhere (all the time), that is known as *pratimukha-(sandhi*). (Tr. P.L. Sharma)

Thus in the drama adversary forces come to hide the original intention and the desired object is lost sight of. It would lead too far to give the definitions of all the five *sandhis* with their examples.

However, not all kinds of dramas should have all the five *sandhis*, some have only four or three. The first and the last have invariably to be present. The order of omission of *sandhis* is also prescribed.

The **Daśarūpaka** gives a definition of *sandhi* which brings out its etymological meaning of relationship or connection:

> अर्थप्रकृतयः पञ्च पञ्चावस्थासमन्विताः ॥
> यथासंख्येन जायन्ते मुखाद्याः पञ्चसन्धयः ।
> अन्तरैकार्थसम्बन्धः सन्धिरेकान्वये सति ॥
>
> DaRū I.22cd-23
>
> अर्थप्रकृतीनां पञ्चानां यथासंख्येनावस्थाभिः पञ्चभिर्योगाद् यथासंख्येनैव वक्ष्यमाणा मुखाद्याः पञ्च सन्धयो जायन्ते । एकेन प्रयोजनेनान्वितानां कथांशानामवान्तरैकप्रयोजनसम्बन्धः सन्धिः ।
>
> Avaloka comm. of Dhanika on the above
>
> The five *artha-prakṛtis* (ingredients of plot) combined with the five *avasthās* (stages of the development of plot) are born as the five *sandhis* starting with *mukha. Sandhi* is the connection of (the components of the plot) geared to one (objective), with another intermediary objective.
>
> Commentary:
>
> From the combination of five *artha-prakṛtis* with the five *avasthās* respectively are born the five *sandhis* starting with *mukha. Sandhi* is the relation of the parts of the plot that are connected with one objective, with another intermediary objective. (Tr. P.L. Sharma)

The idea seems to be that in *sandhi* there is a juncture of the components of the plot with an objective which is intermediary or subsidiary to an objective (*artha*) to which they are already geared. The hero is making efforts to attain an objective and all the components of the plot are connected with that objective which is, so to say, a part of or which leads to or is subsidiary to the main objective. The efforts addressed to the main objective, naturally, have to address themselves to intermediary or subsidiary objectives and *sandhi* stands for the points in the plot where a relationship with the intermediary objective is established. This is an explanation of the initial statement that *sandhi* is the combination of the five *arthaprakṛtis* with the five *avasthās* respectively.

Each of the five main *sandhis* has a number of subsidiary 'limbs', *sandhyaṅgas* which are important for establishing connections between the components of the plot. The total number of these is 64. Abhinavagupta (on NŚ XIX.69-104) gives illustrative examples on each, but it is not possible to reproduce them here. Let us only see Bharata's definition and explanation of these *sandhyaṅgas*:

पुनरेषां तु सन्धीनामङ्गकल्पं निबोधत ॥
सन्धीनां यानि वृत्तानि प्रदेशेष्वनुपूर्वशः ।
स्वसम्पद्गुणयुक्तानि तान्यङ्गान्युपधारयेत् ॥
इष्टस्यार्थस्य रचना वृत्तान्तस्यानुपक्षयः ।
रागप्राप्तिः प्रयोगस्य गुह्यानां चैव गूहनम् ॥
आश्चर्यवदभिख्यानं प्रकाश्यानां प्रकाशनम् ।
अङ्गानां षड्विधं ह्येतद् दृष्टं शास्त्रे प्रयोजनम् ॥
अङ्गहीनो नरो यद्वन्नैवारम्भक्षमो भवेत् ।
अङ्गहीनं तथा काव्यं न प्रयोगक्षमं भवेत् ॥
उदात्तमपि यत्काव्यं स्यादङ्गैः परिवर्जितम् ।
हीनत्वाद्धि प्रयोगस्य न सतां रञ्जयेन्मनः ॥
काव्यं यदपि हीनार्थं सम्यगङ्गैः समन्वितम् ।
दीप्तत्वात्तु प्रयोगस्य शोभामेति न संशयः ॥

NŚ XIX.49cd-55

Again, understand the scheme of *aṅgas* (prescribed) in the *sandhis.* One should incorporate the *aṅgas* of *sandhis* that are *vṛttas* i.e. the parts of the total dramatic composition (to be placed) in different points (of the drama) in a sequence and that are full of the qualities of their own excellence.

Aṅgas are seen, in the Śāstra, to have sixfold objective; viz. 1) the construction or elaboration of the desired objective, (viz. the relish of *rasa*); 2) the 'non-decay' (flow) of the story (i.e. clear exposition of the story so that the story does not become a riddle); 3) bringing delight to the composition; 4) concealment of those things that need to be concealed; 5) delineation of the story with an element of wonder and 6) illuminating the things that deserve to be illuminated.

Just as the man who is devoid of limbs cannot 'begin' or undertake any complete activity, similarly the poetic (dramatic) composition devoid of *aṅgas* is not fit to be performed.

Even if a poetic (dramatic) composition is of a high order, but is lacking in *aṅgas*, it cannot bring delight to the mind of the wise. But even if (a composition) is not of a high order, but is well-equipped with *aṅgas*, it attains beauty (*śobhā*), there being no doubt.

(Tr. P.L. Sharma)

A further subdivision of *sandhi* and *sandhyaṅga* are the *sandhyantaras*, establishing connections within a *sandhyaṅga* (cf. NŚ XIX.106cd). Bharata does not give a detailed explanation of these, but Abhinavagupta has illustrated many of them.

Thus in the context of drama *sandhis* are stages of action joining the whole plot together.

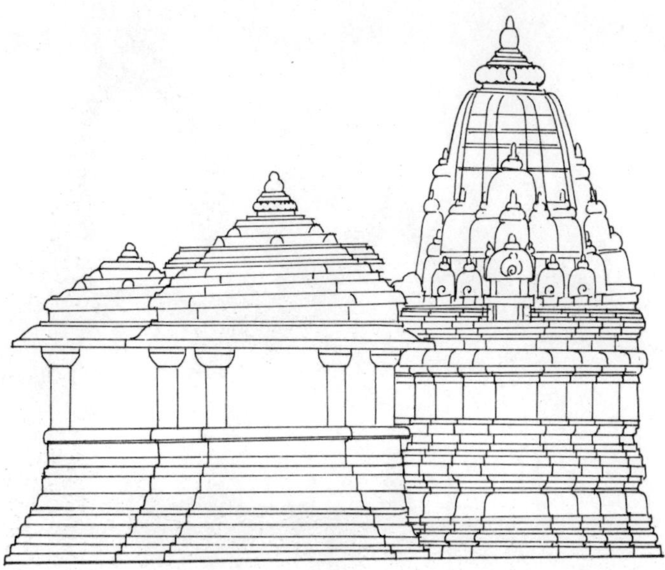

Figure 3: Sandhisthala: joining part between the two parts of the temple (śālā or maṇḍapa and vimāna or śikhara)

In architecture (*vāstu*) there is a certain continuity between the conception of the Vedic altar (*agnicayana*) and the temple. In both, the joining parts and junctures are called *sandhi*. An erotic symbolism is implied when the two main parts of the temple are compared to bride (*mukhaśāla*) and bridegroom (*vimāna*), and the place of junction meeting-place (*milanasthala*) or *sandhikṣetra*:

> राहाभागे प्रस्थदेशे स भागो मिलनस्थलम् ।
> विमानवरश्रेष्ठश्च कन्या च मुखशालिका ॥
> वरकन्या यथास्थाने सम्मुखे सन्धिक्षेत्रजा ।
>
> ŚiPrak II.595-596 ab
>
> That place (on the front) in the width of the *rāhā* is the place of junction (*milanasthala*). The *vimāna* is the best bridegroom and the *mukhaśālikā* is the bride.
> That place in front, where the bridegroom and the bride meet becomes the place of junction (*sandhikṣetra*). (Tr. A. Boner)

Thus it is not by chance that in many temples this place of junction is decorated with erotic figures (→*mithuna*), symbolically indicating the union between the God (the *mukhaśālā* being meant for the devotees and the *garbhagṛha* for the deity).

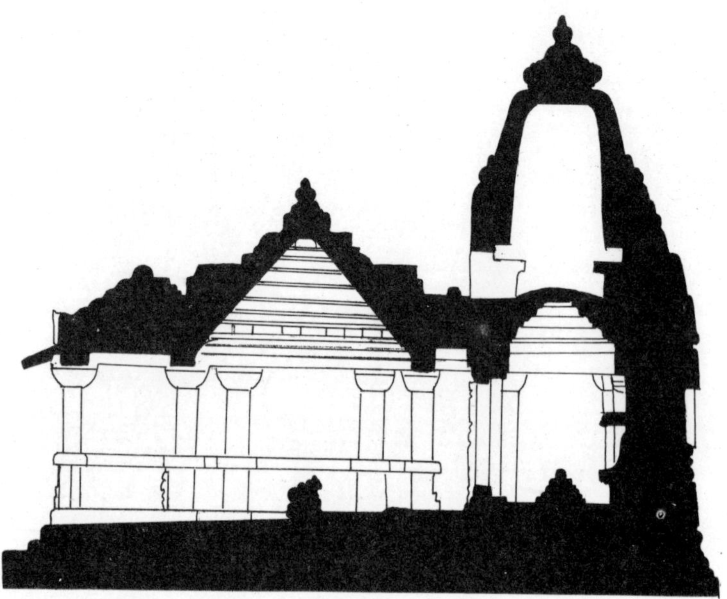

Figure 4: Sandhisthala: section of the above

Technically other junction parts of the temple are termed *sandhisthāna*, as e.g. in the construction of the door:

द्वारशेषं द्विबाहुं च अर्धभागेन वर्धयेत् ।
तत्र जायेत यत्क्षेत्रं सन्धिस्थानं तदुच्यते ॥
सन्धिबिन्दुं समारभ्य त्रिगुणं वेधं वर्धयेत् ।

ŚiPrak I.74-75 ab

The two side-lines from the end of the door-part should be extended by half a unit. Upto where they reach, that part is called place of junction (*sandhi-sthāna*).
From the *sandhi-bindu* the width (of the *mukhaśālā*) is extended (on either side) by three units (*triguṇa vedha*). (Tr. A. Boner)

Such places of junction may be vertical or horizontal divisions. In the vertical the recesses between different parts of the *śikhara* are also termed *sandhi*, as also the interval between the parts of a *gavākṣa* (window):

पार्श्वद्वये समभागे मध्यमा त्रयसन्धिषु ।
प्रतिभागे स्तम्भरूपेण छेदयेत् समभागतः ॥

ŚiPrak I. 367

On either side (of each vertical line) two equal parts should be made (leaving) three intervals in between. Every part should be equally carved into the form of a pillar. (Tr. A. Boner)

The recesses on the *śikhara* are often decorated with the mythical *virāla* figures, as in Orissan architecture (cf. ŚiPrak I.359). In the horizontal, *sandhi* or junctions may be the connecting parts of a pillar.

तद्वुत्सेधे त्रिभागे तु भागेनोत्सन्धिरिष्यते ॥
भागेन वेत्रमंशेन पद्मं पाल्याभमिष्यते ।

Mayam XV.35cd-36ab

(The abacus of the pillar) is three modules high and its height is divided into three (equal) parts: the upper connecting element occupies one, as do the reed and the inverted doucine. (Tr. B. Dagens)

In this context the **Śilpa-Prakāśa** also speaks of *vali-sandhi*, i.e. the junction between the different roll-mouldings (ŚiPrak I.123).

Another technical meaning of *sandhi* in architecture is the assembling of pieces:

पार्श्वगस्थितशयितद्रव्याणां सन्धिरुच्यते ।
एकस्मिन् वस्तुनि द्रव्यैर्बहुभिश्च निघट्टनात् ॥

Mayam XVII.1

Now the assembling of oblique, vertical and horizontal pieces is explained. A single construction (is made) with many pieces (and results) from their being assembled. (Tr. B. Dagens)

Apart from the purely technical meaning, *sandhi* is an important element in architecture/sculpture as the place of juncture between various parts.

The symbolism of erotic images (*mithuna*) being placed on the juncture between *mukhaśālā* and *vimāna* has been described by Devangana Desai, e.g in the case of the Kandariyā Mahādeva temple at Khajuraho. Michael Meister gives another example of the same symbolism: "The priest or architect of Chitor, searching for a scheme within which to place his images, saw the relation between his conjoint images of Śiva-Pārvatī and Śiva-Viṣṇu and the juncture between *prāsāda* and *maṇḍapa* in which to put them. Though no line of similar linkage on temple walls can be shown from the intervening period, architects at Khajuraho have struck on the same location faced with the need to give prominent place to scenes of ritual and physical union" (M. Meister, p. 226-234). Another implication of this placement at the junctures is to protect the temple at this most vulnerable part against obstacles. "But above all these functions, through the content of the scene and its significant placement on the juncture of the hall of devotees (*Paśus, Jīvas*) and the womb-house of divinity (Pati,

Śiva), the juncture of the phenomenal and transcendental worlds, the architect-priest conveys the transcendence of the human condition, the non-dual state of timelessness in which there is neither day, nor night, neither Sun nor Moon." (Devangana Desai, p. 164).

Classification

We find classifications of *sandhis* in various disciplines, as seen above:

1. Āyurveda gives different classes of joints in the human body, of which the most general division is that in movable and immovable (cf. SuSam Śarīrasthāna V.24-25).

Another classification given by Suśruta follows the shape of the respective joints which are compared to different objects:

> सन्धयोऽष्टविधाः - कोरोलूखलसामुद्गप्रतरतुन्नसेवनीवायसतुण्डमण्डल-
> शङ्खावर्त्ताः ।
>
> SuSam Śārīrasthāna V.27
>
> Joints may be divided into eight different classes (named after the objects which they respectively resemble in shape), namely *Kora* (hinged or lap-shaped), *Ulūkhala* (ball and socket), *Sāmudga* (back of the palm), *Pratara* (raft), *Tunna-sevanī* (seam-like or dove-tailed), *Vāyasa-tuṇḍa* (crow-beak), *Maṇḍala* (circular), and *Śaṅkhāvarta* (involutions of conch-shell). (Tr. K.L. Bhisagratna)

2. In grammar (*Vyākaraṇa*) different classes of *sandhis* are given according to the preceding and following vowels or consonants which are joined and whether it occurs in a word or in a sentence.

3. In drama (*Nāṭya*) five kinds of *sandhis* are mentioned which form the structure of a play: *mukha, pratimukha, garbha, vimarśa* and *nirvahaṇa*. Each of these *sandhis* of the plot has a number of 'members'. The total number of these *sandhyaṅgas* is 64 (see above).

Process

Whenever two elements in space or time are joined together, it involves a dynamic process, in which some transformation occurs, mostly leading to a merging or union of the two. A mere static juxtaposition of two elements would not be termed *sandhi*.

Among the different kinds of processes we may mention the following which are all called *sandhi*:

1. The merely physical process of joining, e.g. two metals by heating, of two bricks or stones in a building, or of two architectural parts or storeys in architecture.

2. The medical process of healing in the sense of joining, as e.g. cuts or wounds, fractured bones or disjoined limbs.

3. The religious process of ritual performed at the times at *sandhyā* or *parvan*, destined to 'heal' time, to bridge the gap between day and night, between bright and dark fortnight, between seasons etc. One of the main functions of the Vedic *agnihotra*, of the *cāturmāsya* sacrifices and other forms of *yajña*, of the daily *sandhyā* rites and seasonal festivals, is that of assuring a continuity of time by joining and uniting the otherwise disparate divisions of time.

The ritual performance can be substituted by a purely spiritual process, which always contains the element of unification: *sandhāna, anusandhāna, yoga.* Various yogic methods are applied both, to focus attention on the gaps existing between two breaths or two thoughts, and to assure the continuity of consciousness.

4. The process in Sanskrit drama is marked by the five *sandhis*, whose dynamic nature is also made clear by the plant metaphor used. However, the movement involved is not a linear progression, but a circular – or spiral – development, where the end joins the beginning.

Conclusion

Space and Time would not be structured, and hence could not be measured, without junctures – a bamboo can be measured by the number of knots, time can be measured by the number of days and nights. These junctures are sensitive and important moments or spaces of transition, taking characteristics from both sides, at the same time separating, thus differentiating the two and uniting them, partly overlapping. As in grammar, *sandhis* in every field are essential for the smooth functioning, bridging the gaps without breaks. Ultimately the junctures in any field have the purpose of overcoming the fundamental dualities, without denying differentiation.

Bettina Bäumer

Select Bibliography

Dasgupta, S.: Obscure Religious Cults. Calcutta: Firma K.L. Mukhopadhyay, 2, 1962.

Desai, Devangana: "The location of sculptures in the architectural scheme of the Kaṇḍarīya Mahadeva Temple of Khajuraho: Śāstra and practice," in: Dallapiccola, A.L.: Shastric Traditions in Indian Arts, Vol. 1, Texts, Stuttgart: Steiner Verlag, 1989, pp. 155-165.

Lévi, Sylvain: Le Théatre indien. Paris: Collège de France (L. Honoré Champion), 2, 1963.

Meister, Michael: "Juncture and Conjuncture: Punning and Temple Architecture," in: Artibus Asiae, Vol. XLI, 1979, pp. 226-234.

Vatsyayan, Kapila: The Square and the Circle of the Indian Arts. New Delhi: Roli Books International, 1983.

SŪTRA

Overview

Sūtra has a range of meanings reaching from the thread, the measuring thread to rule and aphorism or concise statement in philosophical and scientific literature. Its metaphorical usage is equally important as the 'thread connecting all the worlds together.'

The origins of the term lie in the realm of textile manufacture, but its development led to a type of scientific activity that is especially productive within the domain of the human sciences.

Etymology

The noun *sūtram* is derived from the verb *sīvyati*, 'sew, join'. It is *sīvyatyanena*, "that by means of which something is sewn" (**Uṇādisūtra** 4.171). It is identified (4.162 and 169) with *tantu* which also means 'thread'. In the **Ṛgveda**, another derivative from the same root, *syūman*, has similar meanings: 'thong, band, belt, chain'.

Wilhelm Rau has suggested that in many early technical works, scientific as well as philosophic, rules are thought of as woven together in the manner in which strands are sewn/woven/turned together into a thread. According to him, it is no coincidence that many basic terms of early philosophy (e.g., *guṇa, tarka, nidāna, bandhu*), and especially terms for scientific works (e.g., *grantha, sūtra, tantra, nibandha, prabandha*), originate in the language of textile manufacture (Rau 1970: 681-682).

Core Meanings

The two core meanings of *sūtra* are 1) Thread and 2) Rule. It is the spatial use of the thread for measuring which leads to the rule as a 'measure' for any activity, ritual, scientific or artistic. Each may be further subdivided, but it is the relationship between these two clusters of meaning that accounts for the productivity of the notion.

Thread as a Metaphysical Metaphor

Two mantras of the **Śāṅkhāyana Āraṇyaka** refer to amulets which consist of a jewel on a string. Amulets are effective because the Self is strung on life held together by food.

पुरुषो मणिः प्राणः सूत्रमन्नं ग्रन्थिः ।

ŚāṅkhĀr XI.8

The jewel is man, the string is breath, and the knot is food.

The other *mantra* is a spell which addresses the Bilva tree:

अमृतं मे मणेः सूत्रमश्विनावपि नह्यताम् ।

ŚāṅkhĀr XII.7

The thread that goes through the jewel is immortality.
May the Aśvins fasten it!

The **Śatapatha Brāhmaṇa** interprets the Sautrāmaṇi ritual, in which the Adhvaryu buys malted barley with wool and fried rice 'with thread,' through an apparent non-sequitur:

ऊर्णासूत्रेण क्रीणाति ।तद्वा एतत् स्त्रीणां कर्म, यदूर्णासूत्रम्; कर्म वा इन्द्रियं वीर्यं, तदेतद्रुत्सन्नं स्त्रीषु, तद्यदेवेन्द्रियं वीर्यमुत्सन्नं स्त्रीषु तदेवावरुन्धे ।

ŚBr XII.7.2.11

With wool and thread he buys – this, to wit, wool and thread, is woman's work; and work, indeed, means energy, or vital power, and this latter is extinct in women: he thus secures (for the Sacrificer) that energy, or vital power, that is extinct in women.
(Tr. J. Eggeling)

Elsewhere the **Śatapatha Brāhmaṇa** comments on the white horse, the sun, that is made to sniff the Naturally Perforated Pebbles of the Agnicayana altar. The rite evokes a vision of a solar system strung together by a thread:

तद्यदवघ्रापयति - असावेव तदादित्य इमाँल्लोकान्त्सूत्रे समावयते । तद्यत्तत्सूत्रमुपरि तस्य बन्धुः ॥

ŚBr VII.3.2.13

Even as he (the Adhvaryu priest) makes it (the horse) smell (the altar), so yonder sun strings these worlds to himself on a thread. And as to that thread, the significance of that (will be explained) further on. (Tr. J. Eggeling)

The explanation is given in the last portion of the **Śatapatha Brāhmaṇa**, more widely known as the **Bṛhadāraṇyaka Upaniṣad**. Uddālaka, son of Aruṇa, asks Yājñavalkya about:

तत् सूत्रं येनायं च लोकः परश्च लोकः सर्वाणि च भूतानि संदृब्धानि भवन्ति ।

That thread by which this world, the next world and all beings are strung together?

Yājñavalkya answers:

वायुर्वै तत्सूत्रम् । वायुना वै ...सूत्रेणायं च लोकः परश्च लोकः सर्वाणि च भूतानि संदृब्धानि भवन्ति । तस्माद् वै पुरुषं प्रेतमाहुर्व्यस्रंसिषतास्य अङ्गानीति । वायुना हि सूत्रेण संदृब्धानि भवन्ति ।

BṛUp III.7.2

Wind is that thread. It is by the thread that is Wind that this world, the next world and all beings are strung together. Therefore they say of a deceased person, "his limbs become unstrung," for they are strung together by the thread that is Wind. (Tr. R.E. Hume)

A late Upaniṣad has an interesting passage on *sūtra*, combining its physical use with its metaphysical meaning.

सूचनात् सूत्रमित्युक्तं सूत्रं नाम परं पदम् ॥
तत् सूत्रं विदितं येन स मुमुक्षुः स भिक्षुकः ।
स वेदवित् सदाचारः स विप्रः पङ्क्तिपावनः ॥
येन सर्वमिदं प्रोतं सूत्रे मणिगणा इव ।
तत्सूत्रं धारयेद् योगी योगविद् ब्राह्मणो यतिः ॥
बहिः सूत्रं त्यजेद् विप्रो योगविज्ञानतत्परः ।
ब्रह्मभावमिदं सूत्रं धारयेद् यः स मुक्तिभाक् ॥

ParabrahmaUp 2cd-5

It is stated to be *sūtra* because it indicates. The *sūtra* is the Supreme state (*padam*). One who knows it properly is desirous of release and a mendicant. He is the knower of the Vedas and follows the right moral laws. He is a wise man who purifies his line. It is that by which everything is permeated like gems remain threaded in a *sūtra*. That sort of thread should be borne by a *yogin*, by the knower of *yoga*, by *brāhmaṇas* and by renouncers. A twice-born should give up the external thread and it should be given up by the one who is well-practised in the truth of *yoga*. This *sūtra* represents the state of *Brahman*. The one who bears it is a person to attain release. (Tr. H.N. Chakravarty)

The image of pearls on a string is used as a metaphysical metaphor in the **Bhagavad-Gītā**:

मयि सर्वमिदं प्रोतं सूत्रे मणिगणा इव ।

BhG VII.7

On Me this Universe is strung like necklaces of pearls on a string.

The Self pervades the universe like a thread runs through a garland and is referred to as *Sūtrātmā*:

एतत् समष्ट्युपहितं चैतन्यं सूत्रात्मा हिरण्यगर्भः प्राणश्चेत्युच्यते ।
सर्वत्रानुस्यूतत्वात् ज्ञानेच्छाक्रियाशक्तिमदुपहितत्वाच्च ।

VedSā II

Consciousness associated with this totality is called *Sūtrātmā, Hiraṇyagarbha, Prāṇa*, etc., because it is immanent everywhere and because it identifies itself with the five great uncompounded elements endowed with the powers of knowledge, will and activity. (Tr. Swami Nikhilananda)

The 'thread' image is retained when *sūtra* is used as 'rule' (see later):

काचं मणिं काञ्चनमेकसूत्रे ग्रथ्नाति बाला नहि तद् विचित्रम् ।
विशेषवित् पाणिनिरेकसूत्रे श्वानं युवानं मघवानमाह ॥

No wonder that the girl strings together glass, gems and gold on one thread. Even Pāṇini, who ought to know better, combined dog, youth and king of the Gods in one rule.

The reference is to **Aṣṭādhyāyī** 6.4.133, which deals with the vocalization of the *-v-* in *śvan, yuvan* and *maghavan* (Chatterji 1957:126).

Measuring Strings, Ritual Threads and Other Uses of Threads

Measurements are often made with a string. The laying down of the measuring line is referred to as *sūtrapātana*, e.g., in the legend of the foundation of Śrīnagar by Pravarasena II:

पार्श्वस्थं तं लग्नमुक्त्वा प्रातर्मत्सूत्रपातनम् ।
दृष्ट्वा पुरं विधेहीति वदन्भूतं तिरोदधे ॥

RājTar III.348

When he stood near, the demon indicated to him the auspicious time and disappeared after saying: "Build (your) town where tomorrow you see the measuring line laid down by me." (Tr. M. A. Stein)

Strings are used in combination with pegs (*śaṅku*; e.g., ŚiPrak I.47). More details are given in connection with construction of a theatre:

शोधयित्वा वसुमतीं प्रमाणं निर्दिशेत् ततः ।
पुष्यनक्षत्रयोगेन शुक्लं सूत्रं प्रसारयेत् ॥
कार्पासं बाल्वजं वापि मौञ्जं वाल्कलमेव च ।
सूत्रं बुधैस्तु कर्तव्यं यस्यच्छेदो न विद्यते ॥
अर्धच्छिन्ने भवेत् सूत्रे स्वामिनो मरणं ध्रुवम् ।
त्रिभागच्छिन्नया रज्ज्वा राष्ट्रकोपो विधीयते ॥

छिन्नायां तु चतुर्भागे प्रयोक्तुर्नाश उच्यते ।
हस्तात् प्रभ्रष्टया वापि कश्चित्त्वपचयो भवेत् ॥
तस्मान्नित्यं प्रयत्नेन रज्जुग्रहणमिष्यते ।
कार्यं चैव प्रयत्नेन मानं नाट्यगृहस्य तु ॥

NŚ II.27-31

Having cleaned the ground one should indicate the measure; one should spread out a white thread at the time of the sixth lunar asterism. The wise should make the thread out of cotton, coarse grass (*eleusine indica*), *muñja* (a kind of rush, *saccharum muñja*) or bark, this thread should be such as would not break or tear. If the thread gets torn in half (of its length), the master's death is inevitable; if torn in one third, the people get agitated; if in one fourth, the performer's end is spoken of. If it slips from the hand, some loss or other evil will occur. Hence the holding of the string should always be done with effort and the measurement of the theatre-auditorium should be done with care. (Tr. P.L Sharma)

Prescriptions for the material from which a thread should be made depend on its uses. For example, when drawing a *maṇḍala*:

... तत्सूत्रं विद्धि पट्टजम् ।
कार्पासमथ वा क्षौमं श्लक्ष्णं दृढमकृत्रिमम् ॥

JaySam XXI.8

The thread should be made from silk, cotton or flax. It should be fine, strong and non-artificial. (Tr. H.N. Chakravarty)

The measuring thread may be called *pramāṇasūtra*:

प्रमाणसूत्रमित्युक्तं प्रमाणैर्निश्चितं हि यत् ॥

Mayam VI.19cd

What is called '*pramāṇa* cord' is determined by the prescribed dimensions (of the intended construction). (Tr. B. Dagens)

Other technical names are used:

तद् बहिः परितो भागे सूत्रं पर्यन्तमिष्यते ।
गर्भसूत्रादिविन्याससूत्रं देवपदोचितम् ॥

Mayam VI.20

The *paryanta* cord goes round the outside of the area determined by the *pramāṇa* cord. The cords which establish (certain placings) such as that of the foundation deposit are spoken of as 'determining' (*vinyāsa*) cords. (Tr. B. Dagens)

There are many ritual uses in addition to measurements. At the beginning of the *Agniṣṭoma*, for example, a piece of gold is offered with a string tied around it (ŚBr III.2.4.14). Special threads are placed on the body, e.g.:

कर्ममायाणुमलिनत्रयं बाह्वौ गले तथा ॥
शिखायां च क्षिपेत् सूत्रग्रन्थियोगेन दैशिकः ।

TĀl XVII 2cd-3ab

The teacher should place the thread on the arms, on the neck, on the tuft of hair which are considered impure because of deeds, *māyā*, and limitedness. These threads should be tied with knots. (Tr. H.N. Chakravarty)

The 'sacred thread' (*yajñopavīta*), sometimes called *brahmasūtra*, consists of several strands or threads:

कार्पासमुपवीतं स्याद् विप्रस्योर्ध्ववृतं त्रिवृत् ।
शणसूत्रमयं राज्ञो वैश्यस्याविकसौत्रिकम् ॥

Manu II.44

The sacred thread of a *Brāhmaṇa* shall be made of cotton, (shall be) twisted to the right, (and consists) of three threads, that of a *Kṣatriya* of hempen threads, (and) that of a *Vaiśya* of woollen threads. (Tr. G. Bühler)

The 'marriage-string' (*vivāhakautukasūtra*) tying together bride and bridegroom is not only prescribed in the ritual manuals, but referred to in literature, e.g.:

अथ तस्य विवाहकौतुकं ललितं बिभ्रत एव पार्थिवः ।
वसुधामपि हस्तगामिनीमकरोदिन्दुमतीमिवापराम् ॥

Ragh VIII.1

After this, the king Raghu delivered also the earth into his hands, as if it were another Indumatī, even while he wore (round his wrist) the elegant marriage-thread-ring. (Tr. G.R. Nandargikar)

बबन्ध चास्राकुलदृष्टिरस्याः स्थानान्तरे कल्पितसन्निवेशम् ।
धात्र्यङ्गुलीभिः प्रतिसार्यमाणमूर्णामयं कौतुकहस्तसूत्रम् ॥

Kum VII.25

She (Menā) also fastened the marriage-string of wool round her (Umā's) hand, which was misplaced as her eyes were filled with tears of joy, but which was being pushed back (to its right place) by the nurse with her fingers. (Tr. M.R. Kale)

Threads or strings are also used like bandages and in combination with a *mantra* for medical purposes, e.g., against rheumatism:

पिशङ्गे सूत्रे खृगलं तदा बध्नन्ति वेधसः ।
श्रवस्युं शुष्मं काबवं वध्रिं कृण्वन्तु बन्धुरः ॥

AV III.9.3

On a reddish string the wise and skilful bind a brush (?). Let the bandages make impotent the flowing and puffing (?) *Kābava* (spirit). (Tr. R.T.H. Griffiths/W.D. Whitney)

or in connection with the removal of lumps:

उदरान्मेदसो वर्तिर्निर्गता यस्यदेहिनः ॥
कषायभस्ममृत्कीर्णां बद्धा सूत्रेण सूत्रवित् ।
अग्नितप्तेन शस्त्रेण छिन्द्यात् ...

SuSam Cikitsāsthāna II.45-46

In the case of a perforation of the abdomen marked by the discharge of lumps or rope-like fat through the wound, the emitted or ejected fat-lump should be dusted with the ashes of astringent woods pounded together with black clay and burnt. A ligature of thread should then be bound round the fat-lump and the fat-lump cut off with a heated instrument. (Tr. K.L. Bhisagratna)

Sūtra as Rule

The notion of *sūtra* as rule, first developed in **Baudhāyana's Śrauta-Sūtra** (see next Section), was employed to the fullest extent in the grammar of Pāṇini. Patañjali places Pāṇini's composition of *sūtras* in their proper context:

प्रमाणभूत आचार्यो दर्भपवित्रपाणिः शुचाववकाशे प्राङ्मुख उपविश्य महता प्रयत्नेन सूत्रं प्रणयति स्म, तत्राशक्यं वर्णेनाप्यनर्थकेन भवितुम् ।

Mahābh I.1.1

The teacher (Pāṇini) functioning as an authoritative means of cognition, used to produce the *sūtra* with great effort: holding a cleansing bunch of *darbha*-grass in his hand, being seated on clean ground, his face turned towards the east. This being so, it is impossible that even one sound be without purpose. (Tr. P. Thieme)

Ojihara (1978:227) has pointed out that this statement does not imply that Pāṇini's rules are beyond criticism, but that they have to be subjected to a thorough examination in order to find out what is their ultimate motivation (*prayojana*). The term *pramāṇabhūta* which here refers to Pāṇini, is also used of the Buddha, e.g., in the **Lalitavistara** and in Dignāga's **Pramāṇasamuccaya** where Hattori translates it as "the personification of the means of cognition." He adds (1968:74) that the term also means "to have come into existence a means of valid cognition," in which sense Jinendrabuddhi uses it to distinguish the Buddha from *Īśvara* and other *pramāṇas* which are maintained (by others than Buddhists) to be eternal.

A *sūtra* is a brief 'rule' which describes the salient features of a field of experience. Because of its succinctness, it generally requires an 'explanation' (*vyākhyāna*) which is provided by a *bhāṣya* or 'commentary'. A number of related technical terms have come into usage, with slightly different meanings in the different disciplines in which they are used. In general, *vṛtti* means 'gloss' but in grammar it can denote 'application (of the grammatical rules)' (*śāstravṛtti*). A *vārttika* is not part of a regular commentary, but is confined to the elucidation of rules that raise specific problems because they seem to be unclear or incomplete.

Patañjali's **Mahābhāṣya** is the first text that discusses these logical and methodological problems in detail, but as we shall see in the next section, the ritual *sūtras* paid attention to them first. Terms that refer to special kinds of *sūtra*, such as *paribhāṣā* 'meta-rule', occurred already in these *sūtras*, but terms such as *vārttika* did not.

In grammar *vārttika* is defined as: "A critique on what has not been said or badly said in the *sūtra* " (*sūtre'nuktaduruktacintākaratvam*)
Kumārila Bhaṭṭa wrote:

सूत्रेष्वेव हि तत्सर्वं यद् वृत्तौ यच्च वार्तिके ।
सूत्रं योनिरिहार्थानां सूत्रे सर्वं प्रतिष्ठितमिति ॥
ये वदन्ति तान् प्रत्युच्यते...तस्मादगमके सूत्रे सति अवश्यं
दोषप्रतिसमाधानार्थं वृत्तिकारादिभिर्यतितव्यम् ।

TantraVā I.3.11

To those who hold "what has been stated in the *vṛtti* or in the *vārttika* is already present in the *sūtras*. All views (propounded by the later commentators) exist in the *sūtra* – have their basis in the *sūtra*" we reply: "... when the *sūtra* fails to express the intended views, it becomes the duty of the *vṛttikāra* and others to solve the defects (to correct the fault) in the *sūtra*." (Tr. R.S. Bhattacharya)

According to the grammarians, 'grammar' (*vyākaraṇa*) is the same as *sūtra*. The relationship between sounds and meanings, however, is not learnt by asking a grammarian 'make words' (*kuru śabdān*) just like one asks a potter: "make a pot" (*kuru ghaṭam*). Instead, one learns that relationship in the market place: *lokataḥ*, 'from the world' (Mahābh. ed. Kielhorn p.7).

Patañjali returns to this topic later in his Introduction (*Paspaśā*):

न हि सूत्रत एव शब्दान् प्रतिपद्यन्ते । किं तर्हि ? व्याख्यानतश्च । ननु च
तदेव सूत्रं विगृहीतं व्याख्यानं भवति । Mahābh (Paspaśā)

...People do not learn words from rules alone. – What then? – From the exposition also. – Excuse me, but the self-same rule when analysed becomes the exposition. (Tr. K.C. Chatterjee)

The final view is given in the following terms:

सूत्रत एव हि शब्दान् प्रतिपद्यन्ते ।... यो ह्युत्सूत्रं कथयेन्नादो गृह्येत ।

Mahābh (Paspaśā)

It is from the rules that people learn words.... he who says something not warranted by the rules, what he says is not accepted. (Tr. K.C. Chatterjee)

In later works, several definitions of *sūtra* are found, most of them similar, e.g.:

अल्पाक्षरमसन्दिग्धं सारवद् विश्वतोमुखम् ।
अस्तोभमनवद्यं च सूत्रं सूत्रविदो विदुः ॥

KāMīm Ch.2

Sūtra-experts know *Sūtras* to consist of few syllables, be unambiguous, to contain the essence, to be open to all sides, without embellishments and faultless.

Development of the Sūtra Style

In a wide-ranging study of 1963, Louis Renou surveyed Sanskrit literature in the *sūtra* style. He showed that the *sūtra* period was initiated when *śruti* had almost been completed and *smṛti* had begun to appear. Only the Kalpasūtras may be regarded as still resorting under the Vedic domain of *śruti.* A *sūtra* is close to a 'formula', a formalized expression that is used for analysis within the context of a scientific discourse, or that enunciates principles upon which a system of thought or enquiry is based. The term refers both to 'rules' and to 'manuals consisting of rules'.

The first *Sūtras* were the Śrauta-Sūtras, and the earliest among these are those of Baudhāyana, author of a ritual manual generally assigned to the sixth century B.C. (Caland 1903:11). Baudhāyana introduced not only the notion of 'rule' but also that of 'meta-rule' (*paribhāṣā*). Meta-rules display a higher level of abstraction and generality than rules; they often specify how rules have to be used. The relation between the Śrauta-Sūtras and the Brāhmaṇas, earlier disputed, was correctly formulated by Caland, tested by Tsuji (1952) and has been expressed by Gonda in terms that are no longer controversial:

"The authors of the Brāhmaṇas endeavoured to explain the origin, meaning and raison d'être of the ritual acts, etc., and to prove their validity; the compilers of the *Sūtras*, on the contrary, aimed at a systematic description of every ritual in its natural consequence." (Gonda, The Ritual Sūtras, p.497).

After the Vedic period, philosophical *Sūtras* come to the fore. The rules of Nyāya and Mīmāṃsā reflect *paribhāṣā* meta-rules (*nyāyasiddhāḥ paribhāṣāḥ*). Many of the Mīmāṃsā-Sūtras are closely related to meta-rules of the Śrauta-Sūtras or to the *vārttikas* of grammar. The philosophical *Sūtras* are followed in turn by *Sūtra* works in the domains of politics, law, erotics, medicine, etc. Many of these *Sūtras*, which were originally descriptive became in due course prescriptive.

It is justified to go beyond Caland's observations, confirmed by Tsuji and Gonda, on the relationship between the *Brāhmaṇas* and the Śrauta-Sūtras that were quoted at the beginning of the section on the *Sūtra* style. The *Brāhmaṇas* do not merely try to explain the rites; their mythical interpretations are in addition often fanciful, arbitrary, inconsistent and ad hoc. The *Sūtras*, on the other hand, do not only offer systematic descriptions; they embody a science.

Conclusion

Both the physical and metaphorical meanings of *sūtra* have deeply influenced Indian culture. The basic idea is that the universe is woven together like a texture, or strung together like a necklace, by an inner connection or immanent principle, often called *sūtrātman*. The function of *sūtra* is both measuring and binding or connecting together. Sanskrit literature is full of similes and metaphors with thread or string, necklace etc. This reflects the general Indian tendency to see connections and inter-relations in the cosmic and human spheres.

Sūtra led to at least three major revolutions in the history of human civilization. The first, which marks its prehistoric origin, led to textile manufacture and included such uses of threads as have been surveyed. These uses occur worldwide and are not confined to India. The development from 'thread' to 'rule' that took place around the seventh century B.C. and that was sketched here, was equally important: it signalled what was probably India's major contribution to science. Equally Indian is the third revolution which belongs to our own times: the moral economic and political threads that Gandhi spun on the traditional Indian *dharmacakra* reconstructed as a spinning wheel.

In the West, the importance of rules was recognized by Aristotle and later logicians and mathematicians. Dionysius Thrax and other Greek grammarians adopted Aristotle's classifications but not his system of logic in which rules played such an important role. Ancient Greece, therefore, did not develop linguistics, and neither did ancient China, despite examples of writing going back to 1300 B.C. In India, linguistics originated not in spite of the absence of writing but because of it (Renou and Filliozat 1953:668). In Western linguistics, the importance of rules was recognized only in the twentieth century. Noam Chomsky's discoveries of the notion of rule and of a particular class of rules, viz., context-sensitive rules, are the same as Pāṇini's discoveries – an extraordinary fact that suggests that these features are universal. Pāṇini also discovered the infinity of language which implies that the rules of linguistics should be recursive. This insight, introduced into Western philosophy by Wilhelm von Humboldt (1767-1835), was illustrated two thousand years earlier by Patañjali in a colourful passage:

> अथैतस्मिन् शब्दोपदेशे सति किं शब्दानां प्रतिपत्तौ प्रतिपदपाठः कर्तव्यः । गौरश्वः पुरुषो हस्ती शकुनिर्मृगो ब्राह्मण इत्येवमादयः शब्दाः पठितव्याः ? नेत्याह । अनभ्युपाय एष शब्दानां प्रतिपत्तौ प्रतिपदपाठः । एवं हि श्रूयते बृहस्पतिरिन्द्राय दिव्यं वर्षसहस्रं प्रतिपदोक्तानां, शब्दानां शब्दपारायणं प्रोवाच नान्तं जगाम । बृहस्पतिश्च प्रवक्तेन्द्रश्चाध्येता दिव्यं वर्षसहस्रमध्ययन-कालो न चान्तं जगाम । किं पुनरद्यत्वे । यः सर्वथा चिरं जीवति स वर्षशतं जीवति ।... तस्मादनभ्युपाय शब्दानां प्रतिपत्तौ प्रतिपदपाठः । कथं तर्हीमे शब्दाः प्रतिपत्तव्याः । किञ्चित्सामान्यविशेषवल्लक्षणं प्रवर्त्यम् ॥
>
> Mahābh (Paspaśā)
>
> Now if grammatical expressions are taught, must this be done by the recitation of each particular form for the understanding of grammatical expressions – for example, should we recite the grammatical forms *gauḥ, aśvaḥ, puruṣaḥ, hastī, śakuniḥ, mṛgaḥ, brāhmaṇaḥ*? No, says the author, this recitation of each particular form is not a means for the understanding of grammatical expressions. For we have a tradition which describes how Bṛhaspati addressed Indra during a thousand divine years, going over the grammatical expressions by enunciating each particular form, and still did not attain the end. With Bṛhaspati as the professor, Indra as the student, and a thousand divine years as the period of study, the end could not be attained; so what of us at the present day, who when we live in full life at most a hundred years? .... The recitation of each particular form, therefore, is not a means for the understanding of grammatical expressions. How, then, must grammatical expressions be understood? Some work containing general and particular rules has to be composed. (The term for 'rule' that is used here is *lakṣaṇa*, a common synonym for *sūtra*.)

The originality of Indian science lies in the discovery and analysis of rule-governed activities like ritual, language and the Arts. These rules express regularities that are similar to the regularities of nature and the non-human universe in general, whether the latter are regarded as 'laws of nature' or as mathematical formulas. In fact, if the latest speculations in theoretical physics are correct, the universe consists of 'strings'. Ancient India did not hypothetize that there are deep or intrinsic differences between the human and the non-human world, or between the human and the natural or physical sciences. Western civilization, with its growing emphasis on non-human science, never produced a science of ritual like that of the Śrauta-Sūtras, and produced a science of language only belatedly, after being influenced by the Sanskrit grammar of Pāṇini. This is largely due to the notion of *sūtra* and it is this notion that will have to be the corner-stone of the human sciences of the future.

Frits Staal

Sūtra in the Visual Arts

by Bettina Bäumer

The physical, the ritual, the metaphorical and the measuring functions of *sūtra* are all present in the Arts of architecture, sculpture, painting, in the drawing of ritual *maṇḍalas* as well as decorative auspicious designs (*ālpanā, kolam, citta*, in various regional languages and styles). The use of a thread for making a straight line, for laying out a ground-plan, for measuring the parts of images, has never been considered a mere technical device in the traditional Arts of India. In any visual art the line is of fundamental importance which alone makes structure and measure possible, leaving aside its symbolic significance. The line itself has been called *sūtra*, and only later *rekhā*, mainly because the method of drawing a straight line has always been to dip a thread in white or red powder and to make it touch the surface, leaving a trace of the coloured powder. But if the traditional artist even today, with the facilities of modern technical means, prefers to follow the same old method, it means that he is conscious of the symbolism implied in the use of the *sūtra*. A kind of play on the three meanings of *sūtra* as line, measuring thread and rule is found in the **Vāstusūtra Upaniṣad**:

सूत्रायने रेखा सुभगा भवन्ति ॥

VSUp II.20

Lines following the *sūtra* become harmonious. (Tr. A. Boner)

In architecture (*vāstu*) at the laying out of the ground-plan, and even before that when the building-site is selected and measured, the thread is used for determining the space-directions, and to get the orientation with the help of the gnomon:

शङ्कुद्विगुणमानेन तन्मध्ये मण्डलं लिखेत् ।
पूर्वापराह्णयोश्छाया यदि तन्मण्डलान्तगा ॥
तद्बिन्दुद्वयगं सूत्रं पूर्वापरदिशीष्यते ।
बिन्दुद्वयान्तरभ्रान्तशफराननपुच्छगम् ॥
दक्षिणोत्तरगं सूत्रमेवं सूत्रद्वयं न्यसेत् ।
उदगाद्यपरान्तानि पर्यन्तामि विनिक्षिपेत् ॥
सूत्राणि स्थपतिः प्राज्ञः प्रागुत्तरमुखानि च ॥

Mayam VI.8-11ab

The line which joins the two points where the shadow (of the gnomon) has touched the circle, in the morning and in the evening, gives the east-west direction. The line which passes through the space between these two points and (which is like that which) connects the head and tail of a carp, is the north-south axis; the sage should draw these two lines. Then the circles which have their centres in the east and west points should be drawn. (Tr. B. Dagens)

One cord is made the measure for the construction, called *pramāṇa-sūtra*:

प्रमाणसूत्रमित्युक्तं प्रमाणैर्निश्चितं हि यत् ।

Mayam VI.19cd

What is called '*pramāṇa* cord' is determined by the prescribed dimension (of the intended construction). (Tr. B. Dagens)

The *sūtra* to be used in the construction of a temple is first consecrated by a ritual:

सर्वें च शिल्पिनः भाटो दैवज्ञश्चोत्तमः तथा ।
सहितं पीठपूजान्ते गर्भसूत्रादिस्थापनम् ॥

ŚiPrak II.179

In a gathering of all the *śilpin*, with the Bhāṭa (singing the praises of the king) and the best Astrologer, after (performing) the *pūjā* of the foundations (*pīṭha*) the measuring string (*garbhasūtra*) and other things are placed. (Tr. A. Boner)

While measuring the site and testing the ground for a temple, good or evil omen is attached to the *sūtra* used:

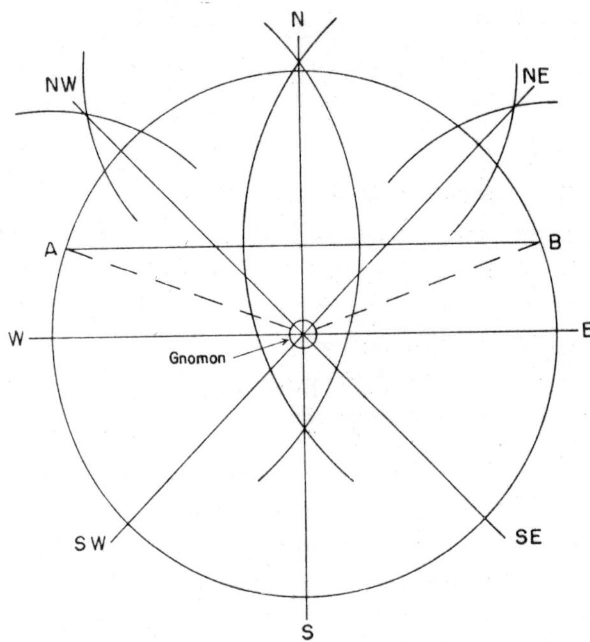

Figure 1: Orientation

केन्द्ररेखोपरि यदि सूत्रं जायेत वर्धितम् ।
तदा ह्याचरते कीर्तिं लेशमात्रं न संशयः ॥
अशुभं यदि तत्स्थाने सूत्रं सङ्कीर्णं जायते ।
परित्याज्या तदा भूमिः नात्र कार्या विचारणा ॥

ŚiPrak I.51-52

If on the radius (*kendra-rekhā*) the string grows longer, then fame will accrue without any doubt. When the land is inauspicious the string in that circle grows shorter; that land should be abandoned without any further consideration. (Tr. A. Boner)

Once the site has been determined, the thread is again used for marking:

वास्तुस्थापनकर्मान्ते भूमिमार्जनशोधनम् ।
करणं सूत्रपातार्थं शङ्कुः मध्यस्थलस्थितः ॥

ŚiPrak I.47

After determining the building site, it should be cleansed and purified. For marking it out with the thread, a peg (*śaṅku*) should be fixed in the centre of the ground. (Tr. A. Boner)

Knowledge of the thread means knowledge of measure, and hence the disciple of the architect is called *sūtragrāhin* (→*sūtradhāra*):

स्थपतेस्तस्य शिष्यो वा सूत्रग्राही सुतोऽथवा ॥
स्थपत्याज्ञानुसारी च सर्वकर्मविशारदः ।
सूत्रदण्डप्रपातज्ञो मानोन्मानप्रमाणवित् ॥ Mayam V.18cd-19

The *sūtragrāhin* is the disciple or the son of the architect and follows his directions; he is skilful in all the Arts; he knows how to make the rod and the rope fly and how to measure length, height and proportions. (Tr. B. Dagens)

Obviously, the elevation of the temple is equally measured by means of a thread, following the fundamental measure (*pramāṇasūtra*).

In the context of sculpture (*śilpa*), the line has two distinct and yet related meanings: One is the composition of the total image or panel which is laid out in a diagram, consisting of the cross of the vertical and horizontal middle lines (*madhyasūtra, prasthasūtra*), other diameters of the circle, the border-lines, inscribed triangles, etc. This compositional diagram is more than a functional structure for the balanced and harmonious placement of the parts of the image. It is a symbolical representation of the cosmos and each line symbolizes a different element.

रेखान्वये सर्वाङ्गाणि न्यासय ॥ ८ ॥
इति भेदनक्रिया एवं वज्रेण शिलायां रेखाङ्कनकरणं ध्येयम्, न भूमौ न वा इष्टके । अथासौ आङ्गिरसो होवाच – ब्राह्मणं भगवन्तं पिप्पलादं द्वौ प्रश्नौ पृच्छामि, तौ चेन्मे वक्ष्यति । का रेखा, कस्तस्या भावः, कति भेदाः, ब्रूहि पिप्पलादेति ।तान् ह स ऋषिरुवाच – आङ्गिरस, शिल्पकाश्यप शृणु रेखाव्याख्यानम्, तथा तासां भावञ्च, रेखा न्यासस्याधारः सा धारेव। सा कर्मप्रतीतेरधिभूतमधिदैवतञ्च ।
तेजांसि सरलरेखाणि ॥ ९ ॥
तद्रेखेण मण्डलं भिन्दन्ति, यथा कर्तारः कर्मणा विश्वं परिभिन्दन्ति, तेभ्यः तद्रूपेण रूपार्थं चाक्षुषत्वेन देशकथानुमतं सर्वाणि रूपाङ्गाणि प्रभवन्तीति । अङ्गसाम्यं प्रभवतीति ।

VSUp II.8-9

Sūtra 8: All limbs have to be set along the lines.
This is the dividing action. The lines are to be drawn with white powder (*vajra*) on the stone, not on earth and not on brick. Then Āṅgirasa said: "I am asking the *brāhmaṇa*, the venerable Pippalāda, two questions, whether he may tell me: What is the line? What is its character (*bhāva*)? How many varieties are there? Please tell, O Pippalāda." To them the Ṛṣi said: "O Āṅgirasa and Śilpakāśyapa, hear the explanation of the lines and their character (*bhāva*). The line is the support (determinant) of the composition, it is like a

> boundary. It is that which corresponds to the fundamental elements (*adhibhūta*) and to the gods (*adhidaivata*) in the realisation of action.
> Sūtra 9: Straight lines are as rays of light.
> By the line they (the *sthāpakas*) divide the circle, as the creators by their action divide the world. From these (lines) in this way all the parts of the image become visibly manifest, for the sake of the whole image, in accordance with the myths of the country and the harmony of the limbs arises. (Tr. A. Boner)

These compositional lines had both, a symbolic as well as practical function, and "for a skilled and experienced Śilpin a few fundamental lines may have amply sufficed to lay out the most complex patterns." (A. Boner, Principles of Composition, p.6).

While preparing the stone for carving, a grid or *koṣṭhaka* was drawn on the surface:

> पालाशदण्डरज्जुसंयोगे रेखामानय ॥१५ ॥
> शैले कोष्ठकानामुत्थानक्रमेण रेखामाचरेत् । पयसा शोणशैलचूर्ण-संयोगेन धीराः कोष्ठकान् प्रकुर्वन्ति । कोष्ठमध्ये पादाच्छिरोऽवधि रूपमुपलब्धव्यमिति ।
>
> VSUp IV.15
>
> Sūtra 15: Draw the lines with a measuring rod of *palāśa* wood and a rope.
>
> The skilful (artists) should draw the lines on the stone for the grid in ascending order, they should make the grid with a mixture of water and red stone powder. Inside the grid the forms are obtained proceeding from foot to head. (Tr. A. Boner)

The more technical use of *sūtra* in sculpture is related to the system of measurement (*tālamāna*, →*māna* in the Arts) where *sūtra* relates to the plumb-lines of the body of the image. In the words of Kapila Vatsyayan:

"Viewed vertically and frontally the human body is conceived as two halves along an imaginary absolute vertical median termed the *brahmasūtra*. This is the constant and invariable and stands for the unchangeable pull of gravity. All movement is visualized in relation to this vertical median, representing the earth-sky-principle. The other four vertical axes enumerated by the canons, with some minor differences, are variable and are drawn from different points of the body in different categories of sculpture. These are the *madhyasūtra*, the *pārśvasūtra*, the *kakṣasūtra* and the *bāhusūtra*. Vertically, the human figure can be measured in terms of these axes and the relative positioning of different parts of the body from the central median can suggest the relative states of dynamism, disturbance and composure. The *madhyasūtra* (the central median)

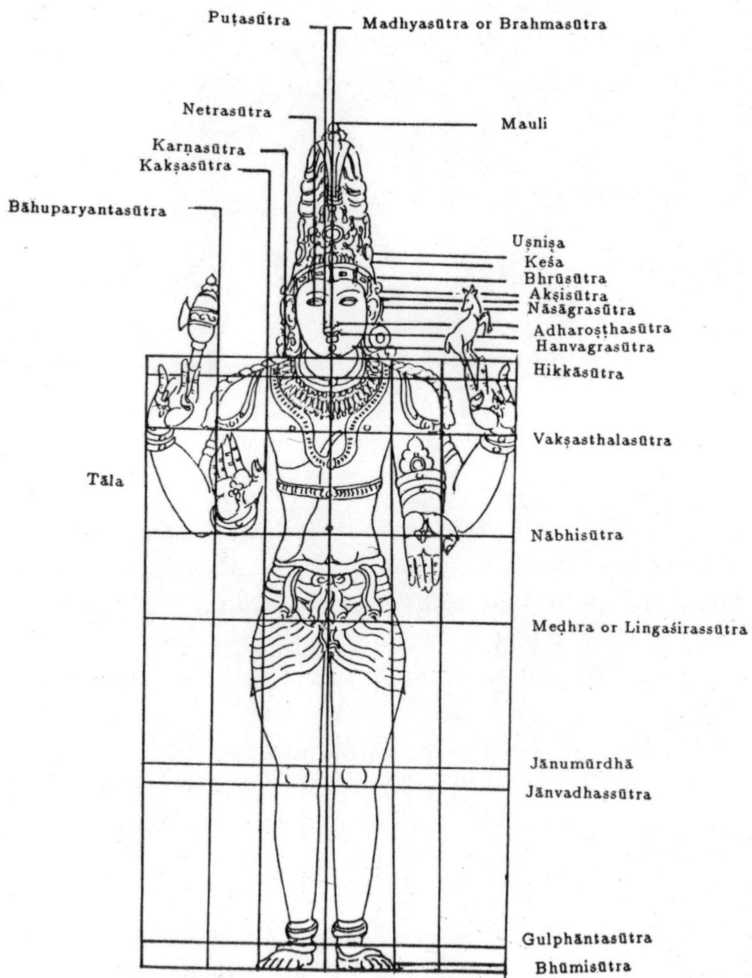

Figure 2: Pratimā with Sūtra-divisions

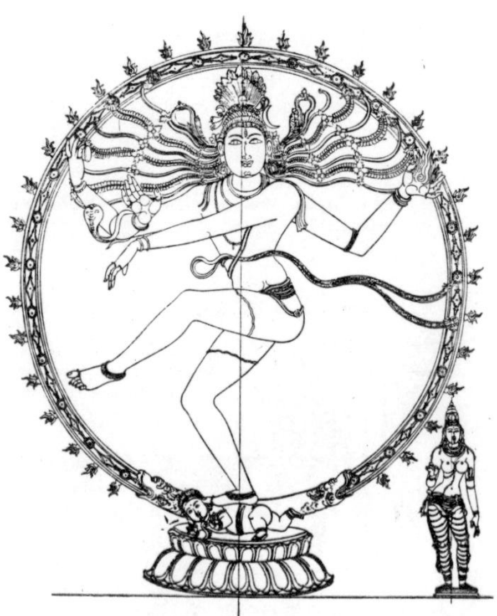

Figure 3: Naṭarāja in *bhujaṅgatrāsita* with *madhyasūtra*

is drawn vertically through the centre of the face and in images where the weight of the body is equally distributed each limb is equidistant from this vertical median. Naturally, it coincides with the *brahmasūtra*, the imaginary absolute central median in these images. The *pārśvasūtra* is drawn from the tip of the shoulders to the ground, the *kakṣasūtra* from the armpit and the *bāhusūtra* from the elbows and finally one from the tip of the hand, with outstretched arms.

Horizontally, the figure is divided into many sections, but the three main divisions are determined by the major joints of the human skeleton and the central point of the body, namely the navel. There is the horizontal axis called the *hikkāsūtra* which passes just above the shoulders and through the pivot joint of the neck; the *bhadrasūtra* or the *nābhyanta* or *nābhisūtra* passes through the navel; the *kaṭisūtra*, the *yonisūtra* in the female figure and *meḍhramūlasūtra* pass through the pelvis touching the root of the penis in the male figure. Finally, two horizontal axes pass through the knees, i.e. the *jānusūtra* and the ankles, the *gulphasūtra* respectively. Other horizontal axes are drawn along the different parts of the face, that is above the *hikkāsūtra*, especially the fore-head, eyebrows and nose; others pass along the chest in the region between the *hikkāsūtra* and the *nābhisūtra* called the *vakṣasthalasūtra*; yet others pass through the thighs the region between the *kaṭisūtra* and the *gulphasūtra*. Finally there is the *bhūmisūtra*" (Fig. 2). (The Square and the Circle of the Indian Arts, p. 107).

The manuals for image-making, the Āgamas and Śilpa-Śāstras, are full of descriptions of these *sūtras* which assume the right proportion of the figure, just as the compositional diagram (*pañjara*) gives a harmonious composition to the image-panel.

Sūtradhāra

by Radhavallabh Tripathi

The word *sūtradhāra* stands for the person holding the *sūtra*. *Sūtra* indicates different meanings in different contexts, viz., a thread, stringline, a cord, a fibre, the string of a puppet, a short rule or a precept, a formula and the work comprising aphorisms or rules on any subject. In general, *sūtradhāra* is the person who has the say in any context, being at the helm of affairs. *Sūtradhāra* however, has a close association with theatre and various crafts. In the tradition of Sanskrit drama, *sūtradhāra* is a combination of a stage-manager, the producer and the director of a stage-performance. **Medinīkośa** gives the following meanings of the term *sūtradhāra*: the sugar-cane called *puṇḍra*, Indra, the main character entering after the *nāndī* (salutary verse in a dramatic performance) and an artisan (*śilpin*): **Medinīkośa** 301, p.144). **Kalpadrukośa** (74, p.425) cites *sūcaka* and *bījadarśaka* as synonymns of *sūtradhāra* and **Vaijayantīkośa** also holds *sūcaka* and *sūtradhāra* as synonyms.

We thus find that etymologically, the term *sūtradhāra* covers a very wide perspective, but in practice it has been related to the world of drama and technical acumen more often. Apte has referred *sūtradhāra* as the "author of a set of aphorisms" (The Practical Sanskrit English Dictionary, p.996), but I am unable to trace any reference to *sūtradhāra* in this sense; the word *sūtrakāra* is more appropriately used for the author of a set of aphorisms. *Sūtradhāra* in the literary tradition has been so famous for his debut in the fields of theatre and crafts, that the term *sūtradhāra* in its wider sense could be used only metaphorically in a secondary sense. Bhoja in this way refers to Almighty God as the "*sūtradhāra* of all the three Worlds" (**Samarāṅgaṇasūtradhāra**, 1.1), while Bhāsa has retained the technical context of the word '*sūtradhāra*' by calling God as:

लोकत्रयाविरतनाटकतन्त्रवस्तुप्रस्तावनाप्रतिसमापनसूत्रधारः ॥

Dūtaghaṭotkaca, 1

'The *sūtradhāra* for the introduction and end of the plot of the play continuously going on in all the three worlds'.

Bhartṛhari in his **Vākyapadīya** has called Time (*kāla*) the *sūtradhāra* of the universe, and in Helārāja's commentary we find an early reference to the puppet-theatre and its string-holder:

तमस्य लोकयन्त्रस्य सूत्रधारं प्रचक्षते ।
प्रतिबन्धाभ्यनुज्ञाभ्यां तेन विश्वं विभज्यते ॥

Vāk III.9.4

यन्त्रपुरुषप्रख्यं विश्वं सूत्रधारपुरुषकल्पकालप्रतिबद्धचेष्टम्। कालेन हि स्वशक्त्या भावानां स्थगनोन्मज्जने जन्मनाशपर्याये विभजता सूत्रधारेणेव यन्त्रपुरुषस्य सूत्रसञ्चारवशेनोन्मेषनिमेषादिक्रियाकारिणा विश्वं प्राप्तपौर्वापर्यप्रविभागं प्रविभागलक्षणाश्चेष्टाः कार्यन्ते ।

Comm. Helārāja

Time has been called the wire-puller (*sūtradhāra*) of the world-machine. It regulates the universe through prevention and permission. (Tr. K.A.S. Iyer)

The universe is similar to a mechanical puppet whose movements are controlled by time representing a puppet-operator (stringholder). As the puppet-operator causes the actions such as the opening and the closing of the eyes etc. of a mechanical puppet by moving the strings, in the same way time, by its own power, divides the concealment and emergence of things which are synonyms for creation and destruction respectively and thus makes the world obtain the division of priority and posteriority.

The references to *sūtradhāra* in **Kalpadrukośa** and **Medinīkośa** indicate that *sūtra* and *bīja* are the key terms for proper identification of *sūtradhāra*. We will revert to these terms shortly. Before that it will be proper to trace the sociological background and the history of *sūtradhāra*.

Basically, *sūtradhāra* and his associates belonged to the *varṇasaṅkara* category in the caste system, and in the Vedic period, they were associated with various subsidiary functions or duties related to the performance of *yajña*. Roughly they could be termed as the *sūtas*. **Yajur-Veda** (XXX.6) prescribes that persons engaged in various professions should be invited to perform their respective jobs for the *yajña* ceremony, *sūta* and *śailūṣa* having been cited there at the very outset in a fairly long list. *Sūta* was to be invited for *nṛtta* and *śailuṣa* for *gīta*.

A person belonging to the *sūta* class could also be engaged for construction of *yajñavedī*. The *vedī* had to be erected strictly in accordance with the measurements prescribed for it. A *sūtra* or cord was used for measurements. It appears from the **Nāṭya-Śāstra** of Bharata and the texts on *vāstuvidyā* that *sūtra* and *daṇḍa* (the measuring rod) were two standard measurements in those days. The *nāṭyācārya* or *sūtradhāra* responsible for construction of the theatre-house himself held the *sūtra* or the cord for measurement, and started measuring the land at the prescribed auspicious occasion:

पुष्यनक्षत्रयोगेन शुक्लं सूत्रं प्रसारयेत् । NŚ II.27

One should spread out a white thread at the time of the sixth lunar asterism. (Tr. P.L. Sharma)

It appears that the *sūta* began to be called *sūtradhāra* also, as he used to hold the *sūtra* or cord for measurement of sites or the plinth for the *vedī* in *yajña*. The **Mahābhārata** treats both the terms *sūta* and *sūtradhāra* as equivalents and identifies a *sūta* as *sūtradhāra*. This stanza occurs in the context of the *nāgayajña* (the serpent sacrifice) of Janamejaya, and describes the *sūta* invited to erect the sacrificial platform (*vedī*) for the *yajña*. The epithets and adjectives used for *sūta* here are very striking:

स्थपतिर्बुद्धिसम्पन्नो वास्तुविद्याविशारदः ।
इत्यब्रवीत् सूत्रधारः सूतः पौराणिकस्तथा ॥

MBh I.47.14cd-15ab

He is said to be the *sthapati* (an architect or master carpenter), *buddhisampanna* (wise), *vāstuvidyāviśārada* (expert in the technique of house-building), the *sūtradhāra*, the *sūta* and the *paurāṇika* combined in one [the last appellation assigning him the great responsibility of reciting and preserving the *Purāṇa* and *Itihāsa* literature].

This is the earliest available reference to *sūtradhāra* in Sanskrit literature, and it identifies one and the same person as a *sūta*, *sūtradhāra*, an architect and a master-builder and also a *paurāṇika* as well.

The *sūtas* had attained a very honourable position in society owing to their immense contribution in various fields that included preparing the *vedī* for Vedic rituals, preparing arms and armaments, chariots and construction of houses or buildings. Over and above all this, they arduously pursued the great task of preserving, collecting and expanding the Purāṇa literature. It was a *sūta muni* who had presented the **Mahābhārata** and eighteen Purāṇas before the august assembly of eighty-eight thousand *ṛṣis* headed by Śaunaka in Naimiṣāraṇya, and it was in the holy place of Naimiṣāraṇya that an infuriated Balarāma had killed a *sūta muni* who was interpreting Purāṇa before the *ṛṣis*. To Balarāma, he was guilty of occupying a higher seat before the sages like Vyāsa. But for committing the gruesome murder Balarāma himself was branded with the heinious crime of *brahmahatyā* by those very sages! The *paurāṇika sūtradhāra* to them was as venerable as a *brahmarṣi*.

In the texts dealing with *Vāstuśāstra*, *sthapati* and *sūtradhāra* are closely linked together, although, unlike in the **Mahābhārata**, they are not treated as synonymous or identical. *Sthapati* is described as the master architect and *sūtragrāhin* as his disciple:

स्थपतिः स्थापनार्हः स्यात् सर्वशास्त्रविशारदः ।
न हीनाङ्गो नातिरिक्ताङ्गो धार्मिकस्तु दयापरः ॥

अमात्सर्योऽनसूयश्च तन्त्रसर्वाभिज्ञानवान् ।
अरोगी चाप्रमादी च सप्तव्यसनवर्जितः ।
सुनामा दृढबाहुश्च वास्तुविद्याब्धिपारगः ॥
स्थपतेस्तस्य शिष्यो वा सूत्रग्राही सुतोऽथवा ।
स्थपत्याज्ञानुसारी च सर्वकर्मविशारदः ।
सूत्रदण्डप्रमाणज्ञो मानोन्मानप्रमाणवित् ॥

VVid p.12-16

A *sthapati* is authorised for performing the *sthāpanā*. He should be well versed in all the *śāstras*. He should not be a disabled man, nor should he have extra limbs in his body. He must be religious and full of pity, devoid of jealousy and envy, adept in Tantraśāstra, free from diseases and carelessness as well as the seven addictions. He should have a good name and strong arms and capable of measuring the great ocean of *Vāstuvidyā*. A *sūtragrāhin* is either his disciple or his son. He is obedient to the *sthapati*, and expert in all acts (pertaining to *vāstuvidyā*). He should understand the measurements by *sūtra* and *daṇḍa*, and should also understand the technique of *māna* and *unmāna*.

The word *sthāpanā* has been a current term in Vāstuśāstra tradition as evinced from the very first line of the above excerpt. This is a very significant term in the context of our theatric tradition also. *Sthāpaka* stands for the actor performing the prologue of Sanskrit drama, and *sthāpanā* is the prologue done by him. Bhāsa's plays have *sthāpanās*, which his successors term as '*prastāvanā*', and in a few cases also '*āmukha*' (as in **Mṛcchakaṭika**).

Sūtradhāra has been referred in **Manusaṃhitā** as *sūtragrāhin* or *sūtrakāra* (Manu, I.4.47-48). He has been called *sūtrakāra* in **Mahāvastu** also. *Sūtradhāra*'s association with both theatre as a performing art and architecture together is clear to Bāṇa, when he eulogises Bhāsa:

सूत्रधारकृतारम्भैर्नाटकैर्बहुभूमिकैः ।
सपताकैर्यशो लेभे भासो देवकुलैरिव ॥

Harṣacarita, I.15

Bhāsa earned fame by his plays which were like temples. Like temples, they were also initiated by the *sūtradhāra*, they also had large *bhūmikās* (roles, foundation) and had the *patākās* (sub-plot, flag).

Thus a *sūtradhāra* was hailed both as an architect and a theatre-director. **Mudrārākṣasa** by Viśākhadatta refers to a *sūtradhāra* called Dāruvarman who had erected a *toraṇa* which would just collapse at the moment Candragupta was to pass beneath it. Cāṇakya however sensed the conspiracy beforehand. Dr. R.N. Mishra has given a number of references from ancient Sanskrit inscriptions where the *sūtradhāras* have been named and have been described as inscribers or temple-builders.

The authors of texts on Vāstu-Sūtra were also known as *sūtradhāra*. The *sūtradhāra* called Maṇḍana has written a number of texts on fine Arts and architecture. His father, named Kṣetra, was also known as a *sūtradhāra* as we come to know from his self-introduction:

श्रीमद्देशे मेदपाटाभिधाने क्षेत्राख्योऽभूत् सूत्रधारो वरिष्ठः ।
पुत्रो ज्येष्ठो मण्डनस्तस्य, तेन प्रोक्तं शास्त्रं मण्डनं रूपपूर्वम् ॥

Rūpamaṇḍana, p.214

There was a senior *sūtradhāra*, called Kṣetra in the country of Medapāṭa. His eldest son, known as Maṇḍana, has composed this *śāstra* called **Rūpamaṇḍana**.

Sūtradhāras were patronised by the kings. Bhoja in his **Samarāṅgaṇasūtradhāra** has extensively dealt with the qualities of *sthapati* to be patronised by the king (SamSū Chapters 44-45). From another work of Sūtradhāra Maṇḍana, named Rājavallabha, we come to know that king Kumbha of Mewar who himself is known as a celebrated author of quite a few works on music, musicology and dance, had patronised *sūtradhāras* (**Rājavallabha**, XIV.43).

Was the *sūtradhāra* a person who manipulated the puppets through strings? Of course, puppets made of wood had come into existence during the period of **Mahābhārata**, as the Great Epic refers to them at least thrice by the way of similitude:

यथा दारुमयी योषा नरवीरसमाहिता ।
ईरयत्यङ्गमङ्गानि तथा राजन्निमाः प्रजाः ॥

MBh III.31.22

O king, as a properly manipulated wooden woman moves its limbs, so do the people.

However, *sūtradhāra* is not known for running the puppet-shows or operating puppets, the existing references right from the **Mahābhārata** to later classical literature always refer to him either as an architect, a theatre-director or a *paurāṇika*; and in fact this tradition recognises *sūtradhāra* as a combination of all the three, and it was with him that Indian classical theatre came into inception.

Samudramathana (Churning of the Ocean), a *samavakāra*, was perhaps the earliest full-fledged drama staged in our country. The **Nāṭya-Śāstra** of Bharatamuni makes a reference to *sūtradhāra* in its description of the premiere of this play. Bharatamuni himself had sponsored and organised the show on the festive occasion of Indramahaḥ (festival in the honour of god Indra). Witnessing the performance, the *asuras* or *vighnas* (the demons) felt offended and out of fury, created pandemonium by overpowering the stage with their *māyā* and rendering the artists almost defunct to disrupt the show. *Sūtradhāra* here comes into the picture:

> तथा विध्वंसनं दृष्ट्वा सूत्रधारस्य देवराट् ।
> कस्मात् प्रयोगवैषम्यमित्युक्त्वा ध्यानमाविशत् ॥
> अथापश्यत् सदो विघ्नैः समन्तात् परिवारितम् ।
> सहेतरैः सूत्रधारं नष्टसंज्ञं जडीकृतम् ॥
>
> NŚ I.67,68
>
> Seeing this sort of injury done to *sūtradhāra* (and his associates), Indra sat in meditation to ascertain the cause behind the disruption of the performance and then he saw the *sūtradhāra* along with the others surrounded on all the sides by the *vighnas* and rendered stupefied and inert.

The **Nāṭya-Śāstra** refers to this as an incident that happened in a mythical time, and we can take it as the earliest reference to *sūtradhāra* in the Nāṭyaśāstra-tradition. Bharatamuni has been referred to as the person responsible for sponsoring and managing the performance of **Samudramathana**, and the *sūtradhāra* has been identified here as an actor, quite different from Bharata himself. This shows that the person actually managing the troupe and directing the play was not required to stage his entry as *sūtradhāra* in the beginning of the play. Abhinavagupta, the commentator par excellence on the *magnum opus* of Bharata rightly suggests here that the performance of *Samudramathana* had been disrupted at the very outset when the *sūtradhāra* was just rendering the prologue of the play. The prologue of the performance of *Samudramathana* was not presented by Bharata himself.

The **Nāṭya-Śāstra** has defined *sūtradhāra* also taking into account what *sūtra* stands for in the context of theatrical arts:

> गीतस्य च वाद्यस्य च पाठ्यस्य च नैकभावविहितस्य ।
> शिष्टोपदेशयोगात् सूत्रज्ञः सूत्रधारस्तु ॥
>
> NŚ XXXV.30
>
> *Sūtradhāra* is designated so because he knows the *sūtra* of theatrical performance – he can impart training to the able disciples in singing, musical instruments and textual recitation imbued with various *bhāvas*.

Owing to his expertise and occupation of training others in theatrical arts, *sūtradhāra* also began to be called *nāṭyācārya* or the master of theatre. Vema, a later theorist in the field of Sanskrit dramaturgy, has identified *sūtradhāra* as *nāṭyācārya*. In **Mālavikāgnimitra** of Kālidāsa, Gaṇadāsa and Haradatta are doing the job of training the maids of royal harem in theatrical arts. They have been designated as the *nāṭyācāryas*.

The person who knows, teaches and also practises the *sūtra* of drama and theatre is *sūtradhāra*. The word *sūtra* here indicates the essence of all the techniques, precepts, maxims and principles involved in the practice of theatre, and *sūtradhāra* is an authority on them.

Curiously enough, this definition of **Nāṭya-Śāstra** does not exactly correspond to the appearance of *sūtradhāra* as described there itself in the context of the production of *Samudraṃathana samavakāra*. Bharata, who is the preceptor and the mentor for this production does not present himself as the *sūtradhāra* of the play. The *sūtradhāra* who performs the prologue of *Samudramathana* must be a member of his troupe – an actor trained by Bharata himself.

This description of *sūtradhāra* in practice as presented in the first chapter of **Nāṭya-Śāstra** just answers the definition of *sūtradhāra* as given by Śātakarṇi, one of the earliest writers on the art of theatre and dramaturgy. He has been quoted by Sāgaranandin:

> आह शातकर्णिः – अनुष्ठानं प्रयोगस्य सूत्रं, तद् धारयतीति सूत्रधारः ।
> पूर्वरङ्गमात्रोपजीवी बहिःपात्रमित्यर्थः ।
>
> NLRKo p.110-11
>
> Śātakarṇi says – *anuṣṭhāna* or the ritual is the *sūtra* of the performance. The person who holds this *sūtra* is the *sūtradhāra*. He is an external character useful for the *pūrvaraṅga* only.

We find that Śātakarṇi has a somewhat different idea of *sūtra* and *sūtradhāra*, taking the former to mean just the ritual of *pūrvaraṅga* (the preliminary rites to be performed before actual presentation of the play), and the latter as the person conducting or performing these rites. This definition rather narrows the function of *sūtradhāra*. A similar definition under attribution to Bharata has been quoted by Jagaddhara in his commentary on **Mālatīmādhava**, but it is not found in the text of **Nāṭya-Śāstra**.

Thus the tradition presents two views about the *sūtradhāra*. According to one, he holds the highest office in the realm of theatre. He is the final authority and the *sine qua non* there. The second view however, just treats him as a person performing the ritual of *pūrvaraṅga*; which extended to the *prastāvanā* (the prologue) of the play or was replaced by *nāndī* (the propitiatory verse) and *prastāvanā* as prefixed to the texts of Sanskrit plays.

Both these views of *sūtradhāra* are correct in their respective context. Bhavabhūti, the most renowned dramatist after Kālidāsa in the realm of Sanskrit drama, uses the word *tauryatrika-sūtradhāra*, where the *tauryatrika* stands for the trio of theatrical arts comprising music, instruments and dance. In **Uttararāmacarita**, the magnum opus of Bhavabhūti, the manuscript of the play prepared by Vālmīki himself on the basis of his own Epic is sent to Bharatamuni, as Lava informs in the IV act:

तस्यैव कोऽप्येकदेशः प्रबन्धान्तरेण रसवानभिनेयार्थः कृतः । तं च स्वहस्तलिखितं मुनिर्भगवान् व्यसृजद्भगवतो भरतस्य तौर्यत्रिकसूत्रधारस्य।

A part of the last portion of the Great Epic has been converted by the sage in the dramatic form full of *rasa*, for performance, and its manuscript written by the sage himself has been dispatched to Bharata – the '*tauryatrika-sūtradhāra*'.

Very interestingly, the play as per the script supplied by Vālmīki is designed for production by Bharata and is presented in the hermitage of the sage; and the **Uttararāmacarita** records this production as a *garbhāṅka* (play within a play) and this *garbhāṅka* starts with the entry of a *sūtradhāra* for the presentation of its prologue. Thus Bhavabhūti has referred to both the *sūtradhāras* in his play – one who is the master of theatre in all respects, and the other who is the *sūtradhāra* for the time being, just for the purpose of presenting the preliminaries or the prologue of the play.

According to **Nāṭyaśāstra** *sūtradhāra* has been defined as:

चतुरो नाट्यकुशलः शास्त्ररीतिप्रतिष्ठितः ।
नानापाषण्डकार्यज्ञो नीतिशास्त्रार्थवित् तथा ॥
वेश्योपचारनिपुणः काव्यशास्त्रविचक्षणः ।
नानागतिप्रचारज्ञो रसभावविशारदः ॥
नाट्यप्रयोगकुशलो नानाशिल्पसमन्वितः ।
छन्दोविधानतत्त्वज्ञः सर्वशास्त्रविचक्षणः ॥
ग्रहनक्षत्रतत्त्वज्ञो देशव्याहारतत्त्ववित् ।
पृथिवीद्वीपवर्षाणां पर्वतानां जनस्य च ॥
प्रमाणाचारतज्ज्ञश्च राजवंशप्रसूतिवित् ।
श्रोता शास्त्रार्थकार्याणां श्रुत्वा चैवावधारकः ॥
अवधार्य प्रयोक्ता च शास्त्र(?)श्चैवोपदेशने ।
एवंगुणस्तथाचार्यः सूत्रधारो विधीयते ॥
स्वाभाविकान् गुणां श्चैव गदतो मे निबोधत ॥
स्मृतिमान् मतिमान् धीर उदारः स्मितवाक् शुचिः ।
अरोगो मधुरः क्षान्तो दान्तश्चैव प्रियंवदः ॥
सर्वदोषविनिर्मुक्तः सत्यवाग् दक्षिणस्तथा ।
अलुब्धः प्रतिमन्ता च स्वाभाविकगुणास्त्वमी ॥

NŚ(KM ed.) XXIV.91-98 (also cf. Mātṛgupta as quoted in the Comm. by Rāghavabhaṭṭa on AbhŚāk p.14)

Now we will describe the qualities of *sūtradhāra*. He is adept in the techniques of the *śāstra* from the very beginning, is gifted with perfection in the cultivation of rhetorics; has to be an expert in the timing of songs and musical notes as well as musical instruments.

He should be wise; a master of theatre; well established by his knowledge of the techniques of *śāstra*; should be knowledgeable in various acts of *pāṣaṇḍa*; should be an expert in dealing with the courtesans; should have the mastery of poetics; should know the stage movements; should be adept in *rasa* and *bhāva*; should be an expert in dramatic performance; should know various arts and crafts; should be equipped with full knowledge of metres and the knowledge of all the *śāstras*.

Besides he should be conversant with astrology, should know the linguistic modes of addresses prevalent in different regions; should know the extent of earth, of islands, of man as well as the customs in practice therein; should be familiar with genealogy of kings; should be a listener of scriptures and should remember their contents and should also be able to impart training in them.

Now I will speak of the natural qualities of *sūtradhāra* – memory, wisdom, patience, sublimity; pleasant speech, piousness, immunity from diseases, sweet nature, forgiveness, restraint, tendency for speaking dear words, being devoid of all the blemishes, truth, generosity, avoidance of greed and allowance for the views of others – these are the natural qualities.

There are definitions of *sūtradhāra* in **Viṣṇudharmottara Purāṇa**, **Bhāvaprakāśana**, **Mandāramarandacampū** and some other works but they merely repeat these ideas.

The series of preliminary rites called *pūrvaraṅga* comprises 19 items and *sūtradhāra* is directly involved with the performance of these items. He faces the audience while conducting the *bahirjavanikāgata aṅgas* of *pūrvaraṅga*, i.e. the items to be performed after the curtain has been removed from the stage; while the first items, called *antarjavanikāgata aṅgas* are performed inside the curtain, under his supervision.

Contrary to the directive of **Nāṭya-Śāstra** that the *sūtradhāra* should recite *nāndī* (V.104), we generally have this conventional dramatic direction in the beginning of Sanskrit plays:

नान्द्यन्ते ततः प्रविशति सूत्रधारः ।

Enters *sūtradhāra* after the *nāndī* is over.

If *nāndī* is an item to be performed after the curtain has been removed, and if *sūtradhāra* is entering the stage after *nāndī* then he is not participating in the recitation of *nāndī*. Commentators like Jagaddhara (on Bhavabhūti's **Mālatīmādhava**), the author of **Candrikā (on Prabhodhacandrodaya**) and the anonymous author of **Abhijñānaśākuntala-carcā** have extensively discussed the propriety of the above dramatic direction and the resolution of its contradiction with the dicta of **Nāṭya-Śāstra**. The author of **Candrikā** opines that this dramatic direction pertains to the *sthāpaka*, and not to the *sūtradhāra*. The former stages his entry after *sūtradhāra*, having recited *nāndī*, has made his exit. This commentator has also suggested an alternative arrangement on the basis of a work called **Sarasvatīvilāsa**. Accordingly, if Kuśīlavas recite *nāndī*, then *sūtradhāra* himself enters on the stage to present the prologue.

This gives rise to the problem of the identity of *sthāpaka* and his relationship with *sūtradhāra*, which we cannot discuss here in detail.

While Sāgaranandin, Viśvanātha, Dhanañjaya and Dhanika, Śāradātanaya and several commentators referred above all agree that according to Bharata's **Nāṭya-Śāstra**, *sūtradhāra* and *sthāpaka* are two different individuals, Abhinavagupta, the best exponent of Bharata, has quite a different view. He holds that the same *sūtradhāra*, who had been observing the items of *pūrvaraṅga* ritual, re-enters the stage as *sthāpaka*:

> सूत्रधार एव स्थापक इति सूत्रधारः पूर्वरङ्गं प्रयुज्य स्थापकः सन् प्रविशेदिति न भिन्नकर्तृकता ।
>
> AbhiBhā I.248
>
> *Sūtradhāra* himself is *sthāpaka*; and this *sūtradhāra* after having performed the *pūrvaraṅga* enters as *sthāpaka*, hence the authorship (of *pūrvaraṅga* and *prastāvanā*) is not different.

There is an important distinction between *sūtradhāra* and *sthāpaka* as they both serve different functions. Since *sthāpaka* is not the real *sūtradhāra*, therefore the whole tradition beginning from the **Nātya-Śāstra** uses the epithet '*sūtradhāraguṇākṛti*' for him. *Sthāpaka* is thus an actor performing the role of *sūtradhāra* in the prologue of the play to be performed on the stage. A study of the *prastāvanās* of various Sanskrit dramas proves that this *sthāpaka* reproduces through *abhinaya* not just the *sūtradhāra* who performs the *pūrvaraṅga* ritual, but the *sūtradhāra* of theatre in the widest sense of the term: a man who is managing the performance, all the affairs of the troupe, and who is responsible for each and every thing that goes on on the stage or behind the curtains. Thus the *sūtradhāra* reproduced by the poet in the *prastāvanā* of his play is one of the dramatis personae, while the *sthāpaka* is just the member of the theatre-group who is supposed to enact the *sūtradhāra*. If the poet himself is writing the *prastāvanā* for his play, there is no question of putting the word *sthāpaka* in the script, the poet names the dramatis personae in the play and he does not name the actors that are going to assume the roles therein.

Sūtradhāra is thus the great master of theatre, the director, philosopher and guide to the artistes. The person assuming certain characteristics of *sūtradhāra* for the time being in a given time-space is also called *sūtradhāra* hypothetically. Our dramatic tradition presents both the views of *sūtradhāra.* In classical Sanskrit drama, the *sūtradhāra* remains conspicuous by his absence on the stage after the *prastāvanā,* but in several traditional folk forms of Indian theatre, he is allowed to move freely between the audience and the dramatic world, to intervene in between and to interpret the proceedings being presented on the stage. Even if *sūtradhāra* remains behind the curtain, as in Kuchipuri dance-dramas, or in Rāsalīlā or Rāmalīlā, the audience is made to feel his presence through his repetition of dialogues spoken on the stage by the characters, announcements, songs or interpretative stanzas recited by him from behind the curtain. We find historicity percolating into mythological world due to such constant outbursts by the *sūtradhāra.* In **Vīthīnāṭakam** (lit. streetplay, a folk form of Tamilnadu), the *sūtradhāra* stands between the mythical time and the audience and makes remarks pertaining to contemporary situations. Even Sanskrit drama was subsequently influenced by this interpretative style introduced by the *sūtradhāra*; and, as a result we have plays like **Pārijātaharaṇa** by Umāpati, where Kṛṣṇa and other characters speak in Sanskrit, while the *sūtradhāra* goes on addressing the audience in Maithili prose and songs. Similar is the case in **Gorakṣavijaya** of Vidyāpati Ṭhākur or Sanskrit plays produced in Assam under the school of Śaṅkaradeva.

Select Bibliography

Caland, Willem: "Über das rituelle Sūtra des Baudhāyana," Abhandlungen für die Kunde des Morgenlandes 12 (1903) 1-65. Reprint 1966.

Chomsky, Noam: "On the notion 'Rule of Grammar"', Structure of Language and its Mathematical Aspects, Proceedings of Symposia in Applied Mathematics 12 (1961) 6-24.

Gonda, Jan: The Ritual Sūtras, Wiesbaden 1977 (O. Harrassowitz) Hattori, Masaaki, Dignāga, On Perception, Cambridge Mass. 1968.

Kuiper, F.B.J.: Varuṇa and Vidūṣaka. On the origin of the Sanskrit drama, Amsterdam, 1979.

Ojihara, Yutaka: "Sur une formule patañjalienne: na cedānīm ācāryāḥ sūtrāṇi kṛtvā nivartayanti," Indologica Taurinensia 6 (1978) 219-234.

Rau, Wilhelm: Weben und Flechten im Vedischen Indien, Wiesbaden 1970.

Renou, Louis: "Sur le genre du sūtra dans la litterature sanskrite," Journal asiatique 251 (1963) 165-216.

Renou, Louis and Jean Filliozat: L'Inde classique. Manuel des études indiennes, Vol.II, Paris, 1953.

Staal, Frits, "The Concept of Metalanguage and its Indian background," Journal of Indian Philosophy 3 (1975) 315-354.

Staal, Frits: "Context-sensitive Rules in Pāṇini," Foundations of Language 1(1965) 63-72. Reprinted in: Universals 171-180.

Staal, Frits: Universlas. Essays in Indian Logic and Linguistics, Chicago, 1988.

Staal, Frits: Rules without Meaning: Ritual, Mantras and the Human Sciences, New York - Bern - Frankfurt am Main - Paris, 1989.

Thieme, Paul: "Meaning and form of the 'grammar' of Pāṇini," Studien zur Indologie und Iranistik 8/9 (1982/1983) 3-34.

Tsuji, Naoshiro: On the Relation between Brāhmaṇas and Śrautasūtras, Tokyo, 1952 (in Japanese, with English summary).

Sūtradhāra:

Kuiper, F.B.J.: "Sūtradhāra and Sthāpaka", ABORI, Diamond Jub. Vol.

Mishra, R.N.: Ancient Indian Art and Art Activity, IIAS, Simla, 1975.

Thieme, Paul: "Sūtradhāra und pūrvaraṅga" in Studien zur Indologie und Iranistik, Reinbek, Verlag für Orientalistische Fachpublikationen, 1987.

TĀLA

Overview

The word *tāla*, of ancient origin and uncertain derivation, has from a very early time served as a basic term for the standard of measure (*pramāṇa*) in the visual and performing Arts, a standard of measure based on either (a) the length or (b) the motions of the human hand. In this concept we see yet another indication of the profoundly anthropomorphic worldview that inspired the thinkers of early India – a worldview that emerges with clarity in the various articles in this and the previous volume of studies in the fundamental concepts of the Indian Arts. With the individual situated at the centre of the universe, his most immediate extensions – his hands – enabled him to measure and thus regulate the dimensions of his existence and his experience, as manifested in the audible and visual Arts.

Although the visual measurements and physical actions of *tāla* were strictly prescribed, meticulously performed, and precisely calibrated, the term signifies something far more meaningful than a set of purely quantitative labels for portions of visible space and audible time: the idea of *tāla* has been invested with a rich aura of metaphysical symbolism and the connotations of solemn ritual, carrying the clear implication that he who measures or performs rightly, by means of *tāla*, becomes a privileged participant in a sacrificial action that is pleasing to the patron deities of the Arts and therefore earns merit for the performer, as well as bringing pleasure to the spectators and auditors. Because the cosmic Man-Body stands as a pervasive and powerful metaphor for the organic formal relationships in the various Arts (see Kapila Vatsyayan, The Square and the Circle of the Indian Arts, pp. 18-19) the components of *tāla* become the means by which a scale of ideal human proportions is imposed upon the artistic substance (sounds and images), thereby regulating and controlling the pulsating audible and visible rhythms. In particular, the complex and multileveled system of *tāla* – by which Indian music has been organized for at least two thousand years – is unique among the world's art musics and must be seen as one of the chief reasons why a large number of brilliant traditions of drumming and improvisation arose and were brought to a high state of development on the Indian subcontinent.

Etymology

What is beyond dispute is that *tāla* is an augmented form of the masculine noun *tala* (surface), and the relationship between the two words constitutes an important key to the meaning of this crucial technical term in the Arts of India. Beyond this, the history of the word is obscure, although each scholar will have his or her favourite explanation. Monier-Williams assigns the derivation of this nominal stem, unconvincingly, to a number of minor, hypothetical roots: (1) *stṛ*– (to spread out, to strew), (2) *tal*– (to establish, to fix), arising perhaps from a causative form of the root *tṛ*– (to attain, to accomplish), and/or (3) *taḍ*– (to strike). A case can be made for each of the preceding, especially if one is willing to overlook phonological obstacles on the grounds of semantic similarities. One can sense a vaguely defined semantic field of the sort that often arises from phonetic concordances (Lewis Rowell, The Subconscious Language of Musical Time, p. 97), but the meaning of the two basic terms begins to clarify in their normal forms.

Tala signifies a flat surface of some kind: the roof of a house, the base or lower part of anything, the sole of the foot, and – most significantly – the palm of the human hand. *Tāla* (note the augmented form) denotes the fan-palm tree (*Borassus flabelliformis*), its leaves; and any of its products – because of the flatness of its leaves; but, more importantly, *tāla* signifies an action applied to such a flat surface: a clap of the hand or hands, a clash of cymbals, the flapping of an elephant's ears, or – still more abstract – a measure of space (as in architecture, painting and sculpture) or of time (as in music and dance).

There are no obvious and popular cognates in the other principal Indo-European languages, although the ancient Greeks knew the *Borassus flabelliformis* by the name of *tāla*. As far as can be determined, the Sanskrit *tāla* is unrelated to the Latin word *tālea*, which means a 'cutting' (of a plant) or a 'bar' (of metal) and is employed in the medieval European isorhythmic system to denote a rhythmic pattern that is superimposed arbitrarily upon a pre-existing plainsong melody and repeated over and over again as the structural framework for a polyphonic composition. This procedure is strikingly similar to the cyclical *tālas* of later Indian music (the *Deśī tālas* and their modern counterparts) and suggests one of those coincidences that ought always to be distrusted. The Latin *tālea* still survives in the English suffix 'tail' – in the sense of 'cut to size' and hence to limit, as in works such as 'tailor, detail', and 'entail'. There may be something to this line of argument, but nothing except wishful thinking can connect *tāla* with the Greek *talantāw* (to sway or oscillate, to measure out).

Little more can be deduced from an etymological perspective, and it is evident that the meaning of *tāla* was established at a very early stage in the evolution of the Indian Arts.

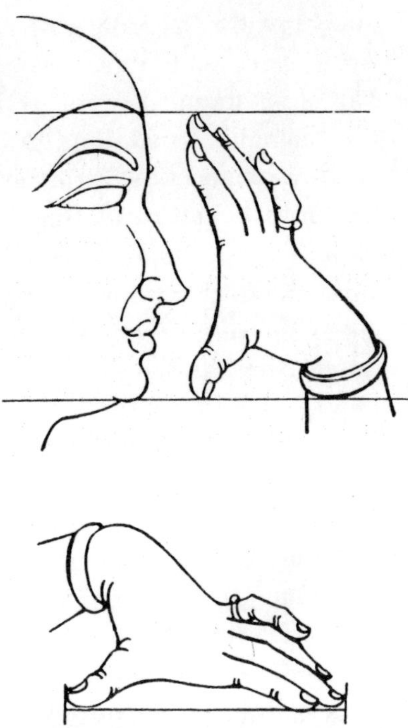

Figure 1: Tāla-measurement

Layers of Meaning

The basic meaning of *tāla*, as an artistic concept, is 'span' – a span of space (as measured from the tip of the stretched-out thumb to the tip of the middle finger, or the length of the face) and a span of time (as marked off and articulated by audible and silent gestures performed by the hand(s)). The former appears to have developed first. The **Saṅgīta Ratnākara** defines the measure of *tāla* thus:

> अङ्गुष्ठमध्यमाङ्गुल्यौ ये हस्तस्य प्रसारिते ।
> तदग्रयोरन्तरालं तालमाहुर्मनीषिणः ॥
>
> SR VII.1036
>
> The thumb and the middle finger of the hand that are stretched, the span of their tips is called *tāla* by the wise ones. (Tr. P.L. Sharma)

At this point it is possible to rationalize Monier-Williams' derivations: first, the metaphor of 'strewing', as in spreading straw for a bed or laying out a sacrificial space, suggests the way in which artistic substance is made to unfold, especially by means of the technique of *prastāra* (permutations), and hence it is easy to imagine the establishment of an hypothetical level space; so one aspect of this complex idea may involve the orderly distribution and disposition of the artistic 'events' in both space and time. Second, the root meaning of 'establish, fix' suggests a way of attaining one's objective, by quantifying and thus rendering the art object amenable to measure. And, finally, the notion of striking or beating has an obvious connection with the physical action of *tāla*, as well as with the ideas of delimiting and regulating.

One can scarcely overemphasize the importance of the idea of measure in the traditional culture of India, and of the principal organ of action. With measurement comes control, and with control comes knowledge – the knowledge that is essential if one is to pierce through the world of illusion to ultimate reality. As Kapila Vatsyayan points out in her perceptive analysis of the doctrines of the **Kena Upaniṣad**: "The actuality of sense perception and its vital role in a framework of discipline, restraint and control is a central pivot around which the (Upaniṣadic) imagery is used" (The Square and the Circle of the Indian Arts, p. 12). With the aid of concrete handspans and their audible/visible motions, visual space and audible time are made manifest to sense perception and brought under control so that their structure may thereby become knowable.

→*Māna* signifies measure, and *pramāṇa* a standard of measure; hence the process of spatial and temporal measuring suggests at the same time the 'right measure', the way in which the arts ought to be measured. *Tāla* thus becomes not merely an objective measure and a means of description, but a standard of proper measure and ideal proportions – scaled to human size. An artistic creation measured by means of *tāla* will look the way in which human beings are supposed to look or move, and will be scaled to the units of human attention and perception. In modern psychology 'chunking' is the somewhat inelegant term denoting the way in which humans group and organize their perceptions, artistic and otherwise; the artists of early India appear to have grasped instinctively a readymade system of 'chunking' that has survived intact to the present day.

Still more needs to be said with reference to the ideas of measure and control. Gonda provides numerous examples of the special significance attached to the act of measuring in Vedic culture (J. Gonda, Vedic Ritual, pp. 251-52): "When one has undertaken a journey one should in the evening before going to sleep measure one's face and in the morning measure the length of three feet or three span: probably with a view to preventing a sort of *deminutio capitis* in the literal sense." The **Sāmavidhāna Brāhmaṇa** (III. 4.7) states that if a stick measured in the morning has become longer during the night one's plans will be crowned with success, reminding us that divination by means of measuring is a universal in world cultures of antiquity. And it need scarcely be mentioned that precise measurement was regarded as essential in all the solemn rites and sacrifices; incorrect measure was sufficient to prevent one from attaining one's objective, just as incorrect or misaccented recitation could destroy the person of the sacrificer, his family, and all his possessions (NārŚik I.1.5-6).

Thus, to summarize, the core meaning of *tāla* is as follows: to measure and thus to control, by means of hand-spans – visibly and/or audibly.

Development of the Concept and References from Literature

It is difficult to establish a meaningful chronology for the development of the term, as the several technical uses of the word *tāla* seem to have become solidly established by the time of their earliest appearance in the extant literature, uses that include but are not limited to the following: 1) medical reference to the therapeutic benefits derived from consuming the products of the palmyra tree; 2) spatial measurements by 'spans' – in building construction, proportions of a statue, and the dimensions of painted images, but also in literary descriptions (as, for example, when describing the length of a hero's stride or the span of his fully-drawn bow); 3) in dance the span between the two feet is prescribed in term of *tāla*, and 4) above all, the conventional references to keeping musical time by clapping the hands, a topic that appears again in literary descriptions of the courtly pleasures of music and dancing. We shall document some representative passages in the following pages.

But if we look for a historical development, that development is rather to be found within the technical details of the particular 'system' of *tāla* referred to and the growing aura of cultural symbolism. Consistent with Indian tradition, such a development is virtually always informed and guided by the core meaning of the term. Hence, the *mārga* and *deśī* phases of the early system of musical *tāla*, which will be detailed in the following section, may differ in structural principles, specific gestures, range of durations, emphasis, and other aspects, but they do not represent an essential change or progression of the underlying idea. The arrangement of the following references will, therefore, be more thematic than chronological, although a rough chronological order will be maintained within the group of references from each field of learning.

Tāla was apparently recognized as a musical term by the time of Pāṇini, who refers (in **Aṣṭādhyāyī** III. 2.55) to keeping time with the hands as *pāṇigha* and also as *tālagha*. On this authority we find etymological explanations such as those of the **Saṅgīta-Ratnākara** and the later **Saṅgītamakaranda**:

तालस्तलप्रतिष्ठायामिति धातोर्घञि स्मृतः ।
गीतं वाद्यं तथा नृत्यं यतस्ताले प्रतिष्ठितम् ॥

SR V.2

The word *tāla* is derived from the root *tala*, meaning the act of establishing; the suffix *ghañ* is added (to this root). (This derivation is true) because song, instruments, and dance are established in *tāla*. (Tr. P.L. Sharma)

तालशब्दस्य निष्पत्तिः प्रतिष्ठार्थेन धातुना ।
गीतं वाद्यं च नृत्यं च भाति ताले प्रतिष्ठितम् ॥

SMak p. 32

The word *tāla* is derived from the root (which means) the base. *Gīta*, *vādya* and *nṛtya* scintillate (when) founded on *tāla*. (Tr. M. Bose)

1) Two references from the medical literature will suffice to illustrate the prescriptions of the Āyurvedic physicians, who recommended the products of the palmyra tree both as analgesics and as agents by which the bodily humours (*doṣas*) could be brought into a healthy state of equilibrium. The second-century **Caraka Saṃhitā** and the fourth-century **Suśruta Saṃhitā**, two of the basic textbooks of early Indian medical practice, are representative of this branch of the scientific literature.

तथा तालप्रलम्बं स्यादुरःक्षतरुजापहम् ।
खर्जूरं तालशस्यं च रक्तपित्तक्षयापहम् ॥

CarSam Sūtrasthāna XXVII. 115-116

Tālapralamba (the tender top portion of the *tāla* stem) alleviates wound and pain in the chest. *Kharjūra* and fruit of *tāla* are useful in the case of internal haemorrhage and wasting. (Tr. P.V. Sharma)

तालनारिकेलपनसमोचप्रभृतीनि ॥
स्वादुपाकरसान्याहुर्वातपित्तहराणि च ।
बलप्रदानि स्निग्धानि बृंहणानि हिमानि च ॥
फलं स्वादुरसं तेषां तालजं गुरु पित्तजित् ।
तद्बीजं स्वादुपाकं तु मूत्रलं वातपित्तजित् ॥

SuSam Sūtrasthāna XLVI. 177-179

The fruits such as the *tāla, nārikela*, and *moca*, etc., are sweet in taste and of digestion, and subdue the *vāyu* (wind) and *pittam* (bile). They are cooling in their potencies, and act as constructive tonics. Of these, the fruit of a *tāla* is sweet in taste and heavy in digestion. It subdues the deranged *pittam*. The pulp found inside its seeds is sweet of digestion and diuretic, and it subdues the *vāyu* and *pittam*. (Tr. K.L. Bhisagratna)

2) In the visual arts *tāla* is a straightforward unit of measure. It also means the storey of the temple, as in Rāmacandra Kaulācāra's **Śilpa Prakāśa**, in relation to the *Vaitāla* style of temple:

तदूर्ध्वे भित्ति यद्भागे तलाकारे च वैतालिकम् ।
कूर्मपृष्ठाकृतौ ताल आदितालः स उच्यते ॥

ŚiPrak II. 56

The wall-portion above this is like a plain, broad roof (*vaitālika*). This roof in the form of a tortoise-back is called the *ādi-tāla* (first storey). (Tr. A. Boner)

We are on more conventional ground in the following three references, which prescribe the relative heights of the images in terms of hand-spans:

एवंविधो भवेद्विष्णोस्त्रिभागेनास्य पीठिका ॥
नवतालप्रमाणास्तु देवदानवकिन्नराः ।

MatPur CCLVIII. 15b-16a

The pedestal of the image should be divided into three parts. The heights of the *devas, dānavas* and *kinnaras* are nine *tālas.*

In another reference from the same work, the proper measurement of the images in terms of *tāla*-spans is said to bring redemptive benefits:

एवं नारीषु सर्वासु देवानां प्रतिमासु च ।
नवतालमिदं प्रोक्तं लक्षणं पापनाशनम् ॥

MatPur CCLVIII. 75

Thus about the images of the goddesses. Their features which have the measure of *navatāla* are destructive of sins.

शृणु प्रसङ्गभेदेन तालमानादिनिर्णयम् ॥
शिष्यबोधाय वक्ष्यामि शक्तिमूर्तिषु केवलम् ।
वसुताले च मुख्येन देवीविग्रहमाचरेत् ॥

ŚiPrak II. 775b-776

In connection with this, hear the description of proportions (*tāla*), measurements (*māna*) and other things. I am explaining the image of the *Śakti* for the knowledge of disciples only. The image of the *devī* is mainly made in *vasutāla* (*aṣṭatāla*, eight spans high). (Tr. A. Boner)

Numerous passages from the epic and *kāvya* literature refer to *tāla*, both as a technical unit of measure and in a more metaphorical sense. In the **Mahābhārata**, Arjuna is described as follows:

य एष मत्तर्षभतुल्यगामी महद्धनुः कर्षति तालमात्रम् ।
एषोऽर्जुनो नात्र विचार्यमस्ति यद्यस्मि संकर्षण वासुदेवः ॥ MBh I. 180.18

That hero there, of tread like that of a mighty lion, who draws the large bow in his hand four full spans in length, is Arjuna. There is no doubt, O Saṃkarṣaṇa, about this, if I am Vāsudeva. (Tr. adapted from P. C. Roy)

The description of a drawn bow measured in *tāla*-spans is a conventional poetic topic, as we find once again in a passage from the **Bhāgavata Purāṇa**:

तालत्रयं महासारं धनुर्यष्टिमिवेभराट् ।
बभञ्जैकेन हस्तेन सप्ताहमदधाद्गिरिम् ॥

BhāgPur X.46.25

Kṛṣṇa snapped the most powerful bow of Kaṃsa measuring three *tālas*, [even] as a leader of elephants would break a sugar cane, and held the [Govardhana] hill with hand for a full week. (Tr. C.L. Goswami)

In contrast to the preceding the following description of Karṇa draws upon the common simile of the palmyra tree:

प्रांशुः कनकतालाभः सिंहसंहननो युवा ।
असंख्येयगुणः श्रीमान्भास्करस्यात्मसंभवः ॥

MBh I.126.5

Tall he stood, like a golden palm tree (*kanakatālābha*), this youth with the hard body of a lion. Innumerable were the virtues of this magnificent son of the sun. (Tr. J. A. B. Van Buitenen)

3) References to *tāla* abound in the *kāvya* literature, particularly in connection with music and dance, and we shall include two such passages before proceeding to explore the concept of *tāla* as a measure of time in the literature of Saṅgīta-Śāstra. In Kālidāsa's masterpiece, the **Meghadūta**, the poet provides a vivid picture of the *yakṣa's* beloved amusing herself by causing her pet peacock to dance, accompanied by the jingling of her many bracelets:

तन्मध्ये च स्फटिकफलका काञ्चनी वासयष्टि-
र्मूले बद्धा मणिभिरनतिप्रौढवंशप्रकाशैः ।
तालैः शिञ्जावलयसुभगैर्नर्तितः कान्तया मे
यामध्यास्ते दिवसविगमे नीलकण्ठः सुहृद् वः ॥

Megh II. 19

And between them [an *aśoka* and a *keśara* tree] is a golden roosting rod with crystal tablet,
Surrounded at its base with gems the color of unripe bamboo shoots,
On which a peacock, friend to you clouds, settles at close of day
After my love made it dance, clapping her hands (*tālaiḥ*) with sweetly tinkling bracelets. (Tr. Franklin and Eleasor Edgerton)

And in the **Raghuvaṃśa** Kālidāsa constructs an extravagant simile that draws upon the many meanings inherent in the word *tāla* – the sound of elephant ears flapping, the reverberant drumming, and the underlying poetic conceit that the *rāgas* of the birds are underscored by the elephants keeping the *tāla*.

उषसि स गजयूथकर्णतालैः पटुपटहध्वनिभिर्विनीतनिद्रः ।
अरमत मधुराणि तत्र शृण्वन्विहगविकूजितवन्दिमङ्गलानि ॥

Ragh IX. 71

Being roused at dawn from his slumbers by the flappings of the ears of an elephant-herd resembling the sound of loud-sounding drums, he amused himself there listening to the agreeable notes of birds (supplying the place of) the auspicious verses of bards. (Tr. R. G. Nandargikar)

Most references to *tāla* as a temporal measure occur in the context of music or dance, but the word was also employed as a technical term in the discipline of yoga. According to the **Yogamīmāṃsā** III. 3-4 (pp. 262-263) the unit of *tāla* is equated with the time taken to touch one's knee thrice, followed by a clap, and the **Agni Purāṇa** provides the following laconic prescription:

तालो लघ्वक्षरो मात्रा ।

AgPur 161.24

[With respect to *prāṇāyāma*, the breathing exercises] The unit *mātrā* is the time taken to utter a short vowel or the time taken in slapping the hands together.

And the following passage specifies three durations of the *prāṇāyāma* – short (*yavīyān*), intermediate (*madhyama*), and long (*jyeṣṭha*) – in a ratio of 1 : 2 : 4 that is reminiscent of the relationship among the three states of the *mārga tāla* system as set forth in the **Nāṭya-Śāstra** and the **Dattilam**: *ekakala, dvikala,* and *catuṣkala.* The proportions of the three yogic *prāṇāyāmas* are as follows: short, 12 *tālas* (that is, circumambulation of the knee 12 times); intermediate, 24 *tālas*; and long, 48 *tālas.*

यवीयान्मध्यमो ज्येष्ठः स तालैर्द्वादशादिभिः ॥
तालो द्वादशभिर्जानुपरिणाहपरिभ्रमैः ।

MṛgĀ yp I.27b-28a

By means of twelve *tālas, prāṇāyāma* is ascertained as short (*yavīyān*), intermediate and long. The measurement of *tāla* [in the shortest of these units] is known by circumambulating the expansion of the knee twelve times.

The remaining references will be taken from the musicological literature (Saṅgīta-Śāstra). The following passage, however, from the second-century classic, the **Cilappatikaaram**, demonstrates that the idea of *tāla* was already among the standard technical concepts in music and dance, and also that it was by no means confined to the central Sanskrit tradition. In C 7:(1) 3-8; 12-20 we find the following dialogue:

> Listening carefully, she [Maatavi] gave the *yaazh* (a plucked string instrument) to Koovalan saying, "I am not commanding you, but may I know the *taaLam* of the piece you are going to play?" And he began to sing and play on the Kaaveeri (river) and the seashore to please Maatavi. (Tr. S. Ramanathan)

And, later in the same work (3:14), different varieties of musical compositions are defined according to their differences in *tāla*:

> *Kantam* is a musical composition (*uru*) set in one *taaLam* with a limited number of feet. *Pirapatam* is a musical composition with no restriction as to number of feet and set in more than one *taaLam*. (Tr. S. Ramanathan)

The opening verse of Bharata's *tāla* chapter provides an appropriate entry into the concept of *tāla* as a controlling system of musical metre, manifested by hand gestures:

> वाद्यं तु यद् घनं प्रोक्तं कलापातलयान्वितम् ।
> कालस्तस्य प्रमाणं हि विज्ञेयं तालयोगतः ॥
>
> NŚ XXXI.1
>
> The *vādya* (form and content of performance) spoken of on the idiophones (*ghana* instruments, especially cymbals), that is composed of *kalā* (unsounded action), *pāta* (lit. 'throwing down,' sounded action), and *laya* (rest), time is known as the measure of that [*vādya*] in combination with *tāla*. (Tr. P. L. Sharma)

The important compound in the above verse (*kalā-pāta-laya*) affirms that the three main components by which musical time is measured are these: inaudible action, audible action, and rest. With the aid of this gesture language the passage of time is made manifest to sense perception and, as an added benefit, the performance is brought under control. Abhinavagupta added an extensive commentary to this verse, which merits quotation in full:

> तत्र हन्यत इति घनः कठिनतैकरूपः । तत एव (इव) नमनोन्नमन-
> शैथिल्यादियोगाभावादक्षरवैचित्र्यं स्वरवैचित्र्यं चानुरुध्यमानमात्रेणोपयोगि ।

कांस्यतालिकादिरुच्यते मूर्तो घन इति मूर्तिकाठिन्यमिति युक्तम् । तस्य घनस्य यदातोद्यं तोदनं हननं तस्य विधिवच्चरतः, शीघ्रत्वसमत्वादिरूपं यद्विकल्पनं विभागस्तत्र चच्चत्पुटादिगतद्रुतलघुगुरुप्रविभाग एवं निमित्तः ... अत्र क्रिया च तालः कालो वा ।... न कालः क्रियाव्यतिरेकः, अपि तु सर्वेषां परिच्छेदहेतुः काल इत्युच्यते । परिच्छेदश्च क्रि(य)यैव ।... अन्योन्यं च विशीर्णरूपतया एकपरिच्छेदात्मकसाम्यादाशा(काङ्क्षा) भावे शास्त्रस्य प्रतिष्ठानविशेषेण यत् प्रतिष्ठानसम्पादनं तत्र हेतुः क्रियाखण्डस्ताल इति तात्पर्यम् । तत्र च घनातोद्यमतिरिच्यत इति । यद् घनं नाम वाद्यमातोद्यं प्रोक्तमुद्दिष्टं तस्य तालेन भाविना शम्यादिसशब्दावापादि-निःशब्दक्रियाविशेषेण योगे सति यस्तालः परिच्छित्यात्मककालखण्डः क्रियारूपो द्रव्यात्मा स एव गीतक्रियाप्रमाणपरिच्छेदोपायः ।... कालः परिच्छिद्यते आवापादिक्रियया सा कला । पात्यते शब्दश्रवणादितोऽपरत्र स कालविशेषो येन शम्यादिपातेन ...। लीङ् श्लेषणे (पा॰ धा॰ VI.31) इत्यस्य लय इति रूपम् । तेन स्वरो वर्णोऽन्यो वा यत्रापादितस्तत्रैव या लीनता विश्रान्तिः ।...स लयः ।

AbhiBhā on NŚ XXXI.1

The *ghana* category of instruments is essentially of the nature of solidity. In it (*ghana*) there is no combination of bending, stretching, looseness, etc. as in the chordophones (*tata*), and hence the variety of syllabic and tonal sounds is not inherent in this category; it (the above variety) is relevant or applicable only through these instruments being struck. Instruments like the *kāṃsya-tāla* (bronze cymbals) are of solid form and hence it is proper to speak of their solidity. The striking or playing of this *ghana* [instrument] in its regulated form is composed of fastness, evenness and the like, and this is made possible by the units like *druta*, *laghu*, *guru*, etc. in (*tālas*) like *caccatpuṭa*.

Here action (of the hands or on the cymbals) is (equated with) *tāla* or time. Time cannot be perceived without action; rather, time is the limiting factor for everything. And the act of limiting is possible through action alone. [The different components of musical performance] are mutually disconnected and their unity of form (limitation) is established by a fragment of time which is *tāla*, and this act of establishing is like the Śāstric establishing of a specific type (the grammatical syntax seems to be implied) by way of meeting the demand of *ākāṅkṣā* (requirement of completion of sense). And in this act (of limiting) the *ghana* instrument excels. The *vādya* (that is, the form and content of instrumental performance) on *ghana* [instruments, that is, idiophones] that has been described, when combined with *tāla*, that is, with specific sounded actions like *śamyā* and un-

> sounded actions like *āvāpa*, [gives rise to] *tāla* which is a fragment of time bearing the nature of a limiting factor and taking the form of action, being in essence a *dravya* (substance) and that (time taking the form of *tāla*) is the means of limiting the measure of musical activity. *Kalā* stands for the (particle of) time that is limited by actions like *āvāpa*. *Pāta* is that specific time where the act of dropping (*pāta*) is performed and a sound is heard, that is, it is a sounded action. The word *laya* is derived from the root *līṅ*, meaning to combine or join or paste together. Hence *laya* is that merging or rest that sticks to the point where a musical note or syllable or something else is performed. (Tr. P.L. Sharma)

In passages such as the preceding, sprinkled liberally throughout Abhinavagupta's commentary on Bharata's chapter, the system of *tāla* found its most penetrating and eloquent exponent. The great eleventh-century Kashmiri philosopher plumbs the most profound depths of the concept of *tāla* as the measure of time in *gāndharva*, the ancient ritual music for the theatre. In the passage cited Abhinavagupta points out that time is itself a substance, thus reflecting the views of the Nyāya system of philosophy in that (a) time cannot be perceived without action, and (b) action is impossible in the absence of some form of substance. Abhinavagupta's analysis is further informed by the concept of time as a limiting power as expounded by the grammarian Bhartṛhari. A fragment of time or a musical duration is meaningless until it is articulated by the combination of unsounded action (*kalā*), sounded action (*pāta*), and rest (*laya*); rising thus to consciousness and becoming manifest to sense perception, it acquires meaning as a part of the domain of *tāla*. Abhinavagupta also stresses that *tāla* is made manifest by the solid instruments, and hence it is equated with the form and content of performance on this special class of musical instruments that lack the variety of syllable and tone arising from other instruments, but excel in manifesting *tāla* when they are struck.

In the **Dattilam**, a manual that is contemporaneous with the **Nāṭya-Śāstra**, we find a clear statement both of the purpose of *tāla* and of its division into standard topics, of which the later will be analyzed in the subsequent section of the present article. Dattila's preamble and *tāloddeśa* follow:

अथ तालं प्रवक्ष्यामि ... ।
तालात् साम्यं भवेत्साम्यादिह सिद्धिः परत्र च ।
तत्र ज्ञेयाः कलाः पाताः पादभागास्तथैव च ॥
मात्रा च परिवर्तश्च वस्तु चैव विशेषतः ।
विदार्यङ्गलयाः पाणिर्यतिः प्रकरणं तथा ॥
... च गीतिर्मार्गश्च शास्त्रतः ।

Datti 109B-112A

> Now I shall expound *tāla* (based upon authentic accounts in the *śāstras*). Through *tāla* is achieved *sāmya* (equipoise (and) *sāmya* is the source of fulfilment here (in this world)) and hereafter.
>
> (In *tāla*) one should know specifically the *kalās*, the *pātas*, the *pādabhāgas*, the *mātrā*, the *parivarta*, and also the *vastu*, the *vidārī*, the *aṅga*, the (different) *layas*, the *pāṇi*, the *yati* and the *prakaraṇa*, the *avayava*, (?) the *gīti* and also the *mārga*. These, according to the *śāstra*, are the topics pertaining to *tāla* the wise should endeavour to understand. I shall now, in brief, decree the precise nature of these. (Tr. M. Lath)

To conclude this brief survey of the ancient and medieval musical texts that deal with the subject of *tāla* in a systematic way, we reproduce a portion of Śārṅgadeva's introductory material from the **Saṅgīta-Ratnākara**:

> कालो लघ्वादिमितया क्रियया संमितो मितिम् ।
> गीतादेर्विदधत्तालः, स च द्वेधा बुधैः स्मृतः ॥
> मार्गदेशीगतत्वेन, ... ।
>
> SR V.3-4a
>
> The time that is measured with actions such as *laghu* and the like, (thus) effecting the measurement of song and the like, is *tāla* and that (*tāla*) is known to be twofold by the wise, in the form of *mārga* and *deśī*. (Tr. P.L. Sharma)

The division of *tālas* that Śārṅgadeva refers to in the above passage – into the two categories of *mārga* and *deśī* – is a consequence of the *deśī* ('regional') movement that swept across Indian musical culture in the second half of the first millennium, a movement in which a large number of local and regional musics and musical preferences were taken up and incorporated into the main central tradition. This influence was felt not only in the field of rhythm, but also in the expansion of the system of *rāgas*, the developing repertoire of art songs and song types (*prabandhas*), and the growing use of the various regional vernaculars. Essentially it marks a broad line of demarcation, a line whose edges are admittedly fuzzy, between the musics of ancient and modern India. The terms →*mārga* and *deśī* are first opposed in this sense in Mataṅga's **Bṛhaddeśī**; one can only lament the loss of the *tāla* canto from this pivotal treatise. Characteristically, the older *mārga* structures were retained as separate categories, although it is not certain that they continued to flourish in practice, nor is it clear that many of their details – as set down in the later treatises – were based on reliable documentary evidence or experience with the living tradition, particularly after the time of Abhinavagupta.

The *mārga tālas* are the group of five described in the **Nāṭya-Śāstra**, each operating in the three *mārgas* (*citra, vṛtti* and *dakṣiṇa* in which the basic duration (the *kalā*) is equated with two, four, or eight *mātrās*, respectively. The names, number, structure, and delineating actions of these ancient *tālas* have remained unchanged. The newer *deśī* category, on the other hand, differs in that 1) the names and numbers of the *tālas* have altered, resulting in an enormous expansion of rhythmic and structural possibilities; 2) the *laghu* unit became variable in duration; 3) newer, smaller durational units were added, and 4) the actions that delineate the various *tālas* were no longer specified, neither the sounded nor the unsounded actions.

The following citation aptly sums up the traditional role of *tāla* in the music of India:

गीतं वाद्यं तथा नृत्यं तालवर्जं न शोभते ।
तालाभावात्र मेलः स्यादमेलादव्यवस्थितिः ॥
न रङ्गमव्यवस्थातो विना रङ्गं कुतो लयः ।
लयं विना न सौख्यं स्यात् तन्मूलं ताल उच्यते ॥

Saṅgitopaniṣadsāroddhāra II.5-6

Gīta, vādya, and *nṛtya* do not appear in their full beauty without *tāla*. Without *tāla* there can be no integration (*mela*), and without integration there can be no method. There can be no music without method, without music there can be no *laya*, without *laya* there can be no delight. The root of all is *tāla*. (Tr. M. Bose)

Application in the Arts

The purpose of this section is to present an overview of the measures and structural principles of *tāla* in the various Arts – as a measure of space (in architecture, sculpture, painting, and physical movement) and as a measure of time (in music and dance). Interestingly, it is in the art of dance that *tāla* is employed as a measure of both artistic dimensions: spatial, with reference to the number of hand-spans between the feet in a particular pose or the length of a step, and temporal, with reference to the rhythmic structure of the accompanying music. Perhaps it is the dancer who knows *tāla* from the most privileged perspective.

With respect to the concept of *tāla* as a spatial measure, the essential point is that the hand-span is a unit of obvious value in a scale of anthropometric units and proportions, especially in that the unit of measure can be established as relative to the scale of the image (as in sculpture and painting) as well as a more or less absolute unit (as in architecture and the preparation of all kinds of consecrated space). In their analysis and prescriptions of the proper dimensions and poses of the human figure, the authors of the Śilpaśāstras visualized their subject as an abstract, conceptual design laid out along a scale of appropriate proportions. The conceptual tools for the process of plastic composition included the following: *pañjara*, abstract design in space; *sūtra*, the several vertical and horizontal axes; *māna*, measurements along the vertical, horizontal, and transverse planes thus established; *bhaṅga*, 'pose,' the result of certain conventional deflections from absolute verticality, frontality, and the like; and the basic positions – *sthāna* (standing), *āsana* (seated), and *śayana* (reclining).

Having thus established the conceptual framework for the design, the *tāla* unit and the various other units of measure were employed to bring the image into the desired scale of proportions. Here once again one notes the prominence of the concept of →*māna* (measure), which is the source of several distinct sets of measurements, including *māna*, measurement along the vertical planes; *pramāṇa*, along the horizontal planes; *parimāṇa*, around the circumference; *unmāna*, along the transverse plane, the depth of the image; and *upamāna*, the measure of space between any two limbs of the body.

Tāla, as a unit of measure, could thus represent either a linear measure or the area of a square. Various scales of proportion were laid down in the early texts, depending upon the type of figure to be represented and the particular *rasa* to be expressed. While we find a certain degree of variation from one text to another, the following general scale represents the consensus: ten *tālas* (in height) for a deity, eight for men, seven for women, five or six for Gaṇeśa, and four for children. This systematic process of elongation and shortening has proved to be a powerful tool for expression in the visual arts, and its main value lies in the establishment of a consistent set of correspondences between (a) the proportions of an image, and (b) the underlying emotion and vital rhythms that the sculptor or painter seeks to communicate.

Several additional anthropometric units combined with the *tāla*-span to provide the basic scale of measure. In particular, the *aṅgula* (the breadth of a finger, or eight barley-corns) served as the standard by which the several other units were reckoned, including the *vitasti* (twelve or thirteen *aṅgulas*, equivalent to the *tāla*), the *pāda* (fifteen *aṅgulas*, the length of the foot), *vyāma* ('fathom,' the height of a man with upstretched arms, equivalent to 120 *aṅgulas*), and *vyāyāma* (96 *aṅgulas*, the height and breadth of a man with arms outstretched). Other units of more or less absolute measure appear in the architectural *śāstras*: in addition to the units mentioned above, now employed in an absolute sense, we find intermediate units such as the *aratni* (the 'cubit,' measured from the tip of the middle finger to the elbow, ca. 17-21 inches), the *hasta* (literally the 'hand,' but here employed as the length of the forearm, equivalent to 24 *aṅgulas*), and the *daṇḍa* ('rod', equivalent to four *hastas*). In the **Nāṭya-Śāstra** the static measures of *tāla* are translated into the proportions of dynamic movement – in Bharata's prescriptions for the various positions and steps (the *cārīs*) of the dancers and actors.

Our brief discussion can only scratch the surface of an immense subject, for which readers may refer to Kapila Vatsyayan, Classical Indian Dance in Literature and the Arts, pp. 12-21, and idem, the Square and the Circle of the Indian Arts, especially pp. 43-46, 53-60, 77-79, and 103-142.

If the idea of *tāla* is a relatively uncomplicated standard of measure for artistic space (especially human space), in music the word signifies a complex, hierarchical system for the generation, measurement, and regulation of musical time. In the early literature of Saṅgīta-Śāstra the word *tāla* appears in two different, and sometimes confusing, senses: (a) as a general term for the entire system of musical rhythm, and (b) as a special term for one of the eight hand gestures, in which the left hand slaps down audibly upon the right palm or the left knee. Although the principal authors are not in agreement upon a canonical order or number of *tāla* topics, we may accept the following set of fifteen as a basis for discussion. The following chart is a display of the standard components of the *mārga tāla* system as presented in **Nāṭya-Śāstra** and **Dattilam**, organized into the various structural levels:

the level of *infrastructure*: gestures, accents, durations, rests, and their timing

1. *kalā*, a basic unit of time, also one of the four silent gestures articulating such a unit
2. *pāta*, one of the four audible gestures, usually a clap
3. *laya*, the rate of gestural succession (that is, 'tempo'), conceived as the intervening rest between actions
4. *yati*, the principle of regulation and rhythmic control; and also, in a more specialized sense, the direction of the temporal flow (whether even, accelerating, or decelerating)
5. *pāṇi*, the principle of phasing or synchronization, by which the entrances of the various performers are regulated

the level of *structure*: phrase, lines and line-divisions, caesuras, formal sections and poetic stanzas	6. *pādabhāga*, one formal unit (equivalent to the Western 'measure' or 'phrase') of a group of four, literally 'a division into (four paws)' (as of a quadruped) 7. *mātrā*, a phrase or line, typically consisting of four *pādabhāgas*; also a time duration in verse; also the smallest unit of time-measure 8. *parivarta*, an obligatory repetition of a formal unit or a portion thereof 9. *vidārī*, a pause or cadence, or the unit thereby terminating 10. *aṅga*, a section consisting of several phrases or poetic lines 11. *vastu*, a longer formal component, a stanza
suprastructure: the level of entire compositions	12. *prakaraṇa*, a collective term for the *saptarūpas* of the ancient ritual music for the theatre – the seven *gītakas* 13. *avayava*, alternate versions of the *gītakas*, arising from the many performance variables
topics that pervade all levels of the hierarchy	14. *gīti*, text-setting, also style in general 15. *mārga*, the relative density of events within a given span of time, the time within which a set of musical actions are deployed

Many of these terms are still in use today, although some of their meanings have altered along with the alterations in the rhythmic basis of the system. The above topics may be profitably compared to the *tāla daśa prāṇās* of later origin (circa 17th century):

1. *kāla*, the twelve divisions of absolute time, from *kṣaṇa* (instant) to *kākapadam* ('crow's foot,' a division 262, 144 times as long as *kṣaṇa*)

2. *mārga*, the density of events within a pattern or a rhythmic cycle

3. *kriyā*, 'action', the collective term for the various hand gestures
4. *aṅga*, the component parts of a given *tāla* cycle
5. *graha*, the point in a cycle where the music begins, replacing the older concept of *pāṇi*
6. *jāti*, expanded versions of the basic *tāla* patterns, produced by counting with the fingers
7. *kalā*, a variable unit of time, establishing the ratio between the melodic/textual activity and the structure of the *tāla*
8. *laya*, the three conventional speeds (slow, moderate, and fast)
9. *yati*, the rhythmic design of a cycle, as manifested by the patterns and relative lengths of its components
10. *prastāra*, the process of permutation

Space will not permit a full analysis of the many technical categories and the differences between the two systems, but we may draw the following conclusions:

The formal basis of the entire system has shifted – from a set of complex, modular structures (the *gītakas*) to an integrated system designed to facilitate improvisation over a repeated rhythmic cycle (a notion that was present only in embryo in the ancient system, in the prescribed *parivarta* repetitions). Structural and suprastructural topics have disappeared from the list, and in their place we see a number of concepts affecting the synchronization, control, and perpetuation of the cycle (*āvarta*), which has become an implicit assumption of the system.

Many gradual transitions separate the ancient and modern rhythmic systems, but in the contrasts presented above we find yet another illustration of the vital differences between the strictly prescribed forms of the early ritual tradition of music for the theatre and the great variety of regional patterns and procedures which began to be codified during the second half of the first millennium. The *deśī tālas* which represent an intermediate step in the historical evolution of the idea of *tāla*, display not only a contrasting method of organization and a different, richer repertoire of structural patterns (expanding from the five *mārga tālas* to the 120 catalogued by Śārṅgadeva), but were probably controlled by a new gesture language. Moreover, they featured a number of shorter durations and a variety of highly-irregular rhythms.

In its musical application, *tāla* functions as a highly sophisticated and a relative measure – in that the sounds and motions of the hand replaced the fixed span of the hand as the *pramāṇa* or standard of measure. In music absolute values are notably hard to measure, and musical time requires all the flexibility it can achieve in order to bring the incredible richness and variety of durations, accents, silences, and groupings under control, and in an integrated manner. One of the crowning achievements of Indian rhythm has been the way in which a number of related concepts (*laya, mātrā, akṣara, kalā, and mārga*) have been deployed to define collectively the set of equations establishing the timing of a composition or performance.

In the ancient *tāla* system, the solution was to fix – if not all of the rhythmic ratios – at least as many as possible (often as many as three or four between the various structural levels: the gestures of *tāla* are the markers of structure, *laya* is the interval between gestures, the *mātrā* was a conventional measure of duration (a conceptual time unit equated with the *laghu* duration and the time taken to articulate five short syllables of text), *akṣara* is a syllabic unit of any kind (a written letter, a *tāla* gesture, or indeed any musical unit that can be represented by a syllable – a dancestep, drumstroke, or one of the seven *svaras*), *kalā* is the relative standard by which rhythmic form is measured (with 1, 2, 4, or 8 *mātrās* assigned to the *kalā*), and *mārga* is the relative density of musical events, as measured by the span of time within which a given sequence is to be completed. The following figure illustrates one such set of rhythmic equations for the *Ṣaṭpitāputraka tāla* in the *citra mārga*: note in particular the discrepancy between the actual durations of the *tāla* and the underlying framework of conceptual rhythm as expressed in *kalās* and *mātrās.*

<table>
<tr><td>6 tāla durations</td><td colspan="3">pluta</td><td>laghu</td><td colspan="2">guru</td><td colspan="2">guru</td><td>laghu</td><td colspan="3">pluta</td></tr>
<tr><td>6 tāla gestures</td><td colspan="3">sam</td><td>tā</td><td colspan="2">śa</td><td colspan="2">tā</td><td>śa</td><td colspan="3">tā</td></tr>
<tr><td>6 kalās</td><td colspan="2"></td><td colspan="2"></td><td colspan="2"></td><td colspan="2"></td><td colspan="2"></td><td colspan="2"></td></tr>
<tr><td>12 mātrās</td><td></td><td></td><td></td><td></td><td></td><td></td><td></td><td></td><td></td><td></td><td></td><td></td></tr>
</table>

In the above counterpoint of conceptual and perceptual time units, we see the essence of Indian rhythm. What can be said about the subsequent development of these temporal concepts in the later musicological literature and musical practice is that (1) their domains narrowed, (2) their variations became more limited, (3) their mutual relationships became more fixed, and (4) some were reinterpreted in order to accommodate the demands of new rhythmic practices. The ancient system depended upon a bewilderingly complex array of rhythmic equivalents that were constantly shifting, almost as if one were concocting a recipe with an assortment of measuring spoons and cups that expanded and contracted when filled with different ingredients ! The system was overly complex, and it was altered drastically in response to new musical needs.

Conclusion

The keywords for the idea of *tāla* have been these: measure, control, integration, and manifestation (of the inner structure, rhythms, and vital energies of the art work). In this we see a remarkable cultural demonstration of the power of an extremely simple idea – the control of artistic dimension (time, space, and the human body) by means of the body's most convenient appendage. In this way artistic units are scaled to human proportions and to the proportions of the forms of human utterance and apprehension, and presented in abstract, idealized designs that reveal archetypal Indian preferences for shape and meaning.

Betty Heimann, in her 1937 book on Indian and Western Philosophy: A Study in Contrasts (London: Allen and Unwin), cited the famous dictum of the ancient Greek author Protagoras – "Man is the measure of all things." – as the cardinal principle of Western thought, in contrast to the motto of the **Bṛhadāraṇyaka Upaniṣad** I.3.22: "This *Ātman* (the vital essence in Man) is the same in the ant, the same in the gnat, the same in the elephant, the same in these three worlds ... the same in the whole universe."

Heimann was both right and wrong. In the world of ultimate reality, such things as measure, proportion, duration, and the like are nonexistent or irrelevant; but in the world of illusion – the world that the Arts inhabit and in which they have their being – proportion and measure are the means by which virtual substance is rendered knowable, and thus beautiful. In this sense, by means of *tāla*, man is indeed the measure – and measurer – of all things.

Lewis Rowell

Select Bibliography

Gonda, Jan: Vedic Ritual. Leiden: E.J. Brill, 1980.

Lath, Mukund: A Study of Dattilam. New Delhi: Impex India, 1978.

— Dattilam. New Delhi: Indira Gandhi National Centre for the Arts, 1988.

Panikkar, Raimundo: "Time and History in the Tradition of India," with an appendix on "Empirical Apperception of Time" by Bettina Bäumer, in Cultures and Time. Paris: Unesco Press, 1976.

Powers, Harold S. "India," in The New Grove Dictionary of Music and Musicians, ed. Stanley Sadie, sec. II, no. 5 (vol. IX, pp.118-125).

Ramanathan, S: Music in Cilappatikaaram. Madurai: Madurai Kamaraj University; 1979.

Rowell, Lewis: "The Ancient Tāla System: A Comparative Approach." Journal of the Music Academy, Madras 57 (1986):83-99.

— "Form in the Ritual Theatre Music of Ancient India." Musica Asiatica 5 (1988):140-190.

— "The Subconscious Language of Musical Time." Music Theory Spectrum 1 (1979):96-106.

Saṅgīta-Ratnākara of Śārṅgadeva, vol. 3 (forthcoming), trans. R.K. Shringy, under the supervision of Prem Lata Sharma.

Sharma, Prem Lata: "Śāstra and Prayoga: Contemporary Tāla Practice vis-a-vis Śāstric Tradition, with special reference to Hindustani Music." Paper presented at the Seventh World Sanskrit Conference (Leiden, The Netherlands), August 1987.

Vatsyayan, Kapila: Classical Indian Dance in Literature and the Arts. New Delhi: Sangeet Natak Akademi, 1968.

— The Square and the Circle of the Indian Arts. New Delhi: Roli Books International, 1983.

MĀNA

I. Māna: Vedic

Overview

The root *mā-* and the noun *māna* denote an activity and its result which generally involve 'construction' and most often, in addition, 'measure' and 'measurement'. Neither term is confined in its use to visible matter; both are also used in a more abstract manner.

Etymology

Vedic and Sanskrit *māna* 'building' derive from a verbal root *mā-* but there are several roots *mā-* in Sanskrit. One reason is that Sanskrit long *ā* developed from two vowels in Indo-European: *ā* and *ē*. These two are kept distinct in some other languages of the Indo-European family, such as Greek, but in Sanskrit they have collapsed into one. While Indo-European *mā-* 'make, produce, create' has developed directly into one Sanskrit *mā-*, Indo-European *mē-* with several meanings, including 'measure', has led to another Sanskrit *mā-*. Some scholars (notably T. Burrow) have argued that there were two Indo-European roots *mē-*, each resulting in a Sanskrit *mā-*, so that we must distinguish three:
(1) IE *mā-* 'to make, produce, create' leading to a Sanskrit *mā-* with similar meanings from which *māna* 'building' (also: 'altar') is derived as well as a noun *mātrā* meaning 'substance, material' related to Latin *materia/materies* from which several modern languages derive terms for 'matter'. By reducing the grade of its first syllable, this root also accounts for the suffix *-maya*, 'made of' in *manomaya, ānandamaya*, etc. This *mā-* is related to Indo-European and Sanskrit *mātṛ* 'mother', a noun that resembles many others with the same meaning found in Indo-European and non-Indo-European languages.
(2) IE *mē-* 'to measure' which led to a second *mātrā* meaning 'measure'. The two meanings of *mātrā* are not always distinguished and the term may be used with a systematic ambiguity. This applies also to the verb *mā-*, or to both at once, as in **Ṛgveda** X.71.11 which refers to the Adhvaryu priest: *yajñasya mātrāṃ vi mimīta u tvaḥ*. This phrase suggests "another produces the material basis of the ritual" as well as: "another lays out the measure of the rites".
(3) IE *mē-* 'to devise skilfully' is not found in Sanskrit as a verbal root, but exists in Greek where it has been very productive. Nouns like *metis* 'wisdom, skill, craft' have been derived from it, and others come from an extended root *med-* leading to 'meditation' and the like. In Sanskrit, this accounts for

māyā- 'skill, craft, contrivance' later: 'illusory appearance'. There are cognates in Greek corresponding to its derivatives *purumāya, māyāvant, māyāvin* and *māyin* (→*māyā*). Although *mā-* possesses distinct etymological backgrounds this does not imply that it has distinct meanings. The importance of etymology, which provides the historical background of a word, should not be overestimated. Forms and meanings of words change, and although these changes are slow and gradual, and take place in accordance with general principles, they may lead to results that are far removed from their original sources. There is no reason to assume that the original meanings of words linger on in the consciousness or unconsciousness of the users of a language, and even less to postulate a collective unconscious in which original meanings are preserved and to which individuals have access. Individuals may gain access to the results of etymology if scholars have found them and made them accessible; beyond this truism, words, meanings and concepts lead a life of their own.

That etymology does not account for meaning is well known. The Mīmāṃsā philosophers and kindred philosophers of language have always maintained that *yogād rūḍhir balīyasī* "usage is stronger than derivation". When Wittgenstein remarked that "the meaning of a word lies in its use " he merely echoed what teachers of Latin had always said, viz., *verba valent usu*, "words derive their validity from their use". This inherent limitation of etymology constitutes a special case of the biological principle that forms and functions, which develop in response to needs, are independent of origins that are due to chance. Striking examples are the human brain and human language which are employed in ways that cannot have anything to do with their origin or origins.

For ultimate origins one may have to go beyond etymology and the Sanskrit root *mā-* provides an apt illustration. It is likely that this root is related to words like *mama* which according to Jakobson precede the first acquisition of conventional speech since they do not at first refer to 'mother' but are used by babies as a general expression of affection. The transition from affective expression to designative language is marked by *papa* who produces "the first distant, merely deictic, rudimentary cognitive attitude in the child's verbal behavior". If this imaginative scenario is to be taken seriously – as I think it should be – we should complete and update it by adding the immediately preceding stage which is set, in Jakobson's words, by "the most natural order of sound production: an opening of the mouth followed by its closure". This is, of course, an apt description of the mantra OM. The verbal root *mā-* has been very productive by taking on a variety of preverbs. We have already noted *pramāṇa*, but special mention should be made of the uses *nir-mā-* as 'creating', especially in connection with the creative activity of Prajāpati as Sylvain Levi, among others, has emphasized. Burrow (1980:316) is worth quoting on the uses of this compound: "The combination *nir-mā-* first appears in the **Atharva-Veda** and in the later language it completely replaces the uncompounded verb in the sense of 'produce, create'. By this means the inconvenient homonymy of *mā-* 'to measure' and *mā-* 'to create' is got rid of. In classical Sanskrit the meaning 'create' is expressed only by *nir-mā-*, while *mā-* by itself, or in combination with other prefixes, means 'to measure' with no trace of the meaning 'create'.

Other prominent compounds are formed with *vi-*, but some of these seem to derive from *mā-* 'make' (e.g., *vimāna* 'palace', 'car', etc.), while others derive from *mā-* 'measure' (e.g., *vi-mā-* 'measure out', the activity of the land surveyor who has been compared with Viṣṇu Trivikrama).

Prati-mā-, 'imitate', 'copy' does not necessarily presuppose the use of a measuring-cord or similar instrument as Gonda (1959:177) has noted with reference to ṚV I.164.24 and other passages.

Abhimāna 'self-conceit', 'pride' can lose its preverb again so that Ḍalhaṇa in his commentary on **Suśruta Saṃhitā** (Sūtrasthāna II.6) is in a position to note:

मानः सर्वत्रोत्कर्षेणात्मनो ज्ञानम् ।

Māna means superiority complex. (Tr. P.V. Sharma)

Māna as 'authority' led to the later →*pramāṇa*, one of the key terms of Indian philosophy and epistemology. This term may also lose its preverb again and be still recognizable as in **Mānameyodaya**, the title of a late work on Mīmāṃsā according to the school of Kumārila Bhaṭṭa of which the first part was written by the Nambudiri Nārāyaṇa Bhaṭṭa who lived in the sixteenth century. This work begins with the following verse:

आचार्यमतपाथोधौ बालानपि निनीषताम् ।
भीमतां कोऽपि गोपालपोतः पोत इवास्तु नः ॥
मानमेयविभागेन वस्तूनां द्विविधा स्थितिः ।
अतस्तदभयं ब्रूमः श्रीमत्कौमारिलाध्वना ॥

To us who lack confidence in our desire to take even youngsters across the ocean of the system of the preceptor,
May that indescribable cowboy be like our canoe.
The existence of things is twofold: means of knowledge (*māna*) and objects of knowledge (*meya*);
Therefore we shall propound both according to the path of the venerable Kumārila. (Tr. after C.Kunhan Raja and S.S. Suryanarayana Sastri)

Layers of Meaning

If there must be one, the core meaning of *māna* would seem to be 'measure', but in Vedic this meaning is displayed in a spectrum of more specialized meanings that range from the concrete to the abstract. The most concrete designations are 'building' and 'place', the intermediate meanings encompass not only visible *sizes* but also, more strikingly, audible *melodies*. The more technical senses of 'measurement' will be dealt with in the next section.

Development of the Concept

In the Ṛgvedic hymns to Varuṇa, the god who is primarily responsible for the cosmic and moral order (*ṛta*) which emanates from chants and recitations, frequent reference is made to Varuṇa's *māna* 'palace', as when Sage Vasiṣṭha says:

बृहन्तं मानं वरुण स्वधावः ।
सहस्रद्वारं जगमा गृहं ते ॥

ṚV VII.88.5ab

I went into your high palace, self-powered Varuṇa,
your house with the thousand doors.

In the **Atharva-Veda**, *mānasya patnī*, 'Lady of the Building' is addressed as a house that is being inaugurated:

मानस्य पत्नि शरणा स्योना देवी देवेभिर्निमितास्यग्रे ।

AV III.12.5

O Lady of the Building, as a sheltering and kindly goddess you were erected by the gods.

The same expression occurs in another similar hymn:

यस्त्वा शाले प्रतिगृह्णाति येन चासि मिता त्वम् ।
उभौ मानस्य पत्नि तौ जीवतां जरदष्टी ॥

AV IX.3.9

He who accepts you, O House, as well as he by whom you have been built, let both of them, O Lady of the Building, attain mature age.

This hymn abounds in rare technical terms derived from *mā-* 'measure', e.g.:

उपमितां प्रतिमितामथो परिमितामुत ।
शालाया विश्ववाराया नद्धानि वि चृतामसि ॥ AV IX.3.1

Of the props, of the supports, and also of the connecting beams
of the house which possesses all desired objects we loosen the ties.
(Tr. J. Gonda)

This architectural hymn plays an important role in the **Kauśika-Sūtra** of **Atharva-Veda** (VI.22). As Bloomfield noted long ago, its various designations of the house "represent a fairly complete summary of the huts and other sheltered places which are needed in the larger Vedic sacrifices" (e.g., *sadas*, *havirdhāna*, etc.).

In later Vedic, *māna* is not a common term for a dwelling, unlike *śālā*, *gṛha* or *āgāra*. The ritual Sūtras add others, e.g., *veśman* 'habitation', *śaraṇa* 'refuge' and *vāstu*.

In the **Ṛgveda**, the connection between 'building' and 'construction' is most clearly alluded to in one of the many hymns where the poet extols the great deeds of Indra:

सद्मेव प्राचो वि मिमाय मानैः

ṚV II.15.3

With measures like those of a house he has measured the forward moving (courses?).

In its most remarkable use, *māna* in the **Ṛgveda** refers to the music of the spheres, as in another Indra hymn:

दिवो मानं नोत्सदन्त्सोमपृष्ठासो अद्रयः ।

ṚV VIII.63.2

Like the melody of heaven, the pressing stones have paused.

In connection with the Maruts, thunder is also implied:

प्र यदित्था परावतः शोचिर्न मानमस्यथ ।
कस्य क्रत्वा मरुतः कस्य वर्पसा कं याथ कं ह धूतयः ॥

ṚV I.39.1

When from a far you project your melody, like a flame (its shadow),
Following what, in what shape, to whom are you protecting Maruts moving?

The poet's activity is compared to the running *Soma* liquid in another verse that contrasts winners and losers in the verbal contest:

प्रत्नान्मानादध्या ये समस्वरञ्छ्लोकयन्त्रासो रभसस्य मन्तवः ।
अपानक्षासो बधिरा अहासत ऋतस्य पन्थां न तरन्ति दुष्कृतः ॥

ṚV IX.73.6

Those who sound the ancient melody, keeping the right rhythm, inventors of a powerful mode –
The blind and the deaf have fallen behind, the wicked do not pass over the path of truth.

Here as elsewhere in the Veda, *śloka* does not denote the banal verse of later times that survives in English *slogan*, but refers to the proper mode of chant or recitation.

In later Vedic, *māna* applies primarily to measurement. In the Śulba-Sūtras, *mānayoga* refers to the drawing of a figure according to a given set of measurements, for example, with reference to the *mahāvedi* or Great Altar Space:

त्रिंशत्पदानि प्रक्रमा वा पश्चात्तिरश्ची भवति षट्त्रिंशत्प्राची चतुर्विंशतिः पुरस्तात्तिरश्चीति महावेदेर्विज्ञायते मानयोगस्तस्या व्याख्यातः ।

BŚulSū I.90

The western side is thirty *padas* or *prakramas* long, the *prācī* (median) thirty-six, the eastern side twenty-four: this is the tradition for the *Mahāvedi*; it has been explained how it is to be measured out. (Tr. G.Thibaut)

The term *māna* is not confined to ritual enclosures and altars; it may refer to the measurement of a chariot (*rathamāna*). The term *pramāṇa* is used like *māna*. Since a chariot is measured in *aṅgulas*:

अङ्गुलैः रथसम्मितायाः प्रमाणम् ।

KātŚulSū II.1

The measurement of (a *vedi*) equal in size to a chariot (is done) by *aṅgulas*. (Tr. S.R. Sarma)

Kātyāyana refers to the relation between *pramāṇa* 'measure' and *pramāṇa* 'authority'.

प्रमाणे शास्त्रं प्रमाणं निर्ह्रासविवृद्धयोः ।

KātŚulSū I.24

On reduction or increase in the measure (of a geometrical figure prescribed in the Śulvasūtras), *śāstra* is the authority. (Tr. S.R. Sarma)

In ritual practice, the basic measure is a *subjective* measure because it is based upon the size of the *yajamāna*. In the *Nambudiri* tradition, before any altar or enclosure is constructed, the *yajamāna* is made to stand with hands raised above his head and the distance from the tips of his fingers to the ground is

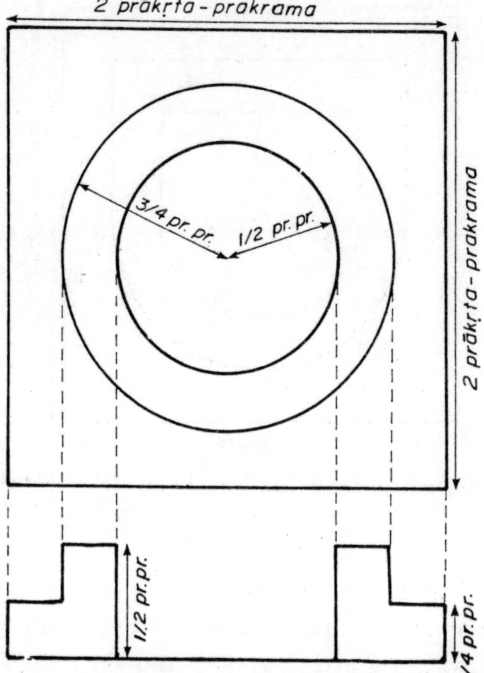

Figure 1: Dimensions of the Domestic Altar (Gārhapatya)

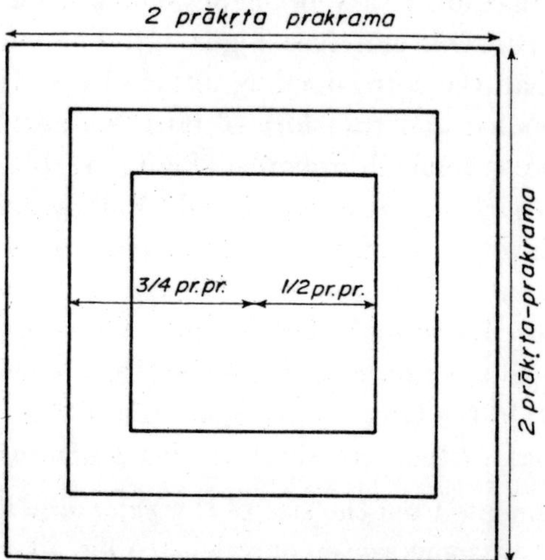

Figure 2: Dimensions of the Offering Altar (Āhavanīya)

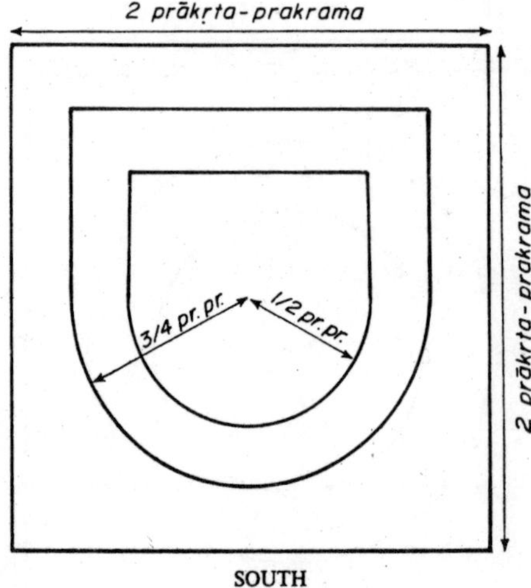

Figure 3: Dimensions of the Southern Altar (Dakṣiṇāgni)

copied on a measuring stick which is then divided in five equal parts. Each fifth (*pañcamī*) is marked and determines the length of one *aratni* of his altar. This measure is extended with a fourth (*sapāda*) and then called *prākṛta-prakrama* – the 'ordinary' *prakrama*: it is used for each of the three altars of the Old Hall (*prācīnavaṃśa*) (Figures 1, 2, 3) and also for the new Offering Altar (*āhavanīya*) of the *Agnicayana* that is built in the shape of a bird. The bricks that are used for the piling up of that altar vary in shape and size, but all their measures are based upon the *pañcamī* unit (see Figure 4). The *Agnicayana* altars are in two cases larger than the corresponding altars of the *Agniṣṭoma*. The basic unit is therefore extended and transformed into two new units, a *madhyama* 'middle' and a *vṛddha* 'extended' *prakrama* (Figure 5). In the *Agnicayana*, the new Domestic Altar (*gārhapatya*) inside the Old Hall (*prācīnavaṃśa*) is a large square consisting of five layers of 3 x 7 rectangular bricks with sides that are one-third and one-seventh of the size of the *yajamāna* (Figure 6). The Old Hall of the *Agnicayana* must therefore be larger and is accordingly constructed from the middle *prakrama* units (Figure 7). Since the bird-shaped altar is even larger and would not fit within the Great Altar Space of the *Agniṣṭoma*, that space is in the *Agnicayana* constructed with the extended *prakrama* (Figure 8).

Deriving measurements from the size of the *yajamāna* is related to the idea that the *yajamāna* is in some sense equivalent to his altar and identical with his ritual. This speculation is found in the Puruṣa-Sūkta and elsewhere in the Brāhmaṇa literature and has greatly appealed to Western and Indian scholars which is due, in part, to its connotation of 'self-sacrifice'. However, the basic idea is as old as measurement itself for measures are almost always derived from the

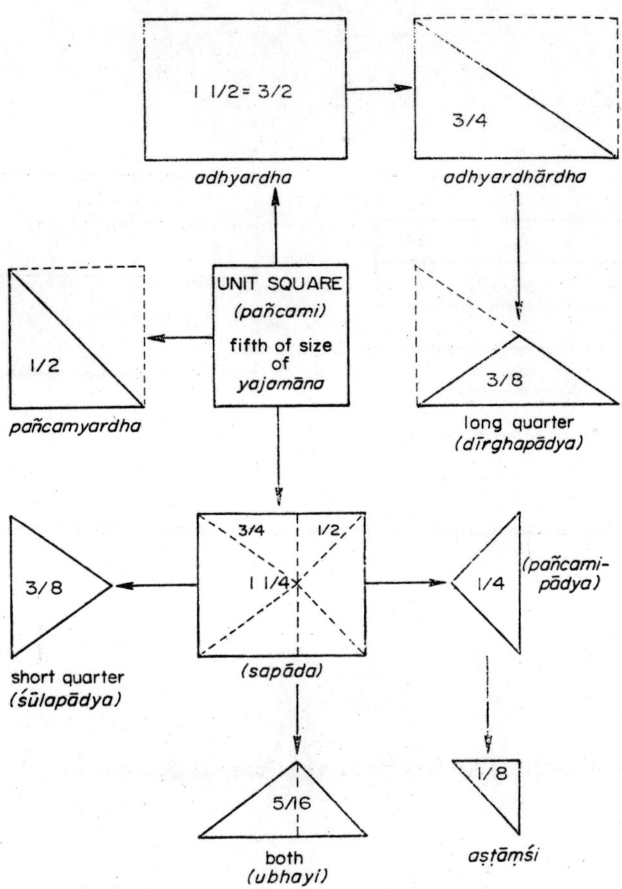

Figure 4: The Shapes of the Bricks

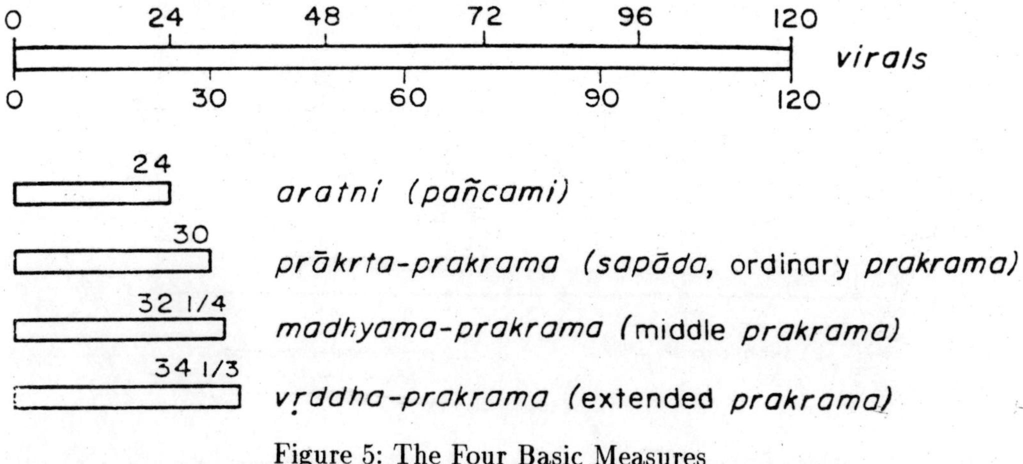

Figure 5: The Four Basic Measures

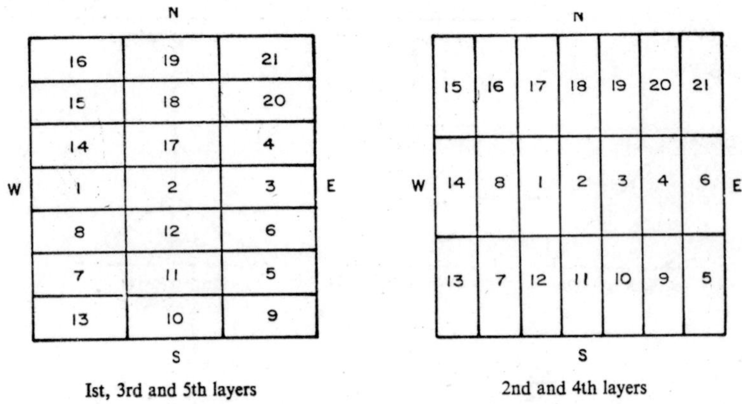

Figure 6: The Bricks of the New Domestic Altar

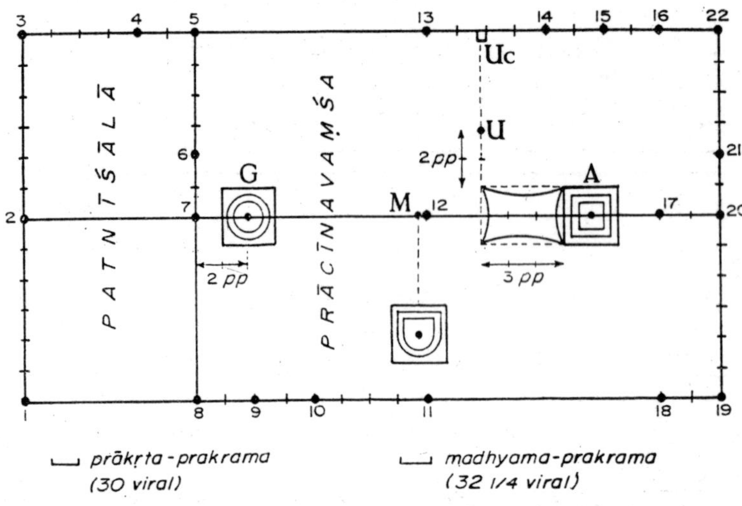

Figure 7: Dimensions of the Old Hall (Prācīnavaṃśa)

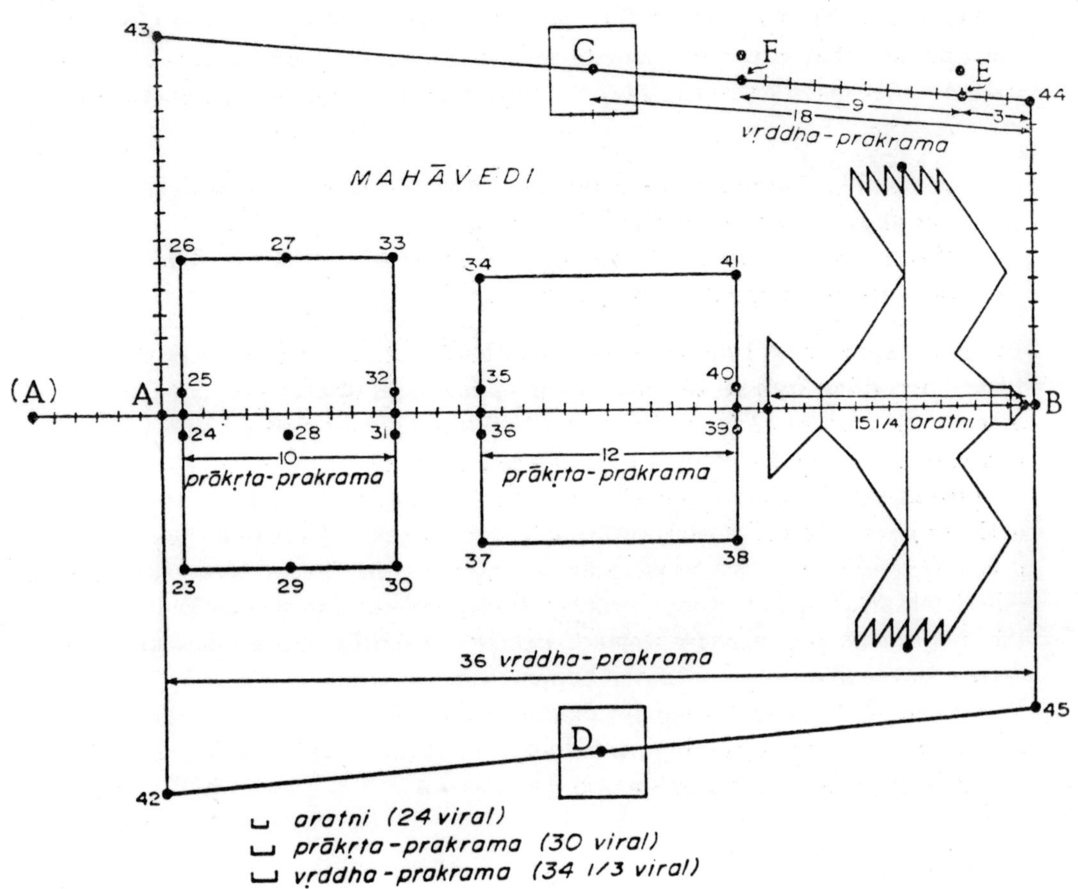

Figure 8: Dimensions of the Mahāvedi

human body. In all civilizations, measurements are based upon fingers, hands, palms, feet, forearms and other bodily parts. Numerical systems such as the decimal system are also based upon the human body.

The idea that man is the basic measure was expressed by the Greek sophist Protagoras in the fifth century B.C. in terms of the Greek term *metron* which corresponds to Sanskrit *mātrā* and derives from the same Indo-European verbal root *mē-* that underlies one form of Sanskrit *mā-*. Plato quotes this doctrine as asserting that:

> *pantōn chrēmatōn metron anthrōpon einai, tōn men ontōn hōs esti, tōn de mē ontōn hōs ouk esti.*
> Man is the measure of all things, of things that are that (or 'how') they are, of things that are not that (or 'how') they are not.

By these expressions, Protagoras seems to have intended a relativistic subjectivism: according to him, any man's perception is in principle as good as any other's, although he seems to have admitted also that a healthy man's perception may be more reliable than that of a sick person.

Protagoras' doctrine is sometimes taken to signify that man is the centre of the universe. Actually, such anthropocentrism is more Christian than Greek, it is expressed in Genesis where man occupies a more central place than any other creature. This is neither Greek nor Vedic, and especially in its Vedic form, the idea of man as a measure seems to indicate primarily that all measurement derives in the final resort from the human body.

[Stages of the later development of *mā-* and *māna* esp. in the Arts will be described in the accompanying contribution by Bruno Dagens, so here mention will only be made of a few important derivatives.]

Conclusion

Māna and the history of the verbal root *mā-* show how profound consequences may result from relatively simple phonological developments that have nothing to do with semantics: the collapse of two Indo-European sounds, *ā* and *ē*, into a single Sanskrit *ā* has led to a realm of ideas in which creative activity is in varying degrees characterized by measure.

A comparison with the ancient Greek is illuminating: for in Greek, the two Indo-European sounds remained distinct and 'measure' was expressed by a separate root from which words such as *mētis* 'wisdom, skill, craft' are derived. This may also have led to an enlarged root *mā-gh-* which produced in due course 'machine' and various other 'mechanisms'. Although Indians were and still are great mathematicians, the science of geometry, literally a 'measure of land', continues to be associated with ancient Greece. It is noteworthy, however, that only Sanskrit suggests the remarkably intellectual conception that there is no 'making' without 'measure'. This fits the historical facts, for Greek and Vedic mathematics are closely related although their relationships are not simple.

The historian of mathematics Seidenberg has shown that both Vedic and Greek mathematicians tried to construct altars in a shape different from a given altar, but with the same surface area. In both traditions, the emphasis is constructive or geometric and not algebraic or computational as it was in ancient Babylonia around 1700 B.C. The Babylonian computational orientation itself depended on geometrical constructions that were even earlier and from which the Greek and Indian traditions derive as well.

Seidenberg's conclusions have been accepted by other leading historians of mathematics such as B.L. Van der Waerden. They are remarkable because they imply that the Vedic Indians, whose Indo-European civilization is generally assumed to have entered India around 1500 B.C., must have imported their geometric rituals.

Old-Babylonian is not an Indo-European language and these conclusions have not been studied within a linguistic perspective. Language and mathematics may develop independently and their relationships are ill-understood, in both historical and conceptual terms. So there is much scope for future research – an observation that provides the final measure which tells us that it is time to stop.

Frits Staal

II. Māna in the Arts: Architecture and Image-making

Introduction

1. *Māna* is an all-pervading concept in the creative Arts such as architecture or image-making. As a matter of fact if one tries to remove from any technical text on such subjects what deals with *māna*, very little will remain if any. Such importance is mainly due to the fact that if *māna* is 'measure', 'measurement', in all the meanings of the terms, it is altogether 'harmony' that is to say one of the basic concepts of any creative work.

2. Measuring for a *śilpin* – whichever his trade: architecture, image-making or the like – is never the mere recording of the size of an already existing artifact. For him, it is to choose, to fix and to ascertain measurements in order to create that is to say to convert into actuality his idea of what he intends to make. One may say that doing so the *śilpin* is following the way of Varuṇa

measuring the earth (ṚV VIII.42.1). Thus ascertaining the measurements of a future measurable feature, he will act in such a way that it will have the right size and the right proportions, that is to say that it will be in harmony with the outside world in which it is to appear and harmonious by itself, in short beautiful.

3. As derivative of *mā-* (see Frits Staal's contribution) *māna* means that by which something is measured. In this sense it is as well the measure of something, i.e. its size than the unit and/or the standard and/or the instrument used to determine that measure or that size. The 'object' being thus 'measured' may be of any kind, the main point being that it is compared with scale of reference deemed as of a known value. Amongst the several other derivatives from *mā-* which may be conceptually correlated to *māna*, one may think, especially when dealing with Arts, of *māyā* – most important on the side of the 'creative' aspect – and of *mātrā*. That last term appears often as a synonym of *māna*; however its meaning seems to be mostly connected with the practical act of measuring; as such it designs as well some specific measurement units.

4. Besides that, a special place must be given to words such as *pramāṇa*, *upamāna*, *parimāṇa* and the like: even if some of them are derived from prefixed forms of the basic root *mā-* as *māna* is derived from its unprefixed aspect, they appear very often to be used more as derivatives from *māna* itself intended to precise the specific kind of measure/measurement/instrument of measure alluded to (see quotations given). However the specific case of *vimāna* may be pointed out here: its various meanings show a constant intermingling of the two basic concepts implied by *mā-* measuring and building according to preconceived measurements.

5. As a whole it does not seem that any word may be deemed as a full synonym of *māna*. The most probable would be *mātrā* but as it has been already said its use is more or less confined to practical operations of measuring and leaves aside the creative aspect of the concept. On the other side one must underline that without getting a proper full-fledged synonym, *māna* itself is widely used in technical texts as a synonym or a substitute for several more specific terms dealing especially with measuring operations. Some of those are the derivatives of prefixed forms of *mā-* already mentioned; others are words such as *utsedha, dīrgha, vistāra* to mention only a few.

Who is measuring?

1. It is useless to try to list what is measured in Arts, for the treatises show well that everything is subject to measurement. This being the case, taking measures or more exactly fixing measures, whichever they may be, is not an easy task. If all the *śilpins* are to be versed in the measurements (*mānavid*, e.g. **Mayamata** XI.18cd), a special emphasis is given on the necessary knowledge

that the architect (*sthapati*) must have in that field and on the accuracy to be adhered by him.

एवमेवं विदित्वा तु स्थपतिर्मानयेद् दृढम् ।

Mayam V.13ab

Thus knowing (the system of measurements), the architect is to measure rigorously.

2. More than that, one of his assistants, the →*sūtradhāra*, is more specially in charge of the measurements: according to the **Mayamata** (V.19cd) he is to know "measures of length and height and proportions" (*mānonmānapramāṇavid*) which are often deemed as the lamp of architecture:

विज्ञेयं सूत्रधारेण हस्तमानं च लक्षणम् ।
मानोन्मानप्रमाणाख्यं वास्तुशास्त्रादिदीपकम् ॥

AparPṛ XLI.2

By the *sūtradhāra* are to be known the measurements in cubits and the characteristics as well as measures of length and height and proportions which are called the luminaries of the treatises of architecture and similar texts.

How to take measurements

1. Plans of any construction, from the smallest building to the biggest town, are established according to diagrams (*pada*) similar to those used in rituals (building itself is a ritual!). Alike those, they are basically drawn according to a perfectly regular pattern, square (or circular). This explains why the basic measurement is always the width (hence *māna,* besides *vistāra, viśāla, tāra...*); should the intended construction be oblong, its length (*āyāma, dīrgha...*) is deduced by the way of proportions from that width; let us add that as a matter of fact the height (*ucca, utsedha...*) also is always deduced from the width.

2. At the time of the laying-out of the construction a regular figure (square or rectangular) will be drawn on the ground with the chosen measurements; its border line does not mark the overall extension of the intended construction but only of its basic plan: it is to be used as a reference line (hence its names: *pramāṇasūtra, mānasūtra;* also *ṛjusūtra* and *ājusūtra*, →*sūtra*) for calculating the projection (*nirgama*) of foreparts or the like added to the basic plan or the recess (*nikṣepa*) of some elements.

प्रमाणसूत्रमित्युक्तं प्रमाणैर्निश्चितं हि यत् ॥
तद्बहिः परितो भागे सूत्रं पर्यन्तमिष्यते । Mayam VI.19cd-20ab

> What is called 'reference line' is determined by the prescribed dimensions (of the intended construction); the overall line goes round the outside of the area determined by this (reference line).

Let us add that several possibilities are given for the use of the reference line; thus for example:

> अन्तःस्तम्भं बहिःस्तम्भमाजुसूत्रं तथा भवेत् ।
> गृहाणां भित्तिमध्ये तु शालानां तु तथा भवेत् ॥
> प्रासादानां तु पादाद्बाह्ये पान्मध्ये शयनासने ।
>
> Mayam XV.57-58ab
>
> The reference line corresponds to the inside or the outside of the (row of) pillars (which surrounds the building); but for houses (it plumbs) with the median axis of the wall; it is the same for halls; for temples (it plumbs) with the outer face of the pilasters and for a sleeping place with their median axis.

3. When dealing with images, the method is slightly different. The reference measurement is generally the height (see below). The positioning of the various limbs of the image is done through reference to a complex set of plumb-lines (*lambasūtra*). The names given to the various kinds of measures in most of the treatises (with some discrepancies between them) are compounds of *māna*. Thus for instance:

> मानं प्रमाणमुन्मानं लम्बमानोपमानके ।
> एवं पञ्चप्रमाणेन व्यक्तलिङ्गं तु कारयेत् ॥
> मानं स्यात्प्रतिमोत्सेधं तद्विस्तारं तु यद्भवेत् ।
> तत्प्रमाणमिति ज्ञेयमुन्मानं तस्य नाहकम् ॥
> लम्बमानं तु सूत्रेण मितं यत्तदुदीरितं ।
> तद् द्व्यन्तरप्रमाणं यदुपमानं तदुच्यते ॥
>
> AjitĀ kp XXXVI.41-43
>
> *Māna, pramāṇa, unmāna, lambamāna* and *upamāna*, those are the five kinds of measurements to be used when making a manifest image. *Māna* is the height of the image; its width is called *pramāṇa*, while its circumference is the *unmāna. Lambamāna* is the measure along a (plumb-)line; the distance between two (plumb-lines) is what is called *upamāna.*

(One may note the various uses of *pramāṇa* in that quotation.)

With what to measure or systems and units of measurements

1. A measurement whichever it is, is the expression of the relation between a known unit and the size of what is to be measured. The unit may be a fixed one which refers ultimately to a standard of universal value. In such case the measurement may be deemed as 'absolute' and gives the true 'size' of the measured object. But the unit may be also a conventional one which has been arbitrarily fixed for the specific object to be measured. In such case measurement will be considered as relative and will give the 'proportions' of the object. By combining the two kinds of measuring the *śilpin* will obtain the inner and outer harmony already dealt with.

2. Units of both kinds are often called by one and the same name: thus for example an image whose height is 96 digits (*aṅgula*: absolute unit) may measure 124 of its own digits (*aṅgula*: relative measure); in the same way a *daṇḍa* is a 'pole', that is to say an absolute unit (= 5 cubits) or a 'module' that is to say a relative one used in architecture. Lastly absolute units of measurement are organized according to systems (*mānakrama*, e.g. **Mayamata** V.11cd; *mānopakaraṇa*, e.g. **Mayamata** V.1ab, **Kāmika** I.16.1ab) wherever in the case of relative units such systems appear only when dealing with image-making.

Absolute units of measurements

1. In most of the technical treatises of architecture as well as in those dealing with mathematics, astronomy as in some other texts a system of absolute units is given which starts from the atom (*aṇu, paramāṇu*), considered as the ultimate natural standard:

> जालान्तरगे भानौ यदणुतरं दर्शनं रजो याति ।
> तद्विन्द्यात्परमाणुं प्रथमं तद्धि प्रमाणानाम् ॥
>
> BṛSam LVIII.1
>
> When the sun passes through a lattice-window, the smallest particle that comes to sight is to be known as an atom for this is the first of (all) the measures.

> परमाणुरिति प्रोक्तं योगिनां दृष्टिगोचरम् ॥
>
> Mayam V.2cd
>
> What is to be seen (only) by the yogins is called 'atom'.

(Let us note that *aṇu* may be used also as a time-unit...)

2. The system is organized on a three-level basis. The first level deals with formless units going by regular steps from the atom upto the barley seed which makes the connection with the second level, that of the linear units of common

use (digit to rope). Lastly are the standards used for measuring distance up to the highest, the *yojana*. The following chart which intends to summarize the main features of the system does not take into account the discrepancies which appear when comparing several texts. While those discrepancies may be taken as mere technicalities, they remind us that each Śāstra has its own coherence and that "one must follow his chosen treatise and not another one" (*svaśāstroktaṃ prakartavyaṃ paraśāstram vivarjayet*). It is to be emphasized that the terminology in such field is very rich and that we are not giving here all the synonyms which may be used in each case:

रत्निश्चैवमरत्निश्च भुजो बाहुः करः स्मृतः ।

Mayam V.8ab

A cubit (*kara*, scil. *hasta*) is known as *ratni, aratni, bhuja* and *bāhu*...

I. Formless units (*amūrta*):

atom (*aṇu, paramāṇu*)	
speck of dust (*rajas, reṇu, ratharenu*)	8 atoms
tip of a hair (*vālāgra*)	8 speck of dust
nit (*līkṣā*)	8 tips of a hair
louse (*yūkā*)	8 nits
barley grain (*yava*)	8 lice

II. Linear units of common use

barley grain (*yava*)	
digit (*aṅgula, mānāṅgula, mātrā...*)	8 barley grains
span (*vitasti, tāla*)	12 digits
cubit (*hasta, kara, ratni, aratni, bāhu..*)	24 digits
pole (*daṇḍa, kārmuka, yaṣṭi...*)	4 cubits
rope (*rajju*)	8 poles

III. Units for distances

krośa	500 poles
gavyūta, goruta	2000 poles
yojana	8000 poles

3. Such a global system allows to measure the size of everything with appropriate units from the infinitesimal to the whole universe. It results clearly from the combination of several clusters of units taken from different usages. Thus the lower units of the middle level (digit, span, cubit) refer clearly to anthropometry with most probably the ubiquitous *aṅgula* as basic standard: it is in fact often deemed as 'the digit which is the measure' (*mānāṅgula*) or even 'the measure' (*mātra*):

परमाणुक्रमाद् वृद्धं मानाङ्गुलमिति स्मृतम् ।

*　　　　*　　　　*

...यवाष्टगुणितोऽङ्गुलम् ।
अङ्गुलं तु भवेन्मात्रम्...

Mayam V.2ab, 4bc

The digit which is the measure (*mānāṅgula*) is a multiple of an atom... by multiplying a barley grain by eight (one gets) a digit (*aṅgula*); a digit is 'measure'...

The crucial position thus given to *aṅgula* is a very significant one for it makes Man the measure of everything. Sometimes this may lead to a very practical use of the human standard:

मध्यमाङ्गुलिमध्यस्थपर्वमात्रायतं तु यत् ॥
कर्तुर्मात्राङ्गुलं प्रोक्तं यागादीनां प्रशस्यते ।
देहलब्धाङ्गुलं यत्तदुपरिष्टाद्विधीयते ॥

Mayam V.11cd-12

The length of the middle phalanx of the middle finger of the officiant is called '*mātrāṅgula'*; it is to be used in sacrifices and the like; that which has been just mentioned is also called 'digit taken from the body'.

We shall see later that this 'digit taken from the body' is of a wide use in image-making, even if the 'body' is, at that stage, the one of the image.

4. The higher units of the middle level (pole, rope) are undoubtedly of agrarian or rustic origin; the same origin is to be found for *krośa* and *gavyūta* while the *yojana* refers clearly to the regular yoking and de-yoking of the bulls during a long-distance trip. As for the first level, the barley grain is the only unit of common practical use and may have been the original lower natural standard. The other ones (louse, nit, tip of a hair, speck of dust) are no more than the necessary steps to allow regression down to the infinitesimal which may be seen only by the best of the yogins; the epithet '*amūrta*' applied to such units by the **Sūrya-Siddhānta** shows well their purely theoretical or, better, intellectual character. They are to be seen as the result of an effort to relate the whole system to what may be considered as the lowest humanly measurable size of fixed value.

5. If we refer to architecture we may see that the barley grain is used very sparingly and only for small objects ("with the barley seed are given the measures of the smallest things", *yavenālpīyasāṃ mānam,* Mayam V.11a) such as the internal partitions of the casket of the foundation deposit:

फेलोच्चार्धत्रिभागैकं कोष्ठमित्त्युच्छ्रयं भवेत् ।
तद्भित्तिघनतां कुर्याद्यवैर्द्वित्रिचतुष्टयैः ॥

Mayam XII.14

The height of the partitions dividing the (internal) compartments is half or one third the height of the casket; the thickness of those partitions is to be two, three or four barley grains.

Amongst the units of the common use level the cubit appears as the main standard in temple and house architecture ("the cubit is for all the *vāstu*", Mayam V.7bc), while the pole is the standard for village and town planning.

एकभौमं चतुर्मानं वक्ष्ये संक्षिप्य शास्त्रतः ।
त्रिचतुर्हस्तमारभ्य नवपङ्क्त्यन्तविस्तृतम् ॥

Mayam XIX.1

Briefly and in accordance with the treatises I present the one-storeyed (temples) (for which there are) four (possible sets of) measurements: their width goes from three to nine cubits (or) from four to ten.

एकद्वित्रिचतुर्भिः पञ्चभिरपि कार्मुकैश्च मार्गततिः ।

Mayam IX.36ab

The width of the streets is of one, two, three, four or five poles (*kārmuka* = *daṇḍa*).

Digit and span are mainly used as submultiples of the cubit; however the digit is the unit for small dimensions (such as the breadth of pillars) and also for corrections as required for *āyādi*-conformity.

6. As far as images or *liṅgas* are concerned, their measurements are generally given with relative units (below), however when absolute measurements are given digits and cubits are used in a pragmatic way, the first for the smallest, the others for the biggest (e.g. Mayam XXXVI.302-303 or XXXIII.49-50ab and 52cd-53).

7. Harmony is a necessity in Art and must be general. The purpose of *āyādi* ("the gain and others") is to verify the concordance of the absolute measurements with auspicious features: the proposed measurements are thus connected with six numerical series (hence the name *ṣaḍvarga* often given to the procedure) certain elements of which are auspicious, the others not. Those series are generally 'gains' (*āya*) and 'losses' (*vyaya*), 'matrices' (*yoni*), 'asterisms' (*nakṣatra*), 'solar days' (*vāra*) and 'parts' (*aṃśa*). The relation is established through a complex sequence of arithmetical operations with which we shall not deal here. Should the measurement correspond to an inauspicious feature it is to be slightly changed, that is to say by one digit.

आयादिसम्पदामर्थं मानादेकाङ्गुलक्षयात् ॥
प्रवृद्ध्योत्तुङ्गमात्तव्यं तत्र दोषो न विद्यते ।

Mayam XXXIII.51cd-52ab

It is not a fault if a height is chosen (for a Liṅga) which is more or less, by one digit, than the heights given above, if this is done for success as regard to 'gains' and others.

Such process is to be applied to the measurements of all works, using in each case the proper standard:

षडेते कल्पनीयास्तु सर्ववस्तुषु देशिकैः ।...
...लिङ्गं तु मेयं मानाङ्गुलेन तु ।
शिविकारथखट्वादि सर्वं तालेन मीयते ॥
प्रासादमण्डपादीनि हस्तमानेन चैव हि ।

AjitĀ kp XXXVI.376ab,379-380ab

Those six (formulas) are to be put in practice by the learned for all the works; ... (for that) *liṅga* is to be measured with the 'digit which is a measure', palanquins, carts, seats and the like with the span and temples, pavilions and others building with the cubit.

Relative units of measurement in architecture

1. Relative units of measurement are used to express proportions, that is to say ratios between two elements or between an ensemble and its components. Good proportions being the base of harmony, they are ubiquitous when dealing with the making of works of art. This being the case they are of two very different sorts and we may define the ones as 'unqualified' or 'fractional' units and the others as 'qualified' or 'modular' units.

2. 'Unqualified' or 'fractional' units are called 'parts' (*aṃśa, bhāga*) or 'measures' (*mātrā*); they are obtained by dividing a known dimension by an arbitrarily chosen number; they are used to express the inner proportions of the feature of which the dimension has been divided or to calculate the dimension of another feature. Thus for instance for fixing the height of the various mouldings (*aṅga*) which ornate the socle (*upapīṭha*) of a building:

उच्छ्रये भानुभागे तु द्व्यंशेनोपानमीरितम् ।
पद्ममंशं तदूर्ध्वेऽर्द्धं क्षेपणं पञ्चभागिकम् ॥
ग्रीवमर्धेन कम्पं स्याद्भागैकेनाम्बुजं भवेत् ।
शेषांशं वाजनं कम्पमष्टाङ्गमुपपीठकम् ॥

Mayam XIII.6-7

The (total) height being divided in twelve parts, the plinth takes up two parts, the doucine one and the fillet which tops it one half; the dado (takes up) five parts, a fillet a half, a (second) doucine one; the remaining part is for the upper string-course (and) the fillet (which tops it); such a socle has eight mouldings.

Else for establishing the size of an image according to that of the sanctum in which it is to be housed:

त्रिभागे गर्भविस्तारे द्विभागेनोत्तमा भवेत् ॥
शरभागयुते गर्भे गुणभागेन मध्यमा ।
नेत्रभागयुते गर्भे व्योमभागेन चाधमा ॥

AjitĀ kp XXXVI.2cd-3

The width of the sanctum being divided into three parts, (that of) the best (image) is of two parts; the (width of the) sanctum being divided into five parts, the medium (image) is of three parts (wide); the (width of the) sanctum being divided into two parts, the inferior (image) is of one part.

3. Another way to establish regular proportions is to take the size of a given element as the reference unit for several others. The most striking example of such 'qualified' or 'modular' units in architecture is the 'module' proper (*daṇḍa*) of which the definition is the following:

पादाग्रविपुलं यत्तु तद्दण्डमिति कथ्यते ।
सर्वाण्यङ्गानि हर्म्याणां मानयेद्दण्डमानतः ॥

Mayam XV.28cd-29ab

The breadth of the pillar at its top, is what is called 'module'; all the elements of the buildings are to be measured according to the value of the module.

Its use is general, especially when dealing with projections and recesses; thus in the description of the attic (*gala*);

...गलं स्यात्प्रस्तरोपरि ॥
तन्मूले वेदिकां कुर्यात्तस्य लक्षणमुच्यते ।
त्रिदण्डं वेजनं तु स्यादुत्सेधं स्याद् द्विदण्डतः ॥

AjitĀ kp XIV.64d-65

The attic is above the entablature; at its bottom there is a stereobate; here are the characteristics (of the attic): its recess is of three modules and its height of two...

In the same way, horizontal proportions of hypostyle structures such as pavilions (*maṇḍapa*) or halls (*sabhā*) are often given using a modular unit called 'division' (*bhakti*) or 'part' (*aṃśa, bhāga*) which value is equal to an intercolumniation. Thus for instance, from the description of a particular type of pavilion:

द्विभक्तिविस्तृतं चैव विस्तारद्विगुणायतम् ॥
त्रिपञ्चाङ्घ्रिसमायुक्तं द्व्यंशैकं मुखभद्रकम् ।

Mayam XXV.143cd-144ab

(The pavilion) is two intercolumniations wide and twice as long. It has fifteen pillars and its front-porch is two intercolumniations (wide with a projection of) one.

Iconometry

1. It is however in the field of image-making that the use of relative units is the more interesting and the more pregnant, for it shows in a perfect manner on one side that Man is the fundamental standard for Art and on the other that precision in measurement is the basis for perfection.

2. Proportions of images are ruled by complex iconometrical canons based on the use of modular units for the oldest treatises such as **Bṛhat Saṃhitā** and of modular-fractional units in the more recent ones (**Aṃśumatkāśyapa Āgama, Ajitāgama**). Let us add that in both cases the units get the same names and that, in both cases too, the basic principle is that the higher ratio between the unit and the size of the image corresponds to the higher hierarchical position of the character represented. The underlying idea of this hierarchical classification being the following: the highest ratio gives the biggest number of units in the whole, which means that unit being smaller, measurements will be more precise. In other terms accuracy in measurement is the criterion of perfection.

3. The main standard is always called *aṅgula* which we may translate for the sake of clarity by 'digit', but which is more precisely the 'finger', as is shown by the self explicative compound *dehalabdhāṅgula* "finger taken from the body". We have already found this "digit taken from the body" in another context; here it does not refer to the body of the *śilpin* but to that of the image; however the parallel is striking and we shall see that the 'human' origin of that digit is certain; other terms to designate it are *aṃśa* ('part') and *mātrā* ('measure'). Other standards used are the 'face' (*mukha*) and the 'span' (*tāla*) which however are clearly seen as multiples of the *aṅgula*. For the *tāla* there is a complex system of ratios (see below), while things are clear for the *mukha*:

स्वैरङ्गुलप्रमाणैर्द्वादश विस्तीर्णमायतञ्चमुखम् ।
नग्नजिता तु चतुर्दश दैर्घ्येण द्राविडं कथितम् ॥

BṛSam LVIII.4

The own digit (of the image) being taken as standard, the face makes

> twelve of them in width and height. However, according to Nagnajit, a height of fourteen is prescribed by Drāviḍa [=Southern] tradition.

The strong connection between *mukha* and *aṅgula* is well expressed in the following description:

> प्रतिमामुखमानेन नवभागान्प्रकल्पयेत् ॥
> चतुरङ्गुला भवेद्ग्रीवा भागेन हृदयं पुनः ।
> नाभिस्तस्मादधः कार्या भागेनैकेन शोभना ॥
> नाभेरधस्तथा मेढ्रं भागेनैकेन कल्पयेत् ।
> द्विभागेनायतावूरू जानुनी चतुरङ्गुले ॥
> जङ्घे द्विभागे विख्याते पादौ च चतुरङ्गुलौ ।
>
> MatPur CCLVIII.26cd-29ab
>
> (The height of the image) must be made up of 9 parts, using the face of the image as unit: neck is of 4 digits, then chest of one unit; perfection is attained by making up of one unit (the distance) from that (chest) down to the navel; then from navel down to the penis there is one unit, the length of the thighs is of 2 units, the knees make up 4 digits, legs are told to be of 2 units and feet of 4 digits.

4. The oldest texts on the subject show well that the images of gods are no more than idealized projections of the human body. For instance the **Bṛhat Saṃhitā** gives thus the human proportions:

> अष्टशतं षण्णवतिः परिमाणं चतुरशीतिरिति पुंसाम् ।
> उत्तम-सम-हीनानामङ्गुलसङ्ख्या स्वमानेन ॥
>
> BṛSam LXVIII.105
>
> The size of the superior, medium and inferior men is respectively of 108, 96 and 84 of their own digits taken as standards.

or elsewhere:

> षण्णवतिरङ्गुलानां व्यायामो दीर्घता च हंसस्य ।
> शश-रुचक-भद्र-मालव्य-संज्ञितास्त्र्यङ्गुलविवृद्ध्या ॥
>
> BṛSam LXIX.7
>
> The height and the span is of 96 digits for *Haṃsa* (type of man) and of three digits more (each time) for those who are known as *Śaśa, Rucaka, Bhadra* and *Mālavya* [thus their respective sizes are of 99, 102, 105 and 108 digits].

Then when dealing with image proportions:

दशरथतनयो रामो बलिश्च वैरोचनिः शतं विंशम् ।
द्वादशहान्या शेषाः प्रवर-सम-न्यून-परिमाणाः ॥

BṛSam LVIII.30

(The height of images of) Rāma, son of Daśaratha, and Bali, son of Virocana, is 120 (of their own digits); heights of others (images) which are superior, medium and inferior are less (each time) by 12 (of their own digits) [thus 108, 94 and 84].

That is to say that the proportions of the best of the gods and the best of the *asuras* are to be more precisely defined, that is to say more perfect than that of the best of the men. This being the case, one may note that here other images are to be made with human ratios.

5. The modular-fractional canons which appear afterwards are far more complex. They multiply the categories in order to refine on the hierarchy. While using the *dehalabdhāṅgula* as the main unit, they give an important place to the *tāla*:

लब्धं बेरेषु यन्मानं तालगण्यं तु यद्भवेत् ॥
अङ्गुलं देहलब्धं तु तत्तालं द्वादशाङ्गुलम् ।
कल्पितं स्यात्सुरश्रेष्ठ तैर्बेरेष्वङ्गकल्पना ॥

AjitĀ kp XXXVI.19cd-20

The measurement used for the images is the number of *tāla*; the digit is taken on the body (of the image) and the *tāla* makes up 12 digits. O best of the gods! it is with such units that are to be calculated the limbs of the images.

This emphasis on →*tāla* may be seen in that the whole system is called *tālamāna* ("measuring by *tāla*") and each category is named according to the number of *tāla* in which is to be divided the height of the images: thus *daśatāla, navatāla* and so on. But the treatises go further by distinguishing three subcategories for the two higher ratios:

रव्यङ्गुलमिदं तालमिति शास्त्रस्य निश्चयः ॥
त्रैविध्यं दशतालस्य नवतालस्य चैव हि ।
उत्तमं मध्यमान्तञ्च तेषां भेदो विधीयते ॥
उत्तमं दशतालं तु चतुर्विंशच्छताङ्गुलम् ।
चतुरङ्गुलहीनं तद्दशतालं तु मध्यमम् ॥
तस्माच्चाधममित्युक्तं हीनं यच्चतुरङ्गुलैः ।
नवतालोत्तमं ज्ञेयं शतं सद्वादशाङ्गुलम् ॥

AjitĀ kp XXXVI.23cd-26

This *tāla* makes up 12 digits, thus affirms the treatise; however

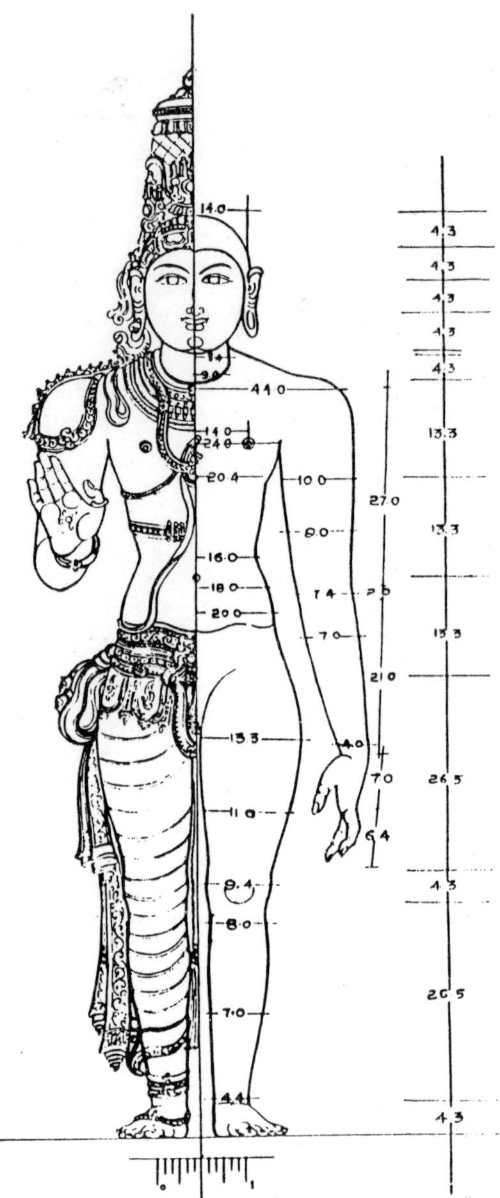

Figure 9: Tālamāna, Measurement of Pratimā

there are three kinds of *daśatāla* and *navatāla* categories, superior, medium and inferior of which the difference is told here: the superior *daśatāla* makes up 124 digits, the medium 4 digits less and the inferior 4 digits less again. The superior *navatāla* is known as making up 112 digits etc..

The result of such oversubtle division is that the value of the *tāla* may vary from 12.4 to 11.6 digits for the *daśatāla* categories and from 12.44 to 11.55 for *navatāla*.

6. The *tāla* system is given by several treatises with lots of small discrepancies. We have summarized in the following chart the way it appears in the **Ajitāgama** which goes down to the three *tāla* categories (some other texts like **Aṃśumatkāśyapa**, go down to one *tāla*). This chart is self-explanatory in that it shows clearly how the precision of the measurements decreases along with the total number of digits.

Tālamāna

(AjitĀ kp chap.36)

tāla:	10/1	10/2	10/3	9/1	9/2	9/3	8	7	6	5	4	3
aṅgula (total):	124	120	116	112	108	104	96	86	72	60	48	36
Top of the head:	4	4	4	4	4	4	2	1	1	1	1	1
uṣṇīṣa	1	}4	}4	}4	}4	}4	}2	}1	}1	}1	}1	}1
keśānta	3											
Face:	13.4	13	12.4	12	11	11	11	11	11	9	12	8
(*keśānta*)												
akṣisūtra	4.4	4.6		4								
nāsāpuṭānta	4.4	4.4	}12.4	4	}11	}11	}11	}11	}11	}9	}12	}8
hanu	4.4	3.6		4								
Neck:		4.4	4	4	4	4	4	3	3	3	2	22
galavṛddhi	0.4	}4	}4	0.4	}4	}4	}3	}3	}3	}2	}2	}2
kaṇṭha	4			3.4								
Torso:	40	39	37.4	36	35	33	32	27	19	21	20	14
hikkānta	13.4	13	12.4	12	12	11	11	}18.4			7	
hṛdayānta	13.4	13	12.4	12	12	11	11		}19	}21	7	}14

nābhi	13	13	12.4	12	11	11	10	8.4			6	
meḍhra/yoni												
Legs:	62	60	58	56	54	52	48	44	38	27	13	11
uru	27	26	25	24	23	22	21	19	15.4	12	5	4
jānu	4	4	4	4	4	4	3	3	3.4	2	2	2
jaṅghā	27	26	25	24	23	22	21	19	15.4	11	4	3
pādatala	4	4	4	4	4	4	3	3	3.4	2	2	2

7. That the *tāla* system is clearly intended to allow the *śilpin* to show in the images the hierarchical order of the beings they represent, appears clearly in the distribution of the images as given in the **Ajitāgama** (see chart below). The lower position of Gaṇeśa and Vāmana (and also Vṛṣendra!) is not surprising, as their anatomical characteristics place them from the iconographical point of view amongst the substandard beings. On the other side one may note the subtle distinction established between the *Mātṛkās*: four of them have been placed in a superior position (*madhyamadaśatāla*) for they are connected with the three heads of the pantheon. In the same way all the *dikpālas* are placed in the *uttamanavatāla* categories, except Indra placed a little higher in the *adhamadaśatāla* one, due most probably to his rank of leader of the gods. As for men, they seem to have been put deliberately below the gods while, as we have seen, they were amongst them in older treatises. However this apparent lowering, due probably to new theological trends, is offset by the fact that, whichever his hierarchical position, Man remains the basic standard for making images of gods...

Distribution of the images (AjitĀ kp XXXVI.27-37)

10 *tāla* (1) Brahmā, Viṣṇu, Maheśvara.

10 *tāla* (2) Umā, Kātyāyanī, Lakṣmī, Cāmuṇḍā, Sarasvatī, Māheśī, Vaiṣṇavī, Brāhmī.

10 *tāla* (3) Skanda, Indra, Āditya, Vīrabhadra, Kṣetrapāla, Śacīdevī, Uṣā, Bhūmi, Vārāhī, Indrāṇī, Kaumārī, Aśvins.

9 *tāla* (1) Vahni, Antaka (Yama), Nirṛti, Varuṇa, Vāyu, Vaiśravaṇa, Īśāna; Ṛṣis, Śāstā, Maṇḍana; the wives of the preceeding; Apsaras, Mahāmoṭī, Vidyeśas, Tārkṣyas, Gandharvas, Yakṣas, Siddhas, Cāraṇas, Nāgendras, Vidyādharas, Gaṇeśa, Rudras, Ādityas, Vasus.

9	*tāla*	(2)	Rākṣasas, Asuras, Kinnaras.
9	*tāla*	(3)	other gods and goddesses
8	*tāla*		men
7	*tāla*		Piśācas
6	*tāla*		hunchbacks
5	*tāla*		Gajāsya
4	*tāla*		Vāmana
3	*tāla*		Bhūtas and Vṛṣendra.

Conclusion

1. The overwhelming place occupied by *māna* in treatises dealing with architecture and image-making is first related to the creative aspect of the concept: one cannot create without first ascertaining the dimensions of what he intends to create. More than that, artistic creation needs harmony which may be obtained through the choice of right dimensions, that is to say of a right size and of right proportions. Such harmony must be found in the work of art but also in the space which surrounds it: the world is a symphony in which each new creation must be able to play its own part without dissonance. Let us add that by prescribing several sets of dimensions for a given element, the treatises leave a wide leeway to the *śilpin*: he can choose whichever seems the best according to his own aesthetic feelings, which feelings cannot be dictated as may be the dimensions.

2. The basic idea of harmony goes beyond the material environment of the intended work of art. As we have seen when dealing with iconometry, measurements are used to express the religious hierarchy which rules the world of the gods. In the same way one may see that when dealing with house-architecture, for instance, the measurements are used as an instrument given to the *śilpin* in order to allow him to materialize and to make visible abstract principles. More than that, accuracy being the scale of perfection, it is only the best of the *śilpins* who will be able to make images of the highest. In the same way, the atom which is the ultimate measure cannot be perceived but by the best of the yogins, amongst whom will be the perfect architect who has mastered his senses (*jitendriya,* Mayam V.16).

3. The various systems of measurements intend to encompass the whole of reality from the infinitesimal up to the whole universe. This being the case, it is clear that they are centered upon Man to whom the most commonly used units are directly related and who, ultimately, appears as the basic standard offered to the *śilpin.*

Bruno Dagens

Select Bibliography

Burrow, T. (1980): "Sanskrit MĀ– 'to make, produce, create'," Bulletin of the School of Oriental and African Studies 43.311-328.

Dilke, O.A.W. (1987): Mathematics and Measurement, Berkeley and London.

Gonda, J. (1959): "The 'Original' Sense and the Etymology of Skt. māyā," in: Four Studies in the Language of the Veda, The Hague, pp.119-194.

Gonda, J. (1965): The Savayajñas (Kauśikasūtra 60-68), Amsterdam

Jakobson, R. (1962), "Why 'Mama' and 'Papa'?" Selected Writings, The Hague, I: 538-545.

Lévi, Sylvain (1898): La doctrine du sacrifice dans les Brāhmaṇas, Paris.

Lévi, Sylvain (1906-1908): "Des préverbes chez Pāṇini," Memoires de la Société Linguistique de Paris 14.276-279.

Renou, Louis (1939): "La maison védique," Journal Asiatique 231.481-504.

Renou, Louis (1955-1969): Etudes védiques et pāṇinéennes, I-XVII, Paris.

Seidenberg, A. (1962): "The Ritual Origin of Geometry," Archive for History of Exact Sciences 1.488-527.

Seidenberg, A. (1978): "The Origin of Mathematics," Archive for History of Exact Sciences 18.301-342.

Seidenberg, A. (1983): "The Geometry of the Vedic Rituals," in: AGNI Vol. II, pp.95-126.

Srinivasan, Saradha (1979): Mensuration in Ancient India, Delhi.

Staal, Frits (1977): "Ṛgveda 10.71 on the Origin of Language," in: Revelation in Indian Thought: A Festschrift in Honour of Professor T.R.V. Murti, Emeryville, pp.3-14.

Staal, Frits (1983): AGNI: The Vedic Ritual of the Fire Altar, I-II, Berkeley.

Staal, Frits (1983): The Science of Ritual, Poona.

Staal, Frits (1989): Rules without Meaning. Ritual, Mantras and the Human Sciences, New York, Bern, Frankfurt am Main, Paris.

LAYA

Overview

Laya, dissolution, absorption, merging, rest, has a wide range of meaning; in music and dance it designates pause and rhythm. The roots *lī-* or *līṅ-* from which the word is derived mean melting, dissolving or merging and embracing, joining, connecting, etc. Both these meanings are inter-connected because melting and merging go together or presuppose each other.

The well-known compounds with *laya* are *pra* + *laya* = *pralaya*, meaning dissolution at the cosmic level, *ā* + *laya* = *ālaya*, meaning 'until *laya*' (dissolution or salvation), dissolution on all sides, or abode, and also forming part of a compound *ālaya-vijñāna* which is a technical expression in Buddhist philosophy. At the microcosmic level, *laya* stands for deep sleep, fainting (one of the eight *sāttvika bhāvas* or involuntary reflexes caused by acute mental states), and liberation or salvation, understood as merging of the individual in the Supreme.

Sāṃkhya and Vedānta systems of philosophy have emphasised the view that dissolution does not mean annihilation or nonexistence, and that it only implies merging in the source, to be followed by re-emerging. Thus dissolution is not an opposite, but a complementary of creation.

In music *laya* is the rest that is inseparably combined with action as its successor and if action and rest are viewed in a cyclic process, rest is both an antecedent and successor of action. The speed of movement in musical time is measured on the basis of the span of rest following each *kriyā*, if the span is long, the *laya* is slow, if it is medium, the *laya* is medium and if it is short, the *laya* is fast. Thus in the textual tradition of Indian music as well as in the older oral tradition, speed is viewed as an effect of the rest-span, rather than the pace of motion, so that medium is the double of fast and slow is the double of medium. But in the current oral and written parlance speed is equated with motion and hence medium is the double of slow and fast is the double of medium. In literature *laya* operates in metre (*chandas*), syllable, word and sentence (the balancing of long-short syllables or *mātrās*, time-units both in poetry and prose).

Etymology and Cognate Words

The word *laya* is derived from three roots viz. *lī dravīkaraṇe* (*curādigaṇa*), conveying the sense of melting, merging, or dissolving, and *līṅ śleṣaṇe/ lī śleṣaṇe* (*divādigaṇa* and *kryādigaṇa*) standing for the act of embracing, sticking, joining or connecting; both these meanings are inter-connected because melting is directly associated with the merging of one thing into another and merging is the culmination of the process of embracing, joining or connecting.

In Vedic literature the word *laya* is used a few times (cf. YV XVIII.7) in the sense of harrow alongwith *sīra* (plough). Breaking the lumps of earth and levelling the ground are the functions of harrow. This specific meaning matches the general meaning of dissolution which also involves levelling or merging of differentiation forming part of creation.

When the prefix *pra-* is added to *laya, pralaya* stands for 1) dissolution or destruction in the context of cosmology (AmKo I.4.22cd); 2) death (AmKo II.8.116) and 3) cessation of activity in a living being i.e. fainting or swooning (AmKo I.7.33d). In **Nāṭya-Śāstra** (VII.94) the word *pralaya* is the last one in the enumeration of eight *sāttvika bhāvas*, the reflex or involuntary manifestation in the body like tears, tremor, choking of the voice etc. caused by intense mental states and it stands for swooning or fainting, the third meaning given in **Amarakośa**. Thus *pralaya* and *laya* are synonymous so far as cosmic dissolution or destruction are concerned, but each word has a very definite usage in music and dramaturgy; only *laya* is used in music and only *pralaya* in dramaturgy. The synonyms for cosmic *pralaya* as given in **Amarakośa** are: *saṃvarta* (lit. proper happening or event), *kalpa* (the time-span of one thousand *yugas*, *kṣaya* (lit. decay), *kalpānta* (the end of *kalpa*). Incidentally, *saṃvarta* pairs with *vivarta* (lit. reflection = creation). Sometimes the word *pralaya* at the cosmic level is used with adjectives qualifying dissolution as being partial and final and this usage takes the form of *khaṇḍa-pralaya* (lit. partial) and *mahā-pralaya* (lit. great). The synonyms for *pralaya* as death have been enumerated in **Amarakośa** as *pañcatā* implying the dissolution of the components of the body into the five *mahābhūtas* (elements), *kāladharma*, the ordained course of time, *diṣṭānta*, the bidden end, *anta*, end, *nāśa*, destruction, and other words connoting death.

The addition of the prefix *ā-* forms the word *ālaya* which is a part of the compound *ālaya-vijñāna* in Buddhist philosophy; *ālaya* also occurs in **Bhāgavata Purāṇa:**

> निगमकल्पतरोर्गलितं फलं शुकमुखादमृतद्रवसंयुतम् ।
> पिबत भागवतं रसमालयं मुहुरहो रसिका भुवि भावुकाः ॥
>
> BhāgPur I.1.3

The Bhāgavata is the ripe fruit of the wish-tree of *nigama* (Veda), it is combined or seasoned with the nectar-fluid from the mouth of the parrot in the form of Śuka-muni (the main speaker of Bhāgavaṭa), O *rasikas* (those who are capable of relishing *rasa*) and *bhāvukas* (those excelling in the experience of *bhāvas* or mental states), drink ye the *rasa* of Bhāgavata again and again in this world, until *laya* (salvation).

The prefix *vi-* is also a common addition forming *vilaya*, but this word does not have a technical connotation; it is used almost as a synonym of *laya*, meaning dissolution.

In cosmology the word *laya* forms part of a triad viz. *sṛṣṭi* (creation), *sthiti* (sustenance) and *laya* (dissolution) or *saṃhāra* (lit. destruction). If *laya* is placed in a pair of complementaries then its counterpart is *sṛṣṭi* or *kriyā*; *sṛṣṭi* would stand for the beginning and *laya* the end, both being components of a cyclic or repetitive process, i.e. two aspects in the cosmic cycle of emergence and merging back that are inseparably related. In the context of consciousness *laya* (merging in sleep) forms a pair with *vikṣepa* (distraction) and both are equally detrimental to *samādhi*. In music *laya* has *kriyā* (lit. action) as both its complementary as well as inseparable 'antecedent', because there can be no *laya* or rest without *kriyā*. The operation of *laya* is channelised by *mārga* (lit. path) and *yati* (lit. control) that prescribes the order of *laya*. These related concepts will be explained in the section on music.

Layers of Meaning

The important meanings of *laya* are 1) dissolution or 'destruction' (*saṃhāra*) at the cosmic level, implying the dissolution of one element into another in the reverse order, with reference to the order of creation; 2) deep sleep or slumber (*suṣupti*) in living organisms where the merging of the faculties of sensation and perception into consciousness is implied; 3) in Haṭhayoga, the state comparable to *samādhi* (deep meditation) spoken of by Patañjali; 4) in music, the *viśrānti* or rest immediately following each *kriyā* or action, spoken of in the treatment of →*tāla*; taking a cyclic view of this action, rest not only succeeds, but also precedes each action.

The core meaning of *laya* is that it is an inseparable antecedent and follower of activity in the macrocosm as well as microcosm; in the former i.e. in the cosmic sphere, *laya* operates as dissolution to be again followed by creation and in the latter i.e. individual life of creatures, it operates partially in the form of deep sleep and fainting and completely in the form of death to be followed by waking up or regaining consciousness or rebirth respectively. In music, it is the inseparable follower of *kriyā* or action, in the form of rest, to be followed again by action. In all the three spheres viz. cosmic, individual life and music, the cycle of 'action' and 'rest' is clearly implied and this fact justifies the use of the same word in these three spheres. The basic idea is that rest is inseparable from activity, both are like reversibles; life at all levels and artistic activity in the form of music exists in the continuum of creation-destruction, waking-sleep, birth-death, action-rest etc.; these twins are really speaking a component unit of a cyclic movement at all the above levels. Thus *laya* is a concomitant, rather than an opposite of creation or activity. It is noteworthy that in the five characteristic features of Purāṇa, *sarga* stands for creation and *pratisarga* (lit. counter-creation) means dissolution.

Development of the Concept

That *laya* or dissolution does not imply complete annihilation, is clarified in the following *sūtra* of the Sāṃkhya system of philosophy:

नाशः कारणलयः ।

SāmSū I.121

Nāśa or destruction of a thing is its merging in its cause.

Thus *nāśa* is not annihilation or non-existence, but the phenomenon of a thing assuming the state of its (material) cause. The root *ṇaś-* also means *adarśana* or non-apprehension and not destruction. The same idea is expressed in the following verses of the **Mahābhārata**.

यस्माद्यदभिजायेत तत्तत्रैव प्रलीयते ।
लीयन्ते प्रतिलोमानि सृज्यन्ते चान्तरात्मना ॥

MBh XII.306.31

A thing merges into the same from where it emerges, all (things) merge or dissolve in the reverse order and are created by the inner *ātman*.

यद्यस्माज्जायते भूतं तत्र तत्प्रविलीयते ।
लीयन्ते प्रतिलोमानि सृज्यन्ते चोत्तरोत्तरम् ॥

MBh XIV.42.4

An element (*bhūta*) merges from where it is born; (the *bhūtas*) dissolve in the reverse order and are created one after another.

The same view is echoed in the following statement of Śaṅkarācārya:

यस्य हि यत उत्पत्तिः तत्र तस्य प्रलयो न्याय्यो मृदीव शरावस्य ।

BrSūBh IV.2.1

A thing can merge into what its material cause is, as for instance an earthen plate into earth.

Laya in the sense of sleep has been paired with *vikṣepa* (distraction) and both are impediments to *samādhi* (deep meditation).

लयविक्षेपरहितं मनः कृत्वा सुनिश्चलम् ।
यदा यात्यमनीभावं तदा तत् परमं पदम् ॥

MaitUp VI.34

By making mind all motionless,
From sloth and from distraction freed,
When unto mindlessness one comes,
Then that is the supreme estate! (Tr. R.E. Hume)

The above idea is echoed in the Vedānta system:

लये सम्बोधयेच्चित्तं विक्षिप्तं शमयेत्पुनः ।
सकषायं विजानीयात् समप्राप्तं न चालयेत् ॥
यदा न लीयते चित्तं न च विक्षिप्यते पुनः ।
अनिङ्गनमनाभासं निष्पन्नं ब्रह्म तत्तदा ॥

MāṇḍKā II.44,46

When the mind gets merged in *laya* (sleep), one should awaken or arouse it (through knowledge, repetitive effort and detachment) and again when the mind is affected by *vikṣepa* (distraction), one should calm it down, knowing that it (the mind) is full of *kaṣāya* (the tinge of attachment). When the mind reaches the state of equilibrium, one should not move or stir it (towards objects of enjoyment). When the mind is not affected by *laya* and not also by *vikṣepa*, (then) it is without movement and reflection and that is the state of *Brahman* attained.

The Sāṃkhya system also expresses a similar view.

ध्यानं निर्विषयं मनः ।
लयविक्षेपयोर्व्यावृत्त्येत्याचार्याः ।

SāmSū VI.25, 30

The state of *dhyāna* (meditation) is the same as the objectless state of the mind... This is (attained) through the elimination of *laya* and *vikṣepa*, so say the *ācāryas* (teachers).

Suṣupti or deep sleep is a state of the mind (*vṛtti)* according to **Yoga-Sūtra** (I.6), but in *samādhi* (meditation) all *vṛttis* (states) have to get dissolved. Thus there is a difference between the *laya* in deep sleep and the *laya* in meditation. Śaṅkarācārya has thus explained this difference.

लीनधीरपि जागर्ति यो जाग्रद्धर्मवर्जितः ।
बोधो निर्वासनो यस्य स जीवन्मुक्त उच्यते ॥

Viveka Cūḍāmaṇi 430.

One who keeps awake (through meditation) during the merging of the movement (*vṛtti*) of the mind during sleep and who, while awake, is free from the *dharmas* (movements of the mind towards objects) and whose *bodha* (understanding) is free from desires, he is known as *jīvanmukta* (liberated while alive).

The state of *laya* (as distinct from sleep) has been equated with *samādhi*, *mukti* and the like.

राजयोगः समाधिश्च उन्मनी च मनोन्मनी ।
अमरत्वं लयस्तत्त्वं शून्याशून्यं परं पदम् ॥
अमनस्कं तथाद्वैतं निरालम्बं निरञ्जनम् ।
जीवन्मुक्तिश्च सहजा तुर्या चेत्येकवाचकाः ॥

HyPrad IV.3,4

Rājayoga, meditation, mindless state (*manonmanī*), immortality, *laya*, *tattva* (thatness or complete identification), *śūnyāśūnya* (neither emptiness, nor non-emptiness), ultimate state, mindlessness, nonduality, supportlessness, thinglessness, liberation during life, *sahaja* or spontaneous state, the fourth state – all these are synonymous.

Layayoga is spoken of in Haṭhayoga.

लययोगश्चित्तलयः संकेतैस्तु प्रजायते ।

Dattātreya Yogaśāstra p.10

The merging of the mind is *layayoga*, which comes into being through *saṅketas* (directions like fixing the gaze on the tip of the nose, or in the middle of the eyebrows).

The state of *laya* is described as one where all desire has dropped away, where the mind is not affected by anything.

लयो लय इति प्राहुः कीदृशं लयलक्षणम् ।
अपुनर्वासनोत्थानाल्लयो विषयविस्मृतिः ॥

HyPrad IV.34

They have spoken again and again of '*laya*'; what is the definition of '*laya*'? It is the total loss of memory of objects brought into being by the absence of the upsurge of desires.

Pralaya or destruction of the macrocosm and microcosm is also known as *laya.*

नित्यो नैमित्तिकश्चैव तथा प्राकृतिको लयः ।
आत्यन्तिकश्च कथितः कालस्य गतिरीदृशी ॥ BhāgPur XII.4.38

Destruction or dissolution is fourfold viz. *nitya* (eternal, daily death of born beings), *naimittika* (lit. occasional, dissolution when a day of Brahmā ends), *prākṛtika* (the merging of elements into one another) and *ātyantika* (lit. final, liberation of the self), thus is the movement of time.

These four types of *pralaya* are also spoken of in other Purāṇas (e.g. ViPur I.7.41-43, VI.3-5, KūrPur II.45; AgPur 368.1,2).

In Buddhist thought the word *laya* is used for the merging of the mind in meditation (cf. **Bhāvanākrama** (Prathama), p. 182). *Laya-auddhatya* (lit. the insolence of *laya*) is considered to be detrimental to meditation and is to be subdued (**Madhyāntavibhāgaśāstram**, p.130).

Ālaya-vijñāna is a central concept in Buddhist philosopy of the Yogācāra school and it has been translated as the 'store mind', being the store-house or container of the latent residues or impressions of previous actions, hence it is a basic layer of the mind. In Vijñānavāda an unbroken stream of a series of *vijñāna* is accepted, even though the existence of an eternal knower, doer and enjoyer is denied. The idea of continuity appears to be conveyed by the word *ālaya*. The following etymological explanation would confirm this view.

तच्च सर्व-सांक्लेशिक-धर्मबीजस्थानत्वादालयः । आलयः स्थानमिति पर्यायौ। अथवा लीयन्त उपनिबध्यन्तेऽस्मिन् सर्वधर्माः कार्यभावेन । यद्वा लीयत उपनिबध्यते कारणभावेन सर्वधर्मेष्वित्यालयः। विजानातीति विज्ञानम् ।

Sthiramati's comm. on VijMSi, Triṃśikā 1-2

It is (called) *ālaya* on account of its being the abode of the 'seeds' of all attributes (*dharmas*) leading to suffering. Or, all attributes remain merged in it as effects; or that which merges in or is related to all attributes as causes is *ālaya*. That which knows is *vijñāna*.

Manifestation in the Arts

Forming part of the treatment of the temporal aspect of music, *laya* is very basic to it, because time is one of the two main components of music, the other being pitch combined with volume and timbre. The following passages from **Nāṭya-Śāstra, Abhinava-Bhāratī** and **Saṅgīta-Ratnākara** explain the concept of *laya* in music.

त्रयो लयास्तु विज्ञेया द्रुतमध्यविलम्बिताः ।
छन्दोऽक्षरपदानां हि समत्वं यत्प्रकीर्त्तितम् ॥
कलाकालान्तरकृतः स लयो नाम संज्ञितः । NŚ XXXI.370-371ab

लय एव ताल इति मनसि कृत्वा तस्यैव प्राग्लक्षणमाह (ना॰ शा॰ 31.5)— कला प्राकृतव्यपदेशतया प्रसिद्धा। अन्योन्यमध्यवर्ती कालः। तत्कालानन्तरं तत्कृतः सम्पादितोऽत्र एव वैकृतस्वभावो लयो नाम संज्ञितोऽन्वर्थलब्धः। श्लेषविश्रान्त्यात्मार्थः स लयः । तस्य च स्थूल-सूक्ष्मकार्यगम्यं स्वरूपमाह। छन्दोऽक्षर इति । यदिति । यस्माद्विश्रान्तिलक्षणाच्छन्दश्छन्दोऽन्तरेण न समं तुल्यकालं प्रयुक्तमिति व्यपदेशो जायते । तेनाक्षरगतः पदगतः सकलवाक्यगतश्च लय इत्युक्तं भवति।

AbhiBhā on above

Three *layas* are known; viz. fast, medium and slow. The evenness or equality (in time-measure) of metre, syllable and word, is known as *laya* that is brought into existence by the difference in the duration of *kāla*.

Commentary:

Laya has been defined in the very beginning (NŚ XXXI.5cd), keeping in mind the fact that *laya* itself is *tāla*. *Kāla* is known as *prākṛta* i.e. as pertaining to nature or being the cause. (The purport seems to be that *kāla* or the standard unit of time is perceived even in life in general termed as *prakṛti* or nature and that is the cause of *laya*). Time is the mutual interval between (*kalās*). *Laya* is of the nature of *vikṛta* (created or effect, as opposed to natural or causal), formed as it is by (or after the formation of) the above time-interval; the meaning of the word *laya* is according to its derivation or etymology. That *laya* is of the nature of embrace or combination and rest. The nature of that (*laya*) as perceived through its gross and subtle effects, is spoken of through the phrase beginning with *chandas* (in the text **Nāṭya-Śāstra**).

Chandas (metre) is (made) of the essence of rest; without metre it cannot be said that there is an evenness or equality in performance. Hence it is being said that *laya* operates in syllable, word and all sentences.

क्रियानन्तरविश्रान्तिर्लयः स त्रिविधो मतः ।
द्रुतो मध्यो विलम्बश्च द्रुतः शीघ्रतमो मतः ॥
द्विगुणद्विगुणौ ज्ञेयौ तस्मान्मध्यविलम्बितौ ।

SR V.44-45ab

Laya is the rest that immediately follows 'action'. That (*laya*) is known to be threefold, viz. fast, medium and slow. *Druta* (fast) is the quickest one, the medium and slow ones are double and again double of the same (fast) (respectively).

The measure of rest immediately following every action determines *laya*. In fast movement, the measure of rest following each action is the minimum, in medium movement the rest is double of that in the medium one. Thus *laya* has been equated with rest in the textual tradition. The same equation holds good in the oral tradition recorded in the song texts of Dhrupad (cf. the following excerpt from a Dhrupad ascribed to Bakhshoo: "*druta madhya vilambita kara dikhāve*", Song-text No. 65).

But in the current oral tradition and the text-books followed in institutions imparting music education today, *laya* has been equated with action, rather than with rest and hence the order of the three *layas* has been reversed i.e. medium is said to be the double of slow and fast is the double of medium.

It is difficult to say when and how or why this change came about. Since action in *tāla* is intermittent, both action and rest are inseparably combined. It does not, therefore, make any basic difference whether *laya* is equated with action or rest. But etymologically *laya* means rest. Thus the current equation is a departure from tradition. When *laya* is equated with rest, fast-medium-slow is the order of double-degrees, but when it is equated with action, slow-medium-fast becomes the order of double-degrees. In the above excerpt from the Dhrupad text ascribed to Bakhshoo, the order of fast-medium-slow is accepted and hence it conforms to the older tradition.

The word *laya* is usually translated as 'tempo', but 'tempo' does not bring out the original meaning of *laya*; it rather corresponds to the current meaning of *laya* viz. speed, whereas *laya* stands for rest which is the basis of speed.

Laya is said to be manifold operating in different degrees of fast, medium and slow.

मार्गभेदाच्चिरक्षिप्रमध्यभावैरनेकधा ॥
लयोऽक्षरे पदे वाक्ये योऽसौ नात्रोपयुज्यते ।

SR V.45cd-46ab

Laya is of different types or kinds through the feeling of slow, fast and medium; according to the difference in *mārga*; that (*laya*) which (operates) in syllable, word and sentence is not useful or applicable here (in music).

The reference to *laya* in metre, syllable, word and sentence in the above passage as not being relevant in music appears to be in contradiction of the passage of **Nāṭya-Śāstra** quoted above where the *laya* operating in these linguistic units is spoken of. This apparent contradiction could be resolved by taking the view that **Nāṭya-Śāstra** is using the *laya* in music. **Abhinava-Bhāratī** (on NŚ 371cd- 372ab, immediately after the passage under reference) clearly refers to *laya* in song and instruments.

Mārga (lit. path) is a special concept of the ancient →*tāla* system. Every *tāla* is accepted to have three *mārgas* or spans of length, according to **Nāṭya-**

Śāstra. Saṅgīta-Ratnākara adds a fourth one. *Mārga* (path) is a term related to space, but is used for denoting the time-span of the cycle of a given *tāla* and this span has basically three degrees, each successive one being the double of the previous one, as follows:

	Name	Measure of basic unit, viz. *kāla*
1.	*citra mārga*	One *guru* or two *mātrās*
2.	*vṛtti* or *vārttika mārga*	Two *gurus* or four *mātrās*
3.	*dakṣiṇa mārga*	Four *gurus* or eight *mātrās*

The fourth *mārga* named *dhruva* has been added by **Saṅgīta-Ratnākara**, the *kāla* being equal to one *mātrā* there, but basically the number of *mārgas* continued to be three. **Bṛhaddeśī** (p.52, 53) mentions a fifth *mārga* named *śūnya-mārga*, which could be understood to be the half of *dhruva-mārga* thus bringing down the duration of *kāla* to one-half of a *mātrā*.

The above verse of **Saṅgīta-Ratnākara** says that *laya* becomes manifold on account of *mārga*. Kallinātha explains this and the gist of his commentary is given below:

Mārga is the equivalent to path and *laya* could be understood to be the pace of the one who treads on the path. If there are three paths leading to a particular place, each one being the double of the previous one, the treader on the shortest path will reach the destination in the shortest time, the one who treads the second path that is double in length as compared to the first one, would take double the time taken by the first one, provided he walks at the same pace. The one who treads on the third path which is double the time taken by the second treader, provided his pace is the same as that of the second treader. Even though all the three treaders are walking at equal pace, the first one reaches first of all on account of the shortness of his path, but he gives a feeling of having reached soon. The second treader gives the feeling of having reached in still longer time as compared to the first one. Thus the length of *mārga* tends to arouse a feeling of slower or faster or medium pace (*laya*) even though in reality there is no variation in the latter. There is also the possibility of the treader on each path walking at fast, medium or slow pace. Thus each *mārga* could have three *layas*: 3 x 3 = 9. The *laya* being manifested in linguistic units like syllable, word and sentence, has been said to be out of context. The idea appears to be that in dialogue or soliloquy (in drama) the length or shortness of rests in-between syllables, words and sentences is definitely perceived, but since there is no *tāla* structure involved there, technically *laya* would not be relevant.

The importance of *viśrānti* or rest in the process of measuring time (→*māna*) is highlighted in the following passage of **Saṅgīta-Ratnākara**:

विश्रान्तियुक्तया काले क्रियया मानमिष्यते ।

SR V.43cd

Māna (measurement) in (or of) time is accepted (lit. desired) through action accompanied by rest.

The concepts of *mārga* and *yati* are directly related to *laya* and they are explained in the following passages of **Nāṭya-Śāstra** and **Saṅgīta-Ratnākara**. Whatever has been said above with regard to music, applies also to dance.

स्रोतोगता च गोपुच्छा समा चात्र विधाय च ॥
लयप्रवृत्तवर्णानामक्षराणामथापि च ।
नियमो यो यतिः सा तु गीतवाद्यसमाश्रया ॥

NŚ XXXI.371cd-372ab

अत्र लये विशेषणतया या यतिः सा त्रिधा ।... गीतवर्णानां स्थाय्यादीनां वाद्ये चाक्षराणां झुण्टुंकटकथादीनां सम्बन्धिनां या लयप्रवृत्तिर्लयविशेषो द्रुतादिस्तयोपलक्षितो यो नियमः सा यतिः । क्रमेण गीताश्रया वाद्याश्रया च ।... तत्र प्रथमभागे विलम्बितस्य यावदन्ते द्रुतस्य नियम इति स्रोतो-वद्गमनात्तथा यतिरुक्ता एतद्विपर्ययाद्गोपुच्छा ताद्रूप्यादेव । यस्तु प्रथमे तावद्यतिनिर्वाहपर्यन्ता स एव लयो नियमः सा समा । तत्रासां क्रमेण द्रुतविलम्बितमध्याः प्राधान्याशयेन विषय उच्यते ।परमार्थतस्त्रिष्वपि तिस्र इति ।एवं नियमविशिष्टो लयस्ताल इति यावत् ।अत एव नियमांशस्यैव प्राधान्याल्लोके यतिरिति ताद्रूप्यव्यवहारः ।

AbhiBhā on above

The regulation of *varṇas* (units of melodic movement) and *akṣaras* (syllables used in identification of the strokes, or instruments) that move in *laya*, is known as *yati* sustained by song and instruments. (This *yati* is threefold; viz.) *srotogatā, gopucchā* and *samā*.

Commentary:

The *yati* that qualifies *laya* is threefold. The specific order of *laya* that is manifested in the *varṇas* (units of melodic movement) in *gīta* (song or melodic content of music) such as *sthāyin* (steady, the first of the four *varṇas*) and instruments through syllable, like *jhuṇṭuṃ kaṭa-katha* etc., starting with *druta* (fast) and the like, is known as *yati* standing for the regulation of that (order). This *yati* is sustained in song and instruments respectively (in relation to melodic unit and syllabic sound). *Srotogatā* (lit. associated with the flow of water) is known as such because of its movement, like the flow of water that begins in slow (speed) and ends up with fast (movement), *gopucchā* (the cow's tail) is the reverse (of *srotogatā*, i.e. fast in the beginning and slow in the end) and is known as such because of identical form (the cow's tail being thin on top and big at the end, implying the cluster of hair). That which implies the continuation of one and the same *laya* from the beginning to the end is *samā*. Thus those three (*yatis*) are said to be associated with fast, slow and medium respectively. But in reality each one of the three *yatis* can be formed in all the three *layas*. The *laya* regulated in this way is *tāla*. Since regulation is predominant here (in *yati*), in general usage (*loka*) the word *yati* is used (for an ascetic who has restrained his passions).

The idea that each *yati* could operate in three *layas* has been worked out in the following passage of **Saṅgīta-Ratnākara**.

लयप्रवृत्तिनियमो यतिरित्यभिधीयते ॥
समा स्रोतोगता चान्या गोपुच्छा त्रिविधेति सा ।
आदिमध्यावसानेषु लयैकत्वे समा त्रिधा ॥
लयत्रैध्यादादिमध्यावसानेषु यथाक्रमात् ।
चिरमध्यद्रुतलया तदा स्रोतोगता मता ॥
अन्या विलम्बमध्याभ्यां मध्यद्रुतवती परा ।
द्रुतमध्यविलम्बैः स्याद्गोपुच्छा द्रुतमध्यभाक् ॥
द्वितीयान्या भवेन्मध्यविलम्बितलयान्विता ।

SR V.46cd-50ab

The regulation of the order of *laya* is called *yati* and that is threefold: viz. *samā, srotogatā* and *gopucchā*. *Samā* is of three types according to the threefold *laya*. (viz. fast, medium and slow), being of identical *laya* in the beginning, middle and end. *Srotogatā* is (again threefold) having slow, medium *laya* (in the beginning and end respectively) and another one having medium and fast (in the beginning and end respectively). *Gopucchā* is formed by (the order) fast, medium and slow (in the beginning, middle and end respectively), its second (variety) is formed by fast and medium and the other one is with medium and slow.

In literature, *laya* operates through metre or through syllable, word and sentence, as explained in **Nāṭya-Śāstra**. In architecture, sculpture and painting, the word *laya* is not used in the texts dealing with these Arts, but the English word rhythm is frequently used by great interpreters of Art like A.K. Coomaraswamy and Alice Boner. 'Rhythm' in this context could stand for *laya* or *chandas*. 'Rhythm' could be roughly equated with *laya* because the latter, being of the nature of the rest merging with action, brings about a regular pattern of pulsation in terms of time which could be extended in terms of space.

The following two extracts would be pertinent as they draw upon a similarity between *laya* in time that operates in music and rhythm in visual arts that operates in space.

"In these passages the spiritual significance of rhythm in art is plainly asserted. Conversely they are also of interest in connection with the problem of the origin of art, all rhythm corresponding in the last analysis to cosmic rhythms." (A.K. Coomaraswamy, The Transformation of Nature in Art, p. 179, note).

"And just as anatomy is expressed in simile, Divinity itself is expressed in an analogy of form, character and movement. Such transfigured form-language cannot be approached either discursively or sentimentally, for it directly touches our inner awareness of cosmic correspondences. Like notes and intervals in music, it awakens a response in us from the irrational depths of our being. Like music, it uses form in rhythmic sequences, in a subtle interplay of parallel and opposite movements, resulting in a closely knit harmony, which instead of evolving in time, spreads itself out in space. In these free rhythms is echoed the rhythm of the universe". (Alice Boner, "The Symbolic Aspect of Form" in Alice Boner: Artist and Scholar, p. 105).

In the creative process of any Art, the contemplative component could be described through the word *laya* implying complete dissolution of all distractions, and similarly in the receptive process also the *laya* or dissolution of subject-object dichotomy is a normal condition.

Process

The process in the context of *laya* could be visualised in 1) the spiritual *sādhanā* prescribed in Haṭhayoga, Vedānta and Yoga, 2) the reverse order of dissolution, as compared to the process of creation described above under 'Development of the Concept' and 3) hastening and slowing down in music.

Conclusion

Thus *laya* as dissolution is an inevitable companion of creation, as death it is an inescapable follower of birth, as sleep it is unavoidable in relation to the state of awakening, and in music it is the rest embracing action, as the state of liberation it is the merging of the individual in the Supreme. Merging is the essence of *laya* in any given context. The above pairs imply a continuum and not a cut-out point at any level.

Prem Lata Sharma

Select Bibliography

Bäumer, B.: Alice Boner – Artist and Scholar. Varanasi: Bharat Kala Bhavana, 1990.

Coomaraswamy, A.K.: The Dance of Shiva. New Delhi: Munshiram Manoharlal, 1974.

Lipsey, Roger (ed.): Coomaraswamy – Selected Papers, Vol. I, Traditional Art and Symbolism. Delhi: Oxford University Press, 1986.

—Coomaraswamy – Selected Papers, Vol. II – Metaphysics. Princeton: Princeton University Press, 1977.

ŚŪNYA/ŚŪNYATĀ

Overview

Śūnya means void, devoid of, empty, zero, and *śūnyatā* denotes the doctrine of emptiness propounded by Buddhism. It is the emptiness of space which is a condition for the appearance of any object, just as the number zero, being no number at all, is the condition for all the numbers. Therefore zero (*śūnya*) and infinite (*ananta*) have been identified.

I. In mathematical usage *śūnya* denotes zero which has been taken as the basis of the decimal system. India's contribution to mathematics and science is the discovery of the zero.

II. In Buddhism, *śūnyatā* does not denote nihilism, but the negation of all affirmative statements about the world. It corresponds to a spiritual experience and to the practice of emptying the mind from all impressions. The doctrine of *śūnyatā* has found its full development in Nāgārjuna.

III. The dominant note of the Vedic religion and thought was that of fullness (→*pūrṇa*), but the idea of the void as a spiritual state is equally present in the Hindu Tantras which describe several stages of *śūnya* in the spiritual development (cf. Śaivāgamas and Kashmir Śaivism).

In the Arts the idea of *śūnya/śūnyatā* is important in the context of the aesthetic experience, and in the creative act. The creation of poetry, of a painting or a musical composition has to come out of a vacant state of the mind of the artist. This corresponds to the visualization of a deity in Tāntric Buddhist practice, as described in the **Hevajra Tantra**:

प्रथमं शून्यताबोधिं द्वितीयं बीजसंग्रहम् ।
तृतीयं बिम्बनिष्पत्तिं चतुर्थन्न्यासमक्षरम् ॥

HT I.3.2

First the realization of the void,
secondly the seed in which all is concentrated,
thirdly the physical manifestation,
and fourthly one should implant the syllable. (Tr. D.L. Snellgrove)

Whether the process is that of representing the deity in an image or of visualizing its form in the inner imagination, the same creative process is involved which starts precisely from the state of the void (cf. also **Sādhanamālā**).

The architect who builds a temple has to deal with and organize empty space. It is not the walls which make a building but the empty spaces created by the walls. As A.K. Coomaraswamy puts it: "In order to understand the use of terms for 'space' (*kha, ākāśa, antarikṣa, śūnya*, etc.) as verbal symbols of zero (which represents privation of number, and is yet a matrix of number in the sense 0 = x - x), it must be realized that *ākāśa*, etc., represent primarily a concept not of physical space, but of a purely principial space without dimensions, though the matrix of dimension." (A.K. Coomaraswamy, "*Kha* and Other Words Denoting 'Zero'...", in: Selected Papers, Vol. 2, p. 225).

Etymology

The word *śūnya* has been derived from *śūna* which Pāṇini recognizes as the past participle of *śvi-*, 'to go, to grow', generally 'to swell'. *Śuna*, then, should mean 'swollen' or 'grown' but in its occurrences in the **Ṛgveda** it also seems to have the sense of 'lack or deficiency'. It is possible that there were two different words originally but being of similar form they were fused giving a single sense of 'absence or emptiness'. But the word *śūnya* does not occur in the classical Upaniṣads except that the probably later **Maitreyī Upaniṣad** (II.27) seeks to identify the *śūnya* with the *pūrṇa*.

The word *śūnya* means void, empty (*śūnyaṃ tu vaśikaṃ tucchariktake*, AmKo III.1.56). The **Amarakośa** gives four synonyms of *śūnya* meaning void, empty, worthless and absent. This is illustrated by Cāṇakya in the following verse:

> अविद्याजीवनं शून्यं दिक्शून्या चेदबान्धवा ।
> पुत्रहीनं गृहं शून्यं सर्वशून्या दरिद्रता ॥
>
> Cāṇakya Śat 47
>
> Life is useless if one lacks knowledge, the direction is aimless if one does not have any friends and relatives, to one who is without a son his house is desolate, everything is void to the poor. (Tr. H.N. Chakravarty)

In the neuter the term *śūnya* denotes the void of the sky (→*ākāśa, kha, vyoman*).

Editor

I. Śūnya: Mathematical Aspect

In Indian mathematics, *śūnya* denotes zero. The nine numbers (*aṅka*) from 1 to 9, together with the zero, constitute the basis of the decimal place-value system which is universally followed today. It is generally agreed that this system originated in India. Likewise the ten numeral symbols emanated from India, though they are now known as Arabic numerals after the chief mediators in the transmission of these symbols from India to the western world.

A discussion of the mathematical aspect of *śūnya* involves three questions: the concept and synonyms of *śūnya* within the decimal place-value system, secondly the symbols used for *śūnya* and thirdly its mathematical functions.

Concept of Zero

While the numbers 1 to 9 are common to many other numeral systems, it is the concept of *śūnya* along with its symbol known as *bindu* that makes the Indian numeral system a truly place-value system, without which the great advances made in modern mathematics are unthinkable. Here *śūnya* denotes the notational place as well as the 'void' or the absence of numerical value in a particular notational place. Consequently all numerical quantities, howsoever great they may be, can be represented with just these ten symbols. Writing in the twelfth century, King Someśvara declares in his **Mānasollāsa** thus:

एकाद्या नवपर्यन्ता नवैवाङ्का स्वरूपतः ।
दशोत्तरक्रमेणैव वर्धन्ते बिन्दुवर्धिताः ॥

Mānaso II.97

Basically, there are only nine digits starting from 'one' and reaching up to 'nine'. By the addition of zeros (*bindus*) these are raised successively to (represent the notational places of) tens, (hundreds) and beyond.

In Vedic literature, there are already several sets of names for the numbers, arranged in a progressive geometrical series where each number is ten times larger than the preceding. Thus the Vājasaneyī recension of the **Yajur-Veda** enumerates in the following passage the names of thirteen decimal places, viz. *eka* (10^0), *daśa* (10^1), *śata* (10^2), *sahasra* (10^3), *ayuta* (10^4), *niyuta* (10^5), *prayuta* (10^6), *arbuda* (10^7), *nyarbuda* (10^8), *samudra* (10^9), *madhya* (10^{10}), *anta* (10^{11}) and *parārdha* (10^{12}) :

इमा मे अग्न इष्टका धेनवः सन्तु । एका च दश च, दश च शतं च, शतं च सहस्रं च, सहस्रं चायुतं चायुतं च नियुतं च, नियुतं च प्रयुतं चार्बुदं च न्यर्बुदं च समुद्रश्च मध्यं चान्तश्च परार्धश्चैता मे अग्न इष्टका धेनवः सन्त्वमुत्रामुष्मिँल्लोके ।

YV XVII.2

O Agni, may these bricks(used in sacrifice) turn into (milk-yielding) cows for me; one(*eka*) and a ten, a ten(*daśa*) and a hundred, a hundred (*śata*) and a thousand, a thousand (*sahasra*) and a ten-thousand, a ten thousand(*ayuta*) and a hundred-thousand, a hundred-thousand(*niyuta*) and a million(*prayuta*), a ten-million (*arbuda*), a hundred-million (*nyarbuda*), a thousand-million (*samudra*), ten-thousand-million (*madhya*), a hundred thousand-million (*anta*), a million-million (*parārdha*). May these bricks become mine own cows in this and in the other world.

Obviously this decuple terminology gave rise to the decimal place-value system, but it is difficult to say how old the place-value system is and when the concept of zero originated. Perhaps the genesis has to be sought in some type of abacus or counting board with columns or spaces for decimal notational places. The word *gaṇitra*, a *hapax legomenon* occurring in the Jyotiṣka story of the **Divyāvadāna** (Darbhanga 1959, p.163) may have denoted such a counting board. Emptiness in any column meant the absence of numerical value in that particular notational place, and this emptiness was indicated by the word *śūnya* or by one of its synonyms.

The synonyms commonly used for *śūnya* in mathematical and astronomical texts are *ākāśa*, *ambara*, *kha*, *gagana* and the like for the *ākāśa* is conceived to be emptiness. Occasionally *ananta* is also used, not in the sense of the infinite but as another synonym for *ākāśa*. Other synonyms for *śūnya* are →*pūrṇa*, →*bindu*, *chidra* and *randhra*. The last three actually describe the symbols used for *śūnya*, viz. a small dot (*bindu*) and a small circle as used today (*chidra*, *randhra*).

The earliest mention of a symbol for zero occurs in the **Chandaḥ-Sūtra** of Piṅgala. In this text, Piṅgala teaches a method for calculating the number of arrangements of long and short syllables in a metre containing a certain number of syllables. In modern mathematical parlance, this is the number of combinations of two things in 'n' places, repetition being allowed, which is equal to 2^n. Piṅgala lays down the procedure in short obscure aphorisms:

द्विरर्धे । रूपे शून्यम् । द्विः शून्ये । तावदर्धे गुणितम् ।

Chandaḥsūtra 8.28-31

(First write down the number of syllables in the given metre and go on halving that number. Each time) when (the number is) halved, (write down in a separate row or column the digit) two.

(When you reach an odd number, subtract one from it.) Whenever one (is subtracted, write down in the separate row a) zero.

(Continue thus until the process stops. Then where you wrote a) zero (multiply by) two.

Where (the number was) halved, multiply (the result of the second process) by itself.

It is beyond the scope of this article to explain Piṅgala's method in detail. What is relevant is the fact that in this computation Piṅgala uses the symbols for zero and two as markers for distinguishing between two kinds of operations. The symbol of two marks the places where there is an even number which is divided by 2 and where squaring has to be done later; the symbol of zero marks the places where there is an odd number and consequently absence of halving, and where multiplication by 2 has to be performed. Thus the two symbols were used here in a meaningful way, but the whole computation can be done without any markers at all or with any two arbitrary symbols. The fact, however, that Piṅgala uses them goes to show the existence of a well-recognised symbol for zero at his time, which is variously placed between 400 to 200 B.C.

Joseph Needham observes that "Place-value could and did exist without any symbol for zero... But the zero symbol as part of the numerical system never existed and could not have come into being without place-value" (Science and Civilisation in China, vol.III, p.10n). We do not know what kind of zero symbol was used at Piṅgala's time, but the invention of the place-value system along with concept and symbol of zero must antedate considerably his mention of the zero symbol. A clear reference, however, to the place-value is made in the Jaina canonical text **Anuyogadvāra** (ca. 100 B. C., but this date is contested) where the number of human beings in the world is stated to occupy twentynine notational places (*sūtra* 142: *egūṇatīsaṃ-ṭhāṇāi*=Sanskrit, *ekonatriṃśat sthānāni*).

Thus there is enough indirect evidence to say that the decimal place-value system with symbols for 1 to 9 and zero developed in India much before the beginning of the Christian era. But in the early centuries of this era epigraphic records still continued to use the old system of numerals without place-value.

In the extant mathematical and astronomical literature, however, place-value is implicit throughout, even if it is not directly employed. Thus in his **Āryabhaṭīya** (A.D. 499). Āryabhaṭa-I uses a complex numerical notation but his method of extracting square-roots and cube-roots is possible only in the decimal place-value system. Again, in the following stanza where he explains his peculiar method of expressing numbers with the letters of the alphabet, he clearly mentions the zero symbol:

खद्विनवाङ्के स्वरा नव वर्गेऽवर्गे ...

Āryabhaṭīya I.2

In the place of two nines of zeros (which are written to denote the notational places), the nine vowels should be written (one vowel in each pair of *varga* and *avarga* places)... (Tr. K.S. Shukla)

Āryabhaṭa's alphabetical system of notation is not of immediate relevance here, but his instruction to write down nine pairs of zeros (*kha*) first, in order to denote 18 notational places is interesting. This alludes to an old practice as Bhāskara-I explains in his commentary on the **Āryabhaṭīya** (II.2). In fact, even in recent times, children were taught the decimal notational places by means of a row of zeros written in the following manner:

0 0 0 0 0 0 0 0 0 0

The teacher pointed to the first zero on the right and explained that it was the units place, the next zero as the tens place, the next as the hundreds place and so on (Datta and Singh, History of Hindu Mathematics: A Source Book, p. 82).

In other texts there are unambiguous instances where the word *śūnya* or its synonyms were used in the decimal place-value system. A few examples may be given here. About a century prior to the **Āryabhaṭīya**, the **Puliśasiddhānta** is said to have contained the following stanza, now available only as a quotation in Bhaṭṭotpala's commentary on Varāhamihira's **Bṛhatsaṃhitā** (Varanasi, Vol. I, p. 27):

ख-खाष्ट-मुनि-रामाश्वि-नेत्राष्ट-शर-रात्रिपाः ।
भानां चतुर्युगेणैते परिवर्त्ताः प्रकीर्तिताः ॥

The sidereal revolutions in four *yugas* are stated to be (the number expressed by) zero (*kha*), zero (*kha*) eight (*aṣṭa*), seven (*muni*), three (*rāma*), two (*aśvin*), two (*netra*), eight (*aṣṭa*), five (*śara*), and one (*rātripa*) (read serially from the left, i.e. 1,582,237,800).

A clear and unambiguous mention of the zero in association with the decimal place-value occurs in Sarvanandi's **Lokavibhāga** (Ch.4, Line 56, p.79):

पञ्चभ्यः खलु शून्येभ्यः ।
परं द्वे सप्त चाम्बरमेकं त्रीणि च रूपं च ॥

After five zeros, there are two (*dve*), seven(*sapta*), zero(*ambara*), one(*eka*), three(*trīṇi*) and one(*rūpa*), (that is to say, 13,107,200,000).

The **Lokavibhāga** mentions the date of its completion as Śaka 380 bhādra kṛṣṇa 15, which corresponds to Monday, 25th August 458 A. D. This, then is the earliest dated occurrence of the zero known to us.

In Varāhamihira's **Pañcasiddhāntikā** (ca A.D. 550), *śūnya* and its synonyms occur often, as in I.17:

मुनि-यम-यम-द्वियुक्ते द्युगणे शून्य-द्वि-पञ्च-यम-भक्ते ।
प्रतिराशि खर्तु-दहनैर्लब्धं वर्षाणि यातानि ॥

Increase the *ahargaṇa* by 2227 and divide (the sum) by 2510; with respect to the (remaining) amount, divide it by 360; the quotient is the number of lapsed years... (Tr. D. Pingree)

In his **Bṛhat-kṣetra-samāsa** (A.D. 609), Jinabhadra Gaṇi Kṣamāśramaṇa offers conclusive evidence of the use of zero as a distinct numerical symbol. When he has to write large numbers such as 224,400,000,000, he expresses them succinctly as "twentytwo, fortyfour, eight zeros" (I.69) or 3,200,400,000,000 as "thirtytwo, two zeros, four, eight zeros"(I.71).

Siddhasena Gaṇi (6th century), in his commentary on Umāsvāti's **Tattvārthādhigamasūtra** (III.11), makes an interesting use of the **inherent decimal** property of *śūnya*:

> शेषमिदं भवति ३,५३४,४००,०००,००० । अस्य मूलमादीयते । शून्याष्टकार्धेन चत्वारि शून्यानि शेषस्य मूलमेकाष्टकाष्टकैर्लब्धमिदं १,८८०,००० ।
>
> ... the remainder is this: 3,534,400,000,000. The square-root of this is extracted; half of eight zeros are four zeros; the root of the remaining part is one-eight-eight; hence the resulting root is 1,880,000. (Tr. B. Datta and A.V. Singh)

This example shows that Siddhasena understood that the *śūnya* is not only a symbol for the absence of numerical value in a particular notational place but that it also indicates the tenth multiple inherent in the notational place.

By the second century A.D., even outside the realm of mathematics the idea of the decimal place-value and consequently of the numerical value of any digit depending upon the notational place was so well rooted that this fact was used to elucidate philosophical notions. In his **Abhidharmakośabhāṣya**, Vasubandhu(fifth century A. D.) cites Vasumitra's view in the following passage (p.296) :

> अवस्थान्यथिको भगन्तवसुमित्रः। स किलाह। धर्मोऽध्वसु प्रवर्तमानोऽवस्थामवस्थां प्राप्यान्यो निर्दिश्यते, अवस्थान्तरतो न द्रव्यान्तरतः। यथैका वर्तिका एकाङ्के निक्षिप्ता एकमित्युच्यते, शताङ्के शतं, सहस्राङ्के सहस्रमिति।
>
> Abhidh Ko Bh V.26
>
> Bhadanta Vasumitra held the view of the otherness of the state. He is reported to have stated (as follows). A dharma evolving in the (three) times is designated as other whenever it enters a different state; (this change in designation is) due to the otherness of the state and not due to the otherness of the substance; just as a marker or counter is called one when it is placed in the unit's place, a hundred in the hundred's place, and a thousand in the thousand's place.

It may be noted that this view is attributed to Vasumitra and the wording purports to be his. According to D. Seyfort Ruegg who discusses this passage, "Vasumitra is ... probably to be identified as one of the leading figures at the time of Kaniṣka's Great Council." ("Mathematical and linguistics Models in Indian Thought," p.173). Accordingly, Vasumitra must have flourished in the last quarter of the first century and the first quarter of the second century A. D.

This metaphor of the changing value of a numeral digit according to its place is employed in several other philosophical texts. Thus it is said in the **Vyāsabhāṣya** (bet. A.D. 650 to 850) on the **Yogasūtra:**

> यथैका रेखा शतस्थाने शतं दशस्थाने दशैकं चैकस्थाने तथा चैकत्वेऽपि स्त्री माता चोच्यते दुहिता च स्वसा चेति ।
>
> YSūBh III.13
>
> Just as the same stroke is termed a hundred in the hundreds place, ten in the tens place and one in the units place, so is one and the same woman referred to as mother, daughter or sister.

Vijñānabhikṣu emphasises the role of the *bindu* in determining the numerical value of a digit in his commentary on the above passage:

> यथैकत्वव्यञ्जिका रेखा अङ्कविशेषो यदा बिन्दुद्वयोपरि तिष्ठति तदा शतमिदं नैकमिति व्यवह्रियते, तयोरेकबिन्दुलोपे च दशेदं न शतमिति व्यवह्रियते, अवशिष्टबिन्दुस्थाने चैकत्वव्यञ्जकरेखान्तरदाने सत्येकादशेदं न दशेत्यर्थः।
>
> Yogavārttika on YSūBh III.13
>
> Just as, when the special stroke denoting the digit one stands to the left of two zeros, it is known as a hundied and not as one, when one of the two zeros is removed, it is known as ten and not (any more) as hundred, and when in the place of the remaining zero another stroke denoting the number one is marked, it is known as eleven and not ten...

Śaṅkara also makes use of this metaphor in his commentary on the **Brahma-Sūtra:**

यथैकोऽपि सन् देवदत्तो लोके स्वरूपं सम्बन्धिरूपं चापेक्ष्यानेकशब्दप्रत्यय-भागभवति मनुष्यो ब्राह्मणः श्रोत्रियो वदान्यो बालो युवा स्थविरः पिता पुत्रः पौत्रो भ्राता जामातेति तथा चैकापि रेखा स्थानान्यत्वेन निविशमानैक-दश-शत-सहस्रादिशब्दप्रत्ययभेदमनुभवति ।

BrSūBh II.2.17

Devadatta, although being one only, forms the object of many different names and notions according as he is considered in himself or in his relation to others: thus he is thought and spoken of as man, *brāhmaṇa*, learned in the Veda, generous, boy, young man, old man, father, son, grandson, brother, son-in-law, etc., so again, one and the same stroke is, according to the place it is connected with, spoken of and conceived as meaning either one, ten or hundred or thousand etc. (Tr. P.J. Deussen)

Symbols of Zero

As we have stated above, of the various synonyms of *śūnya*, *bindu* and *chidra/randhra* refer to two kinds of symbols used for representing the zero. Of these, *bindu* or dot is the earlier one; later its place was taken by a small circle (*chidra* or *randhra*, lit. "hole"). In the case of *anusvāra* also an analogous change occurred in Kannaḍa-Telugu script. In early inscriptions, the *anusvāra* was represented by a small dot, often hardly visible on the copper plates. Gradually it was replaced by the small circle, which is called *sunna* in Telugu (from Sanskrit *śūnya*) since it was identical with the symbol of *śūnya*.

There are no clear evidences to say when the change from the dot to the circle took place. In the extant records, the earliest instance of the zero symbol occurs in the eighth century Rāgholi plates of Jayavardhana II, where a tiny dot was used in writing the number 30. Clearly drawn circles appear in the next century in the Gwalior plates of Bhojadeva belonging to the years A.D. 870 and 876.

Interestingly enough, zero symbols appear some two hundred years prior to this in South-East Asia. In the inscriptions found at Cambodia and Sumatra, the Śaka year 605 (=A.D. 683) is written in the decimal system and the zero is represented by a dot. In another inscription from Banka Island, a small circle was used for recording the date, viz. Śaka 608 (= A.D. 686). Obviously the Indian settlers carried with them both the symbols for zero from India, as they did carry the Sanskrit language, word numerals, decimal system, the Śaka era, and so on.

It may thus be concluded that both the zero symbols were in use in India in the sixth century and that the circular symbol must have been invented by this century at the latest. The change, however, was not simultaneous everywhere.

The dot seems to have prevailed longer in Gandhāra and Kaśmīra regions. Thus in the mathematical text known as the Bakhshālī Manuscript and in the unique manuscript copy of an anonymous commentary on Śrīdhara's **Pāṭīgaṇita**, both written in an early form of the Śāradā script sometime after the ninth century, the zero was represented by the dot.

Even after the dot was replaced by the circle, the symbol continued to be called *śūnya-bindu* or *bindu*, as the passages cited above from the **Mānasollāsa** and **Yogavārttika** show. Therefore, when *śūnya-bindu* is mentioned occasionally in literary works, it is difficult to decide whether the dot or the circle is meant. In Subandhu's **Vāsavadattā** (ca. A.D. 400), we meet with the earliest occurrence of the expression, and here it may have been the dot, since the poet compares the stars in the sky with zeros on a dark writing medium:

> विश्वं गणयतो विधातुः शशिकठिनीखण्डेन तमोमषीश्यामेऽजिन इव वियति
> संसारस्यातिशून्यत्वाच्छून्यबिन्दव इव विलिखिताः ... तारा अराजन्त ।
>
> Vāsavadattā (Chowkhamba edition, p.168)
>
> ... the stars shone forth, ... like zero dots (*śūnya-bindu*) because of the nullity of metempsychosis, scattered in the sky as if on the ink-blue skin rug of the Creator who reckoneth the sum total with a bit of the moon for the chalk. (Tr. Louis H. Gray)

On the other hand, in Śrīharṣa's (12th century) description of the King Nala, the *śūnya-bindus* may be small circles, as here the pores on the skin are seen as zeros:

> किमस्य लोम्नां कपटेन कोटिभिर्विधिर्न लेखाभिरजीगणद् गुणान् ।
> न रोमकूपौघमिषाज्जगत्कृता कृताश्च किं दूषणशून्यबिन्दवः ॥
>
> Naiṣadhīyacarita I.21
>
> Did not the creator reckon his merits with crores of lines, the hairs of the body? Did not the maker of the world put the pores of his skin for zeros to indicate the absence of defects? (Tr. K.K. Handiqi)

Indian numerals reached the Middle East through the mediation of the Arabs, though nothing definite is known about the precise period and the path. Among the Arabs, these numerals were known as *Hindasā*. Already in 662, the Syrian scholar Severus Sebokht speaks highly of the Hindus' "valuable methods of calculation; and their computing that surpasses description. I wish only to say that this computation is done by means of nine signs." The Indian numerals known to Sebokht must have contained the zero also, for without it and without the implied decimal place-value system, the nine signs would not have been any improvement over Roman numerals.

Through his **Liber Abaci** (A.D. 1202), Leonardo Fibonacci of Pisa popularised the Indian numerals including the zero in Europe. In this passage from India to Europe, the word *śūnya* underwent many transformations: it became *aṣ-ṣifr* or *ṣifr* in Arabic, *zephizum* in Fibonacci's Latin and finally gave rise to the forms 'zero' and 'cipher'.

Mathematical Functions of Zero

Sanskrit texts on mathematics usually contain a section called *śūnya-gaṇita*, i.e. computations involving zero. While the discussion in the arithmetical texts (*pāṭīgaṇita*) is limited only to the addition, subtraction and multiplication with zero, the treatment in algebra (*bījagaṇita*) covers also such questions as the effect of zero on the positive and negative signs, division with zero, and more particularly the relation between zero (*śūnya*) and infinity (*khahara* = *ananta*).

Brahmagupta, an outstanding mathematician and astronomer of the seventh century, was the first to discuss exhaustively the mathematical functions of zero in his **Brāhmasphuṭa-Siddhānta** (18.30-35). By treating the zero as a separate entity from the positive (*dhana*) and negative (*ṛṇa*) quantities, he implies that *śūnya* is neither positive nor negative but forms the boundary line between the two kinds. It is the sum of two equal but opposite quantities (*dhanarṇayoḥ samaikyaṃ kham*). Brahmagupta states that a number, whether positive or negative, remains unchanged when zero is added to or subtracted from it. In multiplication with zero, the product is zero. A zero divided by zero or by some number becomes zero. Likewise the square and the square-root of zero is zero. But when a number is divided by zero, the quotient is an undefinable quantity, which Brahmagupta designates elliptically as *taccheda*, "that which has that (sci. zero) as the denominator".

Though his formulation "zero divided by zero is zero" will not be accepted today, Brahmagupta did in fact cover almost all mathematical functions of *śūnya*. Mathematicians who came after him took up his concept of *taccheda* and developed it further. Thus Śrīpati (fl. 1039-1056) replaces the word *taccheda* with a more expressive term *khahara*, "that which has zero (*kha*) as the divisor":

विकारमायान्ति धनर्णकानि न शून्यसंयोगवियोगतस्तु ।
शून्याद्विशुद्धं स्वमृणं क्षयं स्वं वधादिना खं खहरं विभक्तम् ॥

Siddhāntaśekhara XIV.6

Numbers, both positive and negative, undergo no change when zero is added to or subtracted from them. But when substracted from zero, a positive number becomes negative and a negative number positive. (A number) when multiplied (by zero becomes) zero; and when divided (by zero becomes) *khahara*.

The celebrated Bhāskarācārya of the twelfth century explains that this *khahara* is an infinite quantity (*ananto rāśiḥ*). What then is an infinite number? Bhāskara resorts to a significant analogy while elucidating the nature of *khahara*:

अस्मिन् विकारः खहरे राशावपि प्रवेष्टेष्वपि निःसृतेषु ।
बहुष्वपि स्याल्लयसृष्टिकालेऽनन्तेऽच्युते भूतगणेषु यद्वत् ॥

Bījagaṇita, verse 20

In this numerical quantity called khahara, there will be no change whether much is added to it or subtracted from it, just as no change takes place in the infinite and immutable godhead, though numerous beings are absorbed in it at the time of the destruction of the worlds or numerous beings issue forth from it at the time of the creation of the worlds.

Bhāskara's commentator, Kṛṣṇa Daivajña offers, at the beginning of the seventeenth century, the rationale for the multiplication and division with zero. Explaining how in multiplication with zero the product becomes zero, Kṛṣṇa argues as follows:

गुण्यस्यापचयवशाद् गुणनफलस्यापचय इति तावत्प्रसिद्धम् ।...अनयैव युक्त्या गुण्यस्य परमापचये गुणनफलस्यापि परमापचयेन भाव्यम् । परमापचये शून्यतैव पर्यवस्यतीति शून्ये गुण्ये गुणनफलं शून्यमेवेति सिद्धम् ।...एवं गुणकापचयवशादपि गुणनफलेऽपचयाद् गुणकस्यापि शून्यत्वे गुणनफलं शून्यमेवेति सिद्धम् ।

Navāṅkurā Comm. on Bījagaṇita, p.18

It is quite well known that as the multiplicand is diminished, the product also diminishes by the same degree... By this logic, when the multiplicand is diminished to the utmost degree, the product also diminishes to the utmost degree. But the utmost reduction of a number results in its becoming *śūnya*. Hence, when the multiplicand is *śūnya*, it is obvious that the product will also be *śūnya* ... In the same manner, as the multiplier decreases, the product also decreases. Hence, when the multiplier is *śūnya* the product is also *śūnya*.

The same logic applies when a number is divided by zero:

यथा यथा भाजकापचयस्तथा तथा लब्धेरुपचयः । तथा सति भाजकाङ्के परमापचिते लब्धेः परमोपचयेन भाव्यम् । लब्धेश्चेदियत्तोच्येत तर्हि परमत्वं

न स्यात् ततोऽप्याधिक्यसम्भवात् । अतो लब्धेरियत्ता भाव एव परमत्वम्।
तदेवमुपपन्नं खहरो राशिरनन्त इति ।

Navāṅkurā Comm on Bījagaṇita p.19

As the divisor is diminished, the quotient increases in a like manner. This being so, when the divisor is diminished to the maximum limit, the quotient must also increase to the maximum limit. If it is specified that the quotient is so much, then the maximum limit is not reached, for a quantity greater than the (specified one) is possible. Therefore, the quotient reaches the maximum limit only when it is impossible to specify that it is so much. Thus it is established that the quantity called *khahara* is infinity.

Bhāskara's views are not fully developed, however, in one respect. Discussing the multiplication with zero, he states:

...खगुणः खं खगुणश्चिन्त्यश्च शेषविधौ ॥
शून्ये गुणके जाते खं हारश्चेत् पुनस्तदा राशिः ।
अविकृत एव ज्ञेयः ...

Līlāvatī, 45-46

The product of zero is zero. But if there remains an operation still to be performed, imagine (the product) to be a multiple of zero. For, zero having become the multiplier, should zero become afterwards the divisor as well, then the (original) quantity remains unchanged.

That is to say, $\underline{a}.0 = 0$ but $\frac{a.0}{0} = \underline{a}$.
This is based on the wrong assumption that the zero in the nominator and that in the denominator cancel out each other, leaving a unchanged. Modern interpreters like Datta and Singh wish to reconcile this position by treating the zero here as the infinitesimal, i.e. a quantity decreasing indefinitely without actually becoming zero, because while $\frac{a.0}{0}$ is not $\underline{a}$, $Lim_{\Sigma \to 0} \frac{a.\Sigma}{\Sigma} = \underline{a}$.

However, if Bhāskara's intention here is to discuss the infinitesimal, he does not distinguish it from zero, and in any case the whole discussion occurs in the middle of his treatment of zero.

Therefore, Nārāyaṇa Paṇḍita refutes this view of Bhāskara by saying that a quantity, once it becomes zero through multiplication, shall remain in that state even if it is subsequently divided by zero, just as a yogin remains in the state of bliss when once he attains it:

शून्याभ्यासवशात् खतामुपगतो राशिः पुनः खोद्धृतो
व्यावृत्तिं पुनरेव तन्मयतया न प्राकृतिं गच्छति ।
आत्माभ्यासवशादनन्तममलं चिद्रूपमानन्ददं
प्राप्य ब्रह्मपदं न संसृतिपथं योगी गरीमानिव ॥

Bījagaṇitāvataṃsa, p.6

Just as a great yogin, having attained, through meditation on the Ātman, the state of Brahman – a state that is infinite, untainted, blissful and of the nature of pure intelligence –, will not revert to the path of rebirth because he has been absorbed in that (Brahman), even so a (numerical) quantity, having itself become zero after multiplication by zero, will never revert to the original number, for it has been absorbed in that (zero).

S.R. Sarma

II. Śūnyatā: Buddhist

Pūrṇatā and Śūnyatā: Non-dualism and illusionism in Vedic thought

The Vedic ethos was centred in the idea of Fullness (→ *pūrṇa*) while it will be generally admitted that the Buddhist ethos finds its central idea in Emptiness or *śūnyatā*; this contrast often emphasized will be found in the sequel to be at least partly misleading. Vedic literature generally breathes the positive spirit of life-affirmation.

मधु वाता ऋतायते मधु क्षरन्ति सिन्धवः । माध्वीर्नः सन्त्वोषधीः ।

ṚV I.90.6

The winds waft sweets, the rivers pour sweets for the man who keeps the Law. (Tr. R.T.H. Griffith)

Vedic man prays to live a hundred autumns: *jīvema śaradaḥ śatam* (ṚV VII.66.16). The whole world is but a manifestation of the Divine, and God is the one reality without a second, universal being (*sat*) or Spirit (*ātman*), infinity (*bhūman*), bliss (*ānanda*), the Absolute or *Brahman. Pūrṇatā* or Fullness is nothing but the perfection or non-dual infinity of absolute being or *Brahman.* The limited being of Names and Forms is only the self-limitation of the Absolute. The created or phenomenal world is real but real only as an expression of *Brahman.* At least this was the usual understanding in Vedic orthodoxy, although the ambiguity implicit in the situation did lead to the occasional voicing of alternative stands. For the normal Vedic vision, not only is the ultimate reality full or self-sufficient but the phenomenal world too has its own kind of fullness or self-sufficiency wherein each phenomenon is integrated with the whole by a complex web of relationships so that the wise man who knows one thing may know all.

पूर्णमदः पूर्णमिदं पूर्णात् पूर्णमुदच्यते ।
पूर्णस्य पूर्णमादाय पूर्णमेवावशिष्यते ॥

BṛUp V.1.1

That is perfect and this is perfect. From the perfect does the perfect emerge. Although perfection is borrowed from the perfect, the original perfection remains as ever.

Optimism and activism were concomitants of this ethos of *pūrṇatā*:

ब्रह्मैवेदं विश्वमिदं वरिष्ठम्

MuṇḍUp II.2.11

(Brahma, indeed,) is this whole world, this widest extent.
(Tr. R.E. Hume)

को ह्येवान्यात् कः प्राण्यात् । यदेष आकाश आनन्दो न स्यात् ।

TUp II.7

Who would breathe, who would live, if there were not this bliss in space (*ākāśa*).

It is in ritual that the Vedic vision found its appropriate symbol enabling man to participate actively in the cosmic order. Manu says: ***karma-yogaśca vaidikāḥ*****. (Manusmṛti,** II.2d)

Even in Vedic thought *rūpa* had the sense of mere appearance or false appearance: "In every figure he hath been the model... Indra moves multiform by his illusions..." (*rūpaṃ rūpaṃ pratirūpo babhūva... Indro māyābhiḥ puru-rūpa īyate*, ṚV VI.47.18, Tr. R.T.H. Griffith).

Nāma, on the other hand, was an act or product of *vāc*, the primal expressiveness or creativity of consciousness. *Rūpa* or Form is what is determined by the self-affirmation of the Self under the veil of limitation, *per accidens*. *Nāma* and *rūpa*, thus, are tinged with limitation and hence, illusion. Although grounded in *Brahman*, the world presents a delusive appearance. "The modification is merely a verbal distinction, a name." (*vācārambhaṇaṃ vikāro nāmadheyam*, ChUp VI.1.4). "A covering of what is false."(*anṛtena hi pratyūḍhaḥ*, ChUp VIII.3.2). "There is no difference here at all." (*neha nānāsti kiñcana*, KaṭhUp II.4.11).

Since the real is eternal and non-dual, the fleeting world of duality can only be regarded as unreal and illusory. The transcendence of *Brahman* then overshadows his immanence. This tends to devalue empirical life and activity including ritual.

तमेतं वेदानुवचनेन ब्राह्मणा विविदिषन्ति यज्ञेन दानेन तपसाऽनाशकेन ।
एतमेव विदित्वा मुनिर्भवति । एतमेव प्रव्रजिनो लोकमिच्छन्तः प्रव्रजन्ति ।
एतद्ध स्म वै तत् पूर्वे विद्वांसः प्रजां न कामयन्ते । किं प्रजया करिष्यामो

येषां नोऽयमात्माऽयं लोक इति । ते ह स्म पुत्रैषणायाश्च वित्तैषणायाश्च लोकैषणायाश्च व्युत्थायाथ भिक्षाचर्यं चरन्ति ।... स एष नेति नेत्यात्मा ।
BṛUp IV.4.22

> The Brāhmaṇas seek to know It through the study of the Vedas, sacrifices, charity and austerity consisting in a dispassionate enjoyment of sense objects. Knowing It alone one becomes a sage. Desiring this world (the Self) alone monks renounce their homes. This is (the reason for it) the ancient sages, it is said, did not desire children (thinking), 'What shall we achieve through children, we who have attained this Self, this world (result).' They, it is said, renounced their desire for sons, for wealth and for the worlds, and lived a mendicant life.... This Self is that which is described as 'Not this, not this'. (Tr. Mādhavānanda)

Thus while the sense of divine immanence, of God shining through all things, had led to an optimistic and active life-affirmation, the sense of the utter Transcendence of reality turning all things into mere shadows leads to dispassion and renunciation. The former experience is essentially an exalted, intuitive feeling in which the passing and limited object is valued as an experience of what is eternal and unlimited; the latter arises essentially from an intellectual conviction that what is delimited as 'this or this', what passes away, cannot be real, a conviction which is vouched for by the existential sense of dissatisfaction and suffering, the source of '*Weltschmerz*'.

Between these two extremes of Reality and Illusion, Being and Non-being, there was also another point of view which saw their dialectical relationship and sought a formulation beyond it. What is empirically real is determinate, arising and passing away in time. Its original source or matrix cannot be bounded or determinate; it cannot be specified in terms of being or non-being. "There was neither non-being nor being then... In non-being the seers discovered through inward wisdom the kinship of being." (ṚV X.129.1,4). "He neither is nor is not. He is nothing but Peaceful (Śiva)." (ŚvUp IV.8). The ultimate principle lies beyond existence and non-existence, good and evil.

Thus Upaniṣadic *Brahmavāda* or *Ātmavāda* culminated in three distinct points of view viz., that all appearances are expressive of Reality; that all appearances are illusory, reality being transcendent; that the Absolute is indefinable and beyond dialectical opposites of being and non-being.

Buddha, Anātman and Śūnyatā

The transition from the Vedic Age to the Age of the Buddha saw the rise and spread of Śramaṇism characterized by the ethos of renunciation and mendicancy. The early Buddhists found the world devoid of any stable essence or reality, "bereft of the 'self' or what 'belongs to the self' " (*sunnam attanā attaniyena vā*). This devaluing of phenomena as essentially non-spiritual, is generally believed to have been the first stage of the Buddhist doctrine of *nairātmya* or *śūnyatā*. It is generally said that the Buddhists began by opposing the Vedic doctrine of *ātmavāda*, denied the Soul and thus formulated *anātmavāda* or *nairātmyavāda*. At first it referred merely to the absence of a soul in the bodily and mental constituents of man. The human personality is wholly contingent and ephemeral, soulless and valueless, a mere mass of suffering, transmigrating from birth to birth. This concept of experience without an experiencing self, of change without identity, would then seem to be a simple rejection of the Vedāntic and Sāṃkhyan notions of an immutable or mutable identity underlying change in general and the procession of psychic change in particular. This rejection has been termed the denial of eternalism or *śāśvatavāda*. At the same time the acceptance of afterlife, transmigration and the law of *karman* distinguish this view from simple materialism for which mental life ceases with the death of the body. This is termed the denial of annihilationism or *ucchedavāda*. Thus it is said to deny the Spirit without denying spiritual life. As a denial of both the ends of Being and Non-being, it constitutes the Middle Path – *madhyama pratipad*. It is generally believed that this radically heterodox and anti-Vedic doctrine of *nairātmya* and *madhyama pratipad* was transformed into the classical doctrine of *śūnyatā* in Mahāyāna.

This popular understanding of *śūnyatā* as soullessness extended into universal insubstantiality or emptiness suffers from misinterpretation as well as simplification. That the body and mind are not the *ātman* is not a denial of the *ātman* but a widely recognized spiritual truth. Buddha did not deny the *ātman* as such or absolutely but only a conception of it as an object or an individual subject. In this respect he agrees with the Vedāntic conception which declares that the Self is 'Not this, not this.' For him the empirical self realizing its own false self-identification with the changing structure of personality is at last liberated on attaining the vision of *nirvāṇa*. The self is not annihilated, neither in death, nor in *nirvāṇa*. What is annihilated in *nirvāṇa* is the delusive ego-sense. What Buddha inculcated was not soullessness but selflessness.

Of the three Vedic views mentioned earlier, both the second and the third find their echoes in Buddha. He saw that the *nāma-rūpa* is rooted in *avidyā* or illusion. The determinate must be further negated to reach the truth. At the same time he also saw the inherently dialectical nature of reality as well as thought.

Being entails non-being, affirmation negation. Dialectical opposites must be transcended to reach the absolute. Thus in Buddha's *nairātmya* or *madhyama pratipad* one may legitimately see the reflection of Upaniṣadic transcendentalism and absolutism. "I am 'not this', 'not this'." "Being and non-being are two extremes; the truth lies in the middle".

This Middle Path was formulated as *pratītyasamutpāda.* There is a current opinion that *pratītyasamutpāda* or Dependent Origination was originally conceived simply as the principle of causality especially as applied to human life and experience. It has been said that it was in the changed philosophical context of Mahāyāna that *pratītyasamutpāda* was reinterpreted as the doctrine of *śūnyatā.* This opinion like the earlier one depends on confusing the original teachings of Buddha with the scholastic dogmas of Hīnayāna sects. Buddha certainly stressed the universal sway of causality and thus formulated the prime assumption of a science of psychology which would banish explanation in terms of invisible ghosts or unintelligible chance. Nevertheless he was not a naturalist, positivist or agnostic. He banished the spiritual from the causally conditioned realm of empirical phenomena only to recover it in its infinity in the ultimate verity of *nirvāṇa. Pratītyasamutpāda* and *nirvāṇa* were the two aspects of reality he discovered in the experience of *saṃbodhi.* So long the mind is swayed by *avidyā* it phenomenalizes the real as *pratītyasamutpanna*, as determinate and finite, contingent and relative, rent by the contradiction of being and non-being. When enlightened it intuits the ineffable and quiet infinity of *nirvāṇa.*

It is from the original vision of Buddha that the idea of *śūnyatā* derives, though Buddha's teachings were obscured and distorted by early sectarian dogmatists and schoolmen. Buddha had sought to avoid metaphysical dogmas as much as theological dogmas and had preferred the language of a mystical dialectic. The schoolmen, however, insisted on definition and classification of all the constituent elements of experience and thus produced diverse systems of *abhidharma* for which there is no positive reality except the transient, empirical particular. It is obvious that such systems could not fail to be spiritually stultifying for many. It is in Mahāyāna that the original spirit of Buddhism was sought to be rediscovered although Mahāyāna too was in the grip of a distorting force from the very beginning. *Śūnyatā* occupies a central place in Mahāyāna and found its classical exposition in the Mādhyamika school.

Pali Canon and Śūnyatā

In the Pali canon '*suñña*' occurs in the sense of 'empty, void' as, for example, in *suññāgāra*, an empty room. In the *cūla-suññatā-sutta* (MajNik III.21) Buddha declares that he dwells in the *suññatā-vihāra* and explains it in terms of the practice of detaching the mind from many things and concentrating it at one point. This enables him to realize (*suññatā-vakkanti*) the emptiness of the world (*suññāgatam*) in various stages till he reaches the state of objectless concentration (*animitta cetosamādhi*) where his mind is freed from the *āsavas*. This is described as the pure and ultimate emptiness (*parisuddha paramāṇuttarā suññatā*). In the meditative context three types of *samādhi* were mentioned viz., "*suññato samādhi, animitto samādhi, appaṇihito samādhi*". These are recognized in other *abhidharmas* also. Thus the **Abhidharmakośa** (VIII.24-26) mentions them and in explaining them says that the *śūnyatā samādhi* may be characterized by having *śūnyatā* or *anātmatā* as its object. The commentator Yaśomitra says:

> निर्वाणमपि शून्यानात्मलक्षणम् । शून्यता अनात्मता हि सर्वधर्माणां लक्षणमिति ।
>
> AbhidhKoBh VIII.24
>
> *Nirvāṇa* is of the characteristic of void and not-self, void and not-self are the characteristics of all constituents.

It seems that originally *śūnyatā* referred to the sense of abstraction which accompanied growing concentration in meditative practice. In due course the *abhidharmic* theory of soullessness or insubstantiality of the *dharmas* came to be used in the description of what the meditative experience is about. It was unfortunately not sufficiently realized that if the object of meditation is regulated by theoretical preconceptions, the experience of meditation could hardly be described as objective or veridical. If one sets out with the idea that all elements are insubstantial or that there is no soul underlying bodily and mental phenomena, and then reaches a vivid meditative experience of these truths, the experience can only be regarded as imaginative. Now Buddha had practised and preached meditation as a means to the intuition of truth, not as a means of self-hypnosis in the service of preconceived scholastic dogmas. The fact is that the *abhidharmic* notions of *anātma* and *śūnya* were the products of a metaphysical reasoning which found little support in Buddha himself and the meditation governed by these notions was intended in reality to inculcate an attitude of detachment or dispassion towards the world. Even in the **Mahāsuññatā Sutta** one simply hears the admonition that the monk should withdraw the mind from all objects and learn to dwell in the resulting abstraction or emptiness – *sabba-nimittānām amanasikāra ajjhattaṃ suññatām upasampajja vihareyya.* This does not mean that one should contemplate on the 'characterlessness' or insubstantiality of all *dharmas*. It means that to let the innate light of the mind to shine forth, the mind must be withdrawn from all objects. Objectless consciousness is the stepping stone to spiritual illumination. On the other hand, when *abhidhammakathā* is called *suññatāpatisaṃyutta* (MilPañ p.17), the reference is to the metaphysical doctrine of *śūnyatā*, not to a spiritual or meditative experience.

Abhidharma and Śūnyatā

The *abhidharmic* concept of *suññatā* implies that all *dharmas* are devoid of a spiritual substance (*attā*), or of belonging to one (*attaniya*), or of any permanent substance including the individual soul as conceived popularly or by some philosophical schools. A good part of *abhidharmic* theory is swayed by realistic and empiricist presuppositions although these are difficult to reconcile with the concept of *nirvāṇa* except for the Sautrāntikas.

The Hīnayānī monk meditated over a multitude of *dharmas*, real but persisting. Mahāyāna did away with this perishing reality, substituting mind-dependent constructs for independent things. It also re-examined the concept of reality, and placed the concept of the radical *śūnyatā* of all *dharmas* in the centre. It is generally said that Mahāyāna replaced the concept of *pudgala-śūnyatā* by that of *dharma-śūnyatā*. Between the two concepts, however, there is a logical asymmetry. *Pudgala-nairātmya* or *pudgala-śūnyatā* denies the reality of a permanent individual soul but regards the psycho-physical constituents of personality as real elements. This doctrine is simply a radically empiricist dogma which denies the soul as a transcendent entity, replacing it by empirical elements. *Dharmanairātmya* or *śūnyatā*, on the other hand, is an essentially idealistic principle which rejects the independent reality of all empirical objects. Objects are merely appearances for the mind depending on its constructive activity. *Śūnyatā* denies that the *dharmas* possess any innate nature or *svabhāva*.

Mahāyānic Śūnyatā

Three stages may be noticed in the development of the Mahāyānic concept of *śūnyatā*. The first is represented by the Mahāyāna-Sūtras in many of which there is no clear distinction between *Vijñānavāda* and *Śūnyavāda*. It is this stage which is reflected in the earlier Brahmanical critique of *śūnyatā*. In the second stage the concept of *śūnyatā* was diversely developed in the different schools, the formulation of Nāgārjuna being the best known. In the third stage the differences between the schools were to some extent blurred and some synthetic concepts and systems were produced.

Śūnyatā as Prajñā-pāramitā

Prajñāpāramitā-Sūtras in their various versions are among the earliest Mahāyāna-Sūtras and were held in equal esteem by the Mādhyamikas as well as the Yogācāras. *Prajñāpāramitā* is the perfection of wisdom. "It is the non-dual knowledge which is the same as the Tathāgata" (Dignāga, **Prajñāpāramitā-Piṇḍārtha** 1). Its realization is simultaneously the realization of *śūnyatā*. In the **Aṣṭasāhasrikā** Subhūti begins by saying:

नाहं भगवंस्तं धर्मं समनुपश्यामि यदुत बोधिसत्त्व इति । तमप्यहं भगवन् धर्मं न समनुपश्यामि यदुत प्रज्ञापारमिता नाम । सोऽहं भगवन् बोधिसत्त्वं वा बोधिसत्त्वधर्मं वा अविन्दन्ननुपलभमानोऽसमनुपश्यन् प्रज्ञापारमितां कतमं बोधिसत्त्वं कतमस्यां प्रज्ञापारमितायामवादिष्याम्यनुशासिष्यामि ?

AṣṭPrPār p. 4

I do not, O Lord, see that *dharma* Bodhisattva nor a dharma called a perfect wisdom. Since I neither find, nor apprehend, nor see a *dharma* 'Bodhisattva', nor a 'perfect wisdom', what Bodhisattva shall I instruct and admonish in what perfect wisdom? (Tr. Conze)

The mind is not an object or distinct essence. To reach itself it must overreach itself.

तच्चित्तमचित्तम् । प्रकृतिश्चित्तस्य प्रभास्वरा ।

AṣṭPrPār p. 5

That thought is no thought, since in its essential original nature thought is transparently luminous. (Tr. Conze)

This self-transcending nature of the mind cannot be said to be or not to be. It is eternal illumination free from all constructs:

अविकारा आयुष्मन् शारिपुत्र अविकल्पा अचित्तता ।

AṣṭPrPār p. 6

The state of absence of thought is without modification or discrimination. (Tr. Conze)

To dwell in *prajñā* one must realize that nothing has any nature of its own, not even *prajñā*. This is the universality of *śūnyatā*. *Rūpaṃ śūnyatā śūnyatā rūpaṃ*. Nothing has ever been produced. The world is ever unborn. How can one speak of its existence or non-existence? All objects are unreal and imaginary (*asaṃvidyamānāḥ sarva-dharmāḥ kalpitāḥ*). They are just magical, illusory (*rūpam eva Bhagavan māyā, māyaiva rūpam*). Even *nirvāṇa* is like a magical illusion, a dream (*nirvāṇam api māyopamaṃ svapnopamam*).

The Abhidharma had argued that behind empirical phenomena there are causal elements (*dharmas*) endowed with definite and distinct characters or *svabhāvas*. But if one can deny a soul-substance behind subjective phenomena, why need one postulate *dharmas* behind objective phenomena? Although these *dharmas* are not *dravyas* in the Vaiśeṣika sense, they are regarded as *dravyasat*. Although they are manifested for a moment, they have a timeless or perennial subsistence. The point of the Mahāyāna-Sūtra is, why should the reality of the *dharmas* be postulated beyond the appearances which form the immediate content of existence? In their fervour for negation the Prajñā-Sūtras mention as many as eighteen types of *śūnyatā*. Subjectivity, objectivity and their duality, all of these may be relegated to the realm of mere appearance. It is only the illuminative, non-dual consciousness where mind becomes non-mind and which cannot be characterized as existent or non-existent, that is *prajñā-pāramitā.*

It needs to be noted that this *prajñā* doctrine of *śūnyatā* is not nihilism. It does not predicate non-existence of things but the inapplicability of the categories of existence and non-existence to them. Nor is it idealistic in the ordinary sense for while it regards the objects as mere images and constructs, it rejects the attribution of existence or a distinct kind of nature to mind itself. It rejects the experience and world of duality as illusory and for truth would fain seek a '*metanoia*' where the mind becomes non-mind. *Prajñā* as non-dual knowledge is the realization of the *śūnyatā* or illusoriness of all phenomena.

Nāgārjuna is said to have recovered the Prajñā-Sūtras and to have composed the voluminous **Mahāprajñā-pāramitā-Śāstra** (Ta-chi-tu-lun) as a commentary. Even though the ascription of Ta-chi-tu-lun to Nāgārjuna be doubted, there can be no doubt that the *Sūtras* constitute the source of his doctrine. What Nāgārjuna did was to formulate *śūnyatā* as a dialectical principle. He also authenticated his doctrine by appealing to the most ancient and genuine of the *Sūtras* ascribed to Buddha so that all sects and schools should find it acceptable.

Śūnyatā as Pratītyasamutpāda

Śūnyatā was in danger of being interpreted as a nihilism which would be subversive of all practical life including moral and spiritual effort. Nāgārjuna identified *śūnyatā* with *pratītyasamutpāda* and the latter with the Middle Path which lies beyond the duality of existence and non-existence. The eternal unreality of the phenomena does not negate their transient practical efficiency. Rather than construct a new philosophical system on the basis of logical argumentation or scriptural dogma, Nāgārjuna developed the dialectical method to an unprecedented degree. The doctrine of *śūnyatā*, thus, came to stand for a dialectical critique of all doctrines.

Śūnyatā has been diversely interpreted by ancient and modern philosophers. Ancient Brahmanical thinkers have regarded *śūnyatā* as the categorical negation of reality. *Śūnyatā*, thus, would be unreality and *śūnyavāda* the denial of all reality. Śaṅkara describes such a doctrine as manifestly illogical since all negation presupposes some affirmation.

शून्यवादिपक्षस्तु सर्वप्रमाणविप्रतिषिद्ध इति तन्निराकरणाय नादरः क्रियते, न ह्ययं सर्वप्रमाणप्रसिद्धो लोकव्यवहारोऽन्यतत्त्वमनधिगम्य शक्यतेऽपह्नोतुमपवादाभाव उत्सर्गप्रसिद्धेः । BrSūBh II.2.31

> As for the view of the absolute nihilist, no attempt is made for its refutation since it is opposed to all means of valid knowledge. For human behaviour, conforming as it does to all right means of valid knowledge, cannot be denied so long as different order of reality is not realized, for unless there be an exception, the general rule prevails. (Tr. Swami Gambhirananda)

Among modern interpreters, Japanese scholars aware of the living traditions of Mahāyāna have clearly distinguished *śūnyavāda* from any kind of nihilism. Thus, Suzuki held *śūnyatā* to be identical with pure, non-dual intuition or *nirvikalpatā*. Speech cannot really express it as was illustrated by the silence of Vimalakīrti, which was praised by Mañjuśrī by saying, "Well done, well done, non-duality is truly above words." (**Vimalakīrti-Nirdeśa-Sūtram**, p. 152: *sādhu, sādhu, kulaputtra, ayam hi bodhisattvānāṃ advayapraveśaḥ tasmin akṣara-vacana- vijñapti-pracāro nāsti*). Since such knowledge beyond words was no stranger to Śaṅkara (BrSūBh III.2.17), one can only marvel at the failure of communication between Buddhistic and Vedāntic philosophers. Stcherbatsky has explained *śūnyatā* as relativity or contingency. *Śūnya* does not mean 'void' but 'devoid' of independent reality. Nothing short of the whole can be real and the whole cannot be spoken by words or determined by concepts. "The universe viewed as a whole is the Absolute, viewed as a process it is the phenomenal." T.R.V. Murti agrees that *śūnyatā* is absolutism, not nihilism or positivism. At the same time it is not a doctrine or theory but the dialectical critique of all theories. Robinson argues that we must distinguish between the ordinary language in which 'existence' and 'non-existence' are meaningful terms and the 'higher order' language which uses '*śūnyatā*'. "Emptiness is not a term in the primary system referring to the world, but a term in the descriptive system (metasystem) referring to the primary system" (Early Mādhyamika in India and China). Some modern interpreters, however, continue to think of *śūnyatā* as pure nihilism.

In common parlance *śūnyatā* has a negative meaning. In early Buddhist and Abhidharmic usage too it continues to have a negative significance viz., the negation of a changeless and individual soul or of a permanent substance generally. Unfortunately under the pressure of their empiricist realism Hīnayānic thinkers could not get rid of the notion of a plurality of real elements. They did not see that *avidyā* not only creates a false ego on the subjective side but a false world on the objective side. Indeed it is from *avidyā* that the subject-object divide itself proceeds. All practice and theory presuppose the working of this radical Nescience. In the Mahāyāna-Sūtras *śūnyatā* is the denial of the truth of all phenomenal experience and knowledge. Neither the ego nor the world – empirical, logical, theological – has any reality. Since *avidyā* is presupposed in all experience and thought, the falsity of its world cannot be detected as that of a dream while it lasts. Common experience and knowledge use the categories of 'being' (*bhāva*), 'non-being' (*abhāva*), 'own being' (*svabhāva*). Different things have distinct identities or characteristic own-being, they exist when produced by causes and then cease to exist. In the light of non-dual knowledge, however, such descriptions are seen to be illusory. *Śūnyatā* does not describe the world, it is a revaluation of common experience and a critique of philosophical theories about it.

Nāgārjuna clearly states that *śūnyatā* is intended to show a way out of all 'views'. If some one clings to *śūnyatā* itself as a 'view', he is indeed incurable.

> शून्यता सर्वदृष्टीनां प्रोक्ता निस्सरणं जिनैः ।
> येषां तु शून्यता दृष्टिस्तानसाध्यान् बभाषिरे ॥
>
> MaKā XIII.8
>
> Emptiness is proclaimed by the victorious one as the refutation of all view-points; but those who hold "emptiness" as a view-point – [the true perceivers] have called those "incurable" (*asādhya*).
> (Tr. F.J. Streng)

Śūnyatā is *prajñā* or vision while *dṛṣṭi* is view or opinion. The distinction is comparable to that between *episteme* and *doxa*; only, *dṛṣṭi* culminates in learned, rational theories including the *abhidharma* and the various *śāstras.* All this is the realm of *saṃvṛti.* It is through the dialectical criticism of opinions and theories and their consequent abandonment that the vision of *śūnyatā* is inducted. In this negation of *dṛṣṭi* Nāgārjuna follows Buddha himself. In the famous **Brahmajālasutta** Buddha had spoken of the 'net of *dṛṣṭis*'. In the famous parable of the Elephant and the Seven Blind Men in the **Udāna** he had picturesquely illustrated the one-sidedness and folly of speculative opinions. Buddha declared himself free from all such *ditthis* which he divided into two main classes viz., eternalist (*śāśvatavāda*) and annihilationist (*ucchedavāda*). Even the Upaniṣads mention these two points of view affirming Being (*sat*) or Non-being (*asat*) as the ultimate principle. Buddha sought to avoid both the extremes because their distinction is meaningful only with respect to finite objects. Nāgārjuna explicitly quotes Buddha:

> कात्यायनाववादे चास्तीति नास्तीति चोभयम् ।
> प्रतिषिद्धं भगवता भावाभावविभाविना ॥
>
> MaKā XV.7
>
> Analysing being and non-being the Lord has refuted both in the "Instruction to Kātyāyana".

Being and non-being have to characterize some entity which is identifiable in terms of its own-being or nature. If both the contradictory characteristics of being and non-being are seen to belong to it conditionally, neither could really belong to it. Besides the nature or own-being which identifies an entity is itself relative to other entities from which it is distinguished while their otherness itself presupposes the identity of the entity in question. Hence *bhāva, abhāva* and *svabhāva* can only be relational abstractions, not realities.

स्वभावं परभावं च भावं चाभावमेव च ।
ये पश्यन्ति न पश्यन्ति ते तत्त्वं बुद्धशासने ॥

MaKā XV.6

Those who perceive self-existence and other-existence, and an existent thing and a non-existent thing,
Do not perceive the true nature of the Buddha's teaching.
(Tr. F.J. Streng)

The way out of the contradictions of being and non-being is the Middle Path, the principle of *pratītyasamutpāda* which affirms that nothing can be or be conceived except in relation to its 'condition' or *pratyayas.* It is as much a principle of causality as of conceptual relativity. Objects are no more than conventional abstractions and designations.

यः प्रतीत्यसमुत्पादः शून्यतां तां प्रचक्ष्महे ।
सा प्रज्ञप्तिरुपादाय प्रतिपत्सैव मध्यमा ॥

MaKā XXIV.18

That which is *pratītyasamutpāda* we declare to be 'emptiness'. That is a relative designation, that is the 'Middle Path'.

Since their being is dependent on others, objects are devoid of any real nature of their own:

इह हि यः प्रतीत्य भावानां भावः सा शून्यता ।कस्मात्? निःस्वभावत्वात्।
ये हि प्रतीत्य समुत्पन्ना भावास्ते न सस्वभावा भवन्ति, स्वभावाभावात्।
कस्मात्? हेतु-प्रत्यय-सापेक्षत्वात् ।

Vigraha-Vyāvartanī under 22

In this doctrine the existence of beings which emerge depending on others is the void. Why? Because it does not have any content. The entities which emerge depending on something cannot have any real nature, because there is the absence of innateness of beings. Why? For they depend on the chain of causes. (Tr. H.N. Chakravarty)

This does not, however, mean that empirical objects cease to function at the empirical level. Chariots, clothes, pots and the like have a conditioned being and are hence devoid of any real nature; yet they are able to carry goods, protect against cold and wind, contain honey, water and milk. Even the words of Nāgārjuna although unreal have a practical function to perform.

That finite objects are devoid of absolute reality but possessed of a working actuality, is a principle common to Nāgārjuna and Śaṅkara. For both nothing can be real which is not self-existent or self-luminous. But while Śaṅkara uses two terms, *Brahman* and *māyā*, Nāgārjuna is content to use only one viz., *śūnyatā*. This should not mislead one into thinking that for Nāgārjuna there is nothing except a universal illusion, though he does not speak of any ultimate reality which may be regarded as entitatively different from that which engenders the illusion of a working reality. This working reality or *vyavahāra* is negated in its illusory aspect, through *śūnyatā* as *paramārtha*.

व्यवहारमनाश्रित्य परमार्थो न देश्यते ।
परमार्थमनागम्य निर्वाणं नाधिगम्यते ॥

MaKā XXIV.10

The highest sense [of the truth] is not taught apart from empirical life,
And without having understood the highest sense one cannot understand *nirvāṇa*. (Tr. F.J. Streng, modified)

Śūnyatā does not change the nature of things, it transmutes their vision.

य आजवंजवीभाव उपादाय प्रतीत्य वा ।
सोऽप्रतीत्यानुपादाय निर्वाणमुपदिश्यते ॥

MaKā XXV.9

Having regard to causes and conditions (constituting all phenomena, we call this world), a phenomenal world. This same world, when causes or conditions are disregarded (i.e., the world as a whole, *sub specie aeternitatis*) is called the Absolute. (Tr. Stcherbatsky)

न संसारस्य निर्वाणात् किञ्चिदस्ति विशेषणम् ।
न निर्वाणस्य संसारात् किञ्चिदस्ति विशेषणम् ॥

MaKā XXV.19

There is no difference at all between *Nirvāṇa* and *Saṃsāra*. There is no difference at all between *Saṃsāra* and *Nirvāṇa*.
(Tr. Stcherbatsky)

We cling to the empirical world thinking it to be real. *Śūnyatā* changes our attitude towards it by criticising our habitual sense of reality. Established in *śūnyatā* consciousness is transmuted into *prajñāpāramitā*. That by the unreality of the *dharmas* Nāgārjuna does not mean their non-existence, is without doubt. *Śūnyatā* is certainly not non-existence or annihilation. However, even

Vedāntic *māyā* has been distinguished from existence and non-existence. The question is, does Nāgārjuna posit an absolute reality concealed in or behind the world illusion and thereby answer Śaṅkara's obvious charge that there can be no negation without some affirmation? Although the answer must ultimately be in the affirmative, it must be admitted that Nāgārjuna does give some ground for this to be questioned at first sight. While he affirms the unreality of diverse elements or *dharmas* repeatedly, he practically never affirms the reality of anything. He speaks of *paramārtha* as if it is simply the negation of *vyavahāra* and in identifying *nirvāṇa* and *saṃsāra* he raises the doubt that *nirvāṇa* too may be illusory. Like Subhūti he seems to negate everything, but unlike Subhūti he rarely speaks of *prajñā* or non-dual knowledge except as the negation of being and non-being.

The reasons for this negative emphasis, however, are not far to seek. Works like the **Madhyamaka-Kārikās**, or **Vigraha-Vyāvartanī** are essentially aimed against philosophers of Sarvāstivāda, Sāṃkhya and Vaiśeṣika schools. They are dialectical refutations of philosophical theories. The method of Nāgārjuna's dialectic, called *prāsaṅgika*, is wholly negative. It merely attacks the opponent's position without seeking to establish any position of its own. For Nāgārjuna every thesis or *pakṣa* entails an antithesis or *pratipakṣa*. He tries to show the dialectical untenability of all theses. Hence *śūnyatā* refutes the reality of empirical objects or rational constructs but it leads to the eloquent silence of eternal and non-dual truth.

> निवृत्तमभिधातव्यं निवृत्ते चित्तगोचरे ।
> अनुत्पन्नानिरुद्धा हि निर्वाणमिव धर्मता ॥
>
> MaKā XVIII.7
>
> When the object of thought has ceased, nothing is left to be said.
> Truth (*dharmatā*) is like *nirvāṇa* unborn and unceasing.
> (Tr. Stcherbatsky)
>
> अपरप्रत्ययं शान्तं प्रपञ्चैरप्रपञ्चितम् ।
> निर्विकल्पमनानार्थमेतत् तत्त्वस्य लक्षणम् ॥
>
> MaKā XVIII.9
>
> The mark of reality (*tattva*) is this not being dependent on another,
> quiescent, ineffable, unconstricted by thought, non-dual.
> (Tr. Stcherbatsky)

What Nāgārjuna speaks of *dharmatā* or *tattva* here clearly shows that his dialectical exposition of *śūnyatā* needs to be understood in the background of the general Mahāyānic doctrines of *prajñāpāramitā* and *dharmadhātu* which propounded an illusionistic absolutism.

It needs to be stressed that the principal hurdle to the understanding of *śūnyatā* is provided by the instinctive belief that the working reality of common experience is the paradigm of all reality. If this is attacked as untenable, there is an instinctive reaction to jump to the other extreme of nihilism. If my familiar world of pots and pans is unreal, then nothing is real. In his **Ratnāvalī** Nāgārjuna shows considerable apprehension of this kind of misunderstanding (Lindtner, **Nāgārjuniana**, pp.163 ff; **Madhyamaka-Śāstra**, ed. P.L. Vaidya, pp.296 ff.). Philosophers are no better than common people because to the extent to which they are dissatisfied with empirical objects they tend to invoke transcendent principles which, however, continue to derive their reality from their indirect or partial contact with empirical existence. The result is that positivist as well as transcendentalist philosophies fall within the two extremes of the 'speculative net' (*diṭṭhi-jāla*) which Buddha had condemned. Nāgārjuna does not quarrel with the working reality of empirical things, nor does he seek to escape from them or supplement them by an appeal to ideal or transcendental principles. He only shows dialectically the contradictions of instinctive and speculative thought. On the nature of the vision attained when words and thoughts are dropped, Nāgārjuna is studiously silent like Vimalakīrti or the Vedāntin Bādhva, or like the Buddha himself or even Dakṣiṇāmūrti. He, however, makes us see that *śūnyatā* itself is not merely a dialectical negation of *dharmas* and *dṛṣṭis* but something more, an awesome and ineffably holy principle, the highest and the deepest for realization through the total dedication of a Bodhisattva. So he invokes *pratītyasamutpāda* with the negative but highly evocative characterization '*anirodham anutpādam*' etc.

To speak of the Absolute is to relativize it and so Nāgārjuna consistently enough avoids speaking of it. Indeed, in so far as the Absolute is a philosophical principle or concept it has no place in Nāgārjuna's dialectical system. The traditional Buddhist concepts for ultimate reality or the Absolute of some kind were *paramārtha, asaṃskṛta, nirvāṇa, dharmatā* or *dharma-dhātu, tattva.* For Nāgārjuna *paramārtha* is relative to *vyavahāra, asaṃskṛta* to *saṃskṛta, nirvāṇa* to *saṃsāra. Dharmatā* or *tattva* is the same as *pratītyasamutpāda* or *śūnyatā* and is characterized in wholly negative terms of which the most significant declare that here there are no birth and death, words and thought, or any evil. "*Anirūḍham anutpādam... prapañcopaśamaḥ śivaḥ*" is reminiscent of **Śvetāśvatara Upaniṣad** (IV.18b): "*na san nacāsañchiva eva kevalaḥ*". The meaning of *śūnyatā* is conveyed as much through dialectical speech as through the silence where it ends. The repetitive dialectic of Nāgārjuna provides, as it were, a *koan* for Zen meditation.

Śūnyatā and Dialectic

Quite often *śūnyatā* is identified with dialectical reason itself. It is Nāgārjuna's mode of reasoning which has fascinated thinkers through the ages.

Nāgārjuna's method is one of critical examination (*parīkṣā*) of certain concepts of general philosophical significance and of some dogmas current in the Buddhist schools. This critical examination proceeds through the uncovering of contradictions in the position criticised, that is, through *prasaṅgāpādana*, and the method is called *prāsaṅgika*. As is well known, Nāgārjuna follows an ancient scheme of fourfold predication (*catuṣkoṭi*). Affirmation, negation, conjoint affirmation and negation, the negation of both affirmation and negation, these are the four modes of predication or *koṭis* which are considered in turn and found wanting. Thus with respect to the cause-effect relationship examined in the *prakaraṇa* of the **Madhyamaka-Vṛtti**, entitled *Pratyayaparīkṣā*, the four predications are: The effect is identical with the cause, the effect is not identical with the cause, the effect is both identical and not identical with the cause, the effect is neither identical nor not identical with the cause. According to the canons of normal logic only the first two make sense and only one of them could be true. The third is a contradiction and hence false. The fourth is reducible to the third. Thus the tetralemma (*catuṣkoṭi*) of Nāgārjuna appears to violate the laws of Contradiction, Excluded Middle, and Double Negation. Diverse interpretations have been proposed in the defence of Nāgārjuna. Bhāvaviveka and Buddhapālita sought to supplement *prasaṅgānumāna* by *svatantrānumāna* believing that valid negation presupposes some valid affirmation. Attempts have been made to invoke the idea of many-valued logic. Some scholars have interpreted the four *koṭis* asymmetrically (cf. R.N. Ghose, The Dialectics of Nāgārjuna). In fact, the tetralemma was of ancient usage and used differently by different philosophers. The agnostics used it to support the impossibility of definite predication about certain transcendental questions. A similar use was made of it in the *Abhidharma* in the context of the *avyākṛtas*. The Jainas used a more elaborate seven-fold predication in support of their Non-absolutism (*anekāntavāda*), which has even been interpreted as probabilism.

The fact is that Nāgārjuna does not seek to violate any laws of logic. He points out contradictions because they show falsehood. This presupposes the Law of Excluded Middle. The Law of Double Negation is also accepted in his reasoning. He uses common logical devices like simple negation (*prasajyapratiṣedha*), hypothetical syllogism, modus tollens, destructive dilemma, enthymeme. The first two *koṭis* – thesis and antithesis – were used by him to develop a dialectical contradiction. The third was not used for a synthesis but to show the impossibility of a synthesis. The fourth was used to show the impossibility of any logically defensible predication in the case under examination. Nāgārjuna's dialectic is thus simply aimed at showing the impossibility of any rational solution of metaphysical questions. His dialectic is the refutation of Buddhist dogmatics and metaphysical theories, not of logic. Buddhist dogmatics is relevant to the lower truth or *saṃvṛti*. *Śūnyatā* leads one to the higher truth or *paramārtha* which makes *nirvāṇa* accessible. The concept of *śūnyatā* was also endorsed by Yogācāra which declared "*cittamātraṃ yaduta traidhātukam*". The **Laṅkāvatāra** thus reduces the whole universe to a mere dream or mirage. Since mind is the only reality, external objects can only be illusory. Even ideas are illusory because they presuppose the duality of subject and object. It is only pure and non-dual consciousness that is knowledge free from all delusion. The realization of *niḥsvabhāvatā* culminates here (**Vijñaptimātratā-Triṃśikā**, ed. Levy, vv. 23-30). To a modern student of spiritual phenomenology, *śūnyatā*, *prajñāpāramitā* and *vijñapatimātratā* seem to coalesce at this point, although this would not be acceptable to traditional scholastics as may be seen in the divergent interpretations of the **Aṣṭasāhasrikā** in the different schools.

Śūnyatā and Art

Nāgārjuna's *śūnyatā* shows that nothing is real by nature (= *svabhāva-śūnya*) but that everything is illusory (*māyopamā*), merely an image (*pratibimbopamā*). Man is not the dependent creature of a real, hard world of nature. He is the detached spectator and critic of a magical show, a world of images. This transformation of the point of view towards the world and the self has a certain parallel to what happens in aesthetic experience and creation (see Bibliography). There too real objects (*laukikaviṣaya*) become ideal (*ālambana*) within an imaginative experience (*alaukika-pratīti*). Both in the spiritual vision of *śūnyatā* and the aesthetic vision the object is an image (*pratibimba*) and the subject detached from the actual ego. Though both have an axiological dimension the primary context for *śūnyatā* is cognitive while that for art is emotive. Since the understanding of *śūnyatā* moves from dualistic cognition towards a non-dualistic vision and art from mere emotion to its deeper stirrings of truth and value, here too the two domains are not wholly apart. In religious Art especially the philosophical vision of *śūnyatā* and imagination or image-making, the two could well be complementary. Śāntarakṣita described *pratītyasamutpāda* as similar to an image, *pratibimbādisannibham* (**Tattvasaṃgraha**, vv. 1-4). This may be compared to Śaṅkuka's description of the art-object as an image which appears vividly but is neither true nor false. The fact is that idealistic Buddhist thought was undoubtedly used by the aestheticians of Kashmir, which needs to be investigated in detail.

G.C. Pande

Select Bibliography

Śūnya :

Bag, A.K. and S.R.Sarma (ed.), *Concept of Sunya*, Indira Gandhi National Centre for the Arts, Indian National Science Academy and Aryan Books International, New Delhi 2003.

Coomaraswamy, A. K. : "Kha and other words denoting zero in connection with the Metaphysics of Space" in : Selected Papers, Vol. 2 ed. Lipsey, Roger. Princeton: Princeton University Press, 1977.

David Seyfort Ruegg. "Mathematical and Linguistic Models in Indian Thought : The Case of Zero and *śūnyatā." Wiener Zeitscrift für die Kunde Südasiens* 22 (1978) 171-181.

Datta, Bibhutibhusan and Avadhesh Narayan Singh : History of Hindu Mathematics : A Source Book. 2nd edition, Bombay : Asia Publishing House, 1962, 2 parts.

Needham, Joseph and Wang Ling: Science and Civilisation in China. Vol. 3, Cambridge: at the University Press, 1959.

Sarvanandī, *Lokavibhāga*, in Balachandra Siddhānta Shastri(ed.), Sholapur 1962.

Vasubandhu, *Abhidharmakośa Bhāṣya*, in P.Pradhan(ed.); revised second edition by Aruna Haldar, K. P. Jayaswal Research Institute, Patna, 1975. (Tibetan Sanskrit Works Series Vol. 8).

Śūnyatā :

Anesaki, M. : Buddhist Art in its Relations to Buddhist Ideals. New York : 1915.

Ghose, R. N. : The Dialectics of Nāgārjuna. Calcutta : University of Calcutta.

Gnoli, R. : The Aesthetic Experience According to Abhinavagupta. Varanasi: Chowkhamba Sanskrit Series Studies, 1968.

Lamotte, E. : Le Traité de la Grande Vertue de Sagesse de Nāgārjuna (Mahāprajñāpāramitāśāstra). 2 Vols. Louvain : 1944, 1949.

Murti, T. R. V. : The Central Philosophy of Buddhism, Delhi ; 1960.

Pande, G. C. : "Aesthetics from a Buddhist Point of view", in : Buddhist Studies. Vol.I, Delhi : Delhi University, 1978.

—, Foundations of Indian Culture. Vol.I. New Delhi : Books and Books, 1984.

—, Studies in the Origins of Buddhism. Delhi : 1983.

Robinson, R. H. : Early Mādhyamika in India and China. Madison : 1967.

Stcherbatsky, T. : The Central Conception of Buddhism. Delhi : 1970.

Venkata Ramanan, K. : Nāgārjuna's Philosophy as presented in the Mahāprajñāpāramitā śāstra. Tokyo : Rutlan Vermont, 1966.

PŪRṆA

Overview

The Indian, esp. Brahmanical tradition has been obsessed with the idea and ideal of fullness and totality. *Pūrṇa*, both as adjective or adverb, denotes 'fullness', in the sense of content, perfection, completion, and as noun, *pūrṇatā*, it is symbolic of the Supreme Reality, the Absolute in its unalterable fullness.

There are five different dimensions of the concept as it has been used in the different texts, e.g. 1) fullness, abundance, 2) conclusion, 3) sustenance, 4) perfection and 5) auspiciousness, but the derivative meanings of self-sufficient, self-contained fullness and completeness have been retained as the core meanings, permeating all its usages. Though a study of all these usages reveals a kind of evolution in thought this is not a vertical but horizontal evolution. In philosophical texts, it assumes the garb of a distinct philosophical term, pregnant with sublime and abstract meaning, that of *Brahman* or the Absolute, and in the field of Arts, its primary associations are 'auspicious' or 'perfect'. The most common symbol of fullness is the 'vase of plenty', *pūrṇakalaśa* or *pūrṇakumbha* which is a pervasive element in daily life, ritual and the Arts.

Etymology and Cognate Words

Pūrṇa is a p.p.p. of the verb *pṝ-*, (*piparti* or *pṛṇāti*), to fill, to nourish, to satiate. From the same root →*prāṇa* is also derived. The Indo-European cognates are Gr. *pletho*, Lat. *plere*, to fill, and hence Gr. *pleroma*, fullness, Lat. *com-pletus*, 'complete', *plenus*, etc. The abstract noun is *pūrṇatā*, and important compounds are *pūrṇimā*, full-moon night, *pūrṇamāsa*, full-moon, *pūrṇāyus*, 'of full life-span' (name of a Gandharva), etc.

Pāṇini mentions the formation of the word *pūrṇa* by *nipātana* in his Sūtra VII.2.27 (*vā dāntaśānta pūrṇa* etc.). According to the commentator on Pāṇini Sūtra, this word can be derived either from *pūr* belonging to 4th class or 10th class (see comm. **Nyāsa** and **Padamañjarī** on **Kāśikā** VII.2.27), or from *p ṛ-* according to Kṣīrasvāmin (comm. on **Pāṇini Dhātupāṭha**) and Kāśakṛtsna (see Kāśakṛtsna Dhātuvyākhyānam by Yudhisthira Mimamsaka 2.68).

It may be mentioned here that the word *pūrṇa* mostly occurs as adjective or adverb in many hymns of the **Ṛgveda** and the **Atharva-Veda** (e.g. ṚV I.154.4; ṚV I.82.3; AV VII.80.1, etc.), though it is listed in the **Nighaṇṭu-Nirukta** also as noun (neuter), as one of the hundred synonyms of water (cf. **Nighaṇṭu-Nirukta** I.12 No. 75). (cf. also **Nirukta** XIV.11 where it is mentioned as an element, *bhūta*). At both the places, the commentator Durgācārya derives the word *pūrṇa* from *pṛ-* in the sense of *pālana* (sustenance) or *pūraṇa* (filling up).

Thus the core meanings of *pṛ-* from which the word *pūrṇa* is formed to denote sustenance, fullness, self-sufficiency, self-containedness are carried throughout the Indian tradition, overlooking the meaning as water or element (*bhūta*) recorded in the **Nighaṇṭu-Nirukta**.

In some Buddhist texts, however, the word *pūrṇa* is also used as noun to signify 'a monk', implying the idea 'fullnes', 'self-sufficiency', 'perfection'.

The basic meanings that can be gleaned from various usages can be stated as fullness, self-sufficiency, perfection.

The opposite or complementary concept of *pūrṇa* is →*śūnya*, void, emptiness.

Layers of Meaning

The layers of meaning of *pūrṇa* reach from the physical notion of fullness, e.g. of a vessel, or of the moon, to the symbolical, metaphorical, to the notion of perfection and to the metaphysical concept of the Absolute as Totality and all-inclusive Fullness.

The word *pūrṇa* occurs in the older texts as an adjective or adverb, but in later philosophical texts as a substantive or noun, signifying the totality or completeness of the Absolute. In all these usages however the idea of self-sufficiency and fullness (*pūrṇatā*) pervades and remains the core meaning.

The uses of the word *pūrṇa* in the Vedic hymns reveals one dimension of the meaning, namely, full measure.

We see another dimension of the meaning in the philosophical texts, both Upaniṣadic and later speculative texts, where the word occurs as noun, signifying a philosophical concept, an ontological entity.

The use of the word *pūrṇa* to convey the sense of conclusion, (e.g. in ŚBr I.9.3.3: *pūrṇaṃ ninayati, sarvaṃ vai pūrṇam*) or perfection (e.g. in the Saun XVI.90d: *sa pūrṇa eva*) are again conceptual offshoots of the core meaning of 'fullness'.

It appears that the different layers of meanings revealed by the numerous usages in various texts represent only variations of the core meaning of 'fullness', round which all shades of meanings revolve.

Development of the Concept

The earliest usages of the word *pūrṇa* in Vedic texts have been either as adjective or adverb, signifying 'full', 'abundant', 'complete'. For instance, in the **Ṛgveda** (I.154.4) the steps of Viṣṇu (→ *krama*) are described as full of honey, symbolising celestial bliss (*tri pūrṇā madhunā padāni*, three steps full of honey). This hymn also occurs in **Taittirīya Saṃhitā** (III.3.11.2), conveying the same sense.

Similarly, in the hymn occurring in **Kāṭhaka Saṃhitā** the word *pūrṇa* signifies fullness in the material sense.

पूर्णो वै प्रजापतिः समृद्धिभिः ऊनो व्यृद्धिभिः ।

KāṭhSam III.2

Prajāpati is full in wealth (but) deficient on spending.

सुसंदृशं त्वा वयं मघवन्वन्दिषीमहि ।
प्र नूनं पूर्णबन्धुरः स्तुतो याहि वशाँ अनु योजा न्विन्द्र ते हरी ।

ṚV I.82.3

Praiseworthy blessing hast thou laid upon the pair who with uplifted ladle serve thee, man and wife.
Unchecked he dwells and prospers in thy law: Thy power brings blessing to the sacrificer pouring gifts. (Tr. R.T.H. Griffith)

The **Atharva-Veda** gives a poetic description of the fullmoon night:

पूर्णा पश्चादुत पूर्णा पुरस्तादुन्मध्यतः पौर्णमासी जिगाय ।
तस्यां देवैः संवसन्तो महित्वा नाकस्य पृष्ठे समिषा मदेम ॥

AV VII.80.1

To full in the front, full rearward, from the middle the full Moon's Night hath conquered in the battle. In her may we, dwelling with Gods and greatness, feast in the height of heaven, on strengthening viands. (Tr. R.T.H. Griffith)

The fullness of the moon on the fullmoon night (*paurṇamāsī*), when all its sixteen digits are revealed on both the sides, the visible front side and the invisible rearside, is suggestive of complete fullness of the Supreme Being, the embodiment of 'light of knowledge'. Just as the full effulgence of the light of the full moon vanquishes the veil of darkness from the mid-region of the earth, symbolically mentioned as the victory in the battle, the light of the Supreme Being also destroys the veil of darkness on the surface of the earth. The seer therefore prays to the god to enable him to enjoy the same, staying at the height of heaven in company with the gods.

Another hymn of the **Atharva-Veda** seems to use the word *pūrṇa* in a ritual context which has led to the philosophical concept of the Supreme Being who is the embodiment of Fullness.

पूर्णात्पूर्णमुदचति पूर्णं पूर्णेन सिच्यते ।
उतो तदद्य विद्याम यतस्तत्परिषिच्यते ॥

AV X.8.29

Forth from the Full, he lifts the Full, the Full he sprinkles with the Full. Now also we may know the source from which it is sprinkled around. (Tr. R.T.H. Griffith)

As we would presently see, this hymn has been echoed almost in similar words in the **Bṛhadāraṇyaka Upaniṣad** (V.1.1).

There is however one hymn in the **Atharva-Veda** where the *pūrṇakumbha* (vase of fullness) is pregnant with deep symbolic meaning.

पूर्णः कुम्भोऽधि काल आहितस्तं वै पश्यामो बहुधा नु सन्तः ।
स इमा विश्वा भुवनानि प्रत्यङ् कालं तमाहुः परमे व्योमन् ॥

AV XIX.53.3

Above time is set a brimful vessel (*pūrṇa kumbha*);
simultaneously we see Time here, there, everywhere.
Set face to face with all existences,
Time is throned, men say, in the loftiest realm. (Tr. R. Panikkar)

Used here as adjective qualifying *kumbha* (pot or urn) which is imagined here as the repository of Eternal Time, the word *pūrṇa* signifies 'fullness' in absolute terms. The seer employing highly poetical terms imagines the Full Pot "throned on the loftiest realm" above the mundane world and Time, as Eternal Time, filling to the brim the urn overlooking the creation. The Eternal Time is actually the 'Timeless Eternity' (*kālātīta kāla* or *mahākāla*), to borrow a phrase from Sri Aurobindo, the Immutable Being from which flows down the temporal time responsible for universal flux or continuous change. The Timeless Eternity therefore is imagined by the seer-poet to be seen everywhere in the mundane world, engulfing the entire phenomena in the form of phenomenal time or *kāla*.

The word *pūrṇa* occurs at a number of places in the Brāhmaṇas in the context of description of sacrificial rite. The offering with the sacrificial spoon has to be full so that it may lead to completeness.

तां वै पूर्णां जुहोति ।सर्वं वै पूर्णं सर्वेणैवैनमेतच्छमयति ।

ŚBr II.2.1.3

(He) offers it (with a) full (spoon). Everything having been complete, he appeases him with all. (Tr. J. Eggeling)

पूर्णं गृह्णाति ।सर्वं वै पूर्णम् ।सर्वमेष ग्रहः ।तस्मात् पूर्णं गृह्णाति।

ŚBr IV.2.2.2

He (the Adhvaryu) draws it (*agrayāna*) full; for full means all, and

this *graha* is all; therefore he (Adhvaryu) draws it full.
(Tr. J. Eggeling)

पूर्णं निनयति । सर्वं वै पूर्णम् । सर्वेणैवैनमेतच्छमयति ।

ŚBr I.9.3.3

A full (vessel) he (*Adhvaryu*) pours out, (because) full means completion (*pūrṇa*). By means of all, he appeases him. (Tr. J. Eggeling)

In all these passages which occur in the context of offering the final oblation to the sacrificial fire (*pūrṇāhuti*), description of the *Agrayānagraha* rite and the *Darśapūrṇamāsa* sacrifice respectively, the word *pūrṇa* is used to denote 'fullness' of the offering, or 'completion' or 'conclusion' of the sacrificial rite.

The use of the word *pūrṇa* in the Upaniṣads however, marks the shift from the ritual to the philosophical sense in gradual steps.

The invocation of the **Bṛhadāraṇyaka Upaniṣad** marks the transition from a ritual context to the Absolute:

पूर्णमदः पूर्णमिदं पूर्णात्पूर्णमुदच्यते ।
पूर्णस्य पूर्णमादाय पूर्णमेवावशिष्यते ॥

BṛUp V.1.1

The Yon is fullness; fullness, this.
From fullness, fullness doth proceed.
Withdrawing fullness's fullness off,
Even fullness then itself remains. (Tr. R.E. Hume)

Here the word *pūrṇa* refers in symbolic terms to the Supreme Reality which, remaining ever immersed in its integral nature, is always self resting (*svātma-viśrānta*). Gopinath Kaviraj has shed light on the sublime philosophical meaning underlying this verse which may be summarised as follows. This verse attempts to bring out the nature of the Supreme *Brahman* in terms of the integral Whole (*paripūrṇa*) which, as such, is beyond finite mind's comprehension. It is always Full-in-Itself, the one without a second, and therefore does not suffer from any want or deficiency. It exists everywhere, and at all times as the 'one Whole' (*paripūrṇa*), the integral Reality. Being the sole Reality, It is the locus of both creation and dissolution of the world which is going on from time immemorial in the form of the play of its innate power, without affecting in the least its essential integral Nature. Looking from the mundane level, it has two aspects – the aspect which is capable of being apprehended by the mind denoted by the term *idam*, and the aspect which is beyond the reach of the mind that is indicated by the word *adaḥ*. But, as a matter of fact, there is no difference whatsoever between these two aspects, because what once appears as within the reach of the senses due to the expansion of one's capacity may well go out of one's grasp when the powers of senses contract. But the Supreme Reality as such remains the integral Whole (*paripūrṇa*) at all times and at all places. It is beyond mutation or evolution. It is formless yet with form, attributeless yet with all attributes, far yet near, all-pervasive yet transcendent. All contradictions lose their identity in it. All that emerges from It is also of the nature of all-inclusive Fullness. It may be likened to zero which symbolises the infinity in the domain of mathematics (→ *śūnya*). Any addition or subtraction does not make any change in it. It ever remains the immutable infinity. Thus the Supreme Reality is integral Fullness which is a corollary of its self-resting nature as the Absolute.

The word *pūrṇa* figures at one place in the **Chāndogya Upaniṣad**, in a deep philosophical meaning.

यद्वै तद् ब्रह्मेतीदं वाव तद्योऽयं बहिर्धा पुरुषादाकाशः ।
यो वै स बहिर्धा पुरुषादाकाशः ॥
अयं वाव स योऽयमन्तः पुरुष आकाशः ।
यो वै सोऽन्तः पुरुष आकाशः ॥
अयं वाव स योऽयमन्तर्हृदय आकाशः । तदेतत्पूर्णमप्रवर्ति ।
पूर्णामप्रवर्तिनीं श्रियं लभते य एवं वेद ॥

ChUp III.12.7-9

Verily, what is called Brahman that is the same as what the space outside of a person is.
Verily what the space outside of a person is –
That is the same as what the space within a person is.
Verily, what the space within a person is –
that is the same as what the space here within the heart is.
That is the Full, the non-active. Full, non-active prosperity he obtains who knows this. (Tr. R.E. Hume)

In this passage the word *pūrṇa* is used to signify the concept of the Supreme Being who is the embodiment of fullness. As such, It remains immersed in Its integral nature, which also implies total absence of movement or action. For action or movement involve change which means deviation from its self-resting state. This is denied in the immutable *Brahman* on account of its fullness. Also movement presupposes the existence of space surrounding *Brahman*. This is denied because the immutable *Brahman* is beyond space and time. A person who succeeds in realising this nature of *Brahman*, achieves perfect union with it.

The **Taittirīya Upaniṣad** however uses the word *pūrṇa* to denote fullness both in its material and spiritual senses. In the first sense:

तस्येयं पृथिवी सर्वा वित्तस्य पूर्णा स्यात् ।

TUp II.8

Let this whole earth be full of wealth for him (who is well versed in the scriptures and is not smitten with desire). (Tr. **R.E.** Hume)

In the context of the five 'layers' of the person or *ātman*, the same Upaniṣad describes how each layer is filled with the preceding one.

तस्माद्वा एतस्मादन्नरसमयाद् अन्योऽन्तर आत्मा प्राणमयः। तेनैष पूर्णः।
तस्माद्वा एतस्मात्प्राणमयाद् अन्योऽन्तर आत्मा मनोमयः। तेनैष पूर्णः।
तस्माद्वा एतस्मान्मनोमयाद् अन्योऽन्तर आत्मा विज्ञानमयः। तेनैष पूर्णः।
तस्माद्वा एतस्माद्विज्ञानमयाद् अन्योऽन्तर आत्मा आनन्दमयः। तेनैष पूर्णः।

TUp II. 2-5

Verily, other than and within that (i.e. food, the supporting yet consuming substance of all life) one that consists of the essence of food; the *ātman* (self) is different from and more intrinsic than that which is of the nature of breath. By this (breath) is filled up the self.

Verily, other than and within that (i.e. breath) one that consists of breath is a self different from and more intrinsic than that which is of the nature of mind. By this (mind) is filled the self.

Verily, other than and within that (mind) one is that consists of *vijñāna* is a self different from and more intrinsic than that which is of the nature of *vijñāna*. By this (*vijñāna*) is filled up the self.

Verily, other than and within that (i.e. *vijñāna*) one which consists of bliss is a self different from and more intrinsic than bliss. By this (bliss) is filled up the self. (Tr. R.E. Hume)

Here, the Upaniṣadic seer seems to attempt to identify the element that constitutes the real self, removing layer by layer the different shells covering it (following *arundhatī-nyāya*, a popular method or mode for discovering the star Arundhatī adjacent to *saptarṣi-maṇḍala*). The word *pūrṇa* here is used to signify the particular stuff that constitutes the real self.

The use of the word *pūrṇa* in the **Saundarananda** of Aśvaghoṣa, a literary work with plenty of Buddhist concepts presented through literary medium, reveals yet another dimension in the usage of the word. Aśvaghoṣa gives a list of names of many Buddhist monks in a verse who were all contemporaries of the Buddha.

स कप्फिनः काश्यप औरुविल्व महामहाकाश्यपतिष्यनन्दाः ।
पूर्णश्च पूर्णश्च स पूर्णकश्च शोनापरान्तश्च स पूर्ण एव ॥ Saun XV.90

Kapphina, Kāśyapa, son of Uruvilva, Mahāmahā Kāśyapa, Tiṣyananda, monk *pūrṇa*, *pūrṇaka*, Śonāparānta who is also a monk. (Tr. E.H. Johnston)

In the Buddhist religious tradition, a Buddhist monk is called *pūrṇa* on account of his achieving 'perfection' in religio-philosophical sense. It is thus a good example of a word evolving into a technical term on account of extension of its etymological meaning.

Some post-vedic philosophical texts indicate the continuance of the same usage of the word *pūrṇa* which we find in some Upaniṣads. As a matter of fact, some passages from the **Yoga-Vāsiṣṭha** not only reveal the same dimension of the meaning of the word but they also appear to elaborate upon the famous Upaniṣadic *mantra*.

पूर्णात्पूर्णं प्रसरति यत्तत्पूर्णं निराकृतिः ।
ब्रह्मणो विश्वमाभातं तद्धि स्वार्थं विचक्षितम् ॥
पूर्णात्पूर्णं प्रसरति संस्थितं पूर्णमेव तत् ।
अतो विश्वमनुत्पन्नं यच्चोत्पन्नं तदेव तत् ॥

YVās III.10.28-29

From the full, the full emerges. That which it is, it is full and has no form. The universe remains manifest from Brahman and the manifestation is for the purpose of attaining the real nature.
From the full, the full emerges and remains also full. Therefore the universe that is unborn (prior to creation), and that which is born is also that (i.e. full). (Tr. H.N. Chakravarty)

'Fullness' indicates here a perfect equilibrium of the cosmic and the transcendent. The Supreme Being is an embodiment of Fullness on account of its all-comprehensive and all-inclusive nature. He is the one integral Reality from whom multiplicity emerges yet He does not suffer any diminutions but remains the ever one integral Whole.

The philosophical systems continue the same meaning, especially in Vedānta. Thus Śaṅkara says in his **Śārīrakabhāṣya** on the **Brahma-Sūtra**.

परिपूर्णशक्तिकं तु ब्रह्म, न तस्यान्येन केनचित्पूर्णता सम्पादयितव्या ।

BrSūBh II.1.24

The power of Brahman is absolutely complete (i.e. full), (hence) that does not require to be supplemented by any extraneous help. (Tr. G. Thibaut, adapted)

Brahman, the Supreme Reality, is said to be full-in-itself, hence it exists as the absolutely independent Reality. Its fullness in that sense is its intrinsic nature. No doubt this aspect of its nature follows from its being one without a second. The addition of the prefix *pari* to *pūrṇa*, literally meaning fullness on all sides, actually signifies here 'absolute perfection', that is *Brahman*, according to Śaṅkara.

The **Haṭhayoga Pradīpikā**, a sectarian *yoga* text of much later date throws light on the implication of the word *pūrṇa* as 'fullness' from the point of view of yogic experience. When a yogin achieves perfect concentration of mind after controlling all his senses, the true nature of self is revealed to him in his absolutely cleansed mind. He then experiences its presence everywhere, inside himself, and at the same time outside himself. The entire creation appears to him as 'filled with the Fullness' which signalises his union with Supreme Self or *Brahman*.

अन्तः पूर्णो बहिः पूर्णः पूर्णः कुम्भ इवार्णवे ।

HyPrad IV. 56

Full within, full without, full like the pot in the ocean (such is the experience of yogin in meditation). (Tr. S. Iyengar)

The fullness experienced by the yogin is indicative of his union with *Brahman*, the achievement of the state in which one and many coalesce.

A Vaiṣṇava philosophical text talks of degrees of fullness (*pūrṇatva*) in the manifestations of Divinity on earth. The Vaiṣṇavites conceive Lord Hari to be the perfect embodiment of Divinity who is manifested on the earth in full, fuller and fullest form under different situations. He is capable of being represented in these forms through the medium of literature and drama, as is mentioned in the **Bhaktirasāmṛtasindhu**, a Gauḍīya Vaiṣṇava text of late medieval period.

हरिः पूर्णतमः पूर्णतरः पूर्ण इति त्रिधा ।
श्रेष्ठमध्यादिभिः शब्दैर्नाट्ये यः प्रतिपद्यते ॥

BhRSi III.1.104

Lord Hari has three forms, the most complete, more complete and the complete. These forms are signified by the words the best, better etc. in the act of dramaturgy. (Tr. H.N. Chakaravarty)

The Vaiṣṇavites believe that Lord Hari's integral Divine nature cannot be represented in toto through the medium of drama, only a few facets of His total Divine Personality can be shown on the stage. Therefore the author mentions degrees of His Integral nature (*pūrṇatva*) which can possibly be presented on the stage. The zenith of His Divine personality however is to be seen only in the Divine personality of Lord Hari. This no doubt indicates a somewhat new development in the signification by *pūrṇatva* (fullness).

A blending of the Upaniṣadic philosophic connotation of the word *pūrṇa*, however, is carried forward to the highest level of development in the texts of Kāśmīr Śaivism. A more refined dimension is revealed, and deeper metaphysical import is added to the meaning of the word *pūrṇa*. Utpaladeva in his **Īśvara Pratyabhijñā Kārikā** says:

स्वात्मेव स्वात्मना पूर्णा भावा भान्त्यमितस्य तु ।

ĪPKā II.1.7 cd

To the universal subject, the objects shine as identical with itself, and, therefore, as beyond all limitations, like the self itself. (Tr. K.C. Pandey)

The word *pūrṇa* here signifies the 'Fullness' which is the very nature of the universal Subject, the supreme Experiencer. While explaining the metaphysical import sought to be conveyed by this usage, Abhinavagupta in his commentary **Vimarśinī** quotes a line from an unknown source which reads:

अपूर्वापरं हि इदं मूर्तितः क्रियातश्च सर्वं सर्वतः पूर्णम् ।

ĪPKāVịm II.1.7cd

(The eternal subject) has no succession. All are perfect in form and action in Him in every form. (Tr. K.C. Pandey)

This undoubtedly is in conformity with the Śaivite theory of Divine Freedom (*svātantrya*) of the Supreme Lord, a cardinal doctrine of Kāśmīr Śaivism.

In the opening benedictory verse of his **Vimarśinī** commentary on the **Īśvara Pratyabhijñā Kārikā**, Abhinavagupta develops the meaning of *pūrṇatva* (fullness) into a full-fledged concept which he holds to be synonymous with the Supreme Śiva. He is held to be always resting in Himself (*svātmaviśrānta*).

निराभासात्पूर्णादहमिति पुरा भासयति यद्
द्विशाखामाशास्ते तदनु च विभङ्क्तुं निजकलाम् ।
स्वरूपादुन्मेष- प्रसरण - निमेष - स्थितिजुषस्
तदद्वैतं वन्दे परमशिवशक्त्यात्मनिखिलम् ॥

ĪPKāVim I.1.1

I bow to the Absolute which is the unity of Parama Śiva and (His) Śakti, the unity which from its ultimate state, first of all, manifests the pure Ego 'I', and then (through its Will) divides its power into two, the ultimate state which, being without any manifestation, is self-contained (*pūrṇam*), and is responsible for creation (*unmeṣa-prasaraṇa*) and dissolution (*nimeṣa-sthitijuṣām*) through play and suspension of its power. (Tr. K.C. Pandey)

The Supreme Reality is the perfect equilibrium of Śiva and Śakti, the One and the Many, and therefore said to be self-contained (*pūrṇa*), resting-in-itself (*svātma-viśrānta*) and beyond all manifestation (*nirābhāsa*).

Jayaratha gives the following interpretation of the above benedictory verse, quoting it in his commentary on the **Tantrāloka**:

चिन्मात्रस्वभावः पर एव शिवः पूर्णत्वात्, निराशंसोऽपि स्वस्वातन्त्र्य-
माहात्म्याद् बहुरुल्लिलसिषया परानन्दचमत्कारतारतम्येन इत्यादि ।

Comm. on TĀl IX.51

The Supreme Lord Śiva, being-in-essence, pure consciousness alone, is without any desire because of his Fullness. By virtue of His innate freedom of will, (He) becomes intent on manifesting Himself externally, (and) shines in diverse forms in accordance with the comparative difference of tasting His innate Delight. (Tr. H.N. Chakravarty)

In the **Tantrāloka** Abhinavagupta attempts to explain the concept of fullness through an analogy from the actual life of man. He says:

कामस्य पूर्णता तत्त्वं संघट्टे प्रविभाव्यते ।

TĀl. III.170

The perfection or zenith of *kāma* or desire is realised (by all) at the time of union (*saṃghaṭṭe*) (of two partners). (Tr. H.N. Chakravarty)

Jayaratha in his commentary on the **Tantrāloka** elucidates the word *saṃghaṭṭa* saying that it actually signifies mutual agitation with the characteristic of equiflavoured balance at the time of coitus (*paras-parasāmarasyātmasaṃkṣobhāvasare* etc.).

Abhinavagupta describes the Supreme consciousness as perfect Fullness because It always shines by itself.

संवित्तत्त्वं भासमानं परिपूर्णं हि सर्वतः ।

TĀl X.222 cd

The Reality of Consciousness shines in its fullness in every respect. (Tr. H.N. Chakravarty)

It must be noted here that the prefix *pari-* has been added to *pūrṇa* to highlight as it were the independent and absolute nature of supreme Consciousness.

This becomes clear from the following description of the Supreme Lord by Abhinavagupta in his **Tantrāloka**.

तथाहि स्वस्वतन्त्रत्वपरिपूर्णतया विभुः ।
निःसंख्यैर्बहुभी रूपैर्भात्यवच्छेदवर्जनात् ॥ TĀl IX.52cd-53ab

The Supreme Lord, because of His innate autonomy of Will and Fullness shines in myriad forms without undergoing any limitations in His own. That is He ever remains as the highest light (*para-prakāśa*) free from all sorts of limitation. (Tr. H.N. Chakravarty)

He gives a reason for naming the Supreme Lord as Parama Śiva:

तावान्पूर्णस्वभावोऽसौ परमः शिव उच्यते ।

TĀl I.108 ab

He (Supreme Lord), is called Parama Śiva on account of all the Śaktis (numbering twelve) being included in Him, therefore His innate nature is perfect. (Tr. H.N. Chakravarty)

Elucidating this Jayaratha says:

पूर्णे सर्वमस्ति, सर्वत्र पूर्णमस्ति, अन्यथास्य पूर्णतैव न स्यात् ।

In the Full everything has its existence, everywhere Fullness exists, otherwise it would be impossible to designate it as Fullness. (Tr. H.N. Chakravarty)

In the commentary on the **Parātrimśikā**, Abhinavagupta explains the concept of fullness (*pūrṇatva*) which is the very nature of the Supreme Being in this manner (cf. *susampūrṇām* ... PTrī Verse 31):

सर्वतत्त्वैः सुष्ठु अभेदेन सम्यगनपायितया पूर्णत्वम् । सर्वत्र च परमाणावपि यदा समन्तात् भरणं - सर्वात्मीकरणम् । सर्वैर्वा घट-सुख-तिर्यङ्-नर-विरिञ्चि-विष्णु-रुद्र-मन्त्रसदाशिवादिप्रमातृरूपैः अवयवमानैरहमेकरस ... ।

PTrīVi p.97

The Supreme Being exists fully (*samyak*) and invariably (*anapāyitayā*) identified with all the *tattvas*. Then the fullness of the Supreme Divine shines (when) the Supreme Being makes everything in all direction even in the atoms wholly His own. All the external objects, such as jar etc., all (inner experiences) such as pleasure etc., all experiences such as animal, man, Brahmā, Viṣṇu, Rudra, Mantra, Sadāśiva exist (in Him) identified with His self like (inseparable) limbs. (Tr. J. Singh)

Elsewhere in the same text, Abhinavagupta describes the state of Bhairava:

अन्तःकृतसकलमन्त्रमहेशादिभिः स्थावरान्तप्रमातृजालस्याहमात्मनो-ऽस्माकमिति समुचितापतितव्यपदेशस्य भैरवात्मपूर्णतामयम्... ।

PTrīVi p.78

The state of Bhairava reveals the Fullness by withdrawing in Himself the entire creation beginning with *sakala* (limited and embodied experiencers) upto Mantra, Śiva etc., from an immobile object and experiencers whose very life consists of empirical egofeeling and which is rightly designated as ours. (Tr. J. Singh adapted)

The fullness of Consciousness is described in a poetic manner in the same text thus:

संकोचयन्ति हृदयं नहि शास्त्रपाशा
नो संविदं कलुषयेद्यदयं च लोकः ।
सम्यक्स्वभावपदवीपरिपूर्णरूपा
सैवोल्लसल्लयभरा भरिता स्थितिः स्यात् ॥

PTrīVi p.78

Neither the restrictions of *śāstras* (religious texts) can confine the heart within narrow limits, nor can popular views contaminate consciousness. That alone is the state of plenitude which is infused with the joyful condition of absorption or *khecarīsāmya* which is completely replete with the attribute of the essential nature of the Divine (which is Fullness). (Tr. J. Singh)

In all the citations quoted above from the writings of Abhinavagupta, the concept of *pūrṇa* used to signify the integral nature of the Supreme Being or Consciousness has reached its zenith as a philosophical concept. The word *pūrṇa* was no longer a term expressive of an attribute of the Divine Being, it was used as a synonym of the Absolute which according to the Kāśmīr Śaivites is all-inclusive. This is borne out by the spiritual experience of a Śaiva yogin on attaining the highest state of spiritual realisation when the world around him does not 'melt into thin air', he continues to experience the world as an expression of his essential divinity. Abhinavagupta describes this state of Bhairava in the following words:

यस्तु ध्वस्ताखिलभवमलो भैरवीभावपूर्णः ।
कृत्यं तस्य स्फुटमिदमियल्लोककर्तव्यमात्रम् ॥

TĀl II.39cd

But the individual who attains the fullness of the state of Bhairava, the Lord, that is when he realises the identity of his consciousness with Śiva after shattering all the worldly impurities is Śiva himself. Yet obviously (being equipped with body) he still has to perform some work which proceeds from him merely as a duty. (Tr. H.N. Chakravarty)

That the attainment of Sivatva, the highest state of spiritual realisation by a Śaiva yogin when he becomes full-in-himself does not negate his existence as an embodied being engaged in worldly activity, is obvious from the above description of *Bhairavī-bhāva*. This is also in conformity with the philosophy of integration emphasised by the Kāśmīr Śaivites.

Elsewhere the word *pūrṇa* has also been used by Abhinavagupta in an altogether different context as an adjective of *āhuti* to convey the sense of concluding or final oblation as in the Vedic texts. While describing the Tāntric sacrifice in symbolic terms which a spiritual aspirant is required to perform as a part of his spiritual discipline, Abhinavagupta says:

> य ऊर्ध्वे किल संबोधः कुण्डे स प्रतिबिम्बितः ।
> वह्निः प्राणः स्रुक्स्रुवौ च स्नेहः संकल्पचिद्रसः ॥
> इत्थं ज्ञात्वादितः कुण्डस्रुक्स्रुवाज्यमनूभृशम् ।
> द्वादशान्तविबोधाग्नौ रुद्ध्वा पूर्णाहुतिं क्षिपेत् ॥
>
> TĀl XV.429-430
>
> Consciousness which abides above (at the end of the twelve) shines reflecting in the sacrificial pit as fire, the vital energy is the ladles (*sruk* and *sruva*). The clarified butter is the desire with the characteristic of the concept of duality. Conceiving all of them thus from the beginning and calling to mind the *mantras* of each and then leading them to the end of twelve to have their rest of equilibrium there, and then restraining (them) there fully, one should offer the final oblation (*pūrṇāhuti*). (Tr. H.N. Chakravarty)

It may be pointed out here that unlike the Vedic rituals described in the Brāhmaṇa texts, Abhinavagupta does not attach much importance to the actual performance of the sacrificial rite because that does not help the aspirant much in the achievement of his spiritual realisation. As a true follower of Kaula spiritual tradition, he considers every rite to be a symbolic representation of some deeper spiritual thought. He has attempted to explain the symbolism underlying every act of the sacrificial rite of *kulayāga* that an initiated spiritual aspirant is required to perform, including the *pūrṇāhuti*. The main purpose of *pūrṇāhuti* is to first lead all the objects of the phenomenal world to merge into the Supreme Light of consciousness which is the *bimba*, the source of everything, that shines below as its reflection (*pratibimba*). It is therefore enjoined that the spiritual aspirant should seek the merger of the reflection first represented by worldly objects in the Fullness of pure consciousness in such a way that they lose their identities and shine in the equilibrium of the light of consciousness. When this is achieved, the sacrificer offers the last oblation below so that everything gets merged into the Consciousness. This is as it were "Fullness becoming full, from Fullness emerges Fullness".

Elsewhere in the context of Tāntric sacrifice the word *pūrṇāhuti* occurs in other texts too to signify the offering made with a full ladle e.g. *pūrṇāhutiṃ tato dadyāt* (the offering must be made with a full ladle). Thus the ritual-physical and the symbolical-spiritual meaning of *pūrṇāhuti* are two dimensions of the use of the term.

In the Arts

by Bettina Bäumer

The general ideal of fullness and perfection is present in all manifestations of Indian Art, but it comes to bear mainly in two contexts: One is the aesthetic and poetic theory, the other the visual symbolism in architecture, sculpture and painting.

Abhinavagupta describes the fullness of aesthetic experience in the context of drama thus:

> तथा ह्येकाग्रसकलसामाजिकजनेक्षितम् ।
> नृत्तं गीतं सुधासारसागरत्वेन मन्यते ॥
> तत एवोच्यते मल्लनटप्रेक्षोपदेशने ।
> सर्वप्रमातृतादात्म्यं पूर्णरूपानुभावकम् ॥
>
> TĀl X.85-86
>
> The spectators who watch, absorbed in a performance of dancing and singing, feel that it is a sea of nectar. With reference to watching, wrestling and dramatic performance it is taught that in it a state of identity with all knowing subjects occurs, which causes (in them) experience of perfect beatitude.

Jayaratha, the commentator, clarifies the concept of *pūrṇa* thus:

> इयदेव हि पूर्णं रूपं यद् विगलितवेद्यान्तरतया तत्रैवानन्याकाङ्क्षत्वेन परामर्शनम् ।
>
> This verily is the nature of *pūrṇa* in which all the knowables have dissolved and steady reflection (*parāmarśana*) of beatitude continues because it is free from the desire for any other object (as separate from the self). (Tr. H.N. Chakravarty)

The complete aesthetic experience is here clearly related to the identification or merging of the multiplicity of objects and subjects in the one Subject, which is accompanied by freedom from desires due to the bliss experienced.

In works of poetics we find the conception of a perfect simile (*pūrṇopamā*) which consists in the unification of *upamāna* and *upameya*, the object of comparison and the thing to be compared.

> गुणद्योतकोपमानोपमेयशब्दानां सामग्र्ये पूर्णा: ।
>
> KāvyālSū IV.2.2
>
> A simile becomes perfect with the entire assemblage of words, signifying excellence of *upamāna* and *upameya.*

> सा [उपमा] पूर्णा यदि सामान्यधर्म औपम्यवाचि च ।
>
> SāDar X.18
>
> That kind of simile should be considered as perfect which expresses common characteristic (of the two *upamāna* and *upameya*) and also reveals the similarity.

In music too, *pūrṇa* has been used in a technical sense, as the complete series of notes:

> पूर्णाः पञ्चसहस्राणि चत्वारिंशद्युतानि तु ।
> एकैकस्यां मूर्च्छनायां कूटतानाः सह क्रमैः ॥
>
> SR I.4.33
>
> Including the *mūrcchanā*-series (*kramas*) there are 5040 complete permutational note-series in each of the *mūrcchanās.* (Tr. P.L. Sharma and R.K. Shringy)

In the **Saṅgītasudhākara** commentary on the above text, this has been explained thus:

> पूर्णा या मूर्च्छना ग्रामद्वये तासामेकैकान्त्यस्वरापकर्षेण... ।
>
> If the *svara* existing between the two groups of *svaras* are (also) included, then that *mūrcchanā* becomes complete by isolating the last *svara.*

The idea of fullness which had been poetically expressed in the Vedic hymns has found its symbolical representation in the 'vase of plenty', *pūrṇa kalaśa.* P.K. Agrawala summarizes its importance in the visual arts in his monograph: "*Pūrṇa-Ghaṭa*, the Full Vase, is one of the most typical and perfect symbols of Indian Art and mythology. Its names in Indian literature, according to the rich expressiveness of Sanskrit language, are *Pūrṇa Kalaśa, Pūrṇa-Ghaṭa, Pūrṇa-Kumbha, Maṅgala Kalaśa, Bhadra Ghaṭa, Chandana Kalaśa*, etc. The symbol has at its back a long and hoary tradition in literature, Art and real life.

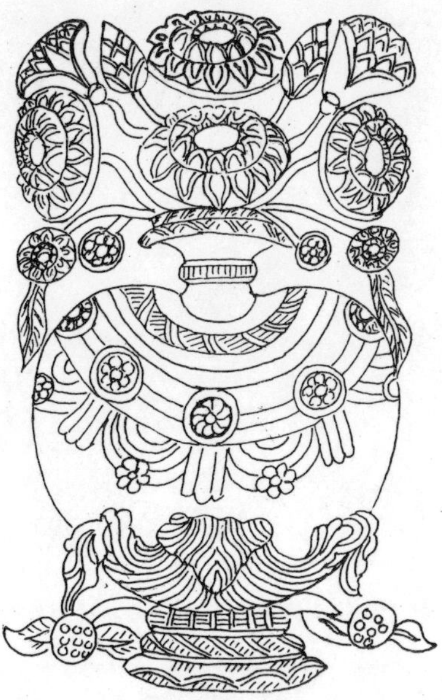

Figure 1: Pūrṇa-Kumbha, Amaravati

Its ritual value is so deep-rooted and ubiquitous even to this day that no religious ceremony can be performed without the installation of the Auspicious Pot. Right from the earliest times onwards it has stood through the ages in Indian civilisation as a visible symbol of the most mysterious life-forces revealed as creation, and as a popular decorative motif of beauty and auspiciousness. It has represented from the time immemorial the plentiful effusion of nature's blessings bestowed upon man. Its form in Art and ritual is the richly decorated pitcher full with water and overflowing with bunches of lotus buds, flowers and leaves. Green foliage vegetating from its mouth make it look extremely charming.

As the highest symbol of plenitude the *Pūrṇa Ghaṭa* stands to be unique, used freely, though meaningfully, throughout the history of Indian Art from the Śuṅga period onwards when stone and other permanent material begin to be used widely for architecture and art. It is accepted not exclusively by one creed, but is common to all religions taking birth and flourishing on Indian soil. It is "employed equally by all sects and occurs not only in India proper, but also in Farther India and Indonesia." It was received as a token of auspicious beauty and welfare from India in the countries coming at one time within the orbit of her cultural expansion, and spread all over Asia and islands where influences of Indian culture were deeply felt.

It is (1) auspicious and apotropaic, (2) embellishing and complementary, as well as (3) indicative and symbolical. It is the emblem *par excellence* of fullness

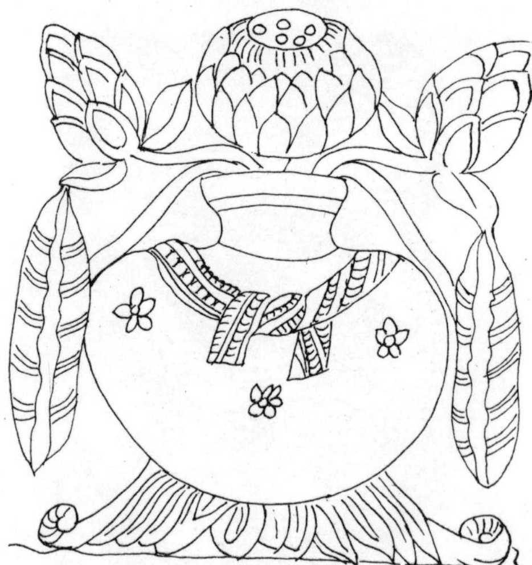

Figure 2: Pūrṇa Kalaśa, Mathura

and prosperity, of life endowed with all gifts, moral, material and spiritual. The full blooming overflowing contents of life are comparable to the plants and foliage luxuriating from the mouth of a jar filled with the life-giving liquid." (P.K. Agrawala, Pūrṇa Kalaśa or the Vase of Plenty, pp.1-3).

The jar filled or overflowing with the pure and auspicious waters is a symbol of fertility on all levels, from vegetal to animal, human and to divine life. It is often associated with goddess Śrī or Lakṣmī, and with the female womb or breasts carrying and giving life. "It is the womb which conceals within it the mystery of the birth of the cosmos." (*Ibid.* p.6). The manifold forms of representing the *pūrṇa kumbha* include the early reliefs at the Sanchi Stupas where rich foliage is sprouting forth from the mouth of the jar, representations of Śrī-Lakṣmī standing on a *kumbha*, the *kumbha* as base or top of a pillar, or as the crowning element of a temple or of other architectural parts of the temple, in the form of friezes etc. In all of Indian Art, whether Buddhist, Jaina or Brahmanical, the *pūrṇa kumbha* is one of the eight auspicious symbols (*aṣṭamaṅgala*), used very commonly in houses, at ritual occasions and at festivals. Without going into art-historical details, a few illustrations may suffice as examples.

Conclusion

Originating from the Vedas conveying the sense of fullness and perfection, *pūrṇa* developed into a symbol of auspiciousness, prosperity and perfection in the Arts. In philosophical texts of later period it was equated with the Supreme Being who also is the embodiment of absolute Perfection, auspiciousness, Fullness, abode of all Powers, the ultimate source of the entire creation. The

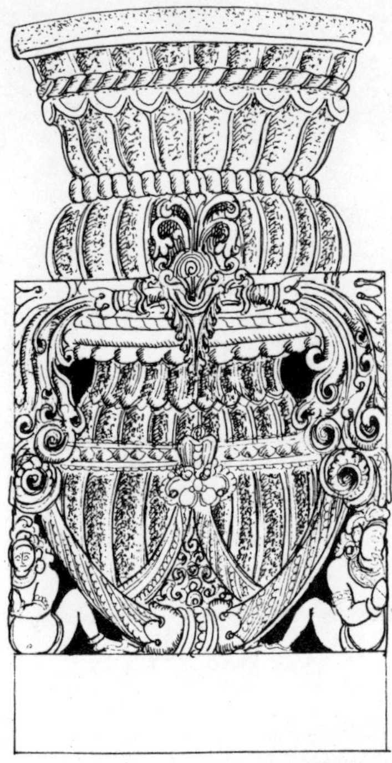

Figure 3: Pūrṇa-Kumbha as pillar-base, Ellora

Viṣṇusahasranāma Bhāṣya summarizes this idea when it describes Viṣṇu as the embodiment of fullness: "(He is) The Plenum, as He possesses all the objects of desire and all śaktis or energies." (*Pūrṇaḥ: sakalaiḥ kāmaiḥ sakalābhiḥ śaktibhiśca sampanna iti pūrṇaḥ* ViSahasrBh 86). This abstract concept of Fullness seems to permeate all the different branches of human thought, religion, philosophy, literature and Arts.

Debabrata Sensharma

Select Bibliography

Agrawala, Prithvi Kumar: Pūrṇa Kalaśa or The Vase of Plenty, Varanasi, Prithivi Prakashan, 1985.

Sastri, S. Kuppuswami: "Pūrnaism in Indian Philosophy – the Wholism of Ancient India" in Philosophical Quarterly, Calcutta, April 1935.

BIBLIOGRAPHY

Abhidhānacintāmaṇi Kośa of Hemacandra: Surat: H.K. Javeri, M.M Chokasi, Jain Pustakoddhāra Saṃsthā, 1946.

Abhidharma Kośa of Vasubandhu: ed. by Swāmī Dvārikādās Śāstrī Varanasi: Bauddha-Bharati, 1987.

— tr. by Subhadra Jha. Patna: Kashi Prasad Jayaswal Research Institute, 1983.

— Abhidharma Kośa Bhāṣya by Louis de lavallee Poussin, tr. by L.M. Pruden. Berkeley: Asian Humanities Press, 1988.

Abhidharma Samuccaya: ed. by Prahlad Pradhan. Santiniketan: Visva Bharati, 1950.

— Le Compendium de la Super-Doctrine (Philosophie) (Abhidharmasamuccaya) d'Asaṅga, traduit et annoté par Walpola-Rahula, Paris: Ecole Française D'Extrême Orient, 1971.

Abhijñānaśākuntalam of Kālidāsa: with the commentary Arthoddyotanikā of Rāghava Bhaṭṭa, ed. by N.B. Godabole; Revised by W.L. Shastri Pansikar. Bombay: Tukaram Jawaji, Nirnaya Sagar Press, 1913 (6th ed.).

— ed. by M.R. Kale. Delhi: Motilal Banarsidass, 1987.

Abhilaṣitārthacintāmaṇi of Someśvara Deva: ed. by R. Samasastry. Mysore: University of Mysore, 1926.

Adhyayanasūtra: ed.by Muni Puṇyavijaya. Bombay: Śrī Mahāvīr Jain Mahāvidyālaya, 1977 (Jaināgama Granthamālā 15).

Aghoraśivācāryapaddhati (Kriyākramadyotikā): with Prabhā Comm. of Nirmalamaṇi, ed. by K. Krishna Sastri and P. Rama Sastri. Tamilnadu, 1927.

Agni Purāṇa: Poona: Ananda Ashram, 1957 (Ananda Ashram Sanskrit Granthavali-41).

Agniveśya Gṛhya Sūtra: ed. by L.A. Ravi Varma. Trivendrum: Trivendrum Sanskrit Series-44, 1940.

Ahirbudhnya Saṃhitā: ed. by M.D. Rāmānujācārya. Madras: Adyar Library, 1966.

Aitareya Āraṇyakam: with comm. of Sāyaṇācārya, ed. by Kashinatha Sastri. Poona: Ananda Ashram, 1979, 2 Vols. (Ananda Ashram Sanskrit Granthavali-32).

— ed. and tr. by A.B. Keith. Oxford: The Clarendon Press, 1909.

Aitareya Brāhmaṇa of the Rigveda: ed. and tr. by Martin Haug. London: Trubner and Co., 1863, 2 Vols.

— Rigveda Brāhmaṇa: The Aitareya and Kauṣītaki Brāhmaṇas of the Rigveda: tr. into English by A.B. Keith. Delhi: Motilal Banarsidass, 1981 (Reprint) (Harvard Oriental Series-25).

Ajitāgama: ed. by N.R. Bhatt. Pondicherry: Institut Français d'Indologie, 1964, 1967, 2 Vols.

Amarakośa of Amarasiṃha: with comm. of Ācārya Kṛṣṇamitra ed. by Satyadeva Misra. Patna: Indira Prakashan, 1972.

Amṛtodaya of Gokulanātha: ed. by M.M. Sivadatta. Bombay: Nirnayasagar Press, 1897.

Anekārthasaṃgraha of Hemachandra: ed. by S.P. Jagannath Shastri Hoshing. Varanasi: Chowkhamba Sanskrit Series, 1969.

Aparājitapṛcchā of Bhuvana Deva: ed. by Popatbhai Ambashankar Mankad. Baroda: Orientral Institute, 1950.

Āpastamba Dharmasūtra: ed. by G. Bühler. Bombay: The Department of Public Construction, 1932 (Bombay Sanskrit Series-44, 50), 3rd edition.

Āpastamba Gṛhyasūtra: ed. by A. Chinnaswami Sastri, and U.C. Pandey. Varanasi: Chowkhamba, 1971 (Kashi Sanskrit Series-59).

Āpastamba Śrautasūtra: ed. by T.T. Srinivasagopalachary. Mysore: University of Mysore, 1953 (Oreiental Research Institute Publications Sanskrit Series-98), Vol. II.

— ed. by A. Srinivasaraghavacharya. Mysore: University of Mysore, 1960 (Oriental Research Institute Publication Sanskrit Series-104), Vol. III.

Āpastamba Śulvasūtra: ed. by Satya Prakash and R.S. Sharma. Delhi: Mahalakshmi Pub. House, 1968 (Ratna Kumari Pub. Series-5).

Arthaśāstra of Kauṭilya: ed. and Tr. by R.P. Kangle. Delhi: Motilal Banarsidass, 1986, 3 Vols.

Arthaviniścayasūtra: Patna: K.P. Jaiswal Research Institute, 1971.

Āryabhaṭīya of Āryabhaṭṭa: ed. by Kripa Shankar Shukla. New Delhi: The Indian National Science Academy, 1976.

Āryamañjuśrīmūlakalpa: ed. by T. Ganapati Sastri. Delhi: Sri Satguru Publication, 1989, 4 Vols.

Āścaryacūḍāmaṇi of Śaktibhadra: with an Introduction by S.Kuppuswami Sastri. Madras: Sri Balamanorama Press, 1926 (Shri Balamanorama Series-9).

Aṣṭādhyāyī of Pāṇini: tr. by S.M. Katre. Delhi: Motilal Banarsidass, 1987.

— ed. by S.C. Basu. Varanasi: Motilal Banarsidass, 1988.

Aṣṭaprakaraṇa: ed. by V.V. Dwivedi. Varanasi: Sampurnananda Sanskrit University, 1988.

Aṣṭasāhasrikā Prajñā Pāramitā: ed. by Rajendralala Mitra. Calcutta: The Asiatic Society, 1888 (Bibliotheca Indica, A Collection of Oriental Works).

— tr. by Edward Conze. Calcutta: The Asiatic Society, 1970 (Bibliotheca Indica, A Collection of Oriental Works No.284).

— Prajñāpāramitā and Related Systems: ed. by Lewis, Lancaster. Berkeley Buddhist Studies Series, 1977.

Āśvalāyana Gṛhyasūtra: ed. and tr. in Eng. by N.N. Sharma. Delhi: Eastern Book Linkers, 1976.

Āśvalāyana Śrautasūtra: tr. and ed. by H.G. Ranade. Poona: R.H. Ranade, 1981, 1986, 2 Vols. (Ranade Publication Series 2, 4).

Atharvaveda Pariśiṣṭa: ed. by J.M. Balling and J.V. Negelein. ed. with Hindi Notes by Ram Kumar Rai. Varanasi: Chaukhamba Orientalia, 1976.

Atharvaveda Saṃhitā: ed. by Śrīpāda Dāmodar Sātvalekar. Paradi: Svādhyāya Maṇḍala, 1985, 4 Vols.

— The Hymns of the Atharvaveda: Tr. by R.T.H. Griffith. Varanasi: Chowkhamba Publication, 1968, 2 Vols. (The Chowkhamba Sanskrit Studies-66).

— Paippalāda Saṃhitā of the Atharvaveda, ed. by Durgamohan Bhattacharya. Calcutta: Sanskrit College, 1970.

Aṭṭhasālinī (on Dhamma Saṅganī): ed. by P.V. Wapot and R.D. Wadekar. Poona: Bhandarkar Oriental Research Institute, 1942.

— The Expositor: Tr. by Pe Maung Tino, ed. by Mrs. R. Devids. Luzac and Co. Ltd., 1958.

Aucityavicāracarcā of Kṣemendra: ed. by R.S. Tripathi. Varanasi: Chowkhamba Sanskrit Series, 1982.

Baudhāyana Dharmasūtra: ed. by A. Chinnaswami Shastri. Varanasi: Chowkhamba, 1972 (Kashi Sanskrit Series-104).

Baudhāyana Gṛhyasūtra: ed. by R., Shamasastri. New Delhi: Meharcandra Lachmandas, 1982.

Baudhāyana Śrautasūtra: ed. by W. Caland. New Delhi: Munshiram Manoharlal, 1982, 3 Vols. bound in 2.

Baudhāyana Śulbasūtra: with Sanskrit Comm. by Dwarka Nath Yajvan, Eng. tr. by G. Thibaut, ed. by Satya Prakash and Ram Swarup Sharma. New Delhi: The Research Institute of Ancient Scientific Studies, 1968.

— Śulba Sūtras of Baudhāyana, Āpastamba, Kātyāyana and Mānava: ed. and tr. by S.N. Sen and A.K. Bag. New Delhi: Indian National Science Academy, 1983.

Bhagavadgītā: with Śāṅkarabhāṣya. Gorakhpur: Gita Press, 1967.

— ed. by W.L.S. Pansikar. Varanasi: Indological Book House, 1984.

— with Sarvatobhadra Comm. of Rājānaka Rāmakaṇṭha. Srinagar : Research Department, Jammu and Kashmir State, 1943 (Kashmir Series of Texts and Studies 64).

— tr. into Eng. by R.C. Zaehner. London: Oxford University Press, 1981.

Bhāgavata-Purāṇa of Kṛṣṇa Dvaipāyana Vyāsa: ed. and tr. by A.C. Bhaktivedanta Swami Prabhupada. Manila: Bhaktivedanta Book Trust, 1982.

Bhaktirasāmṛtasindhu of Rūpagosvāmin: with 'Durgāsaṅgamanī' comm. of Jīvagosvāmin and "Bhaktisārapradarśinī" comm. of Viśvanātha Chakravarti, ed. by Shyamdas. Vrindavan, 1981.

Bhaktirasāyana of Madhusūdana Sarasvatī: ed. by Janardana Shastri Pandey. Varanasi: G.K. Pandey, 1976.

Bharata-Bhāṣya of Nānyadeva: ed. by Chaitanya P. Desai. Khairagarh: Indira Kala Sangita Visvavidyalaya, 1961, 1976, 2 parts.

Bhāsanāṭakacakram: ed. by C.R. Devadhara. Delhi: Motilal Banarsidass, 1987.

Bhāskarīya - Bījaganita with the comm. Navāṅkurā of kṛṣṣna Daivajña, ed. by V.G. Apte, Poona 1930 (Anandasrama Sanskrit Series No. 90).

Bhāṭṭacintāmaṇi of Gāgā Bhaṭṭa: Varanasi: Chowkhamba, 1933.

Bhāvanākramaḥ of Ācārya Kamalaśīla: ed. by Ācārya Gyaltsen Namdol, Sarnath: Central Institute of Higher Tibetan Studies, 1985.

Bhāvaprakāśa of Śāradātanaya: ed. by Yatiraja Swami and K.S. Ramaswami Sastri. Baroda: Oriental Institute, 1986 (Reprint).

Bodhicaryāvatāra of Śāntideva: ed. by P.L. Vaidya. Darbhanga: The Mithila Institute, 1960.

Brāhmasphuṭasiddhānta of Brahmagupta, ed. by Ram Svarup Sharma, New Delhi: The Indian Institute of Astronomical and Sanskrit Research, 1966, 4 Vols.

Brahmasūtra: with Śaṅkarabhāṣya. Bombay: Nirnayasagar Press, 1948.

— with Śāṅkarabhāṣya. Delhi: Motilal Banarsidass, 1985.

— tr. by G. Thibaut. Delhi: Motilal Banarsidass, 1890, 1896 2 vols (Sacred Books of the East Series-34,38).

— ed. and tr. into Eng. by Swami Gambhirananda, Calcutta: Advaita Ashrama, 1983.

— Brahmasūtra-Śrībhāṣya of Rāmānuja: ed. by Uttamur Vira Raghavacharya. Madras: Ubhaya Vedant Granthamala, 1963.

— Vedāntasūtra of Bādarāyaṇa: with the Comm. of Baladeva, tr. by Srisa Chandra Vasu. Delhi: Oriental Books Reprint Corporation, 1979.

— Vedāntasūtra: with the Comm. of Rāmānujācārya, tr. by G. Thibaut. Delhi: Motilal Banarsidass, 1984 (Sacred Books of the East Series-48).

Bṛhaddeśī of Mataṅga: ed. by K. Sāmbaśiva Śāstrī. Trivandrum, 1928 (Trivandrum Sanskrit Series 94).

Bṛhaddevatā of Śaunaka: A Summary of the details and myths of the Ṛgveda, ed. by A.A. Macdonell. Delhi: Motilal Banarsidass, 1965, 2 vols.

Bṛhat Saṃhitā of Varāhamihira: ed. and tr. by M. Ramakrishna Bhat. Delhi: Motilal Banarsidass, 1981, 1982, 2vols.

Buddhacarita of Aśvaghoṣa: ed. and tr. in Hindi by Sūryanārāyaṇa Chaudhurī. Bihar: Saṃskṛta Bhavana, 1948.

Campūbhāratam (Bharatacampū) of Ananta: with the Comm. of Rāmachandrabudhendra, ed. by Kasinath Pandurang Parab. Bombay: Nirnayasagar Press, 1930.

Campūrāmāyaṇa (Rāmāyaṇa Campū) of Bhoja: with the Comm. of Rāmacandrabudhendra, ed. by K.P. Parab. Bombay: Nirnayasagar Press, 1898.

Carakasaṃhitā: English tr. by P.V. Sharma. Varanasi: Chaukhamba Orientalia, 1981, 1983, 1985, 3 Vols.

— with the "Āyurveda Dīpikā" Comm. of Cakrapāṇidatta, ed. by Jadavaji Tikamji Acarya. Delhi: Munshiram Manoharlal, 1981, 4th ed.

Daśarūpaka of Dhanañjaya: with Comm. of Dhanika, ed. and Hindi tr. by Bholasankara Vyasa. Varanasi: Chaukhamba Vidyabhavan, 1973, 4th ed.

Dattilam of Dattila: ed. by Sambasiva Sastri. Trivandrum, 1930 (trivandrum Sanskrit Series 102).

— ed. and tr. into Eng. by Mukund Lath. Delhi: I.G.N.C.A., 1988.

The Dhammapada: Pali text, English tr. and notes, ed. by S. Radhakrishnan Delhi: Oxford University Press, 1950, 8th ed. 1984.

— Dhammapadam: tr. by C. Kunhan Raja. Adyar: Theosophical Publishing House, 1956.

Dhvanyāloka of Ānandavardhana: ed. by Pattabhirama Sastri. Varanasi: Chaukhamba Sanskrit Series Office, 1940.

— Dhvanyāloka or Theory of Suggestion in Poetry: tr. by K. Krishnamoorthy. Poona: Oriental Book Agency, 1955 (poona Oriental Series 92.).

Gāthā Saptaśatī of King Hāla: ed. and tr. into English by Radhagovinda Basak: Calcutta: The Asiatic Society, 1971.

— The Gāhākośa of Hāla (Sātavāhana): Part II, ed. by M.V. Patwardhan. Delhi: Bhogilal Leherchand Institute of Indology 1988.

Gaṇaratnamahodadhi of Vasubandhu: ed. by J. Eggeling. Delhi: Motilal Banarsidass, 1968 (Reprinted).

Gobhila Gṛhyasūtra: with Bhaṭṭanārāyaṇa's comm., ed. by Chintamani Bhattacharya. Delhi: Munshiram Manoharlal, 1982, 2nd ed.

Gṛhya Sūtras: tr. by H. Oldenberg and F. Max Müller. Delhi: Motilal Banarsidass, 1981, 1989, 2 Vols. (Reprint) (Sacred Books of the East-29-30).

Haṭhayogapradīpikā: with Jyotsnā comm. of Brahmānanda, ed. and tr. by Srinivasa Iyangar. Madras: Adyar Library, 1975 (Reprint).

Hevajra Tantra: A Critical Study, with Yogaratnamālā comm. of Kanhapāda, ed. by D.L. Snellgrove. London: Oxford University Press, 1980, 2 Vols. (Reprint).

Īśānaśivagurudevapaddhati: ed. by T. Ganapati Sastri. Delhi: Bharatiya Vidya Prakashan, 1988, 4 Vols.

Īśvarapratyabhijñā Kārikā of Utpaladeva: with Vimarśinī by Abhinavagupta: ed. by M.S. Kaul. Srinagar: Research Department, Jammu and Kashmir State, 1918, 1921, 2 Vols. (Kashmir Series of Texts and studies).

Īśvarapratyabhijñāvimarśinī of Abhinavagupta: with the Comm. Bhāskarī, ed. by K.A. Subramaniya Iyer and K.C. Pandey and tr. by K.C. Pandey. Delhi: Motilal Banarsidass, 1986, 3 Vols.

— Īśvarapratyabhijñāvimarśinī (Bhāskarī): tr. by K.C. Pandey. Lucknow: Superintendent Printing, 1954.

Jayākhya Saṃhitā of Pāñcarātra Āgama: ed. by Embar Krishnamacharya. Baroda: Oriental Institute, 1967.

Kalpadrukośa of Keśava: Baroda: Oriental Institute, 1932.

Kāmakalāvilāsa: with the comm. of Natanānandanātha, tr. by Arthur Avalon. Madras: Ganesh and Comp. Ltd., 1953.

Kāmasūtra of Vatsyāyana: ed. by Gosvami Damodar Shastri. Banaras: Chowkhamba Sanskrit Series Office, 1929.

Kāpiṣṭhala-kaṭha-Saṃhitā: A Text of the Black Yajurveda, ed. by Raghuvīra. Delhi: Meharchandra Lachhmandass, 1968.

— Kāṭhaka Die Saṃhitā der Kaṭha Śākhā: ed. by Leopold von Schroeder. Wiesbaden: Franz Steiner Verlag, 1970, 2 Vols.

— Yajurvedīya Kāṭhaka Saṃhitā: ed. by Śrīpāda Dāmodara Sātvalekar. Paradi: Svādhyāya Maṇḍala, 1985.

Kātyāyana Śrautasūtra: tr. by H.C. Ranade, Pune: Ranade Publication Series, 1978.

— The Śrautasūtra of Kātyāyana: with extracts from the Comm. of Karka and Yājñikadeva, ed. by Abbrecht Weber. Varanasi: Chowkhamba Sanskrit Series, 1972.

Kātyāyana Śulvasūtra: ed. and tr. into Eng. by S.D. Khadilakar. Poona: Vaidika Saṃśodhana Maṇḍala, 1974.

Kauṣītaki Brāhmaṇa: ed. by E.R. Sree Krishna Sarma. Wiesbaden: Franz Steiner Verlag, 1968, 3 Vols.

Kāvyādarśa of Daṇḍin: with Comm. of Jīvānanda Vidyāsāgara Bhaṭṭāchārya, tr. by V. Narayana Iyer. Madras, 1952.

Kāvyālaṅkāra of Bhāmaha: ed. and tr. by P.V. Naganatha Sastri. Delhi: Motilal Banarsidass, W.D.

Kāvyālaṅkārasūtra of Vāmana: ed. by Narayana Ram Acharya. Varanasi: Motilal Banarsidass, 1983.

Kāvyamīmaṃsā of Rājaśekhara: ed. by S.D. Dalal and R.A. Sastry. Baroda: Oriental Institute, 1934 (Gaekwad's Oriental Series-1).

— with Comm. "Prakāśa", ed. and tr. by Ganga Sagar Roy. Varanasi: Chaukhamba Vidyabhavan, 1964.

Kāvyaprakāśa of Mammaṭa: tr. by Ganganatha Jha. Varanasi: Bharatiya Vidya Prakashan. 1967.

— with comm. of Vaman Jhalakikar. Pune: Bhandarkar Oriental Research Institute, 1750.

— with comm. "Saṅketa". Pune: Ānanda Āśrama, 1921.

Kulārṇava Tantra: ed. by Tārānātha Vidyāratna with Introduction of Arthur Avalon and Readings of M.P. Pandit. Delhi: Motilal Banarsidass, 1984 (Reprint).

Kumārasambhava of Kālidāsa: with Comm. of Mallinātha on 1-8 Cantos, and Comm. of Sitaram on 8-17 Cantos, ed. by Wasudev Laxman Shastri Pansikar. Bombay: Nirnaya Sagar Press, 1961.

— ed. by M.R. Kale. Delhi: Motilal Banarsidass, 1986.

Laghuyogavāsiṣṭha of Abhinanda: with "Vasiṣṭha Candrikā" comm., ed. by Wasndeva Laxman Shastri Pansikar. Delhi: Motilal Banarsidass, 1985 (Reprint).

Lakṣmī Tantra: Pāñcarātra Āgama, ed. by V. Krishnamacarya. Madras: Adyar Library and Research Centre, 1975 (Reprint) (Adyar Library Series-87).

— Lakṣmī Tantra: A Pāñcarātra Text, tr. with notes by Sanjukta Gupta. Leiden: E.J. Brill, 1972.

Madhyamaka Śāstra of Nāgārjuna with the Comm. Prasannapadā by Candrakirti; ed. by P.L. Vaidya. Darbhanga: Mithila Institute, 1960.

Mahābhārata: ed. by V.S. Sukhthankar. Poona: Bhandarkar Oriental Research Institute, 19 Vols., 1971, 1974.

— tr. into English by P.C. Roy. Calcutta: Datta Bose and Co., 12 Vols.

— The Mahābhārata: tr. and ed. by J.A.B. Van Buitenen. Chicago: The University of Chicago Press, 1980, 1981, 1978, 3 Vols.

Mahābhāṣya of Patañjali: ed. by F. Kielhorn, revised by K.U. Abhyankar. Poona: Bhandarkar Oriental Research Institute, 1985, 1965, 1972, 3 Vols.

— Mahābhāṣya: Paspaśāhnika: tr. into English by K.C. Chatterji. Calcutta, 1957.

La Mahā Nārāyaṇa Upaniṣad: ed. critique, trad. Française... en annexe La Prāṇāgnihotra Upaniṣad per Jean Varenne. Paris: De Boccard, 1986 (2nd ed.).

Mahārthamañjarī of Maheśvarānanda: with the Comm. Parimala, ed. by V.V. Dvivedi. Varanasi: Varanaseya Sanskrit Visvavidyalaya, 1972.

Mahāvīracarita of Bhavabhūti: with Vīrarāghava Comm., ed. by T.R. Ratnam Iyar, S. Rangachariar and K.P. Parab. Bombay: Nirnaya Sagar Press, 1901.

Mahāyānasūtrālaṅkāra of Ārya Asaṅga: ed. by Swami Dwarikadas Shastri Varanasi: Bauddha Bharati, 1985.

Maitrāyaṇī Saṃhitā: ed. by Śrīpāda Dāmodar Sātavalekar. Paradi: Svādhyāya Maṇḍala, W.D.

— Die Saṃhitā der Maitrāyaṇīya Śākhā, Herausgegeben von Leopold von Schroeder, Wiesbaden: Franz Steiner Verlag GMBH, 1970, 3 Vols.

Mālatīmādhava of Bhavabhūti: with Comm. of Jagaddhara, ed. and English tr. by M.R. Kale. Delhi: Motilal Banarsidass, 1967, 3rd ed.

Mālavikāgnimitram of Kālidāsa: with Comm. of Kāṭyavema, ed. by K.P. Parab. Bombay: Nirnaya Sagar Press, 1918, 5th ed.

Mālinīvijayottara Tantra: ed. by Madhusūdana Kaul Shastri. Bombay: Research Department, Jammu and Kashmir State, 1922 (Kashmir Series of Texts and Studies-37).

Mānasāra: tr. by P.K. Acharya. Allahabad: Oxford University Press, 1933.

Mānasollāsa of Someśvara: ed. by G.K. Shirgondekar. Baroda: Oriental Institute, 1967 (Gaekwad Oriental Series-28).

Manusmṛti of Manu: ed. by J.L. Shastri. Delhi: Motilal Banarsidass, 1983

— The Laws of Manu: tr. by G. Bühler. Delhi: Motilal Banarsidass, 1964 (Reprint) (Sacred Books of the East Series-25).

Mataṅga Pārameśvarāgama: with comm. of Bhaṭṭa Rāmakaṇṭha, ed. by N.R. Bhatt. Pondicherry: Institut Français d'Indologie, 1982.

Matsya Purāṇa of Vyāsa: Bombay, Laksmi Venkatesvara Press, 1980.

— ed. by Nag Sharan Singh. Delhi: Nag Publishers, 1983, 2 Vols.

Mayamata: Critically ed. and tr. in French by Bruno Dagens. Pondicherry: Institut Français d'Indologie, 1976.

— tr. in English by B. Dagens. Delhi: Sitaram Bhartia Institute of Scientific Research. 1985.

Meghadūta of Kālidāsa: with comm. of Mallinātha, ed. and Eng. tr. by M.R. Kale. Delhi: Motilal Banarsidass, 1987.

Medinīkośa of Medinīkara: ed. by J.S. Hoshing. Varanasi: Chowkhamba Sanskrit Series 1968.

Mimāṃsāsūtra of Jaimini: with Śābara Bhāṣya, ed. by Ratna Gopal Bhatta. Varanasi: Chaukhamba Publications, 1910.

Mṛcchakaṭika of Śūdraka: with comm. of Pṛthvīdhara, ed. and Eng. tr. by M.R. Kale. Bombay: Booksellers Publishing Co., 1962.

Mṛgendrāgama (Kriyāpāda and Caryāpāda): with comm. by Bhaṭṭa Nārāyaṇa Kaṇṭha, ed. by N.R. Bhatt. Pondicherry: Institut Français d'Indologie, 1962.

— Mṛgendra Tantra (Vidyāpāda and Yogapāda): ed. by Madhusudan Kaul Sastri. Srinagar: Research Department, Jammu and Kashmir State, 1930 (Kashmir Series of Texts and Studies-50).

Mudrārākṣasa of Viśākhadatta: critically ed. and Eng. tr. by K.H. Dhruva. Poona: Oriental Book Agency, 1923 (2nd ed.).

Nāgānandam of Harṣa: ed. by J.M. Ashar. Bhavanagar: Students Publishing Co., W.D.

Nārada Bhaktisūtra: ed. and tr. by Swami Chinmayananda. Bombay: Chinmaya Mission Trust, 1982.

Nāradīya Śikṣā: with the Comm. of Bhaṭṭa Śobhākar, ed. and tr. by Usha R. Bhise. Poona: Bhandarkar Oriental Research Institute, 1986.

Narāyaṇapaṇḍita's Bījagaṇitāvataṃsa, ed. by Kripa Shankar Shukla, Lucknow: Akhila Bharatiya Sanskrit Parishad, 1970.

Nāṭyaśāstra of Bharata: with Abhinava Bhāratī comm., ed. by M. Ramakrishna Kavi and J.S. Pade. Baroda: Oriental Institute, 4 Vols. (Vol. I-Chapts 1-7, 1956; II Chapts. 8-18, 1934; III Chapts. 19-27, 1954; IV Chapts. 28-37, 1964) (Gaekwad Oriental Series-36, 68, 104-105).

Netra Tantra: with the Comm. by Kṣemarāja, ed. by Madhusudana Kaul Shastri. Bombay: Research Department Jammu and Kashmir State, 1926, 1936, 2 Vols. (Kashmir Series of Texts and Studies).

Nighaṇṭu and the Nirukta of Yāska: ed. and tr. by Lakshman Sarup. Delhi: Motilal Banarsidass, 1984 (Reprint).

— Niruktam (in Bengali): Yāska's Nirukta, ed. by Amareswara Thakur. Calcutta: University of Calcutta, 1955, 1960, 1963, 1970, 4 Vols.

Nīti and Vairāgya Śatakas of Bhartṛhari: ed. and tr. by M.R. Kale. Delhi: Motilal Banarsidass, 1971.

Nyāya Sūtra of Gautama: with Bhāṣya of Vātsyāna; tr. in Eng. by Ganganatha Jha. Delhi: Motilal Banarsidass, 1984 (Reprint).

— tr. in Eng. by Mrinalkanti Gangopadhyaya. Calcutta: Indian Studies, 1982.

Pāṇinīyaśikṣā: ed. by Man Mohan Ghosh. Delhi: Asian Humanities Press, 1986.

Parātrīśikā Vivaraṇa of Abhinavagupta: ed. by M.S. Kaul Shastri. Srinagar: Research Department, Jammu and Kashmir State, W.D. (Kashmir Series of Texts and Studies-18).

— ed. by B. Bäumer, tr. in Eng. by Jaideva Singh. Delhi: Motilal Banarsidass, 1988.

Prabodha Candrodaya of Kṛṣṇamiśrayati: with the Nāṭakābharaṇa of Govindāmṛta, ed. by K. Sāmbaśiva Śāstri. Trivandrum, 1936 (Trivandrum Sanskrit Series-22).

Prakaraṇa Pañcikā of Śālikaṇṭha Miśra: ed. by A. Subramaniyam Shastri Varanasi: Banaras Hindu University, 1961 (Darśana Series No. 4).

Prapañcasāratantra of Śaṅkarācārya: Revised by A. Avalon, ed. by Aṭalānanda Sarasvatī. Delhi: Motilal Banarsidass, 1981, 2 Parts in one Vol. (Reprint) (Tāntric Text Series-19).

Praśamaratiprakaraṇa of Umāsvāti: ed. by Rajkumar. Bombay: Śrī Paramaśrutaprabhāvakamaṇḍala, 1950.

Prasthāna Ratnākara of Puruṣottama Gosvāmin: ed. by Varanasi: Vidyavilasa Press, 1909.

Pratyabhijñā Hṛdayam of Kṣemaraja: ed. and tr. by Jaideva Singh. Delhi: Motilal Banarsidass, 1973.

Priyadarśikā of Śrīharṣa: ed. by R.V. Krishnamachariar. Madras 1906 (Sri Vani Vilas Sanskrit Series 3).

Puggalapaññati: ed. by Bhikkhu J. Kasyap. Nalanda: Pali Publication Board, Bihar Government, 1960 (Nalanda Devanagari PaliSeries).

— Designation of Human Types (Puggalapaññati): Tr. by Bimala Candra Law. London: Messrs Luzac and Company Ltd., 1969.

Raghuvaṃśa of Kālidāsa: with Mallinātha comm., ed. and Eng. tr. by G.R. Nandargikar. Delhi: Motilal Banarsidass, 1982.

Rājataraṅgiṇī of Kalhaṇa: tr. and ed. by M.A. Stein. Delhi: Motilal Banarsidass, 1979, 3 Vols.

Rāmāyaṇa of Vālmīki with the Tilaka Comm. of Rāma: ed. by Wasudev Lakshman Shastri Pansikar. Delhi: Indological Book House, 1983, 2 Vols.

— tr. into English by M.N. Dutt. Patna: Eastern Book House, 1987, Reprint, 4 Vols.

Rasagaṅgādhara of Jagannātha: with the Comm. of Nāgeśa Bhaṭṭa, ed. by Mathurānātha Śāstrī. Bombay: Nirnaya Sagar Press, 1947, 6th ed. (Kāvyamālā-12).

Ratnāvalī of Śrīharṣa: ed. and Eng. tr. by M.R. Kale. Bombay: Booksellers Publishing Company, 1964, 3rd ed.

Rauravāgama: ed. by N.R. Bhatt. Pondicherry: Institut Français d'Indologie, 1961, 1972, 2 Vols.

Ṛgveda Saṃhitā: ed. by Śrīpāda Dāmodara Sātavalekara. Paraḍi: Svādhyāya Maṇḍala, 1985, 4 Vols.

— The Hymns of the Rigveda: tr. with Comm. by Ralph T.H. Griffith, Varanasi: Chaukhamba Sanskrit Series Office, 1971, 2 Vols.

Ṛtusaṃhāra of Kālidāsa: with "Haripriyā" comm., ed. by Laksmīprapannāchārya. Varanasi: Chaukhamba Amarabharati Prakashan, 1977.

Sāhitya Darpaṇa of Viśvanātha: with 'Kusumapratibhā' Comm., ed. by Haridas Bhattacharya. Calcutta: Hemacandra Bhattacharya, 1945.

Samarāṅgaṇa Sūtradhāra of Bhoja: ed. by V.S. Agrawal. Baroda: Oriental Institute, 1966 (Gaekwads Oriental Series-25).

Sāma-Veda: ed. and tr. by Devi Chanda. Delhi: Munshiram Manoharlal, 1980.

Sāṃkhya Kārikā of Īśvarakṛṣṇa: with Yuktidīpikā Comm., ed. by Ram Chandra Pandeya. Delhi: Motilal Banarsidass, 1967.

Sāṃkhya Sūtra with Pravacanabhāṣya of Vijñāna Bhikṣu, ed. by R.S. Bhattacharya. Varanasi: Bharatiya Vidya Prakasana, 1977.

— The Sāṃkhya Philosophy: containing Sāṃkhya Pravacana Sūtram, with the Vṛtti of Aniruddha, and the Bhāṣya of Vijñānabhiksu and extracts from the Vṛttisāra of Mahādeva Vedāntin; Tattva Samāsa; Sāṃkhya Kārikā; Pañcaśikha Sūtram, tr. by Nandlal Sinha. Delhi: Oriental Books Reprint Corporation, 1979 (Reprint).

Saṅgītaratnākara of Sārṅgadeva: with Comm. of Siṃhabhūpāla and Kallinātha, ed. by S. Subramanya Sastri. Madras: Adyar Library and Research Centre, 4 Vols. Vol. I. Chapt. I 1943, II Chapt. II-IV, 1944; III Chapt. V, VI, 1986 Rev. IV Chapt VII, 1953.

— ed. and Eng. tr. by R.K. Shringy and Prem Lata Sharma. Delhi: Motilal Banarsidass, 1978, Vol. I.

— ed. and Eng. Tr. by R.K. Shringy. Delhi: Munshiram Manoharlal Pub. Pvt. Ltd., 1989, Vol. II. and forthcoming Vol. III.

Saṅkalpa Sūryodaya of Veṅkaṭanātha (Vedānta Deśika): with Sanskrit Comm., ed., and Tamil tr. by T. Vīrarāghavāchārya. Madras: India Printing Works. W.D.

Śāṅkhāyana Āraṇyaka: ed. by Sridhar Pathak. Poona: Anand Ashrama, 1987.

— tr. A.B. Keith. London: The Royal Asiatic Society, 1908.

Śāṅkhāyana Brāhmaṇa: ed. by Gulabrao Vajesankara Ojha. Poona: Anand Ashram, W.D.

Śāṅkhāyana Śrautasūtra: with Comm. of Varadattas Anartiya and Govinda, ed. by A. Hillebrandt. Delhi: Meharchandra Lacchmandass, 1981, 4 Vols.

— tr. in Eng. by W. Caland and ed. by Lokesh Chandra. Delhi: Motilal Banarsidass 1980, Reprint.

Śāradā Tilaka of Lakṣmaṇa Deśikendra: ed. by Arthur Avalon. Varanasi: Motilal Banarsidass, 1933.

Sarvadarśana Saṅgraha of Sāyaṇa Mādhava: ed. by T.G. Mainkar. Poona: Bhandarkar Oriental Research Institute, 1978.

Sarasvatīkaṇṭhābharaṇa: ed. by B. Bhattacharya. Varanasi: Banaras Hindu University, 1979.

— ed. by Anundoram Barooah, Assam: Publication Board, 1969 (Reprint).

Śatapatha Brāhmaṇa of the White Yajurveda in the Mādhyandina Recension: ed. by A. Chinnaswami Sastri, Paṭṭābhirām Śāstry and Rāmanātha Dīkṣita. Varanasi: Chaukhamba Sanskrit Sansthan 1984.

— according to the Mādhyandina recension with the Vedārthaprakāśa Bhāṣya of Sāyaṇācārya, supplemented by the Comm. of Harisvami Delhi: Gian Publishing House, 1987, 5 Vols.

— according to the text of Mādhyandina recension, tr. by Julius Eggeling. Delhi: Motilal Banarsidass, 1986 Reprint. (Sacred Books of the East Series-12, 26, 41, 43, 44).

Sātvata Saṃhitā: ed. by V.V. Dvivedi. Varanasi: Sampurnanda Sanskrit University, 1982.

Saundarananda of Aśvaghoṣa: ed. and tr. by E.H. Johnston. Delhi: Motilal Banarsidass, 1975.

Saundaryalaharī of Śaṅkarācārya: ed. and tr. by W. Norman Brown. Cambridge: Harvard University Press, 1958.

Siddhāntaśekhara of Śrīpati, with the comm. of Makki Bhaṭṭa and Babuaji Misra, ed. by Babuaji Misra, Calcutta: University of Calcutta, 1947, 2 parts.

Śilpa Prakāśa of Rāmacandra Kaulācāra: ed. and tr. by Alice Boner and Sadasiva Rath Sarma. Leiden: E.J. Brill, 1966.

Śivadṛṣṭi of Śrī Somānandanātha: with the Vṛtti by Utpaladeva, ed. by M.S. Kaul Shastri. Srinagar: Research Department Jammu and Kashmir State, 1934 (Kashmir Series of Texts and Studies-54).

Śivamahimnastotra of Puṣpadanta: with the Comm. of Jagannātha Chakravarty, ed. and tr. by Arthur Avalon. Madras: Ganesh and Co., 1953, 3rd ed.

Śiva Purāṇa: ed. by Ramtej Pandey. Varanasi: Chawkhamba Vidyabhavana, 1986.

— tr. by J.L. Śāstrī. Varanasi: Motilal Banarsidass 1981-1988, 4 Vols. (Ancient Indian Tradition and Mythgology Series 1-4).

Śiva Sūtras: The Yoga of Supreme Identity, ed. and tr. by Jaideva Singh. Delhi: Motilal Banarsidass, 1979.

Śivasūtravimarśinī of Kṣemarāja: ed. by J.C. Chatterjee. Srinagar: Research Department of Jammu and Kashmir State, 1911 (Kashmir Series of Texts and Studies-1).

Skanda Purāṇa: Calcutta: Manasukharai Mor Prakashan, Vol. I, 1965.

Ślokavārttika of Kumārila Bhaṭṭa: with Comm. "Kāśikā" of Sucarita Misra and Nyāya Ratnākara of Parthasarathi Mishra, ed. and Eng. tr. by Ganganatha Jha. Delhi: Satguru Publications, 1979.

— ed. and tr. by Durgadhar Jha. Darbhanga: Kameshvar Singh Darbhanga Sanskrit Visvavidyalaya Prakashan, 1979.

Somaśambhupaddhati: ed. and tr. by Helene Brunner Lachaux. Pondicherry: Institut Français d'Indologie, 1963.

Spandakārikā: The Divine Creative Pulsation. The Kārikās and the Spanda Nirṇaya of Kṣemarāja, ed. and tr. into English by Jaideva Singh. Delhi: Motilal Banarsidass, 1980.

Śṛṅgāra Prakāśa of Bhoja: ed. by G.R. Josyer. Mysore: International Academy of Sanskrit Research, 4 vols. 1955, 1963,1969, 1977.

Śrautakośa: R.N. Dandekar. Pune: Vaidika Saṃśodhana Maṇḍala, Vol. I, Part I and II, Vol. II, Part I and II, 1962.

Stavamālā: ed. by Bhavadatta Sastri and Sivadatta. Bombay: Nirnaya Sagar Press, 1903.

Śukranītisāra: tr. by Jagadishvarananda Saraswati. Sonipat: Rishidevi Rupalal Kapur Dharmartha Trust, 1983.

Sūryasiddhānta: ed. by Phanindralal Gangooly. Delhi: Motilal Banarsidass 1989.

Suśruta Saṃhitā of Suśruta: with "Nibandhasaṅgraha" Comm. of Śrī Ḍalhaṇācārya and Nyāyacandrikā Pañjikā of Gayadāsācārya on Nidānasthāna, ed. by Jadavji Trikamji Acarya. Varanasi: Chaukhamba Orientalia, 1980 (Reprint).

— ed. with English tr. by K.L. Bhisagratna. Varanasi: Chowkhamba Sanskrit Series Office, 1981, 3 Vols, 3rd edn.

Svacchanda Tantra: with Commentary of Kṣemarāja, ed. by Madhusudana Kaul Sastri. Srinagar: Research Department, Jammu and Kashmir State, 1921-35, 7 Vols. (Kashmir Series of Texts and Studies-31, 38, 44, 48, 51, 53, 56).

Taittirīya Āraṇyaka: with the Comm. of Bhaṭṭa Bhāskara Miśra, ed. by A. Mahadeva Sastri and K. Rangacarya. Delhi: Motilal Banarsidass, 1985.

Taittirīya Brāhmaṇa: with the Comm. of Sāyaṇācārya, ed. by Narayanasastri Godabole. Poona: Ananda Ashrama, (Sanskrit Granthavali-37), 3 Vols.

— with the Comm. of Bhaṭṭa Bhāskara Misra. Delhi: Motilal Banarsidss, 1985, 4 Vols.

Taittirīya Prātiśākhya: with the Comm. Tribhāṣyaratna, ed. by W.D. Whitney. Delhi: Motilal Banarsidass, 1973.

— ed. by R. Samasastri and K. Rangacarya. Delhi: Motilal Banarsidass, 1985.

Taittirīya Saṃhitā of the Black Yajurveda: with the Comm. of Bhaṭṭa Bhāskara Miśra, ed. by A. Mahadevasastri and K. Rangacarya. Delhi: Motilal Banarsidass, 1986, 10 Vols.

— Kṛṣṇayajurvedīya Taittirīya Saṃhitā: ed. by Śrīpāda Dāmodar Sātavalekar. Paradi: Svādhyāya Maṇḍala, 4th ed., W.D.

— Veda of the Black Yajus School entitled Taittirīya Saṃhitā: tr. by A.B. Keith. Delhi: Motilal Banarsidass, 1967, 2 Vols. (Harvard Oriental Series 18-19).

Tāṇḍyamahābrāhmaṇa: with the Comm. of Sāyaṇācārya, ed. by A. Chinnaswami Sastri. Varanasi: Chaukhamba Sanskrit Series Office, 1987, 2 Vols., 2nd ed. (Kashi Sanskrit Granthamala-105).

Tantrāloka of Abhinavagupta: with the Comm. Viveka by Rājānaka Jayaratha; ed. by M.R. Sastri and M.S. Kaul, Srinagar: Research Department, Jammu and Kashmir State, 12 Vols. Vol.I, 1981, II, III, IV 1921; V, VI 1922; VII 1924; VIII 1926; IX 1933;X 1936; XI 1938; XII 1938 (Kashmir Series of Texts and Studies).

— with the Comm. Viveka by Rājānaka Jayaratha, ed. by R.C. Dwivedi and Navajivana Rastogi. Delhi: Motilal Banarsidass 1987, 8 Vols. (reprint).

Tantrasaṅgraha: ed. by M.M. Gopinath Kaviraj. Varanasi: Varanaseya Sanskrit Visvavidyalaya, 1970, Vol. I.

Tantrasāra of Abhinavagupta: ed. by M.S. Kaul. Srinagar: Research Department, Jammu and Kashmir State, 1981 (Kashmir Series of Texts and Studies-17).

Tarkasaṅgraha of Annambhaṭṭa: tr. by M.R. Bodas: Bombay: The Department of Public Instruction, 1930 (Bombay Sanskrit Series No. 45).

Tattvacintāmaṇi of Gaṅgeśa Upādhyāya: with comm. 'Prakāśa'. Darbhanga: Mithila Vidyapith, 1957.

Tattvasaṅgraha of Śāntarakṣita: with the Comm. of Kamalaśīla, ed. by Embar Krishnamacharya. Baroda: Central Library, 1926, 2 Vols.

— tr. by Ganganatha Jha. Baroda: Baroda Oriental Institute, 1937, 1939, 2 Vols.

Ubhayābhisārikā of Vararuci: ed. by V.S. Agrawala and Moti Chandra. Bombay: Hindi Grantha Ratnakara Karyalay, 1959.

Ujjvalanīlamaṇi of Rūpa Gosvāmin: Delhi: Chaukhamba Sanskrit Pratisthan, 1984.

Upaniṣatsaṅgraha: ed. by J.L. Shastri. Delhi: Motilal Banarsidass, 1970.

— Eighteen Principal Upaniṣads (Aṣṭādaśa Upaniṣadaḥ): ed. by V.P. Limaye and R.D. Vedakar. Poona: Vaidika Samsodhan Mandal, 1958.

— Thirteen Principal Upanishads: tr. by R.E. Hume. Delhi: Oxford University Press, 1983 (Reprint).

Uttararāmacarita of Bhavabhūti: with Comm. of Ghanaśyāma, ed. by P.V. Kane and C.N. Joshi. Delhi: Motilal Banarsidass, 1962.

Vaiśeṣika Sūtra of Kaṇāda: with Bhāṣya of Praśastapāda and Comm. 'Upaskara', ed. by Dhundhiraja Sastri. Varanasi: Chaukhamba, 1923.

Vaitānasūtra: The Ritual of the Atharvaveda, ed. by R. Garbe. New Delhi: Mahalaksmi Publication House, 1982.

Vakroktijīvita of Rājānaka Kuntaka: ed. by Sushil Kumar De. Calcutta: Firma K.L. Mukhopadhyay, 1961, 3rd ed.

Vākyapadīya of Bhartṛhari: with the Comm. of Puṇyarāja and Vṛtti, ed. by K.A. Subramania Iyer. Delhi: Motilal Banarsidass, 1966.

Vāstusūtra Upaniṣad: The Essence of Form in Sacred Art, ed. and tr. by Alice Boner, Bettina Bäumer and Sadasiva Rath Sharma. Delhi: Motilal Banarsidass, 1982.

Vedānta Paribhāṣā: tr. by Swami Madhavananda. Howrah: Ramakrishna Mission Sharada Pitha, Belur Math, 1963.

Vedānta Sāra: ed. by Nikhilananda Swami. Calcutta: Advaita Ashrama, 1974.

Veṇīsaṃhāra of Bhaṭṭa Nārāyaṇa: ed. and tr. by R.S. Venkatarama Sastri. Madras: Malati Trades, 1943.

Vibhaṅga Pāli: ed. by Bhikkhu J. Kassapa. Nalanda: Pali Publication Board, Bihar Government, 1960.

— A Book of Analysis (Vibhaṅga): ed. and tr. by P.A. Thittla. London: Luzac and Company Limited, 1962.

Vijñānabhairava: ed. and Eng. tr. by Jaideva Singh. Delhi: Motilal Banarsidass, 1979.

— with the Commentaries of Kṣemarāja and Śivopādhyāya, ed. by M.R. Shastri. Srinagar: Research Department, Jammu and Kashmir State, 1918 (Kashmir Series of Texts and Studies - 8).

Vijñaptimātratāsiddhi: ed. and tr. by K.N. Chatterjee. Varanasi: Kishor Vidya Niketana, 1980.

Vikramorvaśīyam of Kālidasa: ed. by Surendra Nath Shastri. Bombay: Nirnaya Sagar Press, 1942.

Vimalaprabhā of Kalki Śrī Puṇḍarīka: A Comm. on Śrī Laghukāla-cakratantrarāja of Śrī Mañjuśrīyaśa, ed. by Jagannatha Upadhyaya. Varanasi: C.I.H.T.S., 1986, Vol. I (Bibliotheca Indo-Tibetica Series-11).

Vinaya Piṭaka: ed. by J. Takakusu and Makoto Nagai. London: Pali Text Society, 1947.

Viṣṇudharmottara Purāṇa: ed. by Priyabala Shah. Baroda: Oriental Institute, 1958, 1961, 2 Vols. (Gaekwad Oriental Series).

Viṣṇu Purāṇa: Gorakhapur, Gita Press, 1961.

— tr. into English by H.H. Wilson. London: Trubner and Co., 1864, 4 Vols.

Viśuddhimagga: ed. by Dharmanand Kosambi. London: Oxford University Press, 1950.

— ed. by Revatdhamma. Varanasi: Varanaseya Sanskrit University, 1962.

— The Path of Purification: tr. by Bhikku Ñyānamauli. Srilanka: Buddhist Publication Society, 1979 (Reprint).

Vṛttaratnākara: ed. by Aryendra Sharma. Hyderabad: Sanskrit Academy, Osmania University, 1969.

Vyaktiviveka of Rājānakamahimabhaṭṭa: with the Comm. of Rājānaka Ruyyaka, ed. by Madhusudana Mishra. Benaras: Chowkhamba Sanskrit Series, 1936 (Haridas Sanskrit Granthamala No. 121).

Yājñavalkya Śikṣā: with the Comm. Śikṣāvallī, ed. by Amaranāth Sāstri. Kashi: Padmanabha Sharma Diksit, 1937.

Yājñavalkyasmrti of Yājñavalkya: with Mitākṣarā Comm. of Vijñāneśvara, ed. by Umesh Chandra Pandey. Varanasi: Chowkhamba Sanskrit Sansthana, 1983, 2 Vols.

— with Mitākṣarā Comm., tr. by Srisa Chandra Vidyarnava. Allahabad: Panini Office, 1918, Book I.

Yajurveda Saṃhitā: ed. by S.D. Sātavalekara. Paradi: Svādhyāya Maṇḍala, 1957.

— The Text of the White Yajurveda, tr. with Comm. by R.T.H. Griffith. Banaras: E.J. Lazarus and Co., 1957.

Yogasārasaṅgraha of Vijñānabhikṣu: tr. by Ganganath Jha. New Delhi: Akay Book Corporation, 1986.

Yogasūtra of Patañjali: with Comm. of Vyāsa and Gloss of Vācaspati Miśra, tr. by Rama Prasada. Allahabad: The Panini Office, 1924.

— tr. by J.H. Woods. Delhi: Motilal Banarsidass, 1988 (Reprint).

— with the Vyāsa Bhāṣya, tr. by Bangali Baba. Delhi: Motilal Banarsidass, 1982 (Reprint).

Yoginī Hṛdayam: with "Dīpikā" Comm. of Amṛtānanda and "Setubandha" of Bhāskarācārya, ed. by M.M. Gopinatha Kaviraja. Banaras: Govt. Sanskrit Library, Saraswati Bhavan, 1923.

— ed. by Vrajavallabha Dvivedi. Varanasi: Motilal Banarsidass, 1988.

INDEX

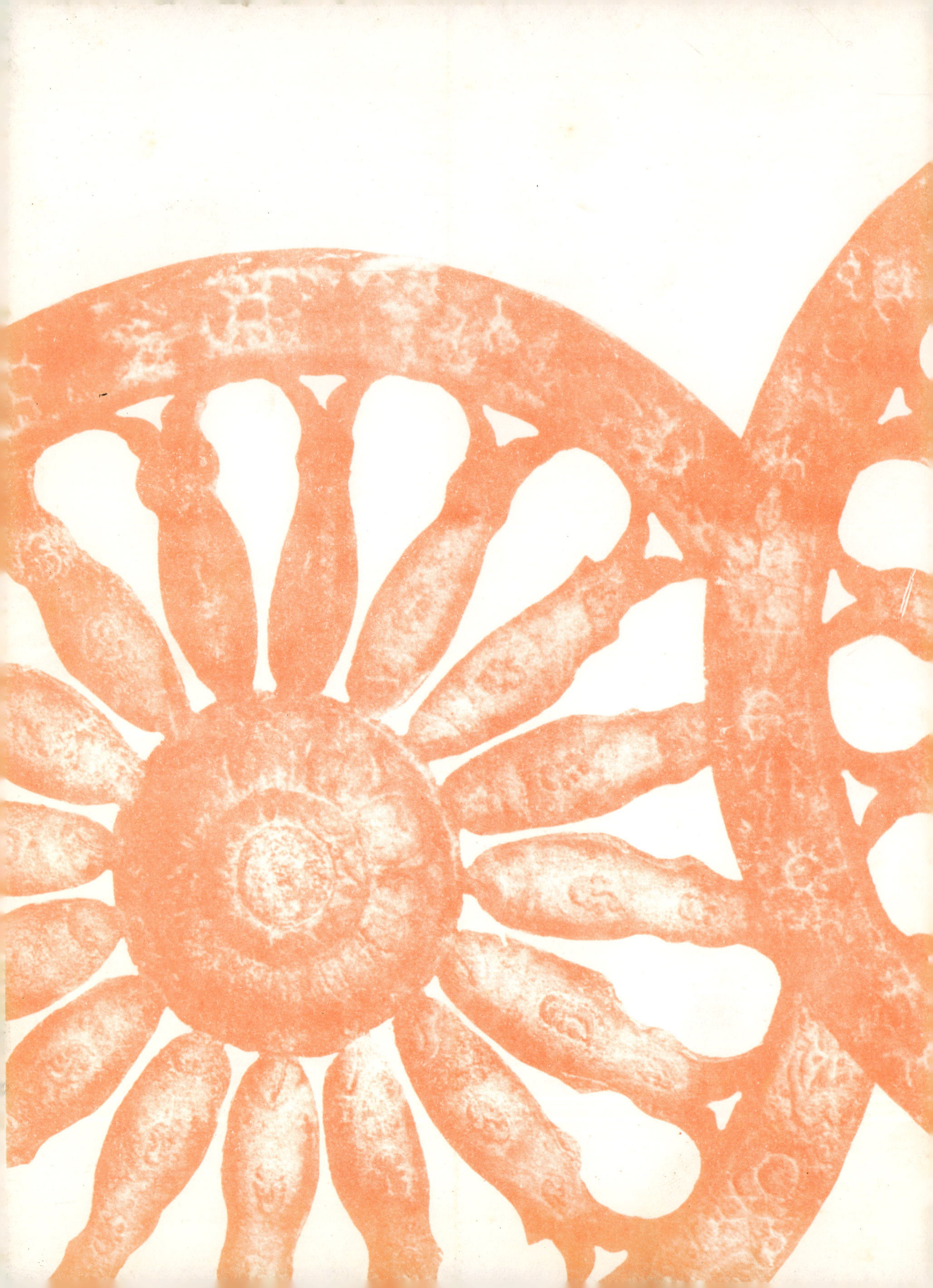